MASS MEDIA VI

Revision developed with James L. Hoyt,
Director of the School of Journalism and Mass Communication,
University of Wisconsin-Madison,
as consultant

MASS MEDIA VI

AN INTRODUCTION TO MODERN COMMUNICATION

Ray Eldon Hiebert........**University of Maryland**

Donald F. Ungurait........**Florida State University**

Thomas W. Bohn........**Ithaca College**

Longman

New York & London

Mass Media VI: An Introduction to Modern Communication

Longman, 95 Church Street, White Plains, N.Y. 10601

Associated companies:
Longman Group Ltd., London
Longman Cheshire Pty., Melbourne
Longman Paul Pty., Auckland
Copp Clark Pitman, Toronto

Credits appear at the end of the book.
Executive editor: *Gordon T. R. Anderson*
Development editor: *Elsa van Bergen*
Production editor: *Dee Amir Josephson*
Text design: *Jerry Wilke*
Cover design: *Kevin Kall*
Photo research assistant: *Karen Presser*
Art Direction: *Kevin C. Kall*
Cover photo: *The Image Bank*

Library of Congress Cataloging-in-Publication Data
Hiebert, Ray Eldon.
    Mass media VI: an introduction to modern communication / Ray
    Eldon Hiebert, Donald F. Ungurait, Thomas W. Bohn.
        p.   cm.
    Includes bibliographical references (p.
    Includes index.
    ISBN 0-8013-0453-9
    1. Mass media. 2. Communication. I. Ungurait, Donald F.
II. Bohn, Thomas W. III. Title. IV. Title: Mass media 6.
V. Title: Mass media six.
P90.H4793   1990
302.23--dc20   90-13463
                                    CIP

ABCDEFGHIJ-VH-99 98 97 96 95 94 93 92 91 90

To
the memory of
Gordon T. R. Anderson,
whose leadership in communications
publishing will long
be remembered

Contents

THE PERSUADERS   **147**

THE MASS-MEDIA INDUSTRIES   **215**

Preface

As we entered the 1990s, dramatic news about the mass media—the media businesses and the programs, publications, films, and recordings they produce—broke all around us. Some analysts suggested that the changes sweeping across the media were so profound that they were shaking the very foundations of mass communications organizations. This prompted Richard Kostyra, director of media services for the J. Walter Thompson advertising agency, to declare, in "In Defense of Mass Media,"

> There have certainly been important changes in the American media during the last decade. The television audience has fragmented, spurred by the proliferation of cable into the majority of U.S. households. Hundreds of new magazines have been launched, the majority targeted to very narrow slices of the consumer base. A national daily has revolutionized the newspaper industry. And we've witnessed the emergence of "new electronic media" such as homevideo, videotex, and even electronic shopping carts.
>
> The consumer press, notoriously introspective, has given these developments a great deal of attention. While the majority of coverage has been "fair," some myths have also been propagated that are clouding our perception of the newly-emerging media environment.
>
> The inevitable decline of mass media is one of these myths. . . .

The basic question is: Do new circumstances, such as more specialized industries, global conglomeratization, splintered audiences, and new media, shatter the picture of the mass media we inherited from the 1970s and 1980s, or do they expand it? Is the media scene shifting so rapidly that no textbook can capture it? We do have to acquire and use new perspectives and a new vocabulary. But it is also true that we have to acquire a sound foundation and to understand where we have come from, in order to appreciate where we are and where we are heading.

The time is ideal for this completely new edition of *Mass Media*. This book was the first introductory text that had the process of mass communication at its core. Its basic holistic, interrelated approach is more appropriate than ever, but now each component, each aspect of the mass media has been freshly examined for this sixth edition. This book is a comprehensive introduction to all the mass media as they have evolved as well as a look at new directions, technologies, audiences, and processes. It is a guide to the new media environment.

This book will serve well the colleges and universities which recognize the need to integrate communication studies. The writing of the unified whole that is *Mass Media VI* itself demonstrated the new, stronger relationships between both industries and parts of the process that had been more distinct. In this book, one chapter builds upon another. From the changed roles of communicators to the global and ethical implications of the new media and changed media structures, we look at how areas of knowledge contribute to a more insightful understanding and use of the complexity known as the mass media. For example:

The lengthening reach of messages and entertainment sent by the media throughout the world does affect how those messages are generated and delivered; movies are planned and marketed for Japanese and East European audiences as well as for Americans.

Technological advancement has forever changed the language that media and we media consumers employ, and it has created subtle new ways to affect our perceptions and our beliefs. Image manipulation has moved out of the darkroom into the discourse about ethics.

Effects of the video revolution are everywhere: video news releases are generated by public relations experts and presented as "objective" news; video magazines and books, interactive video in education, VCR use as an influence on moviemaking are all facts of life.

In this edition, introductions to each major section highlight what is to come and how it links with what we have learned. Part One is a fresh look at the roles today of process and participants. Full of concrete examples, it provides an essential framework for more detailed study of media history and present-day operational strategies, social issues, technical advancement, and the changing marketplace of ideas and images. A new chapter on the effect of media economics on mass communication gives you the tools to judge the structure, conduct, and performance of media industries and includes case studies of movers, shakers, and leaders. The first part concludes with a study of the many audiences we may join—what we bring to communication, what can distort our perception, what is known about our reactions.

Part Two is new to this edition in that new approaches to two key fields—public relations and advertising—have been moved up and given their due, in terms of the broad influences they have on media content (rather than merely providing "support"). These growing areas are closely integrated with the basic media system and mass communication process, and understanding their workings helps prepare us to turn to specific industries.

Part Three, "The Media Industries," looks at the historical development, current organization and operations, basic role, and future trends of seven areas. Each segment has characteristics unique to itself, but we look also at the increasing number of ways in which delineations blur—as program or publication formats merge and as conglomerates gather together separate industries under their umbrellas. We begin with newspapers and television as dominant mass media whose growth led to changes in many others, especially radio, magazines, and motion pictures; lastly we turn to the more privatized or individual-oriented media, recorded music and books.

Part Four investigates the media functions of news and information, analysis and interpretation, instruction and education, and entertainment and art. Chapter 19 offers for the first time in an introductory text the principles by which critical media consumers like you can evaluate what you read and view. In addition, the overlapping of functions, particularly that of entertainment, is explored; this helps us be alert to the ways psychological, social, and political that effects are conveyed.

Part Five brings together many of the themes of the preceding chapters in its focus on the issues that are legal or ethical, that concern individual impact or involve changes in society and public opinion, that reflect global and international communication problems, or that arise from emerging technologies.

Throughout, new case histories, new perspectives, and even new paths of communication have been included. Every chapter has been revised; most of them now include boxed features, new to this edition, to provide supplemental information, interesting profiles, or examples of media in action. To complement a thoroughly updated art program, there are additional displays of data and graphics in the revised and expanded instructor's manual for this edition. (That guide also points out ways instructors can utilize this text as they tailor their introductions to mass communication.) An expanded, indexed glossary and a convenient categorized and annotated bibliography of books and other sources for further study, data, or career information complete the text—which we hope will be only the beginning of lifelong attention to media functions, systems, effects, and issues.

To best present an up-to-date and insightful survey of changing media we have enlarged the team behind this edition of our text. Consultants and researchers in various special fields have contributed their expertise. We are privileged to have benefited from suggestions, research, and content from Arthur Asa Berger, San Francisco State University; Tom A. Bowers, University of North Carolina, Chapel Hill; Pamela J. Creedon, Ohio State University; Lucinda Davenport, Michigan State University; Robert E. Drechsel, University of Wisconsin-Madison; Douglas Gomery, University of Maryland; James L. Hoyt, University of Wisconsin-Madison; and Lowndes F. Stephens, University of South Carolina.

We are grateful for review of the manuscript at various stages of development by Robert Abelman, Cleveland State University; Thomas W. Benson, The Pennsylvania State University; Andrew Chiles, Navarro College; Yvette Guy, Michigan State University; and Lynn C. Spangler, SUNY-New Paltz.

The vision, dedication, and supervision of Executive Editor Gordon T. R. Anderson of Longman and the advisory role played by James L. Hoyt, Director of the School of Journalism and Mass Communication at the University of Wisconsin-Madison, have been important to the effort. The development of the project and coordination of text, art, and ancillaries were handled by Elsa van Bergen, College Development Editing Supervisor of Longman. Research and writing assistance have also been provided by Virginia Blanford, Jeffrey Campbell, and David Fox.

ONE

THE PROCESS AND THE PARTICIPANTS

············ ≡≡≡ ············

Profound and pervasive changes are occurring in the mass media. The concept of "the audience" splinters, media proliferate, formats "blur," technologies advance, globalization grows as a few conglomerates control more categories of media and far-flung markets, and the basic problem of clutter, of onslaughts of communication, overwhelms us. All this is accompanied by an increase in communications *about* mass communications. The covers of newsmagazines increasingly feature not only the stars but the producers, writers, and businesspeople behind the scenes. More cover stories in the nationally distributed *New York Times Magazine* are now devoted to media subjects than to political affairs or other traditional topics, and local papers and broadcasts cover the media issues that were previously the all but exclusive domain of scholarly and professional journals. One medium describes, analyzes, and promotes the operations and output of another as never before.

What also increases, amidst the information overload, is the need for clearer understanding of the communication process. As statistics, demographics, trends, names of industry leaders, names of corporations, and top tens are altered overnight, the study of mass communication as "who tells what to whom with what effect" is perhaps the one constant. The whos, whoms, whats, and hows change, but the basic interrelatedness of these does not.

The chapters that follow provide a framework for closer looks at media systems and effects that will be useful for your own continuing study and/or your consumer enjoyment of the media. They supply the vocabulary, perspectives, and concepts needed to understand media functions and issues. In doing this, they bring the model that *Mass Media* presents into concrete, current terms and cases, to show exactly how the relationships between participants—and even the participants' roles—are continuing to evolve. Knowledge of the process, coupled with constantly amplified research, is vital to a competitive edge in advertising, public relations, and general marketing, as well as survival in the mass media.

We start with an overview of the process and then proceed to explore each of its aspects. The word *communicator* has gained wider meaning, and we

1

describe the diversity of roles, how they must function together, and how new business structures affect the messages we receive. And the *receiver* is ever more elusive, ever more hotly pursued. The attempts and the mechanisms to bring these two components together is the focus of Part 1.

1

The Critical Consumer in the Process of Mass Communication

For many Americans, the day begins with the voice of a local disc jockey or news-person on the clock radio. As we dress, a miniature television set brings us the Cable News Network (CNN) and keeps us "in tune with the world." At breakfast, we speed-read the local newspaper or *USA Today*—the first national capsule-comment newspaper. If we drive, radio "flashes" weather, London and Tokyo stock prices, and fast-breaking stories until we let the tape deck soothe our nerves; if we ride the subway or walk, the Sony Walkman sets the pace. And that's but the beginning of a day. Mass communication consumption, along with sleep and work and school, is the activity that dominates Americans' lives. It is estimated that media fill about one-third of the average day in some way. In the average U.S. household, the TV set is on about 45 hours a week, transmitting 6,000-plus commercials, in that time frame nationally.

There is no doubt that information is power. To compete in acquiring it, individuals and cultures seem to have shifted into "warp-drive," and to compete in delivering it, communicators have assembled—or become part of—vast networks. Central to this age of communication are the institutions known as the mass media. These are less and less distinct industries; they are now components in powerful high-speed information and entertainment systems that bring about change within societies, subcultures, families, and individuals.

Communication informs, entertains, provokes, instructs, and persuades each one of us. Communication links us emotionally and intellectually to other individuals, groups, and institutions. If is often defined functionally as "the sharing of experiences" or the "transfer of meaning or values." The current pace of globalization of media has pushed this to the point where some of those cultures' guardians are protesting and protecting what they view as native.

The communication process is a means to all these ends. It is more than the sum of the parts. Communication is so diverse and complex that it seems to defy definition. In fact, definitions of communication often limit our understanding of the human and technological interactions involved. That is why this book evaluates communication as a complex series of personal, corporate, and cultural actions and reactions that is always moving toward changing goals. And the systems—the complicated and integrated organizations that facilitate communication—are also constantly changing, eluding neat description. Despite the growing complexity

3

Figure 1.1. Mass media means making choices. Inside the NBC remote sports truck, images are being selected, coordinated, and transmitted. In a corner of a suburban supermarket, a teenager punches a code to access the evening's video entertainment.

of mass communication, the basic process by which we relate to others *can* be described. This chapter provides an overview of how a message is delivered and builds a model that will underlie the chapters ahead.

THE FOUR LEVELS OF COMMUNICATION ....

Daily routines involve a variety of communication experiences. These tend to fall into four relatively discrete categories, or levels, of communication.

Intrapersonal communication is one person talking to himself or herself. It is the thought process most of us use before we speak or act.

Interpersonal communication may be dyadic (two persons) or triadic (three people), or it may involve a few individuals communicating with one another. The closer the emotional or physical link, the more personal the communication. Talking on the telephone to someone you love may be a more intense experience than sending that person a letter, but both events are usually less involving than the first face-to-face encounter after a separation.

Group communication covers situations from participating in a business meeting to going to a class to attending a rock concert. As the number of people increases, the level of involvement often changes. Some participants are more active than others; listeners drift in and out; and the total experience is often less immediate and intense than interpersonal communication. Group communication has been

Figure 1.2. This riverboat pilot was aware of the fantastic reach of his voice via early radio. The interviewer for KDKA, Pittsburgh, the first station to be licensed for general broadcasting, was Dave Garroway, who went on to pioneer with a TV invention: "The Today Show."

institutionalized in the world of work as *organizational communication;* work becomes a series of communication events.

Mass communication involves a communicator (almost always more than one person) using a mass medium to communicate with very large audiences. Major changes occur as we move into the process of mass communication:

1. The number of participants increases dramatically. There may be millions of individuals in the audience. But what is just as important is that the *sender* evolves from one person into an organized group whose members take on specialized roles.
2. The message becomes less personal, less specialized, and more general so that it is understood and accepted by the largest possible portion of the public.
3. The audience members become physically and emotionally separated in time and space from each other, from the members of other audiences, *and* from the mass communicator.
4. A mass medium must always be involved for mass communication to occur. Mass communication incorporates complex technologies and never occurs without a complex organization—a newspaper, record company, publisher, or radio station—acting as the channel of communication.

In spite of their differences, intrapersonal, interpersonal, group, and mass communication have a number of similarities. A useful way to analyze commonalities in the process of communication is to examine some of the models that have been developed in the past five decades of mass-communication research.

VISUALIZING THE COMMUNICATION PROCESS ....

At all levels of communication, someone sends something, a message, to someone else. Students of communication use a variety of labels for these components, but essentially they are the same three things. Both the *receiver* and the *sender* must act on the *message* for communication to be successful. The model in Figure 1.3 visualizes the idea that the more the sender (A) and the receiver (B) have in common, the more likely they will understand each other.

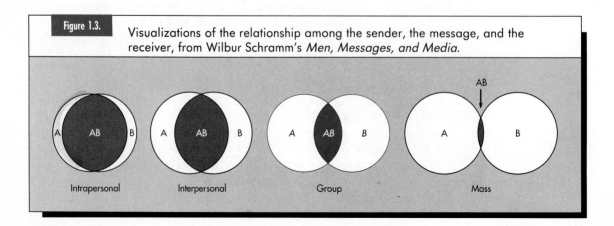

| Figure 1.3. | Visualizations of the relationship among the sender, the message, and the receiver, from Wilbur Schramm's *Men, Messages, and Media*. |

Intrapersonal   Interpersonal   Group   Mass

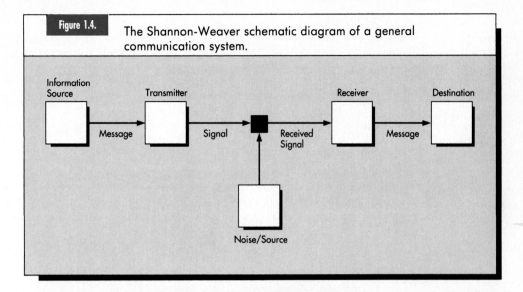

Figure 1.4. The Shannon-Weaver schematic diagram of a general communication system.

One of the basic concerns of communication scholars has been to emphasize that the message sent may not be the message received. In every communication experience, a wide range of factors comes into play. The receiver has frames of reference or personal and cultural perspectives that he uses to interpret the sender's message. The sender, in turn, tries to transmit messages in such a way that they are easily understood and readily accepted by the receiver. By the time we reach mass communication, the two circles in the figure barely touch each other in some cases—for example, in avant-garde foreign films or recordings of Italian operas that are largely outside our experiences.

One of the earliest attempts to model the communication experience was the Shannon-Weaver "mathematical model of communication" (Figure 1.4). This model, developed for the American Telephone and Telegraph Company, identifies a number of elements based on the use of the telephone, which is often referred to as *telecommunication*. The transmitter, signal, received signal, and receiver are part of a system that can have *noise*, or disturbance, anywhere within it. The model emphasizes the movement of a message, using a systems approach to describe the communication process.

The Weaver-Ness model adds further dimensions: *codes*, which are the symbols used to carry the meaning, and *feedback*, which is the response of the receiver to the sender (Figure 1.5). This model emphasizes that communication is a circular, response-oriented activity that allows both source and destination to react, modify, and clarify the communique by using communication pathways, or *channels*. Advertising is a perfect example of the application of feedback, gained through market research, to new and improved products and often to messages that get changed as a result of the feedback.

In formal structured organizations—the military, for example—the group becomes stratified; group members refer to the "chain of command" and "going through channels." The vertical nature of this kind of organization sets up layers through which a message must pass for approval, rejection, or modification. Each level is a "gate" through which a message must pass, and each gate is "guarded" by the next level of authority, the *gatekeeper*. You can imagine what happens to

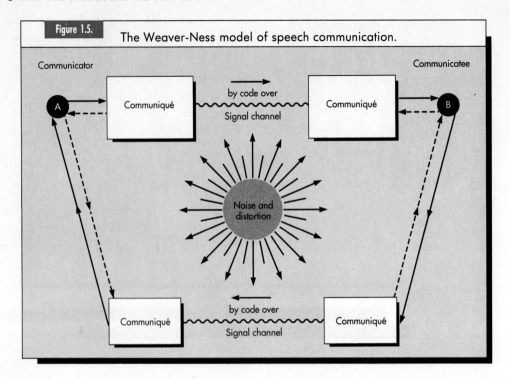

Figure 1.5. The Weaver-Ness model of speech communication.

messages in terms of content modification and time lapse as the message moves from the private up to the general, and then down through the chain of command to the troops. The more complex the organization, the more likely communication breakdown will occur. Memos and meetings become the primary pathways of communication, and these depersonalizes interaction within the corporate setting.

Combining all the elements we have discussed, we reach a model that includes the components that appear in mass communication, albeit modified. Figure 1.6 illustrates nine identifiable elements:

1. An individual acts as the *sender*,
2. who uses a *code* of commonly understood symbols
3. to convey a personal, specialized *message*,
4. over a *channel* that is a pathway (airwave, paper and pencil, memos, or meetings)
5. through one or more members (bosses) acting as *gatekeepers* (if an organization is involved)
6. and passing through the receivers' *frames of reference*, which interpret the message,
7. to another individual *receiver* or a small group,
8. so that the receivers can react and respond in the form of verbal, nonverbal, or written *feedback* to the sender;
9. and, of course, *noise* and distortion can occur at any point in the process and have to be eliminated by the sender, the receivers, or both.

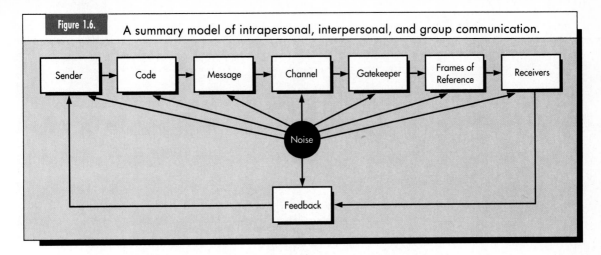

Figure 1.6. A summary model of intrapersonal, interpersonal, and group communication.

The communication process, then, is modular; and individual components can be modified or can take on new variations.

THE HUB MODEL OF MASS COMMUNICATION

When we make the leap to mass communication, the basic elements change significantly, and we add several new components. We need a model that visualizes mass communication as an interactive process. The HUB (Hiebert, Ungurait, Bohn) model describes that process as a set of concentric elements always involved in a series of actions and reactions (Figure 1.7).

The HUB model represents communication as a process similar to that of dropping a pebble into a pool. This action causes ripples that expand outward until they reach the sides of the pool, and then a few bounce back toward the center. Many factors affect that message as it ripples out to its audience and bounces back. The HUB model's rings also reflect the physical processes of sound conduction and electronic transmission. The goal, of course, is to present mass communication as clearly and completely as possible. The term *mass media* appears midway in the HUB model's concentric circles because it is the channel and the most tangible means by which a message is delivered to a mass audience. Mass communication never occurs without a mass medium, but that medium is more than a mechanical device to send messages. The devices and products of the mass media—printing presses, books, newspapers, and magazines; transmitters, radio and television programs; cameras and motion pictures; recording equipment and records and tapes—can be used for several ends, from personal to narrowly organizational to completely mass communication. Books or movies are not in themselves the mass media; neither are computer terminals nor tape decks. Mass media encompass both complex industrial *organizations* (in turn, part of larger organizations) and social *institutions* created to perform the tasks that the society requires of them. These *use* mechanical devices to produce content for consumption by large audiences.

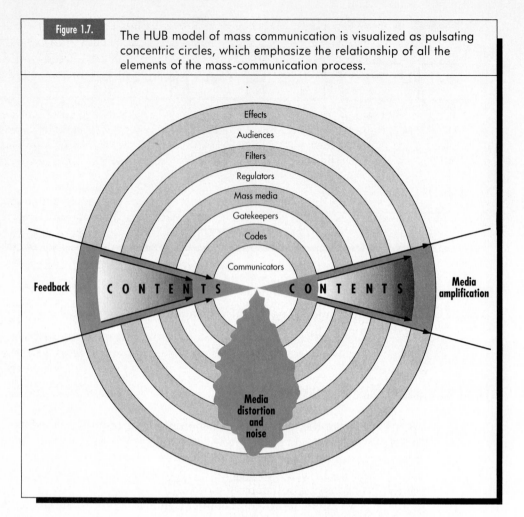

Figure 1.7. The HUB model of mass communication is visualized as pulsating concentric circles, which emphasize the relationship of all the elements of the mass-communication process.

CONTENT

Individuals, groups, and society use mass media to convey content for one or more specific effects. The content of mass communication is dissimilar to that of interpersonal or group communication messages in four basic areas. Mass communication messages are (1) less personal, (2) less specialized, (3) more rapid, and (4) more transient than other messages. Obviously, the number of people involved, the distance covered, and the time span are the overriding conditions that create these differences. There are at least six important tasks or categories of mass-communication content. Increasingly, however, these functions tend to overlap.

Entertainment. Most dramatically shown through the delivery of news, entertainment has become an overlaid or integrated element. The mass media help people relax during their leisure time. The escapist use of the media has encouraged communicators to entertain *as* they inform, analyze, educate, persuade, and sell. This function ranges from tabloid journalism to presentation of literary classics; the mass media contribute to the betterment of our cultural heritage through artistic achievement.

News. The mass media survey events in society and provide reports on those with consequences for the publics they serve. The media's voracious appetite for news content sometimes leads to "news" generated by sources such as advertising agencies and public-relations firms striving to catch a share of attention by controversial or otherwise "newsy" output.

Commentary. The mass media provide us with an evaluation of events, placing them in perspective. In effect, the media take editorial positions and provide insights and analyses beyond the single event. Or media such as books and journals, through the selection of what they issue in the way of commentary, fulfill this role.

Education. The mass media perform a variety of functions that can be called educational. In addition to general edification or enlargement of knowledge and instruction, the media can function as a means of socialization and thus serve to reinforce, modify, and replace the cultural heritage of the present society. This function is either explicit or integrated, as in the case of docudramas.

Public Relations and Advertising. The mass media serve as instruments of propaganda and public persuasion. While public-relations professionals are subdivided into various specialities, media relations is a major role; few of us are aware of the high percentage of the information we receive through news and commentary programs that is generated by public-relations specialists working for governments, business corporations, political action groups, and individuals. Adver-

Figure 1.8. *King*, produced as a special by NBC to celebrate the contribution made by Martin Luther King, Jr., to America, combined several functions. Coretta Scott King was played by Cicely Tyson; King, by Paul Winfield.

tising supports several of the mass media by exchanging money for air time and/or print space. But it is also a source of content since it informs the public about new products, and sells merchandise and services by convincing potential consumers of their value. As contrasted to public relations, the advertiser is *identified* as the source of its message.

COMMUNICATORS

In mass communication, it is extremely difficult, if not impossible, for an individual to be the sender. The mass communicator is a conglomerate or group of individuals, each of whom performs a specialized task. The communicator on "The Tonight Show Starring Johnny Carson" is not simply Johnny Carson but an entire organization involving the network, local station, director, and technical staff, as well as the talent appearing on the show. David Letterman, Arsenio Hall, and all the other late-night talk-show hosts are genuinely funny and intelligent people, but behind them may be small armies of writers. Even a low-budget film will have scores of specialists behind the camera.

In print media, communicators (in *USA Today, People, Mass Media VI*) are not only the writers or authors but also researchers, copy editors, photographers, and many other specialists. *Time* magazine in the mid-twentieth century developed *group journalism,* in which the style and tone of the magazine required individual talents to blend into a successful format. In the electronic media, authors sometimes

Figure 1.9. "Late Night with David Letterman" would not happen without its full complement of writers.

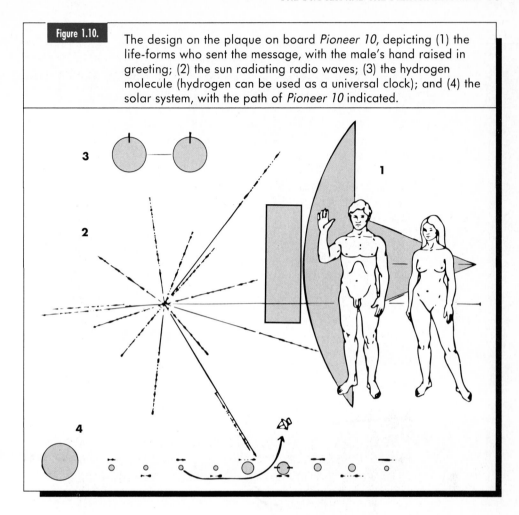

Figure 1.10. The design on the plaque on board *Pioneer 10*, depicting (1) the life-forms who sent the message, with the male's hand raised in greeting; (2) the sun radiating radio waves; (3) the hydrogen molecule (hydrogen can be used as a universal clock); and (4) the solar system, with the path of *Pioneer 10* indicated.

all but disappear in the process. As writer Budd Schulberg noted, in the Cannes Film Festival program for *Casualties of War* director Brian de Palma's name was prominent; in small print was listed the fact that playwright David Rabe wrote the screenplay based on an exposé by Daniel Lang in *The New Yorker*.[1] Although individual personalities may dominate and become symbols for a medium (an actor on TV, a director of a film, the columnist in a newspaper), they are really one part, albeit an important part, of the conglomerate communicator.

CODES

By *codes* we mean the language (verbal or not), and the symbols that are selected to convey best an intended message via a specific medium. In 1983, the *Pioneer 10* spacecraft left the solar system and raced toward the farther reaches of the universe. Before the spacecraft was launched in 1972, scientists had persuaded the National Aeronautics and Space Administration to place a plaque on board (Figure 1.10). The message was coded using a variety of symbols. The earthbound senders assumed that if the message was found by another intelligent life-form, the code could be "broken." This code for inter–life-form communication is not unlike the codes of the mass media, whose messages are cast out and coded in what the sender *hopes* are understandable patterns.

Mass communication has modified and expanded the codes used in other types of communication. For example, in the motion picture, visual symbol systems often replace the verbal. Camera angles, freeze frames, and editing broaden, rather than limit, a film's communicative capacities. Successful coding is a combination of (1) creativity or innovation and (2) understanding the audience's expectation of a format or coding system.

GATEKEEPERS

As in the military, there are gatekeepers within mass-media organizations: individuals such as wire-service editors, television network-continuity personnel, or motion-picture theater managers make decisions about what is communicated and how. They are not usually originators of content; instead, they function internally as creative evaluators. Gatekeepers can be positive forces, improving as well as eliminating content; they can delete, insert, emphasize, or de-emphasize content according to a variety of standards—aesthetic, financial, and those stemming from a professional or organizational code. Regulators, discussed below, are external gatekeepers. Feedback from audiences or market research can in effect serve as a kind of gatekeeping too.

MASS MEDIA

We have already seen what is and is not meant by the term *mass media*. When any mass medium becomes the channel in mass communication, *complex technology* becomes involved and the *amplitude* or potential power of communication increases.

REGULATORS

The regulators of the mass media—courts, government commissions, professional organizations, and public pressure groups—are external in the sense that they function outside the media institution. They have the ability to close down a theater, delete content, influence news coverage, and revoke television or radio licenses. Although these powers are not often used, regulators have considerable impact on decisions of the media because no one wants to incur the "wrath of the regulators."

FILTERS

Filters are the frames of reference that audience members use to understand, accept, reject, or remember mass communication. These frames of reference may be rose-colored glasses, prejudices, cultural preferences, acquired expectations, and many other circumstances we bring to a media experience.

Figure 1.11. The age-old problem of pleasing, or even attracting, audiences touched the dean of American composers, Irving Berlin.

AUDIENCES

Audiences are the most studied components of the process. How do job status and other demographics affect news viewing? What prejudices do preschoolers acquire from the media? How do media appearances by political candidates "prime" people to vote? In other words, what are the filters? Are the codes working? Is the communicator getting through to the targeted audience? And what are the effects?

EFFECTS

The effects of mass communication can be placed into two overlapping categories: (1) the specific impact that mass-communication content has on specific individuals in the audience; and (2) the general effect that the mass media have on society. The effects of mass communication are real, but our ability to study them qualitatively is weak compared with what we can measure in other aspects of the process. Effects will be the central issue in the future of mass communication. Despite attention given to effects in books, journal articles, popular journalism, and broadcasts, this is the least understood, most debated aspect of the mass-communication process.

MEDIA DISTORTION AND NOISE

Many of the sources of noise are physical: static on the radio, a poorly printed newspaper, an out-of-focus motion picture. "Noise" in the mass-communication process can occur at any point, not simply in the channel. Because of its public nature, mass communication allows more kinds of interruption (technical, miscommunication, and misunderstanding) on a far broader level than does interpersonal communication.

MEDIA AMPLIFICATION

The media have the power to intensify messages, first on the immediate level—repetition drives an ad home, for example—so that some messages can overcome noise or get through clutter and filters. The content of communication may also gain in importance by virtue of their very appearance in the media. In other words, the mass media confer status to messages with gatekeepers often determining what should be emphasized. The mass media are powerful persuaders, as political analysts know. Amplification techniques have been misused in conveying propaganda or "hype," but they also have the inherent power to encourage beneficial social action. (Mass media seldom solve problems, unsolved mysteries aside, but they can identify what may need to be done or at least what some who gain access to the media think may need to be done.)

FEEDBACK

Feedback is the communicated response of audience members to a message sent by the system. In interpersonal communication, feedback is immediate. In mass communication, it is delayed and diffused. Even with overnight ratings, TV program producers have little way of knowing if they lost the audience's attention at certain points. Sneak previews are a mechanism for film and broadcast producers to "massage the message" a bit and can affect the content that is later released, but even this comes many months and miles from the creation and packaging of the media product. In mass communication, feedback is often expressed quantitatively: a magazine's circulation figures or a film's box-office receipts.

THE SIGNIFICANCE OF THE MASS MEDIA ....

The mass media bring to the communication process an intensity and complexity that is overwhelming unless examined carefully. The viewpoint of *Mass Media VI* is that every part of the process is influenced by every other part. Therefore, this book strives to be both holistic (to provide an overview) and specific (to isolate each element in order to understand its specific contribution).

All elements of the mass-communication process are valid areas of scholarship. Nevertheless, increased emphasis has been placed on the medium itself (and on the complex business structure supporting it) as an important element in the mass-communication process. Indeed, the medium may be the key component in the process. Marshall McLuhan, in his *Understanding Media: The Extension of Man,* coined the phrase "the medium is the message." What this means is that the carrier of communication—whether human voice or printed page, neon sign or electronic impulse—influences the message, the sender, the audience, and the effects of mass communication far more significantly than was previously understood.

McLuhan later rephrased the statement to read, "The medium is the *massage*." The change serves to emphasize further the carrier rather than the content. McLuhan stated that television itself, not television programs, massages us. Almost any program content is interchangeable, McLuhan argued, and content is relatively unimportant to the impact that this "electronic window" will have on humankind. This concern has prompted much research and commentary. In his thought-provoking book *The Confetti Generation: How the New Communications Technology Is Fragmenting America*, William Donnelly has written:

> *Marshall McLuhan was correct when he said that the medium was the message, and television quickly became our society's central medium of communication. It grew like a weed without the shaping impact of a consciously defined social contract to determine what the medium should be delivering, for what purpose, and with what value. Perhaps it happened too fast, too unexpectedly for constructive reflection; so that the technology shaped us before we could shape it.*[2]

Thus, if we do not understand mass media, we cannot understand mass communication. The mass media speak new languages that we must learn.

The electronic media have homogenized Americans more in the past 35 years than was accomplished by other means in the past. And the nations and people of the world are looking more alike all the time, an effect Marshall McLuhan described when he said we are all becoming residents of a media-created global village. When minuscule groups of terrorists want to emphasize their grievances, they grab us by our international electronic throats. All of us are held hostage on the starship earth because we participate mythically with all the other global villagers in their successes and their sorrows.

The United States is by far the largest producer and consumer of mass communication. American mass media have a great impact not only on our own society but also on the rest of the world. In Africa, for example, one is more apt to hear American than African music on radio and television, in discos and nightclubs, and on home phonographs. In Asia, American movies are shown more often than Asian movies. In Latin America, the *Reader's Digest* is more popular than any locally produced magazine. A U.S. Information Agency survey found that 15 to 30 percent of elite audiences in non-Communist countries read *Time*. More than 200 of the world's leading newspapers subscribe to the *New York Times* or the *Washington Post–Los Angeles Times* news services.

The world's masses are entertained and the "information elite" obtains much of what it feels it has to know from the mass media in the United States. In defending the high prices he has been paying to acquire Macmillan, a U.S. publisher, and other media properties, Robert Maxwell remarked:

> *Information is growing at 20% a year. Communications is where oil was ten years ago. There will be seven to ten great global communications corporations. My ambition is to be one of them. You can't have a world communications enterprise without the U.S., which has 80% of the software and half the scientific information.*[3]

It was announced in May 1990 that American communication entrepreneurship would combine with the vastness of Radio Moscow to build the world's largest radio and television network. Make no mistake; despite inroads made in technology in other parts of the world, despite the pan-European structure of media likely to increase after 1992, American mass-communication industries remain in a leadership position and are a critical force in the world.

If the mass media play such an important role in our lives, are we their victims or their masters? That is, are we managed, manipulated, massaged, and brainwashed by the media, or do the media simply reflect us and our wishes, our purchases in the marketplace, our attention, and our dial twirling and page turning?

The best answer is probably a combination of both. We still do not know enough about the process to make final judgments. Although we speak of communication science, we have far to go to arrive at answers to some basic questions. One thing does seem clear: The more we know about a subject, the less we can be misled about it. The power of print has intimidated human beings for hundreds of years, and the influence of TV images is only beginning to be analyzed. Those with a perspective on the process and an understanding of the increasing interrelatedness of industries and of media formats and functions will be able to discriminate between what is artificial in mass communication and what has value. We begin by bringing our notion of a communicator into contemporary focus.

SUMMARY

Communication is the process that makes us human beings; a day is not spent without being exposed to multiple levels of media input. Communications link us with the rest of the world. But mass communication is not an uncontrollable, mysterious force.

Communication can be best understood as working on four levels: thinking about the first boy and girl you ever had a crush on (intrapersonal communication); talking on the telephone to your mother and father (interpersonal communication); listening to a lecture in class (group communication); and reading this book (mass communication). Remember that a mass medium must always be involved if the process is to be mass communication. A rock concert with thousands in attendance is not mass communication, but a music video of that concert broadcast on MTV is mass communication because a mass medium (broadcasting or cablecasting) is being used. But the mass media are not only channels or devices but the complex institutions that use them.

Visualizing (modeling) the various levels of communication clarifies the relationship among the elements of communication. The HUB model of mass communication identifies 12 components: (1) *content* as media uses and functions; (2) *communicators* as a conglomerate; (3) *codes* as symbol systems unique to each mass medium; (4) *gatekeepers* as checkpoints within the media to start, modify, or stop messages; (5) *mass media* as complex institutions of the host society; (6) *regulators* as external watchdogs that attempt to monitor and change media performance; (7) *filters* as the frames of reference that audiences use to understand or filter out messages; (8) *audiences* as individuals, often in very large aggregates, attending to a particular media event; (9) *effects* as the behavioral reaction of individuals and the impact of the mass media on a parent culture; (10) *noise* as any interruption of the communication process or any media distortion; (11) *media amplification* as the power of the media to focus on an issue, confer status on an individual, or give credence to a viewpoint; (12) *feedback* as the delayed, cumulative, and institution-alized response of the mass audience, usually reported numerically as attendance or monetary figures. If we could present the HUB model in motion, you could see that the concentric circles are not rigid but flex, or pulse, to the beat of a complex interaction of all the elements of the process of mass communication.

Americans produce and consume the most mass communications. People around the world are more likely to watch, listen to, or read products of the American media than their own. Whether you wish to become a media professional or a critical consumer, you must learn to understand and therefore harness the power of mass communication to your needs. You must seek to manipulate the mass media rather than be manipulated by them.

REFERENCES

1. "Auteur!" *New York Times*, December 4, 1989, A23.
2. William J. Donnelly, *The Confetti Generation: How the New Communication Technology Is Fragmenting America* (New York: Holt, 1986), 21.
3. *Time*, November 28, 1988, 82.

CHAPTER 2

The Conglomerate Communicator

When messages are exchanged on an interpersonal basis, the sender and receiver are individual entities. In mass communication, the receiver may be flesh and blood, but a distinct individual sender is more myth than reality. The communicator cannot be thought of as *a* speaker but as a *complex, specialized, and competitive organization.* Let us look at two specific communicators to test this statement.

When Fred Hirsch graduated from Ithaca College in 1975 with a degree in communication, he immediately set out for New York City to climb the broadcast-network ladder. Hirsch is still in broadcasting, but rather than being one of many radio newspeople at NBC, CBS, or ABC, he is the chief reporter and announcer at radio station WDME in Dover-Foxcroft, Maine. Hirsch is also the station's business manager, advertising salesperson, and promoter. Hirsch does not mind all these duties because he owns the station. Fred Hirsch is a communicator who was profiled in the *Wall Street Journal* as being an all-in-one interpreter, speaker, gate-keeper, and manager. But is he an individual or independent communicator? Even Fred Hirsch is only the visible portion of a vast and complex network of people, such as wire services, other media, and advertisers. A mass communicator is somewhat like the conductor of a symphony orchestra. One message comes from many sources, and while the conductor may represent the orchestra, he is not the only communicator responsible for the message.

When Mike Wallace appears as a correspondent on "60 Minutes," for example, the audience may assume that Wallace is the person responsible for the story. Actually, Wallace and the others who are called correspondents—Morley Safer, Harry Reasoner, Ed Bradley, and their colleagues—are primarily performers. They conduct the major on-camera interviews and may suggest and participate in shaping stories, but they have considerable help in compiling the research needed and often may not write their own scripts. The program is written and edited by many others, including its executive producer, Don Hewitt. Indeed, the general rule in TV news is the longer the broadcast, the smaller the role, comparatively speaking, of the on-camera correspondent. Given the system, it could scarcely be otherwise. An average story for "60 Minutes" takes a producer 6–8 weeks to complete, and each "60 Minutes" correspondent appears on about three stories every 4 weeks.

The collaborative nature of broadcasting only increases as the media grow more and more sophisticated and the technology more complex and the conglomerates encourage interaction of individual units. For example, tie-ins (such as simultaneous marketing of the book and screen versions of the same story) have long been common; they are being planned—or orchestrated, if you will—as even more in-

Figure 2.1. Morley Safer, Dan Rather, Harry Reasoner, and Mike Wallace belong to the "60 Minutes" team, communicating their stories and often the words of other mass communicators, such as reporters, researchers, and writers.

tegral to the production of either component now that business leaders like Ted Turner are involved. He has recently started a book-publishing subsidiary of Turner Broadcasting System, Inc., and the first book planned, *Portrait of Great Britain*, was to feature hundreds of photographs taken during production of the Turner miniseries by that name. More and more, the full scope of a communicative effort is carefully laid out in advance and managed throughout the process.

Individuals at times *seem* to function alone as mass communicators. The fresh vision and innovation of filmmaker Spike Lee essentially stem from an individual. But Lee and others, such as Michael Landon, on television who function as writer, actor, producer, are successful because they know how to become part of the media system and work with many different groups, unions, financial backers, and distributors.

Many communicators like Fred Hirsch wear several hats. A survey by Vernon A. Stone of the Radio-Television News Directors Association reports that 48 percent of the TV news directors said they spend more time as managers than as journalists, while 8 percent of radio news directors spend more time managing than they do gathering and reporting news. Mass communicators must effectively interact with scores of other specialists. Too often, aspiring broadcasters, reporters, or filmmakers focus only on performance training. They fail to realize that mass communication is a total process, going beyond any individual. This chapter and the next will study how individuals work together in organizations and how these structures are part of larger networks.

THE CHARACTERISTICS OF THE MASS COMMUNICATOR

Let us look more closely at the features that characterize the mass communicator in the United States. They are competitiveness, size and complexity, industrialization, specialization, and representation.

COMPETITIVENESS

Mass communicators spend huge amounts of money to reach the greatest share of the audience. In interpersonal communication, individuals compete for the attention of another person. Parents of small children are especially aware of this as they try to separate messages from the I-was-talking-first cacophony. All of this is minor, however, compared with the intense competition among mass communicators.

The battle of the TV networks is the most obvious example. In free economies, competition is fueled by media economics in which broadcast media compete for advertising. In order to measure this competitiveness accurately, American mass-media systems rely on companies such as Nielsen Media Research and the Audit Bureau of Circulation to conduct research on comparative standings (see Table 2.1). For television, this is measured in *points* and *share*. A single national ratings

Figure 2.2. Rivals for ratings include Roseanne and Cosby. In late fall 1989 ABC's "Roseanne" had a share of 25.4% of all households with a TV, or 39% of those watching some TV at the time of the Nielsen survey shown in Table 2.1.

Table 2.1.		**Ratings Roundup**	

1	25.4/39	*Cosby Show*	(NBC)
2	24.7/38	*Different World*	(NBC)
3	24.4/37	*Cheers*	(NBC)
4	23.8/37	*Roseanne*	(ABC)
5	21.3/36	*Golden Girls*	(NBC)
6	21.2/33	*Dear John*	(NBC)
7	21.1/33	*60 Minutes*	(CBS)
8	20.2/30	*Murder, She Wrote*	(CBS)
9	20.1/34	*Empty Nest*	(NBC)
9	20.1/34	*L.A. Law*	(NBC)
11	19.9/34	*NFL Monday Night Football*	(ABC)
12	19.0/33	*Barbara Walters Special*	(ABC)
12	19.0/30	*Unsolved Mysteries*	(NBC)
14	18.9/30	*In the Heat of the Night*	(NBC)
15	17.6/27	*ABC Sunday Movie*	(ABC)
15	17.6/28	*Growing Pains*	(ABC)
17	17.4/27	*Wonder Years*	(ABC)
18	17.3/28	*Matlock*	(NBC)
19	16.8/26	*NBC Monday Movie*	(NBC)
19	16.8/27	*Who's the Boss?*	(ABC)
21	16.7/26	*Head of the Class*	(ABC)
22	16.3/25	*CBS Sunday Movie*	(CBS)
23	15.9/26	*Chicken Soup*	(ABC)
24	15.7/28	*Full House*	(ABC)
24	15.7/29	*Hunter*	(NBC)
26	15.1/28	*Midnight Caller*	(NBC)
26	15.1/23	*Night Court*	(NBC)
28	15.0/23	*Doogie Howser, M.D.*	(ABC)
29	14.6/25	*Knots Landing*	(CBS)
30	14.1/22	*ALF*	(NBC)
30	14.1/22	*Jake and the Fatman*	(CBS)

Source: Nielsen Media Research.

point equals 921,000 households, and a share measures a program's draw as percentage of televisions in use. Seasonal ratings (November, February, and May) are crucial in television because they determine advertising rates for the next season and which series will be canceled. Measurement techniques are constantly being refined, with dramatic results. From one day to the next, in September 1987 Tom Brokaw had to bow, much to his surprise, to CBS News's Dan Rather because the means of audience measurement had switched to people meters. Critics say this competitive mode leads to uninspired copycat programming; clearly, the slotting of three strong television talk-show hosts—Oprah Winfrey, Phil Donahue, and Geraldo Rivera—at 4:00 P.M. is an example.

The race is no longer a three-way situation, due to the presence of Turner and Fox Broadcasting and the proliferation of cable channels. Perhaps no other aspect of mass media is getting more attention than cable because of its broad impact on advertising, marketing, programming, and viewer use of TV. Some observers believe that paying for programs by cable subscriptions instead of advertising is diluting the copycat patterns. But competition for market share of revenues is still the name of the game.

No medium is exempt. In the summer of 1989, *Batman* and *Ghostbusters II* competed for box-office receipts. Madonna competes with Paula Abdul for number of records sold. Radio formats change to compete better. The current trend toward more talk radio is driven by the need to have a more inherently exclusive (and therefore competitive) product; as with television talk shows, content and personality can be built and marketed to attract certain audiences, whereas all stations have to offer similar music for the top 40.

SIZE AND COMPLEXITY

Successful mass communicators gain the opportunity to speak out; to be successful, even to survive, they must reach large audiences, and to do this requires large organizations. Size in the context of media requires some clarification, however. Certainly Fred Hirsch's radio station is not large. The average TV station in the United States employs only 60 full-time employees. Of the approximately 2,300 book publishers in the United States, only 425 have more than 20 employees. Nevertheless, all media organizations, regardless of their internal size and structure, rely on networks of specialized people and organizations. Hirsch's radio station, for example, makes use of the vast resources and staff of the Associated Press news service. The smallest book publisher employs artists, copy editors, and other editorial personnel on a freelance basis. Small newspapers use adjunct reporters ("stringers") in the field; while not part of a paper's full-time staff, these people are a necessary part of the organization. If a book or periodical is written by an individual who prints it using desktop publishing and local copy shop, it is not a part of mass media but the "small press": Remember our definition of *mass media* as not simply the means or technology used to communicate but the total, complex institution that delivers a message to a large audience.

Complexity and size are closely related in mass-media organizations. As size increases, complexity emerges. A large daily newspaper has many separate divisions, among them reporting, editorial, advertising, circulation, promotion, research, personnel, production, and management. We tend to think of a musician or singer as the consummate individual, but the recording industry also demonstrates complexity and other mass-communicator characteristics. An album by a rock group will cite not only performers but producer, recording engineer, mixing engineer, assistant engineers, and master disc engineers. Many groups these days are corporations with diversified holdings. This brings us to our next characteristic.

INDUSTRIALIZATION

Competitiveness, complexity, and size form the base from which several other common mass-communicator features emerge. Industrialization is perhaps the most obvious. Each month, it seems, more mass-communication organizations become parts of large conglomerates. This in itself is nothing new. Just after World War I, for example, there was a revolution in moviemaking as consolidation (of production, distribution, and exhibition in theaters) was introduced. As movies became big business, the advantages of controlling all facets of the industry became obvious. Paramount led the way, and by 1920, a number of powerful movie companies fought for dominance.[1]

The current patterns of ownership and the implications of these for the forms and content of mass communication in the 1990s are detailed in the next chapter and in chapters on individual media. A brief overview here will make the point.

Almost all major film studios are subsidiaries of larger corporations. As this text goes to press, Gulf + Western owns Paramount; Warner Brothers films are a part of Time/Warner; and Columbia Pictures is owned by Sony. Traditionally, motion-picture studios were identified with their production executives—Harry Cohn of Columbia, L. B. Mayer and Irving Thalberg of MGM, Darryl Zanuck of Fox, and Jack Warner of Warner Brothers—or with the major stars in their pictures, who were employees under long-term contract. Today, motion-picture stars not only move easily among studios but often form their own companies, becoming conglomerate communicators in their own right.

Studio production heads have been replaced by bankers, investment counselors, and corporate CEOs. When these entertainment corporations allow for artistic freedom, it is through a carefully negotiated business *partnership* with creative people; these are no longer employees. In 1990, Paramount made a deal with producers Don Simpson and Jerry Bruckheimer (*Top Gun, Beverly Hills Cop, Flashdance*) that was "a benchmark for creative and financial freedom" to allow the pair to "operate autonomously from the studio's normal decisionmaking and oversight process."[2] Everyone involved recognized that delivery of "the goods" of box-office successes was expected of such a departure from the norm.

The "sequel syndrome" so common in the motion-picture industry is a good illustration of economic competition fostering a corporate rhetoric based on repetition of a successful format. Consider the *Rocky* series. Focusing on the numbers alone can have a variety of negative consequences as far as creativity is concerned; originality is replaced by reliance on proven themes. But worldwide audiences and foreign investors are increasingly important factors and both groups more readily comprehend a new product when it is like something they have already seen.

Most daily newspapers are part of large chains, such as Gannett, Newhouse, or Knight-Ridder. As with motion pictures, dominant personalities of print media, such as William Randolph Hearst, Henry Luce, Joseph Pulitzer, and William Allen White, have been replaced by the less well known communicators associated with the major chains and communications empires. To be sure, some editors, such as Ben Bradlee of the *Washington Post*, continue to function as public personalities, but the majority of newspaper editors are less interested in their public image and more concerned about their managerial style and productivity.

Book publishers are typically conglomerates with many different imprints: Random House is part of the Newhouse group, and within Random House are Vintage, Pantheon, Knopf, Ballantine, Villiard, and Times Books. Gulf + Western owns Simon & Schuster, Rupert Murdoch's News Corporation owns Harper & Row, Bantam Doubleday Dell is the merged book-publishing unit owned by international conglomerate Bertelsmann, and Longman is one of the diversified holdings of Pearson plc, based in England.

SPECIALIZATION

Specialization is a mass-communicator characteristic that represents *internal* fragmentation. This fragmentation is perhaps nowhere more apparent than in the motion-picture industry, with many of the jobs in filmmaking subdivided by trade unions. For example, painters may include a foreman, a color mixer, a sign writer, and a marbelizer. The photography department of a daily newspaper may have as many as 20 photographers, each one specializing in a content area.

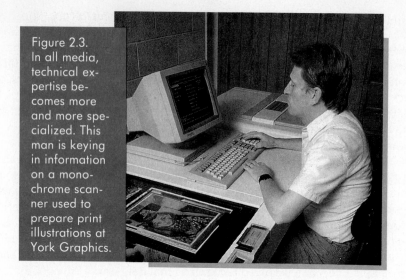

Figure 2.3. In all media, technical expertise becomes more and more specialized. This man is keying in information on a monochrome scanner used to prepare print illustrations at York Graphics.

REPRESENTATION

Representation is basically an *external* fragmentation of the mass communicator. Mass communicators have become so complex and must deal with so many different audiences that they often find it impossible to contact and make arrangements with all the individuals and organizations necessary to a smooth functioning of the organization. Mass-communicator representatives include talent agents, managers, unions, program distributors, broadcast-station representatives, and music-licensing services.

COMMUNICATOR ROLES IN MEDIA ORGANIZATIONS

So that we will be prepared to look more closely at each of the media industries in Part 3, we now turn to the types of specialized roles found in media organizations. We consider three areas covered later—print, broadcast, and motion pictures—and also examine the ways wire services, syndicates, and syndicators function in the communication process. To label these "support systems," as some books do, is not totally inaccurate, but it does misrepresent the integral part they play in both generating and delivering communication.

THE PRINT MEDIA

For years, the "by-line myth" has dominated the concept of print-media communicators. The stereotypes of individual entrepreneurial newspaper reporters created by such movies as *The Front Page* and *All the President's Men* have contributed to this myth. The fact is, a number of people are required to generate a print message.

In the jargon of the newspaper profession, "legmen" are researchers whose main task is to get the facts. They might station themselves at a police headquarters

Figure 2.4. In television news, ongoing communication between the reporter and photographer is essential on every assignment.

and simply telephone leads to the home office. The reporter is usually both researcher and writer. In the magazine or book industry, the researcher is often a fact checker who verifies the authenticity of the work of reporters and writers. Writers play the key creative role in the production of print-media messages, although some magazine and book writers are word technicians who take the ideas of others and dress them in effective language.

The editor—whether specialized as copy editor, assignment editor, or managing editor—is generally more an evaluator of communication, acting as a gatekeeper, than an originator. But all editors are part of the sending process to the extent that they supervise the entire package of communication through imaginative management and evaluation.

The masthead of *Time* indicates the many mass communicators who work on each issue. Much smaller magazines would have a similar division of labor between managers, associate editors, various types of writers, and special editors, often called contributors because they are not on staff but are freelance specialists. One notable difference between the *Time* listing and most other magazines and newspapers is the existence of correspondents. Few publications can afford this depth. We saw that Fred Hirsch and networks alike depend on outside news gatherers.

ORGANIZATIONS THAT CONNECT COMMUNICATORS

Most news media have some sort of network outside of their oganizations and communities through which they gather news, commentary, and entertainment. Some newspapers and radio stations employ homemakers or students as part-time stringers in various neighborhoods. Some have bureaus in state capitals or county seats to report regional-government news. A few large stations and publications

Editor-in-Chief: Jason McManus
Editorial Director: Richard B. Stolley
Corporate Editor: Gilbert Rogin

TIME INC. MAGAZINES
President: Reginald K. Brack Jr.
Executive Vice Presidents: Donald M. Elliman Jr., S. Christopher Meigher III, Robert L. Miller
Senior Vice Presidents: Richard W. Angle Jr., Michael J. Klingensmith

TIME

Founders: Briton Hadden 1898-1929   Henry R. Luce 1898-1967

MANAGING EDITOR: Henry Muller
EXECUTIVE EDITORS: Edward L. Jamieson, Ronald Kriss
ASSISTANT MANAGING EDITORS: Richard Duncan, Karsten Prager, John F. Stacks
SPECIAL PROJECTS EDITOR: Donald Morrison   **EDITOR AT LARGE:** Strobe Talbott
SENIOR EDITORS: Charles P. Alexander, José M. Ferrer III, Russ Hoyle, Walter Isaacson, James Kelly, Stephen Koepp, Johanna McGeary, Christopher Porterfield, George Russell, Thomas A. Sancton, William E. Smith, Claudia Wallis, Jack E. White, Robert T. Zintl
ART DIRECTOR: Rudolph C. Hoglund
GRAPHICS DIRECTOR: Nigel Holmes
CHIEF OF RESEARCH: Betty Satterwhite Sutter
OPERATIONS DIRECTOR: Gérard C. Lelièvre
PICTURE EDITOR: Michele Stephenson
SENIOR WRITERS: David Brand, Margaret Carlson, George J. Church, Richard Corliss, Martha Duffy, Otto Friedrich, Paul Gray, John Greenwald, William A. Henry III, Robert Hughes, Ed Magnuson, Lance Morrow, Bruce W. Nelan, Frederick Painton, Walter Shapiro, R.Z. Sheppard, Frank Trippett
ASSOCIATE EDITORS: William R. Doerner, Nancy R. Gibbs, Marguerite Johnson, Richard Lacayo, Michael D. Lemonick, Richard N. Ostling, Sue Raffety, Ariadna Victoria Rainert, J.D. Reed, Jill Smolowe, Susan Tifft, Anastasia Toufexis, Michael Walsh, Richard Zoglin
STAFF WRITERS: Daniel Benjamin, Lisa Beyer, Janice Castro, Howard G. Chua-Eoan, Philip Elmer-DeWitt, Guy D. Garcia, Christine Gorman, Barbara Rudolph, Michael S. Serrill, Laurence Zuckerman
CONTRIBUTORS: Kurt Andersen, Robert Ball, Jesse Birnbaum, Patricia Blake, Gerald Clarke, Jay Cocks, Ellis Cose, John Elson, Pico Iyer, Leon Jaroff, Stefan Kanfer, Michael Kinsley, Charles Krauthammer, Richard Schickel, John Skow, Richard Stengel, George M. Taber, Andrew Tobias, Denise Worrell
WRITER-REPORTERS: Edward M. Gomez, Alain L. Sanders
REPORTER-RESEARCHERS: Ursula Nadasdy de Gallo, Brigid O'Hara-Forster, Jeanne-Marie North, Jane Van Tassel (Department Heads); Audrey Ball, Bernard Baumohl, David Bjerklie, Rosemary Byrnes, Val Castronovo, Nancy McD. Chase, Oscar Chiang, John E. Gallagher, Lois Gilman, Tam Martinides Gray, Georgia Harbison, Michael P. Harris, Anne Hopkins, JoAnn Lum, Katherine Mihok, Adrianne Jucius Navon, Nancy Newman, Susan M. Reed, Elizabeth Rudulph, Zona Sparks, William Tynan, Sidney Urquhart, Susanne Washburn (Senior Staff); Elizabeth L. Bland, Kathleen Brady, Barbara Burke, Wendy Cole, Tom Curry, Nelida Gonzalez Cutler, Sally B. Donnelly, Andrea Dorfman, David Ellis, Kathryn Jackson Fallon, Mary McC. Fernandez, Cassie T. Furgurson, David M. Gross, Janice M. Horowitz, Jeanette Isaac, Sinting Lai, Daniel S. Levy, Emily Mitchell, Lawrence Mondi, Michael Quinn, Jeffery C. Rubin, Megan Rutherford, Andrea Sachs, Patricia Santella, Sophfronia Scott, David Seideman, David E. Thigpen, Leslie Whitaker, Linda Williams, Linda Young
ADMINISTRATION: Donald Sweet, Alan J. Abrams, Denise Brown, Martha Clark, Helga Halaki, Tosca LaBoy, Katharine K. McNevin, Barbara Milberg, Teresa D. Sedlak, Deborah R. Slater, Rafael Soto
EDITORIAL FINANCE: Eric A. Berk (Manager); Genevieve Christy, Peter Mitchel (Deputies); Patricia Hermes, Camille Sanabria, Linda D. Vartoogian; Wayne Chun, Sheila Greene, Carl Harmon, Gene Isaac, Edward Nana Osei-Bonsu, Esther F. Rodriguez, Katherine Young
CORRESPONDENTS: John F. Stacks (Chief); Barrett Seaman (Deputy); Suzanne Davis (Deputy, Administration) **Special Correspondent:** Michael Kramer **Correspondent at Large:** Bonnie Angelo **Washington Contributing Editor:** Hugh Sidey **Diplomatic Correspondent:** Christopher Ogden
Senior Correspondents: Kenneth W. Banta, Mary Cronin, Hays Gorey, Lee Griggs, William McWhirter, J. Madeleine Nash, Edwin M. Reingold, Alessandra Stanley, Frederick Ungeheuer, Bruce van Voorst, James Wilde
Washington: Stanley W. Cloud, Laurence I. Barrett, David Aikman, Gisela Bolte, Ricardo Chavira, Jerome Cramer, Michael Duffy, Glenn Garelik, Dan Goodgame, Ted Gup, Jerry Hannifin, Richard Hornik, J.F.O. McAllister, Jay Peterzell, Michael Riley, Elaine Shannon, Dick Thompson, Nancy Traver **New York:** Joelle Attinger, Janice C. Simpson, Richard Behar, Eugene Linden, Thomas McCarroll, Naushad S. Mehta, Priscilla Painton, Raji Samghabadi, Martha Smilgis **Boston:** Robert Ajemian, Sam Allis, Melissa Ludtke **Chicago:** Gavin Scott, Barbara Dolan, Elizabeth Taylor **Detroit:** S.C. Gwynne **Atlanta:** Joseph J. Kane, Don Winbush **Houston:** Richard Woodbury **Miami:** James Carney **Los Angeles:** Jordan Bonfante, Jonathan Beaty, Scott Brown, Cristina Garcia, Jeanne McDowell, Sylvester Monroe, James Willwerth **San Francisco:** Paul A. Witteman
London: William Mader, Anne Constable **Paris:** Christopher Redman, Margot Hornblower **Brussels:** Adam Zagorin **Bonn:** James O. Jackson **Rome:** Cathy Booth **Eastern Europe:** John Borrell **Moscow:** John Kohan, Ann Blackman **Jerusalem:** Jon D. Hull **Cairo:** Dean Fischer, William Dowell **Nairobi:** Marguerite Michaels **Johannesburg:** Scott MacLeod **New Delhi:** Edward W. Desmond **Beijing:** Sandra Burton, Jaime A. FlorCruz **Southeast Asia:** William Stewart **Hong Kong:** Jay Branegan **Bangkok:** Ross H. Munro **Seoul:** David S. Jackson **Tokyo:** Barry Hillenbrand, Seiichi Kanise, Kumiko Makihara **Ottawa:** James L. Graff **Central America:** John Moody **Rio de Janeiro:** Laura López
Administration: Susan Lynd, David Richardson, Clementina Allured, Hope Almash, Melissa August, Sharon Boger, Donald N. Collins, Joan A. Connelly, Ann Y. King, Judith R. Stoler **News Desks:** Breena Clarke, Douglas Dale, Brian Doyle, Eileen Harkin, Suzanne W. Marcou, Waits L. May III, Jacalyn McConnell, John F. McDonald, Susanna M. Schrobsdorff, Pamela H. Thompson, Diana Tollerson, Joanne Waugh, Ann Drury Welford, Jean R. White, Mary Wormley
ART: Arthur Hochstein (Deputy Art Director); Linda Louise Freeman (Covers); Steve Conley, Jennifer Napoli, Billy Powers, Irene Ramp, Ina Saltz, John F. White, Barbara Wilhelm (Assistant Directors); Angel Ackemyer, Stefano Arata, James Elsis, Kenneth B. Smith (Designers) **Production:** Paul Dovell (Manager); Carri Marks **Layout:** John P. Dowd (Traffic); Joseph Aslaender, David Drapkin, Victoria Nightingale, Leah M. Purcell, Lisa Sampson, Nomi Silverman, Eugene Tick, Lisa C. Tremaine, Dennis Wheeler **Maps and Charts:** Paul J. Pugliese (Chief); Cynthia Davis, Joe Lertola, E. Noel McCoy, Nino Telak, Deborah L. Wells **Administration:** Carrie A. Zimmerman
PHOTOGRAPHY: Mary Dunn (Deputy Picture Editor); Richard L. Booth, MaryAnne Golon, Rose Keyser, Julia Richer (Assistant Editors); Kevin J. McVea (Traffic); Renee Mancini (Syndication); Arnold H. Drapkin (Consulting Picture Editor) **Researchers:** Dorothy Affa Ames, Martha Bardach, Sarah Buffum, Stanley Kayne, Paula Hornak Kellner, Polly J. Matthews, Gary Roberts, Nancy Smith-Alam, Melanie Stephens, Robert B. Stevens, Eleanor Taylor **Photographers:** Terry Ashe, P.F. Bentley, William Campbell, Rudi Frey, Dirck Halstead, Cynthia Johnson, Peter Jordan, Shelly Katz, David Hume Kennerly, Neil Leifer, Steve Liss, Robin Moyer, Carl Mydans, James Nachtwey, Matthew Naythons, Chris Niedenthal, David Rubinger, Antonio Suarez, Ted Thai, Diana Walker
MAKEUP: Charlotte J. Quiggle (Chief); Eugene F. Coyle (International); Leonard Schulman
TECHNOLOGY: Eileen Bradley (Manager); Alejandro Arce, Kevin Kelly, Michael M. Sheehan, Lamarr Tsufura
COPY DESK: Susan L. Blair (Copy Chief); Judith Anne Paul, Shirley Barden Zimmerman (Deputies); Minda Bikman, Robert Braine, Bruce Christopher Carr, Barbara Collier, Barbara Dudley Davis, Julia Van Buren Dickey, Dora Fairchild, Evelyn Hannon, Judith Kales, Sharon Kapnick, Claire Knopf, Gyavira Lasana, Melinda J. McAdams, Anna F. Monardo, Maria A. Paul, Elyse Segelken, Terry Stoller, Jill Ward, Amelia Weiss
PRODUCTION: Gail Music (Manager); Stephen F. Demeter (Systems Manager); Joseph J. Scafidi (Deputy); Trang Ba Chuong, Theresa Kelliher, Peter N. Niceberg, L. Rufino-Armstrong, Lee R. Sparks (Supervisors); Robert L. Becker, Silvia Castañeda Contreras, Osmar Escalona, Gerry Hearne, Nora Jupiter, Agustin Lamboy, Jeannine Laverty, Marcia L. Love, Janet L. Lugo, Peter J. McGullam, Sandra Maupin, Helen May, Michael Skinner **Graphics Production:** Kenneth Collura, Linda Parker, Lois Rubenstein, Simon Tack
LETTERS: Amy Musher (Chief); Gloria J. Hammond (Deputy); Marian Powers (Administration)
EDITORIAL SERVICES: Christiana Walford (Director); Peter J. Christopoulos, Benjamin Lightman, David E. Trevorrow, Beth Bencini Zarcone

WORLDWIDE PUBLISHER: Robert L. Miller
U.S. PUBLISHER: Louis A. Weil III
Associate Publisher, Advertising Sales Director: Richard Heinemann
Advertising Sales Manager: Stephen J. Seabolt
Associate Advertising Sales Manager: William J. Yonan
General Manager: Barbara M. Mrkonic
Consumer Marketing Director: Ellen J. Fairbanks
Production Director: Martin J. Gardner
Business Manager: Susan F. Sachs
Marketing Services Director: Cleary S. Simpson
Advertising Production Director: Pamela Older

Figure 2.5.
Many individuals, not simply the byline writers, collaborate on the content of an issue of *Time*.

have bureaus in New York, Washington, and one or two other major cities, primarily to report business and financial news, and legislative developments. Only a few can afford the $250,000 a year it costs to maintain a correspondent-at-large or one based abroad. Most newspapers and broadcasters *process* news rather than collect it themselves.

Wire services and syndicates are two types of media organizations that supply news, features, columnists, illustrations, and various services to print, broadcast, and cable media. They may originate content and then represent its creators, but they do not communicate directly to the ultimate audiences. Nevertheless, they display all of the characteristics of the mass communicator.

Wire Services. Independent news services are used widely for the most efficient gathering of general news. The largest American service is the Associated Press (AP), a cooperative that sends news and features to more than 15,000 media outlets around the world, for a total audience of approximately 1 billion. Serving 87.7 percent of daily U.S. papers, representing 98.7 percent of total newspaper circulation, it employs over 3,000 people, including 500 in communications technology alone. AP has 308 news and photo bureaus around the world to serve 112 countries; it provides its own translations in six languages.

AP was founded in 1848 by an association of newspapers in New York City to save on costs of gathering incoming stories from Europe. United Press International (UPI) is an amalgam of the former Hearst International News Service, begun in 1909, and the Scripps-Howard United Press, started in 1908. It was acquired in 1988 by Infotechnology Inc. of New York—which includes Financial News Network. (UPI's new parent company plans to market a variety of types of information such as Securities and Exchange Commission filings, excerpts from trade and professional journals and newsletters, and financial data, and distribute them via its Data Broadcasting Corp.) News services thus target businesses, associations, and government agencies that want increasingly specific kinds of news.

These services transmit about 10 million words a day, thousands of pictures, and hundreds of special broadcast reports. The idea for a 24-hour news channel on TV, CNN, had its origins in the automated continuous service provided by AP, UPI, and others to cable operators for 15 years or so.

News services today are the world's primary news brokers, providing the vast bulk of national, international, and regional news for most media. About 75 percent of the news that most Americans read and hear is provided by the Associated Press and United Press International. In addition, many countries and regions have their own news agencies. For example, the Pan African News Agency (PANA) serves the news media in many African countries. But besides AP and UPI, only three other news agencies have worldwide impact: in England, Reuters; in France, Agence France-Presse; and in the Soviet Union, TASS.

News services provide a variety of coverage, such as a national wire, a regional or state wire, a local wire, business news, or a special radio wire written for broadcast. With the addition of computer technology, they are now capable of providing essentially custom-designed news packages for their media customers. For example, a subscribing television station can decide in advance about how much international news, national news, features, sports news, and business-financial news it would like, and the wire service provides stories consistent with that request. The news services charge their subscribers a negotiated fee based on circulation or station size. A small newspaper of 25,000 circulation may pay as little as $100 to $200 a week, while a large metropolitan daily might be charged as much as $6,000 a week.

Both AP and UPI are staffed by seasoned reporters who work out of bureaus that are organized much like the staffs of daily newspapers, with their own re-searchers, reporters, copyreaders, and editors. Almost every state capital, all major cities, and most foreign capitals have news-service bureaus, and their reporters and correspondents travel into remote and often dangerous areas to collect and interpret the news that is ultimately processed into our living rooms.

In addition to relying on their own reporters to cover stories, wire services also expect their subscribers to provide story coverage if news breaks in their area. For example, when a United Airlines plane crashed in Sioux City, Iowa, in the summer of 1989, initial wire-service accounts relied on newspaper and broadcast reporters from the Sioux City area until they could dispatch their own staff members to the scene.

In addition to AP and UPI, there are a number of smaller supplementary wire services run by larger newspapers or newspaper chains seeking to distribute more widely—and of course to profit from the efforts of their own reporting staffs. Examples are the New York Times News Service, the Christian Science Monitor News Services, Newhouse News Service, and Gannett News Service, among others.

Figure 2.6. Wire services pioneered with delivery of news from the field and front line. A journalist on the northern Gaza Strip takes careful notes of military orders restricting the press on a tour of refugee camps.

Finally, a number of companies whose businesses may be largely outside of the news media provide specialized news services, providing information within their area of operation. These include such organizations as the National Oceanographic and Atmospheric Administration (NOAA), which provides weather information, and Dow Jones, Inc., which provides a variety of packages of stock-market information and financial-business news.

Syndicates. As news services provide for the centralized gathering and distribution of news and information, so syndicates serve as agencies for the analysis and interpretation functions of the media, as well as providing a range of entertainment features and conveniences such as digests of news, graphics as background to news, and cartoons. More than 400 agencies, now basically a larger and more sophisticated version of the type of operation begun in the mid-nineteenth century, hire writers, illustrators, and commentators, and market their work to individual newspapers. Like wire services, they charge on the basis of circulation or size. A popular and widely syndicated columnist like political humorist Art Buchwald can earn well over $250,000 a year through syndication.

The annual Directory of Syndicated Services, published by *Editor and Publisher*, lists more than 2,500 features available from syndicates. Although the best-known staples of syndication are cartoons and columns, the categories of available material include advice, astrology, automotive, beauty, comics, commentary, computers, education, entertainment, etiquette, family, fashion, food, games, gossip, health, hobbies, humor, legal affairs, outdoors, photography, puzzles, religion, sports, and travel. Unless an individual column or cartoon contains the name or logo of the syndicate, newspaper readers are generally unaware of the role played by syndicates. Syndicated communicators are featured on the next pages.

Universal Press Syndicate, for example, offers 11 comic strips, including "Doonesbury" and "Calvin and Hobbes"; 7 comic panels, including "The Far Side" and "Herman"; 6 editorial cartoons, including Jules Feiffer and Pat Oliphant; 11 editorial columnists, including William F. Buckley, Jr., Jeff Greenfield, and Gary Wills; and a wide range of advice, lifestyle, and entertainment columns, including "Dear Abby," Erma Bombeck, Jeane Dixon, and Roger Ebert.

United Media, formed in 1978 when E. W. Scripps Co. consolidated United Feature Syndicate and Newspaper Enterprise Association, has a well-documented history of a century of mergers and acquisitions, and diversified service. Currently offering over 150 different features as well as news digests and regional television listings, it has a past that includes famous correspondent Ernie Pyle, serializations of literature, and the development of a young cartoonist in the 1940s: UFS changed Charles Schulz's strip "Li'l Folks" into "Peanuts," now in more than 2,200 papers and itself a multimedia industry.

THE BROADCAST MEDIA

The radio and TV industries have three basic groups of communicators: *networks*, *independent production companies*, and *local stations*. Within each group are individual communicators who perform a variety of tasks.

Networks. Networks are organizations that provide TV programming, radio news, and special information services. While ABC, CBS, and NBC readily come to mind, there are other significant players, such as Fox, which has been pressuring

Syndicates package, represent, promote, and distribute a diversity of communications that reach us via national and local print and broadcast media. They are also effective communicators *to* the media. Look at this page from *The Primary Source,* a booklet listing United Media features and services. These include not only individual columnists and cartoonists but the supply of eye-catching graphic displays of newsworthy statistics, maps, TV listings, and seasonal special features such as holiday menus.

GARFIELD®
by Jim Davis
He's a legend in just 11 years. *Garfield* joyfully embodies the pleasures of eating and sleeping. He's a fat cat in more than 2,100 newspapers, in best-selling books and in award-winning TV specials.

NANCY®
by Jerry Scott
This sharp little girl is (can you believe it?) 50 in 1990. Nancy has changed with the times. Although she's still wearing the same dress, she's updated her humor and ideas to fit into the '90s and beyond.

MARMADUKE®
by Brad Anderson
Marmaduke became the world's favorite Great Dane by simply being himself—a big, affectionate dog. He behaves like a real dog—no talk, just action.

COUNTER CULTURE™
by Maratta and Maratta
If you think appliances have no feelings, you haven't read this popular new panel. Next time your toaster burns your toast or your TV gives you a blank stare, pay attention. They're telling you something.

OFF THE LEASH®
by W.B. Park
From pompous porcupines to macho roosters, the off-the-wall animals in this daily panel will remind you of people you know.

JUMP START™
by Robb Armstrong
Joe and Marcy are an average, young, hard-working couple, which makes them easy to identify with and fun to follow. He's a cop, she's a nurse and they hope their hectic schedules will give them enough time to see each other.

ASK SHAGG®
by Peter Guren
Shagg E. Dawg answers kids' questions on all aspects of the animal kingdom. Facts and humor combine in Shagg's enlightening and entertaining comic.

DILBERT™
by Scott Adams
Dilbert's a nerd and Dogbert's his snide little dog and advisor. This new comic strip captures both the nagging insecurities and unjustified confidence we all have. Even you.

Via Tribune Media Services comes award-winning creativity. Andy Rooney has won the Writers Guild Award for Best Script of the Year six times. Especially known for his TV essay, which became a regular feature on "60 Minutes" in 1978 and won him three Emmys, he has written, produced, and narrated a series of 1-hour broadcasts on various aspects of American life (which led to a Peabody Award). He also wrote the script for the first Telstar transatlantic satellite broadcast, carried on all three networks and translated into 11 languages. A career reaching deep into radio, books, magazines, and war correspondence includes a syndicated column distributed to more than 300 newspapers by TMS.

Political cartoonist Mike Peters, winner of the 1981 Pulitzer Prize and Sigma Delta Chi Distinguished Service Award, needs little introduction to anyone who reads a daily newspaper or weekly newsmagazine, or watches television. After graduation from Washington University, Peters began to pursue his childhood dream of a career as a political cartoonist by joining the art staff of the *Chicago Daily News*. Later, while with the *Dayton* (Ohio) *Daily News*, he saw his cartoons syndicated; three books followed. His work has been featured frequently in such publications as *Newsweek, Time,* and *U.S. News & World Report,* and on local and national television. Peters was the first editorial cartoonist to author a network broadcast; the long-running animated editorial cartoon "Peters' Postscripts" appeared three times a week on NBC's "Nightly News." His daily cartoon strip, "Mother Goose and Grimm," satirizes not only *the* fairy-tale figure of all time but, more significantly, us and the world we live in.

the Federal Communications Commission to relax its definition of a network as an entity that broadcasts 15 hours of programs a week on at least 25 stations in at least 10 states. Typically, networks enter into contracts with local television and radio stations throughout the country that are known as network *affiliates*. The contract essentially provides that the station agrees to carry the bulk (but not necessarily all) of the programming the network originates in exchange for compensation by the network to cover use of affiliate facilities and right to air network commercials; the figure is largely determined by the station's rate card (based on viewership) and the composition of the station's audience.

Television network-affiliation contracts are generally "exclusive" to a market. There are some exceptions in smaller markets with fewer than three commercial stations, where one TV or radio station may be affiliated with two or more networks.

Despite increasing success in recent years by independent (non-network-affiliated) stations in many of the country's larger television markets, in most cases commercial stations would rather be network affiliates. As affiliates, they receive first-run national programming that has been heavily promoted and advertised by

Figure 2.7. NBC's "Cheers," after a shaky start, grew to be a top-rated, almost cult show. Original cast members Ted Danson and Shelley Long are seen by millions of new and old fans in syndicated reruns.

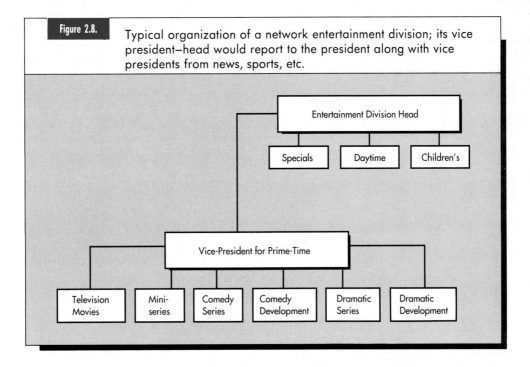

Figure 2.8. Typical organization of a network entertainment division; its vice president–head would report to the president along with vice presidents from news, sports, etc.

the network, and they receive regularly scheduled and on-the-spot news programming from the network's large news department.

On network television, the idea for a prime-time program or a program series can, and often does, originate outside the network, with a program-production company. By the time most programs or series are broadcast, however, they have come in contact with and have been influenced by many network people, all the way from stagehand to chief executive. Figure 2.7 charts the lines of responsibility for programming (maintaining current series and developing new ones, as well as other main segments of activity). The actual chain of power varies; for example, when he was chief executive officer of Capital Cities/ABC, Thomas Murphy was personally involved in picking programs and their time slots.

Production Companies. TV networks have concentrated on producing news, sports, and documentaries. Almost 90 percent of all TV network prime-time entertainment programs come from studios and program-production companies working in conjunction with *network* programmers. The team of creators engaged by a production company does everything short of broadcasting the program. Some production companies produce a pilot program, either independently or after consulting with a network programming department, and then attempt to sell a series to a network on the basis of the pilot. A more common practice is to produce a feature-film pilot, with financial and creative support provided by the network on which the series is expected to appear. (In Part 3 we will look in detail at major film studios as TV producers.)

As the telecommunication delivery system has expanded into cable, video-cassette, and satellite transmission, the number of video communicators has increased. Despite changes in the way content is *delivered* to audiences, the process of production is similar for all programs. In their book *Primetime: Network Television*

Programming, Richard Blum and Richard Lindheim describe why television is considered largely a producer's medium:

> *Consistency, story flow, pacing, production quality, and overall success are dependent on his or her creative ability and supervisory skills. To accomplish these seemingly impossible tasks, a producer relies heavily on an experienced production unit that can deliver under pressure. To be a producer, you must get along with network and studio executives, agents, writers, story editors, directors, casting directors, actors, composers, conductors, editors, and the entire production crew.*[3]

The breadth of creative input and technical capability needed by a production company lead to enormous start-up costs. Most series run in the red, and so subsidiary use of programming is something every producer hopes for. These revenues are generated by syndicators.

Television Syndicators. Television program syndicators (not to be confused with the syndicates that supply news and features to print and broadcast media) are also broadcast communicators. These are companies that produce or obtain television programs and then sell them to local stations on an exclusive-market basis. (If the local station is affiliated with a network, it generally seeks to obtain syndicated programs for those times of day, mainly in the late afternoon, when its network does not provide programs.)

Syndicators obtain their programs from three primary sources: production companies (usually for programs that have already run on a network), film companies (usually for packages of movies that ran in theaters previously), or themselves. This last approach would make them "active senders."

Syndicators are passive senders to the extent that they take off-network programs or feature motion pictures and sell airing rights to them to individual stations in a package. They do not create programs but simply distribute them. Syndicated distribution is done by both satellite and mail through a system known in the industry as "bicycling" in which each station, after airing a particular episode, sends it to the next customer.

Stations in individual markets generally bid against each other to land a contract for a popular syndicated program. A feeding frenzy greeted the first off-network syndication of "The Cosby Show," bringing Viacom Enterprises approximately $700 million. But its client stations exhibited the independence that makes mass communications so complex a business when they rejected a package deal consisting of Cosby and its spin-off sitcom, "A Different World."[4] (Communicators thus deliver feedback to other communicators.) Stations pay for the programs they select by cash or through a "barter" agreement in which the syndicator, in exchange for charging the station less (or nothing), will sell and insert a number of commercials into the available commercial "windows" in the program.

The rapid growth of independent stations in the past few years and a general eagerness to purchase additional strong entertainment in the "access hour" leading into prime time have created unprecedented demand for program content among the 700 stations in the 210 Nielsen markets. The number of program senders is expected to taper off somewhat, but together they spend about $2 billion annually for programming; this figure will continue to increase, and syndicators will continue to be a major factor. More and more affiliates are being attracted away from network programming by a higher-rated syndicated show.

King World Productions has been a noteworthy success. In its fifth year, 1988, it ranked third, with sales of $368 million, just behind Warner and MCA and in

Figure 2.9. "Wheel of Fortune" is a global hit. Hosts Pat Sajak and Vanna White are clearly pleased, as are the network, the syndicators, and the armchair players from Toledo to Tokyo.

front of Paramount, Viacom, Columbia, and Fox. Profits for 1990 were estimated at over $80 million, making it the nation's leading syndicator. Around 90 million people watch its three main offerings—"Wheel of Fortune" (which started out earning no more than $50 a day in license fees), "Jeopardy," and "The Oprah Winfrey Show." Winfrey's own production company went with Roger and Michael King because they are more than distributors; they test-marketed talk-show topics, carefully promoted Oprah Winfrey, and demonstrated her appeal. King World's instincts and staff of researchers led to the development of their first original product, "Inside Edition," which quickly became the leading TV newsmagazine.

Local Stations. A local TV station generally employs its own staff to produce local programs. Staff sizes range from over 100 at major-market stations to fewer than 20 at smaller organizations. Their organizational structures are described in Chapter 10. A large radio station may have around 50 employees; even such stations rely on outside sources for most of their program material. At the local level, radio stations depend on three outside creators for the bulk of their content: (1) the recording industry; (2) jingle-package companies, which produce such items as station-break announcements, weather spots, and station identifications; and (3) format syndicators, which package and distribute specific music and news-information formats. In dealing with syndicates, local stations may use a "representation firm."

The need to reach the right audience and attract the maximum number of listeners has led to extensive program-formula design in local radio. For a number of years, "Top-40" was one of the few formats for local radio; today over 50 major formats exist. Syndicators assist stations during the installation and implementation stage of a format and train operators and other station personnel. Comprehensive operations manuals are provided to ensure proper format procedures, and support includes newsletters and hotlines (see the box in Chapter 11). Such services add additional complexity and structure to the local station.

One of the most significant local-station communicators in radio is the program director (PD). PDs supervise and, in effect, regulate all aspects of a station's programming, including those supplied by syndicators and packagers. Songs, for example, must fit the format, and the quality of the artistry and the audio mix must meet certain criteria. A substandard musical arrangement or a disc with poor fidelity detracts from the station's sound (it provides the wrong kind of noise). The PD helps maintain consistency. Erratic programming in today's highly competitive marketplace is tantamount to directing listeners to other stations.

Despite the increasing influence of format syndicators, radio still retains some attributes of a personal medium through the presence of the news announcer and the disc jockey, the bulwarks of local-radio programming. A good announcer sets the pace—he is the spirit of a radio station. If music is the keynote of the format, the disc jockey represents a harmonizing influence that blends the material supplied by other creative people. Often, her individuality is a major force in the station's popularity. Like the music, the role of the air personality is carefully designed. It is important today, with increased fragmentation and simliar play lists on competing stations.

Each announcer must develop a rapport with the audience. She or he must sound like a "real person," must speak the language of the listener. The day of the contrived hype announcer has passed. Effective communicators on talk radio and the best of the disc jockeys possess an understanding of their audiences and the audience's lifestyle. Their overriding message to the listener must be "I'm one of you."

MOTION PICTURES

The communicator in motion pictures assumes many of the characteristics and performs many of the functions of the broadcaster. The amount of TV production done by motion-picture studios contributes to the similarity of roles. A key difference lies in the fact that although theaters serve as local exhibition outlets for film production, they are primarily passive outlets as contrasted with the more active involvement of networks and independents in production for television.

Motion pictures have grown enormously in terms of production complexity. In the early twentieth century, production involved few people. Often one man— a Chaplin, a Keaton, or a Lloyd—conceived an idea, wrote the script, directed the film, and played the leading role. Only a camera operator and a few extras were needed. The emergence of studios (in the 1920s) changed this pattern, with someone like Woody Allen a notable exception. Huge organizations were built to produce an assembly-line product.

Major motion pictures such as *Batman* (1989) illustrate that American films are still the product of many people working together. The real change in motion pictures in recent years has been the de-emphasis of the studio and the elimination of many elements of general studio overhead that at times cluttered and overburdened a film. However, there is a "downside" to the decline of the studio system. Critics today speak of the new vulnerability of motion-picture directors. They have to find their crew and then train it to their ways, whereas in the past the best studio directors, such as Anthony Mann or Vincent Minnelli, had the advantage of a unit in which there were only occasional changes of personnel. They also had the studio's paternal administration, the cafeteria, the pensions,

Figure 2.10. Richard Attenborough in the key directorial role, on location filming *Gandhi* with Ben Kingsley (right).

and the producers. They did not struggle with the script, audition actresses, and fight over casting. They did not argue for time and money, negotiate with every actor over terms, or handle anxious calls from investors. Those tasks fell to the producer, whom the director was able to despise, resent, and blame if need be. Today's directors, more often than it might seem, do much of the work of producers. Since every film is set up as a one-time deal and most films involve directors far earlier than was the case in the studio era, directors today have to be negotiators, businessmen, and managers.

Each of the major and minor communicators has a separate task, with the producer an organizer who creates a structure in which all the communicators can work effectively. The screenwriter produces a working film script. The film editor reviews the raw footage from the director and assembles the film into a meaningful form. The director has overall artistic control of the film's actual production and is often the one person most closely identified with the total product in the eyes of peers and public.

Motion-picture credits are becoming more complicated each year. *Star Trek II: The Wrath of Khan*, for example, credited Marc Okrand for "Vulcan translation" and Thaine Morris for "pyrotechnics"; *Creepshow* has "roach wranglers" to handle its 25,000 cockroaches. Some Hollywood movies now have technical staffs six or eight times as large as their casts. *Raiders of the Lost Ark* cited 232 technicians, with such esoteric specialties as computer engineering and electronic-system design. The credit lists have lengthened largely because of the sophisticated special-effects movies that have poured out since *Star Wars*. No longer is it enough to have a gaffer (the head electrician), a best boy (the gaffer's right hand), and a number of grips (the equivalent of stagehands). New categories such as synthevision technology, computer-image choreography, and object digitizing are evidence of the computer-generated imagery that is increasingly a part of moviemaking.

THE INDIVIDUAL IN MASS COMMUNICATION ....

Given the enormous industrial complexity of today's mass media, the mass communicator has difficulty being an individualist. Nevertheless, complexity and size do not negate the contributions of the many specialists who make up the conglomerate communicator. We can never overlook the power of personality. When talk-show host Oprah Winfrey revealed how she achieved a much-televised shedding of 70 pounds, the manufacturer of the diet aid she mentioned received 200,000 phone inquiries immediately following the broadcast. When an actress writes about her experiences as an abused child, fellow sufferers in the audience find help and inspiration. And in many other ways, those we hear, see, and read about influence us, subtly or dramatically.

Furthermore, a communications organization is not some sort of infernal machine that runs itself. It is run by individuals who are vital parts of the communication process at *all* levels. At times, the human dimension of even something as vast and complex as network television rears its individualistic head, often in humorous ways. For example, in February 1979, during the showing of the NBC miniseries "Loose Change," a technician at the network inadvertently switched episodes, substituting Part 3 for Part 2. For 17 minutes, a national audience watched with puzzled expressions a drama that was out of sync with its internal reality.

Essential attributes of individual mass communicators are the abilities to think, to see things accurately, to organize their thoughts quickly, and to express themselves effectively. Mass communicators have to be curious about the world and the people in it. Communicators are called on to make judgments, sometimes of vast importance, and they should be able to distinguish the significant from the insignificant, the true from the false. Mass communicators need to have a broad view of the world, but increasingly they must specialize in the communication field. Finally, they must know *how* to communicate. In mass communication, this seemingly simple act becomes exceedingly complex, requiring many kinds of talents, abilities, and specialties. Above all, the sender must understand and respect the medium in which he works.

In his book *The Information Machines: Their Impact on Men and the Media*, Ben Bagdikian writes about "printed and broadcast news as a corporate enterprise."[5] He says that news is both an intellectual artifact and the product of a bureaucracy. Distinguished journalism, he writes, requires strong individual leadership; yet such journalism is often at odds with the demands of corporate efficiency. In a similar vein, Edward Jay Epstein notes in his excellent study *News from Nowhere: Television and the News*, "Before network news can be properly analyzed as a journalistic enterprise, it is necessary to understand the business enterprise that it is an active part of, and the logic that proceeds from it."[6] Both men point to the basic condition of the mass communicator: the ability and need of the individual to function as part of a complex environment, an environment that is competitive, specialized, usually very large, and very often industrialized.

There is both good and bad in the system, but our corporate media enterprises have produced more information and entertainment than any simple, individual, altruistic effort could have achieved. Since one cannot comprehend mass media's communicators without seeing the individual as part of a much larger organism, we now use a wider lens and see how the structure of modern media economics affects the messages we receive.

SUMMARY

The process of communication starts with the communicator. In interpersonal communication, however, mass communicators differ significantly from individual communicators. Mass communicators are characterized by (1) competitiveness; (2) size and complexity; (3) industrialization; (4) specialization, and (5) representation. The impact of these characteristics on mass communicators and, in turn, on mass-communication content, is significant. Mass communication messages are rarely the result of one individual. Media messages are essentially products of a complex communication system, manipulated and massaged by many people. As a result, the rhetoric of mass media is a corporate rhetoric, one shaped by economic competition.

Many people assume that because one person's name precedes or follows a particular article or story, that person alone is responsible for the content. However, print communicators work within large organized, specialized, competitive, and highly expensive environments. Communicators of print messages include researchers and reporters, writers, editors, managers, and a wide variety of syndicated content services.

Wire services and syndicates are two types of media organizations that supply news and other services to print, broadcast, and cable media. They originate material or represent the material's creators, but they do not communicate directly with the ultimate audiences. News services like AP and UPI provide national, international, and regional news to most media. Syndicates serve the same function, except that they distribute entertainment features, graphics, and cartoons.

Each medium has a variety of communicator types. In broadcasting, there are three basic groups: (1) networks; (2) independent production companies; and (3) local stations. In television, the networks are the primary communicators, with local stations assuming a somewhat secondary role. In radio, local stations are the dominant communicators, backed up by the recording industry, jingle-package companies, and format syndicators.

The communicator in motion pictures assumes many of the characteristics and performs many of the functions of the broadcaster, but his or her role is not as complex as that of the broadcast communicator because of the absence of such elements as networks and thousands of individual stations. Motion pictures have grown enormously in terms of production complexity and employ hundreds of people to produce feature motion pictures.

The recording industry also demonstrates many mass-communicator characteristics. On one album alone, in addition to the artists, there are producers, recording engineers, mixing engineers, assistant engineers, and a variety of artistic and technical communicators.

Given the enormous industrial complexity of today's mass media, the mass communicator has difficulty being an individualist. However, complexity and size do not diminish the contributions of the many specialists who make up the conglomerate communicator. Individuals still operate the mass-communication system, and it is important for mass communicators to possess a variety of critical personal and professional attributes in order to succeed.

Ultimately, the mass communicator is a combination of individual and corporate influence and impact. It is important for us to recognize the nature of that communicator and the impact that the mass communicator has on content.

1. Robert C. Toll, *The Entertainment Machine: American Show Business in the Twentieth Century* (New York: Oxford University Press, 1982), 29.
2. Richard W. Stevenson, "Two Producers' Unusual Deal at Paramount," *New York Times*, February 1, 1990, D19.
3. Richard A. Blum and Richard D. Lindheim, *Primetime: Network Television Programming* (Boston: Focal Press, 1987), 22.
4. Steve Brennan, " 'Cosby' Syndication Deal Unpopular," *Boston Globe*, November 24, 1989, 120.
5. Ben H. Bagdikian, *The Information Machines: Their Impact on Men and the Media* (New York: Harper & Row, 1971), 41.
6. Edward Jay Epstein, *News from Nowhere: Television and the News* (New York: Random House, 1973), 216.

The Impact of Media Economics

In profiling the types of mass-media communicators, we have seen that even the more complex of them are part of a still larger system. This chapter focuses on the bigger picture created by the convergence of changes in economic structure, consumption habits, and the new technology. Along with choice of medium and format, these forces control the origination, shape, and delivery of the message.

Mass-media communication is more than large, complex, and specialized; it represents a significant factor in the national economy. The production, distribution, and presentation of radio, over-the-air and cable television, motion pictures, newspapers, books, recorded music, and magazines require great expense and frequently generate enormous profits. We frequently hear critics complain about monopoly newspapers making too much money and holding too much sway in community public opinion. Each year independent filmmakers accuse Hollywood of having all the resources and dominating the movie theater screens in the United States (and recently owning them as well). The budget cutbacks at CBS and NBC News that occurred during the mid-1980s and the introduction of magazine shows such as "A Current Affair" and "Hard Copy" reminded us of the economic constraints inherent in traditional news reporting and presentation.

Among mass communicators there *are* alternatives to these vast enterprises with eyes trained on the bottom line. But in the end, while nonprofit media outlets play an important role in the mass communication in our pluralistic society, they account for little in terms of dollars generated and as economic institutions are dwarfed by their profit-seeking cousins. No analysis of the mass-communication process can be complete unless one addresses questions of financial influence.

THE ECONOMIC PERSPECTIVE

To understand the workings of a media business or collection of related businesses (an industry), to broaden our analysis of the communicator characteristics of size, complexity, and industrialization, we will use three benchmarks: *structure, conduct, and performance.* First, though, we recognize that any media business operates in response to prices and quantities generated by the interplay of *supply and demand.*

Consultant and authority on content for this chapter is Douglas Gomery.

Figure 3.1. Increasing media attention is given to other media because they are big business.

THE POWER OF CONSUMER DECISION MAKING

The whole economic structure of mass communication is rooted in, and best explained as, the audience's purchases of media goods and services influenced by supply and demand. (Simply put, media goods are physical things like TV sets, copies of books, and media services are the content or activities that supplement or supply goods, such as radio programs or magazine articles.)

Consumer demand is the desire to use and the ability to pay for goods and services. *Producer supply* refers to the quantity of goods available for purchase at a particular time and at an attractive price. Media people, like any other businesspeople, seek to supply the demand at the most economically rewarding level for themselves (and sometimes for consumers). Newspapers, magazines, TV broadcasters, and all the other media industries that consistently misread the media marketplace are headed for economic disaster and oblivion.

Record companies, the film industry (with the exception of films made expressly for television), pay-cable-TV services, and book publishers derive practically all their revenue from audiences. The audiences bear the full brunt of the cost of producing these goods and services; other media are wholly or partly supported by advertising. But even then advertisers are attracted on the basis of audience pull. It becomes clear why audience behavior is intensively researched.

Individual decisions to spend money and time on the media are significant because those decisions determine whether a medium will succeed or fail. The audience is made up of consumers who have three basic levels of purchasing power in regard to media consumption:

1. The consumer can choose between media and nonmedia goods and services.

Figure 3.2. Competitors among and within media industries constantly battle for the consideration that precedes consumption.

A family can spend its money on a new living-room sofa, a week's vacation, or a media product.

2. The consumer can choose among various media. The family that decides to spend its money on a media product must determine whether it wants $2,000 worth of books, a stereo system, or a large-screen TV. The person with a free evening can select among going to a film at a multiplex theater, listening to CDs, a stack of magazines by the armchair, and much more.

3. Once the decision is made to purchase a stereo system, for example, the family must then choose among competing brands. For an evening out, the choice may be selecting one of the 10 films at the neighborhood theater.

Rapid turnover is one of the major factors making media businesses viable economic enterprises. Paperback books and magazines are bought and discarded almost as readily as the daily newspaper. Close to 40 percent of a TV network's prime-time programming is changed yearly. The willingness of audiences to spend money and time on short-term media goods and services is one indication of the value they place on them.

THE RELATIONSHIP OF STRUCTURE, CONDUCT, AND PERFORMANCE

Into our economic matrix, then, go two assumptions. We have seen that as users of the media, we seek to maximize our satisfaction, given our available discretionary income. Although the supply increases dramatically and daily, our demand for it is tempered by costs and other demands on our time. At least equal in importance is the fact that media businesses attempt to maximize their long-run profits. In the annual report issued in the year Gulf + Western became known as Paramount Communications Inc. (1989), Martin S. Davis, the chairman and CEO of the diversified entertainment-publishing-finance company, said:

> *Continuing progress in building assets and shareholder values remains our mission, whatever the economic environment portends. Our restructuring since the beginning of 1983 established a framework for our earnings uptrend and parallel rewards for long-term investors. Shareholders who owned our common stock over the five-year period through October 31, 1988, earned a 239% return on their investment (the increase in our stock price plus cash dividends paid). By contrast, the Standard & Poor's Composite Index of 500 Stocks showed a return of 96% over the same period.*[1]

He also pointed out that many of the firm's assets cannot be translated into the usual financial statement terms; they include creativity and capabilities in marketing. Likewise, cable operators do not select programming entirely on the basis of greatest commercial draw but include service and children's offerings. The overriding concern is, however, financial viability and responding to demand.

The structure, conduct, and performance model seeks to answer basic questions about how industries operate and how the business side of media affects both communicators and audiences:

1. The model asks us to analyze the basic *structure* of a set of profit-maximizing firms: Who are they? How big are they? Do some dominate?

2. The structure directly influences the corporation's *conduct* or behavior: How do firms set prices? How do they decide to distribute what they sell?

3. Structure and conduct, in turn, dictate the *performance* of that industry: Are services distributed fairly? How is access determined? At the level of performance, governmental intervention may be used to change conduct or restructure the industry. Economic analysis can help us make more informed choices of appropriate government action and assess the range of possible consequences.

This simple yet powerful framework organizes the large subject of media economics. Case studies from the television (over-the-air and cable), book, magazine, motion-picture, recording, newspaper, and radio industries will make the fundamental principles concrete.

ECONOMIC STRUCTURE

We begin by asking What are the major companies, and who owns them? We might find a single company, such as one newspaper, dominating a specific industry in a city—and that constitutes a *monopoly*. More likely, the industry is dominated by a few companies, or what is known as an *oligopoly*. Familiar examples can be found in the several commercial-television networks or in the seven major movie studios. Rarely are there no dominant players; if that were the situation, a *fully competitive* arena would be possible. An example of this might be the one hundred-plus radio stations available in New York City or Los Angeles. The media industries in the United States tend to be oligopolies, and thus, as can be seen in the boxed chart, prepared by *Channel* magazine, it is fairly easy to identify the most important players in the media business.

But what of the *dynamics* of industrial structure—the rise of new competitors; the effects of owning the means of production, distribution, and presentation (known as *vertical integration*); and the consequences of owning major operations in various media (known as media *conglomerate ownership*)?

CASE STUDY: THE RISE OF RUPERT MURDOCH

The interplay of these factors can be appreciated by looking at one of the most important changes in media ownership that has taken place in the United States in recent years: Australian-born Rupert Murdoch's creation of a U.S. media empire. Through his News Corporation, Ltd., Murdoch has made his mark in this country's newspaper, magazine, movie, home-video, cable-television, and over-the-air-television businesses, and through conglomerate ownership and vertical integration, fashioned a true media powerhouse. Still, it is important to remember that Murdoch's success in the United States represented a *further step* in the development of a global multibillion-dollar media operation that also includes more than 100 publishing operations, a satellite to home-television channels based in Europe, an airline, a major stake in the worldwide Reuters news service, a hotel-reservation service, and even a sheep ranch in the Australian outback.

However strong his operations in Australia and England have been, they did not give Murdoch the media power he sought, so in 1985, he began his serious quest to take a significant place in the media business of the United States: in this country, 1985 operating income was $20,008,000; a year later, it had increased

Name of Company	Projected '89 electronic media revenues (mil.)	Projected '89 revenue breakdown within electronic media	Projected electronic media revenue change ('88 to '89)	Broadcast and cable networks (% ownership)	Network video production, and sampling of shows produced
1. TIME WARNER (a)	$4,650.0	TV Production: 24% Home Video: 17% Programming: 26% Cable: 33%	32.4%	HBO/Cinemax, The Comedy Channel, BET, TBS (part-owner)	Warner Bros. TV: *Murphy Brown, China Beach* Lorimar TV: *Island Son* HBO Pictures: *Perfect Witness, Red King, White Knight*
2. CAPITAL CITIES/ABC	3,875.0	TV Network: 61% TV Stations: 20% Radio: 9% Video: 10%	2.6%	ABC-TV Network, ESPN (80%), A&E (38%), Lifetime (33%)	ABC Circle Films: *War and Remembrance*
3. GENERAL ELECTRIC	3,375.0	Networks: 86% Stations: 14%	−7.3%	NBC-TV Network, A&E (13%), Bravo, AMC, CNBC, SportsChannel America (all 50%)	NBC Productions: *Hardball, Mancuso: FBI*
4. CBS INC.	2,900.0	TV Network: 79% TV Stations: 13% Radio: 8%	4.5%	CBS-TV Network, CBS Radio Networks	CBS Entertainment Productions: *Rescue 911, Wolf*
5. TELE-COMMUNICATIONS INC.	2,082.0	Cable: 100%	22.1%	BET (17%), AMC (43%), Discovery Channel (14%), Home Sports Network (60%), QVC Network (36%). Showtime Networks (50%) (c), TBS (part-owner), other sports nets	Think Entertainment (25%)
6. PARAMOUNT COMMUNICATIONS	1,994.0 (e)	Entertainment: 100%	7.0%	MSG, USA Network (50%)	Paramount TV: *Cheers, Dear John, MacGyver*
7. NEWS CORP.	1,580.0 (e, f)	Filmed Entertainment: 62% Television: 38%	25.1%	FBC-TV Network	Twentieth TV: *L.A. Law, Alien Nation, Doogie Howser, M.D.* STF Productions: *The Reporters*
8. MCA	1,443.8	Television: 42% Home Video & Pay TV: 46% Broadcasting & Cable: 12%	15.1%	USA Network (50%)	Universal TV: *Quantum Leap, Major Dad*
9. VIACOM INTERNATIONAL	1,425.5	Cable: 21% Broadcasting: 10% Networks: 50% Entertainment: 19%	11.8%	MTV, VH-1, Nickelodeon/Nick at Nite, Showtime, The Movie Channel, Lifetime (33%), Pacific Sports Network (50%), Prime Northwest Sports Network (50%)	Viacom Productions: *Matlock, Jake and the Fatman, Snoops*
10. COLUMBIA PICTURES ENTERTAINMENT (g)	1,376.0 (e, h)	Theatrical (Includes Home Video & Pay TV): 55% Television: 45%	43.4%		Columbia Pictures TV: *My Two Dads, Murphy Brown, The Famous Teddy Z*
11. COX ENTERPRISES	1,053.0	Cable: 56% Broadcasting: 44%	9.0%	Discovery Channel (24%)	
12. MGM/UA COMMUNICATIONS (i)	901.9 (e)	Films & Home Video: 90% Programming: 10%	33.7%		MGM/UA TV Productions: *The Young Riders, thirtysomething*
13. WALT DISNEY CO.	882.7	Television: 52% Home Video & Non-Theatrical: 48%	23.4%	Disney Channel	Touchstone TV: *The Nutt House* Walt Disney TV: *The Magical World of Disney*

Domestic syndications and sampling of shows syndicated	Home video labels (% ownership)	Related media interests (% ownership)	TV stations owned, VHF and UHF	Radio stations owned, AM and FM	Cable systems owned (basic subscribers)
Warner Bros. Domestic TV Distribution: *Night Court, Dallas, People's Court, Gumby, Growing Pains*	Warner Home Video HBO Video Time-Life Home Video	24 magazines, Whittle Comm., Time-Life Books, BOMC, Time-Life Music, Warner Record Group, Warner Bros.' Films, other book and magazine publishing	(b)		Time Warner Cable Group (5.8 million)
Foreign only	ABC Video (ABC Distribution Co.)	ABC Publishing, Fairchild Publications, 7 dailies, weeklies, shopping guides, Institutional Investor	VHF: 7 UHF: 1	AM: 11 FM: 10	
Foreign only	RCA/Columbia Home Video		VHF: 7		
Foreign only	CBS/Fox Home Video (50%)		VHF: 5	AM: 8 FM: 12	
		X*Press (videotex service)			TCI Cable Systems (6.5 million) (d)
Paramount TV: *Entertainment Tonight, The Arsenio Hall Show, Star Trek: The Next Generation*	Paramount Home Video	Simon & Schuster, Publishing, Theaters	UHF: 5		
Twentieth Century Fox: *Small Wonder, A Current Affair*	CBS/Fox Home Video (50%)	Salem House, Harper & Row (50%), Triangle Publications (TV Guide), 12 magazines, Deluxe Labs	VHF: 3 UHF: 3		
MCA TV: *Charles in Charge, Out of This World*	MCA Home Video	Universal Pay TV, Universal Pictures, MCA Publishing Group, Universal Studio Tour, MCA Record Group	VHF: 1		
Viacom Enterprises: *The Cosby Show, Superboy, Remote Control*		Viacom Pictures, Showtime Event TV, Showtime Satellite Networks, Viewers Choice (17%), All News Channel (50%), Viacom Licensing and Merchandising	VHF: 4 UHF: 1	AM: 2 FM: 6	Viacom Cable (977,000)
Columbia Pictures TV: *227, Who's the Boss?*	RCA/Columbia Home Video (joint venture)	Columbia Pictures, Tri-Star Pictures, Loews Theaters, Merv Griffin Enterprises			
Television Program Enterprises: *Lifestyles of the Rich and Famous, Star Search*		18 dailies, 10 weeklies, 1 magazine, TeleRep, 100 Blockbuster Video franchises	VHF: 6 UHF: 1	AM: 5 FM: 7	Cox Cable (1.5 million)
MGM/UA Telecommunications: *The New Twilight Zone*	MGM/UA Home Video	MGM/UA Film Group, MGM/UA Distribution Co.			
Buena Vista TV: *Golden Girls, Siskel & Ebert, Chip 'n' Dale*	Walt Disney Home Video Touchstone Home Video	Theme parks	VHF: 1		

Name of Company	Projected '89 electronic media revenues (mil.)	Projected '89 revenue breakdown within electronic media	Projected electronic media revenue change ('88 to '89)	Broadcast and cable networks (% ownership)	Network video production, and sampling of shows produced
14. CONTINENTAL CABLEVISION	868.7	Cable: 100%	5.2%	TBS (part-owner), Movietime (part-owner)	
15. TURNER BROADCASTING (TBS)	840.0	Broadcasting: 36% Cable Productions: 45% Syndication & Licensing: 19%	15.6%	CNN, Headline News, TNT	*Between the Lines, Atlanta Braves Baseball, NBA Basketball*
16. HOME SHOPPING NETWORK	782.5	Cable & Broadcasting: 100%	7.2%	HSN I, HSN II, HSN IV	
17. QVC NETWORK (j)	749.0	Cable & Broadcasting: 100%	39.1%	QVC Network, CVN Network	
18. WESTINGHOUSE	700.0	Broadcasting: 66% Radio: 16% Productions: 9% Satellite Communications: 9%	10.6%	Home Team Sports, Request Television (50%)	NBC/Group W joint venture: *The Open House Show*
19. UNITED ARTISTS ENTERTAINMENT (k)	630.0 (l)	Cable & Programming: 100%	12.3%	TBS (part-owner), Discovery Channel (part-owner)	Think Entertainment (25%)
20. CABLEVISION SYSTEMS	590.7	Cable: 85% Programming: 15%	19.7%	Bravo (50%), AMC (50%), CNBC (50%), SportsChannels (50%), SportsChannel America (50%)	
21. TRIBUNE	547.0	Broadcasting: 73% Entertainment: 17% Radio: 10%	8.2%		
22. COMCAST	498.7	Cable & Programming: 100%	4.4%	QVC Network (20%)	
23. TIMES MIRROR	430.0	Cable: 76% Broadcasting: 24%	12.7%		
24. GANNETT	415.0	Broadcasting & Programming: 100%	6.3%		GTG Entertainment: *Baywatch*
25. KING WORLD	386.4	Syndication: 90% Broadcasting: 10%	38.1%		
26. CABLEVISION INDUSTRIES	355.0	Cable: 100%	13.0%		
27. MULTIMEDIA	325.0	Broadcasting: 44% Cable: 35% Entertainment: 21%	7.4%		Multimedia Entertainment: *Country Music Awards*
28. WASHINGTON POST CO.	320.0	Broadcasting: 59% Cable: 41%	8.3%		
29. ORION PICTURES (n)	319.7	Home Video: 44% Television: 35% Cable: 21%	36.9%		Orion TV Entertainment: *Equal Justice, No Place Like Home*
30. SCRIPPS HOWARD	294.7	Broadcasting: 75% Cable: 25%	7.3%	TBS (part-owner)	Scripps Howard Productions

Revenue projections and breakdowns compiled by *Channels*, using estimates from industry sources. Other company information compiled by Marcy Lerner and Matthew Natale. (a) The Time Warner merger is expected to be complete by year-end 1989. (b) Warner's 40 percent in BHC Inc. will be spun off to shareholders as a public company when the back end of the Time Warner merger is completed. (c) Tentative. (d) Does not include TCI's minority interests in other cable systems. Subscriber total including minority interests is 11.5 million. (e) Includes theatrical revenues. (f) Actual results from the company's annual report. (g) In October, Sony announced its intent to purchase Columbia Pictures Entertainment for $3.4 billion. (h) Columbia's 1989 revenues are compared to 1988 revenues from April 1, 1987 to February 29, 1988, only 11 months. (i) At press time, MGM/UA was seeking a

Domestic syndications and sampling of shows syndicated	Home video labels (% ownership)	Related media interests (% ownership)	TV stations owned, VHF and UHF	Radio stations owned, AM and FM	Cable systems owned (basic subscribers)
					Continental Cablevision (2.5 million)
Turner Program Services: *Secret World, Last Word* Turner Entertainment Co: MGM and RKO films	Turner Home Entertainment	CNN Radio, Atlanta Braves, Atlanta Hawks	UHF: 1		
			UHF: 11		
		QVC Express Catalog			
Group W Productions: *Teenage Mutant Ninja Turtles, This Evening*		Group W Satellite Communications Operations Group, Country America magazine (50%), Premiere Announcement Network, sales and marketing for The Nashville Network and the Prime Network.	VHF: 5	AM: 10 FM: 12	
		Theaters, Corsair Pictures			United Artists (2.5 million)
		Rainbow Advertising Sales, Cable Networks Inc.			Cablevision Systems (1.4 million)
Tribune Entertainment: *Geraldo, The Joan Rivers Show, At the Movies*		Chicago Cubs, 7 dailies	VHF: 4 UHF: 2	AM: 2 FM: 2	
		Comcast Cellular Group, Muzak services			Comcast Cable (1.5 million) (m)
		8 dailies, 13 magazines	VHF: 4		Times Mirror Cable (1 million)
GTG Entertainment: *USA Today on TV*		83 dailies, Gannett News Service	VHF: 8 UHF: 2	AM: 7 FM: 9	
King World Productions: *Wheel of Fortune, Oprah Winfrey*			VHF: 1		
					Cablevision Industries (967,000)
Multimedia Entertainment: *Music City News, Donahue, Sally Jessy Raphael*		14 dailies, 40 non-dailies	VHF: 4	AM: 3 FM: 4	Multimedia Cablevision (320,000)
		2 dailies, Newsweek, Legi-Slate (info. service)	VHF: 4		Post-Newsweek Cable (410,000)
Orion TV Entertainment: *Crimewatch Tonight*	Orion Home Video				
		19 dailies, United Media	VHF: 6 UHF: 3	AM: 2 FM: 3	Scripps Howard Cable (540,000)

partner for a possible merger. (j) The QVC Network-CVN Companies merger is expected to be complete by year-end 1989. In October, CVN announced it would terminate its agreement to manage the Fashion Channel. (k) United Artists Entertainment is 56 percent owned by TCI. (l) United Artists Entertainment's 1989 revenues are compared to combined 1988 revenues of both United Artists Communications and United Cable. (m) Does not include Comcast's minority interests in other cable systems. Subscriber total including minority interests is 2.5 million. (n) Orion Picture's 1989 revenues include third- and fourth-quarter revenues from fiscal 1988 and first- and second-quarter revenues from fiscal 1989. The corresponding quarters are included for 1988.

tenfold and in 1989 had reached $494,051,000. Although his sights were on network television, Murdoch did not initially move directly into that arena but rather into television's source of programming, Hollywood. In March 1985, Murdoch agreed to buy half of one of the major Hollywood studios, Twentieth Century Fox; he purchased full control six months later.

Murdoch knew from his experience in the media business abroad that he needed to control the outlets for Fox's movies and television shows to maximize the profits from his new investment. So in 1985, his Twentieth Century Fox acquired—for $2 billion—six independent television stations from Metromedia, the most powerful collection of TV stations not owned by the three television networks. Murdoch's stations cover more than 20 percent of the households in the United States, broadcasting from New York City (the largest television market in the United States), Los Angeles (the second largest), Chicago (third), Dallas (then eighth), Washington, D.C. (then ninth), and Houston (then tenth). He now had a set of stations providing a reach nearly comparable to the stations owned and operated (the so-called O & O's) by NBC, ABC, or CBS.

To maximize profits from U.S. investments approaching $3 billion, Murdoch hired Barry Diller (for a salary estimated in excess of $3 million per year) to run the newly named Fox, Inc. Diller had the perfect background. He knew how television networks operated; at ABC in the early 1970s, Diller pioneered the made-for-television movie. He also knew Hollywood; running Paramount during the late 1970s and into the early 1980s, Diller created a consistent string of box-office successes.

As the 1980s came to an end, Murdoch continued to invest, to provide Diller with the tools to make millions. In August 1988, for example, in what may have been his boldest move, Murdoch anted up $3 billion for Walter Annenberg's *TV Guide*, the largest selling mass-circulation magazine in the United States (with *paid* circulation of 16 million copies, read by 40 million, in more than 100 separate geographically defined editions) and a power in defining what Americans watched on television. This, with Annenberg's other publications, *Seventeen* and *The Daily Racing Form*, made Murdoch's News Corporation Ltd. the largest publisher of consumer magazines in the United States. Among its other magazines are *New York*, *Star*, and *Premiere*, and having recently acquired *Soap Opera Digest*, it serves well over 1 billion readers. With Murdoch's newspapers that ring the world, News Corporation possesses enormous economic and political power and a base from which to publicize the new offerings of Twentieth Century Fox and its six television stations.

Yet in the 1980s, Murdoch bet billions that in the long run, his U.S. film and television operations would prosper to such a great degree that they would dwarf the profits of his newspapers, magazines, and assorted other businesses. To take full advantage of the film and television capabilities of Fox, he and Diller created a fourth television network by linking up independent television stations (including his own). A network of over-the-air independent television stations, reasoned Murdoch and Diller, could provide an alternative to NBC, ABC, and CBS for advertisers.

The Fox network now reaches 86 percent of the United States through more than 100 affiliates. Securing high ratings proved difficult to accomplish. Only about 5 percent of the U.S. homes using television tuned in. Failure came early and hard. "The Late Show" with hostess Joan Rivers, which telecast opposite "The Tonight

Figure 3.3. Twentieth Century Fox is the production company behind "L.A. Law."

Show with Johnny Carson," lasted only seven months (October 1986–April 1987). Fox's greatest investment (and bust) came with George C. Scott in a situation comedy, "Mr. President." But as the 1980s came to a close, an exceptional hit appeared in the form of Sunday night's somewhat raunchy comedy, "Married . . . with Children." As he entered the 1990s, Rupert Murdoch's ultimate goal remained clear: build a full seven-days-a-week schedule by 1993.

But Murdoch and Diller are skillful businessmen and have always hedged their bets on Hollywood operations. Fox is more than a fourth network. Twentieth Century Fox is the production company behind the hit "L.A. Law" on NBC and syndicator of the off-network syndicated "evergreen" "M*A*S*H." In 1988, Fox penned an agreement to distribute films from its vast feature-film library for telecast in the People's Republic of China. The joint operation, CBS–Fox Home Video, continues to be a major player in the burgeoning videocassette market.

The innovation of the fourth television network symbolized Murdoch's extraordinary efforts to break FBC (Fox Broadcasting Company) into the exclusive three-member oligopoly—NBC, ABC, and CBS—that has been "American network television." It became realistically possible only because Murdoch bought both the means of creation and distribution (Twentieth Century Fox) and an important set of outlets (the former Metromedia television stations). Indeed, the potential for stitching these (and other parts of the News Corporation's vast media empire) together to create a *vertically integrated* corporate empire offers Fox an advantage few other companies have. Consider that a book published by Harper Collins can be excerpted in Murdoch newspapers and magazines, recast as a Twentieth Century Fox film, done again as a television program for the Fox network, and then syndicated around the world. The film can (and will) be reviewed in

Premiere, and the television programs can be promoted in *TV Guide*. Such an effort would provide a vivid example of economic power and the profit potential of vertical integration.

Addressing the International Institute of Communications in Washington, D.C., Rupert Murdoch observed:

> *If in 1980 we had attempted to chart on paper the destiny of our company, we would never have anticipated the 30 very diverse acquisitions we made on four continents, almost all of which arose from unique and unanticipated events. Business situations and business opportunities simply change too quickly for there to be much point in loading ourselves down with piles of strategic speculation.*
>
> *Nonetheless, when I'm asked: Are global communications networks a reality? My answer unequivocally is 'Yes.'[2]*

Using the New Advantages

Two economic motivations spur all forms of vertical integration. First, media businesses can take full advantage of the power that integration offers to reduce costs of sales and transactions. The vertically integrated corporation sells to "itself" and thus does not have to go through bidding procedures. Second, and more important, is *market control*. A vertically integrated corporation need not worry about being shut out of key markets. For example, in the past, Fox had to convince television stations in New York and Los Angeles to buy its films and television shows. Often these stations were already affiliated with NBC, ABC, or CBS and thus had only limited time for Fox products. By vertically integrating, Fox has a guaranteed slot in New York, Los Angeles, Chicago, Dallas, Houston, and Washington, D.C.

During the 1960s and the early 1970s, media corporations began to diversify into many businesses not associated with their core (or founding) enterprise. A *conglomerate* is a large modern corporation not confined to making and distributing a single product but embracing varied lines of business, most likely to be tendered both in the continental United States and throughout the world (the multinational trait). The conglomerate form was rare until the extraordinary merger movement that took place in the 1960s.

The American media business was shaken in 1966 when giant Gulf + Western Industries acquired Paramount Pictures. Gulf + Western manufactured cigars, electrical cable, auto bumpers, and musical instruments; mined zinc; and sold insurance. Founder Charles Bluhdorn then expanded into the entertainment business by purchasing Famous Players, the largest movie circuit in Canada; the book publisher Simon & Schuster; the Madison Square Garden arena in New York City; the New York Knickerbockers Bastketball team; the New York Rangers Hockey club; and the International Holiday on Ice show as well as Paramount. In all, Gulf + Western, in its heyday before its founder's death in the early 1980s, represented more than 60 diverse, often totally unrelated businesses under this one corporate umbrella.

Bluhdorn's successor would strip the company down to a *media-only* conglomerate and in 1989 rename it Paramount Communications, Inc. Indeed, most noted media enterprises did not become pure conglomerates but *media-specialized* conglomerates—with book, magazine, television, and music-recording divisions. Examples included nearly all the Hollywood-based "movie" companies, all three

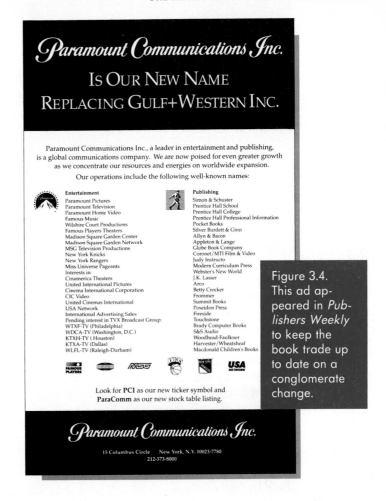

Figure 3.4. This ad appeared in *Publishers Weekly* to keep the book trade up to date on a conglomerate change.

major television networks, newspaper giants such as the Washington Post Corporation and the New York Times Corporation, as well as cable upstarts such as Tele-Communications, Inc.

The original Warner Communications represented the rise of the prototypical media conglomerate. This corporate empire grew out of a 1969 merger between Kinney National Services (which dealt in parking lots, construction, car rental, and funeral homes) and the then struggling Warner Bros. Pictures, a maker of both movies and television programs. In 1971, Warner Communication was formed when Kinney National was spun off to handle the construction, automobile, and funeral businesses. The new Warner Communications empire would grow to include popular music, book and magazine publishing, cable television, and the core Warner Hollywood operations of film and television-program creation. Steven J. Ross, originally of Kinney, was Warner Communications' corporate godfather, Robert Daly, the management maven in Hollywood. The 1989 merger with Time, Inc. simply added to Warner's existing vast range of mass communication and leisure-time businesses.

And then there is Universal Studios, controlled by the conglomerate MCA,

Inc. The *Music Corporation of America* was founded in 1924 as a booking agent for popular swing bands of the era. In the late 1950s, MCA purchased the ailing Universal Studios; faced with a governmental suit because it then both employed and represented the same talents, MCA shrugged off the original talent business and soon began to add television production, theme parks, a chain of gift shops, book publishing, and a popular recording division to its original movie and television operations. In 1986, MCA brought a half interest in Cineplex Odeon movie theaters and became a giant in the movie-theater business in both the United States and Canada. Only Lew Wasserman remained from the talent-agency days, but few doubted that Wasserman had become the most powerful man in Hollywood, indeed one of the most truly powerful men in the world mass-media industry.

Columbia Pictures' experience of the 1980s proved that media, not pure conglomerate ownership, was the true path to long-run riches. In 1981, the mighty Coca-Cola corporation took over Columbia, to ride the wave of entertainment prosperity. Columbia floundered under strict controls of Coke's Atlanta-based M.B.A. cost accountants. With no skill in managing a media company, Coke sold its shares of Columbia to the Japanese electronics giant Sony in 1989. As the 1990s began it was not clear that the melding of Sony, the hardware producer, and Columbia, the creator of the software or programming, could assault both worlds at the same time.

In sum, the prospect is that as the media industries move into the twenty-first century, major participants will function as small parts of only a handful of giant media conglomerates, invariably with names like Time Warner and Sony-Columbia. The economics of mass-media structure will continue to be a *system* that emphasizes vertical integration, conglomeration, world marketing, and billion-dollar size.

ECONOMIC CONDUCT

The structure of a media industry determines the particular characteristics of economic behavior. Since the typical media industry in the United States is an oligopoly (control by a few), we ought to look closely at how such industries operate.

Note that the economic operation of media businesses divides into two types, depending on source of revenue—sales to consumers or advertising fees. The important difference is that the first type, *direct payment*, enables customers to telegraph their preferences to the media company. A hit film such as *Star Wars* sparks a new wave of science-fiction films. But for advertising-supported media, the client of the media company is the advertiser, not the buyers of the newspaper or magazine, or those watching the television show. Advertisers want to hawk their products and so demand media content and style that appeal to audiences who might buy that product. Thus shows go off the air because they do not reach the right audience (for example, ABC's sitcom, "Chicken Soup" in 1989), while low-rated content with the right audiences (for example, those endless golf and tennis tournaments that attract hard-to-reach affluent fans) stays on and prospers.

We have said that critical or informed consumers weigh their options regarding price (the fees for renting a videotape versus subscribing to HBO versus going out to the movies) and types of service tendered (watching half-hour television shows

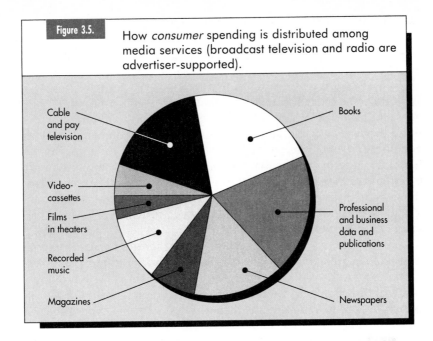

Figure 3.5.

How *consumer* spending is distributed among media services (broadcast television and radio are advertiser-supported).

versus reading various sections of the newspaper versus listening to five minutes of radio news versus listening to an audio tape, over and over again, of a singer such as k. d. lang or Madonna). How does the economic structure affect the array of choices offered to us?

THE MONOPOLY

On one end of the spectrum is the monopoly, a single company constituting the market structure. This is the most concentrated type of media industry, often fostering a message symbolized by the business motto of "we don't care, we don't have. . . ." Such is the case with cable television in any local jurisdiction: Typically, one cable company has been given *the* franchise; no other cable company can move in to compete. Not surprisingly, the monopoly cable company has little incentive to keep prices down or to offer high-quality service; what choice does the sports fan have who wants ESPN? Where can the news junkie turn who cannot live without CNN or C-SPAN?

THE OLIGOPOLY

The typical market structure in the media business, however, is an oligopoly, ownership by a few. Actually, the media business in the United States consists of a set of oligopolies, separate industrial structures, each dominated by a handful of large corporations. The essence of the conduct of an oligopoly is that the number of firms is small enough that all can be cognizant of the others and react accordingly. Take the case of the three major networks' counterprogramming. We all too often see and hear the same kinds of offerings (situation comedies and hour dramas at night, soap operas in the afternoon, news at the dinner hour) presented opposite one another, lending over-the-air television a quality of sameness and repetitiveness.

COMPETITION IN THE SYSTEM

The outcomes of such corporate behavior depend on how many firms there are, how big they are in relationship to each other, past corporate histories, and sometimes the whims of individual owners. To make the most money as a group, oligopolists for some matters ought to cooperate, and they do. They work together to fashion positive governmental policies toward their industry and thus keep out potential competitors. Nothing unites a media oligopoly more than a threat from the outside, as we have repeatedly seen in the cooperation the major Hollywood studios achieve when facing some perceived threat from network television, home video, or cable television.

Once they are able effectively to keep out serious competitors, oligopolists tend to seek and agree upon an informal set of rules for product competition. Then only subtle differences will be tolerated as the members of the oligopoly "compete." In essence, the three major networks have agreed on the rules of the economic game, and *then* seek to differentiate their products to make the most money, always knowing generally what their rivals are up to.

All this does not mean the rules for such decisions are simple or straightforward. They are often a complex set of actions that are simultaneously in the best interest of the oligopolists while permitting some degree of economic struggle. Indeed, we can appreciate the complexities of oligopolistic market conduct for the mass media by looking at one particular pricing and sales problem: bringing feature-length movies to the public.

CASE STUDY: MARKETING MOVIES

Even as late as a dozen years ago, the process of tendering a theatrical feature film seemed one-dimensional. A feature film played in theaters, opening with a lavish premiere and vast publicity campaigns conducted in newspapers and magazines around the country. Once a feature film had "played off" theatrically, it appeared much later on television. Theatrical films earned the bulk of their money in theaters.

The selling and pricing of movies began to change significantly in the mid-1970s. In 1975, one of the major Hollywood studios, Universal, broke fundamentally with tradition, skillfully employing saturation advertising on network television to bring its film *Jaws* to everyone's attention. This use of television advertising was considered an adventuresome, innovative marketing maneuver in 1975, but it worked. During the final six months of that year, this one film earned more than $100 million, easily surpassing *The Godfather* as the all-time Hollywood box-office champion (which has been surpassed since, of course).

Today, theatrical release of feature films requires more and more theater screens, so that Hollywood can take full advantage of the economies of television advertising. Even though the cost of marketing a film can often exceed $10 million, as it is spread over more and more theaters, marketing costs per theater per film remain relatively low. The economies of scale of television advertising of theatrical features provides the foundation of the "multiplex" theater. A shopping-mall multiplex complex with 12 screens is four times more likely to locate a hit than a triplex.

Figure 3.6. The use of television advertising made the opening of *Jaws* an important event and changed the film industry into a machine for the production of blockbusters.

Once the early results set a hit in motion, the blockbuster can be shifted to the largest auditorium in the complex, while new films are introduced in smaller adjacent sites.

A new serious film-viewing market emerged in the mid-1970s. Time, Inc.'s innovation of pay-television's Home Box Office (HBO) added the possibility of millions of extra dollars in a new market. HBO played feature films nearly around the clock and charged subscribers accordingly. Now a movie studio had to consider not only how rivals opened feature films theatrically but also how they maximized sales to Home Box Office, as well as rival pay-television channels—Cinemax, The Movie Channel, and Showtime.

In the mid-1980s, the home-video revolution further complicated a movie company's selling feature films. Suddenly the public could rent or own individual titles, formerly the province of the rich, well-connected, or illegal operator. A decade of underground collectors had bootlegged copies of *Gone with the Wind* and *Vertigo*. Now they could be bought or rented on tape in stores in every village and hamlet across the country.

The growth of the home-video industry was nothing short of astonishing. In 1980, the Hollywood majors collected some $20 million from worldwide sales of videocassettes. In 1987, the monies totaled more than $7 billion. Ten years ago, an average film took in nil from home video; today, that share tops one-third of total revenues (see Table 3.1).

In the beginning, Hollywood loathed the new machine, arguing that home video stole precious dollars from the box office. But during the 1980s, Hollywood

Table 3.1.	Video Marketing Newsletter's Top All-Time Best-Selling Videocassettes*				
Title	Studio	Unit Sales	Highest List Price	Studio Revenue (Millions)	Release Date
1 E.T.	MCA	12,500,000	$24.95	$187	10/88
2 Batman	Warner	9,750,000	24.98	146	11/89
3 Bambi	Disney	8,500,000	26.99	136	9/89
4 Cinderella	Disney	7,500,000	29.95	124	10/88
5 Who Framed Roger Rabbit?	Touchstone	6,800,000	22.99	95	10/89
6 Wizard of Oz	MGM/UA	3,638,559	59.95	51	10/80
7 Land Before Time	MCA	3,600,000	24.95	54	9/89
8 Top Gun	Paramount	3,500,000	26.95	56	3/87
9 Lady & the Tramp	Disney	3,200,000	29.95	58	10/87
10 Crocodile Dundee	Paramount	2,500,000	26.95	38	8/87
11 Beverly Hills Cop	Paramount	2,200,000	29.95	34.8	10/85
Good Morning, Vietnam	Touchstone	2,200,000	29.95	39.5	8/88
13 Star Trek IV	Paramount	2,000,000	29.95	32.7	9/87
14 Indiana Jones Temple/Doom	Paramount	1,800,000	29.95	29	11/86
Raiders of the Lost Ark	Paramount	1,800,000	39.95	26.2	12/83
16 Dirty Dancing	Vestron	1,600,000	89.98	37.6	1/88
17 An American Tail	MCA	1,500,000	29.95	27.3	9/87
Mary Poppins	Disney	1,500,000	84.95	26	11/80
Sleeping Beauty	Disney	1,500,000	29.95	27	10/86
20 Dumbo	Disney	1,450,000	84.95	46.7	6/81

* As of January 1990.
Source: Video Marketing Newsletter, Hollywood, CA.

found a way to exploit the new technology. During the first two years of the decade, the major Hollywood studios tried to sell prerecorded movies to the public for $60 and up, thinking fans would want to accumulate tapes at home as they had with books in forming a library. But quietly, entrepreneurs with no connections to Hollywood began to buy multiple copies of prerecorded movies and offer them for rent for about $2 per day.

Outlets renting videotapes popped up everywhere. Grocery stores, drugstores, convenience chains, gas stations, dry cleaners, and in some locales, even pizza-delivery services, were willing to lease tapes (as the 1980s drew to an end, fully a sixth of all tapes were rented from grocery stores or drugstores). However, Hollywood collects only on the first sale and so has sought to participate more fully in the video riches. To do so, it has lowered prices for tapes, tempting customers to buy rather than rent. With prices falling below $20, customers lined up to buy (not rent) their film favorites. In 1986, Paramount's Top Gun brought in an additional $40 million. E.T.'s heralded release on video in October 1988 set records for multimillion additions to MCA's balance sheet.

The big losers in the home video wars have been NBC, ABC, and CBS. With repeated showings on pay cable and home video, the ratings for theatrical features shown on network television have fallen. So now a network "Night at the Movies" means not reruns of top Hollywood features but a series of films especially made for premiere on television, the ubiquitous "TV movies." These relatively low-budget TV movies thrive by promoting instant controversy; they are often dramatizations of events and crimes sensationalized in tabloids a short time previously. A $20-

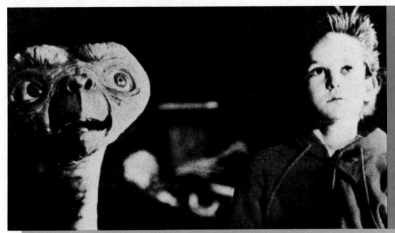

Figure 3.7. *E.T. The Extra-Terrestrial*, Steven Spielberg's fantasy, broke box-office records and was a holdout on video release. Within a short time after its cassette debut, it again made news.

million feature with an orchestrated advertising campaign requires more than a full year of lead time. A TV movie can "turn over" in a matter of months. If ever there was proof of the new movie economics on TV, it came on a Sunday night in February 1984 when CBS first aired *Star Wars*. CBS was so confident that here was a special case that it doubled its prime-time advertising rates. But to nearly everyone's surprise, *Star Wars* was soundly beaten in the ratings by *Lace*, a made-for-TV movie that cost only $3 million to make. Too many folks had already rented *Star Wars* or seen it on HBO to enable that blockbuster to generate sizable network-television audiences. The industry was therefore skeptical when the TV rights to *Batman* went for $70 million in 1989.

In short, because of their considerable market power and adroit conduct, the major Hollywood companies have been the big winners in the world of the new television technologies; they have skillfully learned to take advantage of the new "windows of release" for feature films. They extracted more and more money from their features through a careful use of *price discrimination*. That is, they set different prices for the "same" film. They *segment potential customers* and have each group pay as much as possible for a product, in this case the viewing of a film. Buffs who always want to see a feature right away line up in front of a theater and pay in excess of $6. Those with less interest pay smaller amounts for screenings on pay-television or to rent the video. Millions would remain content to wait until the feature appeared on "free" television. The challenge for Hollywood executives is to set prices at each stage of release to maximize total profits. If they forced theater-ticket prices too high, fans would wait. If they kept theater-ticket prices too low, they would lose possible revenues in the release of pay-television and home video. Recent research is showing that the currently short time lag between theater release and video release *is* keeping many more at home, where they elect to enjoy another medium. Moviegoing has become a more specialized, at times elitist, activity, and the lack of G-rated films clearly reflects this.

Economic conduct is not neutral; it has implications for users of the mass media and how well the media industries serve society as a whole. These and other concerns are *performance issues*.

ECONOMIC PERFORMANCE ....

In the end, what most of us care about are the *consequences* of the economic structure and conduct—economic performance. We encounter specific media complaints every day. Is there some way to improve the quality of television shows? Is the economic structure of the mass media such that the ethics of news coverage are as fair as they might be?

There is comparatively little regulation from without. Even though broadcast radio and television are licensed by the Federal Communications Commission, the actual results of many of the rules differ from the intent. For example, about 20 years ago, the FCC instituted the so-called prime-time-access rule (to mitigate TV network economic power and force better behavior) by requiring that "local" programs be presented in greater numbers in prime time. But to many this policy has backfired; reruns of "Wheel of Fortune" and "Family Feud" (selected by local stations from syndicators' offerings) satisfied the rules but hardly met what policymakers had in mind as "quality local programming." Since the turn of the century, we have relied either on various antitrust laws or on consumer pressure to correct flaws in the economic structure and conduct of these industries. Three criteria can help judge economic performance: *efficiency, use of technology,* and *access.*

EFFICIENCY AS A GOAL

First, the media industry's firms ought not waste resources—in other words, be as efficient as possible. Those promoting free markets, in recent years those associated with the Reagan administration, have argued that a market of oligopolists acts *as if* it were competitive, and so we ought not worry about too much economic power or the actions of a few giant corporations trampling on smaller competitors.

Figure 3.8. Stallone's salaries (such as $20 million for Rambo III) give proof that the star system, begun 70 years ago, is very much alive and well.

The quest for profit maximization, argue those who seek deregulation, guarantees efficient marketplace behavior.

Yet to even the most casual observer, the mass-media industries hardly seem efficient enterprises. Waste seems inherent in excessive salaries paid movie stars or the "limousine culture perks" long associated with the Dan Rathers and Diane Sawyers of the three television networks. With millions clamoring to break into the business, why pay a few so much?

ACCESS TO TECHNOLOGICAL ADVANCES

We would like to see new technologies used as soon as they are available, whether as inputs to the production or distribution of entertainment and news or as delivery systems of the final products into our homes. It has long been known that monopolies and collusive oligopolies resist the innovation of new technologies in order to protect their highly profitable positions. During the 1960s and into the 1970s, the over-the-air broadcasters—as represented by their trade organization, the National Association of Broadcasters (NAB)—lobbied for restrictive regulations governing the then emerging cable-television business. The NAB failed, but for how many years did its actions limit the growth of cable television and thus deny access to the multitude of choices we take for granted today?

In the 1990s, one dominant technological issue concerns high-definition television (HDTV). No one doubts that HDTV offers an image superior to the present television standard, adopted 50 years ago. But as the debate rages on, the over-the-air broadcasters and the cablemasters want to capture HDTV for their own and thus guarantee their future profitability. Dozens of questions surrounding the introduction of HDTV will need to be resolved. Is the new HDTV image so superior that the public can be convinced overnight to junk the old sets and buy new ones? Technological change always offers difficult choices, whether the questions concern HDTV, the use and effect of computers in the covering of news, or how our international relations will dictate the sharing of satellite time.

THE QUESTION OF ACCESS TO COMMUNICATION

Thirdly, we ought to judge economic performance by how well the media industry distributes its products to consumers, both rich and poor. The mass media, because of scale economies and underwriting by advertisers, have long been justifiably praised because their communications are so cheap to acquire. This is not culture and information for the rich only but for even the poorest of society. Over-the-air television is "free" once one has purchased a set. But as more and more of the mass media go to direct payment, how will all citizens be able to pay the ever-growing monthly charges? This is an issue of equity, of access. To be blunt: Will the poor be shut out of the wired world of the next decade?

CRITICISMS OF THE MEDIA

Many grumble that too often television, the movies, even daily newspapers, strive only to appeal to base instincts; they fail to educate or inform. Critics argue television provides only more and more of the *mindless same,* be they situation comedies, news summaries, or professional wrestling matches. Such skeptics seek governmental action to encourage alternative conduct: subsidize educational programs and discourage the profits accorded to run-of-the-mill fare.

We can label a second set of grievances the *wasteland* complaint, which is taken from former FCC chairman Newton Minow's phrase. Critics say the media industries ignore minority cultures and tastes. Although this complaint about economic conduct has been somewhat ameliorated in recent years through the coming of cable television with its black, Spanish, and news channels, the majority of television programs seek a broad-based white-middle-class audience. The government could encourage more diversity, for example, with minority group representatives.

The final grievance lies with market structure, not conduct. This is the problem of *concentration of ownership*. Many feel that the media oligopolies are so few in number, so interested in preserving only their own acquired power, that they do not serve their communities very well. Conservative groups constantly find a "liberal bias" in the coverage by the three network-television news organizations; liberals see monopoly newspaper and television news always supporting the Republicans. Media concentration could be "corrected" by the U.S. Department of Justice's trying to "break up" market structures where too much power exists.

THE INTERPLAY OF STRUCTURE, CONDUCT, AND PERFORMANCE ....

To appreciate fully the interplay of market structure, conduct, and performance we turn to two media industries not yet examined in detail in this chapter. These case studies present the extremes of oligopolistic performance most clearly. On one hand, radio today offers a medium few complain about, a medium that seems efficient and fair, a high-quality sound. With so many radio stations, it is rarely labeled a tight oligopoly. On the other hand, big-city newspapers cause many to complain. They too often operate as effective monopolies. As such, they are not efficient, seek to cover stories that appeal to those members of society attractive to advertisers, and are slow to innovate.

RADIO: MONOPOLISTIC COMPETITION

Radio broadcasting in the United States offers a vast degree of choice. In Washington, D.C., there are nearly 50 local stations plus signals that can be received from nearby Baltimore, Philadelphia, and New York City. Available formats include all news, religious music and talk, country music, adult contemporary music, "beautiful music," soul sounds, urban contemporary music, hard rock, and jazz. As in most markets, the listeners concentrate on the FM band for music, AM for information. Complaints about base appeal, lack of concern for minorities, and too few owners seem to make no sense in today's competitive radio market (see Table 3.2).

Such diversity and choice was not always the rule in radio broadcasting. Into the early 1950s in most radio markets in the United States, three network-affiliated stations dominated the airwaves. But as television diffused fully across the nation, consumers switched to the new medium, and radio broadcasters looked to a new programming strategy, programming music and information keyed to local tastes.

Table 3.2.	Patterns in the New York Radio Market: Owners of Top 20		
Rank	**Station (corporate owner)**	**Frequency**	**Format**
1	WHTZ (Malrite Radio & Television Inc.)	100.3 FM	Top 40
2	WLTW (Viacom International)	106.7 FM	Light contemporary
3	WCBS (CBS Inc.)	101.1 FM	Oldies
4	WINS (Westinghouse Broadcasting Corp.)	1010 AM	News
5	WPAT (Park Radio of Greater New York Inc.)	93.1 FM	Easy listening
6	WNEW (Metropolitan Broadcasting Group)	102.7 FM	Album-oriented rock
7	WRKS (Summit Broadcasting)	98.7 FM	Urban contemporary
8	WQHT (Emmis Broadcasting Corp.)	97.1 FM	Top 40/Urban
9	WOR (Buckley Broadcasting Corp.)	710 AM	Talk/News
10	WNSR (Bonneville International Corp.)	105.1 FM	Soft rock
11	WXRK (Infinity Broadcasting Inc.)	92.3 FM	Classic rock
12	WABC (Capital Cities/ABC Inc.)	770 AM	Talk/News
13	WPLJ (Capital Cities/ABC Inc.)	95.5 FM	Top 40
14	WCBS (CBS Inc.)	880 AM	News
15	WBLS (Inner City Broadcasting Corp.)	107.5 FM	Urban contemporary
16	WQCD (Tribune Broadcasting Co.)	101.9 FM	Contemporary jazz
17	WFAN (Emmis Broadcasting Corp.)	660 AM	Sports
18	WYNY (Westwood One Inc.)	103.5 FM	Country
19	WNEW (Westwood One Stations Group Inc.)	1130 AM	Adult contemporary/MOR
20	WPAT (Park Radio of Greater New York Inc.)	930 AM	Easy listening

Note: Rank is based on Arbitron audience share ratings, 1989.

By the 1970s, the radio business was once again healthy, with millions listening each day.

Most Americans are getting a wide number of choices, limited only by the nature or scarcity of the spectrum band and the size of their market (the bigger, the better). The radio market is technically classified as *monopolistic competition.* Each station is small relative to the total market, and hence (unlike the pure oligopolistic characteristics of the seven Hollywood studios or the five major record companies) most pay attention to the actions of a few close competitors rather than every station in the market. But unlike a truly competitive situation, radio stations do offer differentiated products (their "distinct sounds"). This makes them like oligopolists; hence the compromise nomenclature: monopolistic competition.

It is the rare radio station that is in the long run able to make extraordinary monopoly profits. If one station's sound gets hot (and gives it monopoly or excess profits relative to the others), rival stations immediately imitate, and the temporary advantage disappears. Thus there is frequent movement from one format mix to another.

The performance of the radio market is nearly perfect; only a tiny minority is not satisfied with this system of monopolistic competition. If there are only 25 stations in a sample market, then it is possible, indeed probable, that formats number 20 through 25 on a sample ranking might not be made available; missing might be an all-classical music station. The number of potential listeners who might value such a service might number only a few thousand, but these individuals will be unhappy. Our hypothetical market is clearly not working perfectly, as expected with monopolistic competition, and so we have what economists call a second-best solution.

To encourage the acme of second-best solutions, in 1981 the FCC deregulated radio. That is, it eliminated all restrictions on what programs could be aired, freed stations to set their own advertising schedules, and eliminated the necessity of keeping expensive records for filings with the FCC. The FCC's goal was to cut down the paperwork involved, reduce costs, and let monopolistic competition make *almost* everybody happy. Radio broadcasting offers an example of economic structure, conduct, and performance in which little government intervention (only spectrum regulation) makes the best sense.

NEWSPAPERS: GROWING MONOPOLY

The state of the daily-newspaper industry in the United States causes some legitimate concern. There seem to be fewer and fewer competitors, thus fewer and fewer alternative voices. While more than 500 cities in the United States had two or more competing newspapers in the 1920s (including more than 100 with three), by 1980, only 30 cities had competing newspapers. And the number keeps falling.

This was dramatically illustrated in 1981, when the *Washington Star* ceased publication. Here was a newspaper institution that had served the nation's capital for more than 100 years. To its final decade, the *Washington Star* had seemed to be flourishing with more than 300,000 copies sold each day. And it was owned by Time, Inc., a billion-dollar media corporation with skilled managers and "deep pockets." The closing of the *Washington Star* seemed to set off a wave of closures: the *Philadelphia Bulletin,* the *Minneapolis Star,* and the *Cleveland Press* soon followed. In 1989, a chapter in journalistic history closed with the passing of the *Los Angeles Herald-Examiner,* as we chronicle in Chapter 9.

The newspaper-as-monopoly seems almost inevitable. As one newspaper begins to edge ahead of its rivals, advertisers flock to it to maximize their advertising exposure. This in turn shifts huge cost savings: less need to beat the bushes to drum up advertisers, so a smaller advertising sales staff is needed. The top newspaper gets richer (higher revenues, lower costs) while rivals disappear because of the lack of profits. In the end, a single newspaper remains.

By its very nature, a monopoly newspaper tenders limited performance. The monopoly newspaper, whatever its reporters' skills, sets the agenda for the news in the local area, and with few realistic checks, offers the potential of sidestepping hard-to-handle local issues. Consider that when one newspaper gets all the grocery-store advertisements, it might be less willing to investigate and expose unfair grocery-store pricing schemes and shoddy products.

To promote the economic viability of at least two daily newspapers, the federal government enacted the Newspaper Preservation Act in 1970. This permits two "competitive" newspapers to operate jointly for their noneditorial operations, yet

The Detroit News

COLD SHOTS
Pistons frigid in 102-82 loss **1F**

SPACE STATION
Project planned for 1995 start **1C**

SHOWERS
Low tonight
40°
High Tuesday
Details, page **12F**

Monday
November 27, 1989

15¢

New airline lands at City Airport

Outward bound
Continental Express is planning daily nonstop flights from Detroit to Cleveland Hopkins International Airport, a base for Continental Airlines. Among Continental Airlines' most popular destinations from Cleveland are:
- San Francisco
- Los Angeles
- Denver
- Newport Beach/Orange County, Calif.
- San Diego
- Miami
- Fort Lauderdale, Fla.
- West Palm Beach, Fla.
- Tampa
- Houston

DAVID PIERCE/The Detroit News

PLAN: 5 round-trip flights to Cleveland in February

By Lise Olson
News Staff Writer

A commuter airline plans to provide daily, nonstop service between Detroit City Airport and Cleveland Hopkins International Airport beginning Feb. 1, a spokesman said Sunday.

Continental Express expects to offer five round-trip daily flights between Detroit and Cleveland, Continental Express spokesman Steven E. Mason said. The commuter flights would enable travelers to connect with flights offered from Cleveland by Houston-based Continental Airlines.

Continental Express and Continental Airlines are separate companies. Continental Express manages three of Continental Airlines' subsidiaries — Bar Harbor, Britt and Rocky Mountain Airways.

A move into City Airport requires approval of the Federal Aviation

Please see **Airline/4A**

REACTION: Suburbs upset over expanded service

By Domenica Marchetti
News Staff Writer

Suburban officials are concerned about a commuter airline's plans to provide daily flights between Detroit City Airport and Cleveland.

Continental Express expects to offer five daily, round-trip flights between the two cities beginning Feb. 1, company president Neal F. Meehan said.

But several suburban communities said they fear the expanded service would increase the chance of an accident and lead to additional noise and air pollution, as well as declining property values.

"I THINK I can speak on behalf of the citizens of Warren that any additions of air service at City Airport increases the possibility that an accident will occur," Warren Council President Cecil St. Pierre said.

For the past two years, Warren

Please see **Expand/4A**

GOOD AFTERNOON
BRIEFLY IN THE NEWS

Rose Bowl tickets go on sale at U-M

A limited number of Rose Bowl tickets go on sale at the University of Michigan this week for the Jan. 1 game between U-M and Southern California.

Individual tickets ($43) will be sold to students, faculty and staff members at the U-M athletic department ticket office Wednesday through Friday from 8 a.m. until 5 p.m.

Four-day and six-day tour packages, which include a game ticket, al-

Ready to hunt for flock of faithful

Report: Regulate cholesterol screening

AP and UPI

WASHINGTON — Cha...

Detroit Free Press

LOCAL NEWS
A move is under way to reduce auto exhaust tests.
PAGE 1B

BUSINESS
Companies grapple with the concept of ultimate goal
PAGE 1D

HEALTH & FITNESS
Jane Fonda still works hard for the money
PAGE 1C

THE WAY WE LIVE
TV to air the story of Isiah Thomas' mother, Mary
PAGE 1E

SPORTS
Trail Blazers topple Pistons 102-82
PAGE 1F

METRO FINAL
Rain. High 50, low 36.
Tuesday: Snow showers.
Details, Page 11F ▪▪

MONDAY
November 27, 1989
For home delivery call 222-6500
20 cents

MONDAY MEMO

To our readers

Good morning, and welcome to your new Free Press.

These are some of the improvements and changes you can look for today.

Index on Page 2A

A **summary** and **expanded** index, called Top of the Morning, appear on Page 2A. It's a quick read on the day's news and a guide to the rest of the newspaper. You'll find it on Page 2A every weekday. Also appearing there are the state lottery numbers.

Weather report

Look for the **weather** on the second-to-last page of the paper, its traditional location for many years and one where you'll still be able to find it quickly. Page 11F.

U.S. and world news

PATRICIA BECK/Detroit Free Press
Former Free Press employees huddle Sunday in the Detroit Newspaper Agency composing room at the Detroit News downtown.

Papers avert strike, start JOA

BY JOHN LIPPERT AND WYLIE GERDES
Free Press Staff Writers

The Free Press and News launched their first editions under a joint operating agreement after averting a strike Sunday night when the press operators overwhelmingly ratified a new contract.

Five other unions rejected the offer Sunday but agreed not to strike until at least midnight Wednesday.

The wrangling with the unions

▪ With a 'strange feeling,' former Free Press workers move to News. Page 5B.

came amid the complex launch of the JOA, which officially began with publication of this morning's Free Press.

The unions have been working under a contract with their respective papers that was to expire when a JOA was implemented; new contracts were to be negotiated between the unions

and the new, combined publishing company, the Detroit Newspaper Agency.

Leaders of the five unions representing drivers and circulation workers, editorial employees, typographers, mailers and photoengravers will meet today to plan their next move. The press operators, along with the other five unions, make up the Detroit Newspaper Unions Solidarity Council. It was not known Sunday night how

See JOA, Page 10A

Czech ex-foes discuss reforms

to be free of violating the antitrust laws. The legislation's proponents argued that two editorial voices are better than one, even if jointly operated. The Newspaper Preservation Act, however well it works, operates only as a subsidy to maintain the status quo and hardly leads to aggressive competition for stories.

Consider the case of the *Detroit News* (owned by Gannett) and the *Detroit Free Press* (owned by the Knight-Ridder chain). In August 1988, Attorney General Edwin Meese III, overturning recommendations of his staff, approved the joint operating agreement between these two newspapers owned by two of the largest media corporations in the United States. The U.S. Supreme Court, late in 1989, in a split vote (affirming a lower court's decision), upheld the Meese recommendation. By this governmental action, losses of more than $100 million over the past decade were expected to turn into profits of about $100 million per year for the *Detroit News* and *Detroit Free Press*. It is still too early to determine a stable bottom line, but the first circulation report showed a combined circulation drop of 10.7 percent daily and 16 percent Sunday.

The key question: In such a case, do the citizens truly have two *independent* voices? The record argues that the two subsidized papers will take on a symbiotic relationship, never going after each other too aggressively. Michiganders get different styles of reporting, but not two unique newspapers. But unless we wish to amend the Constitution to permit direct regulation of the press, monopoly newspapers will continue to be the product of today's supply and demand conditions. And less than optimal performance will be the result.

THE CONSEQUENCES OF BUILDING MEGAPOWER

Let us conclude with a case study that pulls together some of the themes of this chapter.

CASE STUDY: TELE-COMMUNICATIONS, INC.

During the 1980s, to the notice of few save media analysts on Wall Street, Tele-Communications, Inc. (TCI) has not only developed into the nation's largest cable franchiser, with nearly 11 million subscribers on line, but also become the nation's largest owner of movie theaters with its United Artists Entertainment division (not connected to Hollywood's MGM/UA—although TCI has been rumored to have an eye on that too); gained power on the board of Ted Turner's well-known networks; underwritten cable's Black Entertainment network, American Movie Classics, the Discovery Channel, and C-SPAN; and purchased a significant interest in Showtime/The Movie Channel. John Malone, quietly and effectively, has made TCI the equal of his more-noted rivals, Time Warner and Fox, Inc. (See Table 3.3.)

Is this good performance? How should we view the changes in the economic structure of the mass-media industries wrought by Malone and company? Their actions surely define the conduct of the new world of cable television. But is this success due to skilled management, operating as well as they can in the wild and woolly world of media competition?

Actually, TCI's power became possible only because of openings provided by the Reagan administration. In 1981, Reagan instituted a major shift in federal policy

Table 3.3.	Programming Investments of Tele-Communications, Inc., 1989	
Programming Investments	**Percent Owned**
American Movie Classics	50
Black Entertainment Television	14
Discovery Channel	49
Prime Time Tonight	35
QVC Network Inc.	27
Think Entertainment	38
Turner Broadcasting System Inc. CNN, Turner Network Television, WTBS	22

Source: Company report.

toward the media by halting all concerns about concentration of ownership and stressing the performance standard of economic efficiency above all. Policymakers argued that media businesses ought to be free from regulation to foster optimum economic growth and choice. "Free competition" was proclaimed the path to economic prosperity. This policy, known as deregulation, saw the FCC drop most rules for regulating television and radio and laws being passed to free the cable-television industry from federal restrictions with the promise of no prosecution under existing Sherman and Clayton antitrust statutes.

In this new open world, Malone seized the day and developed TCI into a power in cable-television programming and presentation, able to dictate the offerings in millions of cable homes throughout the nation. The merger of Time, Inc. and Warner Communications led to their control of 25 percent of all broadcast programming. It also led to a lawsuit by Viacom against Time Warner, charging anticompetitive practices in pay TV. These developments only contributed to a general inclination in Congress to reinstate regulation, limit any one operator's control of the pool of subscribers, and make illegal vertical integration in which cable distributors are also program producers. Malone's response was to announce plans to spin off some of its assets (10 percent of its estimated $13 billion). As this text went to press, talk resurfaced of TCI's efforts to acquire Paramount.

Obviously, John Malone and TCI should not be singled out as the only company creating a diverse media megapower. In the traditional film industry, the Reagan administration freed the Hollywood majors for the first time in 40 years to buy theater circuits. Universal took a major position in Cineplex Odeon; Time Warner and Paramount joined together to form Primamerica; and Sony/Columbia owns the Loews's circuit. In short, deregulation enabled the biggest television and motion-picture companies to integrate vertically to acquire considerable power in the entertainment business. TCI certainly favors its own affiliated program suppliers, so whether customers want the choice or not, on TCI's systems one can be assured of seeing (and paying for) Black Entertainment Television, American Movie Classics, the Discovery Channel, C-SPAN, Showtime, and The Movie Channel, and *then* others if they fit in.

The conglomerate communicator today is in a position to control supply and thus bolster the likelihood of its being the one to focus and answer demand. By remembering the aspects of the structure/conduct/performance model, we may be in a better position to remain critical consumers.

SUMMARY

The economics of the mass media define what we hear, read, and see. And with costs ever rising and new technology appearing, understanding the economics of the mass media will continue to be crucial in making sense of the role the mass media play in our society. The model of structure, conduct, and performance enables us to make sense of the complexities of media economics. We can then grapple with the issues of one-newspaper towns and areas served by only one cable franchise. We can understand how oligopolistic economic structures all too frequently lead movie and television producers to make similar-looking bland products—a problem of economic conduct. And we can rank our alternatives for corrective government action to improve the performance of mass-media industries.

It is more productive to analyze the status and operations of a media industry than to speculate about what we wish. As we form policy responses to the issue of performance, we want to be careful first to understand "what is" and not base our proposals on "what ought to be." We should seek corrective action by government *only if* it can truly help, not because it might fulfill some wish we have for a perfect world.

The giant American media companies defend their creation of vertically integrated media empires and the perfection of news as show business by saying that if they do not do this, foreign companies will. Indeed, the deregulated market for mass media in the United States made foreign companies major players for the first time. In the Reagan years, for example, the West German conglomerate Bertelsmann AG acquired RCA Records and Doubleday. For the first time, pundits have begun to warn United States policymakers about what foreign nations have long understood. It is one thing to have foreign companies own a food or soft-drink industry (Coca-Cola has long had operations in nearly every country in the world) but another to accede to the production, distribution, and presentation of one's popular cultural and knowledge production by foreign owners.

But as we approach the twenty-first century, few doubt that a handful of giant international media conglomerates will dominate film and television. The internationalization of powerful media companies, whether TCI, Paramount, Time Warner, or Murdoch's News Corporation, Ltd., seems to have formed the wave of the future. Their actions will continue to shape and influence the actions of the mass media. But whatever transformations come our way, we must be ever critical of the new forms of mass-media production, distribution, and presentation; the structure, conduct, and performance model of analysis will help us sort out the answers to the troubling questions of proper economic behavior by America's mass media.

REFERENCES

1. Gulf + Western Annual Report, 1989, 3.
2. Speech delivered September 1988.

CHAPTER 4

The Dynamics of Codes and Formats

For all the power of conglomerates to facilitate communication, ideas do not exist until they find appropriate expression. Selecting the most effective "language" or code is the essence of the art of mass communication.

By definition, a *code* is any system of signs or images to convey meaning or content. We've come a long way from cave paintings, however. The process of giving shape to an idea (*encoding*) has become more and more complex. Not only signs but symbols and styles contribute to communication.

The effectiveness of each medium's symbol systems depends on an audience's past experiences with it as well as all other media. Does a particular production elicit reverberations from another? The communicator must find out where the audience is "coming from."

Do codes of individual media interact to produce new possibilities? Consider the addition of sound to moving pictures or the effect of television images combined with radiolike communication. Each mass medium has added its unique contribution to traditional language structure and developed visual and aural systems or formats. The whole is larger than the parts, and the cross-influence of codes continue to be a focus of mass-communication research.

Especially since there is also more and more "cross-media" usage of content material (books become videos, for example) as well as blending of media into new forms (such as MTV), it becomes increasingly important to start with an understanding of the building blocks of communication used *within* each medium. This chapter will introduce the basic coding systems of the media—the characteristics of their symbols, styles, and formats; their traditional uses in print and electronic areas; and their impact on the communication process.

THE RELATIONSHIP OF THE CONTENT, THE CODE, AND THE MEDIUM

The content, the code, and the nature of the medium or channel interact in forming the message unit. The three elements are in fact inseparable in the end result, although each can be analyzed on its own.

Content is the data, the idea, the substance. To the mass media industries, it is the information to be communicated by the message. Content is wedded to the code of a specific medium and its technology, tools, creative process, and business structure. A movie based on a play or a book can never be the same thing as the original presentation. Even if the words are the same, the format—the medium's typical organization of content material—has changed. Each medium makes a statement about reality in its own way, although it may have elements in common with other media. Mass-communication theorist Edmund Carpenter has pointed out that, like theater, film is a visual and verbal medium presented before an audience. Like ballet, film relies heavily on movement and music. Like a novel, film usually presents a narrative that depicts characters in a series of conflicts. Like painting and photography, film is two-dimensional, composed of light and shadow (and, sometimes, color). But the ultimate definition of film lies in its *unique* qualities.

Film is not video. The VCR may have increased the audience of serious and casual consumers of motion pictures, and it certainly has had wide implications for both the media and media economics, but it has not really brought the *essence* of film into the living room. The differences between television and wide screens make all the difference in the world, as those going to theaters to attend rereleases of *Gone with the Wind*, *The Wizard of Oz*, or *Lawrence of Arabia* are seeing for themselves. *New York Times* film critic Vincent Canby explains:

> When I say we don't "see" many details on a television screen that we would see in a theater, I don't mean simply visual details but also all of the other information

Figure 4.1. Although this ad promises heightened excitement in the screen's adaptation of James Ramsey Ullman's classic novel *The White Tower*, it will inevitably lack dimensions the book offered.

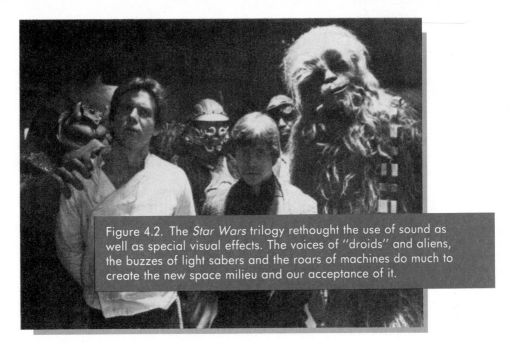

Figure 4.2. The *Star Wars* trilogy rethought the use of sound as well as special visual effects. The voices of "droids" and aliens, the buzzes of light sabers and the roars of machines do much to create the new space milieu and our acceptance of it.

that one absorbs from a movie in a theater without being aware of it. It may be anything from the rhythm of the editing to obvious contortions of plot or just a subliminal sense of esthetic disorder. In the half light of a movie theater, we are sponges.[1]

Recently, well aware of the percentage of revenue coming from post-theater-release videos, Hollywood has sometimes been deliberately shooting motion pictures with the smaller screen in mind (fewer long shots, for example). While there will be some "blurring" of media formats, there will always be creative visions intent on bringing out the best of each medium's capabilities.

Novelists, journalists, copy editors, designers, and artists of the print media choose symbols and develop styles within accepted parameters or common language and send them via well-established book, newspaper, and magazine formats. The range of what appears on the page changes constantly, through innovation, changes in censorship and ethics, and consumer interests. But the basic arrangement of content in these media has remained the same over thousands of years. The writing style as well as the design of the letters used on this page have been selected to enhance and facilitate your perception of the information. That the page is of certain proportions and whiteness and is bound with others on the inner margin are conventions of the English-language book format. On the other hand, the creative partners in the electronic media use sounds, images, contrasts, focuses, movements, to give voice to complex ideas and to share events and emotions. Technological advances create flashy new codes, but it is clear that the interaction of codes with the content and the medium is what gives rise to excellence or mediocrity. Only after a message has been successfully encoded is there any chance that it will ever be *decoded* and thus understood and enjoyed, let alone acted on.

MASS-MEDIA CODING SYSTEMS ....

Communication can occur only when both the mass communicator and the audience *share* a coding system, which we break down into symbols, styles, and formats.

SYMBOLS

Symbols are representations or tokens that individually or in combination carry meaning between sender and receiver. The alphabet and the words using it are sets of symbols. In broadcast and film, the actions of participants communicate every bit as clearly as printed words do; sounds and images are symbols. The vocabulary and grammar of coding can be enlarged to include setting, props, staging, lighting, and actors. The Scarecrow, Tin Man, and Cowardly Lion, Dorothy's companions in *The Wizard of Oz,* serve as symbols for intelligence, love, and courage when they are rewarded for their heroic deeds with a diploma, a heart-shaped clock, and a medal. These signs and characters carry meanings far beyond the words they speak. Audiences are exposed to, understand, and respond to symbols emotionally as well as intellectually. Some symbols become clichés but clearly announce content designed to attract certain audiences (an example would be the artwork on "bodice-ripper" or Gothic novels).

STYLES

Styles are characteristic ways of putting symbols together in meaningful patterns. Styles reflect accepted patterns or fashions of the day. In the 1920s, the surrealist style of painting influenced film artists, who made movies incorporating the style's dreamlike quality. The television series "Miami Vice" was often accused of being all style and no substance. The costumes and sets, which avoided earth tones and were often glaringly lit; the editing techniques; and the popular music of this series developed a way of presenting material more like music videos than traditional police-action shows. It had style as well as *a style.* More recently, "Twin Peaks" set a new standard of Atmosphere over plot. Looking at reruns of the television series "Batman," you will observe the peculiar slant of the camera angle, making everything off-kilter and unrealistic, a technique to bring the comic-book quality more forcefully to mind.

FORMATS

Formats are the frameworks that *house* stylistically similar and dissimilar content units. A format is the general plan or structure of a publication, recording, or program. Music television (MTV) is tightly formatted in terms of which videos are broadcast, how often, when, and in what order. Most magazines format their issues so that they contain a predictable variety of stories and specified topics are adequately covered in each issue, often in a sequence expected by the reader. To some degree, format shapes the substance of each mass medium.

THE IMPACT OF CODING SYSTEMS

The key questions are these:

What do the media add to communication codes that are not found in interpersonal exchanges?
Are there commonly shared symbols among media and groups of media?
Are today's audiences trained to interpret these styles?
Is one format more effective than others with certain content?

While interpersonal communication uses all five senses, the mass media tend to depend largely on sight and sound. Of them, only film, television, and video can be seen as well as heard. The print media are deaf; the phonograph and radio are blind. Let us now take a closer look at the ways communicators work with the characteristics of each medium and overcome limitations.

CODING IN THE PRINT MEDIA

The content of print is "hard copy." It exists in space, unlike electronic content, which exists in time. Essentially, the print media depend on printed words and still illustrations. The print communicator attempts to make the words flow and the visuals move through a design concept wedded to the ideas being presented. Although copy is laid out and white space is used to facilitate flow, the parameters of the printed page are dominant. Professor Walter Ong has written about the feeling of finality and filled space that print conveys:

> A newspaper's pages are normally all filled—certain kinds of printed material are called fillers—just as its lines of type are normally all justified (i.e., all exactly the same width). Print is curiously intolerant of physical incompleteness. It can convey the impression, unintentionally and subtly, but very really, that the material the text deals with is similarly complete or self-consistent.[2]

The special characteristics of print, the conventions used by both sender and receiver of media messages, include its sequential quality, layout grid, and the relationship of typography and illustration.

LINEAR PROGRESSION

The print media depend on a linear progression. The book is the most rigidly ordered of the print media. Content is typically paged in exact order to facilitate a detailed analysis of significant units of information. Exceptions, such as the series that invite you to choose your own adventure or certain self-tutoring educational materials, are actually based on the principle of other interactive forms of communication—video games and computers in these instances.

The magazine presents all or a major portion of a specific article or pictorial essay as a unit, with its conclusion often appearing in later portions of the magazine, to give the advertising more exposure. The newspaper is an information supermarket for news shoppers. Readers are attracted by major stories on the front page or the first page of major sections. They may or may not finish read

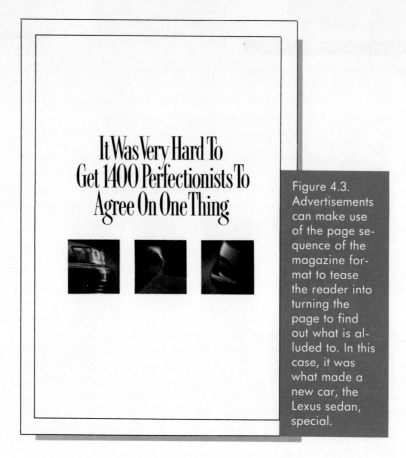

Figure 4.3. Advertisements can make use of the page sequence of the magazine format to tease the reader into turning the page to find out what is alluded to. In this case, it was what made a new car, the Lexus sedan, special.

stories on following pages. Newspapers are the most predictable and magazines the most creative in their design practices. In terms of ideas, books and magazines are flowing space.

PAGE DESIGN: STYLES AND FORMATS

The style of the printed page has been influenced tremendously by major art movements: cubism, futurism, surrealism, art deco, the Bauhaus movement, op art, and the rest. Print designs have their roots as much in graphic design as in information transfer. The print-media designer has to fill the surface with meaning and pleasure for the eye of the reader in a manner appropriate to content. One should be able to distinguish a children's book (and even identify the intended age level) from a gardening book at a distance.

The basic "canvas" in print communication is a two-dimensional space usually higher than wider and almost never square. There is space not only within pages but among pages. The designer gives the page:

1. *Symmetry*, whether symmetrical or asymmetrical;
2. A sense of *proportion*;

3. *Balance*, which gives a feeling of equilibrium;
4. *Dimension*, or a sense of depth as well as height and width;
5. *Contrast*, which is generated by sizes and shapes, spaces, lines and textures, values and colors, and signs and symbols that are recognizable to the reader;
6. A sense of *movement*, which gives the eye visual direction through the page. Pages need to be intellectually and visually joined in the minds of the audience.

All of this takes place within a basic design, the *grid*, on the surface. The typographic grid is the systematic management of physical space. The surface (the page and its size) is a constant within a given publication. But the arrangement of space is creatively variable within certain constraints such as size of type, number and width of columns, and number and size of visuals.

THE BUILDING BLOCKS OF PRINT

Specifically, the building blocks of print communication are (1) type; (2) copy set in columns; (3) headlines, headings, and titles; (4) photographs and illustrations; (5) charts, graphs, and tables; (6) captions; and (7) margins and white space.

Type. Unquestionably, type is the most important creative element in the design of print materials. The selection of type is extremely large and getting larger.

Figure 4.4. Each of these special display typefaces immediately conveys the feeling of a certain time or setting. More conventional typography, when skillfully used, codes a message just as effectively if more subtly.

Type is a tone of voice, the vocal quality of the silent eye. One of the main principles in selecting the type for *Mass Media VI* was readability. Can the pages be read quickly and clearly? The typeface used to set *Mass Media VI* is Palatino. It has a no-nonsense, up-front, scholarly voice.

Type and design have an impact on meaning. Individual pieces of type or letters have shape, size, weight, width, and slope.

1. *Shape* is the essential design of the type face.
2. *Size* refers to measurement of height—for most purposes, from 6 to 72 points (a point is about 1/72 inch); this page is set in 10-point type resting on 12-points of vertical space.
3. *Weight* is the thickness of the stroke.
4. *Width* is the horizontal space the letter occupies.
5. *Slope* is the angle, or lean, of the letter in italic, bold italic, or oblique form.

One expert on typography, D. J. R. Bruckner, states that "thousands of elements of design go into an alphabet to give it strength, grace, balance, and clarity, and a change in any of them affects all the others."[3]

Copy. Print media organize copy in columns because columns make the page easier to read and give it visual rhythm. In magazines and newspapers, columns allow for horizontal and vertical ads. The copy is built out of letters into ever-larger units.

The *word* is a "learned" combination of letters, which when spelled correctly serve as a symbol for an idea or a thing. The *line* is an optical arrangement of words with a spatial potential of less than one sentence to more than one sentence. The *sentence* is a series of words that normally includes a subject and verb. The *paragraph* is a complete idea, except in editorials and historical romances. The *column* is a series of ordered lines with width and height, which are the essential copy blocks and the central style element of the printed page. Both psychological and technological needs dictate the width of columns. For example, there is a limit to how many characters (individual letters, spaces, and punctuation marks) the eye can comfortably and rapidly take in per line of type.

Headlines, Headings, and Titles. Titles, headings, and headlines draw the eye's attention to, and stimulate the mind's involvement with, the information unit. They are the "come-on" for the material they announce. They "shout" at us, but a raised voice must be used sparingly or it will not be listened to. Headlines summarize and analyze content, set a mood or tone for the piece, and index the page for the reader.

Photographs and Illustrations. The key elements of a visual are size; cropping (how much of the original image is deleted); physical relationship to the copy format; intellectual and emotional relationship to the words; physical relationship to other visuals on the page; and direction in which they force the eye. Knowing the significance of the way a book illustration works with the pattern of the type, artists carefully design "dummies," or layouts of each page in the proposed sequence. One, Ben Shahn, once remarked how he discovered "the delights of type: fitness, elegance, tradition, humor, the color of pages, the vast panorama of choices, each with its own peculiar flavor which added so much to the words said." In any printed piece, the purpose of the illustrations is to help carry the information load.

Charts, Graphs, and Tables. In descending order of effectiveness, the chart is best; the graph is better; the table is good. All three data displays must present the minimum data and, if necessary, break down the data into multiple charts rather than one table (*simplicity*), force the eye to help the brain reach the conclusion (*effectiveness*), and isolate the major points from the lesser points (*clarity*).

Captions. The caption is more than a label. Somewhere (and the closer to the visual, the better) the caption must provide any needed explanation or justification for the visual. The problem with caption content is that it tends to be ignored by readers; points made in the caption often go unnoticed.

Margins and White Space. Blank areas set off and highlight all the other elements. Margins and white space are critical in most print-media designs.

All creative designs and decisions in print are for reader satisfaction—and perhaps for writer, editor, publisher, and designer satisfaction as well. Legibility, instant communication, clarity, and simplicity lead to understanding and retention.

INDIVIDUAL PRINT MEDIA

As Marshall McLuhan and others have pointed out, when writing was introduced, it did not simply record oral language; it was an entirely new language. It utilized an alphabet as its code. Nevertheless, bits of alphabets are meaningless in themselves. Only when these components are strung out in a line in a specific order can meaning be created.

Books. The book is basically an extension of the alphabetized code with an even more uniform linear order—an organized logical progression of words and pictures. Because of its coded form, the book is an individual medium generally read silently and in solitude. Tracing the development of mass communication reveals, for example, that the arrival of printed books smaller than previous painstakingly hand-copied volumes changed the nature of reading. Professor Walter Ong describes the manuscript culture as "a social activity, one person reading to others in a group. . . . Print created a new sense of the private ownership of words."[4]

A book is usually conceived of as a "serious" mass medium with a definite author or authority. Whether the content is narrative, descriptive, or chronological, it tends to be read in a standard progression rather than selectively, as are most magazines and newspapers (obviously, anthologies can be resequenced by the reader). The code by which a book is structured also enables the audience to consume content at its own pace, even to reread portions of the content. A book can therefore deal with complex ideas and plots involving many issues or people; its language and code are best able (of the print media) to handle this complexity effectively.

Newspapers. Instead of a line-by-line development of an idea, in newspapers there is an explosion of headlines and stories, all of which are juxtaposed and competing for attention. The front pages of the *New York Times*, the *Daily News*, and *USA Today* give some idea of this simultaneity of ideas. They also suggest that code systems can be manipulated in different ways to reach different readers with different information. The *Daily News* is coded to attract a reader different from the *New York Times* reader and to accommodate the kinds of news it prints. *USA*

Figure 4.5. The public's hunger for war developments led to an extraordinary use of columns and headlines, which would be clearly visible as newsboys held their folded wares aloft.

Today has redesigned the newspaper to fit Americans' new information lifestyle, which seems to survive on "headline news." The colorful design style of *USA Today* uses extensive visuals as well as color photos, graphs, and charts to illustrate the capsule-news style. Through varied page makeup, using multicolumn headlines with stories developed vertically beneath the headlines, all newspapers give readers a choice and encourage selective reading. The inverted-pyramid style of writing a story provides guidelines. Important information is given first; less important items follow in order of descending importance. The reader can stop anywhere and still grasp the essence of the story. (And the editor can cut the story at any point without destroying its meaning.) Newspaper columns are narrow and paragraphs short to speed reading and aid readers in assessing meaning. By breaking up a story, short paragraphs permit an audience to skim and read selectively. Banners and headlines in different type sizes indicate the importance of the articles, and they give the reader a quick summary of the contents.

This coding process and its characteristics extend naturally from the way people read newspapers. They do not generally sit down with a newspaper for hours; they read selectively for short periods of time on the subway, in the office, or over breakfast. Few people read a newspaper from front to back. Some people read only one or two sections, such as sports or the comics.

Magazines. Instead of presenting many stories to the reader simultaneously on any given page or "spread" of two facing pages, magazines publish articles in a sequential plan according to the publication's philosophy. Most magazines print a table of contents, which demonstrates their use of sequential organization, but they also make creative use of juxtaposition—one story versus another, advertisements versus stories, photographs versus print, and color versus black and white.

Magazine readers approach the medium from any one of several predictable points:

A reader who is familiar with the magazine will turn directly to *Time*'s movie reviews or some other priority.

If the cover of *Newsweek* instigated the purchase, the reader will often go directly to the cover story.

The "professional" reader (researcher) will focus on the table of contents of *U.S. News & World Report*.

The reader who is "killing time" will riffle through *People* until something catches her eye.

Because of the specialized nature of magazines, several design-code observations are important.

1. Although each issue's cover is unique, cover design is the visual signature of most periodicals.
2. Each issue has an overriding visual design, but special articles demand individual identity.
3. Pictorial features offer limitless possibilities and are an art form in and of themselves.
4. The typeface becomes the fabric of the periodical and creates an overall gray scale or visual tone.
5. Lines and decorative elements (borders, indentations, and such) serve as fences to separate some ideas and as glue to join others.
6. Single pages are usually vertical, and the spread is horizontal. But both should be laid out horizontally to get the most pleasing visual impression. In effect, layout breaks pages down into horizontal modules.

CODING IN THE ELECTRONIC MEDIA

The electronic media can be divided into two combinations:

Aural media. Radio and sound recording are completely dependent on sound.
Audiovisual media. Motion pictures and television use all the sound techniques of aural media, all the design capabilities of print, and movement. They combine the verbal and the nonverbal.

THE BUILDING BLOCKS OF SOUND

Sound is paramount in aural media, and in audiovisual media, sound must be wedded to the visuals. Orson Welles's training in radio and theatre brought an aural dimension to *Citizen Kane* that has reverberated in films over the past 40 years. Sound is at least as important as sight in creating illusions and realities in motion pictures.

Figure 4.6. *Citizen Kane* is an audiovisual masterpiece. The beauty of the film is that its visual and aural techniques complement each other and advance the dramatic intent of the plot and theme. Orson Welles as Charles Foster Kane stands in front of his larger-than-life campaign poster at a political rally that becomes immense and yet rings hollow because of the sound techniques used. In this scene, the images and sounds contradict each other to dramatic effect.

Essentially, sound can be categorized as voice, music, sound effects, and silence.

Voice. The voice can be that of singer (record), announcer (radio), actor (film), or narrator-commentator (television). All four media, of course, use all four vocal entities.

Music. The music can be vocal or instrumental. The uses of music in mass-media drama include

1. Main-title music over credits, which prepares the audience for the film as an overture does in musical theater;
2. Music to identify characters, time period, and place;
3. Music to support action;
4. Music to establish mood;
5. Music to state themes;
6. Music to reinforce the visual style.

Bernard Herrmann's score for *Psycho* does it all. It literally controls the emotions of the audience and makes them fear for their lives. It is the "music," not Norman Bates's "mother," that slashes at the audience. It meets and exceeds every criterion for the film score: it is the mood, the action, the theme, and the characters. If you have the opportunity to view *Psycho* without sound, the point will be driven home.

Sound Effects. *Star Wars* revolutionized sound even more than special visual effects. Sound effects can be local, identified visually; background, accepted environmental source; and artificial, unique aural identity, as in *Star Wars*'s lasers, spaceships, and so on.

Silence. The tension created by silence is often more effective than jarring sound. The film *2001: A Space Odyssey* is a textbook on the uses of silence. Silence is the electronic equal of print's white space.

THE BUILDING BLOCKS OF SIGHT

All the visual techniques in television and film are built around *movement* because both movies and television are *motion* pictures. The basic principles of still composition—balance, symmetry, line, value, shape, texture, color, dimension, contrast, and the rest—are developed around the basic concepts of movement.

There are essentially two classifications, or elements, in telecommunication and film communication.

Intrashot elements (include movement of the camera; movement of actors, animals, and things; and movement of the background—all within the shot).
Intershot elements (create movement by editing shots together; literally, a visual rhythm is created between shots).

Intrashot Elements. Composition is the overriding visual concern of every shot, and each movement in a shot of camera, actor, or background requires a recomposition of that shot. The *positioning* of all the pictorial elements within the frame shape is the paramount consideration in filmmaking. Every shot must be a whole and contribute to the audience's understanding and enjoyment of the film's themes, ideas, and story lines.

Camera angles determine the viewpoint and area seen by the audience. Basically, *objective* camera angles are the least emotional views of an unseen observer; *subjective* camera angles offer a personal viewpoint and involve the audience emotionally; *point-of-view* camera angles offer a specific character's viewpoint (as though the camera were the actor's eyes).

Subject size depends on the distance from the camera and on the lens used. In descending order, they are extreme long shot, long shot, medium shot, close-up,

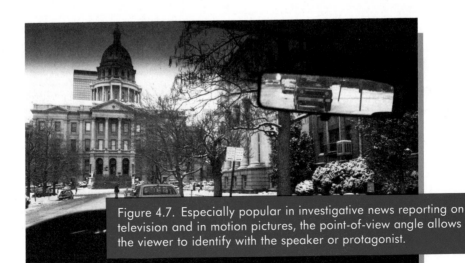

Figure 4.7. Especially popular in investigative news reporting on television and in motion pictures, the point-of-view angle allows the viewer to identify with the speaker or protagonist.

The "audiovisual score" from a film can be precisely diagramed, even though when a work is totally successful, we are unaware of the building blocks that contribute to the final product. In the diagram of twelve shots in *Alexander Nevsky* (1938), directed by Sergei Eisenstein, 17 measures of music by Serge Prokofiev accompany images of knights and troops awaiting the "Battle on the Ice," an especially memorable scene.

Alexander is atop Raven Rock and the Russian army is below on the frozen Lake Chudskoye. There is a sharp rise and then a sudden drop in the music *and* in our visual focus from Shot III to Shot IV for example; this punctuates the shifting

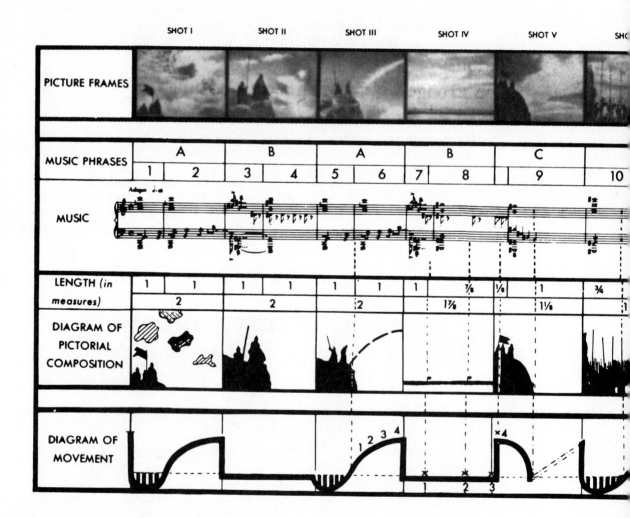

from identification with Alexander and a second knight in the foreground to apprehension of the approaching masses of warriors in the distance, a level line on the horizon.

Eisenstein dissects the fusion of music and image, the spatial relationships, and the psychological effect on viewers in his book *The Film Sense*. In his words, his analysis set out to discover the " 'secret' of those sequential vertical *correspondences* which step by step relate the music to the shots *through an identical motion* that lies at the base of the musical as well as the pictorial movement."

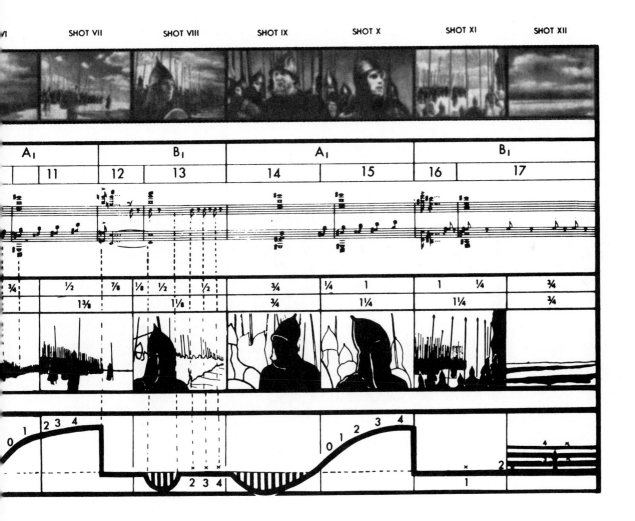

and extreme close-up. The shots also involve more than one subject, and so there are two-shots (two characters), three-shots, and group shots. The shots also have foreground and background treatments.

The lens also has an impact on size. Lenses fall into three general groups: *wide-angle* lenses see more than the eye can; *telephoto* lenses see less than the eye can and are used for close-ups at long distance (as is a telescope); *normal* lenses approximate the eye. These three lenses have fixed focal lengths. The *zoom* lens has a variable focal length and approximates visually all three of the above lenses and incorporates them by zooming in or out. The depth of field (area in focus) also varies with each lens. It is greater with wide-angle (short) lenses than with telephoto (long) lenses.

Lighting is to film what paints are to canvas. The cinematographer paints with four basic lights: the *key light* is the primary light source (the sun or a lamp); the *fill light* softens the effects of the key light by eliminating harsh shadows; the *kicker* or *backlight* separates the actors from the background; the *background light* adds depth to the composition.

Film stock is more than the difference between black-and-white and color. It has to do with contrasts (hardness, softness, hues) and the amount of light (speed), filters, and processing.

Figure 4.8. The dramatic coding effect of lighting is shown here: The fuller lighting of the bottom view makes the candidate appear far more trustworthy.

Intershot Elements. The second category of movement in film (and television) is the movement created by linking one image to the next. The movement between shots, or intershot movement, is an *editorial* function. And for many critics, editing is the heart and soul of audiovisual art. The manipulation of a succession of visual and aural images generates both a kinetic and an intellectual energy, as well as moving forward the dramatic intent of the story line.

Editing manipulates both *real* time (the time the audience spends viewing) and *dramatic* time (the length of the story and the characters that live the drama). Basically, editing moves the story line and facilitates action. *Continuity editing* is storytelling; it is slower and less frantic than *dynamic editing,* which is used in fast-paced action scenes. In both forms, editing establishes direction, controls pace and rhythm, generates spatial and emotional relationships of characters and locations, and reveals details of insights that the audience needs to know.

The building blocks of the art of editing are

1. The *frame*, a single photographic image (sound films are shot and shown at 24 frames per second).
2. The *shot*, an individual moving image or length of film exposed from the time the camera begins running until it ends.
3. The *scene*, a dramatic unit in one place at one time; it consists of one or more shots. If either time or place changes, a new scene begins.

Figure 4.9. In "The Odessa-Steps Sequence" from *Potemkin,* director Sergei Eisenstein used dynamic editing to expand time. Yet by cutting abruptly from image to image he manipulated the rhythm of the film so that the pacing seems to quicken, thereby accentuating the feeling of terror and panic implicit in the narrative.

Figure 4.10. Integration of sound and image is a highly specialized task. At work is sound effects editor Alan Splet, pictured shortly after winning an Oscar for his work on *The Black Stallion*.

4. The *sequence*, a major dramatic unit (made up of scenes) that completes exposition, character development, a theme, or a dramatic action.

Frames, then, are edited into shots, shots into scenes, scenes into sequences, and sequences into films.

Editing "builds" the film. The editing of a scene must be compelling and coherent because the audience must be both involved and able to understand. Editors perform a series of creative steps. First, they select specific shots from those available. Normally, only 10 to 20 percent of the available footage appears on the screen. Second, the selected shots are arranged so that the story line moves forward meaningfully. Third, each component shot is modified into a length that emphasizes the dramatic tone and action of the film.

The available footage is the raw material of the editor, who follows some general principles and some specific techniques to cut a film. For example, the techniques of editing includes *cuts* (one shot changes instantaneously to the next), *dissolves* (one shot gradually recedes as another gradually replaces it), *wipes* (a new shot shoves another off the screen vertically, horizontally, or diagonally), and *fades* (a shot goes to or comes from black). Traditionally, cuts are used between shots; dissolves, between scenes; and fades, between sequences.

As editors move from raw footage to rough cut to fine cut, they must edit not only image to image and sound to sound but also image to sound. Synchronization of image and sound is the basic element (and "sync" was the toughest problem to lick in the development of motion pictures).

Experience Intensified

The mass media "intensify" visual and aural perceptions. Aurally, the recording studio—with "sweetening" techniques, which improve the dynamics of the sound, and 16, 24, 35, 48, and ad infinitum tracks mixed down—can improve live performance to an extent. Color photography is more intense than color in the "real" world. The media codes generate a hyperreality that today is bigger and better and faster and more intense than ever before. We are willing to suspend belief while watching a fantasy like *Return of the Jedi* or the re-created reality of a docudrama like "Holocaust." Media codes transport us to new levels of experience. Certainly, a level of intense participation exists when the media environment, content, and mass communicator's handling of codes take us into the jungles of Vietnam with the "grunts" in *Platoon*, transport us through the pages of Tolkien's *Hobbit*, capsulate the week in *Sports Illustrated*, or rock us to sleep with the newest images in music videos.

Audiences have learned to "decode" new media languages and adjust to new dialects as they emerge. The naive movie audiences of the early 1900s have become

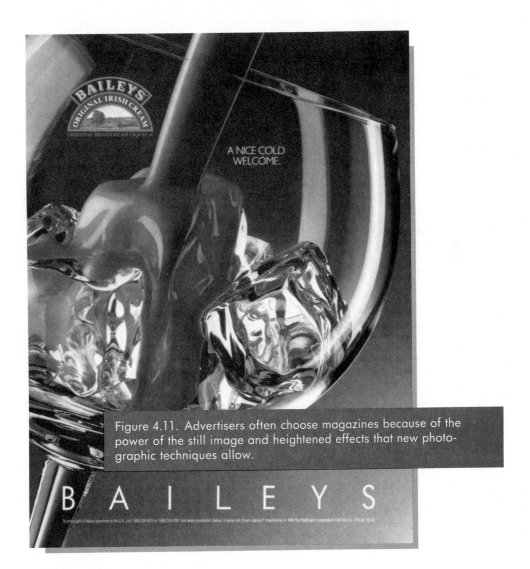

Figure 4.11. Advertisers often choose magazines because of the power of the still image and heightened effects that new photographic techniques allow.

a hardware-oriented generation of "film freaks" who want to know how the special effects work as well as experience the story line. Audiences have grown more "literate," which allows the filmmaker to expand the lexicon of the medium. This is what makes the creative process such a joy. The media are expanding human language.

SUMMARY

The process of coding in mass communication involves three essential elements: (1) symbols, which stand for things, ideas, and emotions; (2) styles, which are characteristic ways we put symbols together to generate meanings; and (3) formats, which are the overall structures or frameworks that organize mass-media content. Three components *interact* as the message unit: codes, contents, and the mass media themselves. Since every mass medium is unique, with coding devices and traditions significantly different from any other medium, the same content will be a significantly different experience, depending on the medium code used.

Codes of the print media vary from one another as well as from those of the electronic media. However, there are similarities in terms of the basic building blocks, if not in the ways the building blocks are manipulated. The print media proceed linearly from letter to letter, word to word, paragraph to paragraph, page to page, section to section. Design considerations on individual pages involve symmetry, proportion, balance, dimension, contrast, movement. Type, headlines, photos and illustrations, charts and graphs, captions, and margins and white space are of prime importance in page design.

In the electronic media, sound and movement are added to the traditional art elements (line, shape, value, color, and texture). Sound is of paramount importance in radio and sound recording but is also an essential element in the talking pictures of television and film. Voices, music, sound effects, and silence contribute to the aural style of a film. The camera, the actors, and the background move within a shot, and the total meaning of a scene is expanded by editing shots together in unique patterns. The cinematographer uses a variety of compositional tools: frame shape, angles, subject size, and depth of field, which are controlled by lenses, film stock, and lighting. The editor then builds frames into shots into scenes into sequences into a film.

Audiences have learned to understand media languages. The content of the mass media are made magical by the manipulation of each medium's codes.

REFERENCES

1. Vincent Canby, "Classics Thrive on Screen Test," *New York Times*, September 10, 1989, H19,24.
2. Walter Ong, "Print, Space, and Closure," in *Communication in History*, ed. David Crowley and Paul Heyer. (New York: Longman, 1991), 111.
3. "How the Alphabet Is Shaping Up in a Computer Age," *New York Times*, September 10, 1989, H42.
4. Ong, 109.

CHAPTER 5

Gatekeepers, Regulators, and Guardians

Do you know at whose directive a textbook is revised to eliminate the labeling of evolution as scientific fact? When a word is "bleeped" off radio or television, do you know who is responsible for censoring it? When you were in your early teens and tried to see an R- or X-rated movie, do you know who kept you out of the theater? When the publisher of *Hustler* is tried in a Georgia courtroom for obscenity, do you know why?

In the first three examples, the media themselves are the censors, even though they may be acting in response to community pressure groups; in the fourth example, a local-government authority has power to regulate *Hustler*'s sale. Many people simply assume that the federal government is responsible for all such restrictive actions. In many countries, the government *is* the chief censor and regulator of mass media. The political upheavals in Eastern Europe, Central America, and elsewhere have had much to do with unleashing governmental constraints. In the United States, however, the government plays a relatively small role in media regulation and control of message content. Only local authorities have the right to censor, and then in very limited ways. Government is but one of several institutions that can apply pressure in some areas of mass communication to influence quantity, quality, and direction.

We can identify six groups that formally and informally regulate the process of mass communication: media gatekeepers, government, content source, advertiser, individual consumer, and consumers joined in pressure groups.

This chapter will describe the role of each of these sources of control. Though often out of public view, they are undeniably a key part of the communication process. The deeper issues that arise as one or more of these gatekeepers or regulators affect the message are explored throughout this book and especially in Chapters 21 and 22.

GATEKEEPERS WITHIN THE MEDIA

The media may submit to self-regulation simply because they do not want to offend their audiences or do not want a public outcry to encourage government to be more restrictive. Most media regulation starts internally, and media's self-censorship can often be more crucial than outside pressures. A chain of assignment editors, reporters, researchers, copy editors, producers, managers, executives, di-

Figure 5.1. From initiation of the communication idea through fine-tuning its presentation, there are media gatekeepers at work: An assignment editor at a news assignment board schedules reporting crews' fieldwork. During the picture and sound-editing process, journalists and their editors can emphasize, reveal, pace, and structure the various elements that make up a television news story.

rectors, and many others control content—news and entertainment alike—in terms of their perceptions of audience interests, filters, and preferences.

Employees and sometimes owners of mass media review the creations and productions of communicators, and exercise final authority over what gets published, broadcast, recorded, filmed, and distributed. Early studies of the gatekeeping role tended to focus on an individual, such as a news editor, but that does not represent the network of specialists who at various points in the production process wield power over communication. As researcher Dennis Howitt observes:

> Certainly some individuals are in a better position to allow the passage of information through the mass communication system than others, but this is too autocratic a conception of what happens. Some people may act as gatekeepers in the day-to-day running of a media organization (e.g., subeditors of a newspaper), but others may only fulfill the function for more crucial decisions. Thus the proprietor of a newspaper may choose to influence the content of the news on rare occasions when it suits his purpose while having no influence at all on its day-to-day running.[1]

Depending on the source of the control, changes in the outgoing message may be demanded either during the creative stages or after the completion of the product.

Some mass media, particularly the broadcast industry, employ internal censors whose sole responsibility is to review all outgoing material to make sure it conforms to standards that those media have adopted for themselves. Gatekeepers may also be lawyers for media organizations who "vet" or review content for libel, invasion of privacy, and other legal problems. Individual newspapers, television stations, or networks may have their own printed code of ethics in addition to tacitly understood standards of responsibility. Parts of CBS's code are included in Chapter 21's discussion of one broadcast controversy.

THE ROLES OF EDITORS

In some mass media, the editor's function is growing simply because the production process is getting more complex. For example, movie directors used to be careful during the shooting of each scene, and the editor merely had to assemble the footage. Now directors tend to retake scenes dozens of times and shoot far more footage than can be used, giving the editor a much more creative role. Editors can affect not only pacing but atmosphere and use of reaction shots. They can make a comedy funnier, increase the suspense in a thriller, double the excitement in a war picture. Good editing can enhance a weak film, and poor editing can ruin an otherwise fine picture. The same problems, of course, occur in the print media.

In the broadcast media, the editor may not be as important as the internal censor. Prime time is particularly sensitive, and each prime-time show has its own internal censor who reads scripts, watches dailies (the raw footage of that day's shoot), and can request changes. If a producer is unhappy about a change, he or she can battle it out with the lawyers and managers, but the latter have the last word.

Of the five areas most under scrutiny at networks—violence, replication (the likelihood that a viewer will learn how to commit a crime from TV, for example), sex, language, and early-evening programming standards with youngsters in mind—violence causes the most headaches and uncertainty. Sometimes a counting system is used to determine the acceptable level of violent acts in a program aired at a certain hour. But exactly what is violent? TV insiders Richard Blum and Richard Lindheim have written that

> the slapstick act of squirting a seltzer bottle in someone's face or throwing food is given the same weight as shooting someone with a gun. Even more surprising, verbal threats often are counted as violent acts, but destruction of property is not. As a consequence, few television characters vocalize their anger with statements like "I'm going to kill you and spread your guts over the living room," but there are seemingly endless car chase sequences in which trash cans fall like bowling pins and cars slip and smash in ballets of destruction. To avoid the censor's wrath, people almost always escape from these spectacular crashes unscathed, a real piece of fiction.[2]

Often media gatekeepers do serve as ombudsmen for audiences and for good taste. It is not always a case of committees of lawyers and managers. Fast-breaking news can call for individual instinct as well as corporate position statements. The videotape of the hanging in 1989 of Lieutenant Colonel William Higgins, purportedly by the Arab Organization of the Oppressed on Earth, is a clear example.

Figure 5.2. Media gate- keepers have become much more liberal in their interpreta- tion of public morals in the 1980s. "Hill Street Blues" ushered in an era of more le- nient stan- dards, al- though its first season saw many battles with the net- work gate- keepers.

ABC anchorman Peter Jennings told viewers that that network declined to use anything other than a still photo because the tape "demeaned Colonel Higgins by having us watch him swing." Each station handled the use of the footage in a somewhat different way.

The communication message may be canceled because of judgments other than those of ethics or taste. The conglomerate communicator may decide there is no widespread interest in the message. For example, the United Nations is not the beat it once was, especially for 25 American journalists, half the number stationed there 45 years ago. "For every one or two stories on the U.N. that get in the paper, there are probably ten out there that won't," observed Peter Spotts, national editor of the *Christian Science Monitor*. "How many of their activities directly address readers' concerns?"[3] Actually, these days, quite a few, but for an increasingly image-oriented audience, the UN "really is not a dramatic and visual story . . . [and] is very low on our list of priorities," according to Tom Ross, senior vice president of NBC News.[4]

To further our information-power theme: The media gatekeepers exert enor- mous influence over us. As David L. Paletz puts it,

> *Depending on what they report, how often and in what way they portray it, and the perspectives they provide, [the media] can variously create, have no effects on, hinder, or even prevent politicization. . . .*
>
> *Relevant here are the backgrounds, values, and socialization of journalists; their definitions of news; their reliance on public officials as sources; and the ways they present news. Editing material, presenting it in brief segments on television news programs or in limited spaces in newspapers, encapsulating it for radio in a narrow frame of reference—all these requirements for presenting news have the effect of altering it or, at best, transmitting only a fragment of what has occurred.*[5]

The Impact of Big Business

We cannot forget the role of economics either. As we have seen, eyes on bottom lines belong to individuals who are interested in best-sellers and high ratings, not peripheral interests or expensive controversy. *Publishers Weekly*, a trade journal of the book industry, frequently reports contracts canceled by publishing giants fearful of lawsuits. The Authors Guild has long been vocal in pointing out that increasingly concentrated ownership among publishers will lead to a different kind of censorship. It is therefore not surprising that books *about* media that are less than positive have difficulties seeing the light of day. None of the large publishers wanted to issue *The Blockbuster Complex: Conglomerates, Show Business and Book Publisher*; based on a *New Yorker* series, Thomas Whiteside's book finally appeared on the Wesleyan University Press list. Ben Bagdikian's *The Media Monopoly* was published by Beacon Press, which is part of the Unitarian Universalist Association.

An article in the Press section of *Time*, May 29, 1989, headlined "The Tarting Up of *TV Guide:* Murdoch brings wrenching changes to an industry watchdog," regretted the passing of enterprising reporting on the TV industry after the magazine was sold by Walter Annenberg, noted for his support of media issues and research, to Rupert Murdoch. One disgruntled employee at *TV Guide* commented: "There's no interest anymore in analysis of the industry or in taking a serious look at the content of TV news." There was also a feeling that the new ownership, more familiar with the British press division into elitist and tabloid publications ("a virgin-and-whore feeling about journalism"), misread the American public's broad-based acceptance of a magazine that falls somewhere in between.

As the well-publicized threats against anyone connected with publishing or selling Salman Rushdie's novel *The Satanic Verses* revealed, some media organizations have to weigh economic and security losses against freedom of expression. The ripple effect of fear that Iranian groups would succeed in their death sentences claimed several casualties: a filmmaker named Cyrus Nowrasteh saw his first feature-length work, a thriller about an American detective amid Iranian political exiles, dropped by the American Film Institute's film festival in Los Angeles and by distributors who had agreed to show the movie in several countries.

Professional Standards

Mass-media organizations and individuals have joined together into associations to protect their rights, collect information, lobby for sympathetic laws, further their interests, and establish uniform codes of conduct to guide individual gatekeepers in performing their internal regulation. In addition to national organizations, such as the American Newspaper Publishers Association, media units often have state, county, or city groups. In broadcasting, the National Association of Broadcasters (NAB) lobbies in Congress on behalf of broadcast stations. And when the NAB radio and television codes were in force, it also monitored stations' observance of those codes. In the film industry, the Motion Picture Association of America (MPAA) has a production-code division that establishes film ratings for all films submitted by its members. The Recording Industry Association of America (RIAA) serves as an arbiter of production standards and controls for the sound-recording industry.

Figure 5.3. Violence on television and in films grew considerably more graphic in the late 1960s and early 1970s. Explicit violence in Kubrick's *Clockwork Orange* (1971) and Coppola's *Godfather* (1972) caused considerable uproar. Both films were powerful works of art. Gratuitous scenes of violence do not appear in these two movies, pressure groups are concerned that these films allow for lesser works that do exploit graphic scenes of violence.

Media workers, too, have professional associations. The largest is the Society of Professional Journalists (SPJ), which has both campus chapters (at colleges where journalism and mass communication are taught) and professional chapters (for those working in the media). Such associations were often started in response to public pressures to regulate or restrict media. For example, the comic-book industry, which grew rapidly after World War II, found itself after the war facing growing public criticism linking comics to the rise in juvenile delinquency. The attacks led to the establishment of the Association of Comic Magazine Publishers (ACMP) in 1947. A code was drafted to safeguard children from comic books that presented nudity, torture, sadism, and frightening monsters. The code also banned racial, ethnic, and religious slurs; negative marital story lines; ridicule of law officers; profanity; and detailed descriptions of criminal acts. The ACMP later became the Comic Magazine Association of America (CMAA) and developed a 41-point code. By the late 1980s, 90 percent of industry members were voluntarily submitting materials for code approval, allowing them to display the code seal on their products.

Especially in the United States, gatekeepers are not legally obligated to accept codes of conduct that act as regulators of their actions; the First Amendment prevents such codes from being binding on the communicator. In Sweden, for example, journalists can be thrown out of the profession for violating a jounalistic standard, but in the United States such codes can be used only as voluntary guidelines. Two examples of important professional codes—"A Statement of Principles" of the American Society of Newspaper Editors and the "Code of Broadcast News Ethics" of the Radio-Television News Directors Association—are reprinted here. The codes for public-relations and advertising specialists are included in the chapters covering those industries, in Part 2.

MOTION-PICTURE GATEKEEPING

Self-censorship has long been an important concept in the motion-picture and broadcast media. A motion-picture code was adopted by the industry in the 1920s in an effort to avert government censorship. The code was extremely restrictive: one could not show on film the udder of a cow, a woman's body in profile, or the inside of a bathroom. But codes tend to reflect public interest, and as Americans became less squeamish about sex in the 1950s and 1960s, administration of the strict movie code became more relaxed. In 1968, the movie industry adopted a more lenient form of voluntary self-censorship, a rating system that allows people to determine for themselves the type of movie they wish to see. G (family), PG (parental guidance), R (restricted from those under age 17 without an accompanying parent), and X (restricted from all under age 17) are ratings that are not required by government but are made by the industry itself.

Sometimes the public does not agree with the ratings. When *Indiana Jones and the Temple of Doom* and *Gremlins* were released in 1984, they were rated PG. But critics and parents reacted negatively to the degree of violence in both films. A new rating, PG-13, was then instituted to warn parents to use extra caution in allowing children to see some films that are sexually innocent but contain much violence.

Filmmakers often object to the ratings received by their productions because such ratings can affect box-office receipts, and producers can appeal the rating. The producers of *Ryan's Daughter*, a period piece based on a best-selling novel, threatened to pull out of MPAA when the film was rated R. Under this pressure, the rating was changed to PG. *Midnight Cowboy*, rated X when it came out in 1969, was rerated to R without changes to the film. *RoboCop* was reedited to avoid receiving the feared X rating. The concern over ratings works in both directions. The 1981 Academy Award winner for best film, *Chariots of Fire*, was originally rated PG, but producer David Puttnam and director Hugh Hudson reedited it to add a number of expletives so it would be reclassified R, as a promotional tool.

THE SOCIAL CONTEXT

Back in the 1960s, CBS censors refused to let the stars of "The Dick Van Dyke Show" sleep together, even though they played a married couple. Twenty-five years later, husbands and wives—as well as lovers—not only share beds but make passionate love. In a 1985 episode of NBC's "Miami Vice," a barechested Philip Michael Thomas rolled around in bed with his barechested girlfriend, Pam Grier, on prime time.

The networks employ many people to perform the gatekeeping function. Since television views itself as a family medium, it has usually adopted stricter standards than the movie industry. In 1976, for example, when CBS showed the movie *Smile*, a satirical comedy about young women embroiled in a California beauty pageant, it had to remove certain scenes and words. A scene in which a plucked chicken gets smooched by hooligans at a fraternity initiation was cut by CBS. The words *sanitary napkin* were censored from a scene in which plumbers are complaining about discarded sanitary napkins clogging pipes. In the 1990s, however, such prudishness seems ridiculous.

American Society of Newspaper Editors Statement of Principles

Preamble

The First Amendment, protecting freedom of expression from abridgment by any law, guarantees to the people through their press a constitutional right, and thereby places on newspaper people a particular responsibility.

Thus journalism demands of its practitioners not only industry and knowledge but also the pursuit of a standard of integrity proportionate to the journalist's singular obligation.

To this end the American Society of Newspaper Editors sets forth this Statement of Principles as a standard encouraging the highest ethical and professional performance.

Article I: Responsibility

The primary purpose of gathering and distributing news and opinion is to serve the general welfare by informing the people and enabling them to make judgments on the issues of the time. Newspapermen and women who abuse the power of their professional role for selfish motives or unworthy purposes are faithless to that public trust.

The American press was made free not just to inform or just to serve as a forum for debate but also to bring an independent scrutiny to bear on the forces of power in the society, including the conduct of official power at all levels of government.

Article II: Freedom of the Press

Freedom of the press belongs to the people. It must be defended against encroachment or assault from any quarter, public or private.

Journalists must be constantly alert to see that the public's business is conducted in public. They must be vigilant against all who would exploit the press for selfish purposes.

Article III: Independence

Journalists must avoid impropriety and the appearance of impropriety as well as any conflict of interest or the appearance of conflict. They should neither accept anything nor pursue any activity that might compromise or seem to compromise their integrity.

Article IV: Truth and Accuracy

Good faith with the reader is the foundation of good journalism. Every effort must be made to assure that the news content is accurate, free from bias and in context, and that all sides are presented fairly. Editorials, analytical articles and commentary should be held to the same standards of accuracy with respect to facts as news reports.

Significant errors of fact, as well as errors of omission, should be corrected promptly and prominently.

Article V: Impartiality

To be impartial does not require the press to be unquestioning or to refrain from editorial expression. Sound practice, however, demands a clear distinction for the reader between news reports and opinion. Articles that contain opinion or personal interpretation should be clearly identified.

Article VI: Fair Play

Journalists should respect the rights of people involved in the news, observe the common standards of decency and stand accountable to the public for the fairness and accuracy of their news reports.

Persons publicly accused should be given the earliest opportunity to respond.

Pledges of confidentiality to news sources must be honored at all costs, and therefore should not be given lightly. Unless there is clear and pressing need to maintain confidences, sources of information should be identified.

These principles are intended to preserve, protect and strengthen the bond of trust and respect between American journalists and the American people, a bond that is essential to sustain the grant of freedom entrusted to both by the nation's founders.

This Statement of Principles was adopted by the ASNE Board of Directors on Oct. 23, 1975; it supplants the 1922 "Canons of Journalism."

Radio-Television News Directors Association Code of Broadcast News Ethics

The responsibility of radio and television journalists is to gather and report information of importance and interest to the public accurately, honestly and impartially.

The members of the Radio-Television News Directors Association accept these standards and will:

1. Strive to present the source or nature of broadcast news material in a way that is balanced, accurate and fair.
    A. They will evaluate information solely on its merits as news, rejecting sensationalism or misleading emphasis in any form.
    B. They will guard against using audio or video material in a way that deceives the audience.
    C. They will not mislead the public by presenting as spontaneous news any material which is staged or rehearsed.
    D. They will identify people by race, creed, nationality or prior status only when it is relevant.
    E. They will clearly label opinion and commentary.
    F. They will promptly acknowledge and correct errors.
2. Strive to conduct themselves in a manner that protects them from conflicts of interest, real or perceived. They will decline gifts or favors which would influence or appear to influence their judgments.
3. Respect the dignity, privacy and well-being of people with whom they deal.
4. Recognize the need to protect confidential sources. They will promise confidentiality only with the intention of keeping that promise.
5. Respect everyone's right to a fair trial.
6. Broadcast the private transmissions of other broadcasters only with permission.
7. Actively encourage observance of this Code by all journalists, whether members of the Radio-Television News Directors Association or not.

Figure 5.4. A drama about incest, "Something about Amelia," broke all the taboos that had been maintained by the gatekeepers at ABC. The success of the show highlighted the changes that had taken place in the public mind.

In the early 1980s, the so-called family-viewing policy of the National Association of Broadcasters provided an interesting example of governmental interference in professional codes. "Family viewing" was pushed by Congress and the Federal Communications Commission. It stated that prime-time television periods should be restricted to programs that are appropriate for a general family audience, including children. Hollywood writers, actors, and program producers were upset, claiming that the concept of "family viewing" limited their freedom of expression. A federal district court in California agreed, ruling that "family viewing" violates the First Amendment and need not be enforced or followed by networks or stations.

THE GOVERNMENT AS REGULATOR ....

REGULATION TO PROTECT SOCIETY AND GOVERNMENT

Although many aspects of our lives are governed by statutes and ordinances, the founders felt that certain liberties were sacred to the democratic process—freedom of speech, freedom of worship, freedom to assemble, and freedom of the press. Those guarantees have made mass-media regulation in America different from media laws in other societies, for few countries have such a sweeping declaration of press and speech freedom. Most American governmental regulations of media, but by no means all, are more concerned with maintaining an environment of free communication and protecting the individual's rights in the communication process than they are with restricting communication.

Figure 5.5. *Penthouse* publisher Bob Guccione, angry that religious groups try to keep such magazines off newsstands, declared he would rather have people buy his competition than no magazine at all.

The First Amendment to the Constitution does not define the *limits* of freedom. Judicial and legislative decisions have defined the meaning of that amendment, usually in the light of current trends and social conditions. The Constitution, as it is interpreted by the courts and lawmakers, controls the *regulators* and determines which of their actions are permissible under the American system. Chapter 20 chronicles landmark decisions concerning the freedom of the press—a term now expanded to include nonprint forms of media expression—and the areas of censorship, pornography, libel and sedition, restrictions on court coverage, and copyright.

THE FEDERAL COMMUNICATIONS COMMISSION

Unlike the other mass media, radio and television stations are licensed by the government, but the government cannot censor or suppress any broadcast once the broadcaster has a license. The government began its regulation of broadcasting in the 1920s when major broadcasters requested help to maintain order in the scramble for limited frequencies and channels. The Supreme Court later upheld the notions that broadcasters use public property (the airwaves) and that government has an obligation to administer property that is not private. In 1927, the Federal Radio Commission was established; in 1934, it became the Federal Communications Commission (FCC), charged with regulating radio, telephone and telegraph, and (later) television.

Like the courts, the FCC interprets rather than makes the law. Congress enacts the law. A broadcast station must be licensed by the FCC, and the license must be renewed (radio stations are now given a seven-year license and television stations, a five-year license). It used to be that the station and its programming were formally reviewed at the time of renewal, and if the commission ruled that the station had not acted in the public interest, the license could be rescinded. These reviews are now greatly reduced under deregulation. The FCC can still levy fines of up to $10,000 for specific violations of its rules and regulations. But these regulatory powers do not give the FCC the right to censor. Few licenses have been revoked, since the burden of proof falls on the FCC, and the definition of *public interest* is vague. Nevertheless, the government does have more power to regulate a broadcaster than to regulate a publisher.

The FCC also has controlled the extent of broadcast ownership so that it could prevent monopolies. Formerly, no one could own more than one AM, one FM, and one TV station in any one listening area, and no one could own more than a total of seven of each of these stations in the entire country. Table 3.2 shows the present distribution in one market. In television, no more than five of these outlets could formerly be very-high-frequency (VHF, channels 2 to 13) stations. Under deregulation, a person or corporation can now own 12 AM, 12 FM, and 12 TV stations, and in 1990, ownership of radio may become unlimited. The FCC has also sought to prevent monopolies in local media by not giving licenses to applicants who already own a daily newspaper in the same market. FCC policies favoring minority applicants for licenses were upheld by the Supreme Court in 1990. (The commission has recently begun fining stations with discriminatory hiring practices.)

The FCC has also regulated some broadcast program content, especially in the areas of politics and public affairs. Section 315 of the FCC Code requires the broadcaster to furnish equal time and equal opportunity to all political candidates for a given office. Excepted were news programs, debates between candidates, news-interview programs, and candidates' news conferences.

A former FCC regulation, the so-called Fairness Doctrine, charged broadcasters with the duty of seeking out and broadcasting contrasting viewpoints on controversial issues of public importance. The Fairness Doctrine was different from the equal-time provision of Section 315; it required broadcasters only to present contrasting views, not to give them equal time on the air. Although the constitutionality of the Fairness Doctrine had been upheld by the Supreme Court in 1969, in 1987, the FCC, in response to the deregulation mood in Washington and to broadcasters' complaints, eliminated it. Congress has recently shown interest in reimposing it.

Until the mid-1960s, the FCC paid little attention to cable TV, regarding it as a passing phenomenon. In 1972, the commission adopted a set of rules specifically for this expanding area of television, but under the Reagan administration, it relaxed many of these rules in an effort to allow cable systems to grow. Feeling that things have gone too far, Congress is again pushing for controls on the vertical integration and concentration of ownership, described in Chapter 3.

By the mid-1980s, radio was the most deregulated broadcasting medium. Stations were no longer obligated to devote a certain percentage of their programming to nonentertainment or public-service programs. They were no longer required to ascertain the interests of their communities, maintain program logs, or produce a limited number of programs on issues relevant to their communities. Perhaps most important, stations were no longer required to limit commercials to 18 minutes per hour; they could run as many commercials as they wanted. Finally, the amount of paperwork required to apply for a license renewal was drastically reduced.

Deregulation of television has not come as swiftly, but by the mid-1980s, Congress and the FCC had agreed to eliminate the restrictions on TV stations and networks that had prevented them from owning cable systems. The FCC voted to reduce the requirement that TV stations broadcast a minimum coverage of public affairs and new programming, and to ease the requirement that stations regularly assess community needs for guidance in programming. The commission had also proposed an end to the 16-minute limit on commercials during each TV hour.

But as the Bush administration replaced the Reagan administration and the 1980s became the 1990s, a new FCC, chaired by Bush-appointee Alfred Sykes, began to address a number of regulatory issues. For example, the new FCC chairman launched an effort to respond to demands to clean up indecency on radio, both by disc jockeys and in record lyrics. A number of states have recently been considering mandatory labeling of records, which some feel approaches censorship.

Technological advances further complicate the issue of regulation for the years ahead. Policymakers at the Congressional Office of Technology Assessment question where the innovations in telecommunications will leave us. Professor Paul Barkan, director of the Center of Science, Mathematics, and Technological Literacy, at Westchester Community College in Valhalla, New York, led a seminar in the fall of 1989 to examine the relationship of the media and the Constitution. He said:

> *Because of the expansion of telecommunications, the old concept of the press as a small organization disseminating information to a large number will change. It will be many people disseminating information to many more and the question of the Government's right to restrict ownership of communications companies, for example, is one issue which will be coming up more.*[6]

THE REGULATION OF ADVERTISING

The courts, including the U.S. Supreme Court, treat advertising as *commercial speech* to distinguish it from noncommercial or political speech. In a series of decisions over the last several years, the Supreme Court has generally held that commercial speech is protected by the First Amendment but that it has less protection than noncommercial speech and is subject to controls for truthfulness, fairness, and health and safety. Chapter 8 treats regulation of the various areas of advertising and promotion activity in detail.

THE CONTENT SOURCE AS REGULATOR ....

The source of information can also be a regulator, providing a form of control at the very beginning of the communication process. Although communication has grown massive and complicated, the forms of regulation that are used by the content source can be assigned to fairly distinct categories.

STRATEGIC RELEASING

The source regulates communication by strategically timing and packaging the message in a letter, publication, or (if the content source has enough money) radio, television, or motion-picture production. Or the source might choose to release the message to the media through a news release, a press conference, or an exclusive interview.

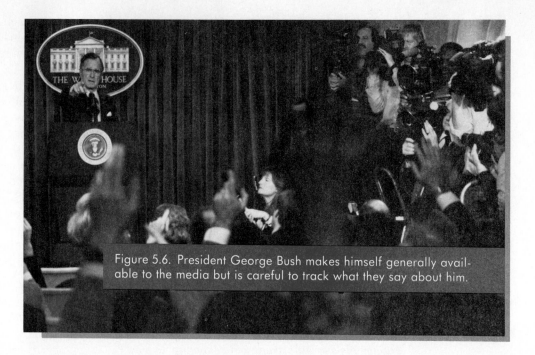

Figure 5.6. President George Bush makes himself generally available to the media but is careful to track what they say about him.

STRATEGIC WITHHOLDING

The source can also regulate the communication flow by blocking the media from getting a certain message or parts of a message. The government can do this by classifying documents or claiming executive privilege. The Freedom of Information Act of 1967 (discussed in Chapter 20) set forth the rationale for what can be legally withheld by the federal government and what cannot, and it established the judicial procedures to make the government prove in court why information should be withheld. Many states have statutes that define the categories of public records to which the media can and cannot have access.

When President Reagan was shot in an assassination attempt in 1981, for example, the White House press office withheld certain details of his injury soon after the shooting. The press office told journalists that the president was only slightly injured, that he was joking and laughing at the hospital, and that he would be back at work soon. Later, the officials admitted that they had withheld information about the gravity of the president's wounds to avoid overreaction.

STRATEGIC STAGING

The source can also regulate the flow of communication by deliberately staging a situation or an event in such a way that a certain kind of message gets into the media. For example, a senator who wishes to express his point of view about a particular issue holds a hearing and calls a group of witnesses, from whom he can elicit the type of testimony that will get news headlines. The president, not wanting to see this point of view emphasized in the media, announces that he is traveling to Europe at the same time that the senator is holding his hearing. The president takes many reporters with him, attracting daily coverage and overshadowing the hearing called by the senator. Meanwhile, a citizen's group holds a rally on the steps of the Capitol to get media (and public) attention for its position.

The terrorists who hijacked a TWA plane in the Middle East in 1985 certainly used that staged event to capture the attention of the American people. Indeed, many people believed that the media, as well as the passengers, were being held hostage by the situation. It was news that could not be ignored. Thus the people who controlled the event also controlled the media.

The Advertiser as Regulator

Advertising support plays a role in the regulation of mass media, but it can be a subtle, unspecific control. David Potter, a historian who has studied advertising as a force in molding the American character, wrote in his book *People of Plenty:*

> *In the mass media we have little evidence of censorship in the sense of deliberate, planned suppression imposed by moral edict (by advertisers) but much evidence of censorship in the sense of operative suppression of a great range of subjects. . . . The dynamics of the market . . . would seem to indicate that freedom of expression has less to fear from the control which large advertisers exercise than from the control which these advertisers permit the mass market to exercise.*[7]

Individual instances can be cited in which advertisers used their economic power to "regulate" the media. For example, advertisers in a Wisconsin town withdrew their advertising from the local newspaper to protest the use of its production shop to print an underground newspaper. Their action could have put the newspaper out of business, but the newspaper stood its ground and ultimately won. News offices of most mass media are separate from the advertising offices; news officials rarely want to accept the dictates of the advertising offices.

Another example is an episode in the life of the television drama series "Desilu Playhouse." In a 1958 program, a military officer was depicted warning the people of Hawaii of an imminent attack by the Japanese prior to the bombing of Pearl Harbor. The army authorities were shown declaring the officer incompetent and removing him from headquarters. But "Desilu Playhouse" was sponsored by Westinghouse, a firm with many government and military contracts. It would not do, cried Westinghouse, to depict the military as blind to the hero's warnings. So CBS network censors cut the show under pressure from the advertiser.

In 1989 a Michigan woman gained national attention for the letters she wrote to advertisers saying she was offended by content on the sitcom "Married . . . with Children." The fact that other sponsors quickly stepped into the breach when some advertising was pulled is not as significant as the growing sensitivity among corporations fighting for their market share. The advertising agencies for many major advertisers use the screening services of Advertising Information Services who report back on sex, violence, profanity, drugs, alcohol, and religion, with eyes ready to pick up homosexuality, child and spouse abuse, and matters that could be embarrassing for specific clients (the use of a phone to plot murders, too much blood—which makes pizza makers nervous, etc.). The "dynamics of the market"

Figure 5.7. "thirtysomething" and other series sometimes have episodes that worry—or scare away—advertisers.

indeed: ABC lost more than $1 million from advertisers that dropped a "thirtysomething" episode showing two men on a bed. Says one screener: "The job has never been as rigorous as it is today."

Theoretically, the more independent the medium can be from advertising, the less power of regulation the advertiser will have. Radio and television, which receive almost all their revenue from advertising, run the risk of great pressures from sponsors. Newspapers and magazines, which, for the most part, receive 33 to 50 percent of their revenue directly from subscribers, have less direct obligation to advertisers. Books, the recording industry, and motion pictures, which receive almost all of their revenue directly from their audiences, can better afford to ignore Madison Avenue; they are not immune to other forces, as we will see.

THE CONSUMER AS REGULATOR ....

No doubt, the greatest area of consumer regulation is in the marketplace. Those publications that sell stay in business, and those that cannot obtain or maintain an audience go bankrupt. Broadcast programs that do not attract large audiences go off the air. Because the media are in business to make a profit, they are usually sensitive to their customers and pay careful attention to the moods and habits of their readers, listeners, or viewers. Of course, what the audience wants may not always be the best or most constructive for the social good. Violence and sex seem to be more popular than news analysis and interpretation of public issues. Thus control by the marketplace has to be balanced with social well-being.

Although mass media are sensitive to individual responses, as media grow the individual voice gets weaker. Increasingly, people have joined together in groups and associations to make their voices heard and their opinions felt. These groups have been able to pressure mass media, thus serving as regulators of mass communication. Nearly every religious, ethnic, occupational, and political group has an association that can speak for the members of the group, exerting pressure on television to stop portraying Italians as criminals, on newspapers to publish stories about gun laws, on radio to present antismoking commercials, on magazines to stop obscenity.

One such pressure group, Action for Children's Television (ACT), petitioned the FCC for a rule barring advertisements on children's shows. The efforts were a major force behind all three networks' appointments of executives to supervise children's programming. Such pressure is also often applied to the media through governmental regulatory agencies.

The National Council of Churches (NCC) has long taken an active role in pressuring the broadcast media about sex and violence in programs. In its latest policy statement, the 260-member governing board of the council said it "recognizes the powerful influence of television, film, cable TV and videocassettes on the opinions, tastes and values of Americans." Citing its first addressing of these issues in June 1963 and in 1972 following the advent of cable TV, the NCC in 1986 issued the following statement to amplify its deploring of violent scenes that "damage the common good and threaten media freedom":

> *We believe that the weight of research over the past thirty years supports the following conclusions about the relationships between televised violence and aggression:*
>
> 1. *Laboratory studies show conclusively that there is a causal relationship between viewing violence on television and subsequent aggressive behavior.*
> 2. *The vast majority of field studies demonstrate a positive association between exposure to media violence and aggressiveness.*
> 3. *The positive association between viewing TV violence and aggressiveness is small but consistent. Looked at across the entire population and over an extended period of time, such a modest statistical relationship implies a substantial negative social effect.*
> 4. *The conclusion that media violence encourages antisocial and aggressive behavior is consistent with accepted theories about the nature of social learning.*
> 5. *Laboratory studies show that violent sexual material stimulates aggression toward women; also, violent material stimulates sexual violence.*
> 6. *Media can and often do create insecurity, vulnerability and dependency, and thereby the overall conditions in which violence is facilitated in society. Most children and adults who are heavy viewers of television express a greater sense of insecurity and apprehension about their world than do light viewers; the "mean world" syndrome.*
> 7. *Because music video often combines teen idols with erotic material and violence in a repetitive context, this new format requires careful research and monitoring. (We believe existing research on media violence in general implies a detrimental effect of violent and sexually violent music video on children and youth.)*
>
> *We oppose compromise with the guarantees of the First Amendment. At the*

same time we deplore the activities of those in the media industries who hide behind these protections to make money at the expense of the public welfare. The public, acting through its governmental institutions, must provide protection for freedom of expression; however, that freedom is not a license to exploit and demean the common good.

We recognize that many professionals within the communication industry are concerned about the amount of exploitative sex and gratuitous violence in the media in which they work, and are doing what they can to serve positively the needs and interests of the viewers. These people deserve and require our support, our encouragement and our commendation. But these individuals are themselves only a small part of a vast and complex system which parcels out responsibility, a little bit to everyone, so that in the end, no one *is ultimately responsible.*

The groups pressuring television broadcasters and advertisers also include angry parents and conservative activists. In 1989, pressure-group protests over provocative storylines on abortion, drug use, and a lesbian character on ABC's "HeartBeat" resulted in sponsor withdrawals. And similar protests led sponsors to cancel spots in NBC's "Nightingales" and "Saturday Night Live" as well as the Fox network's "Married . . . with Children."

Another pressure group that became active in the 1980s was the Parents Music Resource Center, started by a group of prominent Washington, D.C., women who objected to "dirty" lyrics in popular recordings as well as "teen slasher" movies and rock groups' simulation of sexual torture. The women's interest in the issue was sparked particularly by Prince, one of the sultriest stars of the mid-1980s. The women's group was also offended by lyrics in songs by Sheena Easton and Frankie Goes to Hollywood, and by Madonna's gyrating about in a music-video version of her album *Like a Virgin.* The group won the support of the NAB to urge record companies to provide radio stations with advance copies of record lyrics so that the stations could judge the records' suitability for broadcast. They are among those pressing for laws requiring that song lyrics and the label Explicit Lyrics—Parental Advisory be printed on album covers. Record companies and retailers say that a requirement would be possibly a violation of music-publishing rights, but they voluntarily suggested a sticker label when the controversy intensified in 1990.

Books have also suffered from the pressures of public groups that have sought to ban books from libraries and schools. Between 1982 and 1985, there were 22 public book burnings in 17 states. A citizens' review committee in Midland, Michigan, recommended banning Shakespeare's *Merchant of Venice* from the public schools on grounds that it is anti-Semitic. In Waukegan, Illinois, an alderman proposed banning from public schools books that give an unflattering portrayal of blacks, including such classics as *Gone with the Wind, Uncle Tom's Cabin, To Kill a Mockingbird,* and *The Adventures of Huckleberry Finn.* Not only fiction is affected by regional and religious concerns. In the fall of 1989, groups such as the Traditional Values Coalition succeeded in pressuring the nation's largest textbook market, the California Board of Education, to put schoolbook publishers on notice that there should be no mention of evolution as "scientific fact."

One group increasingly applying pressure on all media is women. A number of women's groups have lobbied in various forums for more balanced coverage and an end to employment discrimination by the mass media. In 1976, the National

Figure 5.8.
Record album
showing sexual
explicitness.

Commission on the Observance of International Women's Year produced a set of guidelines for mass-media coverage of and employment of women. Many of these guidelines have been adopted by mass-media communicators and gatekeepers, for the mass media could certainly not continue to be mass if they continued to offend so large a segment of their audience.

We need to take a closer, more analytical look at the individuals and groups that constitute the media audience—or rather, audiences. The pressures and controls they bring to bear on the messages offered by the media have their origins in the ways they perceive those messages. No area of the communication process is more studied today than the filters of the ever more specialized audience.

SUMMARY

The mass media are regulated by internal and external forces, but because of constitutional guarantees of freedom of speech and the press, the media in the United States are subject to less government regulation than in most other countries.

Internal gatekeepers—media editors, producers, directors, managers, publishers, and lawyers—provide preliminary regulation of media content before it is communicated publicly. Organizational codes, professional standards, and possible adverse reactions of consumers or advertisers all influence the content and general freedom of creative expression. Societal standards and degrees of consumer interest in news content and entertainment programming come into play.

Although the government cannot censor, it can restrict the mass media in a variety of ways. It can regulate broadcasting; although that regulation decreased in the 1980s, there is renewed interest in regulatory control. And it can regulate fraudulent advertising, but it cannot regulate taste or moral values expressed in advertising. New forms of media and media use will create new issues.

The source of information can regulate media by controlling the way information is released, withheld, or staged. The advertiser can exercise some regulatory power over the media when the sponsor is more powerful than the medium.

The consumer can control the media's impact on individuals by using the courts to protect against defamation and invasion of privacy. But most important, the consumer can regulate the mass media by deciding which medium to buy in the marketplace. And increasingly, consumers are forming pressure groups to exercise greater power over media conduct and content.

REFERENCES

1. Dennis Howitt, *Mass Media and Social Problems,* vol. 2 of *International Series in Experimental Social Psychology* (Elmsford, N.Y.: Pergamon Press, 1982), 19.
2. Richard A. Blum and Richard D. Lindheim, *Primetime: Network Television Programming* (Boston: Focal Press, 1987), 177.
3. *New York Times,* October 22, 1989, 19.
4. Ibid.
5. *International Encyclopedia of Communication,* vol. 3, 1989, 324.
6. *New York Times,* September 3, 1989, WC5.
7. David Potter, *People of Plenty* (Chicago: University of Chicago Press, 1954), 184.

The Fragmented Audience: Filters and Feedback

Some classic models of the communication process may depict the audience as receiver, but there is very little that is passive about this role. The HUB model presented in Chapter 1 includes it as one of several interacting components of *communication*. This chapter, on the trail of the elusive media audiences, describes the mechanisms of the receiving and reacting stages of the mass-communication process. None of the many audiences that exist can be neatly categorized. Mass-communication audiences are large, impersonal and heterogeneous, removed from the communicator, and changing from medium to medium and from one message transmission to the next. Communicators constantly research their probable audiences to determine the effectiveness of their efforts. The communicators' choice and application of codes and formats, and their prescreening of content through gatekeeping, all constantly interact with unseen individuals and amorphous groups who bring to the communication process their own filters or lenses—their emotions, perception skills, and cultural and social preferences.

THE CHARACTERISTICS OF AN AUDIENCE

As elusive and anonymous as audiences generally are, the concept of *audience* implies a more defined group than does *public*. For the mass communicator, the public, a total pool of available people, is an abstraction; the audience is a reality because audience members actually consume what the media produce. An individual has only to exist to be a part of the public, but a person must take action—read or listen or watch—to become a part of an audience. Audiences participate and respond to the media, and the results are complex and powerful.

In Chapter 2, we saw that when the mass media become involved in the communication process, the receiver changes from one person—who in interpersonal communication remains a discrete, discernible, and recognizable individual in close physical and/or emotional contact with the sender—to part of the total audience for mass communication. Individuals are parts of *aggregates* called readership, listenership, or viewership; they make up mass-communication audiences. Note the use of the plural here. There are many audiences, over time, for any given unit of media content. Mass-communication audiences are complex but do exhibit five basic characteristics.

1. *An audience tends to be composed of individuals who have shared experiences and are*

Figure 6.1.
This family is part of an audience being surveyed by Nielsen Media Research.

affected by similar interpersonal social relationships. These individuals choose the media products they use by conscious selection or habitual choice. Some people react to audiences as unthinking masses, following the line of thought developed by Gustave LeBon in *The Crowd*. The "crowd mentality" and "mass audience" are not well-thought-out concepts. The audience member remains an individual throughout the mass-communication process.

2. *An audience tends to be large.* Charles Wright says, "We consider as 'large' any audience exposed during a short period of time and of such a size that the communicator could not interact with its members on a face-to-face basis."[1] There is no numerical cutoff point intended in the definition of *large*. Audience size is relative. A "large" audience for a hardback textbook might be a "small" audience for a prime-time network series like "The Cosby Show."

3. *An audience tends to be heterogeneous rather than homogeneous.* Individuals in a given audience represent a wide variety of social categories. Some basic media units increasingly seek specialized audiences, but even these groups tend to be more heterogeneous than homogeneous. The audience for *Mass Media VI* is somewhat specialized, but its readers are still part of a mass-communication audience that consumes many different books. Audiences exhibit a "selective heterogenity"; they group themselves in a variety of configurations, often gathering around more than one media offering at a time. You can be in the middle of a novel, pause to read the daily newspaper, and have rhythm and blues playing in the background, not to mention subscribing to five magazines and pay TV.

4. *An audience tends to be relatively anonymous.* Bruce Springsteen, for example, does not personally know the individuals who are listening to his latest record.

5. *An audience tends to be physically separated from the communicator.* The movie *Back to the Future III* was seen by audience members months after it had been shot and miles from the studio where it had been produced. Audiences are separated from the conglomerate communicator in both time and space.

Figure 6.2. Ability to reach target audiences draws potential advertisers.

Audiences are also identified with a variety of subclassifications. We talk about *available* audiences in television (those who have their sets on) versus the *actual* audience (those who are tuned to a specific show). Print readership studies focus on *primary* readers (those who buy the publications) versus *pass-along* readers (those who read publications bought by others). Advertisers are interested in *target* audiences, those individuals who match prospective buyer characteristics or are "heavy users" of a specific brand or product class.

By studying consumer decisions to select one output of the media system, we can describe media-audience interactions in sociological terms and in psychological terms. Let us begin with the first of these approaches.

Sociological Responses to Context

In *Theories of Mass Communication*, Melvin DeFleur and Sandra Ball-Rokeach present three perspectives on how audiences interact with the mass media and the messages that the media carry: the individual-differences perspective, the social-dif-

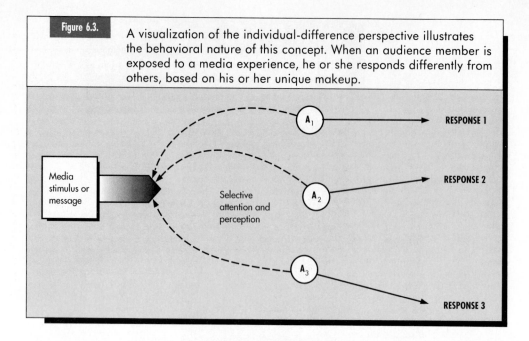

Figure 6.3. A visualization of the individual-difference perspective illustrates the behavioral nature of this concept. When an audience member is exposed to a media experience, he or she responds differently from others, based on his or her unique makeup.

ferences perspective, and the social-relationships perspective.[2] In effect, DeFleur and Ball-Rokeach are looking at the effects of mass-media–audience interaction, or how the audience acts on the content of the media.

THE INDIVIDUAL-DIFFERENCES PERSPECTIVE

The individual-differences perspective describes audiences in terms of behaviorism, or a stimulus-response basis. According to this view, the mass media affect each audience member differently according to that individual's psychological makeup derived from past experiences. In the individual-differences perspective, illustrated in Figure 6.3, audience members (A1, A2, A3) act on the media content by selectively attending to and perceiving the same messages. Therefore, there are separate responses (R1, R2, R3).

THE SOCIAL-DIFFERENCES PERSPECTIVE

If there are social aggregates in American society based on the common characteristics of sex, age, education, income, occupation, and so forth, we can determine broad audience groups (for example, working mothers, males aged 18 to 49, southern white females with two children) that react similarly to specific message inputs.

In this perspective, illustrated in Figure 6.4, the members of the audience (A1, A2, A3) are culturally linked and have a frame of reference in common; therefore, their responses to the same message are similar, given that other conditions remain the same.

The individual-differences and social-differences perspectives, in combination, reflect the "who says what to whom with what effect" approach (visualized in the Shannon-Weaver model in Chapter 1). But DeFleur and Ball-Rokeach observe that

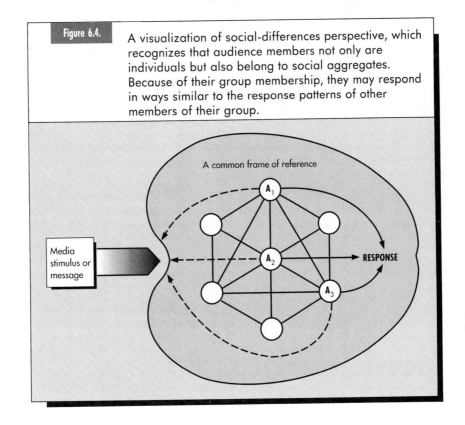

Figure 6.4. A visualization of social-differences perspective, which recognizes that audience members not only are individuals but also belong to social aggregates. Because of their group membership, they may respond in ways similar to the response patterns of other members of their group.

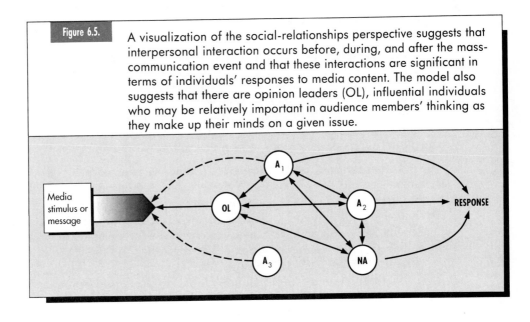

Figure 6.5. A visualization of the social-relationships perspective suggests that interpersonal interaction occurs before, during, and after the mass-communication event and that these interactions are significant in terms of individuals' responses to media content. The model also suggests that there are opinion leaders (OL), influential individuals who may be relatively important in audience members' thinking as they make up their minds on a given issue.

they may not depict the full complexity of audience response; it remains for the third perspective to account for the interactions between audience members.

THE SOCIAL-RELATIONSHIPS PERSPECTIVE

Based on the research of Paul Lazarsfeld, Bernard Berelson, Elihu Katz, and others, this perspective suggests that informal social relationships significantly affect audiences.

In the social-relationships perspective, illustrated in Figure 6.5, the audience members (A1, A2, A3) and an opinion leader (OL) receive a message. According to this view, it is not the media stimulus that has the significant impact; the informal interaction with others creates a common response. Audience member A3 has no observable reaction to the message or others, but an individual (NA) who did not receive the media message yet did interact with audience members now reacts as they do. The diagram also points out the role of a "significant other," an opinion leader (OL) who reacts strongly to the message and then interacts with certain individuals. The interaction, rather than the message in isolation, has the significant impact. Thus from a sociological viewpoint we see that an individual is changed by the total media experience, not just by the content of that experience. Let us now examine the other factors that influence the way we receive messages.

THE ROLE OF FILTRATION IN AUDIENCE RESPONSE ....

Filtration is the process of removing impurities, of separating particles from liquids or gases, or of eliminating certain light and sound wavelengths. When the filtering is over, one is left with less, yet one hopes it is more. In mass communication, messages must struggle one against another because there are so many of them. The average American is involved in thousands of communication exchanges a day. Communication overload is a reality, and our filters help us eliminate the useless, the annoying, and the unwanted. To some extent, filtration is our communication life jacket.

THE CONDITIONS OF FILTRATION

Filters are part of the complex mechanisms that we use to "decode" messages. Your filters are a part of you; they are learned, and they can be relearned. Four basic sets of conditions have an impact on our ability to filter or screen messages: informational or linguistic filters or conditions; psychological filters or conditions; cultural filters or conditions; and physical filters or conditions.

Informational and Linguistic Filters. Each of us has learned a variety of languages and the responses to those codes. When you do not know the signs and symbols, you are at a serious disadvantage. Egyptian hieroglyphs slept for centuries until the work of Jean-François Champollion unlocked the secret of the Rosetta Stone. Champollion discovered that the Egyptian symbols are syllabic and alphabetic rather than pictographic. The mysteries and the glories of ancient Egypt became readable once the message was filterable.

Without accurate informational filters, no positive communication can occur. The specialized codes of science and technology baffle us, not because we are not intelligent but because we do not possess the necessary language skill. That is why

Figure 6.6. Aztec figures illustrate a primitive hand language. Researchers have assigned (a) the ideas of "to favor" and "alliance"; (b) is supposed to demonstrate "virgin" and "wife."

(a)   (b)

in mass communication the primary directive of the conglomerate communicator is to code the content not in a private language but in a symbolic form that the audience can filter accurately and easily. As the world grows more complex, the problems of cross-occupational communication grow greater: Even though communication technology puts us in instant touch with the world, people are becoming more specialized in the functions they perform, and so their filters and vocabulary become more specialized. Engineers do not speak the language of doctors. The people who live in a neighborhood may have less in common with one another than with professional colleagues they meet only occasionally or "speak" with via computer networking. We have to make new maps of the world informationally.

Specialized media have developed to accommodate the growing specialization of society. Almost every day, a new publication is born in America to serve a distinct audience, whether it is a group of prosthetics specialists or an association of terrazzo and mosaic experts. These new media vehicles for new audiences develop new languages, which require specialized informational filters.

Glancing at *Variety* drives the point home: The show-biz jargon is made up of nontraditional symbols. But as one reads along and becomes familiar with its style, one's informational filters "click on." The theatrical nature of the words become not only comprehensible but also more meaningful than standard English. You do not even need a Rosetta Stone. That's show biz!

The Boy Scouts of America spent more than a million dollars in its first paid commercial to dispel its old-fashioned image; it used the hip language preteen boys respond to (the voice-over to a scene of glacier hiking tells the viewer he can "chill out"; another climbing scene, accompanied by loud rock and roll, points out you can "get high" in the Boy Scouts).

Psychological Filters. Our personal receptivity to a specific communication is based on *psychological sets*, or accumulated patterns of experience and habits, which we have in common with others. These sets define other people and events for us. As receivers of messages, we know that certain individuals, interactions, symbols, words, or situations have more impact than others. The power of words depends on the source and the situation as well as the symbol because our psychological filters are discerning. *Rape* is a powerful word psychologically because it connotes one person brutalizing another. Ask a group of men if they have been raped. You will likely receive a perplexed, perhaps incredulous, response. Then ask those same men if they have seen *Deliverance*, a film in which a man is raped by another man. Now the situation changes. Most men understand the terror of the concept, and the psychological impact is sobering. The filter changed with the situation rather than with the symbol or source. Our psychological sets, in effect, are what make us intellectually and emotionally selective regarding the communication process. We *structure* our perception of the world in terms that are meaningful to us according to our frames of reference, or filters. This process has been described as *selective exposure, selective perception*, and *selective retention*.

Wilbur Schramm defined three problems that communicators must expect when they try to communicate meaning. First, receivers will interpret the message in terms of their own experiences and learned response patterns. For example, a jungle tribesman who has never seen an airplane will tend to interpret the first airplane he sees as a bird.

Second, receivers will interpret messages to resist any change in strong personality structures. For instance, a woman who is strongly committed to the Democratic party will tend to ignore the campaign information of the Republicans.

Third, receivers will tend to *group* characteristics on the basis of their experiences to make whole patterns. As is the case when we look at abstract art, we "fill in" the meaning. We add to what the artist provides, based on our individual experiences with other works of art. We psychologically filter the work to give it personal meaning.

The tendency of—indeed, the desire of—the audience to "fill in the blanks" has been studied by Philip Marchand, who observes that people seem to prefer a

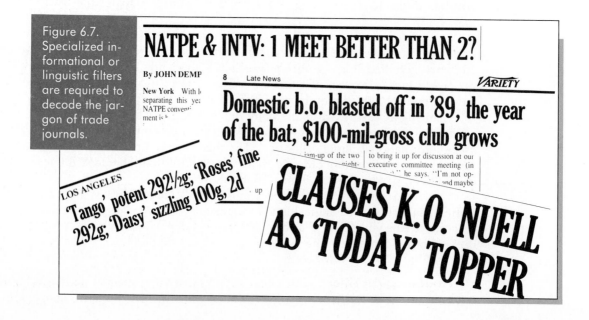

Figure 6.7. Specialized informational or linguistic filters are required to decode the jargon of trade journals.

NATPE & INTV: 1 MEET BETTER THAN 2?

By JOHN DEMP

8   Late News

VARIETY

New York With l
separating this yea
NATPE conventi
ment is l

Domestic b.o. blasted off in '89, the year of the bat; $100-mil-gross club grows

LOS ANGELES
'Tango' potent 292½/2g; 'Roses' fine 292g; 'Daisy' sizzling 100g, 2d   up

iam-up of the two
ght-

to bring it up for discussion at our executive committee meeting (in
" he says. "I'm not op-
and maybe

CLAUSES K.O. NUELL AS 'TODAY' TOPPER

"cool" or more laid-back personality over the long haul: Masks allow "people to imagine a multitude of different personalities behind the mask, including their own. . . . Viewers are never sure they know what is going on behind the knowing smirk, the bemused look on the Carson mask." Ted Koppel, host of ABC's news program "Nightline," explains that the viewer "watches me and he chooses to believe that I believe what he believes."[3]

Cultural Filters. Our personal filters are colored, distorted, and polarized by our culture. In his book *The Silent Language*, Edward T. Hall, a cultural anthropologist, writes of "the broad extent to which culture controls our lives. Culture is not an exotic notion studied by a select group of anthropologists in the South Seas. It is a mold in which we are all cast, and it controls our daily lives in many unsuspected ways."[4] Ten kinds of human activity are "primary message systems": interaction, association, subsistence, sexuality, territoriality, temporality, learning, play, defense, and exploitation (use of materials). These systems vary from individual to individual and culture to culture. They constitute a vocabulary and a language of their own, a silent language of which most of us are not aware.

Consider temporality, for example. To the average American of European origin, time is basically linear and exists as a continuum; there is a past, a present, and a future. Such a person is able to compartmentalize time, to recognize distinctions in time, and to do one thing at a time. However, some American Indian cultures, without written languages, were nonlinear. To the Navajo, time has no limits, no beginning, middle, or end. Time starts when the Navajo is ready, not at a given point.

Territoriality is also a cultural message system. The average American of European origin has a strong sense of space and knows where things belong and to whom they belong. Individuals with this cultural background establish their rights to territory. For example, students take certain seats in a classroom and may well return to the same seats throughout the semester, as if they had established rights to them. But to the Hopi, space does not belong to anyone; they are apt to settle down wherever it suits them, regardless of whose territory they are invading.

We can make an almost endless list of cultural traits and subcultural habits of mind that influence our patterns of communication and our ability to make the act of communication a sharing of an understanding. Cultures are social systems composed of people who have attitudes, mores, beliefs, and opinions in common. In a pluralistic society such as ours, the subgroups to which we belong are often stronger in molding our cultural communication filters than the parent society. The advertising message for Guess jeans is coded to stimulate teens, and communicators wanting to reach the Hispanic market will adapt a format with specialized appeal.

How media address the problem of filters is central to the current apparent splitting of television into broadcasting (programs delivered by the networks we grew up with) and "narrowcasting" (programming to special audiences, largely via cable channels).

Communicators sometimes successfully and profitably reach both specialized and more generalized audiences. Clearly "The Cosby Show" has broad-based appeal, and it was said to be a harmonizing influence in face of social diversity. A pivotal sitcom in this regard was "Sanford and Son," a real departure in the 1970s in its frankness and realism about blacks in this country, specifically an old man and his son who run a junkyard. Some blacks, fresh from years of racial strife,

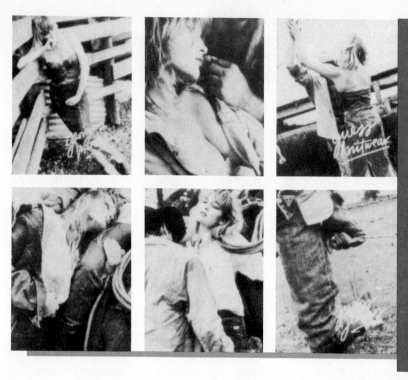

Figure 6.8. The target audience of this ad is the designer-jeans generation. The message is sexy. But the "designer-jeans wars" manage to do it in style. And it seems that the more controversial the ad, the more sensuous the headline, the more titillating the photograph—the better the sales. There is little need for copy in these ads. As they say, "A picture is worth a thousand words," and this six-page spread for Guess is the quintessential example of this style of photographic storytelling and jeans selling.

expected more social commentary, but the basic humor of the show and (in the final analysis) the fact that race was never a burning issue in the series made it widely popular. The coding of the ghetto setting and dialect made it seem contemporary and genuine, but the lack of serious confrontation pulled many subgroups into its audience. Eddie Murphy is a good example of an actor owing his popularity to very different reactions among various audience segments: Some may enjoy and identify with his brashness; others may be amused by qualities that could be labeled catering to stereotypes.

Stereotyping was discussed at length by Walter Lippmann in a pioneering work, *Public Opinion*, originally published in 1922. He borrowed the term *stereotyping* from the printing industry. It refers to the plates, molded from type, that are used to reproduce printed copies, each of which is the same as the original. Lippmann used the term to characterize the human tendency to reduce perceptions to convenient categories, cataloging people, ideas, and actions according to frames of reference for the purpose of easy recognition.

"The pictures inside people's heads," Lippmann wrote, "do not automatically correspond with the world outside." Yet the pictures in our heads are our public opinions, and when those pictures "are acted upon by groups of people, or by individuals acting in the name of groups, they are Public Opinion with capital letters."[5] The Public Opinion is the "national will," which is supposed to inform the public about the truth of the world outside. But communicators themselves cannot keep from shaping the news in terms of the pictures in *their* heads and the stereotypes of their audiences.

Physical Filters. No two people experience the world exactly alike. Our perception is limited or expanded by the way we have conditioned our eyes, ears, fingers, mouths, and noses. Why does one person produce better photographs than another? She has learned to *see* better compositions. Why does a weaver choose the fibers she does? Her sense of *touch* is developed through practice of her craft.

Why does a smoker not realize that his house, car, clothes, hair, and breath reek of cigarette smoke? He has reoriented his olfactory mechanism to disregard or enjoy these *smells*. The nonsmoker has not.

Our physical sensors are the receivers we use to gather in the communication around us. Our sensory perception is heightened, diminished, accepted, or rejected by two sets of physical characteristics: internal physical conditions and external physical conditions.

Internal physical conditions refer to the well-being or health of the individual audience member. A migraine headache, a bleeding ulcer, or an abscessed tooth can radically alter message filtering. In some cases, physical discomfort may heighten the communication experience; for example, a person with an upset stomach may be more than usually receptive to a Pepto-Bismol commercial. Blindness filters motion-picture messages negatively but may increase positively the filtering of phonographic music.

External physical conditions refer to the environment or surroundings in which members of an audience receive messages. If the room in which you are reading this book is too hot, too cold, too dark, or too noisy, the environment will affect your senses and the way you filter the content of this page. Environmental distractions are a frequent source of noise in mass communication. The home television set, for example, often competes with the dishwasher, the telephone, the radio, and even other television sets.

AUDIENCE ENVIRONMENTS

Audiences filter mass-media content in a variety of specialized environments. And when the medium is introduced into an environment, it modifies that environment. Television has changed the living room forever; furniture is often arranged around the TV set, and a separate room was created for it in the American home long before the idea of a "media room" occurred to interior designers. The TV room is often the focus of family activity, and normal distractions and interruptions are accepted as part of the viewing experience. In turn, motion-picture viewing has changed over the years from hushed to vocal as friends have grown used to discussing plot details in the privacy of a home. Still, there are fewer noncinematic stimuli in a theater, and thus we *filter* the two experiences of movie viewing in entirely different physical environments.

The environment for listening to tapes, compact discs, or records depends greatly on whether the player is portable or not. If mobile or equipped with headset, it can be adapted to new environments by means of increased volume. Likewise, our experience of radio varies with the environment. Despite the concentration required by driving, the car radio has a captive audience, a fact responsible for the fact that Los Angeles, our commuter capital, has the nation's largest radio market. The Walkman has revolutionized individual space, creating a jogging companion or a cushion from the jarring quality normally associated with subway travel.

Print media are highly mobile; they can be used almost anywhere if the user is literate and there is enough light. Interestingly, some print-use environments establish physical constraints on the user. When environmental conditions are altered, the audience member may become upset. Today's older generation learned to study quietly, and parents cannot fathom their children's use of rock music as background while doing homework. The retention required affects the reading situation. Reading for pleasure and reading for school are different acts and demand different levels of concentration because each requires us to learn different amounts and kinds of information. The library demands quiet but not restriction of movement; typical concentration levels in a library would make irritating a noise that would be completely unnoticed on the subway. On the other hand, space is usually plentiful in a library, whereas it is at a premium underground. The large amounts of print media consumed in buses and trains have led to changes in format. The changes in size, column length, and layout of daily newspapers that we mentioned in Chapter 4 is but one example.

NOISE

The internal and external physical conditions are part of a major problem that mass communicators must face: *noise*, which encompasses far more than environmental sound. All along the route of a message, from communicator to audience and back, there are many possibilities for distraction, and this element of the communication process should not be minimized. This breakdown in mass communication is called *interference, static,* or *noise*. In person-to-person communication, the listener may look away from the speaker or interrupt the flow of conversation; other people may be talking at the same time. In mass communication, the possibilities of noise are greatly multiplied. Noise can result from *weak signals, clutter*, and *information overload* as well as environmental distractions.

It is important to distinguish between interference, or noise, and filters. Both have the ability to distort the sender's message. The key difference is the ability of senders to control noise, at least partially, and their inability to control filters.

WEAK SIGNALS

Signals can have major effects. Poor sound levels in radio; distorted pictures on television; or poor quality of paper and printing in newspapers, magazines, and books can result in a message reaching an audience in distorted form or not at all. This type of technical noise is the most easily controlled by the sender. The fact that FM radio signals are essentially free from the static found on AM stations has led to the economic and aesthetic success of FM radio. Currently a research-and-development (R&D) priority is a TV set beyond even the high definition that has been in the news, and CDs may soon be supplanted by improved technology.

CLUTTER

Clutter is a broadcasting term that refers to too many bits and pieces of information in a time slot. For example, in the average two-minute commercial break on television, there are four 30-second commercials or even more shorter takes. As the ads in the box show, agencies really have to apply creativity to get a message through. The adult viewer of broadcast television often "shuts down" during the commercial breaks, leaves the room, or (more and more the case) zaps the commericals from his own taping of a previously aired show. It is the opposite with many toddlers, by the way: They play during the show and run in to watch the commercials. Why? Television commercials are intense visuals, with rapid, dynamic editing of both sound and picture.

Clutter may be the jumble of stories splashed on the newspaper page or the profusion of books and magazines lined up on the newsstand rack—all intense competition for the attention of an audience. So many conflicting messages may lead to no messages registering. If we did pay attention to all the messages, if we did not filter out most, we would become victims of information overload.

INFORMATION OVERLOAD

Information overload is a fact of life. The amount of mass communication would overwhelm us if we let it, so audience members at times just shut the mass media off with the switches on the sets and the filters in their heads. Because there is so much to digest in print, we are a society of speed-readers. We physically filter all but the necessary words.

Look at the three triangles in Figure 6.9. There is an "error" in each triangle. Find the error. If you have not found the error, look again. Each triangle repeats a word (snake in the *the* grass; busy as a *a* beaver; Paris in the *the* spring). Because each phrase is so familiar and because we speed-read, we misread. There is too much to read; we cope by deleting what we think is unnecessary. Information overload leads to filtering out some of the wheat with the chaff.

Unfortunately, time has not expanded to meet the demands of increased mass communication, so we physically react with more intense philtering. *Philtering?* You mean *filtering*. No, *philtering* stops you for a microsecond and makes you concentrate. The communicator is trying to combat your filters with philters.

THE AUDIENCE'S DEFENSIVE MECHANISM

Marshall McLuhan described the audience situation in terms of the concept of *implosion*. In this description, the audience is central to mass communication and is under constant bombardment from the media. The media are so pervasive that they are almost impossible for audiences to escape. Since each individual is a

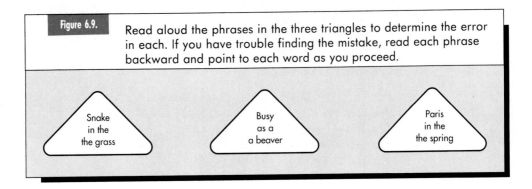

Figure 6.9. Read aloud the phrases in the three triangles to determine the error in each. If you have trouble finding the mistake, read each phrase backward and point to each word as you proceed.

Snake in the the grass

Busy as a a beaver

Paris in the the spring

Advertising agencies have been the most noticeably effective at making a message stand out from the crowd. Consider these examples.

The pink Energizer Bunny ("E.B.") is ever-present in what appear to be other people's commercials—for nasal sprays, cat foods, coffees (bogus)—and thus catch the too-often-turned-off viewer by surprise. Energizer's agency, Chiat/Day/Mojo, did a variation of "book-end ads," where a commercial for one product is split

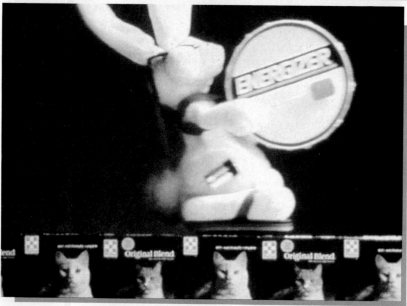

into two parts divided by some other commercial(s). They set up a scenario in which a viewer has to keep watching to get the rest of the story. E.B. has proven so popular, he's appearing as a plush toy too.

"A lot of times, animals are a subtle way to poke fun at some of the more ridiculous things humans do," says Joel Ziskin of Rubin Postaer and Associates, producer of the Bugle Boy ads that got through psychological filters. Austin the chimp is an engaging way of suggesting viewers just might want to dress better in well-fitting Bugle Boy outfits. Spuds, the spokesdog for Bud Light, helped make his product the eighth best-selling beer, and a variety of finny and four-footed friends have been used successfully as promoters.

member of a great number of audiences, thousands of mass messages are sent and received daily. People have developed barriers that resist most communication and filter in those messages that might be helpful for a particular need.

There are informational, physical, psychological, and cultural limits to our ability to perceive and understand. As the mass media provide more and more information and as entertainment and implosion increase, an audience's filtering systems become increasingly taxed, so much so that an individual can or may stop receiving anything at all for a period of time. We daydream, we drift, we lose concentration, we "bail out."

AMPLIFICATION

Those messages that actually get through the maze of mass communication may do so because they are *amplified*, to stand out from the other facts and ideas clamoring for our attention. The very fact that one message gets into the media while others do not serves to emphasize that message and de-emphasize others; gatekeepers play a critical role in this process, as the analysis in Chapter 5 demonstrated. But there are specific techniques of amplification.

Strong signals can amplify the message. Bold type in a front-page headline can make one item stand out more than another. Powerful radio transmission, color television, Technicolor, and stereophonic wide-screen movies, slick paper, and artful typography can add to the effectiveness of a message.

Repetition of the message over a period of time can also amplify it. The name of a person who is mentioned in the headlines day after day becomes a household word and acquires status and prestige; people listen to that person more carefully. Products, ideas, and events can be amplified if they are repeated in the mass media.

Endorsement may be one of the most important elements amplifying a message. An attractive woman is often used to endorse an idea. A baseball hero, movie star, or popular politician can also amplify a message by verifying it for the sender or approving it. Athletes and others are well paid to endorse products in advertisements and commericals. Clever ad agencies seek to get extra mileage from celebrity endorsements. The use of Michael Jackson or a politician in an unexpected setting is a news- and controversy-generating device to pull ads for a certain product out of the commercial clutter; a clip may show up on the nightly news.

As the Eveready bunny engagingly proved, there are all sorts of ways to amplify, some of them using not more but less volume. A 1990 Coke commercial had birds chirping and other nature sounds projected into corners of your living room by a subtle new three-dimensional stereo technology called Q-Sound. Classical music, unusual synthesized sound effects, and even silence are used to attract attention by contrast to the normal commercial blare. Media sound production has exploded as an industry, to the point that there are almost 200 different firms in New York alone.

Mass-media communicators, especially those responsible for economic decisions, must find out exactly what messages get through and to whom. Now that we have seen the mechanisms of common reception, we turn to the ways audiences register reception and their pleasure or displeasure with what they have absorbed.

I'VE NEVER EVER SEEN ANYTHING LIKE IT...

Figure 6.10. Endorsement, repetition, and attention-getting quick takes are elements of Nike's "ultimate sports television commercial," which debuted at the 1990 Super Bowl to show people the "ultimate sports product." Some of those who interacted (clockwise from top left): John McEnroe; Dick Vitale, ABC and ESPN; Michael Jordan; Dick Enberg, NBC; Tommy Heinsohn, CBS; and Wayne Gretzky.

FEEDBACK: CHARACTERISTICS AND MECHANISMS ....

The film *Fatal Attraction*, focusing on the violence simmering under the surface of suburban mores and sexual encounters through an archetypal triangle, is remarkable for several reasons. As we deepen our study of audience participation and reaction, it is especially useful. It invoked newsworthy audience response, remaining the subject of coffee-machine banter for many months. *Time* reported in a cover story, "Killer!": "Like any phenomenal film, *Fatal Attraction* transforms a theater full of strangers into a community: confidant to Dan, cheerleader to Beth, lynch mob for Alex."[6] Alex, the seductress who threatens to shatter an American family, becomes the scapegoat for the audience, who in previews were so incensed at the original ending (an artful suicide, to the music of *Madame Butterfly*) that they demanded, and got, more aggressive punishment. They wanted to participate in revenge; they did not want (as the suicide ending included) a framing of Dan for her murder.

Reliance on preview audiences is nothing new. The Marx brothers tried out jokes that way; Lauren Bacall got a big breakthrough when previewers thought she was worth far more than the small role she originally had in *The Big Sleep*. Who can tell how much the preview dislike of its original title (*Walking on Water*) had to do with the success of *Stand and Deliver*? Studios know that the audience foots the bill and are turning to them for leadership on how to market movies (like *Look Who's Talking*) as well as how to fine-tune them. The power of prerelease viewers to change a production may trouble creative communicators, but the marketplace speaks loudly.

Communication, by definition, is a two-way process, a cooperative and collaborative venture. It is a mutual experience, an exchange between two parties—a sender and a receiver. The communication experience is not complete until an audience is able to respond to the message of the communicator. That response is called *feedback*.

In interpersonal communication, the receiver usually responds naturally, directly, and immediately to the message and sender. We may flutter our eyelids or raise an eyebrow, ask for explanation or repetition, or even argue a point. In this way, a message is shaped and reshaped by the participants until the meaning becomes clear.

On the surface, many responses to mass communication seem to resemble those in interpersonal communication. An audience member may frown, yawn, cough, swear, throw down a magazine, kick a television set, or talk back. None of these responses is observable to the mass communicator, however, and all are ineffective responses unless they lead to further action—writing a letter, making a phone call, canceling a subscription, or turning off the television set. Instead of being individual, direct, immediate, one-time, and personal, mass-communication feedback is representative, indirect, delayed, cumulative, quantitative, institutionalized, and costly.

Despite what seem to be complicating obstacles—obstacles not worth the effort

Figure 6.11. The *Fatal Attraction* triangle: Glenn Close, Michael Douglas, and Anne Archer.

in overcoming—feedback for mass communicators is a vital component in the total process. All of us want our communication to be efficient; mass communicators are similarly concerned. Communicating by mass media involves enormous expense that has to be justified to executives and stockholders. The communicator must make a return on the investment, must demonstrate that her communication is effective, and feedback is necessary to provide the proof. Each TV network pays at least $3.5 million for Nielsen Media Research's basic data. Newspapers and magazines have had their circulation figures verified since 1914 by the Audit Bureau of Circulation (ABC). The cost of this service, at least $5 million a year, is borne by the newspapers and magazines through service fees to the ABC. Add to this the feedback costs for such information as Arbitron (ARB) diaries, Starch reports, and Simmons Market Research Bureau studies, and you have some indication of how important feedback, delivered on a regular basis, is to the mass media. Let us look in more detail at the characteristics of mass-communication feedback.

THE REPRESENTATIVE QUALITY

Since the audiences of mass media are so large, a representative *sample* of the audience is selected for measurement, and the response of this sample is projected scientifically to the whole. A letter to the editor or a change of channels may be noted by the mass communicator, but these responses usually have little significance unless they can be shown to be statistically representative of the feelings and actions of a large portion of that medium's total audience.

Sampling is perhaps the least understood and most controversial aspect of mass-communication survey research. In determining the size of the sample, the idea is to use as few units as possible and still maintain reasonable accuracy. What makes for "reasonable accuracy" varies, but the standard rule of thumb in media-audience research is that samples of fewer than 100 units are often unreliable and samples of more than 1,000 are seldom needed. Nielsen, for example, uses a national sample of about 1,700 households to determine national TV ratings. Like most research companies, it takes great care to create a national sample that is representative of the whole population. It uses a sample drawn from U.S. census

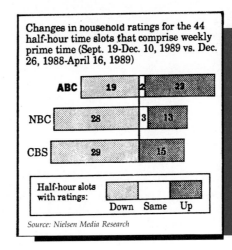

Changes in household ratings for the 44 half-hour time slots that comprise weekly prime time (Sept. 19-Dec. 10, 1989 vs. Dec. 26, 1988-April 16, 1989)

ABC 19 2 22
NBC 28 3 13
CBS 29 15

Half-hour slots with ratings: Down Same Up

Source: Nielsen Media Research

Figure 6.12. Local newspapers, often using wire-service or syndicated graphics, share the bottom line of the Nielsen Television Index National Ratings with readers-viewers.

maps by a method known as *multistage area probability sampling*. Basically, the method guarantees that the number of sample members from each geographical area is proportionate to the total population of the area. For its individual-market ratings, Nielsen uses special current telephone directories.

As developments in media technology expand, especially in television, questions are being raised about traditional sampling methods. Special attention has been focused on the Nielsen national TV ratings because of their effect on the TV industry. The Nielsen sampling process involves a small randomly dispersed sample with no weighting to correct for sample imbalances. The process works when the viewer has the option of choosing among 5 or so programs, but it is overly taxed when the viewer has the option of viewing any of 30, 40, or even 100 channel opportunities. With the advancement of cable and satellite technology, which promises to bring 100 channels and more into the cable-TV household, a much closer look must be given to the sampling process. Today's TV usage can include not only network or nonnetwork broadcasting, or cable, but videocassette recording and/or playback. The need to differentiate accurately among these opportunities grows in importance as costs continue to escalate.

As VCR penetration jumped from 11 percent in 1984 to 70 percent in 1990, the effect of time shifting, fast-forwarding past commercials (known as "zapping"), or not playing the recorded program has become of deep concern to the network broadcaster. In the past, Nielsen credited all VCR taping as viewing, but advertisers recognized that this is not the case and have succeeded in persuading Nielsen to inaugurate a supplementary ratings report that eliminates credit for taping. Any inconsistencies in the composition of the Nielsen sample may well distort audience selection and levels.

Sensitive to such criticism, Nielsen uses people meters (there are 4,000 households with them), electronic devices placed near a family's television set, as shown in Figure 6.1. On the box are a number of buttons; each family member is assigned a specific button. The individual is required to press the appropriate button each time he views, stops viewing, or leaves the room. The people meter, a sophisticated electronic device, can calculate the minute-by-minute viewing of each member of a household, recorded by the members themselves. A further refinement is being developed by Nielsen and the David Sarnoff Research Center. A new totally passive television-viewing measurement system, using "image recognition," would eliminate the need to push buttons. An image recorded by a built-in sensing device would be translated into a set of distinguishing features stored digitally in computer memory. The activities of the viewers would be identified by the computer. Integrated with Nielsen data bases on demographic, lifestyle, and product-purchasing characteristics of sample households, the new data would strengthen the base on which programming and advertising decisions are made in this $12 billion marketplace. Still, the networks, not surprisingly, criticize feedback mechanisms whenever viewership declines.

THE INDIRECT QUALITY

A performer or reporter may occasionally receive a telephone call from a listener or a letter from a reader. In general, however, audience response seldom offers much opportunity for direct interaction or substantially changes specific content unless the response is felt to be representative of the opinion of a large part of the audience. Because mass-communication feedback is filtered through a third party such as a rating organization, there is less variety in form and type of feedback. As we discuss later, one form—quantitative feedback—dominates. In effect, a rating organization such as Arbitron or Simmons acts as a gatekeeper in reverse—altering, modifying, or even preventing feedback from reaching the communicator.

THE DELAYED QUALITY

Mass-media feedback is delayed from the moment of original transmission. Technological innovations are facilitating more personalized use of the media, but so far, things like electronic interaction are a characteristic of audiences so specialized that we cannot call this typical of mass media. Broadcast media allow for the quickest response, but even there, when a network switchboard lights up with viewers' reactions, it's a news-making event. The *Miami Herald* ran an article on November 29, 1989, entitled "*Late Night*'s language gag hits a snag." One Monday night the entire rerun of a David Letterman show was shown in Spanish with English subtitles on WTVJ, Miami. Sixty-nine irate callers accused the NBC affiliate of "pandering to its Hispanic audience"; 35 others inquired about technical difficulties. On a more formal basis, there are overnight TV ratings, but most network ratings are published weekly. Local TV reports are published four to seven times a year, depending on the size of the market. Letters to the editor must go through the mail and face even further delay of weeks or months because of periodical publishing deadlines.

Surveys and polls take time to conduct and evaluate. The reaction of the communicator to feedback from the audience is also delayed by the particular technological and industrial characteristics of a medium. For example, once a motion picture is "in the can," it can be modified in only minor ways after preview screenings. The modifications made to *Fatal Attraction* changed effect significantly, but the reshooting involved a comparatively small section of the film. When preview screenings of Michael Cimino's film *Heaven's Gate*, scheduled to be released in late 1980, resulted in universally negative feedback, the $33-million film was not released. Here was the ultimate consequence of delayed mass-communication feedback: the potential loss of a huge amount of money because the content was completed, at great cost, before significant audience reaction was received. The film was eventually released in 1984 and flopped at the box office.

Before the first episode of a new network-TV series appears in the fall, up to 13 episodes of that series have often been completed. Therefore, because of the financial investment and contractual commitments involved, poor ratings (negative feedback) rarely spell the immediate termination of a new TV program; this usually occurs at the end of the first (fall) quarter, the 13-week period from September to December.

Despite the mass communicator's great concern over efficiency, the feedback delay inherent in mass communication necessitates continuing inefficient communication. In other words, it's a necessary evil. A failed communication can't be fixed unless we know—somehow—that it's broken.

THE CUMULATIVE QUALITY

In mass communication, the immediate and individual response is infrequent and therefore not too important. Rather, emphasis is placed on cumulative and collective responses over a substantial period of time. The communicator stores the

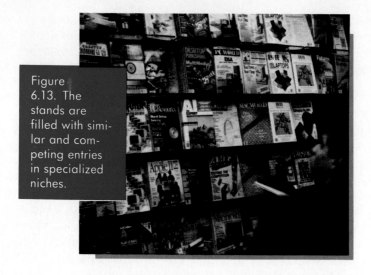

Figure 6.13. The stands are filled with similar and competing entries in specialized niches.

data, and this information influences future decisions, especially concerning what the public wants in content. The spin-off concept in TV programming is evidence of this. "The Cosby Show," for example, has been very successful for several years. This success then resulted in a new program, "A Different World," using characters from the original series. Sequel motion pictures such as *Back to the Future* and *Ghostbusters* are the result of cumulative feedback from the original motion picture. The enormous success of *People* magazine spawned a large number of similar efforts (*Us, We, Self*). For radio ratings, the quarter hour (the standard time unit of measurement) is so short that research organizations such as Arbitron compile audience figures known as *cumes* (see p. 137).

THE QUANTITATIVE QUALITY

Critics provide qualitative judgments through book, photograph, movie, and TV reviews. But the mass communicator is more interested in knowing how many people responded rather than how one person (for example, a critic) responded, unless a critic's view can affect or represent the opinions of a number of people. The review of a book or movie can seriously affect purchases or attendance, but evidence shows that television criticism does not hold similar sway.[7] Little or no consistent critical evaluation of newspapers, magazines, or radio is available, especially to general audiences; more serious analysis of media content is confined to specialized journals. Numbers are what count in mass communication. As the Nielsen Company states in one of its promotional brochures, "These are quantitative measurements. The word rating is a misnomer because it implies a measurement of program quality—and this we never do. Never!"

This fact creates some problems. When you consistently measure the success or efficiency of your message by *how* many responses rather than *what kind* of response, you are severely limiting your ability to judge the quality of your message. A TV program may have a large audience at 9:00 P.M. on Tuesday not because it is a good program but because the competition is weak. Placed in another time slot or on another day, the same program may fail. In network television, for example, Saturday night is known as the "graveyard" because fewer people watch television on this night than on any other night.

The usefulness of quantitative feedback varies with the questions being asked. In terms of *how many people are exposed*, media-research data are excellent within the limits of statistical error. As to *who the audience is*, the feedback is also superior within these statistical limits. In terms of *how messages are perceived* and *the effects of this perception*, reliable feedback is extremely limited. Communication-research firms are sensitive to criticism and are increasingly analyzing the *why* and *who* as well as the *what* of media audiences. Nielsen supplements its people-meter figures with diary responses, and more and more communicators are utilizing interviews and detailed questionnaires to go beyond a simple quantitative measure of response.

Despite a strong quantitative bias, mass-communication feedback is occasionally provided in qualitative measures. The most ambitious attempt to provide qualitative data on a large-scale basis has been the work of a company called Television Audience Assessment (TAA), which developed two measures of viewer response to television programming: program impact and program appeal. Program impact measures the emotional and intellectual stimulation a program provides its viewers, while program appeal measures the overall entertainment value of a program. Both—but especially impact—increase receptivity to commercials. In today's highly competitive media environment, qualitative ratings provide the means for identifying *who* is actually watching, noticing, and reacting favorably to advertisers' messages.

THE INSTITUTIONALIZED QUALITY

Mass-communication feedback is institutionalized. That is, large and complex organizations are required to provide meaningful feedback to mass communicators. Companies such as Simmons Market Research Bureau survey print-media audi-

THE 1989 TIO/ROPER REPORT

If you got conflicting or different reports of the same news story from radio, television, magazines and the newspapers, which of the four versions would you be most inclined to believe—the one on radio, or television, or magazines or newspapers?

Most believable:	Dec. '59	Nov. '61	Nov. '63	Nov. '64 %	Jan. '67	Nov. '68	Jan. '71	Nov. '72
Television	29	39	36	41	41	44	49	48
Newspapers	32	24	24	23	24	21	20	21
Radio	12	12	12	8	7	8	10	8
Magazines	10	10	10	10	8	11	9	10
Don't know/no answer	17	17	18	18	20	16	12	13

Most believable:	Nov. '74	Nov. '76	Dec. '78	Nov. '80 %	Dec. '82	Dec. '84	Dec. '86	Nov. '88
Television	51	51	47	51	53	53	55	49
Newspapers	20	22	23	22	22	24	21	26
Radio	8	7	9	8	6	8	6	7
Magazines	8	9	9	9	8	7	7	5
Don't know/no answer	13	11	12	10	11	9	12	13

Figure 6.14. From Roper, one of many distillations of surveys.

ences. Standard Rate and Data Service provides information on newspaper costs and circulation. In addition, market-research and public-opinion survey groups such as Gallup, Harris, and Roper go directly to the public to find out what messages have come through and what changes have resulted in levels of information, attitudes, and actions. Most media institutions not only purchase the raw data but also seek an analysis of the information by the research organization. In fact, little feedback is interpreted directly by the majority of mass communicators.

This third-party function regarding the indirect nature of mass-communication feedback further complicates the issue. The organization that collects responses and then communicates them to the sender essentially performs a gatekeeping function, with all its potential concerns and problems. The broadcast industry has recognized the potential problems and established the Broadcast Ratings Council. The council functions as an accrediting agency and checks on such areas as sample design, fieldwork, and type of reporting. In essence, mass-communication feedback is mass communication in reverse, containing many of the same elements—complex communicators, specific codes and symbols, gatekeepers, regulators, filters, and so forth.

Cost

Measuring a national audience over a long period of time and with precise sampling methods is expensive. Arbitron prices its service according to a broadcast station's commercial rates. Fees can range from $2,600 a year for small stations to $100,000 a year for large stations, the average for all stations about $20,000. Because of the costs involved, elaborate or qualitative feedback is not common in mass media. Sales figures, TV sets in use, average listeners per quarter-hour, and circulation statistics are relatively gross measures of feedback. Rarely do media communicators know the attitudes or ideas of audience members, even though this information may be important. Cost greatly limits feedback and prevents media communicators from being as efficient and effective as they would like.

TECHNIQUES OF OBTAINING FEEDBACK

Correct sampling procedures are a critical aspect of research. Of the many ways to conduct mass-communication research, five techniques are common to most research organizations: personal interview, coincidental telephone survey, diary, mechanical device, and preview.

PERSONAL INTERVIEW

The personal interview can provide lengthy detailed responses that involve the personal interaction of respondent and interviewer. It offers the greatest flexibility in questioning methods. The drawbacks of this method are that it is time-consuming, relatively expensive, and often depends on recall rather than the immediate responses of audience members. As a result of these and other drawbacks, personal door-to-door surveys have declined in recent years. Focus groups, described in Chapter 8, continue to be used. In broadcasting, only Pulse uses personal interviews as the basis of its reports on local-radio ratings. However, the print media use interviewing for two major forms of feedback: Starch reports and Simmons Market Research Bureau reports.

COINCIDENTAL-TELEPHONE SURVEY

The coincidental-telephone survey provides immediate feedback about what an individual is doing at the time of the call. It is fast, simple, and relatively inexpensive. Extremely lengthy and detailed answers are difficult to obtain, however, and because of the prevalent use of the telephone as a sales tool, many people who are called in such surveys are suspicious and refuse to cooperate. Therefore, coincidental-telephone surveys normally require large samples. This method also automatically limits the sample to people with telephones, those who have not moved recently, and those at home or not using the phone when called. Despite these drawbacks, the coincidental-telephone method provides some of the most accurate information on TV-audience size.

DIARY

The diary method, where respondents keep a log of their family's use of media, has the advantage of providing a detailed record over a substantial period of time (usually a week). Major disadvantages are respondents' failure to maintain the diary (thus depending on recall to fill in data) and to return the diary. The diary method is also more expensive than the telephone technique since it offers a monetary incentive for cooperation but it is not as expensive as the personal interview. Diary keepers are supposed to compile a quarter-hour record of the programs that all family members and visitors have watched for 5 minutes or more during a week (Figure 6.17). The diaries have space to record the names, ages, and gender of participants.

MECHANICAL DEVICE

The mechanical device, such as the people meter used by Nielsen Media Research, records the minute-by-minute use of a TV set. The ability to provide information about specific viewers is a major improvement of the earlier method used by Nielsen, the audimeter, which recorded only whether the TV set was on and which channel it was tuned to. Because of the expense of setting up a people meter in a sample home, the sample, especially in the Nielsen surveys, is relatively permanent.

PREVIEW

Another technique used by a number of mass-communication organizations is the so-called preview theater. Randomly selected people are shown various TV programs (usually pilots) and/or advertisements in a theater and respond to the messages by pushing buttons or turning dials that signal positive or negative feelings. The American Research Institute, of Los Angeles, uses this technique. It is gaining in popularity because it provides data that show how people react at different stages of the message, not simply at its end. Of course, the motion-picture "sneak preview" has existed for almost 50 years. Today, it is used in increasingly sophisticated ways that involve detailed questionnaires filled out by audience members and follow-up interviews with selected viewers. Another technique used primarily by TV production companies is concept testing; sample viewers are asked to respond to a one- or two-paragraph description of a new series or show.

The ways these research methods have been used tend to fall into general patterns. The diary and the mechanical device are used almost exclusively in providing feedback for the broadcast media. The personal interview and the coincidental-telephone survey are essential tools in public-opinion surveys. The coincidental-telephone survey is also used as a fast method of obtaining broadcast-audience information, and the personal interview is used almost exclusively for print-media feedback.

FEEDBACK IN THE MEDIA

MOTION PICTURES AND SOUND RECORDINGS

For commercial films and recordings, box-office receipts and sales provide the most important feedback in determining the kinds of feature-length movies and singles or albums that will be produced and can, more immediately, affect the booking and distribution of a film into theaters and/or the video market. The pattern of spin-off, reproduction, duplication, and sequel is a result of the soaring costs of producing and marketing a feature-length motion picture; few individuals or corporations are willing or able to risk huge sums of money on untried or unproven themes. Only Walt Disney Studios rigorously tests movie concepts before financial commitment to a new project. Despite inroads made on audience-tracking systems by the National Research Group, most feedback on films is delayed.

In addition to gross sales, the record charts reflect movement up and down the list, indicating a record's relative popularity from week to week and its performance against competitors. The *Billboard* "Hot 100" (Figure 6.15) is actually based on feedback from two sources: record and tape sales from the top markets and radio play-lists from major-market radio stations. Most music-oriented radio stations have long obtained some feedback by monitoring best-selling albums and singles at record stores. But statistics on record sales do not always pinpoint favorite songs or match listening patterns.

Recently, with the growth of format syndicators, more sophisticated research programs have been introduced, designed to profile the average listener and provide insight into her characteristics. Research is currently concerned with reaching the "passive" listener, who does not call the radio station's request line or buy many records but listens to radio on a regular basis. A new form of research known as *call-out* involves playing short musical excerpts over the telephone, followed by a series of questions to the respondent. This method is virtually limitless in its potential and can be used to explore listeners' lifestyles. Other forms of research include *auditorium testing,* in which a large group is asked to rate music or other program-related elements. Personal interviews are also frequently employed wherever possible—for example, at shopping malls.

One other form of feedback important to motion pictures and sound recordings is professional recognition, symbolized by awards given by an audience of peers.

FOR WEEK ENDING MARCH 10, 1990

Billboard. TOP POP ALBUMS™

©Copyright 1990, Billboard Publications, Inc. No part of this publication may be reproduced, stored in any retrieval system, or transmitted, in any form or by any means, electronic, mechanical, photocopying, recording, or otherwise, without the prior written permission of the publisher.

Compiled from a national sample of retail store, one-stop, and rack sales reports.

THIS WEEK	LAST WEEK	2 WKS. AGO	WKS. ON CHART	ARTIST — LABEL & NUMBER/DISTRIBUTING LABEL (SUG. LIST PRICE)*	TITLE
1	1	1	86	★★ NO.1 ★★ PAULA ABDUL — VIRGIN 90943 (9.98) 7 weeks at No. 1	FOREVER YOUR GIRL
2	2	2	23	JANET JACKSON — A&M SP 3920 (9.98) (CD)	JANET JACKSON'S RHYTHM NATION 1814
3	4	4	15	PHIL COLLINS — ATLANTIC 82050 (9.98) (CD)	...BUT SERIOUSLY
4	5	5	34	THE B-52'S — REPRISE 25854 (9.98) (CD)	COSMIC THING
5	3	3	51	MILLI VANILLI — ARISTA AL 8592 (9.98) (CD)	GIRL YOU KNOW IT'S TRUE
6	6	6	19	BILLY JOEL — COLUMBIA OC 44366 (CD)	STORM FRONT
7	8	8	44	TOM PETTY — MCA 6253 (9.98) (CD)	FULL MOON FEVER
8	7	7	24	AEROSMITH — GEFFEN 24254 (9.98) (CD)	PUMP
9	10	10	34	MICHAEL BOLTON — COLUMBIA OC 45012 (CD)	SOUL PROVIDER
10	12	12	21	LINDA RONSTADT (FEA. A.NEVILLE) — ELEKTRA 60872 (9.98) (CD)	CRY LIKE A RAINSTORM, HOWL LIKE THE WIND
11	11	11	14	QUINCY JONES — QWEST 26020/WARNER BROS. (9.98) (CD)	BACK ON THE BLOCK
12	9	9	15	BOBBY BROWN — MCA 6342 (9.98) (CD)	DANCE!...YA KNOW IT!
13	19	26	9	ALANNAH MYLES — ATLANTIC 81956 (9.98) (CD)	ALANNAH MYLES
14	15	17	12	TECHNOTRONIC — SBK 93422 (9.98) (CD)	PUMP UP THE JAM - THE ALBUM
15	18	18	25	MOTLEY CRUE — ELEKTRA 60829 (9.98) (CD)	DR. FEELGOOD
16	16	16	81	NEW KIDS ON THE BLOCK — COLUMBIA FC 40985 (CD)	HANGIN' TOUGH
17	13	13	57	SKID ROW — ATLANTIC 81936 (9.98) (CD)	SKID ROW
18	17	14	25	YOUNG M.C. — DELICIOUS VINYL 91309/ISLAND (9.98) (CD)	STONE COLD RHYMIN'
19	14	15	32	BABYFACE — SOLAR FZ 45288/EPIC (CD)	TENDER LOVER
20	21	19	14	KENNY G — ARISTA AL 13-8613 (13.98) (CD)	LIVE
21	21	22	33	GLORIA ESTEFAN — EPIC OE 45217 (CD)	CUTS BOTH WAYS
22	40	42	48	BONNIE RAITT — CAPITOL C1-91268 (8.98) (CD)	NICK OF TIME
23	20	16		ERIC CLAPTON — DUCK 26074/REPRISE (9.98) (CD)	JOURNEYMAN
24	23	23	47	ROXETTE — EMI 91098 (9.98) (CD)	LOOK SHARP!
25	24	25	43	RICHARD MARX — EMI 90380 (9.98) (CD)	REPEAT OFFENDER
26	26	24	16	WHITESNAKE — GEFFEN GHS 24249 (9.98) (CD)	SLIP OF THE TONGUE
27	27	27	19	LUTHER VANDROSS — EPIC E2-45320 (CD)	THE BEST OF LUTHER VANDROSS: THE BEST OF LOVE
28	25	21	36	SOUL II SOUL — VIRGIN 91267 (9.98) (CD)	KEEP ON MOVIN'
29	37	37	30	DON HENLEY — GEFFEN GHS 24217 (9.98) (CD)	THE END OF THE INNOCENCE
30	28	29	26	ROLLING STONES — COLUMBIA OC 45333 (CD)	STEEL WHEELS
31	29	31	17	TAYLOR DAYNE — ARISTA 8581 (9.98) (CD)	CAN'T FIGHT FATE
32	39	39	8	SOUNDTRACK — MCA 6340 (9.98) (CD)	BORN ON THE FOURTH OF JULY
33	30	30	15	BAD ENGLISH — EPIC OE 45083 (CD)	BAD ENGLISH
34	149	—	2	BASIA — EPIC E 45472 (CD)	LONDON WARSAW NEW YORK
35	41	46	16	MICHAEL PENN — RCA 9692-1-R (8.98) (CD)	MARCH
36	32	32	13	SOUNDTRACK — WALT DISNEY 64038* (9.98) (CD)	THE LITTLE MERMAID
37	36	36	6	JOAN JETT — BLACKHEART 45473/EPIC (CD)	THE HIT LIST
38	33	33	51	TESLA — GEFFEN GHS 24224 (9.98) (CD)	THE GREAT RADIO CONTROVERSY
39	38	38	20	SEDUCTION — VENDETTA SP 5280/A&M (8.98) (CD)	NOTHING MATTERS WITHOUT LOVE
40	34	34	34	CHER — GEFFEN GHS 24239 (9.98) (CD)	HEART OF STONE
41	35	35	33	THE 2 LIVE CREW — SKYYWALKER XR 107 (9.98) (CD)	AS NASTY AS THEY WANNA BE
42	49	54		MICHEL'LE — RUTHLESS 91282/ATCO (9.98) (CD)	MICHEL'LE
43	46	47	17	THE SMITHEREENS — ENIGMA 91194/CAPITOL (9.98) (CD)	SMITHEREENS 11
44	31	28	10	JIVE BUNNY & THE MASTERMIXERS — MUSIC FACTORY 91322/ATCO (9.98) (CD)	JIVE BUNNY - THE ALBUM
45	45	45	54	WARRANT — COLUMBIA FC 44383 (CD)	DIRTY ROTTEN FILTHY STINKING RICH
46	42	43	32	NEW KIDS ON THE BLOCK — COLUMBIA FC 40475 (CD)	NEW KIDS ON THE BLOCK
47	52	56	7	KAOMA — EPIC 46010 (CD)	WORLD BEAT
48	55	26	15	ELTON JOHN — MCA 6321 (9.98) (CD)	SLEEPING WITH THE PAST
49	48	48	23	TEARS FOR FEARS — FONTANA 838 730 1/POLYGRAM (CD)	THE SEEDS OF LOVE
50	57	63	6	PETER MURPHY — BEGGAR'S BANQUET 9877-1-H/RCA (9.98) (CD)	DEEP
51	43	40	17	JOE SATRIANI — RELATIVITY 1015 (9.98) (CD)	FLYING IN A BLUE DREAM
52	51	50	37	HEAVY D. & THE BOYZ — MCA 42302 (8.98) (CD)	BIG TYME
53	47	44	31	ALICE COOPER — EPIC OE 45137 (CD)	TRASH
54	53	49	15	RUSH — ATLANTIC 82040 (9.98) (CD)	PRESTO
55	44	41	14	CHICAGO — REPRISE 26080 (9.98) (CD)	GREATEST HITS 1982-1989
56	56	51	30	HARRY CONNICK, JR. — COLUMBIA 45319 (CD)	MUSIC FROM "WHEN HARRY MET SALLY..."
57	69	70	73	FINE YOUNG CANNIBALS — I.R.S. 6273/MCA (9.98) (CD)	THE RAW & THE COOKED
58	58	64	13	THE KENTUCKY HEADHUNTERS — MERCURY 838 744 1/POLYGRAM (9.98) (CD)	PICKIN' ON NASHVILLE
59	59	57	15	3RD BASS — COLUMBIA FC 45415 (CD)	THE CACTUS ALBUM
60	84	86		SOUNDTRACK — ATLANTIC 81933 (9.98) (CD)	BEACHES
61	54	53	6	RICKY VAN SHELTON — COLUMBIA 45250 (CD)	RVS III
62	63	58	14	ROB BASE — PROFILE 1285 (9.98) (CD)	THE INCREDIBLE BASE
63	55	52	15	SCORPIONS — MERCURY 842 002 1/POLYGRAM (9.98) (CD)	GREATEST HITS - BEST OF ROCKERS N' BALLADS
64	62	77	38	PAUL MCCARTNEY — CAPITOL C1-91653 (9.98) (CD)	FLOWERS IN THE DIRT
65	60	65	49	MADONNA — SIRE 25844/WARNER BROS. (9.98) (CD)	LIKE A PRAYER
66	159	—	2	OZZY OSBOURNE — ASSOCIATED 6Z45451/EPIC (CD)	JUST SAY OZZY
67	73	79	19	KISS — MERCURY 838 913 1/POLYGRAM (CD)	HOT IN THE SHADE
68	65	62	16	LENNY KRAVITZ — VIRGIN 91290 (9.98) (CD)	LET LOVE RULE
69	NEW			M.C. HAMMER — CAPITOL 92857 (9.98) (CD)	PLEASE HAMMER DON'T HURT 'EM
70	79	78	20	BIZ MARKIE — COLD CHILLIN' 26003/WARNER BROS. (9.98) (CD)	THE BIZ NEVER SLEEPS
71	80	87	3	HANK WILLIAMS, JR. — WARNER/CURB 26090/WARNER BROS. (9.98) (CD)	LONE WOLF
72	71	69	19	UB40 — VIRGIN 91324 (9.98) (CD)	LABOUR OF LOVE II
73	72	71	40	CLINT BLACK — RCA 9668-1-R (8.98) (CD)	KILLIN' TIME
74	61	60	21	NEIL YOUNG — REPRISE 25899 (9.98) (CD)	FREEDOM
75	74	74	23	MELISSA ETHERIDGE — ISLAND 91285/ATLANTIC (9.98) (CD)	BRAVE AND CRAZY
76	66	61	19	KATE BUSH — COLUMBIA OC 44164 (CD)	THE SENSUAL WORLD
77	70	75	4	EARTH, WIND & FIRE — COLUMBIA 45268 (CD)	HERITAGE
78	87	100	23	JOHN LEE HOOKER — CHAMELEON D1-74808 (8.98) (CD)	THE HEALER
79	64	66	26	JOE COCKER — CAPITOL 92861 (9.98) (CD)	ONE NIGHT OF SIN
80	67	59	15	EDDIE MONEY — COLUMBIA OC 45381 (CD)	GREATEST HITS...SOUND OF MONEY
81	81	85		THEY MIGHT BE GIANTS — ELEKTRA 60907 (9.98) (CD)	FLOOD
82	90	94	4	SLAUGHTER — CHRYSALIS 21702* (9.98) (CD)	STICK IT TO YA
83	76	72	26	RED HOT CHILI PEPPERS — EMI 92152 (9.98) (CD)	MOTHER'S MILK
84	74	67	21	TRACY CHAPMAN — ELEKTRA 60888 (9.98) (CD)	CROSSROADS
85	82	85	22	RANDY TRAVIS — WARNER BROS. 25988 (9.98) (CD)	NO HOLDIN' BACK
86	96	118	3	RESTLESS HEART — RCA 9961 (8.98) (CD)	FAST MOVIN' TRAIN
87	93	93	26	REGINA BELLE — COLUMBIA FC 44367 (CD)	STAY WITH ME
88	86	84	21	BELINDA CARLISLE — MCA 6339 (9.98) (CD)	RUNAWAY HORSES
89	83	82	7	D-MOB — FFRR 828 159 1/POLYGRAM	A LITTLE BIT OF THIS, A LITTLE BIT OF THAT
90	68	68	15	ROD STEWART — WARNER BROS. 4-25987 (39.98) (CD)	STORYTELLER/COMPLETE ANTHOLOGY: 1964-1990
91	77	73	23	BONHAM — WTG FP 45009/EPIC (CD)	THE DISREGARD OF TIMEKEEPING
92	78	76	86	BOBBY BROWN — MCA 42185 (9.98) (CD)	DON'T BE CRUEL
93	94	101	24	ENUFF Z'NUFF — ATCO 91262 (9.98) (CD)	ENUFF Z'NUFF
94	89	92	15	THE STONE ROSES — SILVERTONE 1184-1-J/RCA (8.98) (CD)	THE STONE ROSES
95	88	83	24	EURYTHMICS — ARISTA AL 8606 (9.98) (CD)	WE TOO ARE ONE
96	107	110	4	JULIA FORDHAM — VIRGIN 91325 (9.98) (CD)	PORCELAIN
97	97	90	17	SIR MIX-A-LOT — NASTY MIX 70150 (9.98) (CD)	SEMINAR
98	92	108	6	MCAULEY SCHENKER GROUP — CAPITOL 92752 (9.98) (CD)	SAVE YOURSELF
99	95	95	16		
100	100	106	15		
101	146	138	39		
102	131	—	2	RATTY MATTER — MERCURY 836 950 1 (CD)	WILLOW IN THE WIND
103	91	89	18	LOU GRAMM — ATLANTIC 81915 (9.98) (CD)	LONG HARD LOOK
104	85	80	21	BARBRA STREISAND — COLUMBIA OC 45369 (CD)	A COLLECTION: GREATEST HITS...AND MORE
105	115	127	5	NINE INCH NAILS — TVT 2610 (CD)	PRETTY HATE MACHINE
106	118	125	14	ANIMAL LOGIC — I.R.S. 82020/MCA (9.98) (CD)	ANIMAL LOGIC
107	98	91	37	EXPOSE — ARISTA AL 8532 (9.98) (CD)	WHAT YOU DON'T KNOW
108	111	115	7	SOUNDGARDEN — A&M SP 5252 (8.98) (CD)	LOUDER THAN LOVE
109	101	99	13	XYZ — ENIGMA 73525 (9.98) (CD)	XYZ

Figure 6.15.

○ Albums with the greatest sales gains this week. ● (CD) Compact disk available. ● Recording Industry Assn. Of America (RIAA) certification for sales of 500,000 units. ▲ RIAA certification for sales of 1 million units, with each additional million indicated by a numeral following the symbol. CBS Records and PolyGram Records do not issue a suggested list price for their product. Catalog no. is for vinyl album. *Asterisk indicates catalog no. is for cassette album; vinyl unavailable.

92

BILLBOARD MARCH 10, 1990

Oscars and Grammys can and often do serve as recognition of a specific film or recording, or they reward exceptional careers. The most important effect of this feedback, however, is monetary. An award often brings increased sales for a film or record and gives the performers additional leverage with future employers. A Grammy for Michael Jackson's *Thriller* boosted sales from 25 million to over 30 million. In motion pictures, an already established hit benefits less from an Oscar win, since the audience has already turned out for it. But Woody Allen's *Annie Hall* earned an extra $10 million after it had won the Oscar for best picture in 1977, and *Gandhi*'s Oscar added over $16 million to the $38 million it had already taken in at the box office.

THE BROADCAST MEDIA

As we have discussed, for radio and television, critics' feedback has little impact, and awards in the form of Emmys are often used by actors and others to criticize TV business decisions. Feedback in the form of sales of radio or TV sets as well as subscriptions to cable-television systems also has little direct effect on programming practices of stations or networks because it provides no information about specific content; it merely implies that the medium is popular.

In radio and television, five forms of feedback are dominant: (1) cumulative audience (*cume*), (2) homes using television (HUT), (3) rating, (4) share, and (5) cost per thousand (CPM). HUTs are television-only feedback; cumes are radio feedback.

Cume. For a radio station, cumes can represent many listeners over different quarter hours or the same quarter hour over a number of weeks. *Cume persons* are identified as the estimated number of different persons who listened at home and away to a station for a minimum of 5 minutes within a given daypart (specific time period such as 4:00 to 6:00 P.M.).

Arbitron has long been the dominant organization for radio feedback collecting listening information in 260 radio markets across the country. All markets are measured at least once a year, during the spring; however, larger markets are measured up to four times a year. Radio stations and advertisers study the resulting reports to learn of changes in size of their audience, how their formats stack up versus the competition, what the audience profile is, etc.

Radio feedback has become increasingly sophisticated in recent years. Age and gender represent only a small portion of the information available to agencies and advertisers. Information based on income, marital status, family size, presence of children, occupation, employment status, home ownership, education, race, and "geo-demography" are available. Market reports may contain (1) audience trends, (2) discrete demographics, (3) audience composition, (4) demographic buyer, (5) hour-by-hour average cumes, (6) listening locations, (7) loyal and exclusive cume audience, (8) overnight listening, and (9) ethnic composition. Specific demographic groups are studied by repackaging the information into "clusters"—socioeconomic profiles of prospective product users.

HUT. HUT (homes using television) is the most basic form of television feedback. It is illustrated in Figure 6.16.

Ratings. Ratings are a further refinement of broadcast feedback and are expressed as the percentage of individuals or homes exposed to a particular program (Figure 6.17).

The ratings most of us are familiar with are the national ratings compiled by Nielsen Media Research. Actually, Nielsen compiles four ratings, the most important of which involve network TV programs. The national TV ratings obtained by Nielsen (see Figure 6.12) are a percentage of the estimated number of

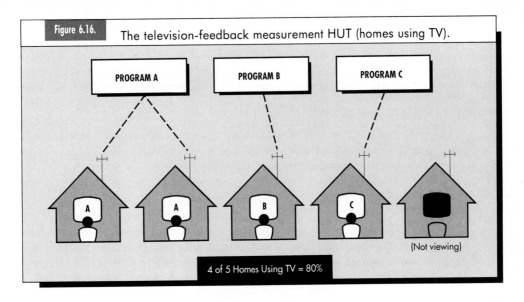

Figure 6.16. The television-feedback measurement HUT (homes using TV).

4 of 5 Homes Using TV = 80%

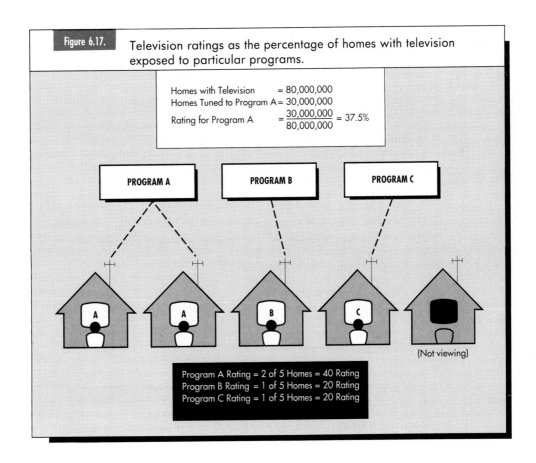

Figure 6.17. Television ratings as the percentage of homes with television exposed to particular programs.

Homes with Television = 80,000,000
Homes Tuned to Program A = 30,000,000

$$\text{Rating for Program A} = \frac{30,000,000}{80,000,000} = 37.5\%$$

Program A Rating = 2 of 5 Homes = 40 Rating
Program B Rating = 1 of 5 Homes = 20 Rating
Program C Rating = 1 of 5 Homes = 20 Rating

American households watching certain TV programs at a particular time. A program rating of 20 means that 20 percent of all American homes equipped with TV sets are watching a particular program. In 1990 there were 92 million TV homes. Thus a rating of 20 means that 18.4 million homes are tuned to that program.

To calculate a rating, two numbers are needed: (1) the total number of homes with television and (2) the number of TV homes watching a certain program. To obtain the rating for a particular program, you divide the number of homes watching a certain program by the total number of homes with television. It should be emphasized that these ratings usually represent households, not individuals; efforts are being made to fine-tune these ratings.

The most specialized ratings are based on product usage, a practice initiated in the mid-1960s by the Brand Rating Index (BRI), for use by advertisers. Viewers of TV programs are reported as percentages (ratings) of users of a product class. This feedback is obtained through personal interviews for product information and diaries for viewer information. Ratings to obtain radio and TV feedback for local markets are also prepared through various methods. Statistical Research uses the coincidental-telephone method for network-radio research. Pulse uses the personal-interview-aided-recall method for local-radio ratings. ARB uses the diary method for local radio and is also the major competitor of Nielsen in providing local-TV feedback.

Local-TV ratings for more than 200 markets are reported nationally from one to seven times a year, depending on market size and demand; the most common time frame is four times a year. In addition, Arbitron and Nielsen provide continuous daily and weekly reports in 14 (ARB) and 23 (Nielsen) major cities.

Share. A share is an equally important measurement of the broadcast audi-

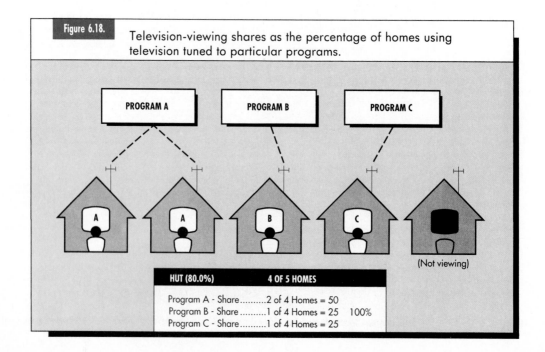

Figure 6.18. Television-viewing shares as the percentage of homes using television tuned to particular programs.

PROGRAM A PROGRAM B PROGRAM C

(Not viewing)

HUT (80.0%)   4 OF 5 HOMES

Program A - Share..........2 of 4 Homes = 50
Program B - Share..........1 of 4 Homes = 25   100%
Program C - Share..........1 of 4 Homes = 25

ence. A *share* is a measure of homes watching a TV program based on homes using television (HUT) at that time (Figure 6.18), whereas a *rating* measures homes watching a program based on all homes with a television set. The percentage of a TV audience accounted for by a share provides a more accurate measure of how a particular program did in competition with other programs broadcast at the same time. To obtain the share for a particular program, you divide the number of homes tuned to a particular program by the total number of homes using television.

Table 2.1 shows feedback in the form of ratings and shares for the top-30 network television programs for one week in the fall of 1989. The table, based on the national Nielsen ratings, lists for each program both its rating (the smaller number) and its share (the larger number). The top-rated program, "The Cosby Show," was viewed by 25.4 percent of all TV households. The 39 figure indicates the percentage of households watching television at that time who were tuned to "The Cosby Show." In using this feedback, mass communicators place as much importance on the share as on the rating because a share indicates how many households watching TV tuned into a program, thus providing a more significant measure of popularity.

CPM. Ultimately, cumes, HUTs, ratings, and shares lead to the most critical form of feedback for media: cost per thousand (CPM). This is the most widely used comparative tool for evaluating the efficiency of a particular medium. A CPM represents the advertiser's cost to reach 1,000 of its target population using a specific medium or combination of media:

$$\frac{\text{cost}}{\text{audience}/1,000} = \text{CPM}$$

As Table 6.1 indicates, CPM is used to evaluate alternatives.

A low rating, share, or cume bumps a program off the air because a program with a rating or share of 10 costs its sponsor twice as much for each home reached as a program with a 20 rating. A television program stays on the air or is canceled almost exclusively according to how much it costs the sponsor of the program to reach 1,000 people (CPM). As long as there is a commercial system of broadcasting in the United States, ratings, shares, cumes, and CPM will play an important role. Broadcasters and advertisers must know what they are getting for their money.

Table 6.1.	We Use CPM to Evaluate Alternatives				
		Delivery (000)		CPM	
	Cost: 30	Homes	Women	Homes	Women
Program A	$30,000	8,000	5,000	$3.75	$6.00
Program B	$40,000	12,000	10,000	$3.33	$4.00
		Delivery (000)		CPM	
	Cost Page 4-Color	Total Women	Women 25–54	Total Women	Women 25–54
Magazine A	$57,270	19,706	11,919	$2.91	$4.80
Magazine B	$45,235	17,498	9,865	$2.59	$4.59

THE PRINT MEDIA

Feedback for books, newspapers, and magazines comes from critics, award committees, and sales. All three provide a good indication of a book's success. For newspapers and magazines, the most important feedback comes from subscription

Figure 6.19. Starch Reports conducts surveys of attention paid to various components of print ads; the stickers record results.

and sales figures. Approximately 5,000 advertisers, ad agencies, newspapers, magazines, and business and farm publications subscribe to the Audit Bureau of Circulation (ABC), which verifies their circulation figures. In 1914 the Advertising Audit Association and the Bureau of Verified Circulation merged to form ABC as a check against deceptive "circulation-boosting" practices. Currently the ABC audits approximately 75 percent of all print media in the United States and Canada through a variety of reports and services. The system requires the cooperation of the print media to submit semiannual paid circulation figures to the ABC, which audits these figures on an annual basis. (In 1990, under pressure from advertisers, ABC branched out into audit of the increasingly popular magazines that do not charge for subscriptions; see Chapter 12.) The critical importance of verified figures is, of course, economic. The ABC figures help determine advertising rates (which are based on the number of readers) and assist the advertiser in creating an appropriate and cost-effective media plan. ABC audits 654 magazines and Business Publications Audit of Circulation monitors 225.

Additional feedback on print media is provided by readership studies conducted by companies such as Simmons and Starch. Simmons provides extremely detailed feedback for the magazine industry similar to that of the ARB radio diaries. Starch measures advertising readership through detailed interviews and then categorizes readers into four groups: (1) *nonreader*, a person who does not remember seeing the ad, (2) *noted reader*, a person who remembers having previously seen the ad, (3) *associated reader*, a person who not only notes the ad but also sees or reads some part of it that indicates the advertiser, and (4) *read-most reader*, a person who reads more than half the written material in the ad. The range of readers provides the advertising industry with information on individual ad effectiveness, including specific layout and copy features.

Telephone calls and letters from readers have not had a significant impact on the print media. These forms of feedback have always been popular with readers, however, and there is a growing sensitivity to readers' opinions, as reflected in letters to the editor. The *New York Times*, for example, receives more than 40,000 letters to the editor a year. Readers' cancellations of subscriptions and boycotts of the shops and products of advertisers are additional means of feedback but are rarely effective unless done by a large number of individuals.

THE IMPACT OF FEEDBACK

Given the reliance on institutionalized and largely quantitative feedback, it is no wonder that the average viewer or reader feels that he does not have an impact on specific television programs, magazines, or motion pictures. Still, individual or group feedback can have an effect if it is directed at the right target, as we saw in Chapter 5. This often takes the form of going beyond the local communicator to other agencies or groups, which, in turn, can exert pressure on the particular medium.

Many dissatisfied audience members of radio and TV stations write to the Federal Communications Commission rather than to the specific station. The FCC, under public pressure, then provides the station with indirect feedback that might be more effective than that of the local audience. For example, WLBT-TV in Jackson, Mississippi, lost its license in 1969 because of indirect feedback on that station's policy regarding racial issues. Action by the FCC can also serve as feedback for other stations, indicating that certain actions are frowned on.

The establishment of the Motion Picture Association of America's production code and a self-regulating agency was a result, in part, of public feedback to Congress, which then transmitted this public opinion to the film industry. In addition, public reaction to increased violence and nudity in film has been communicated to local newspapers and national magazines, which, in turn, transmit it to the film industry.

Letters alone usually cannot keep a TV series on the air or change the content of movies or the lyrics of rock music. But one show, "Remington Steele," demonstrates that a barrage of letters or telephone calls or a boycott by regular users of a medium can have some effect. During the 1985–1986 television season, the NBC program "Remington Steele" ranked 48 out of the year's 82 shows, averaging a 14.4 rating (percentage of TV homes that watched "Remington Steele") and a 25 share (percentage of TV homes watching television that were tuned to "Remington Steele"). On the basis of this feedback, NBC canceled the program. But as a result of a rare instance of direct, personal, qualitative (at least partially), and nonrepresentative feedback, NBC reversed its decision and renewed "Remington Steele" for the 1986–1987 season. The impetus for reviving the show, NBC said, came from over 8,700 calls and letters from loyal fans.

Reform feedback in mass communication must consist of extensive long-term pressure on the appropriate source to be successful in accomplishing major change. Equally important to consistent long-term feedback is the organized group that responds to a specific issue, such as abortion or gun control. What the viewing, listening, and reading audiences must recognize is that like the original media message, feedback must travel through a complex process of communication in order to be heard or read. The simple act of turning off a television or radio or not reading an article or advertisement is not enough.

As we have said in several different ways in this first part of our book, the audience is the prize in mass media. And looking at the HUB model of the communication process, we see that we have come to the outer limits of the pool of human affairs where repercussions then travel inward again, to the heart of the media industries. What we have learned about the process and the participants can now be applied more specifically to the individual (but not separate) components of mass media. None of these has a finger on the pulse of the audience to quite the degree that the public-relations and advertising industries do. They are most keenly aware of the power of public opinion and the influences that can legitimately be brought to bear on audience response. Because of this and because of their increasingly significant role in what the mass media communicate and how the media operate, the next section will present the functions of public relations and advertising.

SUMMARY ....

There is a distinction between the *public* (the total pool of those available to become audience members) and the *audience* (those actually attending the mass medium in question). In fact, there are many separate audiences, and their number and the specialization of their focus increase with the proliferation of media. Any one of us can be a member of several different audiences concurrently.

The audiences of the mass communication media can be described as (1) composed of individuals who may have shared characteristics, (2) large, (3) heterogeneous (rather than homogeneous), (4) relatively anonymous, and (5) physically separated from the communicator. Audiences are also evaluated by the advertisers who buy them, in terms of being available or actual (in broadcasting) and primary or pass-along (in print).

Three theories developed by DeFleur and Ball-Rokeach attempt to describe how audiences respond to media stimuli. The individual-differences theory describes audience members as reacting independently to each media event. The social-differences theory suggests that individuals aggregate and respond similarly based on commonly shared characteristics such as age, sex, education, and income. The social-relationships theory suggests that informal relationships and interpersonal communications before, during, and after media exposure affect the experiences.

Audiences use all their senses to perceive messages and filter those messages with four filters: (1) *informational and linguistic* filters (do we understand the code/language used?); (2) *psychological* filters (how do we selectively expose ourselves to respond to and retain media messages, and how are these behaviors related to our psychological/emotional makeup?); (3) *cultural* filters (how do our upbringing/background associations affect the reception and understanding of mass communication?); (4) *physical* filters (how do our comfort and well-being [internal] and the environments (external) in which we receive messages affect our responses?).

"Noise" can keep a message from reaching its destination, mainly because of: (1) weak signals; (2) clutter; (3) environmental distractions; (4) information overload.

Those messages that actually get through the maze of mass communication do so because they are amplified, primarily through: (1) strong signals, such as bold type in a front-page headline or a powerful radio transmission; (2) repetition of a message over a period of time; and (3) endorsement, in which a message is amplified by a well-known person.

Communication, by definition, is a two-way process, a cooperative and collaborative venture. In order for communication to succeed it is important that feedback take place. Mass-communication feedback is *representative* because audiences of mass media are so large that it is impossible to measure feedback from each member. Instead, a representative sample of the audience is selected. It is *indirect* since it usually comes through a third party, a rating organization or a polling company. Mass-communication feedback is *delayed* from the moment of original transmission. There are overnight television ratings, but most network ratings are published weekly. Letters to the editor must go through the mail and face even further delay because of periodical publishing deadlines.

Feedback in mass media is *cumulative*; emphasis is placed on the collective responses to a program or a periodical over a substantial period of time. Mass-communication feedback is measured, for the most part, in *quantitative* terms, including box-office figures for motion pictures, ratings for television programs, sales figures for records and books, and circulation figures for newspapers and magazines.

Mass-communication feedback is *institutionalized*. Large and complex organizations like Nielsen Media Research, Arbitron, and Pulse are required to provide meaningful feedback to mass communicators. This makes it costly.

There are many different techniques for obtaining feedback in mass communication, but five are most predominant: (1) the personal interview, (2) the coincidental-telephone survey, (3) the diary, (4) the mechanical device, and (5) the preview.

The motion-picture and sound-recording industries depend primarily on sales and box-office receipts to analyze the degree of success of a particular picture or record, even though they do receive some feedback from critics' reviews. In broadcasting, feedback from critics has had little impact. In radio and television, five forms of feedback are dominant: (1) cumulative audience (cume), (2) homes using television (HUT), (3) rating, (4) share, and (5) cost per thousand (CPM). Cumes are especially important for radio feedback, whereas HUTs, ratings, and shares are critical for television feedback.

Mass-communication feedback has a major impact on media programming. Negative feedback results in radio and television stations canceling programs, newspapers and magazines ceasing production, and motion-picture corporations going bankrupt. Even though mass communication is not direct and immediate, it is relatively effective and efficient in determining the ways messages are perceived by audiences.

REFERENCES

1. Charles Wright, *Mass Communication: A Sociological Perspective*, 2d ed. (New York: Random House, 1975), 6.
2. Melvin L. DeFleur and Sandra J. Ball-Rokeach, *Theories of Mass Communication*, 5th ed. (New York: Longman, 1989).
3. *New York Times*, August 13, 1989, H31.
4. Edward T. Hall, *The Silent Language* (Garden City, N.Y.: Doubleday, 1959).
5. Walter Lippmann, *Public Opinion* (New York: Free Press, 1922, repr. 1965).
6. Richard Corliss, "Killer! *Fatal Attraction* Strikes Gold as a Parable of Sexual Guilt," *Time*, November 16, 1987, 74.
7. Richard Pack, "Can Critics Really Influence Television Decision Makers?" *Television/Radio Age*, August 19, 1985, 106.

PART

T W O

THE PERSUADERS

············· ═══ ·············

We have seen that the industries that use the seven broad categories of channels are dependent on many other organizations—wire services, syndicates, syndicators, research firms, and technical and creative production services, to name a few. The subjects of Part 2—public relations and advertising—are other such auxiliary industries, each requiring a full chapter to cover their structures, functions, and roles regarding the media. The fields covered in this part are complex, specialized, and significant: A large percentage of baccalaureate candidates in schools of communications and journalism are hoping to enter one of these media industries. Both these students and those with an eye on writing, production, or performing need to understand the relationships between the persuaders and the mass communicators.

While public relations and advertising each involve areas not directly connected to the mass media, much of what they achieve would be impossible without the links to various publics provided by the media. Public relations and advertising are concerned with *persuasion*, which we have identified as one of the basic functions of the mass media. Advertising and public relations feed messages to the media that are identified or not identified with their sources. In the case of advertising, financial support is also provided to several media. Audiences, as we saw, recognize the influence of advertisers and pressure them when they want to change the messages.

We look at public relations and advertising before studying the evolution, conduct, and contribution of newspapers, movies, or cable TV because they are so integral to the present and future performance of *all* the media. Chapter 3, for example, pointed out that the conduct of the media is dependent on who the clients are, on whether a medium is supported by consumers or advertisers (or both). Public relations supplies content to both print and broadcast media. The influence of these two fields is pervasive.

The two industries now before us are communicators, researchers, and sources of support all at once. They have histories longer than those of most media, a present influence that the critical consumer and the media practitioner need to understand, and a hotly debated future. We begin with a look at the media-relations aspect of public relations.

Public Relations: Shaping Messages for the Mass Media

When President Bush met with President Gorbachev on a ship off the coast of Malta in late 1989, the U.S. media described it as a "PR move." When the tanker *Exxon Valdez* spilled 10 million gallons of oil into Alaska's Prince William Sound, a headline in the *New York Times* described the aftermath as "Exxon's Public-Relations Problem." Today, the use of the term *public relations* abounds in media reports, which suggest that it simply means sugarcoating a problem or capitalizing on opportunities to "look good." Public-relations practitioners are presented as ever-smiling, glad-handing, image makers working secretly behind the scenes, except in times of crisis when they are called upon to perform their magic tricks in public.

The result is that public perceptions of public-relations practices often represent only the proverbial "tip of the iceberg." More often than not, these perceptions are based on media reports that have described the *results* of long-term effective practice such as building goodwill or a positive image rather than the strategies and techniques that make up the *process* of public relations. From a public-relations practitioner's point of view, public relations means much more than this. From a *media* practitioner's point of view, public relations includes great potential influence on the messages sent. Indeed, the issue of ethical dealings between PR specialists and the media is a lively one these days. In order to understand their relationship better, we will look in this chapter at the structure and techniques that have evolved to serve today's public-relations professionals, study several models of practice, reflect on standards and ethics, and look into the future of this special media industry. We should first make an attempt at definition.

Imprecise use of the term in the media leads outsiders (media consumers like you) to believe that there is universal agreement within the practice about what public relations is and what it is not. In fact, when social scientist and public-relations practitioner Rex Harlow conducted a survey in 1976, he found more than 470 definitions of public relations.[1] Even a recent effort by the Public Relations Society of America (PRSA), and of two major professional public-relations organizations in the United States, to reach agreement on a definition ended in a recommendation of not one but two "official" definitions.[2]

Consultant and authority on content for this chapter is Pamela Creedon.

Figure 7.1.

According to Edward Bernays, a pioneer in the development of modern public-relations techniques, the three main elements of public relations are as old as civilized society. They are: informing people, persuading people, and fostering cooperative relationships among people.[3] As should be clear from Part 1, it has become increasingly difficult to get one's point of view expressed or heard. Along with a sound economic base and state-of-the-art media technology, communication experts and specialists are needed today to help individuals as well as groups or corporations to communicate facts, ideas, opinions, and concepts—to gain attention, select effective codes, pass through media gatekeeping and audience filters, and apply the knowledge provided by feedback.

Not only is it a communication facilitator for mass media; modern public relations is itself a media industry involved in a process of sending and receiving messages. The difference between public relations and advertising and media such as magazine publishing or television is that the communicators serve their clients (companies, governments, individuals, etc.) first of all. They are directly fueled by *them* rather than subscriptions, ratings, or end-user purchases.

PUBLIC OPINION AND THE HISTORY OF PUBLIC RELATIONS

Some trace the beginnings of public relations to a farm bulletin archeologists date from 1800 B.C., telling Iraqi farmers how to plant crops, irrigate, and deal with pests.[4] Others begin the history of public relations with the rulers in ancient Babylonia, who commissioned historians to portray them in a favorable light. Educators James Grunig and Todd Hunt suggest that it is ''not stretching history too much to claim the success of the apostles in spreading Christianity throughout the known world in the first century A.D. was one of the great public-relations accomplishments in history. The apostles Paul and Peter used speeches, letters, staged events, and similar public-relations activities to attract attention, gain followers, and establish new churches."[5]

While there is no single event, invention, or uncontested trend that can be labeled as the origin of public relations in the United States, the use of public relations to arouse public opinion is easily traced to the Boston Tea Party and Samuel Adams. We know from our history texts that the American Revolution was not a popular spontaneous uprising but a carefully planned and orchestrated movement by a band of dissidents led by Adams. The Boston Tea Party, perhaps more than anything since, has symbolized the power of staged events to capture public attention, to communicate a message. And then consider the abolitionist movement. We know, for example, that the use of public-relations techniques as political tools, including the publication of *Uncle Tom's Cabin* by Harriet Beecher Stowe, helped to rally support for blacks in the North in the 1850s and 1860s.

Often described as "the oil that makes democracy run," public-relations techniques play an important role in influencing public opinion. Walter Lippmann said that the art of democracy requires the "manufacture of consent."[6] The ability to persuade or convince others of one's point of view is essential in a land where nothing can succeed without the approval of the people. We need only consider the incredible number of communication experts involved in the 1988 presidential campaign: spin doctors, ad makers, speech writers, gesture coaches, and sound-bite writers. Today, we find public-relations techniques used everywhere—by executives coping with industrial accidents, rock stars pitching new albums, television evangelists looking for better fund-raising schemes, or social-service agencies seeking media attention to promote their causes. All over the country, day in and day out, thousands of people are engaged in the business of shaping messages for the mass media.

MODELS OF PUBLIC-RELATIONS PRACTICE

The modern public-relations function has evolved from calling attention to a product or event to a two-way concept of sending messages and listening to feedback. Today, ideal public relations is viewed as a management process in which communication is used to resolve conflict and to improve understanding by assisting an organization to adjust its behavior to the publics on which it depends. Table 7.1 shows the four models.

Table 7.1. Four Model Communication Programs	
Model	**Description**
■ Press Agent	One-way, tells only favorable information
■ Public Information	One-way, uses "journalists-in-residence"
■ Two-way Asymmetrical	Uses strategic messages to persuade. Doesn't seek consensus or accommodate opposing views
■ Two-way Symmetrical	Uses research and communication to manage conflict and improve understanding

Source: IABC.

Press Agentry or Publicity

Have you ever wondered how the MTV veejays know so much about the personal lives of the Beastie Boys or Van Halen? How the sports announcers on ESPN know all about the injuries, statistics, or salaries of the players in the Super Bowl? Or, how the Muscular Dystrophy Association is able to raise so much more for Jerry's kids every year? It's all part of what continues to be the most widely practiced technique or model in the public-relations practice, called press agentry or publicity. In this model, communication is *one-way* (from sender to receiver) and only favorable information is presented.

P. T. Barnum, who started his own newspaper but is best known for his exploits as a circus and museum promoter in the 1800s, is the individual most often associated with the beginnings of press agentry. Barnum, who reportedly once said, "There's a sucker born every minute," is credited with demonstrating how stretching the truth in promotions can pay big dividends at the box office. His promotions of circus attractions—such as General Tom Thumb (a dwarf in a general's uniform) or the 100-year-old woman who claimed she was George Washington's nurse— brought thousands of curious consumers under his big top. Publicity is probably the most visible part of public relations. In fact, Sinclair Lewis once wrote that the art of publicity, next to the talkies and spirituals, was the greatest of all American arts.[7]

Many compare the press agent in public relations to the salesperson in marketing; both jobs are part of a larger function. Others, like Bernays, would prefer to separate modern public relations from the press-agent image. In this view, public relations is not press agentry, flackery, or publicity, but an applied social science in which clients are advised how to inform, educate, and persuade the public to accept their products, services, or ideas.

Public Information

The next model, public information, also uses one-way communication but is more closely allied with journalistic goals like fairness, balance, and objectivity. The development of the model is often associated with Ivy Ledbetter Lee, who is often called the first professional public-relations practitioner. A former *New York Times* and *New York Journal* reporter, he opened his firm in 1904 to counsel such clients and groups as John D. Rockefeller, the Pennsylvania Railroad, Standard Oil, Bethlehem Steel, Chrysler, the American Red Cross, Harvard, and Princeton.

He saw an analogy between the court of law and the role of public opinion, and he saw himself as a new kind of lawyer, one who would represent his client before the court of public opinion by counseling the client on its public communications. Lee regarded his job as one of "adjusting relationships between the clients and their publics"; he spoke of "public relationships," and the phrase *public relations* came into use.

At the federal level, government has not permitted the use of the term *public relations* because some politicians and legislators still believe that the government should not be engaged in persuasion or "propaganda" and that only elected officials should be in direct contact with the public. The executive and judicial branches should only carry out the laws enacted by Congress; they should not be responsive to their publics. So the public-relations function in the executive branch

Figure 7.2.
Ivy Ledbetter
Lee opened the
first firm de-
voted exclu-
sively to advis-
ing clients
about their
public relation-
ships and how
to improve
them.

of government is called public information. During World War I, the United States government officially recognized, for the first time, that it had to organize persuasive communication efforts to win the war. President Woodrow Wilson employed a former Colorado newspaper editor, George Creel, to head the Committee on Public Information. Creel's committee advertised, publicized, and promoted America's role in the war.

Although Creel's committee was disbanded after the war, America's increasing role in international affairs led to the realization that the nation needed to defend itself before the world court of public opinion. When the United States entered World War II, the government established the Office of War Information, headed by Elmer Davis, a former radio news commentator. After the war it evolved into the United States Information Agency (USIA), the official public-relations organization for the U.S. government. The Voice of America was also established, and continues to function as an external broadcast service, using shortwave to beam information, news, and persuasion about America around the world.

While the government produces massive amounts of "information-only" publications, it does not own or publish daily newspapers or own and operate radio or television stations in the United States. The philosophy has been that the media should be privately owned and unrestricted so that they can report the activities of government and keep the bureaucracy from growing too powerful. Nevertheless, it has become increasingly clear that even the government in a free society must communicate vital information to the public. So the government employs public-relations practitioners, to advise government on its public relations and to inform people through the media by using press releases, press conferences, media events, films, brochures, magazines, newsletters, and any other means that prove effective.

TWO-WAY COMMUNICATION

There are two types of *two-way* models of public relations involving sending messages and listening to feedback from the receiver. The first is *persuasion;* the second is *symmetrical communication*. In the persuasive or asymmetrical model, the sender uses feedback to tailor a message to convince the receiver of the sender's point of view. In the mutual understanding or symmetrical model, the sender uses feedback to manage conflict and improve understanding, even if it means changing the sender's behavior.

Chief among those who pioneered in the maturation of public relations and development of two-way models were a husband-and-wife team, Edward L. Bernays and Doris E. Fleischman. Bernays, who taught the first course on public relations at New York University in 1923, and Fleischman, the first woman in the United States to be issued a passport in her maiden name, were equal partners in a public-relations counseling firm. They are even credited with jointly developing the term *public-relations counsel*.[8] Perhaps their most important contribution to the development of public relatioins was their attempt to take public relations out of the realm of art and make it systematic and scientific. Bernays, a nephew of Sigmund Freud, believed strongly in measuring public opinion and in two-way or symmetrical communication.

Bernays and Fleischman counseled literally hundreds of individuals and organizations, including Thomas Edison, Henry Ford, presidents from Coolidge to Eisenhower, Eleanor Roosevelt, opera singer Enrico Caruso, movie magnate Samuel Goldwyn, publisher Henry Luce, George Creel's Committee on Public Information, the NAACP, Procter & Gamble, the United Way, and the United Nations. They were involved in the introduction of radio with David Sarnoff and television with Philco. They even had a hand in making it popular for men to wear wristwatches and making it socially acceptable for women to smoke in public.

In the 1930s and 1940s, the practice of public-opinion polling emerged, pioneered by George Gallup, a former journalism professor, and Elmer Roper, a social scientist. (An example of a Roper report appears as Figure 6.14.) Polling not only provided a mechanism for public-relations practitioners to obtain feedback from their messages but also became a necessary adjunct to tailoring messages to persuade the public.

In the 1950s and 1960s, public-relations professionals turned increasingly to social and behavioral scientists and their theories to help measure public attitudes and test the effects of different ideas and messages on public opinion. By the 1970s and 1980s, public relations had begun to develop its own body of knowledge and research base. Most notable have been the efforts of Dr. James Grunig. This researcher and educator developed a structural view of public relations and also outlined the press-agentry, public-information, asymmetrical, and symmetrical models for public-relations practice that we have discussed.

In addition, two ground-breaking comprehensive studies of the public-relations field, undertaken in the late 1980s, also contributed to enhancing the professional status of the field. The largest, a $600,000 study begun in 1986 to determine the contribution of public relations to organizational effectiveness, was funded by the International Association of Business Communicators (IABC) Foundation. The second, supported by the Foundation for Public Relations Research and Education, provided the first formal report outlining the books, periodicals, data bases, bibliographies, curricula, principles, practices, and ideas that documented and defined the growing body of knowledge in the field of public relations.

PUBLIC-RELATIONS ROLES AND FUNCTIONS ....

Although public relations is often mistakenly viewed only in terms of business and corporate interests, most areas of our society use public relations as a way of maintaining and adjusting relationships with various publics, including local, state, and federal governments; hospitals and schools; volunteer sectors; religious organizations; the arts; the sciences, and even the mass media themselves. In public relations as in other media industries there is a trend toward merging of function.

As the 1990s began, for example, media leaders proposed a public-relations campaign that would bring together a considerable range of roles and functions. To combat the threat of new legislation on the advertising industry, especially its tax deductibility and its beer and alcohol ads, the CEO of Young and Rubicam called for a mammoth "coordinated communications industry campaign of advertising, public relations, mail and belly-to-belly communications." More than 600 people crowded into New York City's Plaza Hotel to hear an emergency panel discussion sponsored by the Ad Club. Alexander Kroll told them: "Bring into being a super-group, with a board of directors. Get them to hire professional communicators, funded by a specific tithing of the membership. That's the dream."[9] *Integrated marketing* is the thing as we proceed into the 1990s. There are nevertheless certain distinct roles.

CORPORATE COMMUNICATIONS

It may be useful to think of public relations simply as *the use of communication by an organization to inform, resolve conflict, and/or improve understanding with its strategic publics.* James Grunig, a leading public researcher, defines public relations as "the management of communication between an organization and its publics."[10] *Public* has two meanings in this book. You will recall from Chapter 6 that there is a general public, meaning all human beings in a given universe, which is not identical with *audience*. Public-relations researchers prefer to define the term *public* as "any group of people tied together, however loosely, by some common bond of interest or concern."[11] Today, most large business concerns, corporations, associations, and institutions with in-house public-relations activities have a person in charge of dealing with publics, often at a vice president level. Communication with and between employees is an essential element, so the person in charge of public relations often has a staff of people who specialize in *internal communication*, producing employee newspapers and magazines. Public-relations directors are also concerned with the owners or principles of their organizations, for whom they may produce stockholders' reports or an *annual report*.

Another side of public relations is the *external public-relations counsel*. Counseling firms, like legal firms, exist to provide independent advice on public-relations problems for clients. Some of these firms undertake the entire public-relations effort of their clients, producing their internal communications as well as providing direction for achieving their public-image goals. Tables 7.2 and 7.3 list the top 20

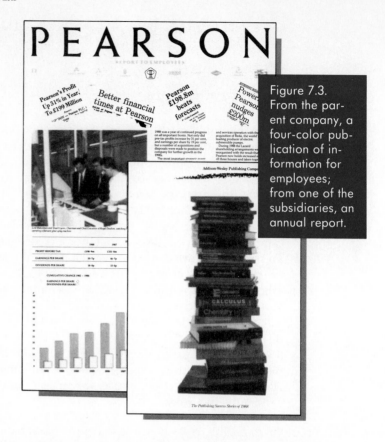

Figure 7.3. From the parent company, a four-color publication of information for employees; from one of the subsidiaries, an annual report.

Table 7.2. Top 20 Firms in Terms of 1988 PR Fee Income			
(A) Means Ad Agency Related	1988 Net Fees	Employees	% Fee Change From 1987
1. Hill and Knowlton (A)	$145,000,000	1,760	+29.6
2. Burson-Marsteller (A)	138,600,000	2,200	+18.0
3. Shandwick	121,880,000	1,610	+86.0
4. Ogilvy Public Relations Group (A)	47,600,000	700	+24.0
5. Rowland Worldwide (A)	41,900,000	614	+46.0
6. Omnicom PR Network (A)	36,080,283	400+	—
7. Fleishman-Hillard	32,500,000	399	+39.0
8. Daniel J. Edelman	31,425,395	391	+25.0
9. Manning, Selvage & Lee (A)	26,874,000	336	+13.8
10. Ketchum Public Relations (A)	26,435,000	334	+20.4
11. Golin/Harris Communications	25,611,000	378	+35.0
12. Creamer Dickson Basford (A)	20,184,286	250+	+20.0
13. GCI Group (formerly GreyCom) (A)	17,322,000	313	+58.0
14. Ruder Finn	15,811,927	232	+17.0
15. Regis McKenna	15,453,000	187	+6.6
16. Robinson, Lake, Lerer & Montgomery (A)	13,500,000	110	+24.0
17. Cohn & Wolfe (A)	10,100,000	110	+16.0
18. Financial Relations Board	7,854,457	93	+7.6
19. Robert Marston and Assocs.	7,500,000	62	−3.8
20. Dorf & Stanton Communications	7,241,623	104	+14.2

Table 7.3.	Largest Independent Public Relations Firms with Major PR Operations in the U.S.		
	1988 Net Fee Income	Employees	% Fee Change From 1987
1. Shandwick	$121,880,000	1,610	+86.0
2. Fleishman-Hillard	32,500,000	399	+39.0
3. Daniel J. Edelman	31,425,395	391	+25.0
4. Ruder Finn	15,811,927	232	+17.0
5. Regis McKenna	15,453,000	187	+6.6
6. Financial Relations Board	7,854,457	93	+7.6
7. Robert Marston and Assocs.	7,500,000	62	−3.8
8. Dorf & Stanton Communications	7,241,623	104	+14.2
9. Gibbs & Soell	5,280,874	70	+24.0
10. The Kamber Group	4,549,000	66	+11.4
11. Stoorza, Ziegaus & Metzger	4,331,047	63	+29.0
12. Cone Communications	4,101,017	47	+11.3
13. E. Bruce Harrison Co.	3,871,478	48	+18.1
14. The Rockey Co.	3,699,894	55	+54.0
15. BMc Strategies	3,458,631	24	+18.7
16. Lobsenz-Stevens	3,418,000	46	+15.0
17. Hi-Tech Public Relations	3,048,967	39	+35.7
18. KCS&A Public Relations	3,042,000	33	+12.6
19. Public Communications Inc.	2,870,826	43	+17.5
20. Hank Meyer Assocs.	2,703,804	27	—

firms according to three perspectives. These cite those firms supplying documentation to the 1989 O'Dwyer's Directory of PR Firms.

The role that the public-relations practitioner plays for an organization is often divided into *manager*, who counsels the organization on strategic decisions, and *technician*, who carries out management directives. However, recent findings have suggested that practitioners can have both managerial and technical responsibilities, especially those who are specialists in large departments or generalists in small departments.

Organizationally, public relations is perhaps best conceived as the total public-communication effort of an operation, the overall umbrella beneath which are advertising, marketing, promotion, publicity, employee communication, community relations, media relations, public affairs and other functions, including public-relations counseling. Of course, not all organizations follow this formula. In some organizations, *marketing* is the umbrella under which advertising and the marketing-oriented functions of public relations like promotion and publicity are found.

Where does public relations end and marketing begin? The boundaries between these two fields have become increasingly fuzzy. *Marketing*, for our purposes, is defined as a direct concern with the distribution and sale of goods or services. The primary audience of a marketing program is the consumer, but other audiences like wholesalers, dealers, and retailers are involved. But today organizations are recognizing that a product-oriented marketing perspective may not be enough. Experiences like those of the Exxon Corporation with the Valdez oil spill, the Johnson & Johnson Company with contaminated Tylenol capsules, and the

Figure 7.4. Tylenol's manufacturer, Johnson & Johnson, quickly responded to a tampering crisis by informing consumers and employees of steps being taken.

Procter & Gamble Company with toxic shock syndrome and Rely Tampons have caused many top executives to reconsider the importance of a strong public-relations program.

The decision whether to run an organization from a marketing perspective or a public-relations perspective promises to have a major impact on the ability of an organization to survive.

How do advertising, publicity, and promotion fit in? *Advertising* is defined as a very specific type of communication effort, one that is based on purchasing time or space in the mass media in order to send out a message. (Chapter 8 will describe the range of advertising activities.) Institutional advertising, which promotes the total institution rather than individual products, and issue advertising, which promotes an organization's point of view on something, play an important role in public relations.

Publicity should be defined in specific terms as free time or space in the communication media to send out a message. In order to get free space in a newspaper, the message must contain some element of media appeal. To get free time on radio, the message must contain some element of news, human interest, or public-service focus because of the long history of public-service requirements for radio and television stations by the Federal Communications Commission.

The main difference between advertising and publicity is that since advertisers pay for the time or space they use, they have more control over what is said. In publicity, since the message is printed, carried, or aired free, the final shaping of it is left in the hands of the media reporters and editors. Of the two, publicity may be more effective because it carries the tacit endorsement of the media and thus may seem to have more credibility or be more impartial.

Promotion means the use of both advertising and publicity over an extended period of time to communicate a specific point. We speak of promotional campaigns, implying that a relatively long period of time is involved over which message senders wage efforts to get their views on the public agenda and into the public consciousness.

MEDIA RELATIONS

Of the functions that PR practitioners perform with the various internal and external publics of an organization—employee communications, marketing communications, financial relations, community relations, and media relations—*media relations* is the one that is central to this book since it communicates the organization's point of view to an external audience, using the channels of mass communication.

Because the world is simply too big and too complicated for the news media to employ enough people to cover every aspect of every activity, media-relations practitioners serve a useful role for the media and the public. In fact, to a large extent, members of each field are mutually dependent. Media-relations people depend on the media to distribute their message to a mass audience. Journalists and other media practitioners rely on public-relations sources for information and access to sources. Actually, a few of us would believe how much of the news we see and hear is a product prepared by media-relations practitioners and served up free of charge to the media. Studies show that anywhere from 10 to 70 percent of daily news content consists of stories either written by or suggested in part by public-relations sources.[12]

Video News Releases. Practitioners are also serving up a regular diet of video news releases to the television news media, compliments of governments as well as corporations. Medialink, a video news-release distributor, reported that 76 million American television viewers saw Colombia's President Virgilio Barco Vargas speak on his nation's war on drugs. Thus the most watched PR video in 1989 originated with a foreign government; second was Sears, Roebuck, explaining its new pricing policy to 70 million viewers. The "top ten" of video news releases drew an average audience of 37.6 million.[13] One recent study showed that nearly 80 percent of news directors and assignment editors at U.S. television stations use video news releases on a regular basis. However, most of the editors said that they modify the release in some way such as retracking it and adding the voice of their own reporter.[14]

Information Subsidies. Researchers use the term *information subsidies* to describe media-relations handouts like these video and print news releases. Throughout this book we will see how the computer is transforming the mass media. Computerization has also changed the way in which public-relations practitioners deliver their information subsidies to the media. Feature and news services, as described in Chapter 2, are easily accessed in computerized newsrooms.

Satellite transmission of news releases is available through a service such as PR Newswire. Founded in 1954, it pioneered simultaneous electronic transmission of press releases to news media. Today, PRN transmits news and information from more than 15,000 news sources to clients that include over 1,500 daily newspapers, wire services, magazines, trade and technical journals, TV and radio stations, 85 percent of the Fortune 500 companies, and leading computer data bases. PRN is used by publicly owned corporations to fulfill "timely disclosure" requirements

Figure 7.5.
The newsroom
at PR News-
wire

and to send financial news directly to the investment community in the United States, Europe, and the Far East. PRN also transmits news for various other organizations such as embassies, universities, state and local governments, nonprofit organizations. Recently it introduced Entertainet, a separate network designed to transmit entertainment news directly to entertainment editors.

Electronic libraries like NEXIS provide instantly accessible background data on an organization, as well as every news release carried by PR Newswire since early in 1980. As cable television and other new technologies offer opportunities for narrowcasting to target audiences, the hunger for specialized news only increases. Public-relations subsidies support the media system by providing information in a usable and acceptable format.

DIFFERING PERSPECTIVES ON THE USE OF THE MEDIA

It is important to remember that the journalist's ideal of objectivity is not an appropriate ideal for the public-relations practitioner. The public-relations practitioner in a media-relations role is consciously presenting information from the point of view of a *client* or an organization. This does not mean that the information is inherently dishonest, unfair, or inaccurate.

Studies show, however, that journalists often view public-relations practitioners in terms of negative stereotypes.

It may be useful to think of media-relations practitioners in two categories—the journalist-in-residence and the organizational communicator. The *journalist-in-residence* is a public-relations practitioner who has practiced for more than a decade but worked at a media job before entering the public-relations field. They believe in dealing openly with the media and telling as much of the truth as is known in all circumstances because of their belief that a reporter will represent the organization fairly when all necessary information is made available. The *organizational communicators* on the other hand believe that their first allegiance is to the organization. They are likely to approach public relations from a business or marketing point of view, to have been employed in the practice of public relations from three to five years, and to have journalism degrees and some media experience. However, these practitioners believe that the press has a bias toward the negative and sensational, and do not think that it is in the organization's best interest always to be completely open with the press. They also think that there are distinct and necessary differences between the roles of journalist and public-relations practitioner, and would characterize relations with reporters as give-and-take.

If we look at these roles in terms of the models of public-relations practice discussed on pages 151–155, we can see that the journalist-in-residence fits closely with the public-information model. The organizational communicator is oriented toward two-way communication and fits best with the asymmetrical or symmetrical models.

Why is this difference in perspective important? We know that the media serve an important role in raising public interest in an issue. The media-relations practitioner is attempting to influence the media agenda and thus the public agenda, and thus the "pictures in our heads." This is notably true for events that most of us cannot experience directly, like the meeting of Bush and Gorbachev at Malta, the invasion of Panama, and the crumbling of the Berlin Wall.

It might appear that organizations with good media-relations programs could use the media to persuade the public about anything. For example, through the use of a carefully planned media-relations program, Ivy Lee succeeded in changing the image of John D. Rockefeller, Sr., from an unscrupulous industrial tyrant to a philanthropist. More recently, the image of the Chrysler Corporation was enhanced through a media-relations program featuring President Lee Iacocca as its spokesperson. However, the relationship between the mass media and persuasion is not clear-cut. Communication research has shown that while it may be possible to change public images such as those of Rockefeller or Chrysler through a mass-media campaign, the image must be matched with action for the public to be persuaded of a change. In the case of Rockefeller, this was accomplished through the establishment of a charitable foundation and subsequent publicity about its donations. For Chrysler, the credibility of the new image rested with the production of a quality product.

Furthermore, research suggests that the mass media can be used to create an awareness of an issue or product, or to communicate information about an issue or product, but that the mass media are not very effective in changing attitudes. We know that an individual is more likely to be affected by messages that reinforce existing or new behavior. For example, an individual who has made a decision to lose weight may be persuaded by mass-media messages about diet programs or products.

Findings such as these have led public-relations practitioners to question whether the use of the mass media to convey persuasive messages in our mass society with its diverse publics is an effective communication strategy. They argue that only with targeted messages designed to reach specific publics can the mass media be effective in helping them reach an audience in our increasingly fragmented culture. Reaching these audience members means developing message strategies that address their needs, concerns, and interests. Most often, this is done through the use of psychographic research based on the values and lifestyles of audience members.

Interestingly, because of the research that has cast doubt on the effectiveness of the mass media to change attitudes, the increasing emphasis on audience segmentation, and targeted messages, some are predicting a decline in the use of the traditional mass media (commercial radio, television, and newspapers) by public-relations practitioners in the future and thus a decline in the media-relations function in public relations.

SPECIAL PUBLICITY AND PROMOTION MEDIA

Brochures, Pamphlets, Graphic Materials. Printed materials other than books and periodical publications are increasing in volume. These are not new media, but they are being put to new use. Essentially they are being used by practitioners for information, publicity, or promotional purposes.

In the case of brochures, booklets, flyers, leaflets, and pamphlets, proper distribution and appropriate content is central to their effectiveness. The use of direct-mail techniques to distribute these reading materials to people on selected mailing lists has vastly increased their utility.

Use of display graphics, one of the oldest forms of communication, is increasing. Earlier societies used wall posters and notices tacked on bulletin boards to inform and persuade. Many countries, particularly China, still use wall newspapers and posters as well as outdoor radio and television sets to inform and persuade their citizens, and in the United States, posters have experienced a rebirth and revitalization. Billboards have been a fixture in graphic display as long as America has had highways and automobiles. Equally ubiquitous but even more effective, according to research findings, are exterior and interior car cards on streetcars, subways, and buses. Today, even the automobile bumper sticker or grocery bag carries a message.

Direct and Electronic Mail. The personal letter can be used to persuade. Direct mail is based on sending a message through the postal system to readers who have something in common. The gathering of names of such readers has become a big business, and one can rent or buy lists of names from a mailing-list company to reach almost any audience.

Today, with the sophisticated computer capability and the development of the word processor and laser printing, letters can be individually addressed with personal messages inserted at key points in the letter and signed with pen and ink by a signature machine. Letters from the president, members of Congress, or business and consumer-group officials are now often handled in this mass-produced manner.

Electronic mail is also growing rapidly in popularity. As more and more individuals and offices link their computers over telephone lines via modems, the potential to transmit personally targeted messages directly to another computer or to send documents via FAX machines has increased dramatically. The potential of electronic transmission of messages promises to revolutionize the technology of communication and the delivery of persuasive messages.

Ketchum Public Relationships

"Without Ketchum we'd have gone nuts trying to promote peanut butter."

Randy Griggs, Director, Peanut Advisory Board

Not that it was time to panic. Peanut butter is an $860 million industry with an American household penetration of 83 percent. In fact, half of America's annual peanut crop becomes peanut butter. But the Peanut Advisory Board was concerned its sales were flat, and for good reason: it's the kids who gobble up peanut butter. Unfortunately, there are 3 million fewer kids in the 5-to-13 year old category today than 10 years ago, a reduction of 10 percent.

Ketchum's analysis of sales trends, demographic studies and advertising campaigns showed that without exception, branded peanut butter marketing dollars were being spent toward kids and their mothers. The Ketchum solution: adults represented a major opportunity for expanding the market.

How simple. Everybody loves peanut butter. Adults could be a primary focus for a public relations campaign in the effort to meet a challenging objective: creating energy for a century-old product.

Then Ketchum went to work. They developed restaurant and hotel chain promotions featuring upscale peanut butter menu items. They conducted events for food editors to sample delicious adult food made with peanut butter. And they even created an "Adult Peanut Butter Lovers Club" as a mechanism to generate adult-level publicity and quickly position peanut butter as an adult food. A special kit was prepared, including official membership materials and a newsletter. To date, more than 15,000 adults have joined, their curiosity aroused by more than 360 newspaper stories, 46 consumer magazine articles, six network television features and 30 network and local radio interviews in one year.

The result of this multi-year effort: adults have rediscovered their childhood favorite and peanut butter sales have rebounded.

The Ketchum team had the initial creative insights, plus the managerial and public relations know-how to follow through with skill and energy on a simple, single-minded idea. For the Peanut Advisory Board the combinations have been as natural as peanut butter and jelly.

For more information about how you can start a Public Relationship with us, write Paul Alvarez or David Drobis, Ketchum Public Relations, 1133 Ave. of the Americas, NY, NY 10036 or call (212) 536-8800. *New York · San Francisco · Pittsburgh · Washington DC · Chicago · Silicon Valley · Atlanta · Philadelphia · Los Angeles*

Figure 7.6. In a series of ads, Ketchum Public Relations has run testimonials from industry leaders happy with the firm's multiyear, multifaceted approach, from market research to media coverage.

Audiovisual Materials. A-V programs are being mass-produced to the extent that audiovisuals almost qualify as mass media. Yet they retain their personal intimacy and allow for easy and inexpensive production of presentations, even by amateurs.

Most audiovisual displays use still photographs, slides, film strips, and motion pictures but may include disc recordings, audiotape recordings, and videotape recordings. Simple systems are now available to program, synchronize, and mix sound and sight. The development of stereotape, tape cassettes, and compact discs has also enlarged the potential of the entire audiovisual field, providing compact and convenient packages of sound that rival the convenience of books for storage, retrieval, and easy access.

Closed-circuit broadcasting and satellite transmission are other forms of audiovisual presentation that are finding increased use in offices, conventions, news conferences, and educational institutions to augment the communication process. Closed-circuit radio and television are being used in home and office and in shops and factories.

Multimedia Presentations. Since person-to-person communication is still the most effective way to send a message, eyeball-to-eyeball conflict resolution has become institutionalized in our mass society. Meetings, seminars, conferences, and institutes have become such successful media for communication that they are now regularized affairs for most groups. Meetings bring together people from diverse geographical locations for interpersonal communication; hotels have become common meeting grounds, and new hotels are equipped with the latest audiovisual equipment. Sometimes the message rather than the audience is moved from place to place. Some meetings are broadcast via satellite with teleconferences held at several locations simultaneously.

The traveling display or exhibition has been used effectively for communicating across cultural barriers. One special display, the NAMES Project AIDS Quilt, traveled across the United States and helped relatives, friends, and loved ones of victims of acquired immune deficiency syndrome (AIDS) express their concern and grief together. Each quilt square memorialized a person who had died from AIDS. Divided into several large sections, each composed of more than 1,000 quilt squares, the sections were finally assembled on the Ellipse in Washington, D.C., on National AIDS Awareness Day in 1989 (see Figure 7.7). As a medium of communication, the quilt promoted awareness and understanding among people who otherwise might have refused to be together because of the disease's association with the issue of homosexuality in our culture.

The grandest expression of multimedia presentation is probably a world's fair. New forms of multimedia presentations, ranging from posters and brochures to light-and-sound shows, from multimedia-screen projections to complicated all-encompassing exhibits through which one rides in a car fitted with audiovisual, ol-

Figure 7.7. The final display of the AIDS Memorial Quilt in its entirety: 10,848 individual 3' × 6' panels.

factory, and sensory mechanisms to massage all the senses provide for total communication. The communication techniques developed for world's fairs have had wide application in other areas, including higher education and popular entertainment, from the multimedia center at the University of Texas to Disneyland in California and Walt Disney World and EPCOT in Florida.

THE PUBLIC-RELATIONS PROCESS

Public relations itself is a process of building *public relationships* through research, planning, implementation, and evaluation. To be successful, campaigns require ongoing attention and follow through; Figure 7.8 lists a wide range of efforts that were commended by the public relations industry.

To carry out an external or internal public-relations program effectively, many public-relations practitioners rely on a four-step interactive process to help them

Figure 7.8

A SALUTE TO EXCELLENCE
45TH ANNUAL SILVER ANVIL AWARD WINNERS

"Title III: The Monsanto Commitment"
Monsanto Company, St. Louis, MO

"Ventura Improvement Project Public Awareness Campaign"
California Department of Transportation, Los Angeles, CA with Manning, Selvage & Lee, Inc., Los Angeles, CA

"This College is the Community"
Macomb Community College, Warren, MI with Bock & Associates, Inc., Northville, MI

"The Searle Program for Patients in Need"℠
Searle, Skokie, IL with Fleishman-Hillard, Inc., New York, NY

"The Drought is Real"
Los Angeles Department of Water and Power, Los Angeles, CA with Gumpertz/Bentley/Fried, Los Angeles, CA

"Made in the U.S.A./Miss America Communications Campaign"
Crafted with Pride in U.S.A. Council, New York, NY with The Rowland Company, New York, NY

"Children's for Children"
Children's Hospital Medical Center of Akron, Akron, OH with Malone Public Relations, Akron, OH

"The Most Widely Witnessed Wedding in U.S. History"
Huntington Hotel and Cottages, Pasadena, CA with Read Communications, Pasadena, CA

"California Vietnam Veterans Memorial"
State of California's Vietnam Veterans Memorial Commission, Sacramento, CA with Stoorza, Ziegaus & Metzger, Inc., Sacramento, CA

"Peanut Butter Lover's Fan Club Reunion"
Peanut Advisory Board, Atlanta, GA with Ketchum Public Relations, New York, NY

"National Cancer Survivors Day"
American Cancer Society, New York, NY, and Coping Magazine, Franklin, TN with GTFH Public Relations, New York, NY

"Harley-Davidson Celebrates 85 Years"
Harley-Davidson, Inc., Milwaukee, WI with Bozell Public Relations, Chicago, IL

"Soviet Trade Exhibition"
U.S.S.R. Chamber of Commerce and Industry, New York, NY with Burson-Marsteller, New York, NY

"California Raisins' Vacation Across America"
The California Raisin Advisory Board, Fresno, CA with Ketchum Public Relations, San Francisco, CA

"The National Geographic Society Centennial"
National Geographic Society, Washington, DC with Porter/Novelli, Washington, DC

"National Student/Parent Mock Election"
TIME Magazine, New York, NY

"The National AIDS Mailing"
Centers for Disease Control, Atlanta, GA with Ogilvy & Mather Public Affairs, Washington, DC

"National Safe KIDS Campaign"
Children's Hospital National Medical Center, Washington, DC, Johnson & Johnson, New Brunswick, NJ, and National Safety Council, Chicago, IL with Greer, Margolis, Mitchell & Associates, Washington, DC

"Improving Water Quality and Public Images"
The Contra Costa Water District, Concord, CA with Solem & Associates, San Francisco, CA

"11th Hour Override of Off-Track Wagering Veto"
Pennsylvania Horse Racing Industry, Grantville, PA with Skutski & Associates, Inc., Pittsburgh, PA

"AARP/VOTE IOWA—The 1988 Presidential Election"
American Association of Retired Persons (AARP), Washington, DC with The FMR Group, Inc., Washington, DC

"Graffiti: It's A Crime"
National Paint & Coatings Association, Washington, DC with Kaufman Public Relations, Washington, DC

"Sea World of Texas' Grand Opening"
Sea World of Texas, San Antonio, TX with Edelman Public Relations, Houston, TX

"INF Treaty Inspections: The Russians Are Coming"
The On-Site Inspection Agency, Washington, DC

"Post-Launch Market Education Campaign"
The Open Software Foundation, Cambridge, MA with Hill and Knowlton Advanced Technology Division, Waltham, MA

"The Crusader Baby Campaign"
General Health Corporation, Piscataway, NJ with Gaston & Gordon Associates, Inc., Flemington, NJ

"Job Corps Recruiting"
U.S. Department of Labor—Office of Job Corps—Region III, Philadelphia, PA with Smith Mead & Associates, Baltimore, MD

"Visa/Worldwide Sponsorship of '88 Olympic Games"
Visa U.S.A., San Mateo, CA with Manning, Selvage & Lee, Inc., New York, NY

"Cleveland Scholarship Programs: Success Story"
Cleveland Scholarship Programs, Inc., Cleveland, OH with Edward Howard & Co., Cleveland, OH

"GE Enters the Professional Custom Kitchen Market"
GE Appliances, Louisville, KY with Burson-Marsteller, New York, NY

"The Jell-O™ Reading Rocket"
Jello-O® Desserts Products of General Foods USA, White Plains, NY with M Booth & Associates, New York, NY

"New Zealand Challenge for the America's Cup"
Fay, Richwhite Co., Ltd., Auckland, New Zealand with Dorf & Stanton Communications, Stamford, CT

"Panama Crisis: The War of Information"
United States Southern Command, APO Miami, FL

"Employee Relations for Princeton Farms"
Princeton Farms, Princeton, IL with Aaron D. Cushman and Associates, Inc., Chicago, IL

"Broadening the Upjohn Company's Shareholder Base"
The Upjohn Company, Kalamazoo, MI with The Financial Relations Board, Inc., Chicago, IL

"Pet Parent Program"
Ralston Purina Company, St. Louis, MO with Fleishman-Hillard, Inc., St. Louis, MO

"Unidos Contra LaDiabetes" (United Against Diabetes)
The Upjohn Company, Kalamazoo, MI with Manning, Selvage & Lee, Inc., New York, NY

PRSA

determine goals and strategic objectives, and then to evaluate their work. Most importantly, when done properly, this process starts with research and ends with research, and uses research throughout the process to assess each phase of the program and to determine if changes or modifications need to be made.

The public-relations process is becoming increasingly important as practitioners attempt to demonstrate their effect on an organization's overall goals and objectives. Whether these goals and objectives are to increase awareness, create goodwill, pass a school levy, raise funds for a cause, make a profit, or influence public opinion in some other way, the four-step process charted in Figure 7.9 helps develop a communication plan that can make them a reality.

The Emerging Profession

The ingredients generally considered necessary for an occupation to be considered a profession are (1) a body of knowledge, (2) a standard for ethical conduct, and (3) controlled access.

Body of Knowledge

The official *Public Relations Body of Knowledge* report, mentioned on page 154, suggests not only that a body of knowledge clearly exists but that what "distinguishes the body of knowledge in public relations from all knowledge is its *application* to achieve public relations goals." What this means is that public relations draws upon primary research from other fields like psychology, sociology, anthropology, communication, political science, management, marketing, finance, economics, and so forth to achieve public-relations goals. Within the field, numerous publications, including *Public Relations Review, Public Relations Research Annual, Public Relations Quarterly, Communication World, PR Journal,* and *pr reporter* routinely include applied research in public relations. Moreover, the report describes the ideal practitioner as a Renaissance person with a strong liberal arts education, combined with excellent communication skills, especially writing. In addition, to recognize and celebrate outstanding efforts by practitioners each year, IABC sponsors a Gold Quill competition, while PRSA sponsors a Silver Anvil Award (see Figure 7.9). Recent winning campaigns have included "California Raisins' Vacation Across America" by the California Raisin Board; "The Drought Is Real" by the Los Angeles Department of Water and Power with the Gumpertz/Bentley/Fried Agency; "National Cancer Survivors Day" by the American Cancer Society with GFTH Public Relations Agency; "AARP/VOTE IOWA—The 1988 Presidential Election" by the American Association of Retired Persons with FMR Group, Inc.; and "INF Treaty Inspections: The Russians Are Coming" by the On-Site Inspection Agency.

Standard for Ethical Conduct

Both PRSA and IABC, the two major professional U.S. public-relations organizations, have had formal codes of ethics for a number of years and have revised them a number of times (see the box). Both codes are enforced by boards of ethics that meet when a practitioner has been accused of violating one of the articles.

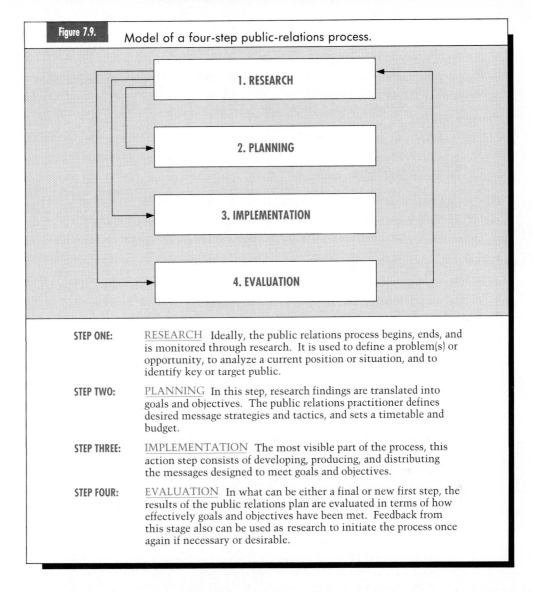

Figure 7.9. Model of a four-step public-relations process.

1. RESEARCH

2. PLANNING

3. IMPLEMENTATION

4. EVALUATION

STEP ONE: RESEARCH Ideally, the public relations process begins, ends, and is monitored through research. It is used to define a problem(s) or opportunity, to analyze a current position or situation, and to identify key or target public.

STEP TWO: PLANNING In this step, research findings are translated into goals and objectives. The public relations practitioner defines desired message strategies and tactics, and sets a timetable and budget.

STEP THREE: IMPLEMENTATION The most visible part of the process, this action step consists of developing, producing, and distributing the messages designed to meet goals and objectives.

STEP FOUR: EVALUATION In what can be either a final or new first step, the results of the public relations plan are evaluated in terms of how effectively goals and objectives have been met. Feedback from this stage also can be used as research to initiate the process once again if necessary or desirable.

The professional public-relations organizations have responded to the increasing awareness of ethical issues throughout the culture by increasing attention to the value system under which its practitioners function and heightening debate about ethical standards. However, not all practitioners belong to PRSA or IABC, the enforcement procedures and penalties for violations have been criticized as weak, and the codes have been criticized for their lack of grounding in ethical theory.

CONTROLLED ACCESS

In the U.S. Department of Labor annual count of workers in various occupations, the category of "public relations and publicity writers" included some 175,000 persons by the end of the 1980s. However, only about 25,000 public-relations prac-

Public Relations Society of America

This Code was adopted by the PRSA Assembly in 1988. It replaces a Code of Ethics in force since 1950 and revised in 1954, 1959, 1963, 1977, and 1983. For information on the Code and enforcement procedures, please call the Board of Ethics Chairman through PRSA Headquarters.

Declaration of Principles

Members of the Public Relations Society of America base their professional principles on the fundamental value and dignity of the individual, holding that the free exercise of human rights, especially freedom of speech, freedom of assembly, and freedom of the press, is essential to the practice of public relations.

In serving the interests of clients and employers, we dedicate ourselves to the goals of better communication, understanding, and cooperation among the diverse individuals, groups, and institutions of society, and of equal opportunity of employment in the public relations profession.

We pledge:

To conduct ourselves professionally, with truth, accuracy, fairness, and responsibility to the public;

To improve our individual competence and advance the knowledge and proficiency of the profession through continuing research and education;

And to adhere to the articles of the Code of Professional Standards for the Practice of Public Relations as adopted by the governing Assembly of the Society.

Code of Professional Standards for the Practice of Public Relations

These articles have been adopted by the Public Relations Society of America to promote and maintain high standards of public service and ethical conduct among its members.

1. A member shall conduct his or her professional life in accord with the **public interest.**

2. A member shall exemplify high standards of **honesty and integrity** while carrying out dual obligations to a client or employer and to the democratic process.

3. A member shall **deal fairly** with the public, with past or present clients or employers, and with fellow practitioners, giving due respect to the ideal of free inquiry and to the opinions of others.

4. A member shall adhere to the highest standards of **accuracy and truth,** avoiding extravagant claims or unfair comparisons and giving credit for ideas and words borrowed from others.

5. A member shall not knowingly disseminate **false or misleading information** and shall act promptly to correct erroneous communications for which he or she is responsible.

6. A member shall not engage in any practice which has the purpose of **corrupting** the integrity of channels of communications or the processes of government.

7. A member shall be prepared to **identify publicly** the name of the client or employer on whose behalf any public communication is made.

8. A member shall not use any individual or organization professing to serve or represent an announced cause, or professing to be independent or unbiased, but actually serving another or **undisclosed interest.**

9. A member shall not **guarantee the achievement** of specified results beyond the member's direct control.

10. A member shall **not represent conflicting** or competing interests without the express consent of those concerned, given after a full disclosure of the facts.

11. A member shall not place himself or herself in a position where the member's **personal interest is or may be in conflict** with an obligation to an employer or client, or others, without full disclosure of such interests to all involved.

12. A member shall **not accept fees, commissions, gifts or any other consideration** from anyone except clients or employers for whom services are performed without their express consent, given after full disclosure of the facts.

13. A member shall scrupulously safeguard the **confidences and privacy rights** of present, former, and prospective clients or employers.

14. A member shall not intentionally **damage the professional reputation** or practice of another practitioner.

15. If a member has evidence that another member has been guilty of unethical, illegal, or unfair practices, including those in violation of this Code, the member is obligated to present the information promptly to the proper authorities of the Society for action in accordance with the procedure set forth in Article XII of the Bylaws.

16. A member called as a witness in a proceeding for enforcement of this Code is obligated to appear, unless excused for sufficient reason by the judicial panel.

17. A member shall, as soon as possible, sever relations with any organization or individual if such relationship requires conduct contrary to the articles of this Code.

(Cont).

Official Interpretations of the Code

Interpretation of Code Paragraph 1, which reads, "A member shall conduct his or her professional life in accord with the public interest."

The public interest is here defined primarily as comprising respect for and enforcement of the rights guaranteed by the Constitution of the United States of America.

Interpretation of Code Paragraph 6, which reads, "A member shall not engage in any practice which has the purpose of corrupting the integrity of channels or communication or the processes of government."

1. Among the practices prohibited by this paragraph are those that tend to place representatives of media or government under any obligation to the member, or the member's employer or client, which is in conflict with their obligations to media or government, such as:
   a. the giving of gifts of more than nominal value;
   b. any form of payment or compensation to a member of the media in order to obtain preferential or guaranteed news or editorial coverage in the medium;
   c. any retainer or fee to a media employee or use of such employee if retained by a client or employer, where the circumstances are not fully disclosed to and accepted by the media employer;
   d. providing trips, for media representatives, that are unrelated to legitimate news interest;
   e. the use by a member of an investment or loan or advertising commitment made by the member, or the member's client or employer, to obtain preferential or guaranteed coverage in the medium.

2. This Code paragraph does not prohibit hosting media or government representatives at meals, cocktails, or news functions and special events that are occasions for the exchange of news information or views, or the furtherance of understanding, which is part of the public relations function. Nor does it prohibit the bona fide press event or tour when media or government representatives are given the opportunity for an on-the-spot viewing of a newsworthy product, process, or event in which the media or government representatives have a legitimate interest. What is customary or reasonable hospitality has to be a matter of particular judgment in specific situations. In all of these cases, however, it is, or should be, understood that no preferential treatment or guarantees are expected or implied and that complete independence always is left to the media or government representative.

3. This paragraph does not prohibit the reasonable giving or lending of sample products or services to media representatives who have a legitimate interest in the products or services.

4. It is permissible, under Article 6 of the Code, to offer complimentary or discount rates to the media (travel writers, for example) if the rate is for business use and is made available to all writers. Considerable question exists as to the propriety of extending such rates for personal use.

Interpretation of Code Paragraph 9, which reads, "A member shall not guarantee the achievement of specified results beyond the member's direct control."

This Code paragraph, in effect, prohibits misleading a client or employer as to what professional public relations can accomplish. It does not prohibit guarantees of quality or service. But it does prohibit guaranteeing specific results which, by their very nature, cannot be guaranteed because they are not subject to the member's control. As an example, a guarantee that a news release will appear specifically in a particular publication would be prohibited. This paragraph should not be interpreted as prohibiting contingent fees.

Interpretation of Code Paragraph 13, which reads, "A member shall scrupulously safeguard the confidences and privacy rights of present, former, and prospective clients or employers."

1. This article does not prohibit a member who has knowledge of client or employer activities that are illegal from making such disclosures to the proper authorities as he or she believes are legally required.
2. Communications between a practitioner and client/employer are deemed to be confidential under Article 13 of the Code of Professional Standards. However, although practitioner/client/employer communications are considered confidential between the parties, such communications are not privileged against disclosure in a court of law.
3. In the absence of any contractual arrangement, the client or employer legally owns the rights to papers or materials created for him.

Interpretation of Code Paragraph 14, which reads, "A member shall not intentionally damage the professional reputation or practice of another practitioner."

Blind solicitation, on its face, is not prohibited by the Code. However, if the customer list were improperly obtained, or if the solicitation contained references reflecting adversely on the quality of current services, a complaint might be justified.

[This code also contains official interpretations of the Code as it applies to political public relations and financial public relations.]

titioners belong to PRSA and IABC. Since only about one in seven people who are classified in a public-relations occupation belong to one of the two organizations with a code of ethics and since there is no requirement for professional training to call oneself a public-relations practitioner, the field falls short on the professional standard of *controlled access*. Public relations can be practiced by anyone. However, today's organizational environment demands that the public-relations practitioner move into roles beyond those of reporter, observer, and writer. He must have a clear understanding of the organization and its mission, be an active participant in policy decisions, be skilled at monitoring and interpreting the organizational environment, and be at ease in a boundary role between the organization and its internal and external publics.

To address this issue, PRSA and IABC maintain a program of accrediting public-relations practitioners through written and oral examinations. Others, most notably Edward Bernays, advocate licensing for public-relations practitioners. Bernays first proposed the idea in 1925, but many practitioners today still oppose the concept on the basis that it infringes on First Amendment rights.

Thus, public relations is best seen as an emerging profession with several organizations working to increase professionalism in the field. Also increasing is the pool of practitioners. By the late 1980s, nearly two-thirds of U.S. journalism and mass-communication schools offered public-relations instruction, and between 3,000 to 5,000 students a year were earning degrees from public-relations programs in these schools.[15] Interestingly, at both the graduate and undergraduate levels, females now outnumber males in journalism and mass-communication programs. For example, for every two males receiving degrees in 1988, three women graduated.

Both PRSA and IABC have developed career ladders to guide practitioners in improving and enhancing their professional skills as they move through their careers. In the chart in Figure 7.10, for example, seven career levels and 65 competency areas are listed. It is important to note that ethics is the one competency expected to span an entire career. Although media ethics is discussed in Chapter 22, here we will consider the special issues arising in public relations.

ETHICS AND PUBLIC RELATIONS ....

The growing power of public-relations practitioners to manufacture consent by influencing public opinion is evident everywhere. We have even added new terms to our vocabulary—like *perception management, spin control* and *plausible deniability*—to describe this power. Doris Fleischman, credited with important contributions to the development of modern public-relations techniques, recognized both the good and the bad inherent in the growing power of public relations to manufacture consent as early as the 1920s. She wrote that

> *public relations was potentially a powerful machine that could conceivably help civilization or wreck democracy, depending on who used it for what ends.*
>
> *Public relations could become a sloganizing machine, a news-mongering device, an instrument for narcissists and exhibitionists. It could become plain silly or it could become a Frankenstein, as it did in Germany and Russia. It could also become a fine tool for education.*[16]

IABC *update*

Figure 7.10.

Plot your career on the IABC matrix

COLLEGE	LEVEL I	LEVEL II	LEVEL III	LEVEL IV	LEVEL V	LEVEL VI	LEVEL VII

T Communication theory
O Writing news
O Writing features
O Newsletter editing and layout
O Magazine editing and layout
O Photography basics
O Graphic design
O Writing for audiovisuals and video
O Law and government relations
O Speakers bureaus
O Event and conference planning/support
O Writing speeches
T Communication ethics

Bars designate time frame when competency generally is acquired during career.

T Writing proposals
  Slide/tape and AV production
  Video production
  Film production
  Print production
O Publications management
  Use of electronic distribution systems
  Basic electronic data processing applications
T General management skills
T Media contact
T Budgeting and cost control
  Personnel supervision/management
T Audience/constituent research
T Feedback systems
T Writing the communication action plan

  O Investor/shareholder communication
    Writing policies and procedures
    Identity programs
  T Time management
  O Member communication
    Personnel interviewing/selection
  T Goals setting
  T Measurement of effectiveness
    Computers in communication management
  O Communication in support of marketing
  T Employee communication program management
  T Organizational culture and politics
  O Community relations program management
  T Project management
  T Public speaking techniques
  T Consulting skills/problem solving

    Financial communication programs
    Managing communication staff/function
    Crisis communication management
    Media relations management
    Labor relations communication management
    Marketing communication function to senior management
    Corporate contributions management
    Accountability management
    Group/meetings management
    Issues management
    Strategic communication planning
    Communication policy formulation

      Organizational design
      International communication management
      Government regulatory affairs and legislation
      Political action committee (PAC) design/management
      Labor relations
      Marketing
      Financial management
      Problem analysis/identification
      Research

T — Included in IABC's accreditation testing
O — Optional in accreditation testing

Fleischman's comment was prophetic. Modern public-relations practitioners find themselves in a delicate balancing act. In corporate public relations, this means maximizing profits and maintaining social responsibility. In nonprofit organizations, it means building financial support and maintaining social responsibility. In government offices and agencies, it means building public support and acting in a socially responsible manner. In public-relations agencies, it means advising clients on various campaigns and advising them on social responsibility. And when the balancing act fails, the consequence is often public embarrassment and loss of credibility. The recent cases of Larry Speakes, Michael Deaver, and Anthony Franco are good examples. In each, the critical issue was not so much legal guilt or innocence but the perception of impropriety by a higher court—that of public opinion.

Speakes, White House spokesperson for six years under President Reagan, claimed that he had simply "exercised his P.R. Man's license" by manufacturing quotes for President Reagan during the Reagan-Gorbachev Geneva summit. Deaver, a former White House deputy chief of staff who advised Reagan on his public image, was caught in a storm over influence peddling after he left the White House and returned to his public-relations/lobbying firm.

The Franco case is perhaps the most embarrassing to the emerging profession of public relations. Franco, the owner of a Detroit-based public-relations agency, was accused of using confidential information to profit by buying stock in a client's firm—better known as insider trading. He later signed a consent decree, which while it does not admit guilt, does require that an individual agree not to do whatever he has been charged with doing henceforth and forevermore. All of this happened *while Franco was national president of the Public Relations Society of America*. He cleverly avoided an appearance before the PRSA Ethics Board by resigning his presidency and membership in PRSA. From the early days of the press agent, ethical public-relations men and women have had to deal with the poor reputation of the thousands of *others* who call themselves public-relations practitioners.

THE FUTURE OF PUBLIC RELATIONS, VIEWED GLOBALLY ....

As the past three decades have shown, Americans are constantly changing and adapting their values and attitudes. There is evidence to suggest that working Americans in the 1990s are putting less emphasis on material success and more on balancing other factors that contribute to success—such as a satisfying lifestyle and involvement in the community. And the traditional American work force will change dramatically. It will be older, more female, and less white. In fact, one study predicts that only 15 percent of those entering the work force by the year 2000 will be white males; and one out of three Americans will be Afro-American, Hispanic, Asian, or American Indian.[17] Change in the student population is viewed by many as an opportunity to move the boundaries of the field toward the ideal symmetrical communication model (see p. 154), which has mutual understanding as its desired outcome.

Looking beyond U.S. boundaries as we approach the twenty-first century, the possibilities of expanded organizational communication for increased sales, more diverse products, and a worldwide exposure and image make participation in international markets appear desirable. Although technology has made international

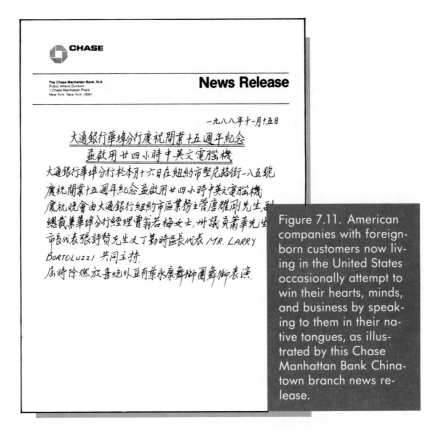

Figure 7.11. American companies with foreign-born customers now living in the United States occasionally attempt to win their hearts, minds, and business by speaking to them in their native tongues, as illustrated by this Chase Manhattan Bank Chinatown branch news release.

communication easier, understanding cultures, regulations, media practices, and government relations from country to country will be essential. Practitioners will need to do more than simply speak another language or find translators for their news releases. In other words, what works with employees, stockholders, neighbors, or customers in Atlanta or Albuquerque may not work in Beijing or Bucharest.

Major economic changes in the West, such as the opening of the borders of Eastern-bloc countries and the dismantling of European economic barriers in 1992, will inevitably result in a need for increased communication efforts. In the East, the planned reunification of Hong Kong with the People's Republic of China in 1997, for example, will bring the active public-relations community in Hong Kong into contact with the world's largest population. Clearly, as we become more interdependent as a world community, we become more dependent on communication to help us understand the new world order. Without a doubt, the role of public relations in this increasingly diverse, interdependent, and global future will grow through the 1990s and beyond.

SUMMARY ....

Public relations is a widely misused and misunderstood term. It is best to think of it in terms of building public relationships through the management of communication to inform, resolve conflict, and/or improve understanding. As the media have grown more and more massive and society has grown more complex, individuals have found it increasingly difficult to express points of view. This led in the twentieth century to the development of public relations.

We know that in a democratic society all citizens have a right to persuade others about their points of view, and public relations often involves persuasion. The public-relations professional serves to persuade the public in much the same way that the legal professional works to persuade in the court of law. No doubt, public persuasion, especially through the mass media, involves two rights that are in conflict: the right of everyone to express herself, whether the expression is honest or not, and the right to have access to the truth. Journalists are essential in solving the conflict between these two rights in the mass media. However, in a democracy, public opinion remains the ultimate arbiter of value and behavior.

Organizationally, public relations represents the total public-communication effort of an operation, under which advertising, marketing, promotion, publicity, employee communication, community relations, media relations, public affairs, and other such functions are located. However, since not all organizations agree on the importance of building relationships, resolving conflicts, and achieving mutual understanding with their publics, some follow a product-oriented marketing perspective and place public relations under their marketing umbrella.

The impact of diversity and global interdependence on public relations will be dramatic. Practitioners are likely to rely less and less on traditional mass communication and more and more on communication targeted toward special audiences and their special needs. Within organizations adopting a strategy to value diversity, the public relations practitioner's role will be critical.

Overall, public relations is an emerging profession that has grown rapidly in the past 10 years. It has also become more scientific and very powerful in influencing public opinion. In the ideal, the goal of public relations is to build mutual understanding. Today, however, practitioners must face and overcome numerous ethical challenges that threaten to undermine public trust of the field.

REFERENCES

1. Rex Harlow, "Building a Public Relations Definition," *Public Relations Review* 2 (1976): 34–42.
2. Philip Lesley, ed., *Report of the Special Committee on Terminology: Public Relations Society of America.* Presented in New Orleans, La., April 11, 1987.
3. Edward Bernays, *The Engineering of Consent* (Norman: University of Oklahoma Press, 1952).
4. Scott M. Cutlip, Allen H. Center, and Glen M. Broom, *Effective Public Relations*, 6th ed. (Englewood Cliffs, NJ: Prentice Hall, 1985).
5. James Grunig and Todd Hunt, *Managing Public Relations* (New York: Holt, Rinehart and Winston, 1984), 6.
6. Walter Lippmann, *Public Opinion* (New York: Macmillan, 1922).
7. Sinclair Lewis, *It Can't Happen Here* (1936), 74.
8. Susan Henry, *In Her Own Name: Public Relations Pioneer Doris Fleischman Bernays*, paper presented at the 71st annual convention for Education in Journalism and Mass Communication, Portland, Ore., July 1988.

9. Randall Rothenberg, "Complaints on Proposed Regulations," *New York Times*, January 19, 1990, D16.

10. Grunig and Hunt, *Managing*, 6.

11. Doug Newsom, Alan Scott, and Judy VanSlyke Turk, *This Is PR: The Realities of Public Relations*, 4th ed. (Belmont, Calif: Wadsworth, 1989), 73.

12. "It's in the Journal. But Is This Reporting," *Columbia Journalism Review* (April/March 1980).

13. "Popular Video from Colombia," *New York Times*, January 19, 1990, D16.

14. "US TV News Directors Say 'Yes' to Video News Releases," *Communication World* (December 1989), 13.

15. Lee B. Becker, "Enrollment Levels Off After Boom Decade," *Journalism Educator* 44(3): 3–15.

16. Doris Fleischman Bernays, *A Wife Is Many Women* (New York: Crown, 1955), 176.

17. William B. Johnston, *Workforce 2000: Work and Workers for the 21st Century* (Indianapolis: Hudson Institute, 1987).

CHAPTER

8

Advertising: Communication and Communication Support

Advertising is essential to our study of the mass media for three reasons. First, it provides financial support for media and vice versa. Indeed, a traditional way of classifying media has been in terms of the relative importance of advertising's support: (1) broadcast television and radio, where advertising basically finances media output; (2) newspapers and magazines, where the burden is shared with subscription and newsstand sales; (3) recorded music, cable, motion pictures, and books, where advertising plays a limited role. However, these distinctions are softening. We are in a transitional phase, with ads appearing with films and videos and even books. Some of this creates problems for those who evaluate media. For example, the *Washington Post*'s book-review editor felt different criteria applied to Whittle Communication's books, which contain advertising, than to others.

Second, advertising is considered by many a significant industry itself and as such is a fascinating subject, with dramatic changes and challenges facing practitioners in this field. Modifications in the way we use the media and the closer scrutiny being given the business and practice of advertising by regulators and action groups have led analysts to reexamine the future of advertising.

Third, advertising is a pervasive part of our culture, a medium for, among other things, the construction of our images of self and society. The messages contained in advertising are of course a form of communication, and scores of books have celebrated and dissected the creativity, persuasion, and impact of its messages.

In this text, our concern is primarily with understanding how this industry operates to make possible much of what we see and hear. This chapter will examine advertising's development, institutions, processes, and effects, particularly as they interact with mass media. But first, as the announcer might say by way of segue into a commercial, an attempt at definition.

What Is Advertising?

Perhaps because we are so surrounded by it, people discuss and study advertising without stopping to define it. (Nor do they realize that advertising is more than

Consultant and authority on content for this chapter is Tom Bowers.

Figure 8.1. One of an effective series of celebrity endorsement ads that feature an understated verbal message, complemented by use of the white space of the newsmagazine page format.

Wilt Chamberlain. Cardmember since 1976.
Willie Shoemaker. Cardmember since 1966.

Membership Has Its Privileges.™

Don't leave home without it.®
Call 1-800-THE CARD to apply.

just the commercials and advertisements they see in newspapers, magazines, and on television.) What sets advertising apart from other forms of communication? For one thing, it is an impersonal message, paid for and controlled by a sponsor.

Impersonal means the sender and receiver of the message do not interact; the advertising message is sent through a medium of mass communication. *Controlled* means the sponsor who pays for the advertising message determines its content. You will recall from the previous chapter that public-relations messages by definition are *not* paid for and can be altered or controlled by the *medium*. Media gatekeepers can reject certain categories of advertising, but accepted sponsors generate and shape their messages.

Advertising agencies and other people responsible for creating advertising do not have independent control over their output. The *sponsor is identified* in the message. Unlike public-relations efforts to send messages, advertisements leave little doubt about the source of the message. That identification is purchased at considerable cost.

TYPES OF ADVERTISING

We can further define advertising by distinguishing among the types of ads produced. Three widely used classifications are type of audience, source of content, and medium.

CLASSIFICATION BY AUDIENCE

Consumer advertising is the type we are most familiar with. It is directed to consumers and deals with products and services used by them. Consumer advertising was always aimed at specific demographic groups, and now increasingly sophisticated market research is attracting a larger market share of audiences such as teens, working wives, or retired persons. The fragmentation of the mass-media audience has hit consumer advertising to the point where many alternatives to traditional uses of media for national marketing are being used.

Most consumers are not aware of *trade advertising.* While consumer-product manufacturers use consumer advertising to increase demand for their products, most of them do not sell the products directly to consumer but to wholesalers or retailers. Trade advertising is placed in appropriate specialized media, usually *trade magazines*, that are read by those "middlemen." They try to persuade them to make the product available in their stores. In trade advertising, manufacturers frequently describe their consumer-advertising campaigns to convince wholesalers and retailers that consumer demand for the product will be high. The manufacturer knows that supermarket managers have limited shelf space and must eliminate some brands. The manufacturer also knows that the store manager is vitally interested in rapid turnover of the product, which will generate more profit for the store. Consequently, the manufacturer will use trade advertising in publications such as *Progressive Grocer* to explain profit margins.

Many companies make products and provide services for nonconsumer businesses. While many of those companies rely on salespeople to sell the products, they are also likely to use *business-to-business industrial* or *professional* advertising. For example, the manufacturer of a prescription drug might use professional advertising to doctors in a publication like the *American Journal of Asthma and Allergy for Pediatricians* and then complement this with a consumer-advertising campaign.

Global advertising is growing as more and more companies around the world try to market their products in several countries simultaneously. In fact, in 1988, for the first time in history, advertising expenditures in other countries exceeded expenditures in the United States, by $3 billion.[1] Advertising agencies have expanded their operations to include branch offices in other countries. Such expansion has sometimes led to problems, however, as when agencies must operate in business cultures where ethical codes are not the same as those in the United States. It may be common practice in some countries to bribe officials who are in a position to select advertising agencies, yet agency officials can be indicted for such action in U.S. courts.

Figure 8.2. Business-to-business advertising placed in *Business Week* to reach persons who might make purchase decisions.

Also, cultural differences and linguistic pitfalls can lead to costly errors. Advertising that emphasizes the female body could not be used in a country like Egypt because of its strong Islamic influence. In Spanish-speaking countries Chevrolet had difficulty marketing its Nova because *no va* means "it does not run" in Spanish.

CLASSIFICATION BY MESSAGE CONTENT

Another way to think about types of advertising is to consider the type of advertising message. *Product advertising* can be like the consumer, trade, business, industrial, and professional advertising just described; it is designed primarily to get product users to buy a specific brand. On the other hand, some companies use *institutional* or *corporate advertising* to improve attitudes toward their company or

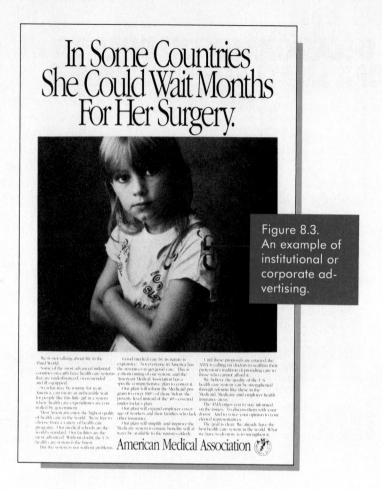

Figure 8.3.
An example of institutional or corporate advertising.

organization or to urge action on social issues. Another term for such ads, which often offer opinion or "editorializing," is *advertorials*. In a recent advertisement, the American Medical Association tried to convince Americans that the U.S. health system, while not perfect, is still much better than systems in many other countries (see Figure 8.3). Such advertising can be aimed at different types of targets, including consumers, potential stockholders, or legislators. Companies frequently use institutional advertising to respond to public criticism after some kind of incident or disaster. After one of its oil tankers ran aground and spilled millions of gallons of crude oil in Alaska, Exxon Oil used full-page advertisements in many newspapers and magazines to apologize for the accident and to assure the public that the company would do all it could to clean up the spill.

Public-service advertising is a special kind of institutional or corporate advertising. It is often done by companies or organizations to benefit social causes or charities. Television viewers see this in action when National Football League players are shown as active in local charitable organizations, to encourage others to support such causes. The *Advertising Council* deserves special mention here. It is a mechanism by which advertisers, advertising agencies, and media donate their services to increase public awareness of the National Negro College Fund, forest-fire prevention, drug-abuse prevention, or the American Red Cross.

Classification by Medium Used

Classification by medium helps assess the relative strengths of the various media. Network radio and television long accounted for practically all advertising for the electronic media, but marketing more narrowly via electronic mail (Prodigy, developed by IBM and Sears, for example) is increasing; a small amount is spent for consumer advertising in motion-picture theaters. Five media account for most of the revenue earned by print advertisers: newspapers, magazines, billboards, transit, and direct mail. In recent years, local advertising, such as store inserts or catalogs with area newspapers, have been dominant over national advertising. It should be noted that such trends must be carefully monitored. A recession that leads to slow business in certain regions or the closing of local stores can quickly make the proportion of ad revenue from nationwide advertising stronger. This was the case in 1990, which was also marked by the beginning of a growth pattern among previously merged national firms.

Every company's media plan begins with an analysis of alternative classes of media. There is no universal rule that stipulates which medium is best, and marketing objectives for most products call for a "media mix" to provide the greatest degree of flexibility.

Any medium remains a substitute for "the real thing"—personal selling, or what politicians call "pressing the flesh." TV and magazine ads for Nissan's Infiniti, with an extremely soft sell of nature images and without a picture of the car, whetted curiosity and effectively drew attention away from the clutter of other car ads (the largest category of advertising in print and on television where it brings in over $3 billion in revenues). Dealers were surprised and pleased by the 60,000 people pulled into showrooms, but the high price kept most at the window shopping level. On the other hand, in some product categories, the medium is replacing the salesclerk to a degree, with catalog showrooms and video terminals in homes becoming retailing facts of life.

Capturing a share of the fragmenting "mature" (stabilized) market requires innovation and specialized approaches such as direct mail to select lists. Too often those starting out in advertising think of the more glamorous and expensive media and overlook the impact of outdoor and transit ads (billboards and car cards) and point-of-purchase advertising.

The overall media strategy is structured around marketing and sales objectives, creative style, target-audience coverage, budget constraints, cost-efficiencies, timing and seasonality of consumption, competition strategy, and availability of media time and space. The media element of the advertising mix is perhaps the most scientific aspect of the total process. It is quantifiable, and evaluation is rigorous. We will explore research into effectiveness under "The Institutions of Advertising"; here, let us put the financial and economic aspects into perspective.

There are several methods of calculating advertising expenditures. Figure 8.4 uses data supplied by one individual in one advertising agency. Other analysts might break spending down according to three segments: (1) only measurable purchases of time or space in mainline media; (2) direct mail, yellow pages, outdoor and local advertising; (3) publicity and promotional efforts, from handouts and flyers to store coupons. Segments (2) and (3), the more personalized or targeted methods of advertising, are rapidly growing because of the overall shift in media audiences' reception of messages (in other words, their avoidance of clutter and their turning away from traditional media).

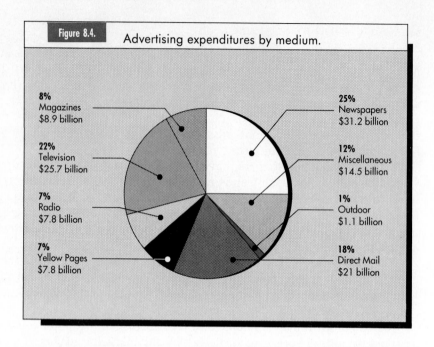

Figure 8.4. Advertising expenditures by medium.

8%
Magazines
$8.9 billion

22%
Television
$25.7 billion

7%
Radio
$7.8 billion

7%
Yellow Pages
$7.8 billion

25%
Newspapers
$31.2 billion

12%
Miscellaneous
$14.5 billion

1%
Outdoor
$1.1 billion

18%
Direct Mail
$21 billion

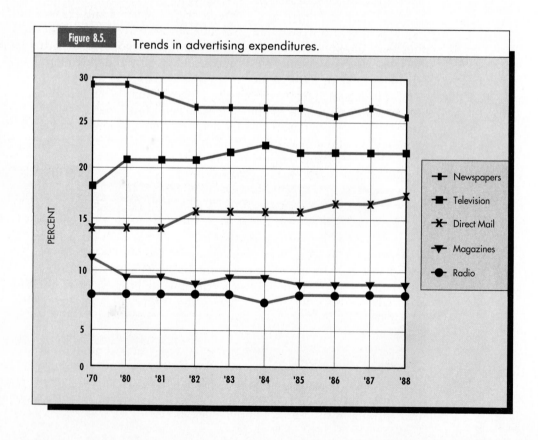

Figure 8.5. Trends in advertising expenditures.

Another factor is the increased importance placed on cost-effectiveness by the conglomerates. As Figure 8.4 illustrates, in 1988, U.S. advertisers spent approximately $118 billion to advertise their products and services. Of that, an estimated $73 billion was spent in newspapers, magazines, television, and radio. Newspapers received the largest share. This may seem surprising; it is due to the fact that the thousands of local advertisers who each spend a few hundred or a few thousand dollars a year outnumber the few hundred advertisers who each spend millions each year in television. There have been notable changes in the percentages of advertising dollars going to each medium, as shown in Figure 8.5. The percentage going to direct mail has increased each year since 1986 because of a desire by advertisers to be more precise in targeting advertising. Some of those dollars have come from newspapers and magazines, and while television's share of advertising expenditures went from 18 percent in 1970 to 21 percent in 1980 as more local advertisers began to use television, it has not increased since then.

Total advertising expenditures have increased every year. However, it should be noted that the *growth rates* of advertising expenditures have not been consistent from year to year. Prior to 1984, that percentage had been steadily increasing.[2] The biggest gains were in 1983 and 1984, but annual growth rates since 1985 have been only about 7 or 8 percent. And advertising is a relatively small industry in terms of persons employed (slightly over 200,000). But as we will see, the influence the TV industry and its practitioners have on our actions and thoughts belies the statistics.

HISTORICAL PERSPECTIVE ....

Almost as soon as people began to buy, sell, or trade goods and services, they used advertising. Crude forms of advertising messages were found in the Roman ruins of Pompeii. When printers in England developed the concept of a newspaper, merchants quickly began to advertise in these new publications, and the advertising revenue helped to support those publications. This was true of the newspapers that were so important as the American colonies grew and sought unity in their struggle against the British. When the Saturday, July 6, 1776, issue of the *Pennsylvania Evening Post* carried the Declaration of Independence on its first and second pages, the text was followed by a series of classified ads directly below.

Nurtured by the need for equipment to replace workers lost during the Civil War, the American industrial revolution in particular was an impetus to advertising. Prior to that time, most craftspeople produced goods primarily for consumers in their immediate area, and their customers knew them personally. The industrial revolution made it possible for manufacturers to produce in such quantity that they had to think about expanding their markets and enlarging their territories. Marketing became more important than production.

THE RISE OF THE AGENCY

Advertising agencies began to appear in the middle of the 1800s. The first ones were actually agents for newspapers and magazines. They purchased advertising

Figure 8.6. Typical nineteenth-century ads.

space at wholesale rates from publications and sold it to advertisers at regular rates. Agencies began performing creative and other services for their clients, but the primary method of agency compensation—discounts from the media—has persisted. (This is explained more fully under "Advertising Agencies.")

The history of American advertising since the 1850s has been shaped largely by agencies and the people who formed and led them, people like Claude Hopkins, Albert Lasker, J. Walter Thompson, Leo Burnett, David Ogilvy, Raymond Rubicam, William Bernbach, Mary Wells, and many others. By the end of the 1980s, however, the force of such dominant personalities in the agency business had faded in light of agency mergers and buyouts in response to increasing demands for profitability. By 1989, two of the most venerable agencies in American advertising history—J. Walter Thompson and Ogilvy and Mather—found themselves owned by the same company, WPP Group of England. Although it is now a worldwide communication company, WPP originally produced shopping baskets and animal cages. By 1988, WPP and its chief rival on the global advertising scene, Saatchi and Saatchi (another British company), together controlled almost 10 percent of worldwide advertising expenditures. As one observer noted, "Madison Avenue has been invaded by an army speaking the Queen's English."[3] Many observers lament this loss of individual entrepreneurship and genius that characterized American advertising throughout much of its history.

ADVERTISING IN THE 1990s

Advertising may be facing a critical turning point, largely because of four factors. The first is a great increase in the number of products and brands available to consumers (think of the number of different cola drinks or bathroom cleansers).

Many brands in some product categories are now virtually indistinguishable from one another, and this has made it harder for advertising to be effective. We are, in addition, past the period of an explosion of new products; advertising as announcement of the latest timesaver, for example, is being replaced by advertising geared to make a personal appeal to one segment of the once potentially large audience. John Philip Jones, a former agency executive, believes that companies in the future will be increasingly likely to reduce advertising expenditures as a way to increase their overall profitability.[4]

The second factor has to do with the mind-boggling array of media choices; this makes it more difficult to reach a *concentration* of consumers large enough to support rising ad costs. On a typical night in 1980, more than 90 percent of American television viewers watched the three commercial networks. By 1988, that percentage had dropped to 67 percent, primarily because of cable TV, independent (nonnetwork) stations, and videocassette recorders.[5] Frustrated advertisers are, according to J. Walter Thompson CEO, Burt Manning, considering a new TV network controlled by the nation's 100 largest companies, who hope to be able at least to control commercial time expenses.[6]

The third factor can be found in supermarkets and discount chains. Electronic scanners that read bar codes on packages give retailers almost instant data about successful products and promotions, and have given retailers added leverage against national manufacturers and their advertising agencies. (Before the availability of such data, advertisers knew more about brand sales and knew it sooner than store managers.) One result has been for advertisers to reduce the proportion of their marketing budgets devoted to advertising and to increase their use of things like coupons and POP (point-of-purchase) displays and radio (radio formats are satellite-beamed into individual stores where promotional messages are dropped in between periods of "elevator music").

All this means that today's advertising majors will be competing for a relatively small number of job opportunities. The job search will widen beyond advertising agencies. The top agencies cut staff by 5 percent in 1987.[7] Growth will probably be stronger in specialized advertising organizations such as those that deal with direct-mail, business-to-business, or industrial clients. Students may also find opportunities in media sales.

The fourth factor is the one cited in Chapter 7's discussion of a coordinated all-media lobbying effort: the regulation of advertising. To understand the changing interaction of advertisers, agencies, the media, and regulators, we must first look at the institutions that create, place, and distribute advertising messages.

The Institutions of Advertising ....

Advertisers

The type of sponsor gives us another way of categorizing advertising.

Retail advertisers are local stores or businesses that sell directly to consumers; more often than not, they do not employ advertising agencies but *deal directly with media*. They range from very large department stores, grocery stores, or banks to very small travel agencies, tailors, or shoe-repair shops. Large advertisers usually have in-house departments to create their advertising. However, the majority of advertising paid for by retail advertisers is produced by the sales departments of newspapers and radio and television stations. Retail advertising is usually concerned with urging consumers to take direct action by visiting the store and buying products available there. The store's image and personality are an important part of the advertising too.

General (national) advertisers normally sell to wholesalers or retailers. Their advertising campaigns are usually designed, executed, and *placed in media by advertising agencies*. Many companies produce more than one brand in the same product category—such as Procter & Gamble's Crest and Gleem—and use different agencies for each brand. Their advertising typically concentrates on creating awareness or increasing knowledge of the brand.

"Co-op" advertising is a special arrangement that sometimes links general and retail advertisers. Under most cooperative advertising plans, a national manufacturer reimburses a retail advertiser for some or all of the cost of retail advertisements that feature the manufacturer's product.

Advertising and Marketing. Marketing activities include all contacts between the organization and the public (consumers), including the product, price, promotion (which includes advertising), and distribution channels between the manufacturer and the consumer. Marketing is also a philosophy that incorporates several important ideas:

1. The organization must be more concerned with satisfying *consumer needs* than addressing its own. The agency or creator of a campaign cannot long afford to be more concerned with aesthetics or creativity per se than persuasion and servicing of needs, whether material or emotional.
2. A company should not be so concerned with short-term sales that it reduces the price of its product and risks its *long-term financial health*.
3. All of the company's activities, including production, finance, and administration, must be *guided by marketing considerations*.
4. To the extent possible, decisions about marketing should be *based on facts* (research) and not conjecture.

Distribution and Advertising. A product's *distribution* patterns (geographic availability) affect advertising in several ways. Many companies do not distribute their product nationwide, so they place advertising emphasis in areas where sales and distribution are strongest.

Personal Selling and Advertising. For some product categories, advertising must presell the product to consumers before they enter the store. This is especially true with foods and toiletries. In other product categories, consumers rely on the store's salespeople, as in the case of some clothing, durable goods (furniture, cameras), or automobiles. Even so, advertising can often presell consumers and even create contacts for salespeople; personal selling efforts must then be *coordinated* with advertising.

Sales Promotion and Advertising. Many companies, particularly those that sell packaged goods such as foods and health aids, are placing increased reliance on *sales-promotion* activities, and those activities must be coordinated with advertising. One of the most common sales-promotion activities is *couponing*, and preprinted print advertising is often used to distribute coupons. Revenue from inserting coupon brochures, store circulars, and catalogs (called ROP, run-of-

"**Money**" **you
can lose
and still have**

No chance for the all-too-short vacation to be spoiled
by a lost or stolen purse if you carry your funds in
American Express Travelers Cheques. Here is "money"
you can actually lose and still have.

When you buy these blue color Cheques, you sign
each one of them and they are *yours* and yours only; and
when you wish to spend them you sign them again.
Without this second signature they cannot be spent by
anyone but you. Should they be lost or stolen, you not
having countersigned them or exchanged them for value,
they will be refunded in full.

Besides, American Express Travelers Cheques are accepted everywhere—in the mountains, in the woods, at
seaside resorts throughout the United States and Canada.
Hotels, garages, stores, and ticket offices, as well as banks
and express offices, have come to expect the tender of
these safe travel funds.

Issued in convenient denominations of $10, $20, $50,
and $100—cost 75c for each $100.

For sale at 22,000 Banks, American Express and Rail-
way Express Agency offices. There is no need to take
any risks when this worry-proof
"money" is so easy to secure.

the new, dollar size
**AMERICAN
EXPRESS**
Travelers cheques

*Steamship tickets, hotel reservations, itineraries, cruises
and tours planned and booked to any part of the
world by the American Express Travel Department.*

Figure 8.7.
American Ex-
press hit upon
a basic human
need with this
1930 ad, es-
sentially say-
ing, "Don't
leave home
without them."
Fear of a ru-
ined vacation
is basic, and
the campaign
lives on.

press, advertising) has in the last 5 years increased to more than four times the
revenue from space advertising in newspapers. Two other sales-promotion activities that require coordination with advertising are *premiums*—additional merchandise items offered to the purchaser to give added value to the product—and
contests and *sweepstakes*—designed to attract attention to the product.

Advertising Expenditures. Who are the major U.S. advertisers and how
much advertising do they do? Table 8.1 shows the top 10 advertisers. The total
for Philip Morris (more than $2 billion) includes its tobacco products (including
Marlboro and Virginia Slims), Kraft General Foods (including Maxwell House, Post
cereals, Jell-O), and Miller Brewing (including Miller Lite and Miller High Life).

Table 8.1.	Leading National Advertisers of 1988: Expenditures in Millions of Dollars and Advertising Expenditures as a Percent of Sales	
	Expenditures in $millions	Percent of Sales
1. Philip Morris Companies	2,058.2	9.9
2. Procter & Gamble	1,506.9	12.8
3. General Motors	1,294.0	1.4
4. Sears, Roebuck & Co.	1,045.2	NA
5. RJR Nabisco	814.5	NA
6. Grand Metropolitan PLC	773.9	NA
7. Eastman Kodak	735.9	7.3
8. McDonald's	728.3	6.4
8. PepsiCo	712.3	6.8
10. Kellogg	683.1	24.7

Source: *Advertising Age*, September 27, 1989.

Grand Metropolitan is a diverse company that markets and advertises such brands as Alpo, Burger King, Pillsbury, Pearle Eyelabs, J & B Scotch, and Absolut vodka. In addition to its soft drinks, PepsiCo markets and advertises Kentucky Fried Chicken, Taco Bell, and Frito-Lay snack foods. Of course, in this era of sudden acquisitions, mergers, and buyouts, all of the above is subject to change.

Advertising and Sales. National advertisers' expenditures do not seem so large when compared to the companies' sales volumes. Table 8.1 shows wide variations ranging from 1.4 percent of sales for General Motors to 24.7 percent for Kellogg. Much of that difference is due to the fact that automobiles are much higher-priced than cereal. The percentages for companies like Philip Morris, Procter & Gamble, and PepsiCo are somewhat misleading because those companies manufacture and advertise a wide range of products. Table 8.2 helps to interpret those percentages by showing percentage-of-sales data for selected industries.

Determining Advertising Expenditures. Companies do not necessarily use a percentage formula to determine the sums they spend on advertising. Those that do, estimate their sales for the coming year and multiply that figure by a predetermined percentage. It's a simple method to use, and it usually means a company will not spend more on advertising than anticipated sales warrant. On the other hand, this method is criticized because it makes advertising dependent on sales. Some experts think a better way to determine advertising expenditures is to ascertain what advertising *needs* to do—such as increasing brand awareness—and then to calculate the cost of accomplishing those tasks.

ADVERTISING AGENCIES

Advertising agencies are specialized companies that plan and carry out advertising work for other companies.

The Major Agencies. There are several thousand advertising agencies in the United States. Many are very small, some with only one, two, or three employees. The agency business is dominated, however, by the very largest agencies, most

Table 8.2.	1988 Advertising to Sales Ratios for Selected Industries	
		Ad Dollars as Percent of Sales
Air courier services		2.1
Beverages		9.5
Cigarettes		5.1
Drugs		4.4
Eating places		3.4
Games and toys, excluding dolls		18.4
Grocery stores		1.4
Hotels and motels		3.8
Malt beverages (beer and ale)		8.7
Motion picture distributors		8.8
Perfumes, cosmetics and toiletries		10.2
Television broadcasting		2.7

Source: *Advertising Age,* October 24, 1988, p. 49.

of which are headquartered in New York or Chicago. There is currently little agreement on the future pattern of agency size. Conglomeration has taken a heavy toll and has led to conflicting situations. A number of advertisers want a return to more personalized treatment and seek the smaller firm; some hire groups they find innovative and efficient, and make them their house agencies. However, few smaller agencies will be able to survive competition with global giants. The 20 largest agencies are listed in Table 8.3. They are ranked by their *billings,* a term that refers to the value of the advertising they place for their clients.

Table 8.3.	The 20 Largest Advertising Agencies in 1990, World Wide Ranked by U.S. Billings ($Million)
1. WPP Group plc	$16,100,000
2. Dentsu Inc.	8,884,023
3. Omnicom Group	8,645,433
4. Young & Rubicam	6,300,000
5. Backer Spielvogel Bates WW*	5,100,000
6. Saatchi & Saatchi Advertising Intl.	5,035,000
7. McCann-Erikson WW*	4,772,000
8. Oglivy & Mather WW*	4,700,000
9. Foote, Cone & Belding	4,600,000
10. BBDO WW*	4,550,000
11. Hakuhodo	4,449,200
12. J. Walter Thompson Co.*	4,407,500
13. Lintas: WW*	4,122,756
14. DDB Needham WW*	4,095,000
15. D'Arcy Masius Benton & Bowles	3,360,801
16. Grey Advertising	3,267,000
17. Leo Burnett Co.	3,245,464
18. EWDB WW	2,700,000
19. HDM	2,499,411
20. Saatchi & Saatchi Advertising*	2,300,000

* *Member of larger group.*
Source: *Standard Directory of Advertising Agencies, No. 220,* June-September 1990.

Have you ever wondered how copywriters and art directors judge advertisements? In 1989, members of the One Club for Art & Copy, the leading organization for advertising creative people, selected their top ads of the 1980s.

The winner? Federal Express's 1982 "Fast-Talker" commercial, in which a fast-talking man demonstrated the speed of Federal Express delivery.

Other favorites:

2. The *1984* commercial for Macintosh computers. Agency: Chiat/Day of Los Angeles. 1984. (A moment of it is shown here.)

3. *Rolling Stone*'s "Perception and Reality" ads aimed at advertising decision makers. Agency: Fallon McElligott of Minneapolis. 1986.
4. Three commercials ("Dumbwaiters," "Rock Drills," and "Furniture Stripping") for Nynex Yellow Pages. Agency: Chiat/Day of New York. 1988. (One of the scenarios is shown here.)
5. The Bartles & Jaymes introductory campaign. Agency: Hal Riney & Partners, San Francisco. 1986.
6. Levi's "501 Blues" campaign. Agency: Foote, Cone & Belding, San Francisco. 1985.
7. The "Helloooo Federal" campaign for Federal Express. Agency: Ally & Gargano. 1980.
8. The outdoor campaign for Nike. Agency: Chiat/Day of Los Angeles. 1984.
9. (tie) "California Coolers" television campaign. Agency: Chiat/Day of Los Angeles. 1987.
9. (tie) Nike's "I Love L.A." commercials. Agency: Chiat/Day. 1985.
9. (tie) Commercials for Miller Lite beer, featuring Boog Powell, Bob Uecker, Dick Butkus, and Bubba Smith. Agency: Backer & Spielvogel of New York. 1984.

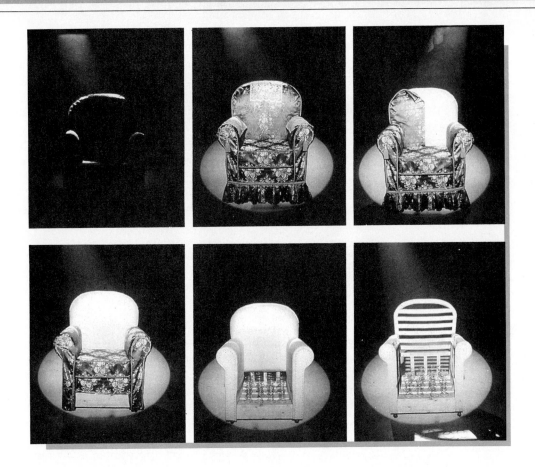

10. "Where's the beef?" commercial for Wendy's. Agency: Dancer Fitzgerald Sample of New York. 1984.

There are various other industry awards, such as Clios and Effies, that recognize creativity and effectiveness. Of course, when everything is working right, cleverness or aesthetics is matched by the hard facts of positive marketplace reaction and action. For example, the *Rolling Stone* series of business-to-business ads pairing an image of the supposed stereotypical *Rolling Stone* reader and the reality reflected by readership demographics (not hippies but serious consumers from all age groups) made a difference. The magazine's research indicated that pages of ads increased 82 percent and that revenues from ads increased 191 percent in the first three years of the campaign.

Source: Jon Lafayette, "Fed Ex Has Best '80s Ad," *Advertising Age,* November 13, 1989, 12.

Reasons for Using Agencies. Many advertising tasks, such as copywriting or media planning, are best carried out by experts. Such experts command high salaries, and most advertisers could not afford to pay such salaries; most companies' advertising tasks would not keep such an expert busy all the time.

An agency's outside or second-party viewpoint contributes to the success of a marketing plan. It is widely believed that an advertiser or its employees cannot take the objective perspective required whereas an agency executive would not be reluctant to criticize or reject an idea or strategy, even if it came from the advertiser's president.

Agency advertising does not cost a company any more than placing the advertising itself. This argument is based on the way agencies are compensated (see p. 195).

What Agencies Do for Clients. An agency's clients are the companies it works for; the agency also refers to these clients as accounts. Many agencies bring employees with special responsibilities together to coordinate the agency's work for that account.

Each such *account group* performs certain major functions for clients:

1. *Account management:* The account group is usually headed by a person with the title *account executive* (AE), who works closely with his counterpart at the client company, often called a *brand manager*.
2. *Creative* work: Someone from the agency's creative department might be called the group's *creative director*, and she often supervises creative specialists such as copywriters (print or broadcast or both), art directors, and television producers.
3. *Media planning and buying: Media planners* select appropriate *media types* (such as consumer magazines) and *media vehicles* (such as *Vanity Fair*) for the advertising. At some agencies, other specialists called *media buyers* do the actual purchasing of television time from networks and stations.
4. *Research:* The account group will probably include a *research analyst* or specialist. In some cases, the agency itself may conduct research for the client, and in other cases the agency will hire independent research firms to provide valuable guidance for the agency and client as they work together to plan, evaluate, and execute the advertising campaign.

As the changes occurring in the mass media are assessed and assimilated, there will undoubtedly be significant changes in agency structure and performance. Because the consumer is affected by so many different media, DDB Needham chairman Keith L. Reinhard has proposed eliminating the traditional media planning function. Instead of buying media time and space as main resources, marketers need to find new ways to map the individual's personal "network" of message boards (billboards and blimps as well as soft-rock radio) and to develop flexible strategies to get into target audiences' "apertures of receptivity."

Agency-Client Relationships. One of the functions of an advertiser's own advertising department is to select, work closely with, and evaluate the work of the agency. Many agency-client relationships are stable and cordial; enduring agency-client partnerships have included Marlboro with Leo Burnett or Eastman

Kodak with J. Walter Thompson. Nevertheless, agencies live with the constant threat of losing a major account, which often means that some agency personnel lose their jobs.

An agency has to drop one account whenever it acquires a larger account that competes with an existing one. Agencies have a policy that they will not work for competing accounts; the fear is that one client's secret or confidential advertising plans might be leaked to the competitor.

A number of other companies or organizations are often involved in the relationships between agencies and clients. For example, agencies usually do not produce television commercials. They write the scripts and plan the commercials, but the filming, editing, and production are done by a *commercial film producer*, who is hired and supervised by the agency. The actors and actresses who appear in the commercial are usually hired through an outside *talent agency*. Contests, promotions, and direct-mail advertising are usually "farmed out" by the agency to companies that specialize in such work. Some copywriting is done by *freelance* writers.

How Agencies Are Paid. The basis of an agency's compensation is the 15 percent media commission. Here's an example of how it works: The agency prepares a magazine ad for the client and arranges to place the ad in a consumer magazine. The cost of the magazine space is $50,000 for a full-page color ad. The magazine runs the ad and bills the agency (not the client) for the cost of the ad ($50,000), less a 15 percent commission ($7,500) for the agency. In turn, the agency bills the client for the full $50,000, the price the client would have paid if it had dealt directly with the magazine. The commission system seems unusual because it means the agency works for the client but is paid by the magazine. The practice dates from the early days of advertising agencies when agencies acted as brokers of advertising space, buying space from newspapers at discounted rates and selling it to advertisers for the full price.

The commission system is sometimes criticized because it seems to encourage agencies to spend too much of their clients' money (the agency commission depends directly on the cost of the advertising placed for the client). Most advertisers, however, are very conscious of how their money is being spent and keep tight reins on their agencies. A rapidly growing field is that of *cost consultancy*. American Express, Ford, Procter & Gamble, and other major advertisers engage specialists to challenge and monitor budgets from agencies and outside production companies, to bring efficiency to the creative process.

Critics also say the agency's compensation is not necessarily related to the cost of its services but rather to the cost of the ad. Because of some of these criticisms and because an agency's commissions are no longer sufficient to cover all of its costs for the client's work, many agencies and clients supplement the commission with other forms of compensation, including fees based on the time the agency spends on an account.

An *in-house agency* is a special type of agency that has been created by some advertisers. It is part of the advertiser's company, and agency workers are employees of the advertiser. Companies usually form in-house agencies to retain the agency commission from the media and therefore save money. The downside is the lack of objectivity in dealing with the parent company.

THE MASS MEDIA

The media that carry the advertising prepared by agencies for their clients are the third major institution of advertising. Ad revenue is extremely important to several media. It provides virtually all the revenue for the typical radio and television station, approximately 75 percent of the revenue for the typical newspaper, and 60 percent for the typical magaine.[8] Some publications are free to readers and thus receive all of their revenue from advertising.

Figure 8.8 illustrates the circular relationship among ad revenue, audience, and content of the mass media. A media vehicle's audience (both its size and the kind of people in the audience) is what interests advertisers. In Chapter 6 we saw the importance of the efficiency factor in selecting a certain medium. Advertisers seek to reach the largest number of consumers *for their product* at the lowest possible price, measured in CPM, or cost per thousand members of a target audience.

As a vehicle's audience gets larger, the vehicle will attract more advertising revenue as long as the quality (the demographics identifying such characteristics as age, job level, income, location of residence) is there. The increased revenue will help to pay for improved news or entertainment content that will attract larger audiences of the same quality, and the circle keeps repeating itself. The relationship *tends* to mean that larger, more financially stable vehicles tend to get stronger and that the smaller, less financially secure tend to get weaker. The closing of one or more of several competing newspapers has been the most frequent example of this survival of the fittest in recent years. Lost ad revenue leads to diminished content, and the spiral continues until the weaker newspaper goes out of business. Chapter 12, on magazines, points out that less (smaller circulation) can be more if the remaining audience fragment coincides with the advertiser's target.

Media Sales. Because advertising revenue is so important to media vehicles, they place considerable emphasis on selling advertising space and time. Many newspaper, radio, and television companies have marketing departments that use

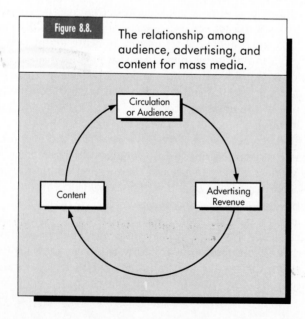

Figure 8.8. The relationship among audience, advertising, and content for mass media.

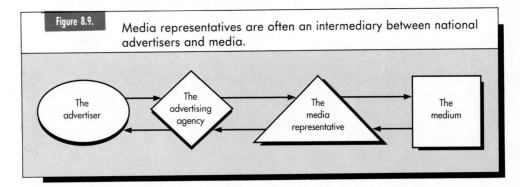

Figure 8.9. Media representatives are often an intermediary between national advertisers and media.

expensive research studies to document the case for their vehicle's advertising power (see Table 9.3). Magazines and broadcast networks pursue the same efforts with clients (advertisers and agency media buyers) at the national level, including advertising-agency personnel who recommend and select media for their clients.

You will recall that a characteristic of mass-media communicators is representation. Most broadcast stations and newspapers that seek advertising by national advertisers cannot afford to maintain constant contact with advertisers and agencies. Consequently, they use the services of *national representative* (*"rep"*) firms that act as their agents and try to persuade national advertisers and agencies to place advertisements in those local media. The relationship among media vehicles, media reps, agencies, and advertisers is illustrated in Figure 8.9.

THE ADVERTISING PROCESS ....

Advertisements do not just magically appear; they are conceived, altered, molded, executed, and placed by many people over long periods of time. That process includes situation analysis, objectives, strategies, tactics, and evaluation.

Advertisers always think in terms of *campaigns,* a series of different advertisements in different media. Those individual advertisements constitute a campaign because they are guided by a central strategy and are organized around a *consistent theme.* At least they are supposed to be; consistent appearance and theme is a characteristic of good advertising.

SITUATION ANALYSIS

Advertising campaigns are not based on hunches or conjecture but on information—about consumers, the brand itself, competing brands, and the media—so a very important first step is to gather as much information as possible about the product's situation, to provide a *definition of the problem* the advertiser faces.

Sources of Information. Some of the information comes the company itself: product test results, distribution (the extent of the product's availability in stores), and reports from consumers who have used the product. Other data might come from *secondary research,* often published and available in libraries. An example is the *Survey of Buying Power,* an annual compilation of statistics about markets (cities) in the United States that is published by *Sales and Marketing Management* magazine.

Syndicated research, described in Chapter 6, is that gathered and compiled by research companies and made available to advertisers, agencies, or media vehicles willing to pay for it. Examples include information about individual product sales and share of market, television audience research or one or more parts of a new full-service marketing-information offering from the Arbitron Company.

Begun in 1949 as American Research Bureau, a television audience-measurement service, Arbitron is the largest local-market radio and television audience-information source in the United States. Of special interest to advertisers are its services that monitor commercials, provide transcripts of radio and TV programming to advertising and public-relations specialists, track acquisition and use of products in participating households, and conduct test marketing, market modeling, and copy testing. Arbitron serves 1,824 radio stations, 3,500 radio advertisers and agencies, 650 television stations, 1,974 television advertisers and agencies, and 390 manufacturers of consumer goods. It sends out 1,525,782 radio diaries and 2,685,539 television diaries; collects 1,357,200,000 scanner records; monitors 62,400 newspapers and 16,621,833 broadcast spots for 75,000 brands, 12,597 TV sets, 106,080 store displays, and warehouse-withdrawal records; it monitors product performance in 18,630 supermarkets, 109,594 grocery stores, and 43,306 drugstores.

Some companies or agencies may also conduct original research for their own purposes. This is sometimes called *proprietary research*. An example of such research would be tests of television commercials conducted among shoppers at a shopping mall.

	Updated Census*	Metro %		Updated Census*	Metro %
1 ▶ Total Households	6,452,800	100.0	**6 ▶** Seasonal Households	54,899	.9
2 ▶ Income of Households			**7 ▶** Education Persons 25+		
Under $10,000	1,074,006	16.6	Elementary 0-8 Grd	1,949,466	18.9
10,000-14,999	577,353	9.0	High-School 1-3 yr	1,508,341	14.7
15,000-19,999	563,186	8.7	High-School Grad	3,432,540	33.3
20,000-29,999	972,349	15.1	College 1-3 yr	1,410,014	13.7
30,000-39,999	855,730	13.2	College 4+	2,000,039	19.4
40,000-49,999	663,953	10.3	Total Persons 25+	10,300,399	100.0
50,000-74,999	1,060,788	16.5			
75,000+	685,435	10.6	**8 ▶** Colleges & Universities*	229	
Median Income	$30,462		Total Enrollment	800,021	100.0
			Full Time Enrollment	458,641	57.3
3 ▶ Value of Owner-Occupied Households			**9 ▶** Occupation		
Less than $30,000	112,866	1.9	Managerial	1,962,655	27.0
30,000-49,999	521,520	8.7	Technical	2,533,998	34.8
50,000-79,999	786,129	13.2	Service Worker	926,595	12.8
80,000-99,999	231,502	3.8	Farm Worker	42,225	.6
100,000-149,999	199,802	3.4	Precision Production	734,849	10.1
150,000+	94,044	1.5	Operators	1,072,260	14.7
Median Value	$62,900				
4 ▶ Monthly Contract of Renter-Occupied Households			**10 ▶** Farm Residents	11,778	
Less than $150	594,569	10.0	**11 ▶** Transportation to Work		
150-199	667,195	11.1	Public	2,075,616	29.3
200-299	1,171,480	19.6	Driving to Work	3,244,087	45.8
300-399	487,288	8.2	Car Pool	1,034,582	14.6
400-499	143,541	2.4	Other	728,219	10.3
500+	131,244	2.2			
Median Rent	$229		**12 ▶** Car Ownership by Household		
5 ▶ Household Size			0 Cars	2,204,300	34.2
1 Person	1,825,500	28.3	1 Car	2,199,300	34.0
2 Persons	1,823,600	28.3	2 Cars	1,500,600	23.3
3-4 Persons	2,076,400	32.1	3+ Cars	548,600	8.5
5+ Persons	727,300	11.3			

*except where noted (see text above)

ARBITRON RATINGS

Figure 8.10. In the Metro Market Profile, Arbitron accumulates data on ethnic populations, households, employment, etc., and breaks them down, using the chart's 12 categories of census data, to analyze a market.

Consumer Behavior and the Purchase Process. Advertisers want to know as much as possible about what consumers think about the product and what it *means* to them. Advertisers want to learn about consumers' actions leading up to purchase, including their motivation for seeking such a product and how they use advertising to learn about product features and competing products. A popular research technique for finding such information is a *focus group*, which involves 8 to 10 consumers who gather in an informal setting. The focus group's discussion is guided by a trained researcher, who encourages participants to talk freely about the product, and records the discussion so the comments can be analyzed and used by the advertiser and agency.

Awareness and Knowledge. Some research measures awareness by giving consumers the name of a product category (such as toothpaste) and asking them to name the brand names that come to mind. Also measurable is consumer knowledge of product features (What is it about this product that prevents plaque from building up on your teeth?) or advertising themes or slogans (What product category and advertiser do you associate with the expression "Just do it"?).

Heavy Users. In almost all product categories, a small share of the users of that product account for a disproportionately large share of the consumption of that product; these people are called heavy users. For example, 30 percent of the users of sore-throat remedies account for more than 95 percent of the usage of those products. Most advertisers target heavy users because they know it is easier to take advantage of their predispositions and purchase behavior than to get light users or nonusers to increase consumption. Some syndicated research, such as that coming from Simmons Market Research Bureau, tells advertisers about the demographic and psychographic (lifestyle) characteristics of heavy users.

New Markets. With more and more brands available and some markets saturated or shrinking (such as cigarettes and alcohol), advertisers have to open new markets both internationally and domestically. Some agencies specialize in ethnic marketing. One, Paul Sladkus International, has found that the number of Asians in this country will grow to 10 million by the year 2000, from 3.7 million in 1980. Greg Sullivan, president of Asian Television Sales, Inc., says, "We are in the beginning stages of an entirely new media trend, particularly on the West Coast. . . . Asians represent a major niche market with a huge amount of disposable income, and this is a real opportunity for any advertiser."[9] There are currently approximately 20 million people in this country who identify themselves as Hispanic. Twenty-seven persent of the households in the Los Angeles area are Hispanic, and here and elsewhere in the United States 25 percent speak only Spanish. Advertisers and media are keenly interested in the new technology being developed by researchers to track minority audiences more accurately.

Capital Cities/ABC's study shows that blacks represent a $700-million market, but it is more fragmented and complex than the two groups just mentioned. Some black advertising leaders are pointing out the need to shift from black to urban as the target. For one thing, the growth rate of advertising for blacks alone is slowing, due in part to the steady assimilation of black Americans into the mainstream. Conversely, advertising using black celebrities and black themes is part of the mainstream consciousness. Also, fashion, music, and other cultural aspects that might first have had the strongest appeal to blacks, or even originated with them, are widely popular.

Although forging into new territories is never as easy as building on an established base, the need to attract new audiences is pressing and it provides a chance for media, advertisers, and consumer groups to work together, and it provides new career paths for today's communications students.

Research about the Competition. Advertisers do not operate in a vacuum; they are always concerned about what their competitors are doing or might do. One important kind of information is *market share*, the percentage of total sales in a product category accounted for by an individual brand. For example, in 1988, Kellogg's Frosted Flakes led the cold-cereal category with a 4.8 percent market share, which made it a slight leader over General Mills's Cheerios (4.6 percent). Those percentages may seem small, but they are significant for a highly competitive product category that had total sales of $6.7 billion.[10] (Frosted Flakes's 4.8 percent market share amounted to more than $320 million in sales.)

Advertisers also want to know about the media expenditures of their competitors, and they get that information from syndicated research companies that measure and report *competitive media-activity data*. (They do this by watching television broadcasts or reading newspapers and magazines.) Most advertisers tend to follow the strategies of their competitors, or at least those of the leading brands in the category.

OBJECTIVES

Situation analysis helps determine advertising goals or objectives, to distinguish advertising objectives from marketing objectives. *Marketing objectives* are basically about product sales and market share. For example, a company's marketing objective might be to increase its total product sales (in dollars or product units) by 5 percent over the previous year. Many activities besides advertising contribute to a product's sales success or failure—including distribution, product characteristics,

Figure 8.11. One of the top 10 advertisers, PepsiCo is also one of those corporations with a variety of product lines to market through research, planning, and evaluation of tactics.

competition, price, and sales promotion—so it is *not* appropriate to use product sales or market shares as advertising objectives or as criteria for advertising success.

Instead, *advertising objectives* should relate to things that advertising can accomplish. An advertising objective might be to increase brand awareness by 20 percent. A creative objective might be to inform consumers that a certain brand of laundry detergent is particularly effective at removing grass stains. A media objective might be to deliver the advertising message to heavy users in northeastern states during the peak sales periods.

The J. Walter Thompson agency uses a continuum to distinguish several possible objectives or purposes of advertising. Ranging on the continuum from the most direct objective to the most indirect are (1) stimulate action, (2) provide information, (3) relate to needs, (4) recall satisfactions, (5) modify attitudes, and (6) reinforce attitudes.

STRATEGIES AND TACTICS

Advertising *strategies* are the broad actions advertisers take to accomplish their objectives, and advertising *tactics* are the execution of the strategies. For example, a company might pursue a strategy of using a well-known celebrity as a spokesperson. The tactics or execution of that strategy would be the selection of the actual celebrity and the writing of the commercials. One strategy to achieve the delivery of an advertising message to upper-income males in the 20 largest markets (cities) in the United States would be to buy advertising time from television stations in those markets during telecasts of a major golf tournament. The tactics would be the selection of the actual stations, perhaps using an Arbitron report, and the negotiations to purchase the time.

Advertising media are carefully selected as part of a specific strategy. Television is sometimes chosen because of its ability to demonstrate a product's benefits vividly and convincingly. Newspapers are sometimes used when advertisers want to announce news of a new and improved product. Magazines are selected because of their ability to reach specialized audiences and to reproduce excellent color. New technology allows inclusion of ads or changes in ad copy to suit very localized audiences. Radio is sometimes used because of its sound qualities or because of its ability to reach consumers on the go. Direct mail is used to target heavy users precisely, and outdoor advertising as a last reminder to consumers on their way to the store.

EVALUATION

Advertisers and agencies use a variety of research techniques to assess how well the campaign realized its objectives. To measure awareness, for example, researchers could ask consumers to list brand names they associate with a particular product category. The percentage that name the advertiser's brand first could be compared to the percentage before the campaign began; the difference would be presumed to be caused in part by the advertising.

Figure 8.12 shows an ad that performed well. R. R. Donnelley & Sons, a leading printer, is pleased with the performance of its "Less Is Not More" eye-catching use of print technology to promote its consolidated manufacturing system as well as the advantages of going to a larger format. Shown is the front, expanded middle, and back of a pop-up–style trade-journal ad. Comments Gordon Hochhalter, creative director:

It dramatizes how larger page sizes allow publishers to tell a more complete story without sacrificing detail or scope. Although this advantage is important to many different kinds of publishers, we believe the point will not be lost on those who create juvenile books. And just to be sure, the illustration of this ad comes right out of the pages of Jack and the Beanstalk. By adding the image of the giant climbing down the stalk to the cover image of the castle, the whole story becomes clear—as well as the reader's perspective on the story. The selling proposition of ''Jack'' is: You can add more impact to your books without adding extra expense.

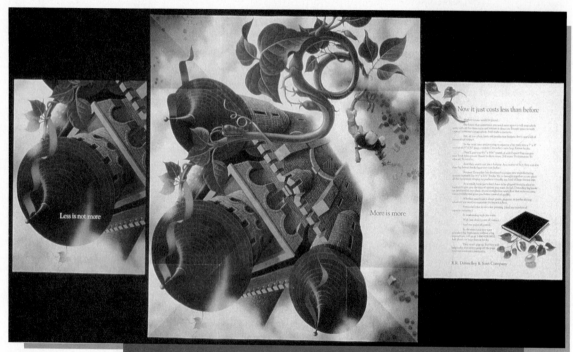

Figure 8.12. The copy for this fold-out ad compares the problem of having more content/story than a normal-sized page can accommodate to Mother Goose's children living in a shoe. The ad actually expands to dramatically show the impact of the printer Donnelley's larger format books: "They'll give you $8\frac{1}{2}$" × $10\frac{7}{8}$" worth of added space that can give your book extra power. Power to show more. Tell more. To dramatize. To educate. To involve."

Assessing the size and composition of media-vehicle audiences is another important aspect of evaluation research. Agencies purchase advertising for their clients with the expectation that the audience will be of a certain size, so it is important to ascertain that the audiences were in fact that large.

The advertising process should never end. Information gained from the evaluation stage is applied to the advertiser's next campaign, and the process starts over again.

CRITICISMS OF ADVERTISING ....

Advertising is a frequent target because it is so pervasive. Some of the criticisms are deserved, but others fail to recognize advertising's purposes and limits. For example, in 1967, Lever Brothers launched a new advertising campaign for Wisk, a liquid laundry detergent. Lever wanted a memorable advertising campaign that would convince skeptical consumers that a liquid detergent could remove tough stains from clothing. The result, the theme line "Ring around the collar" was ridiculed by consumers, who repeatedly cited the campaign as their least favorite and most obnoxious. Many consumers wondered why Lever would continue to use such advertising when it seemed so bad. They did not realize that the campaign had almost immediate positive results for the company, whose sales doubled. Wisk used the theme until 1989; then it changed the theme in response to intense competition from other brands, not because of negative consumer reacton to the campaign.[11]

Advertising is criticized on both economic and social grounds. There are too many criticisms to deal with in detail here, but a few deserve discussion.

ECONOMIC CRITICISMS

Advertising is wasteful because it emphasizes trivial differences between products or brands. Many believe that advertising costs are passed along to consumers. Critics believe that many competing products (such as cola soft drinks) are very similar and that the advertising for those brands wastes money because it emphasizes insignificant differences. If that advertising was reduced or eliminated, the argument continues, prices could be lowered.

Advertising's supporters counter with the argument that advertising can reduce the prices of products in some cases by stimulating mass demand for the product that will lead to lower production costs and lower prices. Other supporters might argue that some product differences created or emphasized by advertising are nevertheless important to some consumers. Advertising for expensive automobiles give the buyers of those automobiles a sense of prestige.

Advertising is wasteful because it makes people buy things they do not need. This assumes that advertising is all-powerful and can manipulate people who are defenseless against its exhortations. Critics ask: Who *needs* a compact-disc player? Or a leather jacket? Or the latest Paris fashions?

Advertising's supporters say it is too difficult to distinguish between essential and nonessential consumer needs. Who is to say that some consumers do not have a real need for the entertainment of a compact-disc player? Advertising's supporters also say advertising does not create needs but only *suggests ways to meet existing needs.* Furthermore, living in a democracy means that consumers have the right to make economic choices (product consumption) as well as political choices (voting). Professor of media studies Stuart Ewen, commenting on contemporary culture for a PBS series, remarked that as we get the feeling more and more political decision

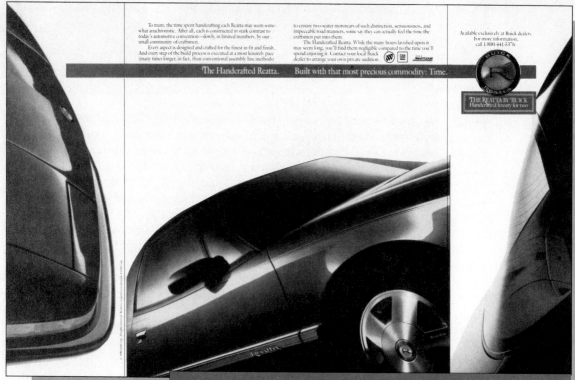

Figure 8.13. The graphic design impact of this Buick ad suits its placement in the upscale *Architectural Digest*. The stylish interior designs featured in the magazine lend prestige to 8 advertisements for cars.

making is made by elites, the "democracy of images" afforded us through mass media, and particularly advertising, has become more valued.

Advertising is irresponsible because it encourages people to consume resources that are scarce or that are depletable. Advertising for large gas-guzzling automobiles is a target for this kind of criticism because it fosters the wasteful use of petroleum products. All of us need to monitor our consumption patterns with regard to certain products. However, is it proper to blame advertising for the problems? The roots lie in our consumption patterns and the production and marketing decisions by manufacturers. Advertising is but a tool of those companies.

SOCIAL CRITICISMS

Advertising does not accurately reflect the diversity of the real world of consumers. This criticism says that advertisements do not feature enough minority persons, women, or older persons. Further, these groups (and others) are often portrayed in inaccurate and demeaning ways. It is a difficult charge to refute, but several studies have documented that advertisements are showing greater diversity and less stereotyping than they used to. More needs to be done, but certainly it will be part and parcel of the effort to reach minority audiences appropriately and effectively.

Advertising exploits minorities. Several of the criticisms already cited occasionally come together in an accusation that advertisers, in an effort to bolster sagging markets, try to influence the disadvantaged, minorities, or children to make unwise consumer decisions. RJR Nabisco was criticized early in 1990 for its campaign to introduce a cigarette, Uptown, to appeal strongly to blacks. The American Cancer Society saw the effort as an "alarming escalation in cigarette marketing" increasing the health and economic woes of the ghetto poor. Mary L. Clarke, president of a branch of the NAACP, called the targeting of blacks "unethical."[12]

Newspapers and magazines slated to carry ads for Uptown found themselves caught in the middle, with the president of the *Philadelphia Tribune* stating, "We don't have the right to make a choice for our readers." Even Jeff Burns, vice president of Johnson Publishing Co., which issues *Jet* and *Ebony*, said, "This is just another product." Estimated cigarette advertising revenue in 1989 for the two magazines was set, respectively, at 7 percent of $35 million and 10 percent of $16.4 million. And RJR's position was that with the shrinking cigarette market, the only viable campaign is increasing market share by attracting smokers away from competition.

Growing criticism pressured RJR to withdraw the product from its test markets. Months later the issue reemerged when clergy and residents of New York City's Harlem neighborhood took up paint buckets and rollers and covered over billboards advertising a range of products they felt harmful. Although the police intervened because the action was a misdemeanor, at least one liquor company immediately promised not to renew its outdoor display contract in the area. Rarely is there such a visual demonstration of audience feedback nor such a speedy response to it.

Advertising directed to children is inherently unfair and harmful because children are too susceptible. The harshest critics clamor for a ban on all advertising—particularly television commercials—directed to children. Other critics would be satisfied with a limited ban on advertising for products that might be considered unhealthful, such as presweetened cereals and candies. In addition to concern about possible harm, such critics believe children are too vulnerable to advertising appeals and that it is unfair to advertise to them.

According to research provided by Michael D. Forzley's *American*, a newspaper directed at children, kids receive over $6 billion in allowances from parents and an additional $9.5 billion in other spending money yearly; by age 12, they are independent shoppers, account for more than $8 billion in fast-food sales, and spend $30 per week on discretionary purchases. About $500 million is spent yearly on advertising to children, and groups such as Action for Children's Television urge parental, educational, and marketer responsibility. Congress has been urged to reimpose FCC limits on advertising on children's television and to monitor program-length commercials or cartoons designed to sell and sometimes misrepresent toys.

Political advertising is demeaning and harmful to the political process. Political advertising has come under increased criticism as candidates at all levels have used more and more advertising, and especially when they have used vicious negative attacks on their opponents. Critics say the expense of political advertising has made candidates too dependent on large financial contributions and subject to undue influence. They also say it is not proper to advertise political candidates in the same manner that one would advertise mouthwash or hemorrhoid remedies. Thirty- or 60-second commercials are not long enough to give voters meaningful information, so the critics charge that candidates rely on meaningless trivia or harsh personal attacks to make their advertising memorable.

On the other hand, political advertising can and does provide some information about candidates that voters would not otherwise receive, primarily because many voters do not pay much attention to political communication through news programs. In their extensive analysis of political advertising, Diamond and Bates conclude that political advertising is probably most effective as a reinforcement of voters' existing beliefs and that voters do learn from political advertising's informational content. They also conclude that unknown candidates can use television commercials to increase name recognition or to polish an image but that negative attacks are very risky because they might backfire. Finally, Diamond and Bates cite several examples to demonstrate that even very good political commercials cannot make losing candidates into winners.[13]

THE REGULATION OF ADVERTISING

Advertisers are not free to do or say what they please. Governmental agencies, primarily on the federal level, regulate advertising, primarily to make sure it is not misleading and is not harmful to consumers or competitors. The extent of regulation at any given period depends on whether a particular administration believes in tight controls and formal protection or in a free and relatively unregulated economy and upon the personal zeal of persons charged with regulatory responsibility.

Most advertisers are honest and careful, and take great pains to make sure their advertising is not misleading and does not violate regulations. However, there is no denying that a few advertisers are not so conscientious; liberties are at times taken with the truth. It is also impossible for any regulatory agency, regardless of the existing regulatory philosophy, to monitor all advertising and to prosecute all alleged cases of abuse.

THE ROLE OF THE FTC

The Federal Trade Commission (FTC) was established in 1941 to regulate unfair competition in business. Through court interpretations, practices, and additional legislation, the FTC's role in advertising regulation has been expanded to include protection for consumers as well as competitors.

The commission does not have to prove any consumer was deceived to take action against an advertiser; it has to show only that the advertising has a tendency to deceive. The FTC does not have to prove that the advertiser intended to be misleading. Finally, the commission says it is not enough for an advertiser to be able to substantiate advertising claims *after* they are made; the advertiser must have substantiation for the claims *before* the advertising appears.

The commission requires that all *demonstrations and visuals* in advertising must be accurate. In a celebrated case involving this principle, the Campbell Soup Company was found guilty of putting glass marbles in the bottom of a bowl of soup to keep the soup's solid particles from sinking to the bottom. The FTC ruled that the television commercials were deceptive because the marbles made viewers think the soup had more solid particles than it actually did. When an advertiser uses a *celebrity spokesperson* to endorse a product—such as former politicians who extol the benefits of a credit card—FTC rules say the celebrity must actually use the product.

The FTC has several *remedies or corrective actions* for misleading advertising. Some actions are proscriptive, designed to prevent advertisers from engaging in certain practices. A commonly used proscriptive action is a *trade regulation rule* about advertising of products in an entire industry (such as the requirement to put health warnings in advertisements for cigarettes). Advertisers who are convicted of violating these rules are subject to fines and imprisonment.

The FTC uses consent decrees and cease-and-desist orders as punitive actions for advertising that has already appeared. Under a *consent decree*, the advertiser agrees to stop the advertising but does not admit any guilt. If the FTC and the advertiser cannot come to terms in a consent decree (which they do most of the time), the FTC can file a formal complaint against the advertiser, and the matter can go all the way to the Supreme Court. When the final decision is against the advertiser, it usually results in a *cease-and-desist order*, which requires the advertiser to stop the practice, usually within 60 days. Violation of such an order can bring a $5,000 fine, 6 months in jail, or both. In some cases, the FTC has also required advertisers to engage in *corrective advertising*. In one such case, a mouthwash manufacturer was required by the FTC to say in subsequent ads that its previous claims (that using the mouthwash could prevent the common cold) had been misleading.

One case illustrates the FTC's actions in regulating advertising. In 1985, the R. J. Reynolds Tobacco Company placed a "public-issue message" advertisement in selected mass media, stating that a medical study had shown there was no proof that smoking increases health risks. "This controversy over smoking and health remains an open one," the ad concluded. But the FTC issued a complaint against Reynolds, accusing the company of deliberately misrepresenting both the purpose and the results of a 10-year study by the National Institutes of Health, which had concluded that smoking is hazardous to one's health. The FTC charged that the Reynolds ad was fraudulent. But Reynolds contended that it had a First Amendment right to express its views. The case, complicated by the fine line between product and institutional advertising, was settled late in 1989, with R. J. Reynolds promising not to misrepresent scientific studies. The firm denied wrongdoing and did not acknowledge its editorial-style statement as advertising.

It should be noted that the FTC is concerned *only* with fraudulence in advertising. It is not a protector of the public's morals or tastes, as reflected in advertising.

OTHER FEDERAL REGULATORS

Other government agencies have more specific tasks in the regulation of advertising. The Food and Drug Administration controls labeling in the important area of food and drugs. The FCC does not regulate advertising on radio and television but it has some indirect power over advertising through its power to grant and renew broadcast licenses. Certain FCC regulations apply to advertising: Sponsors must be identified, profane or obscene material is prohibited, advertising must be sold to political candidates at the station's lowest rates, and stations are prohibited from carrying advertisements for private lotteries. The Postal Service controls fraudulent advertising sent through the mails. And the Securities and Exchange Commission regulates advertising about stocks and bonds. In all these cases, there is no censorship on the part of the government. In the Treasury Department, the Secret Service, under its powers to protect the currency and prevent counterfeiting, prohibits the use of photographs of paper money (shown in actual size and color) in advertising, and the Bureau of Alcohol, Tobacco, and Firearms has rules about the advertising of alcoholic beverages: It cannot feature active athletes, cannot suggest intoxication, cannot imply drinking by underage persons, and cannot make any health claims for alcohol products.

One of the most far-reaching federal controls over advertising, of course, is the ban against cigarette advertising on radio and television—the result of congressional legislation, not agency rules. In recent years, there have been attempts in Congress to enact a total ban on all cigarette advertising. There is strong opposition by persons who believe such a ban would be an infringement on advertisers' rights of free speech.[14] A ban on the advertising of liquor on radio and television is the result of self-regulation, not government rules.

OTHER LEGAL PROBLEMS FOR ADVERTISERS

Advertisers cannot use a person's name or picture in advertising without that person's consent. They also must be careful about the unlawful use of copyrighted

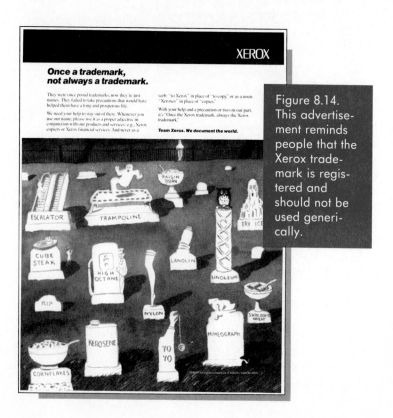

Figure 8.14. This advertisement reminds people that the Xerox trademark is registered and should not be used generically.

material in advertising. (Ads themselves can be copyrighted.) The other side of the coin is that some advertisers must take action to protect their right to their trade names, or those trade names may become "generic." There are many examples of this happening, including such former trade names as aspirin, linoleum, and thermos. As a matter of practice, companies like Coca-Cola and Xerox use advertising to remind people (especially media writers) that their names are registered trademarks (see Figure 8.14). Such ads may not prevent consumers from indiscriminately using terms improperly, but the companies' efforts help to prevent the loss of rights to the names.

SELF-REGULATION OF ADVERTISING

Efforts at self-regulation are not nearly as effective in preventing abuse as government regulations because the self-regulation efforts lack any enforcement power. They rely instead on voluntary cooperation and the threat of negative publicity. Most of those efforts occur at the national level.

The Council of Better Business Bureaus created a National Advertising Division (NAD) to handle complaints about allegedly misleading advertising. In the few cases in which the NAD ruled against advertisers, it has asked the advertisers to correct or stop their advertising. Virtually all have complied, primarily because they were ready to cease the advertisements anyway. In a recent case, the NAD concluded that Blistex lip ointment did not have enough proof to back up its claims of "faster relief" and "stimulates healing." Blistex responded that it would conduct additional tests and then review its original claims.[15]

Some media vehicles and groups have rules prohibiting certain advertising practices (see the box). The national television networks preview all commercials and frequently require advertisers to remove objectionable material.

Network and newspaper policies tend to be somewhat rigid regarding certain categories of advertising, but signs that those standards are being relaxed in response to changing public attitudes. For example, media policies about the advertising of condoms have been loosened in light of the rising incidence of AIDS and the growing acceptance of condoms as protection.

ADVERTISING AS A CULTURAL FORCE ....

In addition to its support of the mass media and its existence as an important mass-media industry, advertising is a pervasive part of our culture. Some experts have estimated that the typical person is exposed to more than 1,500 advertising messages each day, including newspaper and magazine ads, radio and television commercials, outdoor billboards, direct mail, calendars, and matchbooks.

Advertising is an important element of social discourse. People talk about advertising, make jokes about it, criticize it, and praise it. In the summer of 1989, superstar athlete Bo Jackson hit a monumental home run in the All-Star game. However, media coverage and public discussion of that feat was almost overshadowed by coverage and discussion of a television commercial for Nike athletic shoes starring Jackson that was first shown during the telecast of the baseball game.

We hold that a responsibility of advertising agencies is to be a constructive force in business.

We further hold that, to discharge this responsibility, advertising agencies must recognize an obligation, not only to their clients, but to the public, the media they employ, and to each other.

We finally hold that the responsibility will best be discharged if all agencies observe a common set of standards of practice.

To this end, the American Association of Advertising Agencies has adopted the following Standards of Practice as being in the best interests of the public, the advertisers, the media owners, and the agencies themselves.

These standards are voluntary. They are intended to serve as a guide to the kind of agency conduct which experience has shown to be wise, foresighted, and constructive.

It is recognized that advertising is a business and as such must operate within the framework of competition. It is further recognized that keen and vigorous competition, honestly conducted, is necessary to the growth and health of American business generally, of which advertising is a part.

However, *unfair* competitive practices in the advertising agency business lead to financial waste, dilution of service, diversion of manpower, and loss of prestige. Unfair practices tend to weaken public confidence both in advertisements and in the institution of advertising.

1. CREATIVE CODE

We the members of the American Association of Advertising Agencies, in addition to supporting and obeying the laws and legal regulations pertaining to advertising, undertake to extend and broaden the application of high ethical standards. Specifically, we will not knowingly produce advertising which contains:

a. False or misleading statements or exaggerations, visual or verbal.
b. Testimonials which do not reflect the real choice of a competent witness.
c. Price claims which are misleading.
d. Comparisons which unfairly disparage a competitive product or service.
e. Claims insufficiently supported, or which distort the true meaning or practicable application of statements made by professional or scientific authority.
f. Statements, suggestions or pictures offensive to public decency.

We recognize that there are areas which are subject to honestly different interpretations and judgment. Taste is subjective and may even vary from time to time as well as from individual to individual. Frequency of seeing or hearing advertising messages will necessarily vary greatly from person to person.

However, we agree not to recommend to an advertiser and to discourage the use of advertising which is in poor or questionable taste or which is deliberately irritating through content, presentation or excessive repetition.

Clear and willful violations of this Code shall be referred to the Board of Directors of the American Association of Advertising Agencies for appropriate action, including possible annulment of membership as provided by Article IV, Section 5, of the Constitution and By-Laws.

2. CONTRACTS

a. The advertising agency should where feasible enter into written contracts with media in placing advertising. When entered into, the agency should conform to its agreements with media. Failure to do so may result in loss of standing or litigation, either on the contract or for violations of the Clayton or Federal Trade Commission Acts.

b. The advertising agency should not knowingly fail to fulfill all lawful contractual commitments with media.

3. OFFERING CREDIT EXTENSION

It is unsound and uneconomic to offer extension of credit or banking service as an inducement to solicitation.

4. UNFAIR TACTICS

The advertising agency should compete on merit and not by depreciating a competitor or his work directly or inferentially, or by circulating harmful rumors about him, or by making unwarranted claims of scientific skill in judging or prejudging advertising copy, or by seeking to obtain an account by hiring a key employee away from the agency in charge in violation of the agency's employment agreements.

These Standards of Practice of the American Association of Advertising Agencies come from the belief that sound practice is good business. Confidence and respect are indispensable to success in a business embracing the many intangibles of agency service and involving relationships so dependent upon good faith. These standards are based on a broad experience of what has been found to be the best advertising practice.

* First adopted October 16, 1924—most recently revised April 28, 1962. Copyright 1962, American Association of Advertising Agencies, Inc.

Advertising slogans often become part of popular and contemporary culture, and are used in other contexts. In a 1984 television debate, presidential candidate Walter Mondale questioned the substance of an opponent's argument by asking, "Where's the beef?" Virtually all viewers understood his strange question because it was a well-known slogan for a fast-food company.

Advertising is also a reflection of society's values, a mirror of what society considers important. Magazine advertising reflects our tastes in fashion, food, and drink. Television advertising mirrors how we work and how we interact with others. Hundreds of years from now, archaeologists and other social scientists will no doubt analyze advertisements as an important source of knowledge about life and culture in the last decade of the twentieth century.

Sociologist Michael Schudson concludes that advertising is an art form, one that idealizes consumers and is often more successful aesthetically than commercially.[16] And it is a medium that influences other forms of art. Many techniques developed and perfected for television commercials have been adapted to commercial films. The artistic value of ads may become more pronounced as globalism increases. In England, film and commercial directors have long been one and the same; in Japan, graphic and photographic creativity are highly valued.

Recently media and social critics alike have been taking a fresh look at the relationship of art and advertising and the place of each in our daily lives. Many, like Mark C. Miller of Johns Hopkins University, feel advertising is by nature more entertaining than it is art:

> Advertising is engineered to one end—to sell the product . . . the product becomes the moral to the story, the happy ending. Advertising is too simple in its aims and too materialistic in its message to be deemed art.[17]

Others find there's a danger in underestimating the effect of the aesthetic. Ads that invite us to identify with a celebrity are really inviting us to make ourselves into an image. Ads may be fun; ads may bring us desirable media content. Above all, however, they are powerful persuaders.

SUMMARY

Although advertising is a relatively small industry in number of employees, it is important in expenditures and support of the media. In 1988, U.S. advertisers spent an estimated $118 billion, and the bulk of it went to newspapers, television, and direct mail. Advertising revenue provides virtually all of the financial support of commercial radio and television stations, and more than half of the support for newspapers and magazines.

Most advertising that the public is aware of is consumer advertising, but trade advertising, business-to-business advertising, and corporate advertising are also important. International advertising is becoming increasingly important as more and more companies engage in global marketing and advertising.

Advertising appeared almost as soon as people began to manufacture and sell products. The industrial revolution increased companies' manufacturing capacities and made advertising increasingly important as a way to reach new and larger markets. While U.S. agency leaders once dominated world advertising, increasing globalization and other factors have led to the consolidation of several agencies and the lessening of American influence.

Advertising has three major institutions. (1) Advertisers use advertising to help them market their products and services. A few large advertisers spend more than $1 billion a year for advertising, but these totals often represent only a small percentage of their total product sales. (2) Advertising agencies are specialized companies that plan and execute advertising campaigns for most national advertisers. Their work includes account management, creation of advertising, media planning, and research. (3) Advertising media carry advertising to consumers and are dependent on advertising revenue.

Advertisements do not magically appear; they are conceived, altered, refined, and finally executed in a long process that includes situation analysis, objectives, strategies, tactics, and evaluation. The situation analysis includes analysis of research, leading to a definition of the advertiser's problem. The objectives or purposes of advertising can range from creating awareness to urging purchase. Strategies and tactics are the actions needed to achieve the objectives. Evaluation is the process of assessing whether the campaign achieved its goals.

Advertising—as commercial speech with limited protection under the First Amendment of the Constitution—exists in a regulatory environment. Federal agencies, mainly the Federal Trade Commission, have the power to regulate advertising content but do not always exercise that power. Several advertising and media groups also provide self-regulation, although it is not very effective because it has no coercive powers.

Advertising is a frequent target of economic and social criticisms, including the charge that it is wasteful, that it makes people buy things they do not need, that it conveys inaccurate and demeaning stereotypes of certain groups of people, that it fosters advertiser control over media content, that it is inherently unfair and deceptive to children, and that it demeans the political process. Some or all of these charges may be true to a certain degree, but on balance, advertising makes a positive contribution to society and the economy.

References ....

1. Randall R. Rothenberg, "Change in Consumer Markets Hurting Advertising Industry," *New York Times*, October 3, 1989, 1.
2. Ibid., 1.
3. Randall Rothenberg, "Brits Buy Up the Ad Business," *New York Times Magazine*, July 2, 1989, 14.
4. Randall Rothenberg, "An Iconoclast Takes a Look at the Future," *New York Times*, August 1, 1989, 17D.
5. Rothenberg, "Change in Consumer Markets."
6. David Kalish, "A Surprisingly Good Year for the Masses," *Channels*, December 1989, 32.
7. Rothenberg, "Change in Consumer Markets."
8. John M. Lavine and Daniel B. Wackman, *Managing Media Organizations: Effective Leadership of the Media* (New York: Longman, 1988), 25.

9. Michael Lev, "Asians in U.S. Get Attention of Marketers," *New York Times*, January 11, 1990, D19.

10. John C. Maxwell, Jr., "Cereal Market Up, No. 1 Kellogg Down," *Advertising Age*, September 25, 1989, 27.

11. Laurie Freeman, "Wisk Rings in New Ad Generation," *Advertising Age*, September 18, 1989, 1.

12. Anthony Ramirez, "A Cigarette Campaign Under Fire," *New York Times*, January 12, 1990, D1.

13. Edwin Diamond and Stephen Bates, *The Spot: The Rise of Political Advertising on Television*, rev. ed. (Cambridge, Mass.: The MIT Press, 1988), 351–68.

14. Michael G. Gartner, *Advertising and the First Amendment* (New York: Priority Press Publications, 1989).

15. Richard L. Gordon, "NAD Won't Let Butter, Blistex Slide," *Advertising Age*, September 18, 1989, 67.

16. Michael M. Schudson, *Advertising: The Uneasy Persuasion* (New York: Basic Books, 1984), 223.

17. Randall Rothenberg, "Commercials Examined as Artform," *New York Times*, September 8, 1989, D5.

THREE

THE MASS-MEDIA INDUSTRIES

············ ≡ ·············

The interrelationships of the mass media have reached a point where it is difficult to talk about one industry in isolation. However, each of the media industries has evolved in its own way to some extent and has a variety of characteristics that set it apart from others. The chapters that follow study the past, present, and future of seven major areas, and in so doing we make an effort to cite the impact of "outside" influences and that of the significant trends toward conglomeratization, globalization, and blurring of old delineations. In this section we see more concrete examples of specific components in the modern communication process.

The order in which to view the media industries is a problem for textbooks like this one. We could take them chronologically, as they emerged. We could group all print and all electronic media. Instead, we use a sequence that we feel provides the clearest sense of the organic, dynamic, and interrelated nature of the mass media.

We begin with two media—one print, one electronic—that have had great influence on other media. The first is newspapers, which were indeed the first to attain mass-media status; their history and current direction bring together many of the factors basic to any media industry. Chapter 9 is followed by a survey of the medium that continues to have the most dramatic impact on all of us—television. How it has matured and how it faces challenges and opportunities make for fascinating study.

Television's impact on society is rivaled only by its impact on other media, including radio, magazines, and motion pictures. When the growth of the television industry was unfrozen in 1952, none of the mass media were the same again. Radio, magazines, and film each responded to television's growing power by becoming more specialized and target-oriented.

The comparative degree of privatization is another way to categorize the mass media, and we conclude our survey with two industries that some scholars feel are so privatized that they hardly are typical mass media—recorded music and books. We will show how their evolution to their important roles in communications conglomerates, their economics, and their impact have earned them a place among the mass media. Part 3, then, focuses primarily on the mass media as *industries*. Part 4 will further develop the roles and interrelated impact of the mass media from the perspective of functions, of what the content of the mass media does for us. The larger issues their content and their development pose will be explored in Part 5, which concludes with an examination of what effect emerging technology might have on the mass-media industries. Some of the comparatively "new" technology has already served to revolutionize existing industries; thus the videocassette recorder, for example, plays a part in several of the following chapters.

CHAPTER 9

Newspapers

As various scholars have demonstrated, a new means of communication is usually introduced for a small elite, then becomes a mass medium, and finally develops into more specialized channels. Although television has become the dominant mass medium in our society, newspapers were the first to go through the full cycle of development—to become a true mass medium.

Each day, more than 113 million Americans (64 percent of the households) rely on newspapers to provide accurate, timely, and useful information. Newspapers attempt to provide the facts and analyses that allow informed citizens to make effective and responsible decisions in a complex, information-saturated society. The role of newspapers has evolved in response to the changing needs of their readers and is currently going through a "softening" of the news in reaction to other media's coverage of lifestyles, entertainment, and so on. But throughout its long history, the newspaper has been the means by which citizens protect their rights and liberties in a free and democratic society.

Because information is powerful, various authorities have tried to suppress it. Publishers often feel it is their duty to challenge the government's assumptions and conclusions, and in some parts of the world, they have given their lives for this right. In the United States, newspapers have become the "fourth estate" of government (next to the executive, legislative, and judicial), and their power to mold opinion is substantial.

The Founding Fathers, hoping to establish a democratic society, knew that the free flow of information was essential to citizens who were seeking their rights and freedoms. They knew that newspapers were the key, so they insisted on the right of newspapers to pursue the truth and publish it, whether or not the government agreed with their perception of the truth. Thomas Jefferson summed up his political philosophy when he said:

> *The basis of our government being the opinion of the people, the first object should be to keep that right; and were it left to me to decide whether we should have a government without newspapers, or newspapers without a government, I should not hesitate a moment to prefer the latter. But I should mean that every man should receive those papers and be capable of reading them.*[1]

Today, with circulation and advertising revenues totaling over $43 billion annually, newspapers are the largest medium. Not surprisingly, such wealth is not evenly distributed. In the case of the top 20 papers (see Table 9.1), five conglomerates account for more than half of those revenues, mainly because they dominate sizable regional markets. Critical consumers must be watchful and may question whether the economics inhibit the free flow of information newspapers have charged themselves with defending.

Table 9.1.	Top 20 U.S. Newspapers (for 6 months ended March 31, 1990)				
Newspaper	Average daily circ. 10/1/89 to 3/31/90	Change from same period a year ago	Average Sun. circ. 10/1/89 to 3/31/90	Change from same period a year ago	Ownership
1. The Wall Street Journal	1,935,866	+0.2%	NA	NA	Dow Jones & Co.
2. USA Today	1,387,233[1]	+3.4%	NA	NA	Gannett Co. Inc.
3. Los Angeles Times	1,210,077	+8.1%	1,504,540	+5.7%	Times Mirror Co.
4. (New York) Daily News	1,180,139	−4.1%	1,461,316	−4.3%	Tribune Co.
5. The New York Times	1,149,683	+2.9%	1,706,013	+2.6%	The New York Times Co.
6. The Washington Post	824,282	+1.5%	1,154,420	+0.4%	Washington Post Co.
7. Chicago Tribune	740,713	+0.1%	1,141,455	+0.4%	Tribune Co.
8. Newsday	711,264	+2.0%	713,779	+0.8%	Times Mirror Co.
9. Detroit Free Press	639,767	NA[2]	1,270,420	NA	Knight-Ridder Newspapers
10. San Francisco Chronicle Sun.: w/Examiner	569,257	+2.3%	713,172	+1.7%	The Chronicle Publishing Co.
11. Chicago Sun-Times	532,678	−4.0%	566,808	−4.8%	Chicago Sun-Times Co.
12. The Detroit News	526,147	NA[2]	1,270,420	NA	Gannett Co. Inc.
13. The Boston Globe	522,981	+2.6%	787,858	+0.1%	Affiliated Publications
14. The Philadelphia Inquirer	522,020	+4.4%	994,539	−1.6%	Knight-Ridder Newspapers
15. The Atlanta Constitution/ Journal	505,372	+8.2%	682,001	+2.5%	Cox Enterprises
16. New York Post	504,720	−5.7%	NA	NA	New York Post Corp.
17. The (Newark) Star-Ledger	470,045	+2.6%	687,054	+1.6%	Newhouse Newspapers
18. Houston Chronicle	449,755	+5.1%	620,752	+6.0%	Houston Chronicle Publishing Co.
19. The Miami Herald	443,216	+0.1%	551,027	+0.8%	Knight-Ridder Newspapers
20. The (Cleveland) Plain Dealer	438,066	−2.2%	561,150	−1.7%	Newhouse Newspapers

[1] USA Today's daily circulation is Monday through Thursday. Friday circulation of 1,753,537 (+5.1% vs. one year ago) is counted separately because ABC rules require separate reporting when sales of one day exceed others by more than 15%.
[2] After a joint operating agreement began Nov. 27, 1989, the Detroit Free Press switched from a primarily afternoon newspaper to a morning newspaper. The Detroit News switched from a morning newspaper to a primarily afternoon one. The News and Free Press now publish a combined Sunday edition.
Source: Audit Bureau of Circulations.

We will now trace the development of the newspaper and look at how it continues to redefine its role in an increasingly crowded information marketplace, one in which the stakes are as high as the chances for failure. New formats and technologies, changed demographics, and fundamental changes in marketing approaches are a few of the factors.

HISTORICAL PERSPECTIVE

The regular publication of news goes back more than 2,000 years to 59 B.C. when the Romans posted public news sheets called *acta diurna*. The word *diurna*, meaning "daily," has been an important part of news ever since. The words *journal* and *journalism* have their roots in the same word, and the daily, current, or timely aspect of news has always been an essential factor in newspapers.

Through most of the years of the Roman Empire and the Middle Ages, the distribution of news came under the strict control of both secular and ecclesiastical authorities. Even after the development of the printing press in the mid-fifteenth

Figure 9.1. Even though the earliest printing presses were simple, the words printed on them were so powerful that they often struck terror in the hearts of kings.

century, it took another 150 years before the political climate changed sufficiently to allow the beginnings of the modern newspaper.

THE DEVELOPMENT OF THE NEWSPAPER

In Europe printers had to fight monarchs for the right to publish. William Caxton, the first English printer, set up his press in 1476 and, largely because he did not print any news, worked in relative freedom until his death 15 years later. When Henry VIII came to the throne of England, he feared the power of the press; by 1534, he had established strong measures to control printing. For more than 100 years after that, the British authorities maintained repressive restrictions on printers.

As Michael and Edwin Emery point out in their history of journalism, *The Press and America*, "It is significant that the newspaper first flourished in areas where authority was weak, as in Germany, at that time divided into a patchwork of small principalities."[2] The first prototype newspaper, a rudimentary version to be sure, was published around 1609, probably in Bremen, Germany. By 1620, simple newspapers were being printed in Frankfurt, Berlin, Hamburg, Vienna, Amsterdam, and Antwerp.

The first English prototype newspaper was printed in London in 1621. The production of tracts and broadsides accompanied a growing freedom from governmental control, climaxed by the ringing declarations of the poet John Milton. In 1664, in his essay "Areopagitica," he expressed the basic rationale of a free press in a democratic society:

> [T]hough all the winds of doctrine were let loose to play upon the earth, so truth be in the field, we do injuriously by licensing and prohibiting to misdoubt her strength. Let her [truth] and falsehood grapple; who ever knew truth put to the worse, in a free and open encounter?[3]

In 1665, the first true English-language newspaper, in form and style, was published in Oxford, then the seat of English government. When the government moved to London some months later, this *Oxford Gazette* moved, too, and became the *London Gazette*. Thirty-seven years later, in 1702, the first daily newspaper, the *Daily Courant*, was published in London. In those 37 years, English printers of newspapers had won many rights, including the freedom to publish without a license.

THE NEWSPAPER IN THE UNITED STATES

Newspapers in Early America. In the colonies of British North America where people did not have full British citizenship, printers did not yet enjoy press freedom. The first newspaper in the colonies, *Publik Occurances, Both Forreign and Domestick,* published on September 10, 1690, was banned after the appearance of its only issue because its printer, Benjamin Harris, did not have an appropriate license from the British authorities.

Fourteen years later, the *Boston News-Letter* was started, published under the authority of the Massachusetts governor. Nevertheless, in its lifetime, from 1704 to 1776—when it ceased publication because of the outbreak of the American Revolution—it was rebuked by the government on many occasions, and publication was suspended several times.

Most early colonial newspapers, like their European counterparts, existed primarily for the purpose of spreading information about business and commerce. Produced by printers, not journalists, they contained some local gossip and stories, but many of them were dominated by advertising and often had the word *advertiser* in their title. But the colonial printers who published these newspapers could not

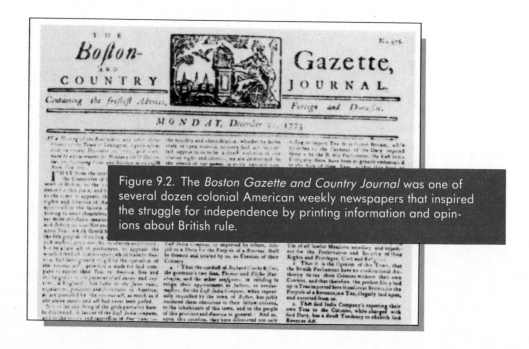

Figure 9.2. The *Boston Gazette and Country Journal* was one of several dozen colonial American weekly newspapers that inspired the struggle for independence by printing information and opinions about British rule.

help but inject stories about political conditions that affected their businesses, and they expressed their opinions on such matters.

In 1721, James Franklin, a colonial printer, began publication of the *New England Courant*, without featuring a "by authority" label. When he published a sarcastic comment about the British governor of Massachusetts, he was thrown into jail; his 13-year-old brother, Benjamin, took over the printing of the newspaper. This started Ben Franklin on a lifetime of writing, printing, and publishing. Later Franklin went to Philadelphia to start his own printshop and newspaper, and before he was 40, he had become the first "press lord" in America, having founded a chain of printshops and newspapers in which he held partial ownership.

Another colonial printer who ran afoul of the British authorities was John Peter Zenger, printer of the *New York Weekly Journal*. In 1734, Zenger was thrown into jail for having libeled the British governor of New York. But a jury of colonists ultimately freed Zenger when a shrewd Philadelphia lawyer, Andrew Hamilton, made a convincing argument that Zenger's facts had been true and that people should be free to print the truth, even if damaging. This case has given journalists an unprecedented power in the modern world.

Increasingly, political activists used the pages of the colonial newspapers to arouse public opinion against the abuses of British authority. After the Revolution, the newspapers again served to encourage social action, helping to persuade the citizens of the newly independent nation to ratify the Constitution and adopt a democratic form of government. Historian Allan Nevins in his essay "The Constitution Makers and the Public, 1785–1790" describes how James Madison, Alexander Hamilton, and John Jay sent letters to the newspapers urging support for the Constitution. Today, we know those "press handouts" as *The Federalist Papers*, classics in the theory of republican government. It was, says Nevins, "the greatest work ever done in America in the field of public relations."[4]

The Penny Press: The First Mass Medium. Although the first American daily newspaper, the *Pennsylvania Evening Post and Daily Advertiser*, was started in 1783, it was not until half a century later that newspapers began to reach a mass audience. The industrial revolution and the growth of urban centers created a new audience for newspapers. Until the 1830s, newspapers were fairly high-priced, aimed at a relatively elite group of merchants and influential politicians, and often functioned as organs for a particular political party or viewpoint. The technical advances in printing in the early nineteenth century included the development in England of an iron press (to replace wood) and the use in Germany of steam power (to replace hand production) and a cylinder that pressed the paper against the type (to replace the flatbed press). In 1846, an American invented the rotary press, in which the type also was put on a cylinder, and in 1865, another American put paper rolls together with a rotary press for the first high-speed printing. Type continued to be hand-set until 1884 when Ottmar Mergenthaler of Baltimore perfected the Linotype to set type by machine: the modern age had arrived.

One New York printer, Benjamin Day, used the new faster press to begin a trend in journalism. In 1833, he started the *New York Sun* and sold papers for a penny rather than the usual six cents. By hiring newsboys to hawk the papers on the streets, he succeeded in making up in volume what he lost in individual sales. The mass audience attracted new advertisers, and the revenue they contributed

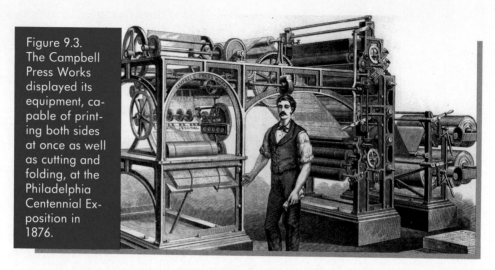

Figure 9.3. The Campbell Press Works displayed its equipment, capable of printing both sides at once as well as cutting and folding, at the Philadelphia Centennial Exposition in 1876.

was key to the survival of these new newspapers. The success of the *New York Sun* initiated the era of the "penny press."

In order to sell penny papers on a mass basis, the newspapers had to contain material of interest to many people. This economic factor led to the development of the profession of news gathering. The man most responsible was James Gordon Bennett, a printer like Day, who started the *New York Herald* in 1835, two years after Day had started the *Sun*. At first, such papers sensationalized and exaggerated the news in a bid for readers; they entertained as much as informed, and presented news in a flashier, easier-to-read format for the growing class of businesspeople and commuters. As the new audiences became more demanding, newspapers responded by becoming more responsible.

With Bennett the modern news reporter was born. He sent men to police stations to get stories about crime, to city hall for stories about politics; he also began the coverage of sports. He sent reporters into New York harbor in boats to meet ships coming in from Europe, so that his paper could be the first with foreign news. And when the telegraph came into use in the 1840s, he was the first newspaper publisher to station a correspondent in Washington, D.C., to telegraph to New York City stories about Congress and government.

Other newspapers, such as Horace Greeley's *New York Tribune* and Henry Raymond's *New York Times*, were started and became powerful forces in mid-nineteenth-century society, playing influential roles in the Civil War, the emancipation of the slaves, and westward expansion. The Civil War had its own role to play in the development of American journalism. Sunday papers were not popular in churchgoing America before the newspaper owners began to issue special editions of war news on that day. Acceptance grew into a special audience: By 1889, the circulation on Sundays passed that on weekdays, and this continues to be more and more often the case.

THE BEGINNINGS OF THE BLACK AND FOREIGN-LANGUAGE PRESS

This period saw the emergence of the first examples of the specialized press. A few years before the advent of the penny press, in 1827, John B. Russwurm and the Reverend Samuel E. Cornish published the first issue of *Freedom's Journal*, the

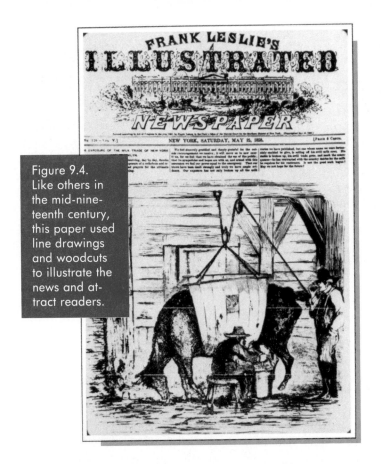

Figure 9.4.
Like others in the mid-nineteenth century, this paper used line drawings and woodcuts to illustrate the news and attract readers.

first black newspaper. They stated: "Too long have others spoken for us. Too long has the public been deceived by misrepresentations in the things that concern us dearly." Though this newspaper lasted only 2 years, before the Civil War more than 40 newspapers were being published for blacks, nearly all of them concerned with the abolitionist movement. Many of them were short-lived; all suffered extreme pressures. The most prominent was *North Star*, founded and edited by Frederick Douglass to "attack slavery in all its forms." By 1890, there were 575 black newspapers in America.

Waves of immigrants came to America's shores during the nineteenth century, and by 1880, there were approximately 800 newspapers publishing in German, French, Italian, Scandinavian, Spanish, and Polish. These newspapers mostly attempted to preserve "old-country" ways and culture in the New World. The most successful of them, *New York Staats-Zeitung*, was founded in 1845 by Herman Ridder; his name is perpetuated in the important Knight-Ridder chain.

Foreign-language newspapers and the black press were at their height at the turn of the century. Strong contemporary voices in the black community rose up, including the *Baltimore Afro-American* in 1892, the *Chicago Defender* in 1905, the *New York Amsterdam News* in 1909, Norfolk's *Journal and Guide* in 1909, and the *Pittsburgh Courier* in 1910. Ironically, the technologies and social conditions that allowed newspapers to become a mass medium eventually led to segmentation and decline of these specialized markets. Advancing technology led to a proliferating of news-papers and newspaper profiles, so that the audience broke down more and more along personal preferences rather than racial and national lines. Simultaneously assimilation of diverse groups into the melting pot of American culture lessened the attractiveness of old ways and roots.

Yellow Journalism and the Muckrakers

Mass-circulation newspapers had become big business by the end of the nineteenth century. The papers were highly competitive, for the most part independent, and no longer tied to any one political party or social group. The number of English-language dailies more than doubled between 1880 and 1900, from 850 to 1,967; circulation exploded from 3 to 15 million daily. Journalistically, two major aspects of the times were the resurgence of sensationalism and, a little later, the emergence of aggressive investigative reporting. Newspapers featured bold headlines, more pictures, and extra editions carrying the latest news. The first photograph was printed in a newspaper on March 4, 1880, in *The New York Daily Graphic*.

"Newspaper barons"—men who had built journalistic empires through ag-gressive promotion—emerged toward the end of the nineteenth century. Joseph Pulitzer developed the strong *St. Louis Post-Dispatch* and then bought the *New York World* in 1883. The *World* had a circulation of 20,000 when Pulitzer took it over; less than a decade later, by 1892, he had raised its readership to 374,000. Pulitzer stressed sound news coverage combined with crusades and stunts to win his read-ers; in 1889, he sent a young reporter with the pseudonym Nellie Bly around the world to beat the record of the fictitious Phineas Fogg, hero of Jules Verne's *Around the World in Eighty Days*. Nellie completed her trip in 72 days, and circulation of the *World* soared as readers kept up daily with her reports. That Pulitzer led the way into modern business practices for newspapers is shown by his changes in advertising. He started using circulation figures to regularize advertising space rates and made it less difficult for advertisers to custom-design ads with their illustrations. The result was a marked increase in the amount of advertising com-pared with news and editorial material in any given issue; it crossed the 50 percent barrier by 1900.

Another businessman, William Randolph Hearst, entered journalism as the student business manager of the *Harvard Lampoon* and then received the *San Fran-cisco Examiner* as a gift from his wealthy father. In 1895, he purchased the *New York Journal* and copied many of Pulitzer's techniques to compete with the *New York World*. Knowing that headlines would sell papers, Hearst not only reported news but also sometimes created news to get banner stories.

In an editorial a year after taking over the paper, Hearst stated: "It is the *Journal*'s policy to engage brains as well as to get the news, for the public is even more fond of entertainment than it is of information."[5] The credence paid to this view today is reflected in the importance of entertaining content and approach in broadcast and print news, as described in Part 4. In 1889, the same year that Nellie Bly circled the globe, Pulitzer's *World* produced the first regular comic section in a Sunday paper. Comic strips became extremely important in building newspaper readership and circulation, especially among immigrants, who used the picture stories to help them learn English. Five years later, they were printed in color,

Figure 9.5. William Randolph Hearst's *New York Journal* typified the yellow journalism of the 1890s. As this issue illustrates, to build circulation, Hearst treated the discovery of a dismembered corpse as a mystery game whose solution would be rewarded with a prize. Later, his reporters caught the murderers.

thanks to the installation of web presses and photoengraving equipment in newspaper printing plants. The success of such features led to the creation of the major syndicates. The comics included "The Yellow Kid," a very popular feature that gave the name *yellow journalism* to this era's newspaper practices.

According to newspaper historian Frank Luther Mott, yellow journalism was based on sensationalized coverage of crimes, scandal and gossip, divorces and sex, disasters, and sports; photographs, stunts, and faked stories were also featured. One of the papers competing with the *World* and *Journal* deliberately took a different path; it ran a contest for a slogan describing its position. The winner was "All the World's News but Not a School for Scandal," but finally the editors decided to keep "All the News That's Fit to Print," and in 1897 it became the enduring tagline of *The New York Times*.[6]

As yellow journalists began to use their influence for the public good—crusades for the downtrodden and the lower classes—newspapers found that they could not only sell more papers but also perform a service to society. A new breed of reporter began to develop, one who was interested in investigating the sins of society, the hidden perversions of power, and the abuses of industry. These men, to use Teddy Roosevelt's expression, "raked the muck of society."

The so-called muckrakers included writer Lincoln Steffens, who exposed graft and corruption in city governments and helped bring about municipal reform. Ida Tarbell's exposé of the Standard Oil Company helped strengthen antimonopoly laws. Samuel Hopkins Adams's investigation of the patent-medicine business led to federal food and drug regulations. These writers worked in the magazine and book fields as well as on newspapers, but they typified the new newspaper journalist, who helped make the daily paper a communicator with unique and unprecedented powers of persuasion and influence.

THE TWENTIETH CENTURY: THE NEW GENERATION OF BUSINESS

The first 30 years of the twentieth century saw great changes in American society and consequently in the shape of the newspaper industry. Many of the business and journalism trends established in this period have continued and grown more pronounced to the present. Circulation increased as the population expanded. Economic pressures and mounting competition spurred the consolidation of ownership, exemplified by the newspaper chain. And, finally, industry-wide standards of journalistic and ethical conduct began to be established.

The years leading up to World War I saw the peak in the number of daily newspapers, with 2,200 in 1910. By 1930, there were only 1,932 dailies, and that number would continue to fall as new ventures failed to keep up with unsuccessful ones. However, during those same 20 years, newspaper circulation nearly doubled, to 40 million copies daily. Business for surviving newspapers was never better; total advertising revenue tripled between 1915 and 1929, from approximately $275 million to $800 million.

Perhaps most significantly, there was a sharp decline in the number of cities with competing daily newspapers. In 1910, of the cities with daily newspapers, 57 percent had two or more separately owned competing dailies; in 1930, only a little over 20 percent. In 1890, New York City had 15 English-language dailies, representing 12 owners; by 1932, there were only 9, representing 7 owners. It was not only that "little" newspapers died; some of the newspaper giants of the nineteenth century declined and fell, including the *New York World* and the *New York Sun*. In *The Compact History of the American Newspaper*, John Tebbel says this marked "the transition from propaganda and personal journalism to the conservative newspapermaking of a new generation of businessmen soon to rise."[7] As the twentieth century progressed, corporate caution replaced flamboyance.

One of the reasons for the change was the high cost of running a business. James Gordon Bennett had started the *New York Herald* in 1835 with an investment of $500. By 1900, it would have taken $1 million to start a New York newspaper; the investment required for a large metropolitan newspaper plant today is usually tens of millions of dollars. The rising cost of newsprint became an enormous burden. Competition for circulation and advertising created other economic pressures. The product began to become standardized in content and similar in format, decreasing the social need for or reader interest in some newspapers.

Figure 9.6. The *Los Angeles Times* has grown since World War II to become a major newspaper. This is how the *Times* covered the end of the war in 1945. In 1989, its competitor, the Los Angeles *Herald-Examiner* folded, symbolic of a nationwide trend toward single-paper dominance.

Sensationalism made a resurgence in the 1920s and was known then as jazz journalism before another, more responsible trend in journalism followed. Jazz journalism was marked by a rise of tabloid newspapers, which are physically smaller than regular "blanket" newspapers, and by the extensive use of photographs. Once again, sex and violence were splashed across front pages. Begun in 1919, the New York *Daily News* used this formula to grow swiftly in the 1920s and become the largest-circulation daily in the country, a rank it held until the late 1980s when it fell to third. At nearly the same time, in 1923, the American Society of Newspaper Editors formulated their Canons of Journalism, which developed during the following decades into the codes of objectivity, truth, and balance that guide newspapers today.

THE STRUCTURE AND ECONOMICS OF THE INDUSTRY TODAY

After World War II, radio, television, and motion pictures grew to challenge the premier position of the newspaper as mass communicator. Television especially affected newspapers, attracting large segments of the population and advertisers away from them. The latter half of this century has seen an exodus of people leaving the city and moving into the suburbs—and newspapers have followed to serve them. Small suburban dailies and weeklies have grown tremendously, as have specialized newspapers attempting to serve a diverse population and specific interests. For many of the newspapers that survive, business is only fair. Ad revenue rose in recent years, mainly through classified ads, which suddenly declined, and inserts. Preprinted or inserted advertising revenue rose from $1.09 million in 1977 to $6.3 million in 1989. But the health of newspapers reflects any current economic climate and at present independent papers feel vulnerable; chains and conglomerates dominate the industry. Many challenges face newspapers, for example, the possibility of being eclipsed by new technologies or the dependence on soft or at least unreliable advertising income.

Declines and Rises

While total circulation has risen to over 63 million, with double that number in actual readership, the number of English-language dailies in the United States dropped to 1,643 in 1989, down from 1,932 dailies in 1930. Total numbers rarely tell the whole story. For one thing, morning papers and Sunday editions are strong and generally becoming more so while circulation of evening papers has declined by 5 million in the past 5 years (see Figure 9.7). Newspapers are shifting to morning editions as America's work force has moved from early rising blue-collar jobs to more white-collar work; in the evening many people tend to turn on the television set for the day's news. In 1950, morning circulation was only two-thirds afternoon circulation; 40 years later morning circulation was double that of afternoon newspapers.

One statistic that worries many newspapers is that while the population nearly doubled from 1930 to 1980, from 122 million to 226 million, newspaper circulation grew at half that rate in those 50 years from 40 million to 62 million daily. *Penetration,*

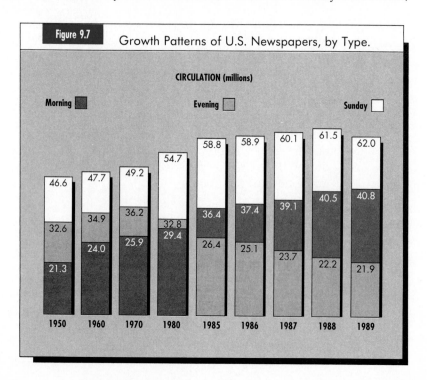

Figure 9.7 Growth Patterns of U.S. Newspapers, by Type.

the number of households receiving a daily paper, is down, as is readership among the young and nonwhites. Weekly newspapers have experienced the most growth. Circulation has risen between 1965 and 1990, from 25 million to 55 million copies, and in 1990 there were 7,600 weeklies being published. Also, average per paper circulation peaked in 1990 to 7,309.

NEWSPAPER ECONOMICS

The cost of running a newspaper has increased greatly. As our newspapers grow in heft (a typical metropolitan daily averages 88 pages, 351 pages on Sunday, according to a 1987 survey), Americans have become the largest consumers by far of newsprint, the paper on which newspapers are printed, followed by the Japanese, who purchase one-quarter of what we do. A newspaper like the *Los Angeles Times* uses approximately 450,000 tons of newsprint a year. After labor, newsprint is the next largest expense—averaging 25 percent of cost. The *Times* also estimates that it has more than $100 million invested in printing equipment alone. Other supply costs have risen, as have wages and salaries.

In 1987, the minimum salary for a *New York Times* reporter who had served her apprenticeship was $929 a week, about $48,400 a year. That same reporter would have made $120 a week, $6,240 a year, in 1950.

The American Newspaper Guild, the chief labor union for reporters, copy editors and other nonmechanical employees, had 33,000 members in 1989. In general, it is felt that membership is not keeping up with growth in the industry and that its power to strike is eroding. (The suburbanization of newspapers has cut into the influence of unions as well, scattering the work force in small pockets.) Such actions as byline strikes (where writers withhold their bylines from stories) have done little more than embarrass publishers. Other unions, such as those for pressmen and drivers, tend to have more influence.

Some unions' clout can become a matter of life and death for a paper. One major reason for the demise of the Los Angeles *Herald-Examiner* in 1989 was a 10-year strike over wages by the American Newspaper Guild, begun in 1967. The Guild was eventually joined by 11 other unions. By 1977, the *Herald*'s circulation had been cut in half, to 330,000, a financial loss from which it never recovered (see the box). The fate of the nation's second largest metropolitan newspaper, the 70-year-old New York *Daily News*, was at stake as management began a collective-bargaining process in January 1990 with hopes that tighter rein on traditional over-manning, featherbedding, and other wastages could get the percentage of revenue going to salary and benefits (50 percent) down to a more workable figure (25 percent is an average for papers of similar size).

Circulation —subscription and newsstand—is important to attract advertisers, but the revenue from it is insignificant in the face of the cost of each edition; its contribution is about equal to the cost of newsprint. (See Figure 9.9.) Analysts and publishers point out that the price of a newspaper is not only too low in real terms but represents our culture's biggest bargain.

Although newspaper advertising spending continues to increase, the growth rate—even for classifieds, which grew less than 3 percent in 1989—has been flat of late. This reflects the general economy, especially slow house and car sales, but the breadth of the problem is alarming the industry.

As a result of rising costs and the suburban exodus, the number of cities with

"A losing business, but a winning newspaper."
—Robert J. Danzig, general manager of
Hearst newspapers

The November 2, 1989, issue of the Los Angeles *Herald-Examiner* was its last. The history and the reasons for the closing of a major paper in the Hearst chain tells us much about the newspaper and the media conglomerate in the United States today.

Its genesis was the Los Angeles *Express,* dating to 1871, and the *Herald* (1877), acquired and merged in 1922 by William Randolph Hearst, and Hearst's *Examiner,* founded in 1903 to help Hearst's bid for the Democratic presidential nomination. Its highlights included a scoop on the explosion of the first H-bomb, the hiring of the first woman city editor (in 1937); crusades, especially for the working class; and its status as the nation's largest afternoon paper (at one time it had 12 editions, and 1 million copies daily). Its problems started in 1962: The Hearst Company merged the morning *Examiner* with the less successful *Herald-Express* to focus on an afternoon edition after the Times Mirror Co. closed its afternoon paper. The *Los Angeles Times* was thus the sole morning paper at a time when the trend we've noted—toward consumer attention to newspaper news on the way to work and TV news in the evening—had begun.

Over and out: Editorial employees gather outside the Herald Examiner building yesterday afternoon to say one last goodbye, just for the record, before getting to work on the newspaper's final edition.

The paper and its ornate building, once including Hearst's hideaway apartment, and providing a model of the Spanish Renaissance architecture that would be used in his famous home, San Simeon, were symbolically important to the Hearsts; attempts to sell the *Herald-Examiner* came too long after the paper's decline and following a years-long strike that cost $15 million, a drop of 400,000 in circulation, and reduction of staff from 2,000 to 700. In its last five years, the paper lost $85 million and a lot of ground to the *Times*, the San Fernando Valley-based *Daily News*, and an increasing number of suburban papers while the inner city ethnic mix steadily fragmented to leave little sense of community identity or reliable readership for local news. In a belated effort to bolster circulation, the Hearst Corp. bought a chain of 28 suburban weeklies and 2 small dailies in 1981.

As the paper closed in 1989, media analyst John Morton observed that 40 percent of *Herald-Examiner*'s circulation would "disappear": "These are blue-collar types, the *Herald*'s traditional audience. They have been drifting away to television and are not reading newspapers at all." Only 62 percent (the lowest in the nation) of people in L.A., the nation's largest radio market due to the automobile-driving commuter, read newspapers according to market researchers at Scarborough Associates.

A major city lost a voice and its journalism an edge. As Ben Bagdikian, of the University of California's School of Journalism, said, "Competition . . . has always meant an improvement in the quality of reporting." And the paper's TV critic, Mark Schwed, summed up his colleagues' feelings: "The bad part is that the *Herald-Examiner* was a real newspaper, not the insurance office that so many papers today are becoming. You could smell the ink. It was old, run-down, stinky, and it was staffed by the young and eager and underpaid. It bled tradition."

The only "winner" was the Hearst Corp., a privately held company that thus disposed of its last losing paper after shutdowns or sell-offs in Baltimore, Boston, Cleveland, New York, and other cities where the affluent were fleeing to the suburbs. It is now a $2 billion-a-year conglomerate—the United States' ninth-largest media group—with 13 money-making papers (including joint operating agreements and at least one whose future is said to be uncertain), 14 consumer magazines, 6 TV stations, 7 radio stations, book publishing, and cable-program companies.

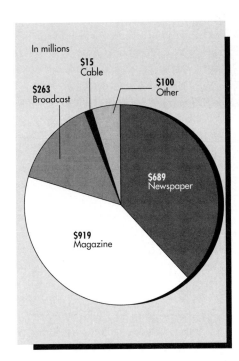

In millions

$15 Cable

$263 Broadcast

$100 Other

$689 Newspaper

$919 Magazine

competing dailies, which began to diminish at the turn of the century, has continued to fall. Of the 1,516 U.S. cities with a daily newspaper only 93 have competing dailies. In 1987, of the top 25 cities, ranked by size, only 12 had two separately owned dailies. New York City, which had nine dailies in 1932, now has four separately owned dailies. Table 9.2 illustrates the importance of chains.

A number of management and production efficiencies are possible with group ownership. In a way, it is the print version of broadcast networks: Advantages include an edge in national advertising marketing, great coverage, economies in purchases (like that of newsprint), and the introduction of professional management personnel. Those who fear the impact of the concentrated ownership of chains today will be interested to learn that at this time, Gannett controls less total newspaper circulation than Hearst did at his peak. In 1910, there were 13 groups, and together they owned a total of 62 newspapers. By 1990, groups owned 1,233 papers, 76 percent of all American dailies. Al Neuharth, the retired chairman of Gannett, built a media empire by buying newspapers across the country—totaling 89 when he stepped down—as well as 10 television stations, 16 radio stations, and a program-production company. The *New York Post* was owned by British media mogul Rupert Murdoch until 1988 when he was forced to sell it because the Federal Communications Commission prohibited "cross-ownership" of more than one medium in a specific market; he also owned a New York television station. As this book goes to press, Robert Maxwell is reported planning the purchase of the New York *Daily News* to complement his European newspaper. Nearly half of all newspaper groups own only two or three dailies each. While individually no one group threatens to have undue influence, collectively the top five groups control about half the total daily circulation.

Table 9.2.	20 Largest U.S. Newspaper Groups			
	Daily Circulation[1]	Number of Dailies	Sunday Circulation[1]	Number of Sunday Editions
Gannett Co. Inc.	6,022,929	82	5,689,876	64
Knight-Ridder Inc.	3,794,809	28	4,681,411	24
Newhouse Newspapers	2,997,699	26	3,784,926	21
Times Mirror Co.	2,626,259	8	3,144,142	7
Tribune Co.	2,608,222	9	3,428,671	7
Dow Jones & Co. Inc	2,409,955	23	495,665	14
Thomson Newspapers Inc.	2,127,123	122	1,681,684	70
The New York Times Co.	1,919,094	27	2,461,966	17
Scripps Howard	1,570,957	21	1,755,627	11
Cox Enterprises Inc.	1,280,040	18	1,654,123	17
Hearst Newspapers	1,207,089	13	2,349,064	10
Media News	1,123,552	19	1,117,436	13
Freedom Newspapers Inc.	938,862	27	959,740	18
Capital Cities/ABC Inc.	898,927	9	931,852	5
The Washington Post Co.	826,871	2	1,187,863	2
Central Newspapers Inc.	824,782	7	968,534	4
Donrey Media Group	790,982	57	786,146	49
Copley Newspapers	767,955	12	768,725	6
McClatchy Newspapers	753,558	11	855,726	8
The Chronicle Publishing Co.	742,410	6	902,238	3

[1] Average for six months ended September 30, 1989.
Source: Morton Research, Lynch, Jones & Ryan; Audit Bureau of Circulations.

The joint operating agreements (JOAs) studied in Chapter 3 are one strategy that has been employed to save financially troubled city dailies and thereby preserve a competitive news environment (a JOA allows separately owned newspapers legally to share business and production facilities if one newspaper would fail otherwise). Under the agreement we have previously described, the *Detroit News* stopped delivering its morning edition, which forced it to bow for the first time in 30 years to its fierce rival for circulation dominance, the *Detroit Free Press*. But while there were inevitably various adjustment and technical problems, there may ultimately be enough benefits to justify the risk of losing a voice in a metropolitan market. The papers can now work to improve features and formats, and expand local coverage.

Though the government allowed JOAs as early as the 1930s, they were not used extensively until the 1970s. They have also been employed successfully in Seattle, between the *Post-Intelligencer* and the *Seattle Times*, and in San Francisco, between the *Chronicle* and the *Examiner*. There is considerable debate over the effect of JOAs. Similarities between two jointly owned papers may stem from the nature of competition among communicators; all papers vie to attract advertisers and thus aim to build strong readership statistics; because of this, they may not promote alternative points of view. Ironically, the existence outside of the JOA of minority, alternative, suburban-oriented, or other special-interest papers gives these leading papers a run for their money. All this was a factor in the demise of the *Herald-Examiner* in Los Angeles, and across the country weeklies and shoppers take advertising dollars away from the major dailies. The shopper pictured in Figure 9.8

Figure 9.8. This shopper evolved from a two-pager to a substantial monthly. Shown is the last issue as an independent paper.

can be called a newspaper due to the proportion of editorial columns to the ads that support the publication. The unusual front page format reflects this division; this last issue before the paper joined a conglomerate shows the storefront from which publisher and sales reps worked. *The Country Shopper* began in 1976 as a one-sheet flier mailed monthly to 4,500 households in a town 50 miles north of New York City. In 1990 the paper, then averaging 61 pages with a circulation of 34,000, was sold to Add, Inc., a Wisconsin-based owner of 50 newspapers in 11 states. These free shoppers compete strongly with paid weeklies.

ADDRESSING A NATIONAL AUDIENCE

While the most growth in the newspaper industry is occurring in smaller daily and weekly community papers, several other newspapers have found economic success by reaching for a national audience. These are also some of the great papers of the past several decades, the ones that mold public debate and set the agenda for other newsmakers. For almost a century, *The New York Times* has maintained its reputation as the national newspaper of record (it is kept in libraries as the official record of the day's events). In 1987, it began a slightly revised national edition, which now accounts for 16 percent of its total circulation and is doing well with advertisers. The *Wall Street Journal* has become the nation's largest daily, highly respected for the quality of its journalism. It is one of the biggest success stories, transforming its circulation of 153,000 in 1950 to just under 2 million in 1990. Though it was never intended to turn a profit and hasn't, the *Christian Science Monitor* is widely praised for its coverage of national and international events. The *Washington Post* has maintained a reputation it achieved in the 1960s and 1970s for excellent hard-hitting coverage of the government, and the *Los Angeles Times*, under the leadership of Otis Chandler, has grown to be a respected voice and a financial success.

The major national newspaper is *USA Today*, launched by the Gannett publishing group in 1982. By 1989, it had become the second-largest daily, even though in 1988 it had failed to turn a profit for the sixth straight year. *USA Today* has had a profound effect on the industry, drawing many detractors and imitators. The newspaper is edited in Washington, D.C., and transmitted by satellite to 33 Gannett printing plants around the country. Regional issues contain some regional content. Citing research that showed that Americans are spending less time reading the paper, *USA Today* combined state-of-the-art color printing, graphics, and photographs with a quick survey approach to news reporting. Gannett has also begun the publication of European and Pacific editions in an attempt to make *USA Today* an international newspaper.

At this point, the jury was still out on the *National*, the newest publication aimed at national distribution. Its turf being sports, this tabloid had to confront the strong coverage of local (and national, international) sports coverage of local papers and the uncertainty among potential advertisers that readers buy the *National* every day or only to get news of specific interest. If any focused coverage (other than money or financial news) has a chance at national distribution, it would be sports. Since Pulitzer introduced a separate sports section in the New York *World*, the public's appetite for news of sports (especially the pros, with the advent of television) has steadily grown.

The Changing Characteristics of Newspapers

The need to attract advertising has also meant a general shift in publishing philosophy that affects the character and content of newspapers. Although the newspaper has advanced enormously in ability to transmit news quickly, it is no match for radio and television and their 24-hour capability of broadcasting developments and bulletins. The "extra" edition, which typified newspaper publishing through World War II, has all but vanished. Newspapers competed with broadcast journalism by doing more than skimming the surface. They have tried to provide analysis, depth, and a context for understanding the significance of events, and they remain unsurpassed at providing a forum for readers' comments and opinions. They have had an edge in investigative reporting; budget and time constraints of radio and television generally restrict such investigation and crusading to brief local series or dramatized and even sensationalized tabloid journalism.

However, the comparative expansiveness of newspapers is undergoing change. Although the *USA Today* approach—designed to serve commuters—may have been criticized when it debuted on September 15, 1982, it is being widely adopted. In 1989, the *Christian Science Monitor* introduced an all-color format and cut its news coverage so that it could be read in 30 minutes, the time its average reader spends with any newspaper. Even *The New York Times* has responded, asking reporters to cut story length by as much as 30 to 50 percent, in general.

Newspapers have adjusted to compete with television by covering every conceivable topic and relying on syndicates to fill any gaps. Daily and weekly newspapers provide all the small details of day-to-day life. They announce births, marriages, and deaths; advertise local sales, employment opportunities, real estate, used cars, local sports, school news; profile the family next door; record civic meetings; carry public and legal announcements. And then there's the comics, one of the most frequently read parts of most papers. On Sundays more than 100 million people turn to the comics supplement.

The newspaper also has the advantage of being a better bulletin board for news. Readers can find the information they need at a glance, flipping immediately to the same section or page every day. They have better control, choosing what news items they would like to read and for how long.

Advertising now takes up about 60 percent of the space in an average daily newspaper, up to 70 percent on Sundays. In 1988, total ad revenue in newspapers reached a high of more than $31 billion, some $16 billion more than television ad revenue. Over $27 billion of it came from local advertising. Many publishers adopt a "marketing strategy," attempting to gain readers who are attractive to advertisers. This usually means trying to attract better-educated, upscale white-collar workers, since television has become the medium through which advertisers reach lower-class and blue-collar audiences. Many publishers are concerned about the implications of this philosophy, fearing that unpleasant news will be downplayed or ignored. However, nearly all newspapers try to carve out a definable market niche—be it a national, regional, or local readership. Metropolitan dailies are now beginning to create separate zoned editions of their newspapers to win over readers and advertisers who moved to suburban papers. This has many implications for the running of the paper. More local coverage means more tight-deadline articles as opposed to pieces that can be prepared in advance, and personnel expansion

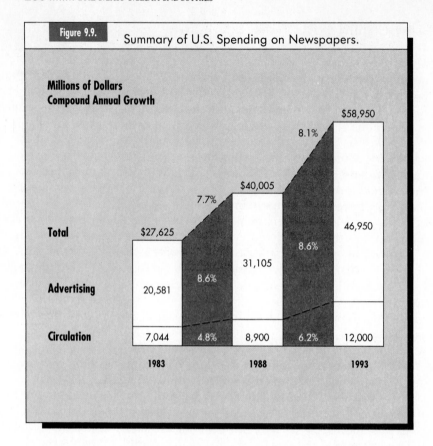

Figure 9.9. Summary of U.S. Spending on Newspapers.

is often required. But it allows a paper to build on the profitable trend of increases in local ads and inserts of preprinted store fliers and catalogs for targeted areas.

THE NEWSPAPER AUDIENCE TODAY

Newspapers reach at least 110 million Americans every day, almost 120 million on Sunday. Nine out of 10 adults read at least one newspaper every week. An average of 2.2 people read each newspaper delivered to a household. The average news-paper reader is more likely to be "mature" rather than either young or old, a college graduate rather than a high school dropout, higher income rather than lower, white rather than nonwhite, and stable rather than mobile. Newspaper-reading habits usually develop in early adolescence and continue to grow until the retirement years when they decline slightly. Newspapers carefully research just who is read-ing their paper, especially to prove to advertisers that they reach markets adver-tisers desire. Finding accurate research methods has become very important to publishers since major decisions are often based on the results of relatively small audience samples. The *Miami Herald* is one of a number of papers that issue an annual booklet of readership statistics, broken down and graphed in various ways (according to county, in comparison with the competitive paper). We have included a sample of their demographics (Table 9.3), which in some ways differ from the above generalizations.

The New York Times was involved in 7 years of litigation with independent dealers who deliver that paper to New York–area homes, to obtain information

Table 9.3.	Miami Herald Reader Demographic Profile Dade County		
	Miami Herald		
	Total Adults	**Avg. Issue Weekday**	**Avg. Issue Sunday**
	1,440,900	841,100	988,600
SEX			
Male	46%	47%	46%
Female	54%	53%	54%
	100%	100%	100%
AGE			
18–24	13%	11%	12%
25–34	20%	19%	21%
35–44	19%	18%	20%
45–54	14%	16%	15%
55 and over	34%	36%	32%
	100%	100%	100%
EDUCATION			
College Graduate	19%	23%	23%
Some College	20%	22%	22%
High School Graduate or Less	61%	55%	55%
	100%	100%	100%
OCCUPATION			
Professional/Managerial	19%	22%	22%
Clerical/Sales	20%	20%	22%
Other Employed	23%	20%	21%
Not Employed	38%	38%	35%
	100%	100%	100%
HOUSEHOLD INCOME			
$50,000 or More	20%	25%	24%
$35,000–$49,999	21%	22%	22%
$25,000–$34,999	26%	25%	26%
Under $25,000	33%	28%	28%
	100%	100%	100%
ETHNICITY			
Hispanic	40%	31%	32%
Non-Hispanic	60%	69%	68%
	100%	100%	100%

How to read chart:
For example, 20% of adults in Dade County have household income of $50,000 or more. This compares to 25% of *Miami Herald* weekday readers and 24% of *Herald* Sunday readers who earn $50,000 or more.
Source: Birch/Scarborough—Multimedia Study 1988.

about the location of the households; advertisers demand detailed demographics, and the *Times*, like the *Washington Post* and the *Baltimore Sun*, no longer could afford to hand over the "nuisance job" of distribution wholly to outsiders.

THE SPECIALIZED PRESS

There is often a grey area for what could be considered a special publication. For example, the *Washington Times*, begun in 1982, is published by a group with backing from Sun Myung Moon, the Korean religious leader who founded the Unification

Church. The *Washington Times* is a daily which is attempting to compete against the *Washington Post*, and the *Times* editor maintains its owners do not influence news coverage.[8] It is generally regarded, however, as having a slant toward the politics and philosophy of the Reverend Moon and the Unification Church. As a consequence, its circulation and advertising revenue are far behind the *Post*'s, and it is financially unstable.

Other specialized papers fall into categories. A rapidly growing type is the sensational, often sexually explicit national tabloid. Examples are the *National Enquirer*, the *Globe*, and the *Star*. They thrive on exaggerated gossip about the rich and the famous, as well as tales, sometimes tall, of freaks and unfortunates and extraterrestrials. They constantly push the scandal that is their stock in trade to the limits of libel and slander, but make up for the legal suits they inspire by the money they make from the millions of readers to whom they appeal.

THE SUBURBAN PRESS

As people have moved out of the central city and into the suburbs, they have sought smaller newspapers with news about their local communities. In the typical suburban communities of Washington, D.C., for example, dozens of weeklies emerged in the 1960s and 1970s—a time when the development of inexpensive printing technologies made the publication of small newspapers for specialized audiences economically feasible. One company, the Army Times Publishing Company, by using a central plant with automated equipment, was able to start five suburban weeklies in the Washington area in a short time—the *Montgomery Journal*, *Prince Georges Journal*, *Alexandria Journal*, *Arlington Journal*, and *Fairfax Journal*.

With the closing of the *Washington Star*, the suburban *Journal* newspapers decided to publish 5 days a week as the need arose for better coverage. Local advertisers have been strong supporters of small dailies and weeklies since they reach the readers they want.

Communication groups are eagerly buying up weekly papers—or better still, numbers of them. Chains own about half of the nation's 7,600 weeklies. In 1988, 200 weeklies changed hands. In 1989, California-based Freedom Newspapers paid an estimated $20 million to Media General for 30 local weeklies. Capital Cities/ABC, Forbes, Inc., CBS, and the Chicago *Sun-Times* (out to beat its rival *Tribune* at its game of attracting suburban readers) paid $60 million for 38 suburban weeklies. Prices in such deals used to be the amount of 1 year's revenues; now they average two times that base because circulation growth of weeklies at 3.3 percent is far stronger than that of dailies; advertisers now direct $5 billion of ad spending toward weeklies, and this will surely increase.[9] The stronger regional papers try to buy out smaller competitors while they're still small.

THE "ALTERNATIVE" PRESS

The "alternative" press is usually meant to describe publications that deal with controversial subjects or viewpoints—sexual, social, or political. They differ from other small newspapers in tending to have little advertiser support; to be sold on the street rather than by subscription. However, a whole range of publications falls under this category, some little more than photocopied sheets and others more closely resembling magazines in format.

Figure 9.10. Many areas are seeing a strong growth in alternative and neighborhood papers.

By their nature, there is considerable flux in the fortunes of the alternative press. Rising to a position of some influence a century and a half out of antislavery and then prosuffrage causes, and also known as the "underground" press, they proliferated in the 1960s. The *Village Voice* was founded in Greenwich Village in 1955; it has since become so successful, as *Rolling Stone* has, that it can hardly be considered alternative anymore. Both are now part of the establishment press. Many publications folded, however, as the social and political movements that spawned them changed. Today, newspapers such as the *Guardian*, in New York City, and *I. F. Stone's Weekly* carry on the tradition.

Editors on both the left and the right of the political spectrum often argue that the mainstream press is guided by an unstated ideological agenda that belies their claim that they report events objectively. The aim of many alternative presses is to expose that hidden bias and to reinterpret events from their perspective. Although some publish material designed to shock, many cover news that never finds its way into regular newspapers.

THE BLACK PRESS

According to Michael and Edwin Emery, in *The Press and America*, the black press peaked at the end of World War II. The largest three black newspapers could be purchased across the country: The *Chicago Defender* had a circulation of 257,000;

the *Pittsburgh Courier* had a circulation of 202,000; and the *Afro-American* of Baltimore had a circulation of 137,000. By 1970, increased racial integration, economic pressures, and the rise of community and radical newspapers caused a serious decline (the circulation of the *Defender* had fallen to 33,000, for example).

Since the publication of *Freedom's Journal*, more than 3,000 black newspapers have been founded in the United States. Today, around 200 are still being published, mostly as weeklies. There are only three dailies: the *Chicago Daily Defender*, the *Columbus Times*, and the *New York Challenge*. The *New York Amsterdam News* remains one of the most successful black newspapers. A weekly with a circulation of around 40,000, it had a peak circulation in the 1950s of nearly 100,000.

Many black newspapers still see their mission as calling for racial equality and integration; they also feel black communities will always have needs the mainstream press will not fill. The somewhat older, more conservative black newspapers were most hurt in the 1960s when radical newspapers found audiences looking for more urgent calls for change. The mainstream newspapers have in turn attempted to attract black advertisers and readers as a result of societal pressures and economic reasons. The increasing affluence of minorities makes them attractive to advertisers. Though coverage of minority issues has increased somewhat in the mainstream press, it has not opened its doors for job opportunities, by and large. A 1987 survey by the American Society of Newspaper Editors found that only 3.6 percent of the newsroom work force were blacks. Industry leaders have set diversity in the workplace as a major goal.

THE HISPANIC AND FOREIGN-LANGUAGE PRESS

Most foreign-language presses declined in the twentieth century, but the Hispanic press has been an exception. Asian publications have also been on the rise, reflecting the strength and autonomy of their communities. Overall, by 1986, there were fewer than 40 foreign-language dailies and approximately 200 other newspapers representing about a dozen languages. As immigrants became settled and many children grew up speaking English as well as a native tongue, they abandoned special publications for those in the mainstream.

Hispanics are the fastest-growing minority population in the United States; from 18.8 million persons in 1988, their numbers are calculated to nearly double over the next 30 years. In 1985, the National Association of Hispanic Publishers found that there were 10 Hispanic dailies, 140 weeklies, and 76 that published less frequently. Today, while nearly 80 percent of Hispanics regard themselves as bilingual, Spanish-language newspapers are popular with English-language publications geared toward an increasingly affluent Hispanic audience.

In 1976, the *Miami Herald*, owned by Knight-Ridder, began publishing a Spanish-language section, but when this failed to attract large segments of the Hispanic population in Miami, Knight-Ridder began publication of a Spanish-language edition of the whole paper, *El Nuevo Herald*. In 1988, it boasted a circulation of 90,000. Gannett purchased *El Diario-La Prensa*, a New York City daily, in 1981; it had a circulation of 60,000. Two important dailies are published by Hispanic owners: *La Opinion* was founded in Los Angeles in 1926 and now has a circulation of 62,000; *Diario de las Americas*, founded in Miami in 1953 by a Nicaraguan exile, now has a circulation of 67,000. Three other major Spanish-language dailies were *Noticias del Mundo* (New York), the *Manana Daily News* (Chicago), and the *Times* (Laredo).

Figure 9.11. The *Miami Herald* researches and serves its bilingual constituency. The front pages of the same day reflect varying emphases of coverage and treatment.

Vista is an English-language weekly magazine aimed at Hispanics that, in 1988, was inserted in 27 mainstream dailies across the country.

MANAGEMENT AND TECHNOLOGY IN A NEWSPAPER

Like all the other mass media, the newspaper is a highly structured, carefully organized, and exceedingly complex mechanism. Literally millions of words come into the large metropolitan daily each day, from many sources. These words must be sorted, selected, checked, evaluated, edited, rewritten, typeset, laid out, made up into pages, printed, and distributed to readers, all in less than 24 hours. In order to accomplish this task with a maximum of reader interest and a minimum of error, the newspaper mechanism must work like a well-oiled machine, with each part running in its place and operating in a smooth relationship to the next.

The operation of a newspaper is usually divided into three parts: editorial, business, and production.

The editorial side of the typical daily newspaper with a circulation of 100,000 has about 75 full-time editorial staff members. The main function of the editorial department is to gather information, judge its importance, evaluate its meaning, write and display it in ways that will attract and hold the attention of readers, and put it through the cycle of production until it reaches the printed page. Editorial personnel typically make up only 15 percent of the newspaper's total work force.

The important decisions are often made in committee. The editors meet at the start of each news day to draw up a list of assignments based on their knowledge of events that have taken place or will soon occur. As the reporters complete their assignments, they and the editors meet in conferences during the day and develop the way the news and opinions will be played in the newspaper. This kind of constant team effort is an essential aspect of newspaper work.

The business manager is in charge of both classified and display advertising. The business manager is also in charge of selling or promoting the newspaper and is responsible for getting it properly distributed, through a circulation department, which is usually made up of independent distributors and a network of newspaper carriers. Finally, the business manager is in charge of the bookkeeping and accounting for the entire organization.

The production manager is in charge of the printing plant, which usually includes composing or typesetting, engraving or photographic-plate making, and printing itself, usually on a gigantic press with more than 1 million moving parts.

A TIME OF PROFOUND CHANGE

How does the idea of teamwork translate as intradepartment cooperation? Journalists have expressed a concern that the newspaper is becoming just another business. In an article, "When MBAs Rule the Newsroom," former reporter Doug Underwood, now with the University of Washington, described the reorganization of the newsroom directed by Michael Fancher, executive editor of the *Seattle Times*:

> In [his] memo, Fancher talked about . . . establishing priorities for the development of senior editors, and serving as liaison with the circulation department to help the Times *meet its circulation goals. Forty percent of his time, he said, would be spent coordinating the news department's role in making and keeping the newsroom budget in line.*
>
> *Nowhere in the memo did Fancher talk about the news—either overseeing the direction of the newspaper's coverage, participating in news decisions, or helping to develop story ideas.*
>
> *Welcome to the world of the modern, corporate newspaper editor, a person who, as likely as not, is going to be found in an office away from the newsroom bustle, immersed in marketing surveys, organizational charts, budget plans, and memos on management training.*
>
> *It's not surprising that, as corporations have extended their hold on U.S. newspapers, the editors of those newspapers have begun to behave more and more like the managers of any other corporate entity.*[10]

C. K. McClatchy, editor of the family-owned, 133-year-old company that owns *The Sacramento Bee*, voiced similar concerns:

> *More than anything else, the factor that seems to be essential for the making of a good newspaper is having individuals in charge who understand the special role newspapers play in keeping the public informed and the absolute importance of that role.*

Figure 9.12. The publication of the modern newspaper requires computers for typesetting and control and more than 1 million moving parts for printing. A huge room is needed just to store rolls of newsprint.

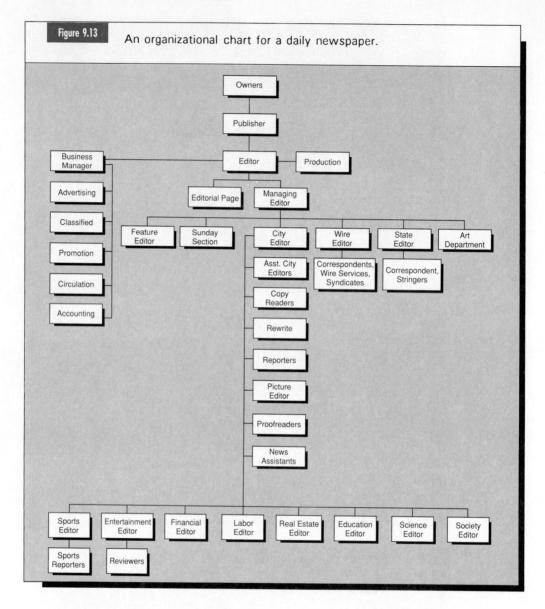

Figure 9.13 An organizational chart for a daily newspaper.

Newspapers are different from other businesses. To be a good newspaper person you must have skills that cannot be learned selling real estate or making a bank loan.[11]

As we proceed through surveys of other media industries, we will hear various versions of the fear that "newspaper people are no longer in charge of newspapers." Sometimes, when those people realize they are not the ones in charge of decisions affecting the news, they withdraw. The other side is that to make papers competitive for the advertising revenue being lured away by other media, to survive rising costs, and to remain healthy components of growing conglomerates, editors have to realize that the practice of newsroom management has dramatically and irreversibly changed.

Technological Advancement

By the mid-1980s, almost every daily newspaper was being printed by photo-offset lithography, a technique of printing from photo-sensitive plates rather than raised letters. Type was being set by simple photo composition rather than casting with hot metal on a Linotype machine. Optical character readers were being used to scan letters on a page or video screen and to set the material in type automatically.

Most major newspapers have already revolutionized their newsrooms with word processing and use computers for circulation, accounting, and advertising tasks. Figure 25.2 illustrates newspaper technology at work.

The news story ultimately goes to the automatic typesetter, which can produce camera-ready copy in the prescribed typeface and size with a headline, to be pasted up for a negative, from which the final plates are made for printing. The CPU, or central processing unit, has an error rate of 1 in 250,000 lines of type.

Computer data bases have profoundly changed the work of the newspaper communicator. Using them, reporters can retrieve, collate, and examine vast amounts of information that would be nearly impossible to process using physical files. On-line data bases are more common; they require a computer phone link to an external computer that holds the information. In-house data bases are also being used as the "morgue" for old stories. One survey estimated that use of data bases had quadrupled between 1982 and 1986. In 1988, Dwight L. Morris, an assistant managing editor for the *Atlanta Journal and Constitution*, which won a Pulitzer Prize for its investigation of a home-loan scandal that would not have been possible without data bases, had this to say:

> The news isn't just fires. The news is information. I think the whole business has to start looking at information differently. It's a matter of finding interesting patterns in life.[12]

The Future Newspaper

Innovative uses of technology may be the way to fend off the approaching challenges of the twenty-first century. Addressing the Newspaper Research Council in late 1989, Richard L. Vaughn, corporate director of research and planning at Foote, Cone and Belding Communications, warned that traditional print media will have a diminishing role:

> Consider a late-1980s futures-oriented comment of just one Cassandra, Nicholas Negroponte of MIT's Media Lab: "Newspapers as we know them won't exist. The whole concept of newsworthiness will change. Newspapers will be printed for a readership of one." Apocalyptic? Unrealistic? Premature speculation? Possibly, but what if he's only 10% right? or 25%? That could matter quite a lot. . . . [The newspaper's] separate sections and discrete information also make it a "niche" medium, which quickly, simply and affordably allows consumers to customize and control their exposure and fulfill their needs. This is true, and it should continue for some time to come. But electronic incursions are going to capture some of your reader base unless you make changes.[13]

Vaughn sees future generations interacting with electronic words, but this does not necessarily mean the death of the newspaper. It will, however, need to become "a communicator not anchored by pulp and ink, but in fact able to reach and be reached by millions of consumers who want what you have, but want it on their terms—not yours."[14]

The newspaper could remain a leading mass medium. There are, according to Vaughn, several things newspaper management can be working on right now:

1. Be aggressive about data-based marketing; go beyond traditional segmentation and research and develop a subscriber-information system that is constantly updated and used in planning of news and features.
2. Promote the paper to advertisers as an efficient direct-marketing tool.
3. Develop new ways to shape products to meet the paper's clients, the advertisers.
4. Develop the capabilities of electronic makeup so that the newspaper of the future is something ever in flux, accessible in different forms to a network of consumers. There is a belief among media experts that while videotex did not take off when first introduced, that might have been because it was ahead of its time.

The paper that could evolve from the above would complete the progression of this medium from elitist to mass to specialized. Let us now see how the other mass media follow or find variations on this theme.

SUMMARY

The newspaper is the oldest mass medium and still one of the most important. The role of the newspaper has evolved in response to the changing needs of its readers, softening the news in exchange for more information on lifestyles, entertainment, and other "feature" sections. Yet newspapers are still the means by which citizens protect their rights and liberties in a democratic society.

Newspapers began in America as a means of communication for an elite audience, the wealthy and politically active upper middle class (mainly because they were the only ones who could read) in early-nineteenth-century America. The era of the "penny press" began in 1833 when development of faster, cheaper presses allowed publishers to aim their newspapers at a mass audience. At the end of the nineteenth century, Joseph Pulitzer and William Randolph Hearst, with their sensationalist "yellow journalism," made newspapers into a truly mass medium. They were also the first to realize the press's potential as a watchdog for the public good. In the twentieth century, newspapers became big business. The rising costs of printing and more intense competition for advertising made newspaper publishing a corporate undertaking.

Newspapers rely on advertising to make a profit; circulation prices barely cover the cost of printing the paper. The development of television forced newspapers to shift to morning editions to catch readers at breakfast or on the train, instead of after work when they go home and turn on the television. While circulation has risen, the number of newspapers has dropped. This may reflect the growing cost of publishing a paper—expensive newsprint, increased labor costs, and competition for advertising from the other media. Chain ownership developed to offset the rising costs, at the expense of competition between papers in the same market.

Most growth in the industry is occurring in smaller daily and weekly community papers. Some newspapers have found success by reaching for a national audience. The *Wall Street Journal* and *New York Times* are examples; *USA Today* was the first newspaper to be published with a national audience in mind. *USA Today* combined color printing, graphics, a light approach to reporting, and satellite transmission to match reader habits and achieve truly national distribution.

Changing readership has greatly affected the way newspapers are put together. Papers have lightened the amount of news coverage in exchange for more feature-type information about lifestyles or entertainment. Newspapers publish editions aimed at a surrounding suburban community, in some cases, printed in other languages. Specialized and alternative presses with small circulations publish papers cheaply, each aimed at a different interest group. The newspaper's role has changed. Unable to compete with television in getting the news out quickest, publishers are now concerned with being the most complete news source and being able to reach specialized audiences.

REFERENCES

1. Thomas Jefferson to Edward Carrington, January 16, 1787, in *A Jefferson Profile as Revealed in His Letters*, ed. Saul K. Padover (New York: John Day, 1956), 44–45.
2. Michael and Edwin Emery, *The Press and America: An Interpretive History of the Mass Media*, 6th ed. (Englewood Cliffs, N.J.: Prentice-Hall, 1988), 5.
3. John Milton, "Areopagitica," quoted in *Prose of the English Renaissance* (New York: Appleton-Century-Crofts, 1952), 766.
4. Allan Nevins, "The Constitution Makers and the Public: 1785–1790," *Public Relations Review* (Fall 1978): 5–6.
5. Editorial, *New York Journal*, November 8, 1896.
6. Michael Schudson, "The New Journalism," in *Communication in History: Technology, Culture, Society*, David Crowley and Paul Heyer, eds. (White Plains, N.Y.: Longman, 1991), 142.
7. John Tebbel, *The Compact History of the American Newspaper* (New York: Hawthorne Books, 1969).
8. David Johnson, *The New York Times*, October 15, 1989.
9. Howard Rudnitsky, "Why Weeklies Are Hot," *Forbes*, February 5, 1990, 100.
10. Doug Underwood, "When MBAs Rule the Newsroom, *Columbia Journalism Review* (March/April 1988): 23.
11. C. K. McClatchy, "How Newspapers Are Owned— And Does It Matter?" *Nieman Reports* (Summer 1988):22.
12. Tim Miller, "The Data-Base Revolution, *Columbia Journalism Review* (September/October 1988): p. 35.
13. Debra Gersh, "Looking Ahead," *Editor & Publisher*, November 11, 1989, 20.
14. Ibid., 33.

Television: Network, Cable, Public

The word *television* still means, through its Greek and Latin roots, "farseeing." The fact that this meaning is expanding—with globalization and increasingly sophisticated satellite distribution of images—is part of the extensive and fundamental changes sweeping the industry. If its refusal to sit still for a portrait is frustrating for those of us who describe and analyze the medium, it nevertheless clearly makes for fascinating study—and open-ended career opportunities.

Television no longer means ABC, CBS, and NBC. Networks, along with affiliates, independents, syndicators, cable operators, and programming and video producers, are in a state of flux, forging new interacting working relationships amid ever fiercer competition for viewers. Early in 1990, a new wrinkle was added with the announcement that four media powers were joining to create Sky Cable, a satellite service that would by 1993 beam television programs on 108 channels directly to homes through a breadbox-size unit. This alone promises to revolutionize further traditional network and cable TV.

Cable has introduced narrowcasting to special-interest audiences. The videocassette recorders that are in almost 70 percent of American homes have made all television viewing a more privatized experience. We seem to have more control over what we see and when we see it. But we may not have much control over, or even understanding of, the impact of what we see on us and our world. Scholars, researchers, and critics closely study television, which is, for all the proliferation and distraction of other media, *the* national mass-communication channel. This chapter provides some perspective by giving a sense of the history and the present direction of the various aspects of television today, details the underlying structure of the industry, looks at the effects of merging organization function, and reveals something of television's power to affect other media.

HISTORICAL PERSPECTIVE

Television, despite its dominant position in our lives, is a young medium—still growing, still developing, still becoming. To begin to grasp where the possibilities of television might lead us, it is important to understand where this ubiquitous medium has come from.

PREHISTORY: 1884–1925

Television grew out of the intense experimentation with electricity in the late nineteenth century. Basic research led to more practical experimentation, which culminated in the work of Guglielmo Marconi. Coincidental with research in wireless communication in the 1880s was the work of Paul Nipkow, who experimented with mechanical scanning-disc methods of sending pictures by wire. The word *television* first appeared in 1907, in *Scientific American* magazine.

Most of the early experiments in television employed the *mechanical* method, including work in the 1920s by Charles Jenkins in the United States and John Baird in Britain. In the United States Philo T. Farnsworth and Vladimir K. Zworykin contributed basic inventions for an *electronic* system, including, most significantly, Zworykin's camera tube, the iconoscope, which he patented in 1928.

EARLY DEVELOPMENT: 1925–1947

Barely 3 years after radio broadcasting became a reality in 1920, a crude, all-electronic TV system was available. The first real transmission of television occurred in 1925, using Jenkins's mechanical method. Zworykin's method of electronic scanning was simpler, however, and eventually produced a better picture. Experiments with electronic television were conducted throughout the world in the 1920s. Shortly after the Russian Revolution, the Soviets had solved the basic problems of mechanical television.

The Federal Radio Commission (later the Federal Communications Commission [FCC]) granted the first experimental license for visual broadcasting to the Radio Corporation of America's (RCA) station W2XBS in April 1928. That same

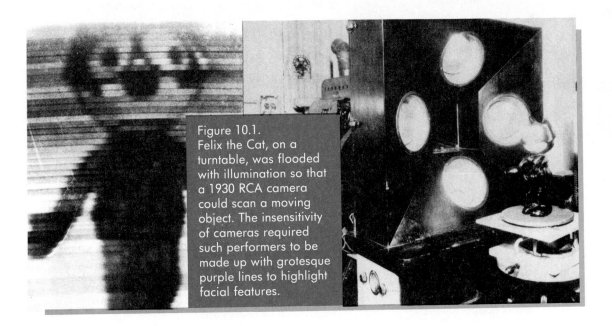

Figure 10.1.
Felix the Cat, on a turntable, was flooded with illumination so that a 1930 RCA camera could scan a moving object. The insensitivity of cameras required such performers to be made up with grotesque purple lines to highlight facial features.

The attention currently given the emergence of a "fourth network" (Fox) or even a fifth overlooks the fact that there was an alternative independent network from television's early days—DuMont. Various circumstances kept it from developing with its competitors, but its legacy is a little-known series of firsts.

Dr. Allen B. DuMont's experiments for the DeForest Radio Company included the first broadcast of synchronized picture and sound as well as the long-lasting cathode ray tube essential to television. From DuMont came the first all-electronic television receiver for the commercial market, the first movable camera dolly, the first camera with a zoom lens, the development of equipment to record broadcasts, and much else.

Shortly after introducing the first set available to the public at the 1939 World's Fair (the choice was between an 8" × 10" or a 20" round screen), DuMont established a New York City station in competition with NBC and CBS to test equipment and induce TV sales. Early programs ranged from reports of World War II to demonstrations of Ping-Pong, to primitive forms of the variety show.

Without a radio network in its pocket, and because one of the owners, Paramount, already had several major-market television station licenses, DuMont was not qualified under federal regulations to be awarded VHF affiliates, could not offer advertisers national coverage, and thus declined during the 1950s until it folded, parts becoming Metropolitan Broadcasting (later the conglomerate Metromedia)—with WNEW-TV channel 5, a major independent television station. Channel 5 is now WNYW, a Fox station.

Jackie Gleason first developed his character repertory at DuMont, until he and

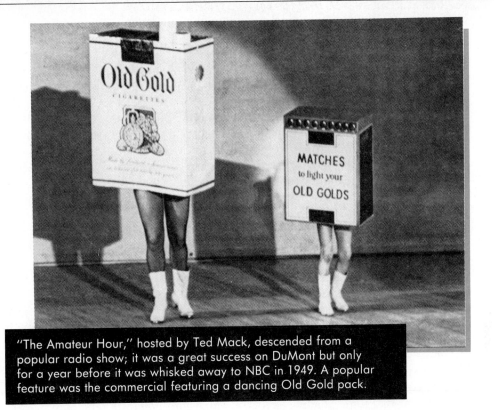

"The Amateur Hour," hosted by Ted Mack, descended from a popular radio show; it was a great success on DuMont but only for a year before it was whisked away to NBC in 1949. A popular feature was the commercial featuring a dancing Old Gold pack.

the Poor Soul, Joe the Bartender, and the Honeymooners went to higher pay at CBS. Other highlights include

First network coverage of professional football and basketball;
First soap opera on network TV ("Faraway Hill");
Its 7:00 A.M. news and weather show, a prototype of the genre;
"Black News," the first news/public affairs series with a minority focus;
"Captain Video," the first space opera (its low-budget set had spaceship controls painted on a wall in the studio atop Wanakmaker's department store);
"The Small Fry Club," the first successful children's program;
First live telecast of an opera from Europe by satellite;
First spot-interview show of passersby"
"Night Beat" (with Mike Wallace, 1955), first of the in-depth interview shows;
"Focus," the first forum for community residents to present views and public-service announcements.

Its programming spanned from slapstick to classical music and drama, and led a *New York Times* critic to reflect: WNEW-TV was "a fascinating illustration of how it is possible to be part of a commercial business and also gain a formidable reputation as a purveyor of outstanding culture in prime evening time."[1]

year, the General Electric Company broadcast the first TV drama over W6X in Schenectady, New York.

Great Britain was first with scheduled programming in November 1936, for 2 hours a day, 6 days a week; 2,000 people saw the first broadcast, which opened with the song "Magic Rays of Light." Germany had TV as early as 1935, though oddly enough Hitler did not utilize it for Nazi propaganda. The 1936 Olympics in Berlin were televised, and in England that year, the coronation of George VI was broadcast, demonstrating, in the words of media commentator Edwin Newman, "the real job of television." Experimentation continued throughout the 1930s. The first major public demonstration of television in this country occurred at the 1939 World's Fair in New York City, with President Franklin D. Roosevelt's appearance on television the hit of the fair.

The start of commercial telecasting was actually July 1, 1941. On that date, both the DuMont and the CBS stations aired programs. Dumont was the fourth network during television's formative years and was the source of many firsts, as chronicled in the box. (For a detailed look at the evolution of broadcasting networks, see Chapter 11's historical perspective on radio.)

It was RCA's station WNBT that ran the first commercial (Bulova Watch Company) and the first sponsored programs, including Lowell Thomas's news program (Sunoco) and "Uncle Jim's Question Bee" (Lever Brothers). By the end of 1941, some 10 commercial stations were serving 10,000 to 20,000 television homes, half of them in New York and half in Chicago, Philadelphia, and Los Angeles.

World War II interrupted TV's growth and delayed its national appearance. The war had some positive effects on television, however. Chief among them was the development of better electronic techniques and equipment, especially the image-orthicon tube.

During the war years, the single most important event affecting TV's future was a duopoly ruling in 1943 that forced NBC to divest itself of one of its two radio networks. This decision created ABC, another economically strong national radio operation that enabled the ABC-TV network to evolve and survive.

TV stations are grouped according to where their signal falls in the electromagnetic spectrum. The two bands into which all TV signals are placed are very high frequency (VHF) and ultrahigh frequency (UHF). Channels 2 to 13 are VHF. Channels 14 to 83 are UHF. Stations located in the VHF band reach a greater geographical area with less power and a clearer signal than stations in the UHF band. Thus almost without exception, VHF stations are more powerful, better established, and more profitable than their UHF counterparts.

Following World War II, the development of television was further retarded by problems involving the placement of television in the electromagnetic spectrum and the $1 million price tag attached to building and equipping a TV station. Many broadcasters thought that FM radio would be the next important medium.

More and more receivers were appearing on the market, however, and more than 1 million sets were sold in 1948 at an average price of $400. The rush for TV facilities was on. AT&T began to install intercity coaxial cable, making possible network interconnection. By early 1948, 19 stations were on the air, 81 stations had FCC authorization, and 116 applications were before the FCC. It became obvious that the commission would have to reevaluate TV broadcasting to prevent station interference, since only 12 VHF channels were available to serve the total system. Recent growth patterns of broadcast television stations are shown in Table 10.1.

THE FORMATION OF THE AMERICAN TELEVISION SYSTEM: 1948–1952

Between 1948, and 1952, three major factors significantly affected the future of video broadcasting: (1) the Federal Communications Commission's "freeze" on TV station allocations; (2) the development of TV networks; and (3) the evolution of video-programming formats.

The Freeze. By the fall of 1948, there were 36 TV stations on the air in 19 cities and another 73 licensed in 43 more cities. In order to solve technical-interference problems, provide for the increased demand for licenses, and study color-television systems, the Federal Communications Commission froze allocations for new stations from September 30, 1948, to July 1, 1952. During these years, the RCA compatible-color system was adopted. UHF channels 14 to 83 were added to VHF channels 2 to 13, and 242 station allocations (frequencies on which stations broadcast) were reserved for educational television.

While the freeze was on, 108 of the 109 commercially licensed stations went on the air, and TV homes jumped from 1.5 million to 15 million. Between 1948 and 1952, one of every three American families bought a TV set at an average cost of $300. Although no new licenses were being granted, growth was possible during this period because almost every major population area was being served by at least one TV station.

The Networks. The generally accepted date for the inauguration of national television networking is the 1948-1949 TV season. In January 1949, the Midwest and the East Coast were linked by coaxial cable. The West Coast linkup occurred in September 1951. Since not every station was able to carry live feeds, however, many new stations had to depend on kinescopes (films of electronically produced pictures) for network programming.

The birth and survival of the television networks depended on four factors: (1) a financially sound parent company that could survive the lean years of television development; (2) ownership of key stations in the largest population centers to provide local revenue and to guarantee that the network's series would be aired in those markets; (3) expertise in national radio operations that provided both financial support and a ready-made line-up of affiliates to carry programs; (4) a backlog or quick development of talent and programs that would attract large audiences for national advertisers. ABC, CBS, and NBC were able to meet these

Table 10.1.	Broadcast Television Stations, by Type				
	VHF	UHF	Network Affiliates	Independents	Total
1977	515	196	623	88	711
1987	524	444	631	337	968

criteria, and they survived. The key, of course, was financial strength. NBC lost over $18 million in its first 4 years of network-television operation.

Programming. In these early years of network and station development, most of the content of television came from radio-programming formats such as quiz shows, suspense programs, Westerns, variety shows, soap operas, and comedies. Indeed, most of TV's early hits were exact copies of radio series transposed intact to television, such as "Suspense," "The Life of Riley," "The Aldrich Family," "The Lone Ranger," "Break the Bank," and "Studio One." Television's first stars were radio personalities, including Red Skelton, George Burns and Gracie Allen, Arthur Godfrey, Jack Benny, and Edgar Bergen.

Television, like newspapers and radio before it, was initially not a household medium. As newspapers were first read in coffeehouses, television was first viewed in local bars and taverns. This pattern and television's inherent visuality were strong reasons that sports programming made up as much as 30 percent of all sponsored network evening time in 1949. As the TV set became more a household item, children's and women's programming became more important, as did variety shows.

Local stations provided programming to fill the gaps left in the network schedules. Much of it was poor quality, however, and as a result, the syndicator emerged early as an important source of TV content. In 1950, the first package of theatrical films found its way into the local marketplace.

The financial base of television was clear from the start. The public was acclimated to radio commercials and accepted them as the means of paying for their programs. Also, the networks had contractual agreements with sponsors. Structurally, TV economics was simply an extension of radio economics, and because of this, television developed much faster than expected.

THE PERIOD OF GREATEST GROWTH: 1952–1960

This slice of television history contained the most fantastic growth spurt ever experienced by a mass medium. By 1955, there were 439 stations on the air. The 15 million TV homes in 1952 expanded to 26 million in 1954, 42.5 million in 1958, and 45 million in 1960. During these 8 years, the percentage of TV-equipped homes in the United States grew from 33 to 90. Station and network profits kept pace with this growth, as gross industry revenues increased from $300 million in 1952 to $1.3 billion in 1960.

The dominant networks were CBS and NBC, primarily because of their network-radio experience, available capital assets, top-quality talent, and large number of affiliated stations. ABC had many problems, primarily the lack of affiliates, but the death of the DuMont Television Network in 1955 eased to a limited degree ABC's need for more affiliates. The merger of ABC with United-Paramount Theaters also helped increase its competitiveness, but throughout the 1950s, it ran a poor third to CBS and NBC.

Color television in the form of RCA's electronic system began to emerge slowly following FCC approval in 1953. The first color sets were manufactured in 1954 and sold for about $1,000. The season of 1954-1955 was the first color season, with NBC programming 12 to 15 hours a week. The high cost of both receivers and broadcast equipment dictated a slow growth, however. Other factors were the refusal of ABC and CBS to move into color programming because such a move would have given NBC the competitive edge; most compatible-color patents were held by NBC's parent company, RCA. Also, the electronics industry already had a thriving business in black-and-white sets, and it too would have had to do business with RCA. Many manufacturers chose to experiment with rather than produce color sets, and so as late as 1960, there were no color series on ABC or CBS.

By 1966, however, all three networks were running a complete color prime-time schedule. This led to a boom in sales of color sets, and by 1972, 50 percent of American homes with television had color receivers.

Another important technical development that occurred in the 1950s was the move toward film and videotape programming. With the development of videotape in 1956, live telecasting, with the exception of sports events, specials, and some daytime drama, soon became a thing of the past. Two reasons for the rise of recorded programming: (1) errors can be corrected before a show is broadcast, thus improving the artistic quality of the program; (2) the program can be rerun, thus recouping some of the skyrocketing costs of program production. Let us take a closer look at the quality of programming itself.

THE GOLDEN AGE BECOMES ONE OF COMPETITION AND CRITICISM...........................

The 1950s are widely known as the golden age of television. Much of the programming then continued the trends of the early years, with a mixture of sportscast, family situation comedies, and variety-vaudeville shows. The magic of live moving images in living rooms had enough impact and novelty for first-time television owners that few artistic demands were put on producers.

HIGHLIGHTS OF THE GOLDEN AGE

The first huge success of commercial television was indeed in the vaudeville format—"The Texaco Star Theatre" led by "Mr. Television." Beginning in 1948, Milton Berle captured the screens of American households every Tuesday night. Ed Sullivan, with the "Toast of the Town" (later "The Ed Sullivan Show"), was a stone-faced newspaperman who gained fame as host of a saner and more broadly entertaining variety show that lasted for more than 20 years. Today it is perhaps best known for introducing the Beatles to this country.

One of the most creative comedy-variety shows of the time, a classic of this golden age that lives again in video cassettes, was "Your Show of Shows," starring Sid Caesar and Imogene Coca. In 1951, "I Love Lucy" arrived, combining the visual jokes of the vaudeville format with the family-neighbors sitcom style to set the dominant standard for the genre and to live on through reruns.

Children's programming was led by "Howdy Doody," which ran from 1947 to 1960, featuring a puppet created by a Buffalo disc jockey, Bob Smith, the mute clown Clarabelle, and a peanut gallery always packed with an audience of youngsters. NBC once figured that the last children on the waiting list to get into the show would reach college age before they would get to see their heroes in person. Burr Tillstrom's more sophisticated puppet show, "Kukla, Fran, and Ollie," starring Fran Allison, originated in Chicago; there were also many network entries in

Figure 10.2. The popularity of Milton Berle (seen here dancing with Beatrice Lillie) in his variety show of the early 1950s earned him the nickname "Mr. Television."

the formal preschool classroom milieu, including "Miss Frances' Ding Dong School," and older students saw "Mr. Wizard" conduct science experiments.

Although Westerns and quiz shows had been on radio, television took these genres and made them something new and extremely successful. "Gunsmoke" arrived on television in 1955 and by the 1959-1960 season there were 32 prime-

Figure 10.3. Former disc jockey Buffalo Bob Smith (right) created the golden age's most popular children's show. Millions waited each afternoon for "It's Howdy Doody Time."

time Westerns. Some analysts attribute this popularity to the escape it provided from outside tensions of the cold war: Old-fashioned American values and clear-cut morality, with obvious good guys and bad guys, were reassuring. It has been pointed out that the traditional family sitcoms reached their peak just as the American nuclear family had begun to disintegrate, and the emerging slew of extremely fantastic comedies (featuring a talking horse, a gorgeous genie, cartoon monsters, and a talking car) were the antidote for growing social turmoil in the United States.

The action-packed Western with its outdoors vistas was also a result of a shift of the heart of the television industry from New York to Hollywood and filming facilities. In retrospect, live drama, originating with the talent of Broadway theater, remains an enduring contribution of that age, something that went beyond popular culture into art. Mostly in series identified with important advertisers, such as the Kraft Television Theater, important original dramas were aired.

Paul Newman was one of scores of later film stars who came to us each week in dramatic works that stressed subtle characterizations (effectively communicated through the tight shots typical of studio productions) and classic human problems. "Marty" went on to become a popular Hollywood movie; its author, Paddy Chayevsky, recently commented that what the golden age gave us was "the marvelous world of the ordinary." By the mid-1950s, drama on television was increasingly innovative—writers, technicians and actors had to learn on the job as they put together an incredible amount of new material: One study estimated over 300 original hour-long plays were written and produced for only three weekly series between 1950 and 1955. But they could not overcome the problems of mounting expense and aging studios; the medium turned to film so that a show could be copied and distributed to many stations later for needed additional revenue. Today,

Figure 10.4. "Robert Montgomery Presents" was one of many live television dramatic series that flourished in the mid-1950s.

with the exception of "The Hallmark Hall of Fame," British Broadcasting Corporation (BBC) imports, cable's A & E Network, and limited network specials, quality drama on television is rare.

Program experimentation began to dwindle as network competition heated up. In the late 1950s, Westerns, situation comedies, and crime-detective dramas accounted for over 50 percent of all prime-time programming. Producers seemed to be jumping on various bandwagons, duplicating whatever was popular at the moment.

By the late 1950s, according to the Tenth Annual Videotown Report published by Cunningham & Walsh in 1957, television had become accepted as a routine part of life and had lost much of its novelty and excitement. A public-opinion poll taken in 1959 revealed a sharp drop in the public's estimation of television following scandals over the rigging of popular quiz shows. Congress began a series of investigations that focused particular attention on the relationship among advertisers, agencies, and broadcasters. Much of this concern was strikingly capsulated by FCC chairman Newton Minow in 1961, when he criticized television and called it "a vast wasteland."

The 1950s were a time of experimentation and change for television. By 1960, television was ready to settle down and grow up. The tensions created by these two trends would highlight TV's maturing years.

GROWTH OF TELEVISION'S IMPACT: 1961–1980

Growth and progress were television's two most dominating characteristics in this period. Criticism of television also became popular as politicians, educators, social scientists, members of minority groups, and parents took turns attacking the medium as 90 percent of American homes became equipped with television sets and viewing levels reached 6 hours a day in the average TV household.

Television's impact on the political process became apparent in the 1960s, beginning with the Nixon-Kennedy debates in 1960. The role of television in political campaigns grew tremendously and stimulated concern about packaged candidates and election by commercial slogan.

Violence on television was attacked following the assassinations of President John F. Kennedy, Martin Luther King, Jr., and Robert Kennedy. An overhaul of Saturday-morning cartoon shows occurred in the 1970-1971 season to appease critics, although this area of programming remains heavily criticized. Perhaps the most dramatic and effective action came against the cigarette industry by the surgeon general's office, with its claims that cigarette smoking is dangerous to a person's health. Pressure by the surgeon general resulted in all cigarette advertising being taken off the air on January 2, 1971. A "family hour" was implemented in 1975-1976 in which the first hour of prime-time programming was limited to material suitable for the entire family. The result was a mishmash of weak comedies and variety programs that proved to be poor lead-ins for later programs, and it was phased out in 1976.

Any historical overview of television in the 1960s finds itself overwhelmed by the sheer number of events, people, and issues in the TV spotlight. In this decade, four events stand out: the Vietnam War, the assassination and funeral of President Kennedy, the Civil Rights movement, and the *Apollo 11* moon landing. The American public was able—through television—to witness and participate in these events as they were happening. At times, this witnessing was inspiring, as when television went to the moon. We will look more closely at the impact of television on individuals and society in Part 5.

NEW MEANINGS FOR "ENTERTAINMENT"

Whatever else television was in this period, it was programs. The ABC network broke new ground by showing *The Bridge on the River Kwai* in 1966, and by the 1970s, the networks were engaged in a furious bidding war for recent and successful motion pictures. Situation comedies formed the single strongest genre of the period. "The Beverly Hillbillies" and "The Donna Reed Show" were but two of the good-natured domestic situations that had little relationship to the reality of the turbulent decade.

However, the 1970s witnessed an abrupt and dramatic shift in the situation comedy to more "adult" themes and topics. Over 25 percent of the network's prime-time schedule in 1976-1977—such programs as "Maude," "Soap," "Sanford and Son," "Alice," "Mary Hartman, Mary Hartman," and "Three's Company"—regularly used abortion, premarital sex, narcotics, bigotry, and adultery as comic material. The most dominant sitcom of the period and a classic to rival "I Love Lucy" was "M*A*S*H." Critics and audiences loved the program, which wove the delicate threads of realism and humor into a rich, touching, intelligent, and very funny picture of life in a combat surgical unit during the Korean War. Its black humor, revolving around the futility of patching up soldiers so they could return to the front lines, was something different, but it worked because a war-weary citizenry identified with the characters' recognition of the insanity of it all. When it went off the air 11 seasons later, still popular, 77 percent of those watching television were tuned in.

Satire came to other genres too. The big break with the Sullivan tradition occurred with such programs as "The Smothers Brothers Comedy Hour," "Rowan and Martin's Laugh-In," and "That Was the Week That Was." Not only was the content adult, often satirical and political, but also, especially with "Laugh-In," the style changed dramatically from that of the vaudeville stage to an edited style that emphasized rapid pacing and strong visual appeal.

Finally, the genre evolved in October 1975 into its last (to date) stage with "Saturday Night Live" (SNL). Because of its late-night time period, the success of "Saturday Night Live" was due to its controversial topics as well as to its genuine and occasionally unique talent. The Not Ready for Prime Time Players cast of Dan Aykroyd, Chevy Chase, Bill Murray, Gilda Radner, and John Belushi ultimately became a program unto itself, and all of the actors ultimately left the show to assume star status on their own. Looking back on 15 years of SNL, *Time* said it "was not just another television show; it was the show that changed television . . . [and] burst onto that scene with a countercultural whoop. It brought to TV, for the first time, the comic sensibility of the '60s generation: anti-Establishment, idol-smashing, media savvy."[2]

Prime-time drama became less theater and more television with such programs in the 1960s as "Alfred Hitchcock Presents," "Perry Mason," "The Defenders," "Dr. Kildare," "Peyton Place," and "The Twilight Zone." More realism and adult themes began to appear in such programs as "Lou Grant," starring Ed Asner as the tough managing editor of a newsroom.

Figure 10.5. Originating as a feature film, M*A*S*H gained a wider following by hitting American viewers where they agonized about the Vietnam War—and let them laugh.

The 1980s brought stronger realism in such programs as "Hill Street Blues" and "St. Elsewhere." These entered new realms, both in subject matter and tone, and in the presentation of several plot lines at once. This was an extension of the soap-opera genre; there were also globally popular shows that were unabashed prime-time soaps, with "Dallas" leading the pack.

Not to be outdone by their prime-time counterparts, daytime soap operas assumed major cult status in the late 1970s and early 1980s. Targeted primarily at women, soap operas achieve remarkable viewer loyalty; note the 30-year life span of such programs as "As the World Turns." One of the secrets of the longevity of soaps in a medium where few shows survive a half season lies in their ability to work around the "noise" and distraction of the typical daytime routine. Soap operas can artificially stretch a conversation over several episodes so that a viewer can miss a program because of household or other demands and still catch up easily (of course, the digests of soap plots, available at any newsstand or supermarket, help too).

The major trend in soap operas of the past 5 years has been the "heating-up" of content. Dialogue, situations, and scenes that would have been unthinkable 20 years ago are standard fare. Today the soaps "suggest" very little and "reveal" a great deal—from a man's bare chest to an "active" bedroom scene. Murder, adultery, and rape, while not exactly everyday events, occur with startling regularity and in fairly graphic detail.

Like talk shows on radio, "talk TV" has emerged as a strong form, primarily in syndication during the daytime. "The Phil Donahue Show" is a good example of the standard formula. The key to the success of such programs is the host's manipulation of the relationships among guest, audience, and host. In recent years, competition for late-night talk-show viewers demonstrates a splintering of the audience once held captive by Johnny Carson.

MADE FOR TELEVISION

Two other types of programming require at least passing attention because of their special, almost symbiotic, relationship to television.

Sports. The first is sports—primarily football. Professional football has become the national TV pastime. The Super Bowl stopped being a football game years ago and is a media event in its own right, with all the accompanying ritual.

It's hard to believe, but in 1936, CBS was actually paid $500 by the Orange Bowl Committee to air the game on radio. By 1965, the rights to that game, televised by NBC for the first time, cost $300,000. In 1972, ABC won rights to the Olympics for $13.5 million, a price doubled by the next Olympic Games. In 1989, a new record for NFL games was set at $3.6 billion, with NBC, CBS, ESPN, ABC, and Turner Entertainment Television involved. Each team made about $32 million before a seat was sold. In the early 1990s, the bidding war continued. With CBS having locked up several sports, NBC bought 4 years of NBA basketball for $600 million, or $62,500 per minute of play.

Although there are elements of risk, sports has the best chance to "boost a network's cachet, shore up ratings, please affiliates, entice advertisers and allow heavy promotion of primetime shows. 'In an uncertain world, it's about as certain as you can get,' says Robert Wussler, a former president of CBS Sports."[3]

Neal H. Pilson, currently president of CBS Sports, put it this way:

> *Increased competition has forced CBS to re-examine what we feel makes network television unique and determine how we can best serve a changing audience. Network television remains the only system that can deliver programming simultaneously to all 92.1 million television homes in the United States. EPSN, the largest*

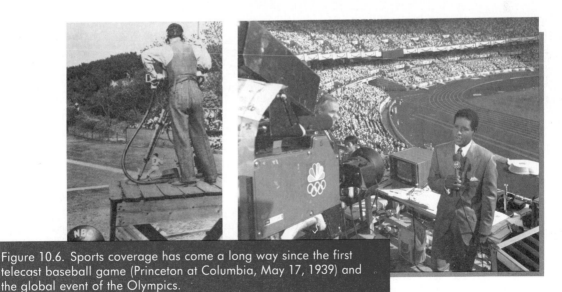

Figure 10.6. Sports coverage has come a long way since the first telecast baseball game (Princeton at Columbia, May 17, 1939) and the global event of the Olympics.

cable service, reaches only 55 million. It is therefore far more economical for the networks to reach all of the television homes with one event than it is for cable services to distribute two, three, or four events at one time.

As a result, I think the networks will be concentrating on marketing national games to the widest possible audience. It is our strongest suit. . . .[4]

News. Network news on television began in 1948 with a 15-minute program on CBS, "Douglas Edwards with the News." This program length remained the standard until 1963, when all three networks expanded to a 30-minute newscast. Along with the increased time devoted to it, news grew in prestige and as a source of revenue. A star system soon developed in network news, led by the anchors for the network-news evening program. Walter Cronkite of CBS became the dominant broadcast journalist of the 1970s.

On the local level, the commercial success of news programs led to a show-business style aptly dubbed "happy talk." Everywhere, news became choreographed and packaged, like any other entertainment program, much to the chagrin of critics and journalists. In 1968, CBS News tried an experiment. During the 1950s and 1960s, the most respected of network news departments had produced its share of award-winning prime-time documentaries. Yet these attracted small audiences and failed to contribute to the network's profitability. The 30- or 60-minute programs were typically devoted exclusively to one topic and relied on one correspondent or reporter to appear on camera. The 1968 experiment changed this tradition. A new program, one hour in length, was devoted not to one topic but to at least four stories, some features, some interviews, some investigative pieces—which relied on a new use of "remotes," and even some hard news. It was "60 Minutes," which became one of the most watched and imitated shows on television. But success did not come easily, or quickly. In the 1970–1971 television season, its third on the air, "60 Minutes" ranked 101 in the network prime-time ratings. Changes were ordered.

The on-air reporters, at the time, including Mike Wallace and Dan Rather, were promoted more as personalities. The pacing of the show was quickened, with most stories limited to 10 minutes. Producers skillfully developed the stories to have dramatic impact and leave little doubt about the evil or wrongdoing being reported. And importantly, the program was eventually, in 1976, given a permanent time slot of its own on Sunday evening, immediately following NFL football.

By the 1975–1976 season, "60 Minutes" was rated 52 among network programs. And by November of 1978, it had climbed to first place, at least for one week. The program had hit on a format and a formula. The *types* of stories and *lengths* of stories were predictable from week to week. "60 Minutes" had the components of good theater—characters, drama, plot, suspense, and resolution. As a result, "60 Minutes" moved from also-ran to top-ten program.

Imitators were not far behind. A notable example of news as entertainment is "Prime Time Live," highly hyped, which debuted with a live studio audience, a "video wall" for location shots to be shown to that audience, town debates, interviews with an unpredictable roster of rock stars, world leaders, serious coverage, humor, and conversation between the star hosts. Although it later became more like the established "20/20," "48 Hours," and "60 Minutes," it was still packaged to intrigue and divert. Elsewhere, attempts at re-creations of news events were actually created by network *entertainment* divisions. The idea, said NBC executive producer Sid Feders, is to tell "people stories." In more than one case, the "simulation" format was dropped, reportedly because it confused viewers; adverse feedback and the question of ethics played a part.

A steadier, if more modest approach to news that amuses is the local TV news program. For decades, the managers of local television stations considered their local newscasts a public-service responsibility. Some high-rated local newscasts earned profits for their owners, but most didn't. And management didn't seem to care. After all, newscasts were viewed as something you did to maintain credibility in your community and to impress the Federal Communications Commission.

This scenario changed dramatically in the mid-1970s. Prompted by a few large national-news consulting firms, the general managers of local stations began to view their newscasts as profit centers. Quite suddenly, previously sleepy news departments found themselves with new equipment, additional staff members, more news time, and a station management paying close attention to the ratings.

Controversies over cheapening the newscasts and pandering to the audience developed around the country as stations selected new anchors more for their appearance than their journalistic talent and selected stories more for viewer interest than for journalistic merits. The consultants advised their client stations on

Figure 10.7. Journalists Sam Donaldson and Diane Sawyer became highly paid and highly publicized stars with the debut of "Prime Time Live."

such traditionally entertainment aspects as hairstyles and wardrobes for news "talent," humorous news stories and quips to be exchanged between anchors, weather forecasters with distinct personalities, theme music and titles, and the appearance of the studio.

How successful were these efforts? Although there was considerable evidence that such changes in newscast format could lead to larger viewing audiences, it appeared that audiences initially attracted by these changes needed to be satisfied with the information conveyed by the newscasters to remain loyal to the station. Nevertheless, ever since the mid-1970s, local television news has been at least a hybrid of information and entertainment.

The technical requirements and opportunities of television have affected the news messages we receive. Images rule the airways. The total verbal content of a typical evening-news program would not fill a newspaper page. And the increasing sophistication of viewers require ever-livelier "sound bites," or nuggets of journalism. Talking heads won't do. Since the media consumer cannot scan or flip a "page" of television news, the show must always move along to avoid the dreaded channel changing. As *New York Times* critic Walter Goodman remarked, "All journalism is part entertainment; the problem for television journalists is to keep that aspect of their profession from taking command."[5]

The author of a book chronicling the recent history of CBS News, Peter Boyer, wrote for the *New York Times* op-ed page:

> *With the arrival of Loews at CBS, Capital Cities at ABC and General Electric at NBC, there emerged the proposition that news was, after all, a business like any other, and as such could reasonably be expected to pay for itself.*

Figure 10.8. "Speaking of what qualifies him to be a network anchor, [Peter Jennings of ABC] will say that, to him, his journalistic credentials are all that count. He'll also say, 'Anybody who pretends they've got here on that—minus the cosmetic features—is kidding themselves.'

"And sometimes he'll think how ironic it is that his reward for establishing himself as more than a face and a voice is a job that makes so much of both."
—Elizabeth Kaye, "Peter Jennings Gets No Self-Respect," *Esquire,* September 1989, 160.

It was a facile, compelling premise that neatly voided a key component of network television's unarticulated charter, which held that news is a public service partly paid for by profits from entertainment shows.

The consequences of so fundamental a shift were huge and inevitable. Imagine the effect upon a newspaper if it were suddenly decreed that the news section had to operate profitably on its own, apart from the revenues generated by the more commercial sections of the paper, such as sports, comics and entertainment news.[6]

It was the costs of network news programs, which involve huge centers of interacting equipment and personnel, which eventually caused the competing networks to cut back, to depend more on local feeds, and to encourage the news divisions to develop prime-time entertainment-oriented formats. The trend toward minimizing the costs of newsgathering was blamed for many of the problems the networks had in getting prompt, smoothly delivered coverage of the San Francisco earthquake in 1989 and other fast-breaking stories.

Meanwhile, local stations have been finding that their straight-news programs can with proper management be profitable with as little as 4 percent of households watching. As part of the changing relationship between networks and affiliates, which we will turn to shortly, individual stations are currently exploring other sources of news content, such as CNN, news services, and syndicators, and dictating their independence from the traditional network news.

THE STRUCTURE AND ORGANIZATION OF NETWORK TELEVISION . . . .

Television's basic function is programming, and the ways programs are produced, distributed, and exhibited are the basis for the organization of the TV industry. In terms of these functions, it is an industry in turmoil.

Program production is traditionally the responsibility of networks, stations, and program-production companies. Distribution is the critical function of the networks, using the ground facilities of AT&T and satellite transmission. The exhibition of programs is the primary role of local stations.

THE NETWORKS

The networks are organized much like stations into four main areas: programming, sales, engineering, and administration. Within each of these major divisions are many units, such as news and sports, each with a separate administrative structure. At CBS, for example, the CBS/Broadcast Group has six major divisions: CBS Radio, CBS Television Stations, CBS News, CBS Television Network, CBS Entertainment, and CBS Sports. Within the CBS Radio Division, there are 15 discrete units, among them Engineering, Program Practices, and Network Sales.

Networks exist only to the extent that they provide a service to stations through an affiliation contract. This contract sets the terms by which the network pays the station for the right to use the station's time to program its offerings. Stations, in effect, *clear* time from their own schedules and sell it to the networks for a price based on the individual station's local rate for one hour. Rates range from $10,000 an hour at the network-owned-and-operated (O&Os) stations in New York City to under $100 at stations in small markets.

The key function of the TV networks is to provide their 700 affiliated stations with programming that will be viewed by a large aggregate audience. The network makes its money by selling this aggregate audience (measured by ratings) to advertisers. Without broadly successful programs, the networks would not survive. The networks get most of their programming from the major Hollywood studios (70%) and independents (14%). For an annual program season, more than 30 separate production companies had been preparing programs for the networks, which spend in excess of $1 billion a year for the right to broadcast the programs. This is changing, however. Small independents cannot compete with the majors, and a number of syndicators and cable companies, on their own or in combination with networks, have become more active as producers (also, in a join-'em-if-you-can't-beat-'em attitude, networks are cooperating in joint programming ventures). Commenting on an ABC/NBC cooperative effort, Brandon Stoddard, head of ABC Productions, said it was one of the signs of "a movement away from the network system as we have traditionally known it—a distribution system for programs provided by the studios . . . what you are going to see happen in the next five to seven years is a movement toward a kind of network studio system."[7]

Certainly Hollywood studios have been a leading source of programming for some time; Universal, Warner, and others have produced shows for every network and have specialized in the made-for-TV films and miniseries that were prime fare until they outdid themselves. They are, however, only one segment of the 200 companies that display new shows for the thousands of local station executives that flock to the industry's annual convention. It is not only the end users, consumers like us, who are inundated by media offerings.

In the 1970s the networks had a 90 percent share of TV viewers; in the 1990s, they can count on considerably less than 70 percent. To keep stations happy, networks these days must be highly innovative and forge new relationships; an example is NBC working with Cablevision to create local cable-news outlets for network O&Os and NBC affiliates. Summing up the trend, *The Wall Street Journal* announced "Broadcasters, Cable Enter 'Era of Blur.'"

To strengthen their financial position, the networks are seeking a change in some basic FCC regulations. The FCC set up strict rules to prevent networks (it defines a network as an entity broadcasting 15 hours of programming weekly on at least 25 stations in at least 10 states) from wielding too much power. To prevent a monopoly, networks could not have financial interest in programs from other production companies and could not themselves syndicate programs they produce. With the entry of so many competing players, many of them vertically integrated and thus possessing widespread media influence, and with the reduced dominance of networks in share of audience, a call for a change in the rules was heard early in 1990. The major networks, along with Fox, which had an eye on establishing its role as the fourth network, felt they would not be able to compete with the proliferating media companies, especially those outside the United States.

To win viewers in a fragmented marketplace, major networks are taking a page from the cable channels and taking aim at targets. For networks, including newcomer Fox, the filter of audience expectations remains crucial. Cable may cater to specialized tastes, with offerings from nightclub comics or serious drama on the Arts & Entertainment Network, which startled those more familiar with television catering to short attention spans. On the major networks, successful shows innovate by building on existing formats. Fox Network's introduction of *The Tracey*

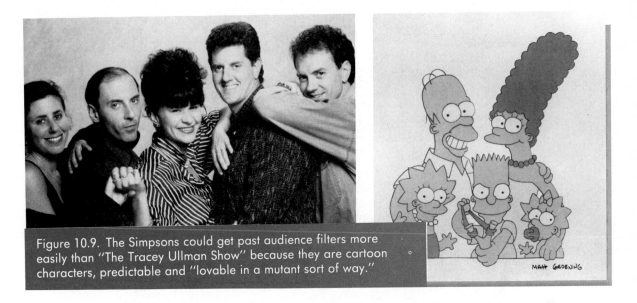

Figure 10.9. The Simpsons could get past audience filters more easily than "The Tracey Ullman Show" because they are cartoon characters, predictable and "lovable in a mutant sort of way."

Ullman Show was not met with high ratings, some felt, because it lacked a reliable core of one central character and situation, which mass media audiences have come to rely on. The comedienne's unpredictable repertoire was unique. One segment of her show, a cartoon sitcom about the Simpson family, spun off into its own series and became an instant mass-media and merchandising success. More of the public "got" that unusual series because of its predictable characters.

THE STATIONS

The actual broadcasting, or airing, of programs is done by local stations. The schedule of the local network-affiliated station generally consists of 65 percent network shows, 25 to 30 percent syndicated programs, and 5 to 10 percent locally produced shows. The syndicated programs are dominated by feature-movie packages, old network series, game shows, and talk shows. Locally produced programming consists primarily of the six o'clock and eleven o'clock news, and noon and morning talk shows.

The local station's role, then, is primarily as an exhibitor of programs created by someone else. Administrative personnel of a station seldom preview the episodes of a series before they are aired, and in effect, stations have little control over many of the programs that they telecast. Despite this fact, the station is held legally accountable for the content.

In a typical commercial TV station, there are four primary activities: programming, sales, engineering, and management. (The organization of a noncommercial station is the same, except for the replacement of a sales operation by an underwriting and grants operation.) Programming incorporates the greatest diversity of any of the units because it includes on-air personalities, writers, producers, directors, and editors, among others. In a small station, one person may constitute a whole sales department or may handle programming in addition to sales. Engineering involves all personnel used to run cameras, slides, and film projectors,

Figure 10.10. The media have always provided subject matter for entertainment. The popular TV series "Murphy Brown" includes inserts of references to latest news in its depiction of life in a TV newsroom.

as well as those used to maintain technical engineering standards. The typical television station employs 70 people. Of its operating budget, 35 percent is spent on administration; 25 percent, on programming and production; 14 percent, on sales; 12 percent, on engineering; 12 percent, on news; and 5 percent, on advertising and promotion.

Unlike radio stations, all TV stations are classified as local outlets. As local outlets, they can be typed according to several classifications: type of frequency (see page 252), market size, and network affiliation.

Market size is vital in TV broadcasting. National advertisers buy time on stations according to market size; stations in major markets get most of the national advertising dollar, while stations in small markets must depend heavily on local advertising. In order to be consistent about the meaning of market size, advertisers use the Arbitron Area of Dominant Influence (ADI). The ADI concept divides the country into 209 markets, each made up of the counties that cluster around the signal of a particular TV station. Generally, there are three basic market-size groups: (1) major, the 100 largest ADIs in the country; (2) secondary, ADIs with populations ranging from 50,000 to 125,000; (3) small, ADIs with less than 50,000 population.

The other important basis for TV-station classification is whether the station is independent or network affiliated. While many TV stations want network affiliation because networks are capable of providing popular types of programs and therefore of attracting a large audience, the number of independent stations has grown significantly—from 73 in 1972 to 230 in 1985 to 401 in 1990. And because of changes in marketing and programming, even long-established independents have experienced increases in ratings. In 35 large markets surveyed by Nielsen, the independents' share of the 24-hour viewing audience has increased from 17 to 22 percent since 1972, while the network share has dropped to 56 percent.

THE SKIRMISHES FOR INDEPENDENCE

The independents have made their headway in the face of an economic mismatch. Networks have the money to underwrite programs. Independents have to shop for every program and then shell out money for the rights. Network affiliates have "availabilities"—commercial slots—that are presold to advertisers. Independents must go out and hustle to fill their accounts. And the 85 percent of independent stations that broadcast on the weaker UHF frequencies suffer the additional disadvantage of lesser audience reach.

Given these problems, how did the independents manage to build up as much combined audience share as a network? Part of the answer is that they specialize. Many independents with specialized formats also emphasize local flavor.

Meanwhile, independents are relying less and less on off-network reruns and movies. Cheap satellite transmission offers an unprecedented variety of material, while serious and costly efforts by independents to create original programming have won over advertisers as well as viewers.

Channels magazine editors have been closely watching the trend away from network dominance, and the intensification of syndication, and predict that the future of local television lies *with* local television:

> [S]tations continue to choke down escalating prices and barter demands by syndicators, especially for choice first-run and off-network half hours. Then there's the indignity of being forced to swallow less desirable programming—or early renewal on an existing show—in exchange for a hot strip. It's called "packaging." It's also illegal. But tell that to a station just dying for that one hit to put it over the top in access. . . .
>
> Surviving, much less prospering, is no sure thing, but stations that work more for themselves and less for national syndicators will be the innovators of the '90s.[8]

Even the affiliates are making new rules. For decades the four time blocks of programming were all but sacred: prime time (8:00–11:00 P.M. EST, dominated by major networks and the entertainment genres we are all familiar with); weekday daytime (7:00 A.M.–5:00 P.M., Monday to Friday, taken up with game shows, soaps, reruns, and news–talk shows; weekend daytime (children's programs, sports, films, and public affairs in the "dead zone" of Sunday morning); fringe time (5:00–8:00 P.M. and 11:00 P.M.–1:00 A.M., consisting of network and local news, talk shows, movies, syndicated programs). Fringe time was the first to acquire new meaning; as the demand for TV time by advertisers increased, this block became more important to the networks. But each of the above has begun to be modified by local stations. Channel 4, NBC's New York City station, began in 1989 to schedule soaps earlier and shift game shows to lead into local news, hoping to increase ratings. Across the country, NBC affiliates have been pressing the network to start weekday prime time at 7:00 P.M. since for many of them 11:00 P.M. represents "the good-night hour" and they need an earlier start on revenue. The late 1980s were also marked by affiliates' increasingly loud protests in specific programming areas, from dismay at their network's coverage of fast-breaking news to criticism of morning-talk-show talent.

The Age of Cable: Television Since 1980 ....

Television today must come to grips with its past and confront new technologies that threaten the basic structure of the industry. In 1985, James Rosenfield of CBS saw that television was facing its fourth major trial—the "trial of technology." Indicating that television had survived three previous trials—acceptance as a medium, cultural integration, and maturity—he expressed deep concern about what he called "unregulated competitors" for the TV audience.

The recent major changes in television have not been in programming but in the manner programming is distributed to and received by the American public. The technological developments of the 1960s and 1970s, together with broadcast-industry deregulation, have spawned a new era in program-delivery systems that involve satellites, cable television, and videocassette players.

Various ramifications of the rise in VCR use on motion pictures, the industry it has greatly affected, will be discussed in Chapter 13. The major impacts of videocassette recorders on television are the ability to record a program for viewing on demand, often without commercials, thanks to zapping or fast-forwarding, and the inexpensive film rentals, another source of competition for consumer attention.

Any summary of television must include the tumultuous events of 1985 and 1986, which saw the greatest economic restructuring of the broadcast industry since the early 1950s.

The deregulation of the industry by the Federal Communications Commission, the growing realization that broadcast properties were more valuable than the stock market recognized, and the emerging specter of hostile bids from corporate suitors—all converged to turn 1985 into a time of takeovers.

In February, Taft Broadcasting Company purchased six TV stations and eight radio stations from Gulf Broadcasting Company for $755 million.

In March, Capital Cities Communications bought the American Broadcasting Company for $3.5 billion—at the time, the largest merger in the United States outside the oil industry and the first time in more than 30 years that a television network had been sold.

In April, cable-television entrepreneur Ted Turner filed a plan with the Securities and Exchange Commission to purchase two-thirds of CBS, Inc., using "junk bonds"—high-interest, high-risk debt—as well as stock in his Turner Broadcasting System Company.

In May, Australian media mogul Rupert Murdoch, along with oilman partner Marvin Davis, bought Metromedia's seven television stations, making him the nation's largest independent television broadcaster.

Meanwhile, the Tribune Company, owner of television stations in New York City and Chicago, paid a record $510 million for KTLA in Los Angeles—making Tribune the most potent rival to Metromedia, renamed Fox Broadcasting.

And finally, in the biggest merger of the year, General Electric acquired RCA and its NBC-TV network.

What is occurring today is the simultaneous activity of programming, new technologies, and regulatory actions, creating an unpredictable marketplace. As Gene Jankowski of CBS remarked:

A good symbol for this new order might be the "double helix"—the famous model of the DNA molecule. It looks like a spiral staircase without the steps. We still have discrete industry segments—stations, networks, production companies, agencies, clients and so on at the core, but the functional elements of our business no longer relate themselves to these segments in the traditional manner.[9]

SATELLITES

When the Communications Satellite Act was passed in 1962, the United States officially got into international television. The first satellites, *Telstar* and *Relay*, were launched in 1963 and provided intercontinental coverage of the funerals of Pope John XXIII and President Kennedy, among other events. In 1965, the first commercial satellite, *Early Bird*, was launched by COMSAT. By 1969, satellite usage had increased, much of it for coverage of the Vietnam War via *Lanai Bird*, the Pacific counterpart of *Early Bird*. By 1971, a full-scale international communication system existed, with three synchronous satellites in fixed positions over the Atlantic, Pacific, and Indian oceans, as well as a large network of earth stations.

The United States began domestic satellite transmission in 1973 when RCA leased time on Canada's *ANIK II* to relay signals between the East and West coasts. In 1974, ABC Radio began transmitting service to its four radio networks via satellite.

As network distribution costs via AT&T land-based long lines increased steadily in the 1970s, the use of domestic satellites increased as well. In 1976, KPLR-TV in St. Louis was granted an FCC license for a satellite receiver, and other stations soon followed suit. In 1977, the Public Broadcasting Service (PBS) began construction of a satellite-interconnect system that eventually would provide direct satellite-to-earth distribution for all PBS television stations and National Public Radio (NPR) radio stations. By the early 1980s, satellite distribution of programs was being used by a wide variety of networks, production companies, and even local stations.

These satellites are a far cry from the tiny *Telstar*: Bristling with antennas and packed with electronics, they are relaying cable-television programs, digital data, and voice traffic to more than 1 million earth stations via 252 channels. Local television stations in the United States have equipped themselves with satellite-transmitting dishes mounted on trucks, with which they relay remote news feeds to their studios.

The current and coming state of the art will be explored in Chapter 25, which deals with the new technology of mass media. Here we will simply point out that with each new development comes an impact on other forms of communication. Satellites compete directly with AT&T's ground networks and, in the case of direct transmission to individual receivers, with local stations and cable systems. The economic consequences of direct satellite-to-home (or to-business, as described in Chapter 18) transmission, especially, are great. Nevertheless, the potential for expanded program service at a reduced cost makes the risk worthwhile.

CABLE TELEVISION

Cable television (CATV, Community Antenna Television) has made even more dramatic strides than the use of satellites. In 1960, there were 640 basic cable systems in the United States with a total of 650,000 subscribers. By 1970, cable had grown to almost 2,500 systems and 1.3 million subscribers. In 1986, over 6,500 systems were serving more than 41 million TV households (47.4 percent penetration). Today it is closer to 10,000, with cable reaching 57 percent of the population. Some analysts predict there will be a gradual consolidation of the smaller systems, but this might well mean greater strength in fewer numbers. As it is, about one-third of the systems originate programming in their own studios, at an average of 25 hours weekly. A subscriber on average devotes more than one-third the total viewing hours to cable. Advertisers are responding, directing $1.8 billion toward cable time in 1989; *Advertising Age* predicts this figure will be $4 billion by 1995. In turn, the cable industry is reacting by offering (through Cablevision Advertising Bureau or Group W's rep firm) assistance to advertisers as they plan expenditures. The use of people meters is a boon here, allowing measurement of cable viewing on a par with that of broadcast. Cable has developed a programming life of its own by augmenting its local-station service with distant-signal imports (such as Atlanta's WTBS-TV), local origination programs, and special services (such as Home Box Office [HBO]). With FCC deregulation of cable in the early 1980s, cable is now free to compete in the open marketplace. Growth in cable penetration and programming (see Figure 10.11) has been adding subscribers to the industry roll at a rate of 250,000 per month. Experts believe cable will level off in the middle of the decade.

THE ECONOMICS OF THE AGE OF CABLE

Cable operators are building supersystems in the new markets. The first was Ted Turner's WTBS. Many will offer 50 channels, and some more than 100. The cable operators are also upgrading existing cable systems and expanding channel capacity to 20 or more channels to increase services and revenue and to make the systems less vulnerable to competition.

The widespread introduction of satellite-delivered pay television revolutionized the industry in the latter half of the 1970s, providing an enormous leap in revenue without significant additional capital investment. Multipay, the selling of two or more pay services to the same home, has proved viable and is counted on to fuel the construction and operation of the high-capacity urban systems. Pay-per-view pay television (PPV) and advertising are regarded as the most immediate sources of additional revenue. And the so-called two-way services—videotex, security, teleshopping, telebanking—although slow in developing, promise new revenue for the future.

Cable has become the medium of choice. Operators (and, ultimately, subscribers) have a panoply of programs to choose from, all delivered conveniently to their backyards by satellites. In 1975, RCA's *SATCOM I* satellite was sent into space, enabling HBO and, later, two smaller rivals, Showtime and the Movie Channel, to transmit movies to local cable systems. Since then, and with the growing presence of VCRs, the living room has rapidly been supplementing the theater as an arena for watching motion pictures.

Programming on pay cable typically includes first-run motion pictures and sports events. A greater variety is emerging, however, including X- and R-rated films on "adult cable" and cultural programs provided primarily by the BBC over cable rather than through its traditional American outlet, the PBS stations. Prices for pay TV vary according to the system.

Over-the-air pay-TV, or subscription television (STV), has had mixed success in recent years. As a result of FCC deregulation in 1977, STV finally got off the

▰ Channel directory ▰

CABLE GUIDE	Port Chester	Y'ktown Putnam	Bedford Mt. Kisco	Yonkers	Comm-Unity Cable	Oss	Peek	C-Tec	Para-gon	U.A. Col-umbia	U.S. Cable
BROADCAST TELEVISION											
WCBS (New York City)	2	2	2	2	2	2	2	2	2	2	2
WNBC (New York City)	4	4	4	4	4	4	4	4	4	4	4
WNYW (New York City)	5	5	5	5	5	5	5	5	5	5	5
WABC (New York City)	7	7	7	7	7	7	7	7	7	7	7
WWOR (Secaucus, N.J.)	9	9	9	9	9	9	9	9	9	9	9
WPIX (New York City)	11	11	11	11	11	11	11	11	11	11	11
WNET (Newark)	13	13	13	13	13	13	13	13	13	13	13
WTXX (Waterbury)					20			10			
WLIW (Garden City)	21	21		21		21	21		32/S	21	
WNYE (New York City)	25					24					
WNYC (New York City)	25	31	31		10	24	18		20/G	23	
WXTV (Paterson, N.J.)	41	32	33	57		39	39		34/U	37	30
WNJU (Newark)	47		-58			30	19		34/U	12	
WEDW (Bridgeport)	49	33		58				12	33/T		
WTZA (Kingston, N.Y.)											8
BASIC CABLE CHANNELS											
A&E (Arts & Entertainment)	16	16	16	16	28	3	14	36	14A	20	22
BET (Black Entertainment TV)								18	31/R		
CBN (CBN Family Channel)	26	26	26	26	36	32	32		24/K	3	34
CNBC (Consumer News Channel)	24		21	24						30	
CNN (Cable News Network)	8	8	8	8	23	22	22	28	6	10	10
CVN (Cable Value Network)						23	23	22	25/L	27	26
ESPN (Ent/Sports Network)	15	3	3	15	26	8	8	8	8	6	3
FNN (Financial News Network)	19	30	30	33	37	29	29	19	10	30	33
LIFE (Lifetime)	23	19	19	23	33	36	36	27	12	15	23
MSG (Madison Square Garden)	3	15	30	30	47	12	12	40	10	12	32
MTV (Music Television)	29	29	29	29	25	35	35	34	30	32	19
NASH (Nashville Network)	18			18	30		24	39		1	35
NICK (Nickelodeon)	22	18	18	22	27	17	17	29	29/P	18	31
SPAN (Cbl. Sat'lite Pub. Affairs)	40	6	6	30	16	40	40	26	23/J	28/34	
TDC (Discovery Channel)	30	10	10	10	34	31	31	21	15/B		28
TNT (Turner Network TV)	44	20	20	20	19			15		29	
USA (USA Cable Network)	17	17	17	17	24	33	33	32	3	31	17
VHI (Video Hits One)	28	28	28	28	32	37	37	33	16/C	33	6
WGN (Chicago Superstation)	20	20	20		22	25	25	37			
WSBK (Boston Superstation)										25	
WTBS (Turner Broadcasting)	27	27	27	27	17	10	10	35	18/E	17	
PAY-TV CHANNELS											
AMC (American Movie Classics)	32	38	14	32	42						
BRAV (Bravo)	33	39	35	33	43	18	18	47	27	23	
DIS (Disney Channel)	31	22	22	31	40	20	20	52	28/O	40	25
HBO (Home Box Office)	6	23	23	6	38	14	3	43	17/D	14	5
MAX (Cinemax)	35	24	24	35	39	19	16	48	26/M	38	21
PLAY (Playboy)	37	14		37	45	29	29	49			
PPV (Pay Per View)	24	15	15	38	46	60	60	42		22	
SC (SportsChannel)	10	6	6	3	44	28	28	50	20/G	24	18
SCA (SportsChannel America)	12	12	32	12		38	38	51	19/F	33	33
SHO (Showtime)	36	37	60	36	41	16	61	41	21/H	39	24
TMC (The Movie Channel)	34	25	25	34		61	30	45	16		
Cooper Wireless (SelecTV)	Satellite dish required										

Figure 10.11.

ground with two stations, one in Los Angeles and one in New York. By the early 1980s, more than 25 stations were operating, all located in large urban areas. Programming on STV is similar to that on cable, but because STV can offer only one channel to a subscriber (versus the tiered service possibilities of cable), many feel that its future is limited to areas that do not have cable. Indeed, by mid-1983, STV subscribership had slipped from a high of 1.4 million to 1.1 million. The Entertainment Channel, a pay-TV network created by RCA, folded in 1983 after only 9 months of operation and more than $80 million in losses. The problems of STV merely underscore the challenges facing other pay-TV delivery systems, such as multipoint-distribution services (MDS) and direct broadcast satellite (DBS). The formula for success in pay-television is no longer simply offering people the latest *Star Wars* or *Indiana Jones* blockbuster. Pay-cable services will need to offer viewers more variety and choice in order to compete.

Many factors cloud the future of cable, the most important being financial. While cable's rapid expansion into a $7-billion industry has secured a foothold in TV's future, the growth has strained resources on every level.

Until stricter regulation is in place (a bill to limit rates was before Congress as this book went to press), there is great potential for cross ownership in the cable industry; one company can own several systems, and cable operators can form cable networks. To look again (see Chapter 3) at Tele-Communications, a major multiple-system operator, TCI owns part of Discovery Channel, Black Entertainment Television, and American Movie Classics. There is obviously an interest in vertical integration as well as generating programming for the channels and having a bigger piece of the pie. The dimensions of the competition are clear: There are over 150 sitcoms running on cable; the break-even point for cable networks is about 30 million homes; the end user is offered more and more choices, with finite amounts of time and money.

Equally finite are the number of fixed, readily accessible positions on the cable converter box. Juxtapose this with the approach of Sky Cable's direct sending of 105 channels into the home. And then look at the telephone companies who are trying to get into the act; they are working to have regulations changed and to forge connections with broadcast and cable groups with an eye to possible partnerships in television. Former CBS executive Gene Mater feels the next few years could bring a new scenario to the industry:

> *It remains uncertain whether the telcos will simply be competitors of cable or the television networks of the future. If negotiated properly, the telcos could conceivably co-opt all the other players. The networks would handle national and international news, national sales and some programming. Stations would focus on local news and advertising. The cable folks would provide the expertise in packaging and deal with the viewer at home, while continuing to serve as the cable programming conduit. And the telcos would be the distribution arm for one and all with nothing going out over the air.*[10]

The key is the fiber-optics system, discussed in Chapter 25.

Meanwhile, production costs of original cable programming have risen, and local cable operators are squeezed between programmers who are demanding higher prices for their product and subscribers who are demanding more service for the same fee. Most of the problems have originated with cable's high hopes for itself. To support the promise of something for everybody, many companies promoted market projections to unrealistic levels.

For all the dramatic growth, cable is an industry for the long haul. It took ESPN (originally Entertainment and Sports Programming Network) 10 years to become the largest cable system in the United States. Eighty percent owned by Capital Cities/ABC, it now has an estimated worth of $1 billion, reaches about 58 percent of TV households, and showed a $1 million profit in 1989; it did not break even until 1985, after losing more than $100 million from 1979 to 1984. Financial analysts recommend many cable stocks but caution that a close look has to be given their acquisitions as well as the future likelihood of continued growth in programming.

THE PUBLIC BROADCASTING SERVICE

After languishing for over a decade, educational television (ETV) began to flex its muscles in the 1960s. The pivotal event in ETV's growth was the passage of the Public Broadcasting Act of 1967. In effect, it provided for the first interconnected network of ETV stations. Most important, it provided educational television with the financial support necessary to become a creative force in American life.

The act established the Corporation for Public Broadcasting (CPB), which, in turn, established the Public Broadcasting Service (PBS) in 1970. After a lengthy and damaging struggle between CPB and PBS for control of the system, PBS emerged in 1973 as the creative controller of the system, with CPB continuing its role as program funder. PBS manages TV programming, production, distribution, and station interconnection, which is primarily by satellite. The most important single programming development during the early years of the PBS system was the creation of the Children's Television Workshop (CTV), producer of "Sesame Street" and "Electric Company," among other programs. An independent non-profit corporation, CTV's only ties to public broadcasting are partial funding by CPB.

Another important programming source is the British Broadcasting Corporation, which has supplied such series as "Civilization" and "Upstairs, Downstairs." In 1980, however, the BBC entered into a 10-year agreement to sell its programs in the United States to a cable network, threatening one of PBS's best sources of prestige programming. By 1989, it could be reported that public TV once "had a lock on all the fare in short supply on commercial television. Cable has not only broken the lock, but stolen plenty of the merchandise."[11] Examples: Arts & Entertainment Network got first dibs on BBC drama, arts, music, and entertainment; Turner Broadcasting could offer the BBC $3.3 million, more than twice the amount

Table 10.2. Public Television Income		
Source	Dollars in Millions	Percentage of Total
FEDERAL GOVERNMENT	$186.4	18.1%
CPB (TV only)	147.6	14.3
Education & Commerce Depts.	38.8	3.8
(NEA, NEH, etc.)		
NONFEDERAL	$843.7	81.9%
Subscribers	222.0	21.5
State Govts.	196.9	19.1
Businesses	160.4	15.6
State Colleges	68.1	6.6
Foundations	41.7	4.1
Local Governments	33.5	3.3
Private Colleges	23.0	2.2
Auctions	22.5	2.2
Other Public Colleges	9.3	0.9
All Others	66.3	6.4
TOTAL	$1,030.1	100.0%

Source: Facts About PBS, August 1988, 7.

public-television funding could provide, for David Attenborough's science series, "Life on Earth."

Financing is at the heart of public broadcasting's future role. Throughout the Nixon administration, there was controversy resulting primarily from CPB's increasing development of public-affairs programming, including several controversial programs and series. Legislation passed under President Ford provided for a federal matching plan and 5-year financing. This $634 million bill became law in 1976 and ensured public broadcasting of a relatively stable financial base for the first time in its history. An analysis of all income for public television for FY87, as estimated by the Corporation for Public Broadcasting (CPB), is given in Table 10.2. The data show that viewing members, organized through the approximately 330 local PBS stations, are now vital to the continuing existence of public-television programming. It must fight for its share of the market, just as the networks do. To win, it may well have to become more active in generating alternative programming that is *not* the natural fare of cable.

THE ROLE OF TELEVISION

The medium is the costliest of the electronic media because of the demand placed on it by the 18-hour daily schedule of most stations. But since only television among the advertising media has sight, sound, motion, and color, it is the most dynamic sales tool available. The appeal of television accounts for the fact that it costs advertisers an average of $150,000 for 30 seconds to advertise on network prime-time television.

With virtually the entire population having access to television 18 hours a day, 365 days a year, television is the mass medium for reaching most of the people most of the time. Because of this, it has less flexibility than we may realize. It is a large, complex *business*. While it can and does provide instant coverage of many important national and international events, the majority of TV time is taken up with programs and schedules that have been researched, marketed, and put together a year or two in advance.

Television has a number of primary social roles, two of which stand out. It has been observed that television's most common role is one of many windows through which we observe, transmit, and reflect society to one another. But television has been criticized strongly for assuming this primarily passive role. Too often, critics say, television is simply a conduit, neutral to a fault and rarely engaging and challenging its audiences. Television has another role, however, and on occasion plays it. Despite its essentially passive nature, television, at times, does act in its own right and uses its power of communication not merely to convey other people's images but also to make its own statement. Many people feel that the TV coverage of the assassination and funeral of President Kennedy and of the *Apollo 11* moon landing were times when television did create genuine statements, perhaps not so much because of its particular design or structure but merely because of its ability to record the event as it was happening.

The future of television seems to rest in the ability of audiences to control and use it for their own purposes. The technological revolution will have a major impact on traditional broadcasting. Broadcasting as we have traditionally defined it is being partly replaced with *narrow*casting, in which producers will send out messages to small clusters of demographically linked groups, who, in turn, will manipulate and "massage" the content for their own purposes. The television marketplace is in transition. The new technologies offer many opportunities for producers and consumers alike. Les Brown, as editor-in-chief of *Channels*, made an observation that is still valid:

> *In the end the revolution may not be technological in nature but cultural. The lag is classic: The delivery systems have arrived well ahead of the product. And in the long run the art of communication, rather than any of the technological miracles, may shape the electronic landscape.*[12]

SUMMARY

Television today, much like radio, is searching for a new identity and function. Despite its dominant position in American society, television is still a young medium, growing and developing.

The development of television can be divided into several distinct periods. From 1884 to 1925, basic research in electromagnetic theory led to more practical experimentation with radio waves and, ultimately, with television signals. From 1925 to 1947, there were experiments in television transmission, and in 1940 commercial television operations began. World War II, however, delayed the commercial development of television.

From 1948 to 1952, three factors significantly affected the future of video broadcasting: the FCC's "freeze" on television station allocations, the development of television networks, and the beginning of video programming formats. The golden age of television occurred in the years from 1952 to 1960. During this time television developed into a mass medium. Color television and videotape were invented and most of the major program forms were developed.

Next came a period of growth, progress, and criticism—1961 to 1980. Television took on a major role in American society, with network television, especially, assuming dominance as a mass medium. Viewing levels exceeded 6 hours per day and strong criticism began to emerge concerning television's impact on and role in society. Television program forms continued to evolve. Network and local television became more important.

The television industry is composed primarily of networks, local stations, syndication companies, network-owned and -operated stations, station groups, cable operations, and public television. The ways programs are produced, distributed, and exhibited are the bases for this organization. The networks provide most of the commercial programming seen by Americans, and the actual broadcasting is the function of the stations in each market. Most local stations are affiliated with one of the three major networks and receive the bulk of their programming from that network. However, other programming sources and independent stations not affiliated with networks are becoming more important in television programming.

The 1980s have been a time of intense change and competition in the television industry. Much of this change is technological and threatens the basic structure of the industry, especially the distribution and transmission of content by satellites, cable television, and videocassettes.

Public television has continued to grow but is experiencing increasing financial problems. Nonbroadcast television is expanding rapidly and the world of business video is emerging as a major communication medium.

Despite increasing competition and criticism, television today is a huge, complex, costly, continuous, and competitive medium. It is society's mass entertainer, mass informer, mass persuader, and mass educator. It is a universal medium. More than 98 percent of American homes have television, and television viewing is the dominant leisure-time activity in American society. Television is the costliest of all the electronic media.

The future of television rests on the ability of audiences to control and use it for their own purposes. The television marketplace is in transition and is being reshaped by a variety of technological and social forces.

REFERENCES

1. Jack Gould, quoted in the retrospective exhibit booklet "Metromedia and the DuMont Legacy" (The Museum of Broadcasting, 1985), 7.
2. Richard Zoglin, "At 15, *Saturday Night* Lives," *Time*, September 25, 1989, 75.
3. Joshua Hammer, "Betting Billions on TV Sports," *Newsweek*, December 11, 1989, 66.
4. Neal H. Pilson, "TV Cash Can Give Colleges High Marks," *The New York Times*, April 1, 1990, S10.
5. Walter Goodman, "When Pictures Dictate the News," *The New York Times*, November 19, 1989, H32.
6. Peter J. Boyer, "When News Must Pay Its Way, Expect Trivia," *The New York Times*, October 2, 1989, A19.
7. Quoted by Bill Carter, "In First for TV, NBC Wants ABC to Produce Show for It," *The New York Times*, September 6, 1989, D1.
8. "9 Rules for the '90s," *Channels*, December 1989, 18.
9. Speech, January 15, 1986.
10. Gene P. Mater, "TV, Cable & Telcos: Future Partners?" *Washington Journalism Review* (September 1989): 50.
11. Judy Flander, "Public Television Hits a Midlife Crisis," *Washington Journalism Review* (July 8, 1989): 32.
12. *Channels*, November/December 1985, 4.

CHAPTER 11

Radio

Radio has entertained and informed American society for over 70 years, a period that has seen it achieve unchallenged prominence, a nearly disastrous decline, and a transformed rebirth. There are now over 11,000 radio stations, reaching almost the entire population, whether at home or in cars or as portable companions. At age 12, we spend about 3 hours daily listening to the radio, seeking assistance with planning our day (how to dress for the elements, how to travel, how gloomy to be about the economy), hearing late-breaking news, feeling part of a nation of call-in participants on a talk show, or shifting moods with the help of our own kind of music.

During its golden age, radio was unsurpassed, bringing families and the country together to listen to "Amos 'n' Andy" and "The Shadow," or scores of other serial shows. Thanks to carefully selected announcers, radio has brought us American English at its spoken best, not an insignificant contribution. In the 1920s, the impetus for many families to get electrical hookups was the desire to be in communication with far-off sources of culture and entertainment.

Radio seemed solidly entrenched as the national mass medium, and then television—"radio with pictures," some called it—arrived to present a very real threat and to make good on it. In response to television's capturing the flag, radio has taken on a new role, one played by no other medium. Radio is adaptable and personal, and potentially as responsive to privatization as recorded music but with far greater variety of content. It is a portable and supplementary medium, not as demanding of undivided attention as television or books. Once the odd-looking toy of amateur enthusiasts, radio continues to have a special place in our communication-rich society.

Now that we have seen how television sprang from radio, we backtrack briefly to trace radio's own colorful past. Then we look at how this medium has grown steadily as an increasingly specialized, target-driven form of mass communication.

HISTORICAL PERSPECTIVE

EARLY HISTORY: 1840–1919

Radio developed out of scientific advances made in the fields of electricity and magnetism. The first transmission of an electromagnetic message over wire was made in 1844 by Samuel F. B. Morse, and by 1861, a transcontinental, high-speed electric communication system was signaling coded messages across the United States. The first transatlantic cable was laid in 1858, and by 1870, a web of undersea cables linked the Western world and its economic outposts. The replacement of

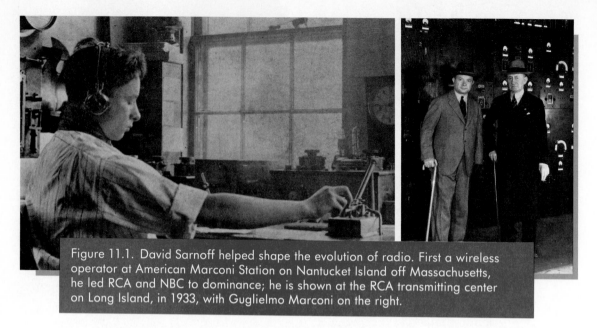

Figure 11.1. David Sarnoff helped shape the evolution of radio. First a wireless operator at American Marconi Station on Nantucket Island off Massachusetts, he led RCA and NBC to dominance; he is shown at the RCA transmitting center on Long Island, in 1933, with Guglielmo Marconi on the right.

Morse code with voice transmission occurred in 1876, when Alexander Graham Bell used undulations in electric current to produce vocal communication by wire. The telephone's ability to code, transport, and decode voice transmissions personalized electric communication in a way that was impossible with the telegraph.

James Clerk Maxwell predicted (1864) and Heinrich Hertz demonstrated (1887) that variations in electric current produce waves that can be transmitted through space *without wires* at the speed of light. These theories stimulated much experimentation, the most successful being Guglielmo Marconi's work in the late 1890s. Marconi received a patent for his wireless telegraph in 1897 and by 1901 was sending wireless dot-dash transmissions across the Atlantic. The work of such men as Reginald Fessenden and Lee De Forest—high-quality voice communication carried by electromagnetic waves—set the stage for radio broadcasting. Until 1940, it would be entirely on AM frequencies. AM stands for "amplitude modulation"; these frequencies bounce off the ionosphere and can travel for great distances.

For the most part, no one thought of using radio to *broadcast* to a mass audience; it was thought of as a tool with specific uses. Again, a medium begins as elitist. RCA, where Marconi continued to work, developed a virtual monopoly on *radiotelegraphy*, which the U.S. Navy rapidly adopted; GE and AT&T pushed forward with experiments in *radiotelephony*, hoping to find a better way to transmit the human voice than over their static-filled wires. The word *broadcast* was originally a naval term meaning to broadcast or disperse orders to the fleet. Eventually, all the new experiments led to a stalemate of competing patents between four major companies (including Westinghouse), which would not be resolved until 1920.

Two major laws concerning the use of radio were the U.S. Wireless Ship Act of 1910, which required all passenger ships to carry radio-transmission equipment, and the second was the Radio Act of 1912, which required all radio operators to be licensed by the Secretary of Commerce. Enacted in the year that a young wireless operator named David Sarnoff demonstrated the importance of radio when he picked up signals from the sinking SS *Titanic* and helped save hundreds of lives, the 1912 act was the first comprehensive attempt to regulate all phases of radio communication.

Public and industrial appetites were whetted. David Sarnoff was one of the visionaries of the medium. In 1916, he wrote a memo to his boss at American Marconi proposing a new use for radio.

> *I have in mind a plan of development which would make radio a "household utility" in the same sense as the piano or phonograph. The idea is to bring music into the house by wireless. . . . The receiver can be designed in the form of a simple "Radio Music Box" and arranged for several different wave lengths.*[1]

Sarnoff's foresight would eventually result in his emergence as president of the Radio Corporation of America (RCA) and one of the most powerful leaders in broadcasting.

THE FORMATION OF THE AMERICAN RADIO SYSTEM: 1920–1928

After World War I, an organized attempt was made to develop radio broadcasting as opposed to point-to-point communication. Though several claim to have made the first broadcast, credit is usually given to KDKA in Pittsburgh when it broadcast the Harding-Cox presidential election returns on November 2, 1920. KDKA was owned by Westinghouse, which hoped to sell radio receivers as a result of that and following hourly broadcasts. During the first year only nine new stations were in operation. But as radio sales increased, convincing the initially timid companies that they were on the verge of an entirely new industry, the number of stations exploded to 600 by the end of 1922, and radio sales rocketed to $60 million. Radio sales doubled in 1923 and doubled again in 1924 to $358 million; audiences gathered

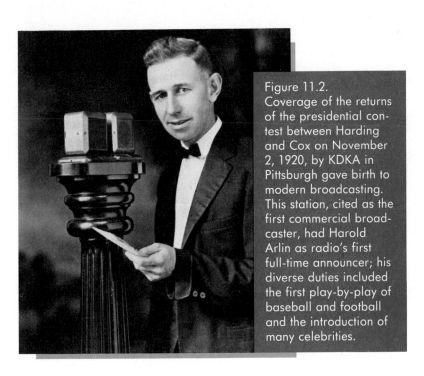

Figure 11.2.
Coverage of the returns of the presidential contest between Harding and Cox on November 2, 1920, by KDKA in Pittsburgh gave birth to modern broadcasting. This station, cited as the first commercial broadcaster, had Harold Arlin as radio's first full-time announcer; his diverse duties included the first play-by-play of baseball and football and the introduction of many celebrities.

by the millions, reacting with wonder and awe to the new technology that allowed the message to travel faster than the messenger.

Initially, stations broadcast anything they could get their hands on—music, sports, news, weather, drama, concerts. As programming expanded, and audiences grew more discriminating, production costs could not be covered by the sale of radios. However, companies were reluctant, even opposed, to turn to advertising as a source of revenue. As Secretary of Commerce Herbert Hoover said in 1922: "It is inconceivable that we should allow so great a possibility for service, for news, for entertainment, for education to be drowned in advertising chatter." Slowly, radio advertising did evolve.

Another cost-saving development was the networks. The first network was created in 1923 by AT&T and radio set manufacturers in order to expand each station's programming. It asked merchants to support the system by becoming *sponsors* of particular programs: Their names would be mentioned in connection with the program, though no direct selling would be allowed. This led to such popular shows as the "A&P Gypsies" and the "Lucky Strike Orchestra."

AT&T withdrew from program distribution in 1926, and a new corporate giant, RCA, took over. Formed in 1919 as a sales outlet for radio manufacturers, RCA now consolidated its position and formed the National Broadcasting Company (NBC). In 1927, William S. Paley formed the Columbia Broadcasting System (CBS), and network broadcasting was off and running.

As more and more stations went on the air, they began to interfere with one another's signals. It was obvious that legislative action was needed if broadcasting was to survive.

We have seen that broadcast media are physically limited by the number of channels or spaces available in the radio spectrum. The Berlin Conference (1903)

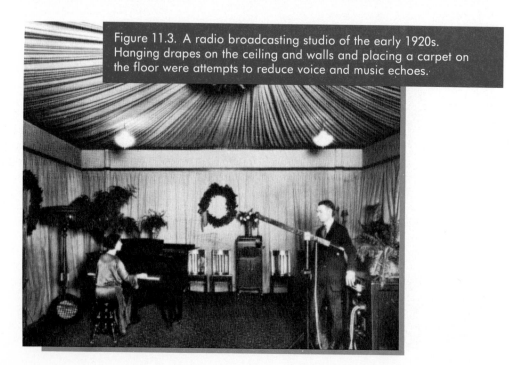

Figure 11.3. A radio broadcasting studio of the early 1920s. Hanging drapes on the ceiling and walls and placing a carpet on the floor were attempts to reduce voice and music echoes.

and the Havana Treaty (1925) established international rules for using radio frequencies, but internal domestic use of the allocated channels was left to individual governments. A growing awareness that the airwaves were a natural resource that belonged to the public also began to affect the legal decision-making process. A milestone was reached when Congress passed the Federal Communications Act of 1934, which established the Federal Communications Commission (FCC) to regulate telephone, telegraph, and radio-communication systems in the "public's interest, convenience, and necessity." (See Chapter 5.) This act remains in effect, modified, of course, by prevailing political, social, and economic conditions.

THE GOLDEN AGE OF NETWORK RADIO: 1929–1945

With its technical problems solved, radio was free to grow almost unrestricted. By the late 1920s, the medium achieved a high degree of program sophistication and financial stability. The nation was in love with radio, and one program perhaps exemplified and brought on these changes more than any other—"Amos 'n' Andy."

"Amos 'n' Andy" began in 1928 and would continue for three decades, broadcasting for 15 minutes every weeknight. "Amos 'n' Andy" did three things: It established the serial or situation comedy as the new format for programming; it brought life to a standstill as, during 1931 and 1932, nearly 40 million people, or one-third of the U.S. population, stopped to listen; and it proved to network sponsors that radio advertising worked. British playwright and critic George Bernard Shaw is said to have remarked, "There are three things which I shall never forget about America—the Rocky Mountains, Niagara Falls, and 'Amos 'n' Andy.'" The Great Depression of the 1930s played a role in radio's boom: A nation squeezed by financial hardship found entertainment virtually free. And it did not take long

Figure 11.4. The broadcasting of the radio series "Gang Busters" illustrates how live radio drama was created. The entire cast gathered around one microphone while the sound-effects men fired safety pistols.

Figure 11.5.
No program before or after "Amos 'n' Andy" captured one-third of the population. Freeman H. Gosden and Charles J. Correll were dialect artists and makers of phrases and expressions still a part of our language as they depicted two southern blacks transplanted to a large city.

for advertisers to make the connection between Pepsodent's sponsorship of "Amos 'n' Andy" in 1929 and its almost immediate rise in toothpaste sales. Advertisers clamored to sponsor shows, and advertising revenue grew to over $25 million in 1930.

Indeed, the network economic picture was so good in 1934 that a fourth radio network, the Mutual Broadcasting System (MBS), was formed to challenge NBC-Red, NBC-Blue, and CBS. (NBC-Red and NBC-Blue were separate systems, each with its own affiliates. Legend has it that their names derived from the color of the string that was used to map out the two systems.) By 1935, MBS had 60 affiliates competing with the 80 to 120 affiliates of the other networks. As network competition intensified and program costs increased, broadcasters needed to know more about the size of their audience. By 1935, a number of research organizations were providing data on the composition of radio audiences. With more than 22 million American radio homes, programming successes became advertising bonanzas.

The second half of the 1930s was a time of refining and polishing established formats. The networks continued to dominate, especially in advertising revenue and program production. More than 50 percent of all radio advertising dollars went to the four national networks (compared with 1 percent today).

Major legal actions also occurred at this time. In 1935, the American Bar Association, in Canon 35, ruled that at the discretion of the presiding judge, broadcast journalists could be prohibited from using radio equipment in courtrooms to cover trials. In 1941, the FCC's "Mayflower decision" forbade broadcasters to editorialize. These two actions reflected to some extent the media bias of society, which identified print as information media and radio (and later, television) as entertainment media. The Mayflower ruling was overturned later in the decade.

Of the 850 stations on the air in 1941, 700 were affiliated with one of the four major networks. Only three corporations made up the network oligopoly at that time, however, since NBC had both a Red and a Blue network. The Federal Communications Commission, recognizing the long-range consequences of the situation, forced NBC to sell one of its networks. NBC sold its Blue-network operation to a group that formed the American Broadcasting Company (ABC) in 1943.

Despite the decline in the production of radio receivers during World War II, advertising revenue continued to climb. The public's demand for war information and mistrust of newspaper publishers doubled the number of news programs in the first half of the war. Ed Murrow transfixed the nation with his live broadcasts from London during the Blitz, bringing home the sounds of war. President Franklin Roosevelt also used radio to communicate personally and intimately with millions during his Fireside Chats. Yet, toward the end, war weariness set in, and entertainment began to dominate again, allowing Americans an escape from the realities of battle.

Radio dramas were performed live until the late 1940s when networks lifted their ban on recordings. Groups such as The Mercury Theatre of the Air and Columbia Workshop produced many memorable programs, including Orson Welles's famous 1938 Halloween presentation of "The War of the Worlds" (see page 418 for a look at this now-classic demonstration of radio's psychological impact). In addition, playwrights such as Norman Corwin and Arch Obler wrote material specifically for radio.

THE DECLINE OF RADIO: 1946–1959

When World War II ended, radio broadcasting quickly resumed its prewar pace. During this time, however, television viewing began its phenomenal rise to preeminence as America's major leisure-time activity. We have seen that when the general audience moved to television, so did general programming—the sitcoms and dramas that had been radio's lifeblood. (In 1950, there were more than 100 series that had been running for at least 10 years.) Radio had to change or die. Slowly, it adopted music almost exclusively, developing sounds and formats that would appeal to specific segments of a local population.

Other changes were also taking place that would affect radio. The first change made FM frequencies available for commercial use in 1940. (FM, or frequency modulation, is signals directly sent on a line of sight, reaching only the horizon or under 100 miles. This limitation is balanced and overcome by the vastly superior quality of reception.) By 1948, over 600 FM stations had been licensed. With the growth of television, however, FM was put on hold until 1958, when the number of FM stations again began to expand. The second change adjusted the distance required between AM stations to allow for multiple use of frequencies previously used by clear-channel stations (stations that operated on an exclusive "clear" frequency). As a result, when the 4-year "freeze" on TV's growth was removed by the FCC in 1952, radio's economic situation was further strained by the fact that 3,000 stations were now competing for audiences and revenue.

Network programming lost its economic base as reduced audience size brought in fewer advertising dollars. Also, the networks were busy establishing themselves in TV programming, and radio was quickly moved to the back burner. By 1960, the last of the networks' major programming forms, the daytime soap opera, went off the air. The only major network programming innovation of the period was NBC's "Monitor" weekend service, which was basically a modification of the disc-jockey format for a national audience.

Local stations quickly moved into this vacuum, and local-station programming

Figure 11.6. "Cousin Brucie" Morrow, one of the celebrities among disc jockeys and talk-show hosts who develop intensely loyal followings.

rapidly developed, primarily around a disc jockey, a stack of records, and a skeletal news-and-sports operation. Total advertising revenue stumbled along from 1953 to 1960 as local salespeople attempted to make up the slack created by the continued slide of network revenue, which hit an all-time low of $35 million in 1960. Despite the network crash, additional AM stations plunged into the business, so that by 1960, 3,500 AM stations were on the air. The number of FM stations grew to almost 700, but they were used primarily as an auxiliary service that simulcast AM programming.

THE RENAISSANCE OF RADIO ....

GROWTH SINCE 1960

Despite the extensive and swift decline in network radio, the 1960s were a period of great economic growth for radio. More than 150 million radios were sold at a retail value of $6 billion. Advertising revenue totaled more than $8 billion during the decade. Network radio stabilized, and revenue increased slowly.

FM radio grew at a phenomenal rate to almost 2,500 in 1970. By 1989, there were 5,576 FM stations on the air as an audience appreciative of the superior technical quality increased. By the mid-1960s, more than 50 percent of all FM stations were stereo operations. In 1965, the FCC ruled that AM–FM combinations in cities of over 100,000 population could no longer duplicate more than 50 percent of either station's programming. This "50-50 ruling," as it was called, affected approximately 330 stations and greatly opened up the FM market. As a result, a wide variety of station formats appeared in the late 1960s. There were stations that broadcast nothing but classified ads, stations with programming for the blind, stations that play only "golden oldies," all-talk stations, and all-news stations. Today, FM is by far the more profitable band.

AM radio has grown too, but more slowly, partly because of a freeze on new AM license awards from 1962 to 1964 and from 1968 to 1973. As a result, AM's share of total listenership has declined steadily, from 60 percent in 1977 to 26 percent in 1987. During that period, FM's listenership share increased from 40

Table 11.1.	Preferences of Listeners According to Age Group	
Age	FM	AM
12–24	84%	16%
25–34	73	27
35–49	59	41
50+	44	56

percent to 74 percent. FM became the band for music while AM became the band for news, talk, sports, and some forms of music, such as big-band and country. A whole generation of listeners has grown up with rock and roll on FM radio, and demographics reveal this split (see Table 11.1).

On a weekly cumulative basis, AM radio reaches about 25 percent of the population, while FM reaches 75 percent. However, it is interesting to note that though FM dominates in total listening, AM still receives about half of radio-station advertising.

As noted earlier, radio is a widespread medium. It is in 99 percent of all American households and 95 percent of all cars. Fifty-seven percent of adults have radios at work. There are estimated to be over half a billion radio sets in the United States.

Radio's weekly cumulative audience is 183 million, or 95 percent of the total U.S. population. Ninety-six percent of men 18 and older listen every week, as do 93 percent of women 18 and older, and 100 percent of teenagers 12 to 17. The amount of time that people listen to radio rose slightly in 1988, reversing a mild decline of the previous 5 years; it hovered around 3 hours a day.

Total advertising, radio's major source of revenue, remains steady and reached $7.9 billion in 1989; the continuing dominance of local advertising is shown in Figure 11.7. It is projected to grow at a rate of 8 percent through most of the 1990s.

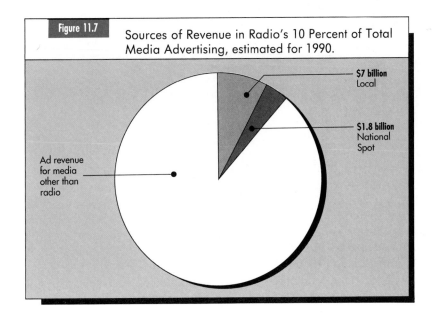

Figure 11.7 Sources of Revenue in Radio's 10 Percent of Total Media Advertising, estimated for 1990.

$7 billion
Local

$1.8 billion
National
Spot

Ad revenue for media other than radio

Radio receives a little more than 10 percent of the total amount spent on all media, which, given the ups and downs of the mass media, is a positive sign. Here too, advertiser-driven strategies completely dominate the field, relying on audience research and "niche" programming for success. We will take a closer look at formats later in this chapter.

Network radio has made a slow but steady climb out of the abyss of the late 1950s. A major innovation occurred in 1968 when ABC Radio developed four separate radio services for affiliates. Recognizing that the audience for radio had become increasingly segmented by age group and lifestyle, ABC offered radio stations both news and public-affairs features that were fine-tuned to particular audiences.

As Walter Sabo, vice president of ABC Radio Networks, said, "The key to success for any network is to provide stations with services they can't do themselves."[2] Network radio will continue to exist as long as it lives by this idea. Rather than *broad*cast, radio networks now *narrow*cast, linking specific audiences with programs that speak their "language."

In the mid-1950s, few people would have predicted even moderate success for radio. But, 40 years later, radio has emerged from the ashes to assume a new identity as a tough hybrid capable of not only competing with television but also, in many cases, surpassing it.

THE SCOPE OF RADIO TODAY

When we compare contemporary radio with radio 40 years ago, we see several major differences:

1. *Organization and Industrial Structure.* Radio has changed from a national-network system with a wide range of programs (most with national sponsors) to a local operation with limited network service. Smaller in scale, it has succumbed to the widespread acquisitions and mergers that have affected other media.
2. *Content.* Forty years ago, radio's content was made up of stories (including soap operas, situation comedies, Westerns, drama) and variety. Today, radio's content is primarily recorded music and disc-jockey talk, along with some news and issues-oriented programming.
3. *Function.* Radio has changed from an in-house, sit-down, communal storyteller to a nonhome, mobile, personal informer and entertainer. Radio rarely assumes the role of a cultural flashpoint today; it supplements our other activities.
4. *Style.* Radio has moved from narrative, linear, dramatically structured 15–30-minute "programs" to nonnarrative, nonlinear, 1–3-minute content units. News, interviews, and talk are largely descriptive rather than dramatic.

Perhaps the most significant trend of the past 20 years has been the sheer increase in the number of stations, increasing competition and pushing to the limit the physical capabilities of the airwaves. There are several causes for this. First, it is now easier than ever to receive a license and have it renewed since there is very little a broadcaster must do to prove that he is operating in the public's "interest, convenience, and necessity."

Deregulation of the broadcast industry in the 1980s has also had a marked effect, allowing companies to own more stations and sell them sooner, creating what one Congressman called a "casino marketplace." In 1985, the FCC raised the total number of stations a company could own to 12 AM and 12 FM (in addition to 12 television stations, up from 7-7-7).

In 1983, there were 9,678 stations, and by 1990 they had surpassed 11,000. Most of the growth continues to be on FM. (However, an international agreement to expand the AM dial in 1990 should begin a spurt in AM growth.) Stand-alone FM stations, those without a sister AM, have seen a steady increase of revenue, and the average price for an FM station has risen by 20 percent. The average price of an AM station has fallen by 4 percent in the past decade. Individually, there are many strong AM stations making a profit, but the overall trend is away from AM and toward FM.

Though few broadcasters have reached the new FCC limits, they have encouraged purchasing and increased the value of stations. In 1987, the FCC relaxed its "antitrafficking" regulations, reducing the time a company was required to maintain ownership of a station from 3 years to 1. While the ability to sell a station quicker increases its value, this creates pressures on the new owner for a greater profit margin to pay for the purchase. This is seen vividly in the 1989 purchase of a classical-music station, KFAC-FM in Los Angeles, for $55 million (the highest price for a station to that date was $79 million). In 1986, it had been bought for only $34 million. The new owners, however, found that classical music was not profitable enough and switched to a rock format to increase advertising. This format switch left L.A. without a classical-music station—one that had served it for 58 years. Nevertheless, the radio companies that have become leaders in growth in recent years have done so through acquisitions of other stations. Without rampant acquisitions by companies such as Westwood One, Sage Broadcasting, and Jacor Communications, the overall revenue picture would look worse than it is.

THE STRUCTURE AND ORGANIZATION OF RADIO

The local radio station is the basic media unit responsible for almost all content, but several media service units are deeply involved in radio programming. The recording, or music, industry provides the majority of most stations' programming at little or no cost for the records, although stations are charged an annual fee for music rights by Broadcast Music, Inc. (BMI), and the American Society of Composers, Authors, and Publishers (ASCAP). Closely allied with the music that most stations play are syndication and format companies that supply a variety of program services, primarily play lists and specific musical formats or schedules. Networks provide a service of national news and features. The wire services provide the bulk of the news information for most stations.

The use of satellites for program distribution, the rise of automated broadcast technology, and the widespread use of computers have added programming options and have improved stations' ability to improve operations and control costs. Approximately 15 percent of AM and FM stations are fully automated.

Station organization varies greatly, depending on the size of the station, type of programming, size of the market, and amount of competition. At very large stations, specialized tasks and departments exist in the news, sales, and programming areas. At medium-size stations, announcers double as newspeople, salespeople, or engineers, as well as entertainers. At small stations, the program manager may also be the sales manager; there is often no news staff, and, usually, all announcers are licensed engineers.

Radio stations are highly competitive, especially in big markets, and pay scales reflect this competitiveness and the size of the station's market. High salaries and specialized roles exist in only very large stations, however. The vast majority of people working for radio stations earn modest salaries.

KINDS OF RADIO STATIONS

Technically, there are two kinds of radio stations: AM and FM. The standard bank of frequencies (535–1,605 kilocycles) is used for AM broadcasting, while FM broadcasting occurs on frequencies between 88 and 108 megacycles (1,000 kilocycles equals 1 megacycle).

AM Classifications. Because about 5,000 AM stations are licensed for broadcast on 107 channels, an intricate system of accommodation has been established based on three major variables: power, signal direction, and hours of operation. AM stations are divided into four classes, according to the power, in watts, of the station. There are over 1,000 AM stations that have a maximum power of 1,000 watts and operate on one of the six local channels. Sixty of the 107 channels are classified as clear, 41 as regional, and 6 as local.

In 1979, it was decided at the World Administrative Radio Conference to expand the AM band from 1,605 kHz to 1,705 kHz, thereby adding 10 channels. Since

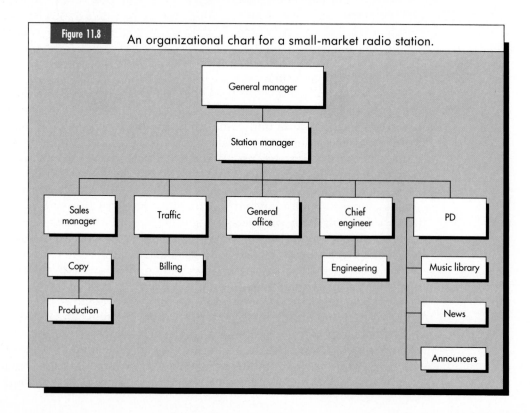

Figure 11.8 An organizational chart for a small-market radio station.

then, the FCC has been deciding how to allocate those channels. Many day-only stations would like to be "homesteaded" to the new channels, which would allow them to expand to full-time. This would also help relieve congestion on current channels. Minorities and noncommercial broadcasters are also petitioning for new space, saying they are not adequately represented on radio and deserve the access.

Another change that may benefit AM in the near future is the development of a continuous-tuning radio. If manufacturers market these, FM listeners will not need to switch bands to hear what's on AM; they can just tune through. Many say this would help raise awareness of AM programming.

FM Classifications. There are three classes of FM stations in operation today; they are defined primarily by power and antenna elevation. The maximum combination of power and antenna height is 100,000 watts and 2,000 feet. Class A stations have an effective coverage area of 15 miles; Class B stations cover 30 miles; and Class C stations broadcast up to 60 miles. The exceptionally high antennas and power are due to the fact that FM signals are direct signals that reach only to the horizon.

The FM signal is 20 times the width of an AM channel, which makes stereophonic sound possible through *multiplexing*. Over 93 percent of FM stations now broadcast in stereo. AM stereo became a reality in 1982, but it has yet to become widespread. This is partly because the FCC has refused to dictate an industry standard, and two competing AM stereo systems have been fighting to dominate the marketplace. Though stereo would improve the quality of music on AM, it is not generally regarded as a panacea for AM's ills.

Other Classifications. Radio stations in the United States are identified by call letters beginning with K or W. Except for a few early stations, such as KDKA in Pittsburgh, stations east of the Mississippi River have call letters beginning with W, while K is assigned to stations west of the Mississippi. Most early broadcast call signs used three letters, but they were quickly exhausted; today, most stations have four-letter call signs.

One additional classification for radio stations is as commercial and noncommercial or educational. Of the more than 1,100 educational radio stations today, only 24 are AM; they date from the early years of radio. In 1945, the FCC reserved 20 FM channels between 88 and 92 MHz for noncommercial educational stations. Since then, the number of noncommerical stations has grown slowly but steadily to over 1,400.

KINDS OF NETWORKS

The past decade of mergers and acquisitions has transformed the structure of the radio industry. Hundreds of smaller networks have come into existence, some of whom—such as Satellite Music Network and Transtar—have been swallowed up by larger players. Unistar is an example of a constructed network. In 1985, United Stations bought the RKO Radio Network, then merged with Transtar in 1989 to create a network with 3,000 station affiliates and with an estimated 64 million listeners. ABC is still the number-one network in ad revenue, and in 1989 purchased the Satellite Music Network. Westwood One has become one of the network revenue-growth leaders in the 1980s through its acquisitions of the Mutual Broadcasting System and three NBC radio networks—National Radio Network, The

Source, and TalkNet. The larger commercial networks—such as CBS, NBC, Mutual, Unistar, Westwood One, and ABC—offer multiple programming services, in effect creating internal multiple networks.

Networks provide a national news service to their affiliates, as well as sports programs, features, commentaries, and music programming. Programs are delivered simultaneously by satellite to all stations, which can tune in at any time during the day, though they are usually obliged to run network commercials. Affiliates usually sign on for 2-year renewable periods and are generally charged for the network's services. A typical music service could cost between $600 and $1,000 a month.

In 1985, a peak year, 58 percent of all commercial radio stations were affiliated with a network, but since then, networks' audiences have dropped by nearly 15 percent. Predictions are that the networks will be relatively stable in the next decade, neither losing nor gaining very much in audience or advertising.

In 1972, National Public Radio (NPR) began the development of a network-radio service designed to provide programming for noncommercial educational stations. It is funded by the Corporation for Public Broadcasting and private donations, distributes programs 24 hours a day, and in 1990 had more than 380 member stations. Public radio offers a unique programming alternative to commercial radio, though it is not financially as stable. Its role is discussed more fully in Chapter 18. NPR has shown innovation and resiliency, recently offering more options and new programs, such as "Fresh Air," an arts interview show that has been picked up by 150 stations, and "Afropop Worldwide," a mostly non-English music show that is sent to 170 stations.

In addition to the major national networks, hundreds of smaller regional and specialized networks either interconnect stations for a specific program (a football

Figure 11.9. Vertamae Grosvenor, host of National Public Radio's award-winning weekly series "Horizons," has produced important documentaries, such as "Slave Voices: Things Past Telling," and provides commentary on NPR's newsmagazine "All Things Considered."

game) or provide various special programming (black news or religious information).

SYNDICATORS

The major difference between networks and syndicators today is the type of contract. Stations usually pay syndicators on a per-program basis for a show that may air a couple of hours a week or for most of every day. But also, syndicators offer to tailor programming to suit the individual station's audience, which is something the networks can come close to but cannot match.

These format specialists use satellites to deliver the programming or market tapes of selected music that will be programmed for up to 24 hours. The tapes may change hourly to provide different moods, rhythms, and styles. They even incorporate seasonal changes. The box illustrates the variety of formats offered by Broadcast Programming, in addition to customized services.

Fees for syndicators' services vary; some are fixed and others are based on a sliding scale, depending on a station's revenue and the size of its market. Per-show costs usually exceed $1,000 a month, while customized services usually push costs over $10,000 a month and more. For stations in large markets, this can be more economical than on-air talent. Over 83 percent of all radio stations, both FM and AM, use some syndicated satellite-delivered music and talk programming.

FORMATS AND THEIR TARGETS ....

Programming the right mix of music, news, talk, and commercials is the key to success for today's radio stations. This means targeting a specific segment of the community (such as baby boomers aged 25 to 45) and attempting to attract them throughout the day. Research is used to discover exactly who is listening, how many there are, and when they are tuning in. Because markets are so crowded, a market share of 6 percent is usually as much as a station needs to become number one. Arbitron and Birch are the two major research organizations in radio today. Accredited by the Electronic Media Rating Council, Arbitron issues a 300-page survey report each quarter and presents its findings in a number of ways:

Metro-audience trends
Target-audience estimates
Specific-audience estimates
Audience composition
Hour-by-hour estimates
Listening locations
Exclusive audience
Overnight-listening estimates
ADI Target-audience estimates

"Narrowcasting" would seem to create a great diversity on radio, and in fact there are scores of formats serving virtually every demographic group, from the young to the old, from the city to the country. Yet within each of the highly specialized formats there is a remarkable sameness and a fear of diversity lest

Based in Seattle, Broadcast Programming is one of the syndicators that are helping local stations do what, in this sophisticated marketplace, they can no longer do for themselves. It offers over 30 different formats and backs up its client services with detailed information on demographics, delivery of reels in convenient form for use in various specific dayparts, and a monthly 12-page newsletter. In addition to industry news, it offers tips on better station management, called Thought Starters; a sharing of affiliate success stories, service awards, and so on; forecasts of trends; and advice on working with prospective advertisers. Regional managers help keep the network of their affiliates in touch.

If you have wondered where radio patter comes from, much of it originates with such a syndicator. Broadcasting Programming supplies weekly information about concert tours, flashes of stars' or composers' birthdays, a toll-free hotline of consultation, and customized copy. And to give affiliates the essential added edge in their market, the organization provides up-to-date analyses of what the competition's up to.

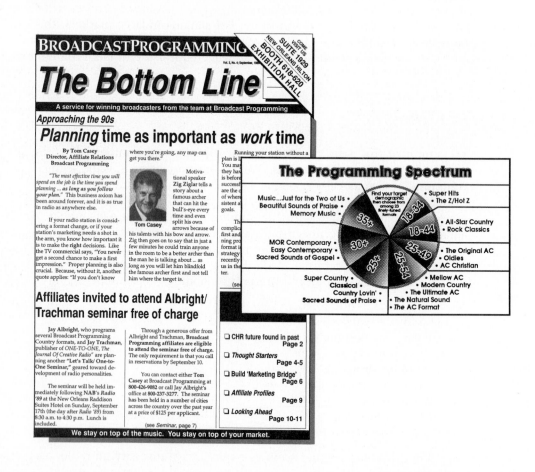

programmers dilute or even lose the audiences advertisers desire. As one broad-caster said, "It's a narrowcast world. [The audience] ought to know exactly what they're going to get when they come to your radio station. If you do something in [the evening] daypart, and they hear you, they may think you've changed. It's a dangerous thing do to."[3]

Program directors have developed program wheels or format disks. These care-fully designed "clocks" ensure the effective presentation of on-air elements. Figure 11.11 on page 299 presents a typical morning-drive-time CHR clock. It reflects a 9-minute commercial load per hour and very detailed "instructions" about what to play when. Stations often have many program wheels, each of which represents specific content. A news clock provides instructions from the news director in concert with the program director on how to format the news to achieve the best integration of news with the other program elements. In all such clocks or wheels, balance is the key.

Table 2.1 ranked the most common formats. Other "specialty" formats include all-sports, polka, multi-ethnic, new age, and all-finance. Formats are somewhat misleading in that they often represent a much wider variety of individual sounds and styles. There is fragmentation within specific formats. For example, urban contemporary ranges from rap to dance to pop music. As some stations adopt "crossover" formats, those that mix two different formats such as country and adult contemporary, the differences become indistinguishable. As audiences age and evolve, so do radio formats. Some leading formats are described below.

Adult Contemporary. A/C is the most listened-to format on the FM dial, but it is fragmenting to adjust to changes in its audience. Traditionally akin to a quieter, top-40 presentation for 25- to 34-year-olds, it now is also soft to create a "re-laxing" atmosphere with 60s and 70s music and very few contemporary hits.

Contemporary Hit Radio. It used to be called top-40, but CHR now fills particular niches, leaning toward dance, urban, or other forms. The current best and fastest selling *singles* are targeted to 12–18-year-olds, featuring a tight fast pace with little if any "dead air." More and more stations are adopting prepro-grammed syndicated shows that emphasize almost nonstop music.

Album-Oriented Rock. AOR plays the hottest *albums*. CHR is still its closest com-petitor, but AOR attracts a slightly older listener, mostly males 18–34. Relying on a steady diet of rock 'n' roll, it has fragmented into three separate categories: classic, mainstream (also dubbed rock 40), and current-based or progressive. Shock radio also falls into AOR, enhancing its aggressive image, though the FCC is currently cracking down on indecency, and shock radio's future is unclear.

Classic Rock. Many in the radio industry feel the classic-rock format is a fad, but programmers are getting listeners. Somewhere between AOR and A/C, and feeling some competition from CHR, it plays late 1960s, early 1970s rock on the assumption that listeners who cut their teeth on the Beatles and the Who will keep listening into their forties, fifties, and sixties. Classic rock offers a full-service format; it provides news, national and local sports, occasional com-edy, and good personalities.

Easy Listening. Call it elevator music or rest-room radio, if you will, but "beautiful music," as it is also called, remains a highly popular format. Featuring mostly instrumentals, with a vocal every 10 or 15 minutes, it appeals to the upper end of the 25–54 group. There is minimal talk, and many stations are computer-operated, using syndicated blocks or shows. Soft A/C is seen as a threat to easy listening. New-age formats tend to find a home here or on classical stations.

Country. The top format on AM today, country is also the most listened-to, overall, although talk radio is gaining. Today, cities from Phoenix to Detroit are successfully finding audiences and offering them a diversified selection of music, from Willie Nelson, Conway Twitty, and the Judds to Randy Travis, Lyle Lovett, and K. D. Lang. Aimed primarily at the 25–54 age group, it has traditionally been popular with blue-collar workers.

News/Talk. Under this generic title fall all-news formats, all-talk formats, and, most commonly, formats that mix the two. This is currently the fastest-growing format, primarily on AM, with an increase of 150 stations between 1988 and 1989. All-news is easily the most expensive format, and many stations are part of a network to maximize resources. The formats are also highly structured, emphasizing traffic reports, weather, frequent time checks, and story repetition during the important morning and afternoon drive times.

News/talk formats are being helped by a decrease in such services on all-music FM stations and by the impact of television talk shows, which have increased the general interest in the form. Also, all-talk programmers cite the increasing number of Americans living alone as another reason for their success.

Urban Contemporary. Though not large in sheer numbers, UC is one of the strongest formats in metropolitan areas, next to CHR and AOR. It is a highly fragmented and evolving format that is similar to CHR and features black artists, rap, and accessible dance music. Disc jockeys are especially important to this format, providing a glue for a wide range of music.

Figure 11.10. The television series "Midnight Caller" stars Gary Cole as the host of a late-night call-in talk show that serves as a forum for discussion of social issues, unpredictable adventure, and dramatic bonding between communicator and radio listener.

Nostalgia/Middle-of-the-Road. MOR, or oldies, format is primarily heard on AM. It concentrates on the pop tunes of the 1950s and 1960s. Its target audience, understandably, is adults 45 and older, and it was the only AM music format to show any significant increase in the past few years. MOR as a *distinct* format is in sharp decline, having lost 73 stations between 1988 and 1989. Many of those stations are converting to talk formats or are blending MOR into other formats. One AM broadcaster said this fragmenting of nostalgia is the "same thing that happened to adult contemporary, which was the same thing that happened to top-40. We'll probably end up being niched to death like other formats depending on the number of signals available."[4]

Hispanic/Ethnic. There are hundreds of ethnic stations in America. Most numerous by far are Hispanic stations, closely followed by black stations. In 1989, there were 237 Hispanic stations, mostly on AM, with formats ranging from CHR, AC, dance, and news/talk. One difficulty for Spanish-language broadcasters has been getting English-language advertisers, who have little feel for this audience. Another difficulty is the preference for English among the second generation of immigrants when it comes to news and information.

Black. As with Hispanic broadcasting, a variety of black stations are connected by issues common to the black experience. However, there has been a recent decline in stations designated as black on both AM and FM, from 202 to 186 between 1988 and 1989. This is due in part to UC, CHR, and dance formats attracting black audiences. Music on all-black formats ranges from pop, jazz, rap, and rhythm and blues, to African, classical, and gospel.

Religious/Gospel. There are over 1,000 stations broadcasting a full-time religious format, and their numbers continue to grow. The format breaks down into stations that broadcast music and those that do not. Stations are divided about 60-40 between AM and FM, respectively. Many operate on low budgets and, like many radio stations today, rely on promotions and sponsorship of community programs to advertise their presence.

Classical. Although there are only about 40 full-time classical stations, no other format can claim a more loyal audience or one more attractive to upscale advertisers. Listeners tend to be wealthy, 25 to 49, and college-educated. *Broadcasting* magazine lists 355 stations that use the format (defined as at least 20 hours per week). Almost exclusively on FM, the number of classical stations has remained relatively stable; however, some are now beginning to adopt a common programming technique that they used to disdain—*dayparting*, or the playing of certain music at certain times to appeal to certain listeners.

Below are the radio stations available in the greater New York area, which takes second place to the car-bound Los Angeles market. The top 10 are ranked according to Arbitron, 1989.

AM Stations

	WABC	770	Talk/News
	WADO	1280	Spanish Language
	WALK	1370	Adult Contemporary
	WBAB	1240	News/Rock
(3)	WCBS	880	News
	WEVD	1050	Big Band/Nostalgia

	WFAN	660	Sports
	WFAS	1230	Westchester News
	WGSM	740	Adult Contemporary
	WHLI	1100	Oldies
	WICC	600	Adult Contemporary
(4)	WINS	1010	News
	WLIB	1190	Talk/Caribbean
	WLIM	1580	Big Bands/Talk
	WMCA	570	Talk/News
(6)	WNEW	1130	Adult Contemporary
	WNJR	1430	Rhythm and Blues
	WNYC	830	News/Talk
(9)	WOR	710	Talk/News
(5)	WPAT	930	Easy Listening
	WQXR	1560	Classical
	WRHD	1570	Nostalgia
	WVOX	1460	Talk/Nostalgia
	WWDJ	970	Christian Music
	WWRL	1600	Gospel

FM Stations

	WALK	97.5	Adult Contemporary
	WBAB	102.3	Rock
	WBAI	99.5	Varied
	WBAU	90.3	Adelphi University
	WBAZ	101.7	Adult Contemporary
	WBGO	88.3	Jazz
	WBLI	106.1	Adult Contemporary
	WBLS	107.5	Urban Contemporary
	WCBS	101.1	Oldies
	WCTO	94.3	Easy Listening
	WDRE	92.7	New Music
	WEBE	107.9	Adult Contemporary
	WEZN	99.9	Easy Listening
	WFAS	103.9	Adult Contemporary
	WFDU	89.1	Music/Public
	WFMU	91.1	Varied
	WFUV	90.7	Fordham University
	WHFM	95.3	Adult Contemporary
	WHPC	90.3	Nassau Comm. College
(1)	WHTZ	100.3	Top 40
	WJAZ	96.7	Jazz
	WKCR	89.9	Columbia University
	WKJY	98.3	Adult Contemporary
	WLNG	92.1	Oldies/Contemporary
(2)	WLTW	106.7	Light Contemporary
	WNCN	104.3	Classical
	WNEW	102.7	Rock
(10)	WNSR	105.1	Soft Rock

	WNWK	105.9	Multi-ethnic
	WNYC	93.9	Classical
	WNYE	91.5	Community Services
	WPAT	93.1	Easy Listening
	WPLJ	95.5	Top 40
	WPLR	99.1	Comedy/Rock
	WQCD	101.9	Contemporary Jazz
(8)	WQHT	97.1	Top 40/Urban
	WQXR	96.3	Classical
	WRCN	103.9	Rock
	WRHU	88.7	Hofstra University
(7)	WRKS	98.7	Urban Contemporary
	WRTN	93.5	Big Band/Nostalgia
	WSOU	89.5	Seton Hall Univ.
	WUSB	90.1	Public Station
	WWHB	107.1	Top 40
	WXRK	92.3	Classic Rock
	WYNY	103.5	Country
	WZFM	107.1	Top 40

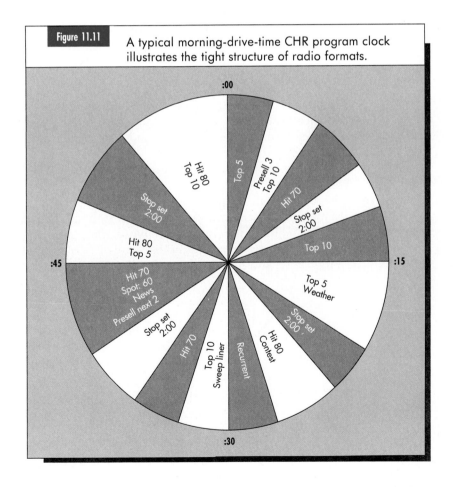

Figure 11.11 A typical morning-drive-time CHR program clock illustrates the tight structure of radio formats.

THE CHARACTERISTICS AND ROLES OF RADIO ....

At present, radio is a mass medium with a highly *fragmented audience* and revenue base. Radio is a *local* rather than a national medium, in terms of both its audience and its income. Radio-listening habits are *personal*, and stations program *selectively* to satisfy individual needs within a relatively homogeneous group. Radio, adapting to the nature of our society, has used technological advances to become *mobile*. People listen to radio as a *secondary activity* to accompany the work or play of the moment, and advertisers use radio to supplement the primary medium in their advertising mix. Many broadcasters and the FCC say radio has a social responsibility; indecency standards and the Fairness Doctrine are ways they have tried to regulate this.

LOCAL

Local stations attract the audiences and earn the revenue. Local disc jockeys, news announcers, and other personalities operate within a local frame of reference, and stations promote community events to increase station awareness and provide a sense of loyalty among listeners. Program sources, however, are increasingly national.

Until the 1950s, radio was the prestige mass medium, controlled by national advertisers and networks. With some 83 percent of all stations now using syndicated material, *local* is an adjective with relative meaning.

FRAGMENTED AND SELECTIVE

Format radio continues to become increasingly specialized, selling its particular audience to advertisers. Top-40 stations, for example, hold a virtual monopoly on the teenage and subteen groups, and advertisers wanting to reach that audience must go to the top-40 stations.

A handful of formats have proved most successful—A/C, CHR, country, AOR. Others are viable but less profitable, and still others have a hard time getting advertising at all. This can be especially true of minority stations. To compensate for the relative lack of minority-owned stations, the FCC grants a preference to women and minorities in comparative-hearing cases (when two or more applicants want the same frequency in the same area). This policy is currently being reviewed in the courts and may become a landmark affirmative-action ruling.

PERSONAL

Closely allied to radio stations' selective programming is the fact that listening to radio has become a personal activity. No longer does the family gather around the radio to be entertained as a group. People tend to listen to the radio as individuals, and radio-station announcers attempt to develop "personal" listening relationships with radio audiences. Song-identification contests, morning wake-up calls, and other call-in promotions giving away cash, cars, trips, and concert tickets are used to develop this sense of involvement, in addition to the traditional dedication and request lines. The talk-show host builds a loyal audience of individuals with whom he disagrees. Entire formats are now built around the talk-show concept.

Much of radio's personal orientation is possible because of the number and variety of radio sets available. In kitchens, radio is listened to for weather reports in order to send children off to school properly dressed. Upstairs, perhaps in the shower, teenagers tune in to hear the latest number-one hit in the country. On the way to work, people listen to traffic reports on the automobile radio. The jogger tunes out the outside world and tunes in a Walkman radio. In all these cases, the individual listens in relative isolation, seeking to gratify a personal entertainment or information need of the moment.

MOBILE

The United States has been called a "society on wheels," and radio has the ability to get out and go with its audience. Automobiles are the fastest-growing location for radio listening, and in 1988, 52.4 percent of all radio listening occurred outside the home.

The trend toward increased mobility began immediately after World War II, although the production of car radios had been an important part of total radio production as early as 1930. By 1951, auto-set production exceeded that of the home-receiver class for the first time, and car radios have continued to be the leading type of set manufactured for the past 15 years.

During the 1950s and 1960s, portable-radio production also topped home-receiver production, excluding clock radios. The tremendous surge in portability was made possible by the transistor. Today, manufacturers seem obsessed with making radios smaller and more portable. Several companies are producing credit-card-size radios weighing 1 ounce. Sony has taken its Walkman under water where it can be submerged for up to 30 minutes and still play your favorite tune.

SOCIAL RESPONSIBILITY

From its inception, radio was seen as a way to educate, to spread common cultural values, and even to teach a common language. Those goals may have been unrealistic, but today the government and the FCC still debate whether they should legislate a sense of social responsibility.

In 1989, the FCC unanimously adopted a policy of prohibiting "indecent" broadcasts 24 hours a day. Previously, indecency standards were relaxed in the evenings when most children would be asleep. To emphasize its crackdown, the FCC had fined six stations in the first year with as many more being threatened; the highest fine was $10,000. Indecency standards are notoriously hard to define, however, and several broadcasters and public-interest groups are currently protesting the policy.

SECONDARY AND SUPPLEMENTARY

The final characteristics of radio are its use as a secondary activity by listeners and as a supplementary medium by advertisers. Radio is used as background or goes along as a companion for the activity of the moment. An automobile radio is secondary to the prime function of the car itself—to go somewhere. We need traffic reports to get there, and radio provides them. Another development that enhances radio's usefulness as a secondary item is the clock radio. It does not jolt you awake;

it sings or talks you out of bed and into the day. Its primary function is not to entertain or to provide information; it is basically an alarm clock.

National and local advertisers with sizable budgets use radio to supplement the major medium of an advertising campaign. Most local advertisers use newspapers primarily but keep the campaign supported with radio ads. Major national advertisers usually spend only a small portion of their total budget on radio. Nevertheless, Radio Advertising Bureau studies have shown that radio can effectively and efficiently reach consumer prospects that television misses.

Radio has clearly survived the competition from television and has evolved into a new and remarkably solid medium. Radio is now a companion medium, fine-tuned to meet almost any need. This unique ability will continue to provide it with the audience and revenue needed to sustain future expansion.

SUMMARY

As a mass medium, radio's story has been one of rapid and tremendous growth, a golden renaissance, a decline, and a rebirth that finds it transformed from its beginning 70 years ago. Radio has proved a resilient medium, one that provides entertainment and information to the whole of American society.

The development of radio can be divided into several periods. The years from 1840 to 1919 were characterized by a number of scientific advances and inventions in the fields of electricity and magnetism. These experiments culminated in the late-nineteenth-century work of Marconi, which gave us the wireless telegraph. The early years of the twentieth century witnessed intense amateur experimentation in both code and voice transmission.

The second major period of radio development—the formation of the American radio system—occurred from 1920 to 1928. Regular radio broadcasting began in 1920 when presidental election returns were broadcast over KDKA in Pittsburgh. By the end of 1922, hundreds of stations were started, broadcasting music, sports, drama, and vaudeville. It was during this period that the industry developed and networks were formed. Laws were passed to govern the industry, and the economic structure of radio was established.

The golden age of network radio was the years 1929 to 1945. Following the success of "Amos 'n' Andy," situation comedies and serial dramas flourished as did advertiser sponsorship of those programs. Network radio became a cultural center for American society.

Radio experienced a period of decline from 1946 to 1959. The decline was primarily in network radio, as network television quickly took over the prime-time evening-programming function. Local stations began to develop original and profitable formats based primarily on recorded music. Since 1960, however, radio has become revitalized and has experienced great economic growth; in the past decade, it has been fueled by acquisitions and mergers as a result of deregulation.

A current statistical profile of radio reveals a strong, vigorous, and dynamic medium, meeting a variety of listener needs and interests. There are more stations on the air, more sets in use, and more listeners than ever before. FM programming and stations dominate radio broadcasting.

There are three major components in the structure and organization of radio:

(1) the local station, (2) the networks, and (3) program suppliers, primarily the recording industry. Stations are categorized by FM and AM frequencies, by commercial and noncommercial status, and by signal strength and signal location. There are a variety of radio networks and syndicators providing an array of program services, including music, sports, features, and commentary.

Most radio programming today is based on format broadcasting, in which a station selects a segment of the audience and attempts to reach that segment throughout its entire schedule. There are a wide variety of radio formats, but we have identified 13 as most important: (1) adult contemporary, (2) contemporary hit radio, (3) album-oriented rock, (4) classic rock, (5) easy listening, (6) country, (7) news/talk, (8) urban contemporary, (9) nostalgia/middle-of-the-road, (10) Hispanic/ethnic, (11) black, (12) religious, (13) classical. These formats are continually evolving as audiences change. Syndicates offer to provide customized formats for individual stations based on audience research.

Contemporary radio is a local rather than national medium in audience and income. Radio-listening habits are personal, and stations program selectively to satisfy individual needs. Radio is a mobile medium. Radio has a social responsibility, though today the FCC regulates this responsibility less than it used to. People listen to radio as a secondary activity, to accompany the work or play of the moment, and radio is used by advertisers to supplement their advertising mix.

Radio has clearly survived the competition from television and has developed into a new and aggressive medium. Radio is a companion medium fine-tuned to meet a variety of needs.

REFERENCES

1. Quoted in Archer Gleason, *History of Radio to 1926* (New York: American Historical Society, 1938), 85.
2. *Variety*, January 8, 1986, 196.
3. Bob Laurence, of Noble Broadcasting, quoted in "NAB Focuses on Formats," *Broadcasting*, October 2, 1989, 47.
4. Phil Hall, of KRTH-AM, Los Angeles, quoted in "NAB Focuses," 44.

Magazines and Periodicals

The French word *magasin*, from which the English *magazine* derives, means "store" or "shop," and indeed, the earliest magazines were simply inventories of French booksellers' storehouses. But over the 300 years of their history, magazines have come to be storehouses of another sort—compendiums of information, articles, stories, poems, drawings, photographs, cartoons. Begun in the early eighteenth century as publications for the elite few, magazines had by the end of the nineteenth century taken advantage of advances in print technology and a rise in literacy to reach out to broader audiences. Indeed, while newspapers were limited to local and regional audiences, magazines became the first truly national medium. A handful of large general-interest publications brought quality fiction and useful nonfiction to audiences throughout the country. In the past decade of their history in this country, the storehouses that are magazines, in response to competition from broadcasting and with a little help from modern technology and marketing techniques, have changed in a number of significant ways.

More than 11,000 magazine titles—general-interest or consumer, business, and literary—are produced on a regular basis annually in the United States. Almost 500 new titles appear every year, of which only some 10 percent can expect to survive.[1] With the recent explosion of desktop publishing, which enables a single individual to write, edit, design, and produce an entire set of pages for reproduction, we can expect to see the number of small publications proliferate.

Only a decade ago, magazine publishers expected the spread of other media to undermine their role as suppliers of information and carriers of advertising, and to some extent those fears materialized. Some of the biggest general-interest magazines—*Collier's*, *The Saturday Evening Post*, *Life*, and *Look* among them—went out of business or were restructured to meet more specialized audience needs.

The situation proved less dire than publishers first thought. The magazine industry has had to respond with widespread consolidations, and certain segments, such as general women's interest, are extremely competitive and facing hard times. But targeted publications remain profitable. As industry experts point out, consumer magazines in particular have done the best job of any major medium in appealing to "niche" audiences.[2] Magazines have developed sophisticated editorial and technological abilities for reaching audiences targeted by interest, income level, ethnic heritage, and zip code. Magazine advertising and circulation revenues moved steadily upward in the 1980s—with consumer magazine advertising revenues up 11 percent in 1989, for example;[3] business magazines' ad spending was up 6 percent.

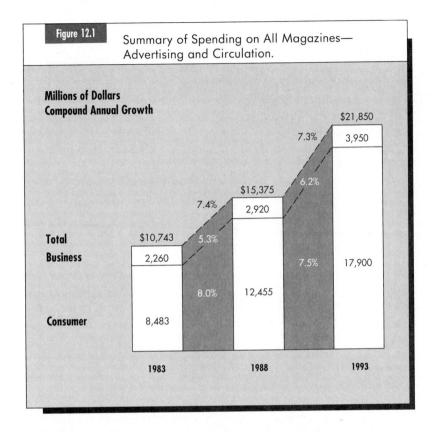

Figure 12.1 Summary of Spending on All Magazines—Advertising and Circulation.

In this chapter, we will look closely at the history of magazines in this country and the present state of the magazine industry. In particular, we will focus on current trends in magazine and periodical publishing—the increasing emphasis on targeting particular audiences, and the technology that enables publishers to accomplish that.

Historical Perspective

The First Magazines

The first English-language magazine was really little more than a newspaper printed on slightly heavier stock. Founded in 1704, the *Review* was published, edited, and for the most part written by a young Dissenter named Daniel Defoe who went on to become one of Britain's most celebrated men of letters. The *Review* carried news and articles on domestic affairs and national policy, as well as essays on literature, manners, and morals.

In 1709, Defoe's most successful imitator appeared. Richard Steele, later joined by Joseph Addison, brought out the *Tatler*; the two men also published the *Spectator*. They printed political, international, and theatrical news, coffeehouse gossip, and moral essays. They also carried advertising, a feature that was to become a vital ingredient in almost all magazine publishing thereafter. Addison and Steele provided a number of important contributions to British literature through their magazines, primarily informal essays.

The first English publication to pick up the French word *magasin* in its title appeared in 1731: the *Gentlemen's Magazine*, founded by Edward Cave. Cave printed a variety of reading in his magazine, but his most important contribution may have been his inclusion of parliamentary debates, making the internal workings of Parliament accessible for the first time. One of Cave's parliamentary reporters was Dr. Samuel Johnson, the lexicographer, critic, and poet, who eventually founded his own magazine, the *Rambler* (1750–1752). By 1750, the *Gentlemen's Magazine* had an amazing circulation of 15,000, and a number of imitators had appeared in London. Only half a century after the first magazine appeared, England was home to more than 150 periodicals.

EARLY AMERICA

About 35 years after the first English magazine was published, the new medium made its debut in the American colonies. In 1740, Benjamin Franklin announced plans to publish the *General Magazine and Historical Chronicle, for All the British Plantations in America*, but another Philadelphia printer, Andrew Bradford, rushed his own magazine into print and beat Franklin by 3 days. American magazine journalism was thus born in a state of intense competition and this has marked its progress ever since.

Bradford's *American Magazine, or a Monthly View of the Political State of the British Colonies* lasted for only three issues, and Franklin's *General Magazine* for six. But these two efforts inspired more than a dozen others in colonial America. None of these first American magazines lasted more than 14 months. The average circulation was about 500 copies (although then, as now, each issue was often passed among many readers), and advertising support was scarce. Magazines covered a wide range of general topics, including religion, philosophy, natural science, political affairs, and literature. These magazines, despite their short lives, were a unifying force in the new nation. They numbered among their contributors and editors many of the great names of colonial American literature, including Franklin, Noah Webster, Philip Freneau, and Thomas Paine as editors; and Alexander Hamilton, John Jay, John Hancock, and even George Washington as authors. Paul Revere was the foremost magazine illustrator of his day. The genre lives on, through journals of social sciences and literature, the so-called little magazines, and many other vehicles of influence and scholarly contribution if not of mass circulation.

THE NINETEENTH CENTURY

After the turn of the century, magazines blossomed into a national force. Some would last a century and a half. They influenced education, spreading the new nation's ideas and culture, building literacy, and shaping public opinion. From the 1820s through the 1840s, magazines played much the same role that radio would play a century later; they brought the nation together into a "national culture." "This is the age of magazines," remarked a poet in the *Cincinnati Literary Gazette* in 1824, and Edgar Allan Poe, himself a magazine editor in the 1830s, wrote: "The

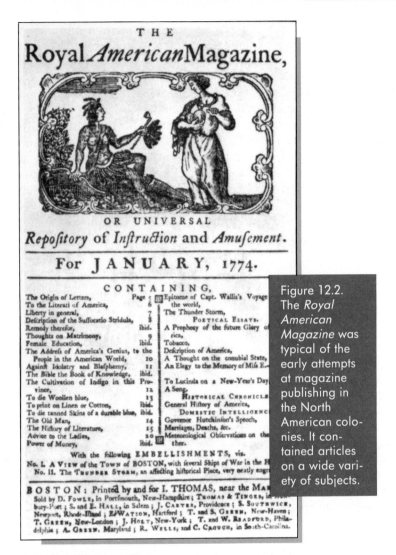

Figure 12.2. The *Royal American Magazine* was typical of the early attempts at magazine publishing in the North American colonies. It contained articles on a wide variety of subjects.

whole tendency of the age is Magazineward. The magazine in the end will be the most influential of all departments of letters.''

Most famous among these national magazines of the nineteenth century was the *Saturday Evening Post*. Founded in 1821 (although it claimed lineage back to Franklin's *Pennsylvania Gazette* of 1728), the *Post* was in continuous publication until 1969 when it fell victim to high production and mailing costs, and, perhaps more importantly, competition for advertising from television and specialized magazines. The *Post*'s circulation had remained high, around 4 million, but advertisers lost interest in its demographics. In the mid-1970s it was resurrected by a new publisher as a ''nostalgia'' monthly. With covers designed to reflect the immensely popular covers Norman Rockwell had painted for the *Post* in earlier years and with a distinctly conservative editorial slant, the new *Post* itself became a specialty item targeted at the audience it had been drawing before its demise.

Niles Weekly Register (1811–1849) covered American political affairs and foreshadowed the weekly newsmagazines of the twentieth century; the *North American Review* (1815–1938) offered more intellectual and literary fare, akin to today's "little" magazines. Perhaps the most widely read of all the early magazines was *Godey's Lady's Book*, established in 1850 and edited for most of its life by Boston feminist Sarah Josepha Hale. *Godey's* used hand-colored engravings of women's clothes along with fiction and poetry to reach a circulation peak of 150,000 copies.

Harper's Monthly and the *Atlantic Monthly*, both founded in the 1850s, were among several dozen widely influential literary magazines. These publications provided a launching pad for most American literary giants of the time, including Washington Irving, Edgar Allan Poe, Harriet Beecher Stowe, Mark Twain, Herman Melville, Nathaniel Hawthorne, Walt Whitman, Ralph Waldo Emerson, Henry David Thoreau, Henry James, Emily Dickinson, and Sarah Orne Jewett.

THE MAGAZINE AS A NATIONAL MEDIUM

With the outbreak of the Civil War, magazines informed citizens—and influenced public opinion. Magazines were widely used by antislavery groups; most famous among these was William Garrison's *Liberator*, started in 1831, which ceased publication in 1865 when its goal of emancipation had been achieved. *Harper's Weekly* (founded in 1857 as a sister publication to *Harper's Monthly*) sent a staff of writers and artists to the battlefields for firsthand coverage of the war; among these was photographer Mathew Brady who produced Civil War pictures that are still regarded as among the best in photojournalism. During Reconstruction, magazines were in the forefront of the fight against political corruption, led by such publications as the *Nation*, whose militant editor, E. L. Godkin, shaped his magazine into a leading commentator on current affairs and a fighter for democratic principles.

The role of magazines in Civil War reporting led to a broader readership, and after the war, magazines—particularly those designed for special-interest groups—began to reach a national audience. Farming magazines had already emerged as a separate publishing field; among these was *Tribune and Farmer*, published by Cyrus H. K. Curtis, who would go on to establish one of the largest magazine empires in history. Magazines for women also came into their own, particularly with the 1883 founding of the *Ladies' Home Journal*, published by Curtis and edited by Edward Bok, and included *Good Housekeeping*, *Woman's Home Companion*, *McCall's*, *Harper's Bazaar*, *Vogue*, and *Vanity Fair*.

By the end of the century, magazines were a mass medium. Improvements in printing dramatically increased production speed. Prices were lowered, and the "nickel magazine" became a counterpart to the penny press and the dime novel. The number of magazines increased by almost 500 percent in a 20-year period, from 700 in 1865 to 3,300 in 1885. By 1900, at least 50 titles were nationally known, many of which had circulations over 100,000. Curtis's *Ladies' Home Journal* topped 1 million, and by 1908, another Curtis publication, the *Saturday Evening Post*, which Curtis had taken over when it was failing, was also selling 1 million copies per issue.

The muckrakers also wrote for magazines, which eventually moved ahead of newspapers in exposing crime and scandal, fraud and manipulation. An example was *McClure's Magazine*, founded by S. S. McClure in 1894, which exposed oil monopolies, railroad injustices, political corruption, life-insurance fraud. McClure was so successful, both in winning audiences and in achieving societal reform, that other magazines, including *Cosmopolitan*, *Munsey's Magazine*, *Collier's*, and *Frank Leslie's Popular Monthly*, followed his example.

Between 1894 and 1904, the American magazine came of age. It proved itself not only a powerful communicator but also a powerful source of influence in American society.

THE CONTEMPORARY AMERICAN MAGAZINE

Magazines have changed substantially in the twentieth century. They have both enlarged their scope and narrowed their focus. As in the earliest days of magazine publishing, innovation in this century seems often to have come from individual genius—the vision of the young with new ideas, fresh talent, and frequently very little money. Categorizing contemporary periodicals is not a simple matter, but analysts generally suggest that most fall into either the consumer (with over 1,900 titles) or the business category (4,200 titles). The consumer category includes all those general-interest and special-interest magazines that we are used to seeing on the newsstand, everything from *People* to *Tennis Today*; the business category includes not only those major financial publications with which most of us are familiar—*Business Week* and *Forbes*, for example—but the myriad trade journals that are circulated within industries or businesses.

Magazines have greater flexibility than most other media. Publishers can create a magazine "package" in almost any size, shape, or dimension, and can achieve change and variation with ease. Some magazines have the luxury of a greater "lead time" than newspapers or television and thus can afford to take a longer look at issues and penetrate problems more deeply, providing more interpretation and analysis. Others, especially the newsmagazines, have brought such sophistication and speed to their reporting, editing, and decision-making processes that they can now feature a cover in television commercials that air before the issue is off press and on the newsstand.

Magazines, unlike books, are usually timely enough to deal with a flow of events, and they have the power to sustain a topic over time in a series of issues, unlike most newspapers and broadcast media. They can custom-tailor their ability to communicate. Magazines do not have the permanence of books, but neither are they as disposable as newspapers or as fleeting as broadcast messages. Weekly magazines are often passed from hand to hand over a period of several weeks; monthlies for several months; and quarterlies are often bound and kept permanently.

The biggest American magazine success story of the first two-thirds of the twentieth century was the digest form, and in particular *Reader's Digest*, which by mid-twentieth century had the biggest circulation of any magazine in the world. Founded in 1922 by DeWitt and Lila Wallace, both children of poor ministers, the *Digest* was passed in U.S. circulation by both *TV Guide* and *Modern Maturity* when it deliberately lowered its guaranteed circulation base by 1.8 million in 1988, to better manage total costs (see page 321), but it remains the circulation leader worldwide. A pocket-size compendium of inspirational nonfiction and condensed books,

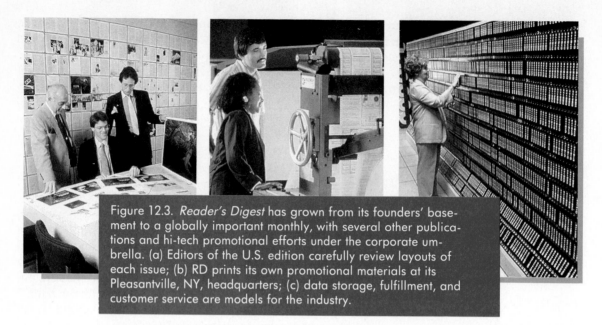

Figure 12.3. *Reader's Digest* has grown from its founders' basement to a globally important monthly, with several other publications and hi-tech promotional efforts under the corporate umbrella. (a) Editors of the U.S. edition carefully review layouts of each issue; (b) RD prints its own promotional materials at its Pleasantville, NY, headquarters; (c) data storage, fulfillment, and customer service are models for the industry.

Reader's Digest is now the centerpiece of a publishing empire that in 1989 reported $1.8 billion in worldwide revenues and $207 million in total operating profit.[4]

Other examples of the digest form share one basic purpose: to save readers time by providing a logically organized, easy-to-read synopsis of information. The newsmagazines perform this function to some extent, as do such specialized periodicals as *Soap Opera Digest* and many of the thousands of industry and professional newsletters.

NEWSMAGAZINES

Another far-from-wealthy son of a missionary, Henry Luce, founded the empire that now includes *Time, Life, Sports Illustrated, Fortune,* and *People*. Luce was a young man just out of Yale when he put together the first issue of *Time* in 1923. Originally the newsmagazines—*Time* and its imitators and competitors, including *Newsweek* and *U.S. News & World Report*—provided readers with a unique service: a weekly summary of major events, with enough interpretation and "color" to allow readers a clear perspective on the news, as well as "back-of-the-book" sections on movies, books, art, and other cultural areas.

In a way, newsmagazines suffered from their own success. They have drawn heavy competition from week-in-review and specialty sections ("Science Today," "Sports Monday") in newspapers, and from television talk and "magazine" shows. Advertising pages in newsmagazines have slipped by 20 percent in the last decade.[5] "One thing became remarkably clear in the 1980s," says Walter Shapiro, a senior writer at *Time,* formerly of *Newsweek,* "and that was that what the newsmagazines were doing was all-consumingly boring."[6] The newsweeklies have responded by experimenting with new formats (less text, more graphics, more particularized personalities), sometimes to the dismay of their staffs. With its larger margins and hyped-up graphics, "there's just less in *Time* than there used to be," one editor complains. "I get through the magazine and I feel hungry."[7]

The challenge of the 1990s and beyond for the newsmagazines will be to make readers feel that the weeklies are indispensable for sorting out the explosion of news and information we face daily. Maintaining readership in the coming decade will "require an insistent focus on content," says one industry expert, and an incorporation of technology such as satellite transmission that enables the weeklies to be as current as daily newspapers.[8]

CITY AND REGIONAL MAGAZINES

Once a primary form of magazine, the city magazine has come back into its own in the twentieth century. Although the *New Yorker*, founded by Harold Ross in 1925, might be considered the first of these, it really fits more easily with other sophisticated national periodicals like *Harper's* and the *Atlantic*. In fact, the first and one of the most successful of modern city magazines is *Los Angeles*, founded in 1960 and noteworthy in that it focuses on a city often accused of having no center. "It was such a hard city to figure out, even when you're living here," explains publisher Geoff Miller.[9] *Los Angeles*, owned by Capital Cities/ABC, Inc., has maintained its circulation (over 170,000) and its profitability in the face of new competition and at a time when the regional publication is having financial problems, in part because it "follows the trends," but also, according to an industry analyst, because it attracts national advertisers. Typically such magazines offer micro-marketing, "taking the focus away from the national level and addressing the local level, where the action is. The fact is that local publications [do that] more definitively than the nationals."[10]

City and regional magazines depend on local economies, which means falling revenues for magazines in Boston and Philadelphia, among others, in recent years. By the mid-1980s, however, virtually every major city, most states, and many regions had magazines of their own. Washington, D.C., boasted half a dozen, and New York City even more. Regional and city magazines can offer local advertisers an audience that is demographically attractive in several ways, and they can offer national advertisers audience *segments* that may well be attractive as well, high in both education and income. Their uniqueness in this area is rapidly being undercut, however, by advancing technology that allows national periodicals to publish "local" issues targeted and delivered to particular geographical areas.

WOMEN'S MAGAZINES

Long the centerpiece of American magazine publishing, women's magazines worked with new formats, new audiences and new challenges in the last decade. Unlike earlier magazines designed for women (particularly those known in the trade as the "seven sisters"—*Good Housekeeping*, *Ladies' Home Journal*, *McCall's*, *Woman's Day*, *Family Circle*, *Better Homes and Gardens*, and *Redbook*), the magazines that began appearing in the 1970s and 1980s do not focus on woman as homemaker. Rather, they target the "new woman" who works outside the home and wants advice not only about cooking, sewing, and housekeeping, but about career development, juggling children, work, marriage, and sex. Magazines like *Self* and

New Woman for younger readers, *Working Woman* and *Working Mother* for career women, and *Lear's*, edited by and targeted at women "of a certain age," have carved out respectable niches in the marketplace, with circulations ranging from 350,000 for *Lear's* to almost 1.3 million for *New Woman*.

The fastest-growing segment of "women's" publishing, according to the *Columbia Journalism Review*, is the regional magazine. Some 50 such publications appeared in the latter half of the 1980s, including titles like *New York Woman, Boston Woman, Michigan Woman*, and so on.[11] A few of these are thick and glossy, but most are tabloid giveaways, with circulations ranging between 10,000 and 50,000.

Perhaps the most competitive battleground in the "women's magazine" category in the 1990s is the upscale fashion and home magazine. Once this turf was the almost exclusive property of S. I. Newhouse's Condé Nast, which has owned *Vogue, Vanity Fair*, and *House and Garden* (now *HG*) since the early years of this century and acquired *Glamour* and *Mademoiselle* several decades ago. But "white-glove" fashion publishing, as the Condé Nast empire was once called, ended in the early 1970s with the arrival of feminism, the new career woman, and *Ms.* magazine. Signs of change were the dismissal of *Vogue's* legendary editor Diana Vreeland and the American debut of the French blockbuster *Elle* in 1985. All women's magazines have in recent years been hurt by their dependence on cigarette advertising and supermarket sales, both sharply down.

GENERAL-INTEREST MAGAZINES

The segment of magazine publishing that has suffered most from the competition of other media in recent years has been the traditional general-interest magazine. Along with *Collier's* and the *Saturday Evening Post*, both of which disappeared in the 1970s, the popular photojournalism periodicals *Life* and *Look* ceased publication—although *Life*, like the *Post*, eventually reappeared as a monthly and in 1989

Figure 12.4. The *Ladies' Home Journal* was the first American magazine to reach a circulation of 1 million. Indeed, women were one of the first groups targeted for specialized magazine publishing. One hundred years after this LHJ issue, targeted women's magazines still provide images of fashion and lifestyle.

boasted a circulation of 1.7 million. *Life* was the first to use photography as a regular journalistic tool to inform, entertain, persuade, and sell.

The twentieth century has seen the rise of "high-end" general-interest magazines that feature articles on art, science, history, philosophy, and current affairs—similar in content, if not in design, to some of America's earliest magazines. A few of these, like *National Geographic* and *American Heritage*, have been around for many years; others, like *Smithsonian* and *Psychology Today*, have appeared in the last few decades and have grown remarkably, *Smithsonian* to a circulation topping 2 million.

People magazine, another Time product, brought together much of what general-interest magazines had done before, covering a wide range of subjects with text and photos. But *People* keeps the text brief, the graphics jazzy, and the costs down (by using only black-and-white photos). *People* and its competitor *Us* have provided a singular success story for new general-interest magazines in the last two decades; they boast circulations of 1.3 million for *Us* and 3 million for *People*,

Figure 12.5.

and they seem to confirm Andy Warhol's often-quoted remark that in years to come, everyone will be famous for 15 minutes.

A final group of survivors in the general-interest category is the Sunday supplement magazines, the color periodicals, often unstapled, that accompany Sunday newspapers. These are distributed "free" with newspapers (although the "granddaddy" of these, the *New York Times Magazine*, is also for sale throughout most of the country on its own). Two major supplements, *Parade* and *In the U.S.A.*, are purchased by hundreds of newspapers that cannot afford or choose not to produce their own supplements. According to advertising analyst Richard Kotyra, "Sunday supplements consistently reach more Americans than any other media outlet."[12] *Parade*, for example, reaches an estimated 66.4 million people each week.

SPECIAL-INTEREST MAGAZINES

Undoubtedly the most significant movement in consumer magazines in recent years has been the tremendous increase in special-interest journals targeted at specific audience segments. Large divisions of the population—ethnic and age groups—are being served more and more by their own magazines. Smaller groups—based on income, for example, or profession—are redivided into more and more specifically targeted audiences.

John H. Johnson, whose Johnson Publishing Company had by 1983 become the largest black-owned business in the United States, has long attributed his success as a magazine publisher (*Ebony, Jet, EM*) to the provision of a unique service for a particular audience. When asked why his *Life*like *Ebony* continued strong when its prototype collapsed, Johnson responded, "What you found in the old *Life* magazine you could find elsewhere. That's not true of what you find in *Ebony*."[13] By the year 2000, when blacks and Hispanics will constitute a majority in one-third of the nation's major cities (according to a survey prepared for *Ebony* in 1983), Johnson Publishing will be strongly positioned to take advantage of this growing audience.

Surely the most remarkable success story of the last decade is *Modern Maturity*, published by the American Association of Retired Persons and now the U.S. circulation leader, with total paid sales topping 20 million. Given the rapidly expanding older population in the United States, magazines targeted at senior citizens would appear to be a good bet for expansion into the twenty-first century.

Age and ethnicity are only two of the characteristics to which publishers now target magazines. Where once a handful of national publications dominated a given field, dozens of smaller, more narrowly focused titles now proliferate. General fan magazines like *Photoplay* and *Modern Screen*, for instance, have given way to the likes of *Tiger Beat*, which features only teenage record and TV personalities; *Soap Opera Stars*; and even "fanzines," underground publications now numbering over 1,000, geared to the alternative music scene and often focusing on individual groups.

Special-interest magazines demonstrate not only range but flexibility. When home computers first became popular, a number of magazines described particular systems and software to consumers; as the market became more sophisticated, the magazines became more specialized. Recently many computer magazines (see Figure 6.13) have concentrated on the "glamour" field of desktop publishing. Special groups of many kinds have turned to magazines for communicating with those

Figure 12.6. Overall circulation remained relatively stable in the 1980s, but the number of magazine titles grew by almost 1,000. The difference was that magazines were aiming more at specific groups and not at mass circulation.

who share their interests, including cat lovers (*I Love Cats*), inn owners (*Innsider*), and counterculturists (*High Times*). One publisher of niche magazines, Diamandis Communications (*Car and Driver, Stereo, Flying*) could boast of $63 million in retail sales before it sold its list to French publisher Hachette. Indeed, concentration on special-interest and international appeal magazines led that firm to put its flagship publication, *Woman's Day*, up for sale in 1990. Established in 1937, its circulation has been dropping as supermarket sales rivals increase.

Specialization in magazine publishing has been a response to a number of factors in American life, including the increasing specialization of jobs, the assertion of new freedoms and tastes, the spread of education, the growth of consumerism, increased opportunities for individuals to pursue interests outside the workplace, and desktop publishing.

Travel

The fastest-growing segment of American magazine publishing at the end of the 1980s was travel. The potentially rich stakes—advertisers spend almost $300 million each year, only about 20 percent of which is now allocated to travel magazines[14]—

Table 12.1.	Top 20 Magazines in the United States, 1989	
Title	Adv. Rate/Guar. Circ. (millions)	Total Paid Circ.
Modern Maturity	19.4	21,430,990
Reader's Digest	16.2	16,343,599
TV Guide	15.8	15,867,750
National Geographic	10.5	10,890,660
Better Homes and Gardens	8.0	8,005,311
Family Circle	5.75	5,461,786
Good Housekeeping	5.0	5,152,525
McCall's	5.0	5,088,686
Ladies' Home Journal	5.0	5,038,297
Woman's Day		4,705,288
Time	4.3	4,339,029
Guideposts		4,203,934
Redbook	3.8	3,901,419
Sports Illustrated	3.15	3,424,393
Playboy	3.4	3,421,203
People	3.0	3,270,835
Newsweek	3.1	3,180,011
Prevention	2.9	3,134,914
Cosmopolitan	2.5	2,702,125
Smithsonian	2.1	2,342,443

Source: Audit Bureau of Circulations, FAS-FAX Report-December 31, 1989.

have attracted a number of big-time players. Publishing czar Rupert Murdoch bought *European Travel and Life* in 1986; in 1989, its subscriptions grew by 25 percent. Also in 1986, Condé Nast paid $25 million for *Signature,* a membership publication for Diner's Club cardholders, and turned it into the colorful *Condé Nast Traveler.* Overall, the travel category of consumer magazines added 25.4 percent new advertising pages in the first 9 months of 1989, a solid 6 percent more than the next leading category of magazines, parenting.[15]

BUSINESS AND PROFESSIONAL JOURNALS

The Audit Bureau of Circulations tracks almost 300 business periodicals, ranging from *Locksmith* to *Poultry Times* to *Chain Store Age Executive.* In addition, hundreds of academic and professional journals, often published by universities, industry councils, or professional organizations, serve readerships in particular fields. Everyone from the courtroom lawyer to the English professor has available a half-dozen or more journals relevant to the profession in which she is engaged. Media practitioners' bibles include *Publishers Weekly, Billboard, Advertising Age, Broadcasting,* and many more. There are about 4,000 trade publications and newsletters.

NEWSLETTERS ....

The newsletter is one of the oldest forms of journalistic communication. The Fugger newsletters, produced in several German city-states in the fifteenth and sixteenth centuries by the Fugger banking house, were among the forerunners of the modern newspaper. Written in letter form, they contained financial information that helped spread the mercantile revolution in middle Europe. The modern newsletter is a strong publishing category.

Not counted in the thousands of commercial newsletters are all the subsidized newsletters used to promote or persuade, and internal organs of communication within organizations or groups; they are essentially products of public relations.

The father of the modern newsletter was probably Willard M. Kiplinger, who began the *Kiplinger Washington Letters* in 1923. A Washington reporter for the Associated Press, Kiplinger was hired by a New York bank to produce reports on government information vital to banking and business interests. Kiplinger reasoned that he might sell the information in the letters he wrote to his employers to other banks and to business people.

Kiplinger typed his four-page letter on his own typewriter and had it mimeo-

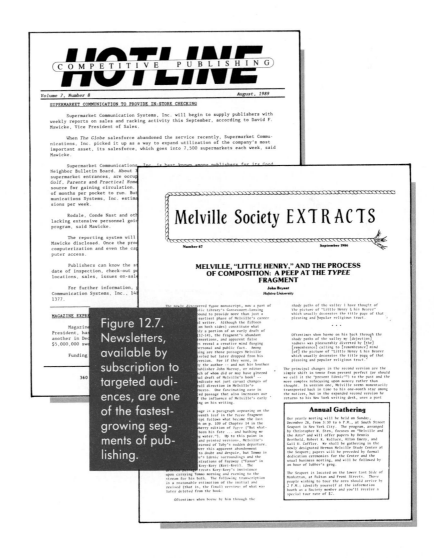

Figure 12.7. Newsletters, available by subscription to targeted audiences, are one of the fastest-growing segments of publishing.

graphed (later, printed by photo offset); underlining and capitalization provided the only graphics. Kiplinger's primary aim was to *distill* information. He typed each complete thought on a separate line, so that each line would be easy to read and remember. He felt no constraints to follow normal journalistic restrictions of objectivity and attribution to sources; rather, he made analyses and predictions for his readers, taking them into his confidence as if he were addressing old friends. The *Kiplinger Washington Letter* continues to appear, in 1990 at a cost of $58 annually; in addition, Kiplinger publishes separate newsletters on agriculture, taxes, and the states of California, Florida, and Texas.

Commercial newsletters generally do not carry advertisements since their central feature is the personal relationship between author and reader. Publishers, as a result, depend on income from subscriptions—and if the subscription list is small and the information of vital importance, the price is very high. Some newsletters, particularly those providing financial advice, cost up to $1,000 per year.

A typical newsletter publisher is Phillips Publishing, of Washington, D.C. In 1974, only 6 years out of journalism school, Thomas Phillips began publishing consumer newsletters offered at relatively low subscription rates and aimed at general audiences, but he soon discovered another, perhaps better market: professionals and business executives willing to pay relatively high subscription rates for current and important information in their specialized fields. Phillips now publishes more than 30 newsletters in two divisions, consumer and professional. The consumer division concentrates on financial and health-related issues, and aims newsletters, priced between $50 and $100, at general audiences. The professional division publishes in four highly specialized and somewhat volatile areas—defense and aerospace, telecommunications, banking, and data—and aims newsletters, priced from $295 to $1,000 (for their daily summary and analyses of developments in defense) at business executives in these fields.

The newsletter is quick, inexpensive, easy to produce, and useful. Just about anyone with a computer and a mailing list can get into the newsletter business. Succeeding at it is not so simple, however; many newsletters are short-lived and make only fleeting impressions.

THE COMICS

One popular periodical that deserves special consideration is the comic book. Of the several forms of comics that appear regularly—single picture and multipanel newspaper comics, for example—the only ones that legitimately fall under the magazine and periodical rubric are the multipage color action or humor narratives that are issued monthly, bimonthly, or quarterly by such comic conglomerates as Marvel and D.C. Comics, and the antiestablishment, sociopoliticoeconomic commentaries that appear irregularly from "underground" sources.

The comic book emerged during the Depression, first as reprints of the newspaper strips that had begun appearing regularly in newspapers in the early part of the century. *Detective Comics* (1937) was the first set of comic books to structure its content on one theme. In 1938, the most popular superhero of all time, Superman, began appearing in *Action Comics*. By 1940, there were more than 40 comic-book titles, and by 1941, 168 titles. At U.S. Army bases during World War II, comic books outsold all other magazines 10 to 1. *Classics Comics*, which first appeared in 1942, provided young readers with faithfully rendered plots of major works of literature. While most comic-book publishers print about 200,000 copies of a given issue, *Classics Comics*, which became *Classics Illustrated* in 1947, stay on the news-stand indefinitely and sometimes sell 1 million or more. The *Classics* version of *Moby-Dick*, for example, was reprinted 13 times between 1942 and 1954, and an-other 10 times after the art was redrawn in 1956. *Ivanhoe* and *Robin Hood*, the two best-selling *Classics*, went through 26 printings each.

More than 100 comic-book companies now publish over 300 titles and sell in excess of 250 million copies annually. But even that figure doesn't provide an accurate picture of comics readership; the industry estimates that every copy, on the average, has three readers in addition to the buyer. Most comic book readers are between 7 and 14, and most are good rather than poor readers, according to research in the area. Longer versions of comics, "graphic novels," have long been popular in other parts of the world and are beginning to appear in the United States. Both graphic novels and comic books are increasingly being printed on higher-quality paper and provided with more sophisticated illustrations in an effort to attract more adult readers.

THE STRUCTURE AND ORGANIZATION OF MAGAZINES

Because magazines come in different sizes and shapes—from pocket-size literary journals to the hardcover coffee-table-size *American Heritage*—and because they are aimed at very different kinds of readers, no one organizational or operational pattern fits them all. Each magazine develops its own way of organizing to get its special job done. Periodicals that deal heavily in news and timely subjects are organized much like daily newspapers; others work on more leisurely publishing schedules and are organized much like book-publishing firms.

The editorial staff of a magazine generally includes an editor as chief executive, with overall responsibility for establishing policies and making final decisions. The managing editor or executive editor carries out the editor's policies and runs the day-to-day operation; staff editors typically head various departments or handle various functions (photo editing, copyediting, layout, or production), and staff writers, often called editors, produce copy.

Many magazines also have contributing editors, who work either full- or part-time in the office or in the field; they are often specialists in particular areas and help the magazine discover material, find appropriate writers, approve the au-thenticity of copy, or actually write. Some magazines also use editorial boards composed of leaders in the field to which the magazine is directed to give the magazine direction and authority.

Magazines traditionally depended largely on freelance contributions. The ed-itor waited for the mail to come in and then published the best of what arrived.

Increasingly, magazines are using staff-developed and staff-written material. Only a handful of professionals make a substantial salary from freelance, full-time magazine writing. Schedules are too demanding and story development too com-plicated to allow editors to rely on unsolicited contributions. Editor and staff gen-erally determine the audience they are reaching, the type of material the audience

*S*py magazine cofounder Kurt Andersen revealed the origins of this offbeat publication in an article written for the *Gannett Center Journal*.

According to him, *Spy* originated because both he and coeditor Graydon Carter had run out of favorite magazines. Both had loved the early *New Yorker, Esquire* in the 1960s, and *Rolling Stone* and *National Lampoon* in the 1970s. But by 1980, they found little to like. "What disappointed us in contemporary magazines," he says, "was what you might call the *People* factor. In the 15 years since *People* was started, general-interest magazine journalism has become almost entirely a matter of personality profiles. In the 1960s and 1970s magazines . . . had an intelligence driving the choice of stories, a conception that involved more than 'Hmmm, Melanie Griffith, she's hot.'"

So Andersen and Carter, along with cofounder and publisher Tom Phillips, set out to concoct the editorial equivalent of "Saturday Night Live" and "The David Letterman Show"—a stylish, intelligent, satiric, ideologically unpredictable, and (most of all) funny stealth bomber of a magazine. "Our idealized reader," Andersen says, "is the caricature of a yuppie, ambivalent about his or her very yuppiness and eager for intelligent, entertaining critiques of himself and his generation."

The money the three men raised in late 1986 and 1987, $2.8 million, was a pittance by Murdoch or Hearst standards, but their timing was perfect. *Spy* appeared just as 1980s glitz was beginning to fade. The first issue—64 pages, 25,000 circulation, a dozen staff—appeared in October 1986, and within 3 years the magazine averaged 110–170 pages and a circulation of 130,000.

The secret of *Spy*'s success lies in its commitment to "literate sensationalism," its ability to blend *National Enquirer* outrage with *New Yorker* sophistication. It relies on public-domain information for much of its "gossip"—checking gun-permit records for names of prominent people and Pulitzer Prize nominations for journalists who have nominated themselves—and its "Separated at Birth?" feature has taken on a life of its own, with book spin-offs and newspaper syndication through United Features.

needs and wants, and the subjects available for development into appropriate magazine articles and stories. Then they produce the material to make sure it fits their editorial needs and time schedule. A case history is featured in the box.

NEW DIRECTIONS

In the 1950s and 1960s, magazines first fought back from television's threat by playing what they called "the numbers game"—building circulation figures artificially by offering giveaways or unrealistically cheap prices to offer advertisers a larger guaranteed audience. Some magazines turned from their traditional newsstand sales to concentrate on subscriptions; they hired sales organizations that used high-pressure techniques and gifts of merchandise to attract subscribers at any cost, with long-term bargain prices or package deals of many periodicals for the price of one. In effect, magazines *bought* subscriptions. They earned very little money from subscriptions; in fact, they often lost money, but publishers hoped to make up the difference through advertising.

By the latter part of the decade, however, publishers recognized that "buying" circulation to attract advertising was a volatile and often self-destructive move; accepting slightly lower circulation figures at substantially higher single-copy prices often made better economic sense. Publishers have increasingly realized that income from circulation can be stabilized while income from advertising cannot. Circulation, in other words, can be profitable. "We have been able to get the average rate per copy up and our costs down enough so that now we make a profit from each copy, regardless of what happens with advertising," according to Newsweek, Inc., Senior Vice President Harold Shain.[16]

TARGETING

What makes the focus on circulation even more attractive now is the ability to select audiences more and more carefully. Increasingly, magazines are using computers and demographic data to make their advertising and their editorial content more selective. When a national magazine's production and circulation can be coordinated so that circulation is broken up into perhaps 25 *megamarkets*, 50 *megastates*, and a group of top-spot zip codes, the advertiser is then able to reach a more appropriate market on either a regional or a reader-interest basis. Perhaps the most sophisticated of these systems is offered by R. R. Donnelley & Sons, the nation's largest printer, in Chicago. Donnelley's printing and binding technology can actually insert single pages or subscription cards into individual copies of magazines so that a clothing company can offer a discount to you on lingerie while offering your next-door neighbor a discount on hunting jackets in the same issue of the same magazine.[17]

As we have seen, national magazines like *Newsweek* and *People* routinely target editions to geographic regions of the country. Each can offer advertisers more than 100 editions of the same issue (the smallest reaching about 25,000 subscribers) in which to advertise hotels, retailers, and other local businesses. Threatened by that kind of pinpoint segmenting, regional and city magazines that prospered in the 1980s responded by forming a network in the 10 largest metropolitan markets, offering national advertisers a package deal on their 1.9 million subscribers. Regional women's magazines have done the same. This kind of cooperative effort can offer convenient alternatives to national publications—and often a demographically desirable audience.

CONTROLLED CIRCULATION

The ability to target an audience by zip code, interest, or income level has made possible another kind of magazine publishing—the *controlled-circulation* periodical, which is sent, often free of charge and unsolicited, to a carefully selected audience. Two Washington, D.C.-area magazines, *Regardie's* and *Washington Dossier*, are sent free to households and businesses targeted by market research and demographic studies as "active" and economically successful. These are consumers that advertisers are eager to reach and for whom they are willing to pay, whether or not the "targets" have indicated any interest in the publications.

Perhaps the ultimate in controlled-circulation magazines are those that exclude competition from other publications. Christopher Whittle, who likes to boast that his Tennessee-based Whittle Communications specializes in "guerrilla media," angered much of the industry in 1988 when he announced his intention to offer doctors a free line of monthly publications for their waiting rooms *if* the doctors agreed to cancel their waiting-room subscriptions to all other periodicals. Whittle offers a similar plan to salons, as does Communications Venture Group Ltd., whose *Confetti* consists of six bimonthly issues, each devoted to a subject of interest to salon customers. Salons that agree to receive *Confetti* are permitted to display up to three other subscription periodicals.

Although Whittle argues that his waiting-room publications are designed to serve both physician and consumer by saving the doctor money and time and providing patients with current reading matter, Whittle has been criticized for producing magazines in which editorial copy is often designed to promote the interests and products of the advertisers.

ADVERTISING VS. EDITORIAL

The blurring of lines between editorial and advertising content has been one of the more controversial developments in magazine publishing in the last decade. In the four top high-fashion magazines (*Vogue, Elle, Mirabella,* and *Harper's Bazaar*) major editorial content routinely begins only after 300 to 600 pages of ads, and increasingly the advertising pages are dominated by long sections that uncannily resemble regular editorial pages in layout and type design and on which the word *advertisement*, required by law, is printed in very small letters. This same kind of lengthy insert is also found in newsmagazines (and newspapers), often extolling the virtues of investment in a foreign country.

GROWTH AND DECLINE

Magazines, which seemed threatened on several fronts at the beginning of the 1980s, actually grew in circulation and advertising income from 1983 through 1988 by 8 percent, and industry analysts expect the growth to continue (see Figure 12.1). Although the consumer-magazine audience has traditionally been concentrated in the 18–35 group, which will substantially decline in the next 30 years in proportion

Figure 12.8. Each quarter, Whittle Communications issues a line of focused *Special Reports*—Health, Personalities, Fiction, Sports, Family, and Living. Subscriptions are for single categories or the whole line. Not available on newsstands, they are a clear example of controlled-circulation publishing, available for browsing at doctors' offices.

to the rest of the population, the success of *Modern Maturity* and other magazines targeted at older readers suggests that new audiences can profitably be brought into the readership circle. In 1989, magazines that showed the fastest-growing ad-page counts included *Longevity* and *Lear's*, both aimed at older readers; *Condé Nast Traveler*; and such "money"-oriented periodicals as *Entrepreneur*, *Harvard Business Review*, *Forbes*, *Fortune*, and *Business Week*. Certainly the death knell for magazines in the mid-twentieth century was premature.

Magazine growth and decline can provide an interesting index of America's changing interests and lifestyles. The rise in popularity of magazines focusing on personal improvement reflected a preoccupation of the 1980s. *Ms.* magazine, which was founded in 1973 as the flag carrier for the feminist movement, gained steadily in circulation and advertising through the 1970s and then began losing readership as feminism faded. *Ms.* was bought in the fall of 1989 by Dale Lang, who also publishes *Working Woman*, *Working Mother*, and *Sassy*, and after a hiatus of 8 months, was reborn in 1990 under the guidance of founder Gloria Steinem and feminist Robin Morgan as one of a handful of national publications that do not carry advertising. It was a risky venture, but as Lang points out, two of America's top-selling periodicals—*Consumer Reports* and *Guideposts*—do very well with only reader support.

Perhaps the most graphic example of shifting American tastes is in the rise, fall, and reemergence of men's magazines since World War II. *Esquire*, a sophisticated publication that often included fiction by writers like Hemingway, Truman Capote, and John Updike, gave way in the mid-1950s to *Playboy*, which demonstrated considerably more license in its sexual attitudes. *Playboy*, which first appeared in 1953 and reached an American circulation high of 6 million readers by 1980, was threatened by competition from the even more graphic *Penthouse* and *Hustler*. In the mid-1980s, however, *Playboy*'s circulation declined by only 2 percent (and in 1990 it claimed a worldwide circulation of 15 million), while *Penthouse* fell by 15.9 percent from 1984 to 1986 and *Hustler* fell off the list of the top 200 magazines by 1986, although it had appeared in the top 50 only 2 years earlier. Today, several new men's magazines are being planned, focused not on sexuality but on men who are "not hip, not downtown" and have "decent" jobs and a "decent" education.[18] One publisher calls his new effort "the Boy Scout handbook for the '90s for the 32-year-old man."[19]

VIDEO MAGAZINES

An excellent example of the blurring of media formats is the video magazine, still in the experimental stage. Actually the first electronic publication in this area was launched in 1977 by Nick Charney, who also founded one of this century's magazine successes, *Psychology Today*. His *VideoFashion Monthly* is still going strong, at $9.95 per monthly issue that goes mainly to the trade. Its offering to the public follows a method of direct-response mailings and ads in targeted print magazines. *RC Video Magazine*, established in 1984, provides its quarterly on radio-control cars to 2,000 subscribers, and a surfing annual video publication sells to 1,000 who pay $29.95.

Only recently has there been a more forceful effort to build a cross-media industry. *The Wide World of Golf* is a bimonthly published by Video Magazines in partnership with ABC Sports and Jack Nicklaus Productions; its goal is 40,000 subscriptions at $99.95 each. Most analysts of this emerging medium say the road to success is definitely niche markets—those *less* serviced by print magazines than golfers. As far as the eye can see, dependable consumer bases for any video magazine will remain small, and the pitfalls and special problems are many.

Apart from the fact that a video magazine might at best reach a universe too small to support the high costs of production and distribution, publishers need a sophisticated computer setup to keep track of subscribers. Many titles will depend on developing small retail sales outlets or distribution through fairs and conventions; direct marketing costs and risks are high; sophisticated marketing know-how is as important as editorial and production skills; and fulfillment (the delivery of the product to subscribers) must be flawless. Advertiser response is spotty; consumer understanding of the product concept uneven. Still, there are some success stories, including video magazines for amateur pilots, and entrepreneurs are optimistic:

"I believe it will be the new printing press," says VideoFashion's Charney, *echoing the sentiments of many. "Over the long haul, the costs of delivering information by video are going down, and publishers don't have to deal with union problems at printing plants. Video magazines are going to sprout up in virtually all trade and consumer special-interest areas. And they'll also be video complements to most major consumer magazines. It's a natural evolution."*[20]

A logical next step in technological development will be the portable CD/electronic book players, which we describe later in this book.

SUMMARY

Like newspapers, magazines have evolved from an elite to a mass medium over the 300 years of their history in this country. In the nineteenth century, they nurtured a national culture; now they are designed to appeal to regional, hobbyist, professional, or other interests represented by current demographics, and most are targeted at specific audiences.

Some 11,000 periodicals are published in the United States, of which fewer than 2,000 are consumer publications and the remainder are professional or business journals. General-interest publications, long the mainstays of magazine publishing, suffered most in the face of increased competition from other media in the past two decades, and respected names like *Life* and the *Saturday Evening Post* disappeared, at least temporarily, from the fray. The built-in flexibility of magazines, however, has been reflected in their ability to adapt. Special-interest magazines and newsletters in particular showed increasing strength in the last decades of the twentieth century.

Increased competition has brought many changes to the magazine industry, not the least of which is the rapid consolidation of ownership under communications giants like S. I. Newhouse, Hachette of France, Rupert Murdoch, and Robert Maxwell. New technology permits publishers to *target* specific audiences on an ever more sophisticated scale, and new audiences are continually being developed. The most impressive success story of the first half of the twentieth century was *Reader's Digest*; the most impressive success story of the second half may well be *Modern Maturity*, published by the American Association of Retired Persons specifically for an aging American population.

Magazines have traditionally drawn young entrepreneurs with more creativity than money, and innovations in technology continue to provide opportunities in magazine publishing not available in other media. Find a topic and a mailing list, and someone will create a magazine around it. Magazines at the end of the twentieth century remain financially and editorially healthy. The number of titles continues to grow, as do total revenues from both advertising and circulation. When we include in the ranks of periodicals such diverse and thriving categories as comic books, newsletters, desktop publications, and video magazines, we find a mass medium that is capable of reaching an audience of immense proportions and providing messages of considerable interest, power, and importance.

REFERENCES

1. "Magazine Executives Celebrate Their Industry's Revival," *The New York Times*, October 24, 1989, D20.
2. Veronis, Suhler, & Associates, *Communications Industry Forecast*, Summer 1989, 133.
3. "Advertising," *The New York Times*, February 7, 1990, D17.
4. *Reader's Digest Global Facts*, January 31, 1990.
5. Bruce Porter, "The Newsweeklies: Is the Species Doomed?" *Columbia Journalism Review* (March/April 1989): 23.
6. Ibid., 24.
7. Ibid., 25.
8. "Media Business," *The New York Times*, November 10, 1989, D5.
9. "Media Business," *The New York Times*, January 5, 1990, D5.
10. Ibid.
11. Pamela Black, "Who's the New Woman in Town?" *Columbia Journalism Review* (May/June 1987), 53.
12. "Advertising," *The New York Times*, August 25, 1989.
13. James Speigner, "John Johnson Says Get Smart, Not Mad," *Madison Avenue Magazine*, December 1984.
14. John Peter, "Travel Magazines Are Taking Off," *Folio*, June 1988, 153.
15. *Competitive Publishing Hotline* 7 (12) (December 1989): 4.
16. "Magazines," *The New York Times*, October 23, 1989.
17. "Donnelley Develops a Way for Magazines to Get Personal," *The New York Times*, November 19, 1989.
18. "Media Business," *The New York Times*, March 26, 1989, D12.
19. Ibid.
20. Paul Taublieb, "Vid Magazines Aim to Carve Niche," *Billboard*, March 10, 1990, 60.

Filmed Entertainment

Individual films continue to have great individual impact and widely felt societal effect. As mass entertainment, they constitute a significant component in the issues of global communication; the motion picture is perhaps the most international of the media. Also, the film has a significant role interacting with the other mass media. This chapter is entitled "Filmed Entertainment" to reflect the scope of the usage of the motion picture via box-office receipts, programming for television, and as videocassettes. For these reasons alone, it is useful to have an appreciation of this form of communication. Above all, however, the dominant aspect of movies today is the part they play in the conglomerate communicators' business plan. This chapter is thus especially industry-oriented.

Like magazines, movies were for a time profoundly affected by the advent of television. They have come into their own again. Few dramas *on* the screen compete with the adventure of the high stakes, wheeling and dealing, or international ventures that are the keynote of life behind the scenes in Hollywood at this time. The importance of filmed entertainment to video companies, television, and syndicators—as well as cinema owners—seems to command ever higher sums and greater attention in the popular press, the financial pages, and trade papers.

Although the medium has progressed to products aimed at specific splinters of the public, the targeted genres are potentially so enormously profitable that they still belong to the mass media. In this chapter we trace in detail the development of the motion picture. We then attempt to describe the structure of an industry in flux. The change in location of consumption, from theater alone to a large measure of end-user in the living room, is distinctive to this medium and is also a factor in the changing organizational and financial structure of the industry. While this medium may not beckon a large percentage of journalism and communications students and unemployment rates are high in comparison with the other mass media (CPAs may find more open doors), no picture of the growth, interrelationship, or globalization of the media can omit a serious look at film.

HISTORICAL PERSPECTIVE

The motion picture is a child of science. A number of discoveries, inventions, and theories have occurred throughout history and demonstrated a continued fascination with reproducing motion. By the early twentieth century, the entrepreneur had joined the scientists and technicians.

THE PREHISTORY OF THE MOTION PICTURE: 1824–1896

Across the centuries, Europeans had invented a number of camera-projection devices, including Leon Alberti's *camera lucida*, Giambattista della Porta's use of Leonardo da Vinci's *camera obscura*, and most important, Athansius Kircher's "magic lantern," developed in 1646, which provided a crude form of projection. Nevertheless, none of these devices went beyond the ability to project *drawn* pictures of *still life*.

Before motion pictures could exist, several discoveries had to take place. The scientific base of cinematography evolved in the nineteenth century with (1) the discovery of the persistence of vision; (2) the development of photography; (3) the invention of the motion-picture camera; (4) the development of motion-picture projection techniques; and (5) the integration of motion, persistence, and photographic concepts into cinematography.

Advancement of projection techniques beyond the magic lantern culminated in 1853 when Baron Franz von Uchatius projected *moving* images visible to a large number of people. In the 1890s, the motion-picture projector as we know it today developed out of experiments by Thomas Edison and Thomas Armat in the United States and August and Louis Lumière in France. But the pictures used to simulate motion were still being drawn. The next step was the invention of photography, resulting from the efforts of Nicephore Niepce and Louis J. M. Daguerre, who presented copperplate photography to the public for the first time in 1839.

In order for these developments in motion, projection, and photography to be integrated, special cameras faster than the still camera, film, and projectors were needed. Eadweard Muybridge's famous motion studies were a primitive form of

Figure 13.1. In the early form of slide projector developed in the seventeenth century, the light from a flame projects an image on a glass plate onto the screen outside the magic lantern. The praxinoscope, a nineteenth-century parlor toy, provided the illusion of motion; figures in various stages of movement were viewed in the mirrors at the center of the revolving drum.

the motion picture, capturing, in 1877, the gait of a galloping horse. A more successful step came in 1882, when Dr. E. J. Marey developed what he called a "photographic gun," which could take a series of pictures in rapid succession. But his camera still used individual plates.

It remained for William Dickson, an assistant of Thomas Edison, to perfect the first motion-picture camera using roll film, which had been invented by an American, a preacher, Hannibal Goodwin. In 1891, Edison applied for patents on the kinetograph as a photographing camera and the kinetoscope as a viewing apparatus, and soon afterward began producing short film strips.

Edison's kinetoscope was a "peep-show" device that allowed viewing by only one person at a time. These tall wooden boxes into which an individual peers are found as antiques in amusement parks and museums. Edison was slow to realize the importance of projection. Eventually taking advantage of the efforts of the Lumière brothers in France and of American inventor Thomas Armat, he developed the Vitascope projector. On April 23, 1896, in Koster and Bial's Music Hall in New York, Edison's Vitascope projector was used for the first public showing of motion pictures in the United States.

BEGINNINGS AND NARRATIVE DEVELOPMENT: 1896–1918

The first subject matter of the newly developed art of motion pictures was simple pictorial realism. Such films as *Arrival of the Paris Express, Kaiser Wilhelm Reviewing His Troops,* and *Feeding the Ducks at Tampa Bay* emphasized the camera's ability to record reality with a minimum of artistic distortion or interpretation. Few of these films ran for more than 1 minute, and they were often run backward to pad the presentation and amaze the audience.

Despite the initial excitement, people soon tired of various versions of Niagara Falls and fire engines racing down a street. Motion pictures began to develop themes involving a sustained narrative.

As early as 1896, the French filmmaker George Meliès began to create motion pictures with a story line. Meliès discovered new ways of seeing, interpreting, and even distorting reality. He contributed much to the development of many standard optical devices, such as the dissolve, split screen, jump cut, and superimposition. Unfortunately, he was unable to move beyond his theatrical and magical background, and his films, such as *Cinderella* (1899) and *A Trip to the Moon* (1902), were always a series of artificially arranged scenes shot from the fixed view of a spectator in a theater.

The Constructed Film. Edwin S. Porter, an American, is credited with the initial development of narrative film. In two films, *The Life of an American Fireman* (1902) and, more important, *The Great Train Robbery* (1903), he demonstrated the power of editing as a means of film construction. Porter was the first to cut from one point of view to another within a scene. *The Great Train Robbery* went beyond Meliès's trick photography for a new approach—a realistic plot line—and offered excitement as entertainment.

The years between 1906 and 1916 were the most important period of motion picture firsts: The feature film evolved, and the world saw the first film star, the first distinguished director, the first picture palaces, a place called Hollywood, and, above all, the development of film as a unique and individual means of expression.

Figure 13.2. George Meliès was the first artist to incorporate dramatic narrative into filmmaking, as illustrated in these scenes from *A Trip to the Moon* (1902). Note the superimposition of objects as a special effect. The face in the moon talked. Meliès is regarded as an originator of the expressionistic film, which stressed imaginary events and personal interpretations of the real world.

Figure 13.3. Edwin S. Porter explored the techniques of film editing to provide dramatic continuity in several key films of the early twentieth century, including *The Great Train Robbery* (1903).

Some historians have aptly labeled these 10 years "the age of Griffith." It was David Wark Griffith who took the raw material of film and created a language, a syntax, and an art. His contributions were many, but more than anything else, Griffith made film into a dynamic medium. He took the technique of editing and cutting for purposes of interpretation to new sophistication.

Beginning with *The Adventures of Dolly* (1908) and culminating with *The Birth of a Nation* (1915) and *Intolerance* (1916), Griffith freed the motion picture from strictly theatrical bounds. He pioneered a more natural acting style, better story organization, and, most important, rather than simply using film as a moving photograph or portable theater, he developed a language that emphasized the unique characteristics of the film medium, such as editing, camera movement, and camera angle. These years also saw the emergence of other notable film styles and important artists. Mack Sennett and his Keystone company developed their special brand of slapstick comedy. Charlie Chaplin went beyond Sennett's slapstick into humor with a deeper, more philosophical edge. William S. Hart made realistic Westerns, and Mary Pickford was the screen's most popular personality.

The Arrival of the Entrepreneur. Since most inventors of cinematic devices did little to exploit their devices commercially, it remained for individual entrepreneurs to bring showmanship to the motion picture. The early commercial development of motion pictures began in vaudeville houses. Films started out as "headliners" but ended as "chasers," which moved patrons out of the theater between shows. Motion pictures then moved to slightly more permanent homes when projectors were installed in empty stores and music halls. There were also

Figure 13.4. From its earliest days and the likes of the Keystone Kops, the motion-picture format and the chase sequence of the action film have made a successful partnership.

a number of traveling film shows, "electric theaters," as they were called. In his history of the mass media, *The Entertainment Machine*, Robert Toll writes:

> *Many average Americans, seated in the comfort of theaters caught their first glimpse of the wonders of the world through the wonders of film. Capitalizing on the early appeal of these realistic pictures, George C. Hale in 1903 outfitted a small theater like a railroad car, dressed the ticket-taker as a conductor, and took patrons on "Hale's Tours and Scenes of the World" by projecting films that had been shot from the front of a moving train. Beginning in 1903, Hale's Tours traveled the country for years and earned Hale some two million dollars.*[1]

In 1905 appeared the first permanent motion-picture theater, the nickelodeon— so named because a nickel was the price of admission. By 1907, there were more than 3,000 of these small theaters, and by 1910, over 10,000 nickelodeons were scattered throughout the eastern half of the country.

Making motion pictures became a thriving enterprise. Edwin S. Porter's *Dream of a Rarebit Fiend* (1906), for example, cost $350 to make and grossed more than $350,000. The Vitagraph Company, which started in 1896 with capital of $936, showed profits of over $900,000 by 1912. The trappings of an industrial empire were not yet apparent, however. There was no star system, no Hollywood. These would all come about as a reaction against a monopoly called the Motion Picture Patents Company (MPPC). Formed in 1909 through the pooling of 16 patents, it controlled virtually every aspect of motion-picture production, distribution, and exhibition in the United States for more than 3 years.

A savage war erupted between the MPPC and independent and foreign producers. It was a battle with one of these producers, Adolph Zukor, that precipitated the final development stage. Zukor acquired the rights to the French film *Queen Elizabeth* (1912), starring Sarah Bernhardt. In order to exhibit it, he had to apply to the MPPC for permission. It refused, so he went to an independent exhibitor. The picture was a success, and the experience led Zukor to form his own company, Famous Players in Famous Plays—the forerunner of Paramount Pictures. Heartened by Zukor's stand, other independent producers began showing films without the permission of the MPPC. Pressure was applied by the MPPC, and as a result, many individuals moved west to escape its control. The move to California came gradually, but by 1914, the state had attracted such men as Cecil B. De Mille, Jesse Lasky, and Zukor. By 1917, the MPPC had been dissolved by the courts.

Its legacy included the introduction of feature-length films, the rise of the star system, and the construction of elaborate motion-picture theaters. For obvious financial reasons, the MPPC had limited all films to one reel and had blocked actor identification. For the independents, longer films and stars became an effective way of attracting customers. To accommodate the influx of star-studded, feature-length films, new theaters were constructed.

The Growth of Hollywood: 1919–1930

International Awakenings. World War I further strengthened America's position in the international film market because virtually all the major film industries of Europe either were shut down or had their production severely curtailed. By 1919, 80 percent of the world's motion pictures were made in southern California.

By 1920, average weekly movie attendance in the United States was 40 million and growing rapidly.

Following World War I, there was a great deal of international development in film. The war-ravaged film industries of Germany, Russia, and France were quickly reconstructed and began producing films important for their contributions to film theory and aesthetics. In Germany, for example, two types of film were dominant: expressionistic and street films. Street films brought to film a new sense of naturalism and realism. Style is less obvious in realistic films. Nevertheless, the camera began to be used with a new sense of personal perspective and movement. Important films of these two movements included *The Cabinet of Dr. Caligari* (1919) and *The Joyless Street* (1925).

The Russians, most notably Lev Kuleshov, Sergei Eisenstein, and V. L. Pudovkin, contributed greatly to the theory of film editing (see the boxed feature in Chapter 4). The Russian concept of *montage*—the creation of meaning through shot juxtaposition—had a significant impact on Russian film and was used by Eisenstein and Pudovkin, especially, to produce films of stunning force and deep meaning. Key films here were Eisenstein's *Potemkin* (1925) and Pudovkin's *Mother* (1927).

In France, motion pictures displayed abstract and surrealistic forms through the work of intellectuals and creative filmmakers such as René Clair, Jacques Feyder, and Luis Buñuel. In such films as *Entracte* (1925) and *Un Chien Andalou* (1929), these men extended the boundaries of film beyond narrative into a world of deep symbolism and pure form.

All this foreign energy had a distinct yet diffused impact on the American film industry. Few of the actual film forms and theories were incorporated by Hollywood; however, the talent that produced them was absorbed: Such directors and film stars as Emil Jannings, F. W. Murnau, Greta Garbo, and Marlene Dietrich came to the United States to make films.

The 1920s. Meanwhile, Hollywood was busy producing films that were a reflection of the Roaring Twenties. Companies became studios, which grew in size and power. Studios that had been solely producers were attracted by the profits to be had through distribution. Paramount led the way toward consolidation on integration of functions. Zukor built a threatening base of theater chains, forcing independent owners to agree to take a year's worth of Paramount films (in 1920 one-third of the movies shown were from that one studio).[2] Salaries rose, huge stages were constructed, and many backlots contained entire towns. By the mid-1920s, 40 percent of a film's budget went for studio overhead.

Three kinds of films dominated the decade: the feature-length comedy, the Western, and the comedy of manners. In such films as Chaplin's *The Gold Rush* (1925), Buster Keaton's *The General* (1926), and Harold Lloyd's *The Freshman* (1925), silent comedy reached the pinnacle of artistic film achievement. The Western matured with the development of the "big" feature, which was best represented by John Ford's *The Covered Wagon* (1923), James Cruze's *The Iron Horse* (1924), and William S. Hart's *Tumbleweeds* (1925). The "B" Western, especially the romantic melodramas that starred Tom Mix, also became prominent, providing contrast to the spectacular Westerns of Ford and Cruze, and the stark realism used so effectively by Hart. The third film form was a direct result of the social conditions of the time. The mores of the country were more free and open than at any time in its history. The comedy-of-manners film was a reflection of this increased sophistication, since it concentrated on high society, glittering wealth, and personal freedom.

The Arrival of Sound. The end of the decade found the motion-picture industry in trouble. As a result of a series of major scandals in the early 1920s, a motion-picture-code office was formed to police both the content of films and the behavior of the people who made them. And the increasing popularity of radio and the automobile created attendance problems. In order to win back the lost audience, something new was needed.

Warner Brothers was a small studio on the verge of bankruptcy in 1926. Having little to lose, it invested its remaining capital in a new sound system called Vitaphone. On October 26, 1927, it presented the first talking feature—*The Jazz Singer*, starring Al Jolson. In 1925, its assets were $5 million. By 1930, its assets of $230 million made it one of the world's largest studios. The motion-picture industry, reluctant at first to abandon silent films completely, soon recognized the public's acceptance of "talkies" as permanent and moved to total sound production.

Sound's impact on content was evident from the start. Swept aside in the rush were many unique forms, most notably silent comedy. Individual stars were also greatly affected. Silent comics, whose basic style was visual, were especially hampered. In addition, many stars found that their voices were displeasing to audiences; the careers of such major silent-film stars as Charles Farrell and Norma Talmadge were curtailed.

The impact on movie attendance and movie economics was undeniable. In 1927, an average of 60 million people attended motion pictures every week. By 1929, this figure had risen to over 110 million. This success gave the industry a tremendous financial boost and helped it over the worst years of the Great Depression.

Furthermore, the expense of making sound films brought financial domination in the form of such companies as Western Electric, RCA, and their respective financial backers, Kuhn-Loeb and the First National Bank of New York. RCA, which made sound equipment, bought a film company and theater corporation and set up a powerful new studio, RKO. The eastern banking interests gained a significant hold on the entertainment industry and its products. Despite Hollywood's domestic success, its dominance of the world market diminished for a time because sound films—unlike silent films, which speak a universal language—required dubbing of foreign languages for overseas distribution, and this was initially expensive.

THE GOLDEN AGE OF HOLLYWOOD: 1930–1946

Like other institutions of the time, film reflected the tensions, crises, and deepening social awareness in the United States. Responding to the time were films such as *The Public Enemy* (1931) and *I Was a Fugitive from a Chain Gang* (1933), which asked their audiences to view people and their actions as a part of or the result of the social conditions of the time. Another response was escapism. As the economic depression deepened, the studios turned toward more musical and comedic themes in an attempt to provide their audiences with another reality. Hollywood produced a wave of Busby Berkeley (including *Footlight Parade* [1933]) and Fred Astaire and Ginger Rogers singing-and-dancing spectacles (*Flying Down to Rio*

Figure 13.5. Busby Berkeley's spectacular musicals often included dancing pianos or other objects; in this *Gold Diggers* sequence we get a bevy of chorus girls with violins—and, of course, the fantastic staircase.

[1936]). These musicals were soon joined by "screwball" comedies, such as *It Happened One Night* (1934), directed by Frank Capra, and *The Thin Man* series, starring William Powell and Myrna Loy.

The 1930s were also the golden age of the studio system. Production was almost completely centered in seven dominant companies: MGM, Paramount, Warner Brothers, RKO, Universal, Columbia, and 20th Century-Fox. Each studio had its own stars and unique style. Until the 1950s, the studio "look" or style was more dominant than the style of a single director.

Toward the end of the 1930s, with war imminent in Europe, American studios began to produce strongly patriotic films, and some cautious steps were taken in portraying future allies and enemies. Until the bombing of Pearl Harbor, the United States was technically a neutral nation, and most film companies were wary of economic reprisals by the Axis governments. After the United States entered the war, Hollywood began to produce war films in which Japanese and Germans immediately became stereotyped villains. The image of the American fighting man was equally stereotyped. American audiences did not want realistic war dramas that detailed the horrors they read about in newspapers or heard about on radio. As the war continued to wear on, the studios turned to more and more escapist fare. More than one-half of the 1,300 films produced from 1942 to 1944 had themes unrelated to the war. As a result of a war-weary civilian population's search for escape, the studios enjoyed enormous success and earned their highest profits ever.

Before we leave Hollywood's golden age, it is interesting to note that it produced a good number of the films chosen by the Library of Congress to be placed on the National Film Registry in their first list of 25, in 1989. The following have been deemed "culturally, historically, or esthetically significant":

Best Years of Our Lives   1946
Casablanca   1942

Citizen Kane	1941
The Crowd	1928
Dr. Strangelove	1964
The General	1927
Gone with the Wind	1939
The Grapes of Wrath	1940
High Noon	1952
Intolerance	1916
The Learning Tree	1969
The Maltese Falcon	1941
Mr. Smith Goes to Washington	1939
Modern Times	1936
Nanook of the North	1922
On the Waterfront	1954
The Searchers	1956
Singin' in the Rain	1952
Snow White and the Seven Dwarfs	1937
Some Like It Hot	1959
Star Wars	1977
Sunrise	1927
Sunset Boulevard	1950
Vertigo	1958
The Wizard of Oz	1939

POSTWAR DECLINE: 1946–1962

The story of film in the years following World War II is essentially a chronicle of decline and frustration for Hollywood and the major studios but of rebirth and growth for foreign and independent films. After the war, American studios resumed standard operating procedures, producing a steady supply of films designed for the mass public's tastes and habits. Soon, however, four events occurred that forced major changes in the traditional Hollywood structure:

1. the rise of television;
2. the hearings before the House Un-American Activities Committee (HUAC);
3. the Supreme Court's divorcement ruling; and
4. the emergence of a vigorous international film movement.

The advent of network television in 1948 diverted much of the audience from its traditional twice-a-week motion-picture habit. Between 1950 and 1960, the number of TV sets in the United States increased by 400 percent, while motion-picture attendance fell by 50 percent.

The fear of communism in the United States, the "Red Scare," had a number of effects. The most devastating was the blacklist, in which many talented craftsmen and artists were labeled as Communists because of alleged left-wing activities and were banned from the motion-picture industry. Experimentation and initiative in content were discouraged, and producers either fell back on old patterns or grasped at experimental technological straws.

The third blow was the decision of the Supreme Court in the *Paramount* case (1950), which forced the Hollywood studios to end vertical integration—by which one corporation produced, distributed, and exhibited films. Film companies were forced to divest themselves of one of the three operations. Most major companies sold off their theater chains and stayed in production and distribution. This, in effect, caused the collapse of the absolute control that the major Hollywood studios had held on the American film market for 30 years.

Coincidental to these domestic happenings, and to a certain extent because of them, a strong international film movement emerged. A variety of styles, collectively known as the New Wave, had in common dedication to esthetics and the idea that style is part of the message, or content, of film. (Chapter 4 surveys the cinematic elements.) American audiences suddenly became aware of non-Hollywood sources of motion pictures. Foreign films were available not only from Japan, but also from England, France, Italy, Sweden, and India. Yet another aspect of studio monopoly was undermined.

In the 1950s, the future of the motion picture as a mass medium looked shaky. As attendance dropped off sharply, the industry frantically responded with such technological innovations as stereophonic sound, wide screens, and 3-D effects. These attractions were built on passing fancies, however, and the basic fact of a changing audience was ignored. Attempts to inject new vigor or new themes were fought consistently. This is clearly illustrated by Otto Preminger's unsuccessful fight to obtain the industry's seal of approval for two films: *The Moon Is Blue* (1953), an innocuous comedy about adultery, and *The Man with the Golden Arm* (1956), a film about drug addiction.

Hollywood tried to win back its lost audience and to regain some of its former prestige by emphasizing size. The spectacle had been a part of Hollywood ever since *The Birth of a Nation* (1915), and in the 1960s, the form was looked on as the savior of the Hollywood system. *Cleopatra* (1963) should have been a warning signal; it was the most expensive and most publicized film made to this time, and it was a monumental box-office failure. But two years later, *The Sound of Music* (1965) became one of the biggest box-office successes in history. The major studios, with their confidence bolstered, set into motion a series of spectacles, among them *Dr. Doolittle* (1968) and *Tora! Tora! Tora!* (1971). All were failures that plunged many of the studios to the point of bankruptcy and led to their eventual takeover by non-Hollywood business interests. Cracks began to appear in Hollywood's facade. The roots of a "new American cinema" emerged from the reorganization of United Artists. Originally organized in 1919 as an independent outlet for the films of D. W. Griffith, Charlie Chaplin, Douglas Fairbanks, and Mary Pickford, United Artists was revamped in 1951 to provide again distribution of independently produced films. With such films as *The African Queen* (1951) and *Marty* (1955), United Artists began to provide new hope for the independent filmmaker.

THE FILM REVOLUTION: 1963–1975

The new cinema that emerged to take the place of Hollywood's traditional picture values is difficult to characterize except, perhaps, in terms of what it rejected. The films of the 1960s and early 1970s were the products of a changing society, a society in which *relevance, awareness,* and *freedom of expression* became watchwords. New filmmakers were searching for new audiences, which, in turn, were seeking a new kind of involvement in the film experience. What surfaced used to be called underground films, films that have been regarded as art, avant-garde, experimental, "new wave," or even pornographic. Perhaps the major film trend of the 1960s was that motion pictures acquired a legitimacy that allowed them to be exhibited virtually without restriction.

One of the first underground features to receive wide public distribution was Shirley Clarke's *Connection* (1961), and Dennis Hopper's *Easy Rider* (1969) was the watershed of this trend, for it finally convinced the major studios that a low-budget ($370,000) independently produced film could be a blockbuster (over $50 million in theater rentals). The significance of *Easy Rider* was not in its artistic merits, although it certainly possessed them, but in the fact that talents outside the Hollywood mainstream (Dennis Hopper, Peter Fonda, Jack Nicholson, and Karen Black) could produce and star in a small-budget film that had wide appeal, especially to the new youth market.

A new awareness, coupled with formal instruction in film production and critical theory, produced an audience that was more perceptive and more knowledgeable about film than ever before. People went to a movie; they no longer went to the movies. Motion pictures were no longer appealing to an audience composed of a cross section of the American population. Almost 75 percent of the film audience of the 1970s was between the ages of 16 and 30, and its effect on motion pictures was dramatic. Many moviegoers demanded that film do more than simply provide escape; it should make statements, take sides, and promote causes. *They Shoot Horses, Don't They?* (1969), for example, revealed the sordid side of the often fondly remembered dance marathons of the 1930s. The outstanding success of such films as *Tell Them Willie Boy Is Here* (1969), *Five Easy Pieces* (1970), *Z* (1969), *Joe* (1970), *M*A*S*H* (1969), *Little Big Man* (1970), *Dirty Harry* (1971), *The Last Picture Show* (1971), *A Clockwork Orange* (1972), and *Cabaret* (1972) pointed to an increased awareness of film as a medium for social comment. Nevertheless, what was thought to be a permanent trend turned out to be simply another cycle. The social-consciousness film movement that had begun with *Easy Rider* quickly faded.

By 1973, a new cycle of films had appeared—the disaster film, headed by *The Poseidon Adventure, Earthquake,* and *The Towering Inferno.* But soon audiences grew tired of being guinea pigs for ambitious special effects artists who filled vapid plots and surrounded dull acting with all sorts of magic tricks. Aside from this minicycle, the mid-1970s was a time of great diversity.

While the content of films took new paths, the basic change of this period was

Figure 13.6. *Easy Rider,* with Dennis Hopper and Peter Fonda, was important in the emergence of the "new American cinema."

in the way films were produced. With 75 percent of box-office revenue coming from an audience under the age of 30, it was the independent talent, often young itself, that was succeeding. Directors such as Francis Ford Coppola, Robert Altman, Martin Scorsese, Steven Spielberg, and George Lucas formed their own production companies, and the studios became the bank and the distribution system. Because of individual successes, such as Michael Cimino's *Deer Hunter* (1979), many directors persuaded the studios to allow them almost total artistic and budgetary control. With Cimino's $30-million disaster *Heaven's Gate*, however, *accountability* once again became a key word.

THE CREATIVE CONFORMITY TAKEOVER

Jaws in 1975 opened the era of the megafilms. The industry generally became entrenched in the bandwagon mentality. As Chapters 2 and 3 warned us, this continues to be a significant component of the competitiveness and globalization of the conglomerate communicator role.

In 1977, *Star Wars* exploded previous box-office records. The success of this film immediately revived the long-dormant science-fiction genre as part of a new cycle that continues to this day; it was less one of content or style, more one of formula and financial success characterized by the obsessive use of sequels and reissues. A result has been fewer films and bigger budgets, especially for advertising and publicity, as hype often substituted for quality.

Among other "sequel sires" was *Rocky* (1977). As the second most popular film of the year, it inspired (some would say "conspired to") a succession of baby *Rocky*s that is still going strong. *Jaws II* and a reissue of *Star Wars* made the top-10 box-office list in 1978. *Superman* led the way in 1979; it was quickly followed by the Steven Spielberg–George Lucas dynasty, beginning in the 1980s. *The Empire Strikes Back* more than doubled the box-office rentals of the number-2 film, *Kramer vs. Kramer*, in 1980; *Raiders of the Lost Ark* and *Superman II* held forth in 1981. The year 1982 starred *E.T.*, as well as *Rocky III, Star Trek II: The Wrath of Khan*, a reissue of *Raiders of the Lost Ark*, and Spielberg's third film in the top 20, *Poltergeist*. In 1981 and 1982, sequels and follow-ups to major films (9 and 11 titles, respectively) accounted for 12 percent of all domestic rentals in each of those years. This is a startling performance, given that over 500 new and reissued pictures are released each year. If one looks at top-10 box-office films of 1985, the continuation of the pattern becomes obvious. The top film, *Back to the Future*, represented some originality with glimmers of early Steven Spielberg shining through (five years later and we are seeing *Back to the Future III*). *Rambo: First Blood, Part II* and *Rocky IV* as numbers 2 and 3 speak for themselves; in 1990, Sylvester Stallone was out promoting *Rocky VI*. *Beverly Hills Cop* was primarily a vehicle for the run-to-the-bank humor and appeal of Eddie Murphy. *Cocoon* was a charming offbeat comedy fantasy, but it was vaguely reminiscent of Ron Howard's previous hit, *Splash*. *The Goonies*, following the success of *The Gremlins*, was simply another Spielberg formula. Rounding out the top 10 were two sequels, *Police Academy 2—Their First Assignment* and *National Lampoon's European Vacation*, and the latest James Bond adventure, *View to a Kill*.

Among the Hollywood studios and independent production companies, *strategy in production* has replaced style. When one looks at films in the last few years, the only word that comes to mind is *conformity*. One of the significant effects of

The crucial planning basically involves:

Concept/acquisition of content, such as a published book

Research and development

Concept conferences with producers and backers

Scriptwriting

Story conferences

Location scouting

Budget planning

Finetuning the shooting script and assessing physical needs

Staffing

Production scheduling

The actual making involves most of these individual communicators—or still other specialists:

Actors, dancers, musicians

Director

Producer and associates

Director of Photography

    Camera operators, focus pullers

    Chief electrician (Gaffer), 1st assistant (Best Boy), crew

Grips (manual laborers)

D. W. Griffith pioneered most modern filmmaking techniques. His *Birth of a Nation* (1915) ushered in the epic scale feature-length film.

Composer
Production Designer
   Set decorator, propmaster
Casting groups
Sound Designer
   Boom operators, sound engineers, recorders, mixers
Lighting technicians
Visual Effects Team, as well as special effects and stunt personnel
Video and Graphics Effects Supervisor, and scores of technicians from ani-
   mators to computer experts to modelmakers to engineers to. . . .
Script Supervisor
Technical Advisor
Costume Designer
   Costumers, wardrobe staff
Hair stylists
General Editor and assistants, as well as separate Film Editors, Sound Editors,
   Music Editors
Location Coordinator and Transportation Department
Production Coordinator and Accountants
Marketing Director, Publicists
Still photographers

Figure 13.7. *Raiders of the Lost Ark*, starring Harrison Ford, is typical of the megahit-and-sequel syndrome.

this trend has been the decline of the foreign film. By 1972, Ingmar Bergman's *Cries and Whispers* could not find an American distributor. None of the films starring such French superstars as Jean-Paul Belmondo that are popular in France have shown up on American marquees, as have few, if any, of the many comedy hits from Italy. The current practice of major American distributors is to concentrate on importing primarily European art films or fantasy and sex films, letting the middle range of popular hits remain at home.

The key to understanding the conformity and noticeable absence of individuality in American films is simple economics. As the average cost of producing a feature film has risen to $20 million, the small film—financed, made, and distributed outside the major studios—is a rare commodity.

The stylistic and thematic freedoms of the early 1970s have given way to the domination of action. Film critic Richard Schickel laments the loss of the traditional function of narrative, with dramatic incidents evolving naturally out of the story and interaction of characters:

> *Now everyone, everything must serve the pitchable, promotable showpiece sequences, never mind the cost in believability, genuine feeling for characters or a satisfying sense of closure. A screenplay today . . . is now merely a power line, transmitting without too much resistance the juice generated by one "wow" sequence onto the next. And the next. Until the whole work short circuits, with flashing, crashing and bashing. Hmmm. Looks like an ending. Must be one.*[3]

While small, personal films like *Diner* (1982), *Mask* (1985), and *Driving Miss Daisy* (1989) are still made, they represent a dying breed. Why this is so, and what impact this is having on the lively art that has been such a prominent fixture on the cultural landscape, is explained by action far from the cameras and lights. Our look at the economics of the motion-picture industry today is preceded by a survey of its basic organizations.

THE STRUCTURE OF THE MOTION-PICTURE INDUSTRY ....

For many years after the Supreme Court ruled that the practice of vertical integration—whereby production, distribution, and exhibition were controlled by one company—restrained free trade, most companies only produced and distributed films; exhibition was controlled by individual theaters or chains. As part of the relaxation of regulation under the Reagan administration, unified control has returned to some degree. Let us examine the function of each segment.

PRODUCTION

The making of films is a complex operation that involves the talents of many people, including directors, cinematographers, producers, editors, lighting and sound crews, designers, musicians, costumers, makeup crews, choreographers, and actors.

The Process. The traditional sequence of events in filmmaking is (1) the development of a story idea into a script; (2) casting and financing (these days, more and more intertwined); (3) shooting the film, overseen by the director; (4) image and sound editing; (5) marketing, which with today's globalization and the general insistence on planning for success (these days a hit must bring in $100 million at the box office) may be the first arena of activity. It is the producer's job to find content and facilitate its development, gather backers, hire a director, and supervise the entire process. As you know from screen credits, there is a further specialization among producers mainly centering on who controls the purse strings.

In 1989, Columbia's new owner, Sony, paid a widely reported $500 million for the producer team of Jon Peters and Peter Guber, even giving Columbia Records to Warner so that they could break their contract there. The team had a stellar track record (including *Rain Man* and *Batman*), and as writer Diane Shah remarked, "Power in Hollywood is the ability to get movies made, and at the moment two of the town's hottest wires are plugged into the . . . offices of the Guber-Peters Entertainment Company."[4] Part of their attraction came from an ability to divide the production tasks, with Guber ferreting out a story and pitching five films in 5 minutes to a director, and Peters performing miracles in the trenches of shooting.

Both aspects of the job are crucial to moneymaking and budget keeping, but both present enormous challenges. Story development—the R & D of the movie business—is often what separates the survivors from the rest. There may be 20 releases by a studio in a year, pictures that may start to earn back their investments. But there are in the same year perhaps 10 times that number somewhere between concept and shoot-ready script, each costing $100,000 or more. Small companies cannot afford this expense and risk, and thus many of them are disappearing or being absorbed into the conglomerates.

Shooting Costs. The average cost of producing a feature film by the major American companies has increased many times since the beginning of World War II, when the average cost per feature was $400,000. Five years ago a comedy could be made for $10–12 million; now it can cost $25 million, largely due to salaries. The average production budget is divided as follows:

Story costs	5%
Production and direction costs	5%

Sets and other physical properties	35%
Stars' and cast salaries	20%
Studio overhead	20%
Income taxes	5%
Contingency fund	10%

In recent years, the industry's unions, long one of the prime contributors to exorbitant production costs, have relaxed some of their requirements to allow skeletal crews and lower minimum wages for low-budget films. This shift in policy was forced on the unions. If Hollywood was to survive, labor costs had to be reduced. One of the peculiarities of the film industry is the large number of specialized unions and work rules, such as Local 659, the cameraman's union, telling producers they must hire a director of photography, a camera operator, a first assistant photographer, and a still photographer. Other rules strictly delineate what worker does what task on the set; a lamp used to light a set must be moved by the gaffer, the stagehand responsible for lighting, not someone responsible for the set.

Because of rising personnel costs, filmmakers have been forced to cut back their expenses wherever they can. In the 1940s, almost 40 percent of a film's budget went to cover studio overhead, which involved the upkeep of the back lots and equipment and an extensive bureaucracy of production and nonproduction personnel. Today, the heart of the motion-picture business lies beyond the studio gates. More and more films are being shot on location in the United States and Europe rather than on Hollywood back lots. With the advent of portable equipment, location shooting is much easier and less expensive than in the past. For most films, the sound stage has become unnecessary, especially since the devel-

Figure 13.8.
On-set conference between actors, producers, and director of *Gone with the Wind*.

opment of the Cinemobile Mark IV in the 1960s. This studio-bus contains dressing rooms, bathrooms, space for a large crew, and a full complement of lightweight equipment. Even so, the increasing appetite for visual effects and action films keeps shooting costs high. And here too the key to survival is the diversified conglomerate.

Changes in the Process.   The studio moguls have been replaced by corporate presidents and boards of directors. Despite many industry people's feelings about the controversial authoritarian studio heads of the past, not everyone agrees that growth of the conglomerate is a positive trend. Of her father, a production pioneer at Paramount, Betty Lasky commented: "Movies were his life." Media critic Neal Gabler explains:

> It is this, most likely, that modern filmmakers are invoking when they wax nostalgic about the studio system. In those days, and presumably not in these, power was at some level a function of, . . . well, of love.
>
> And so when Louis B. Mayer got down on his knees and turned on his spigot of tears to coax a reluctant star to behave, or when Harry Cohn hollered at some poor underling or when Daryl Zanuck smacked a riding crop on his desk before a quivering writer or director, it wasn't just an assertion of authority over the hired hands—though even these assertions seem somehow truer and more human to nostalgists than the cold implacable power of what might be called "corporate" Hollywood today. It was the behavior of men caught up in an obsession. Even their detractors had to concede that Mayer, Warner, Zanuck and Cohn were, in their heavy-handed way, enforcing aesthetic edicts. They wanted the movies to look, sound, fell a certain way: their way.[5]

Now Hollywood is, or attempts to be, audience-driven. As Will Tusher wrote in *Variety*:

> The more conglomerates take over, the more likely that Hollywood will rely increasingly on audience and marketing research, less on instinct or taste. A new takeover-era corporate conceit appears to be taking hold—the notion that high tech readings of the public pulse make it possible to know what the public wants. . . .
>
> [In] the 1960s . . . large conglomerates bought up several film companies to become relatively small cogs in their corporate rosters: Avco Financial Services buying Embassy Pictures; Gulf & Western buying Paramount Pictures; Transamerica purchasing United Artists and Kinney buying Warner Brothers/7 Arts.
>
> In each case, the acquired motion picture company was in a different line of business than the new parent outfit.
>
> Another round of takeovers began in 1981–82 with oilman Marvin Davis buying 20th Century Fox and taking the company private; MGM buying UA from Transamerica; Coca-Cola Co. buying Columbia Pictures Industries; Orion buying Filmways (which earlier had swallowed up American Intl. Pictures); and from TV, Norman Lear and Jerry Perenchio purchasing Embassy from Avco.
>
> During 1985, major takeovers and mergers involved entertainment companies consolidating or expanding their interests. Transplanted Aussie media baron Rupert Murdoch bought out Marvin Davis' interest in 20th Century Fox. Ted Turner and his Turner Broadcasting System sealed an agreement to buy MGM/UA for $1.5 billion and in turn resold a revamped version of United Artists. The new entities

MGM and UA would continue to run the distribution company MGM/UA as a joint venture.

Coca-Cola purchased Embassy Communications. It promptly sold off the Embassy library and film distribution arm to Dino De Laurentis, who renamed it Dino De Laurentis Entertainment Group and disclosed plans to enter domestic theatrical distribution personally with a full slate of 1986 releases.[6]

The trend continues. Sony bought Columbia for $3.4 billion, primarily to have a vast library of cassettes to inspire sales of its hardware products.

Before turning to the distribution function, we point out two of the results of the recent conglomeratization:

1. There is escalating bidding for top talent and thus *new financial arrangements* in which stars and directors take a percentage of a film's potential profit rather than a high salary up front, making them partners in a collaborative enterprise and often giving them power over a film's narrative and presentation.

2. The *package* rules American filmmaking today. The package of various creative communicators rather than the story idea is the key to getting a film made.

Figure 13.9. Although it won no Oscars, *Raging Bull* was judged best film of the 1980s by 54 nationally published critics polled by *American Film* magazine. Martin Scorsese, who directed this United Artists release and was named best director of the decade, feels the big-studio system works when it can do films like his but realizes they go with him as a known quantity.

The idea is a starting point, but preferably it should be "high concept"—readily understood by foreign and domestic investors, easily marketed, and capable of being presold to the widest audience. The concept must be complemented by a director, screenwriters, and stars who have solid track records. Today, risks are left to a few independent filmmakers.

DISTRIBUTION

The primary distributors of motion pictures are the major studios, which have traditionally produced films. Most independent producers also release their films through one of these established studios in two major markets, foreign and domestic.

The foreign market can account for 50 to 75 percent of the annual revenue for many American films. The popularity of American films is so great that some European nations limit the number of weeks that these films may be shown in local theaters.

Domestic distribution of films involves the normal channels that are used to move any product from producer to consumer. Seven major studios dominate film distribution in the United States: Columbia, MGM/United Artists, Warner Brothers, 20th Century-Fox, Paramount, Universal, and Disney. A group of minor studios is also important, especially in the distribution of low-budget independent films. The majors and minors account for 80 to 90 percent of annual film revenue in the United States.

Film-distribution operations involve the booking of films into theaters. Licenses between the distributor and the exhibitor include both price and nonprice agreements. The process of block booking—requiring theaters to buy groups of films rather than individual films—has been outlawed, so every film is leased separately. Local theater owners bid competitively for films. This usually involves a specific guaranteed minimum against a percentage of the gross receipts. For example, the theater owner pays an amount ($1,000 a week) or a percentage of the gross receipts (60 percent of 1 week's ticket sales), whichever is higher. This procedure saves the exhibitor from losing too badly if the film is a flop and helps the distributor if the film is a major success.

The distributors are still the major risk takers because they are the prime borrowers of funds to produce films. If the cost of the movie exceeds production estimates, the distributors provide the necessary capital to complete it. Because of this, the distributors receive their return before the producers do. One-third of the distribution *gross* (total receipts minus the exhibitors' share) is retained to cover distribution costs; the remainder goes to the bank to retire the standard 2-year loan. Before the producer earns any sizable sum, the film must earn roughly 2.5 times its production costs. In effect, interest and distribution costs of a film run about 150 percent of the production costs. Marketing costs in film are among the highest—if not *the* highest—for any major consumer product. The risk in film is increased by the fact that the economic life of a film at the box office is extremely short; for most motion pictures, about 25 weeks account for two-thirds of the total gross revenue. Maximum gross in the shortest time is a critical aspect of film distribution. This is why sustained life through videocassettes has become an integral part of this risky business.

Exhibition

The local theaters and drive-ins are the final link in the structure of the motion-picture industry. As with production and distribution, concentration of ownership is dominant. More than 50 percent of the theaters in the United States are owned by 700 theater chains, and recently the larger studios have acquired some of these. Some 70 percent of an average film's gross revenues comes from 1,000 key theaters. The larger theaters (over 400 seats) account for 90 percent of the total dollar volume of most features and are owned by the theater chains.

Films are exhibited in either roadshow, popular-release, or four-walling patterns. *Roadshow* is used for only blockbuster films, such as *E.T.*, or *Batman*. It requires a large marketing investment and must have a good long-run potential. Tickets are usually sold at only one theater per market. If the film does not do well in this hard-ticket exhibition, it is immediately changed to *popular release*, in which the film is booked in as many theaters as possible. The trend today is toward limited popular release and, in most instances, saturation booking. Several years ago, studios typically released their movies to 900 theaters across the country. But when revenues declined, they adopted a new strategy, "bursting," under which films are distributed to more theaters (1,200) for shorter periods of time. One consequence of this saturation exposure has been the slow strangulation of second-run and drive-in theaters. Another exhibition pattern is *four-walling*, whereby the film's producer bypasses normal distribution channels and contracts directly with the local theater owner. For low-budget, limited-audience-appeal films, this is a popular method because the money usually given to the distributor is put into local advertising.

Success in film exhibition depends on a number of factors, including trade advertising, word of mouth, critical reviews, the weather, local publicity, previous box-office receipts, the season of the year, the number and quality of competing films in the area, the content of the film, and the film's rating by the code of authority. Thus the predictability of a film's success is difficult to assess until the film is released for public appraisal, and the exhibitor often assumes great risk.

Newer movie theaters in the United States reflect the changes taking place in our society. They are often twin theaters or multicinemas with 200 to 500 seats per theater, are located in shopping centers or malls, are leased rather than owned, gain maximum traffic and exposure and share one concession stand (a stand can account for over 50 percent of theater revenues) and one projection booth to cut costs. The theaters can cater to different audiences by showing several films at the same time.

Economic Factors and the Future

The number of drive-in screens and the number of films released annually are the only statistics *not* on the rise for the motion-picture industry. Stars' salaries are commonly $5 million or $6 million; average production costs increased from 1988 to 1989 to reach $23,453,500; features grossing $20 million or more went from 18 in 1988 to 30 in 1989, a year when seven films *each* sold over $100 million in tickets and *Batman* alone grossed over $250 million.

It is well known that box-office receipts have been rising because of increases in admission prices, but there is also renewed public demand for films in addition to those viewed on home videos (more and more as second viewing) and television. In the past 2 years, 43 new movie screens have opened in Manhattan alone, reflecting the record $5 billion taken in by domestic exhibitors in 1989. While it is still tough sledding for the small or marginal film, the pressure is on for major studios to get more in the pipeline. Joe Roth, one in a series of people hired to head Murdoch's Fox Film Corporation, was charged to triple production: "The game plan is increasing production and distribution in all media all over the world."[7]

To conclude our survey of the film, we look at the trends in audiences, video use, television, and the global marketplace.

TRACKING THE AUDIENCE

Early in its history the motion picture was distributed nationally and retailed at prices within the reach of all. For immigrants in the early twentieth century, the larger-than-life stars were valued as modern extensions of the folk heroes they had known in the old country. Motion pictures retain a unique position in American leisure patterns. Film's high technical quality stimulates strong involvement. The theater is designed to encapsulate the viewer: It is dark; the chairs are comfortable; there are relatively few interruptions and little "noise" to detract from content, and food is available. Every aspect of filmgoing is designed to heighten the impact of film experiences.

The nature of the motion-picture audience has changed considerably over the past 20 years. What was primarily an adult audience became a youth audience, although as the baby boomers mature the studios' core audience has shifted from 12–20 to 20–35. Seventy-five percent of the total annual admissions are generated by moviegoers under 40.

Some 60 percent of American moviegoers attend a neighborhood theater; 80 percent consider the subject matter of a film important in deciding what to see; 30 percent consider the actors important; 70 percent prefer American films to foreign films; 83 percent prefer color films to black-and-white films; 39 percent are influenced by movie critics; 47 percent of drive-in admissions are from the suburban market; and 87.5 percent of moviegoers are aware of the MPAA ratings.

Such statistics and the use of them in marketing are crucial to the success of a film in a time when most movies do not break even. Along with the package, in which actors are products, a copycat mentality reigns currently. No one wants to be first to take a chance. The most successful stars are those who do not stray from their image: Clint Eastwood and Sylvester Stallone are examples, and in marketing a rather savage comedy of divorce, *War of the Roses*, it was emphasized that Kathleen Turner and Michael Douglas would be all that we expect them to be from previous roles.

Demographics are the thing. Hollywood still caters largely to the tastes of the young, and it pays attention to the black audience (who represent 13 percent of moviegoers, but 30 percent are frequent moviegoers, compared with 24 percent of the white population). Some analysts feel the black audience helped rescue the failing industry in the 1970s, although many of the films viewed would be considered black-exploitation pictures. This base has in recent years been broadened

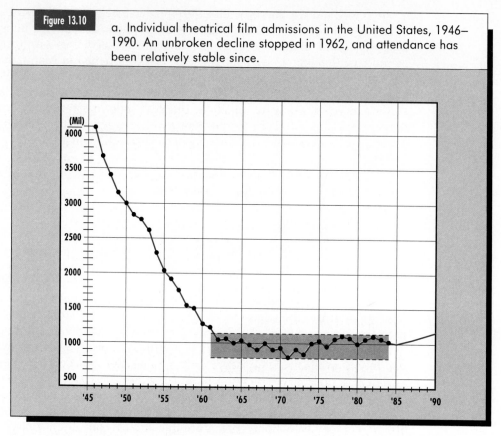

Figure 13.10

a. Individual theatrical film admissions in the United States, 1946–1990. An unbroken decline stopped in 1962, and attendance has been relatively stable since.

by a sizable portion of whites who enjoy black performers. As with books, the financial health of films relies on a rather small percentage of the available public that will support a rather small number of releases, often returning to a favorite production.

The motion picture continues to be a primary recreational outlet, although it is not nearly as significant as it was 40 years ago. The industry peaked in 1946, with estimated box-office receipts of $1.7 billion from 4.1 billion admissions. The decline was precipitous until 1962; admissions have been relatively stable for more than 20 years, as Figure 13.10 shows. Seasonal swings in the domestic box office have long been a fact of industry life. An analysis of week-to-week fluctuations, created by analyst A. D. Murphy, shows a remarkably steady and recurring annual profile of film attendance in the United States.

THE INDEPENDENT FILMMAKER AND THE NICHE

If the major studios' focus is on market research and jockeying for a competitive slot for a predictable movie, the independent filmmaker might be best typified as an individual anticipating what we might respond to. Despite the odds and the economics, there are considerable numbers of independents, often working in the documentary genre. We tend to become aware of them when one breaks through to box-office success and critical acclaim—that is, by reviewers other than the elitist circle writing for specialist publications. As Robert Redford observed of his Sundance Festival for independent films, the real challenge is maintaining noncommercial values and not being co-opted by success.

In 1989–1990, *sex, lies and videotape*, a first film by a 26-year-old director outside the Hollywood establishment, won the grand prize in the Cannes International Film Festival and a box-office gross of $16 million (the film cost only $1.6 million to make). *Roger and Me*, a feature-length documentary written by, directed by, and starring Michael Moore, centered on the effects in Flint, Michigan, of General Motors' closing of a plant there and on Moore's unsuccessful attempts to interview GM chairman Roger Smith as part of his "mission" to elicit corporate responsibility. It cost $260,000 to produce, and part of that money was raised in bingo games in Flint. It was shown at three film festivals and went on to worldwide distribution, a sale to Warner, and lengthy controversy. At the heart of the criticism: (1) a questioning of Moore's ethics in manipulating the picture of GM's total role in Flint for the sake of black humor and satire; (2) his artistic use of Smith's not incomprehensible refusal to see Moore; (3) the blurring of lines between the film that entertains and the documentary, a genre we have associated with straightforward, serious, almost public-service programming (see Chapter 17); it is perceived to be journalism by many, and while it may be subjective, it must be, ultimately, fair. Independent filmmakers recognize and communicate what the establishment has not—especially that there is often a very fine line between reality and imagination, nonfiction and fiction.

Neither Moore nor Spike Lee was nominated for a 1990 Oscar, to the consternation of many who pointed a finger at the Hollywood power structure. Spike Lee started out using the limit of several credit cards to make his first film; now a communicator to contend with, he insists on playing the Hollywood game with his rules and not content formulas. Spike Lee finds that "the most important thing is vision." Profiling him and his production company, Forty Acres and a Mule, for *Newsweek*, David Ansen writes:

> He's subverting the conventional ways Hollywood has programmed us to read movies. He doesn't give us good guys and bad guys; he doesn't provide role models and handy resolutions; his movies don't fall into neat generic categories. In Lee's films, realism and cartoon brush wings, and the narrative flow will suddenly break for a dance . . . a rant directed straight at the camera. Propelled by music, his

Figure 13.11. A scene from *Roger and Me*.

Figure 13.12. Successful documentary maker Karen Goodman's 30-minute film on street entertainers (shown is C. P. [Crowd Pleaser] Lacey), *No Applause, Just Throw Money*, was acclaimed at film festivals from Sundance, Utah, to Leningrad and aired on PBS. Goodman also works on HBO projects. An Oscar nominee, she comments: "I'm not a fan of the broadcast-journalism style, and I don't believe in preaching. I like my statements to be visual."'

rough-edged, seam-showing movies have the urgency of rap, the rhythms of the inner city and the revelations that only an insider can know.[8]

Do the Right Thing was a hotly debated film—the "black experience" from a distinctly black perspective, concluding with explosive racial violence. That it grossed $25 million did not hurt in fostering a heightened interest in black and "crossover" audiences and minority talent.

Not all independents are making documentaries and message films. A few

Figure 13.13. Spike Lee is one of the talented black filmmakers insisting that the black experience must be communicated by those who live it.

carry on the tradition of the 1970s and early 1980s, putting together films designed as commercial hits, outside the major studios. The survivors among them are careful to concentrate on certain niches and not get overly ambitious, especially because $10-million marketing costs loom large for a small company trying to win screen space. (Although films generally earn enough to earn back production costs, they usually go into the red after paying for prints for exhibition and advertising.)

New Line Cinema Corporation, based in New York City as many independents are these days, has two prime targets: young audiences and young blacks. Their *Nightmare on Elm Street* series did well internationally, but *Teenage Mutant Ninja Turtles* was the real breakthrough. Earning the standard fee of 30 percent of box office for distributing it, New Line surpassed *Dirty Dancing*'s record first 3 weeks' $63.4 million to pull in $72.9 million, along with the distinction of being the biggest independent movie ever. It cost only $12 million to make.

Another independent, Carolco, which gained fame through its *Rambo* series, has been hedging its bets by buying control of a videocassette business, a television production company, and another independent company. It is to this kind of synergy that we now turn.

THE VCR REVOLUTION

The late 1970s witnessed a tremendous surge in new forms of video technology, and the 1980s carried this surge to the media revolution. Home video recording dates back to the 1960s, but it was not until 1972 that Sony produced the first videocassette recorder (VCR) for business and education. VCR unit sales increased by 250 percent to 2 million in 1982 and doubled the next year. The rate of recorder sales outdistanced the pace of color TV sales in the 1950s. VCRs have been installed in over 70 percent of American households (some of which have two or more sets) and have become an integral component of the home-entertainment system; they used on average 6 hours a week for recording and more hours for playing. The VCR boom is being fed by lower prices and added features such as advance programming, scanning, and zapping to eliminate commercials. Also fueling this expansion is the growth of the "software" or program content.

The crystal-ball gazers are not in total agreement about the impact of VCRs on the motion-picture industry. On the one hand we read:

> While VCR growth will proliferate, [John Sie, senior vice president of Telecommunications, Inc.] contended that . . . "there is a finite limit" to the viable material that programmers can supply, and it's not enough to sustain the rental business over time.[9]

Actually, Hollywood has been highly responsive to the revolution. Many filmmakers have been shooting their movies with a smaller screen in mind. Studios have also planned video release soon after introduction of a film at the box office. Today, the ancillary market for films is video, and studios' responses include low cassette prices to encourage purchases rather than rentals as the VCR revolution approaches maturity, novelty wears off, and rentals slow down. *E.T.*, at $24.95, started the ball rolling. Some observers feel that the majors also want to put the rental stores out of the business they want for themselves.

Sometimes normal theater distribution is bypassed altogether by what John Hartl, *Seattle Times* columnist, has called "made-for-video movies." They are often not insignificant entries. On the other hand, some of the new video companies were drawn into moviemaking in the late 1980s but soon found pitfalls in the now crowded VCR segment of the filmed entertainment industry. The problem, according to a *Wall Street Journal* analyst, is that the video market had generally polarized into expensive blockbusters and budget flicks that "are so bad they're good."[10] A flatter rental market encourages more diversity.

Conglomerization has given the studios broad control, additional media sources of revenue for films, and, best of all, treasure houses of programming through acquisitions. NBC, owned by General Electric, and Columbia established a joint home video venture in 1982; in 1989, it had revenue of $470 million and profits of $74 million. Film libraries are gold. In 1990, Warner offered to assist an entrepreneur's attempt to finance a purchase of MGM/UA because if he defaulted, Warner would get access to United Artists' 1,075 films, including James Bond, *Pink Panther*, Woody Allen, and *Rocky*.

Can there be a downside to the VCR revolution? Here is one man's view:

> *Nobody can yet assess the ultimate effect of these radical and unprecedented transformations. Some sociologists have expressed concern that the privatization of arts and entertainment, delivered directly into the home, may subvert their traditional role as communal events and agents of social cohesion.*[11]

FILM AND TELEVISION

Television has had a changing but enduring interaction with the motion-picture industry. In the mid-1970s, the relationship begun in the 1950s intensified and solidified. Feature films made up an important block of network schedules, with all three networks running multiple "nights at the movies" and "movies of the week." As motion-picture attendance decreased and the number of TV homes increased, the competition between the two media became cooperation and ultimately coexistence. What once appeared to be a destroyer has turned out to be a savior. Without television, Hollywood would not have survived. Of the approximately 20,000 jobs in Hollywood, 10,000 are in television.

Television provides the function for the motion-picture industry that "B" movies have always provided—a reliable, steady income. New markets in cable and pay-television hold great potential, and it is clear that television and film are firmly and permanently linked. Today, motion pictures are made with both eyes focused on television and video as a source of income, perhaps not as movies of the week but in various other forms.

Many production companies make considerable numbers of made-for-television movies, and these have had both commercial and societal impact. The miniseries phenomenon, which ushered in a new look in network programming, would not have been possible without Hollywood expertise and talent. Interestingly, it was when the miniseries concept ballooned into maxilength blockbuster budget productions that the differing support bases of the two media were evident. Network television is not financed by admission revenue, and when the small-screen epic stopped attracting a large enough share of audience to satisfy advertisers, the genre collapsed, and there was no ancillary market support. Other film revenue arises when feature films are reworked into TV series; the fact that first-run films frequently have vague, indecisive endings is due to potential repackaging as a sitcom or drama series.

As Figure 13.14 illustrates, less than 50 percent of a movie's gross revenue comes from the box office, the remaining dollars coming from some form of television and/or video source. In 1978, 80 percent of a film's earnings came from theaters; by 1985, the box-office take was 43 percent and heading downward. The studios thus aggressively market to all forms of television, including syndication. The syndication market is especially strong since independent stations are not network-affiliated and need "product," and theatrical film packages fit their needs.

There are two ways studios provide programming for television. They can simply finance shows that are made by independents and look to syndication reruns for their profits. Or the studio takes over all roles of producing, from concept to casting to dealing with networks. Disney has recently become very active in this second approach. Its corporate structure includes many successful entertainment units, and their emphasis currently is going beyond delivering sitcoms and individual cartoons to syndicating whole packages of children's programming such as "The Disney Afternoon." Its "Duck Tales," the most successful animated show ever, appears in 56 countries and is seen by 25 million children a day. All this leads to our final aspect of movie economics.

THE GLOBAL FACTOR

No other medium illustrates better the importance of content that is globally useful. The issues accompanying this situation are covered in Chapters 3 and 24; here we touch upon dimensions that affect the industry.

The motion-picture industry is one of America's strongest competitors in the

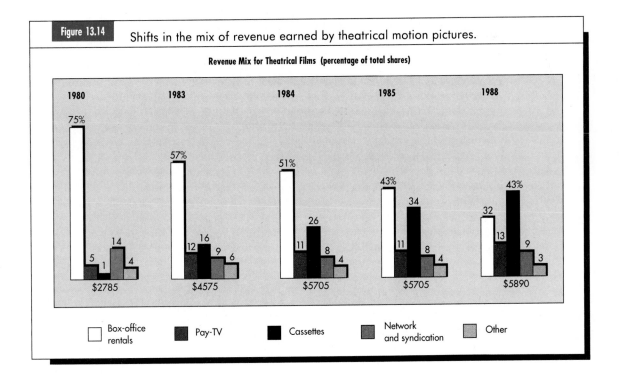

Figure 13.14 Shifts in the mix of revenue earned by theatrical motion pictures.

Revenue Mix for Theatrical Films (percentage of total shares)

global marketplace. Only the aerospace industry ranks above it as an exporter. Overseas box office accounts for more than 50 percent of the total grosses of many U.S. releases, and films such as *Fatal Attraction* and *Who Framed Roger Rabbit?* earned far more abroad.

Foreign exhibitors recognize the superiority of Hollywood know-how, for all its overspending and films that fail. Sony is only one of the Japanese firms to play on our turf. JVC, a consumer electronics company, gave a former president of 20th Century-Fox freedom to control a $100-million investment in Largo Entertainment, a new filmmaking unit, and plans to acquire a major studio. Again, a prime motive is getting content for videocassettes and the rapidly growing foreign market for cable and movie theaters. *Variety* found that in 18 European countries, sales and rentals of home videos were 40 percent above box-office receipts.

Demand abroad and foreign investment here are having their influence, even though the American reaction is of first importance to studios and video companies. Studios hire marketing consultants to do exhaustive research on local market tastes. Japan is especially name conscious, and this preference has to be served by delivering proven concepts and stars (often later in person to do the important promotional tour). One industry insider observed that Hollywood is more and more into the "transportation business."

To get close to the audience, save U.S. production costs, and package internationally attractive films, studios are setting up production units abroad. Warner has opened multiplexes in Europe, and others plan to do so (Warner also has a joint venture with the Soviet film industry to open theaters in Moscow and Leningrad, complete with concession and gift stands and air-conditioning for the first time). Universal and Disney are into theme parks. The pan-European market of 1992 and the opening of Eastern Europe promises a developing audience of at least a billion. Since television is no longer government-controlled in that part of the world, broadcast groups are beginning to be significant players in the auction of rights to American films. The international film festival at Cannes is clearly a mega-event. Covering the dealings at the 1989 bazaar of talent, one observer stated:

> *Foreign advances in Hollywood ownership, the prospective emergence of internally aggressive American megacompanies like Time/Warner Inc. and Paramount Communications Inc., and the birth of pan-European television are creating a brave new world that will increasingly favor U.S. pictures with crossborder appeal. Whether global marketing will be reshaped entirely or merely refined by the new order is a question as open-ended as the future.*[12]

SUMMARY

The place of motion pictures in contemporary society, although diminished, remains strong. The motion-picture medium has experienced significant change in its history.

The development of motion pictures can be divided into several periods. From 1824 to 1896, the many discoveries, inventions, and theories demonstrated a continuing fascination with reproducing motion. This period of intense experimentation culminated, in the late 1880s, in Thomas Edison's invention of a motion-picture camera. During the period from 1896 to 1918, the first subject matter of motion pictures was developed, the first artists began to experiment with the medium, and D. W. Griffith emerged as a pioneer of the motion-picture art. An industry developed to produce, distribute, and exhibit motion pictures.

From 1919 to 1929, intense artistic and creative experimentation occurred in Russia, France, and Germany, resulting in significant films and movements that affected the course of motion-picture history. Concurrent with this international movement was development in the United States, primarily in Hollywood in the 1920s. During those years, the American film industry became firmly established and American film forms—particularly the feature-length comedy, the Western, and the comedy of manners—began to emerge as dominant genres.

The next significant period in motion-picture history occurred with the arrival of sound. From 1927 to 1930, the motion-picture industry underwent a great upheaval—sound film quickly and permanently replaced silent film, resulting in a significant impact on content, individuals, and the industry.

The golden age of Hollywood—1930 to 1946—was a period of intense industrial and creative development in American film, characterized primarily by the work of seven major studios and the artists working for them. World War II did little to diminish the structure of the industry, as Hollywood entertained audiences, both military and civilian, with great success. Following World War II, the American film industry went into a period of decline. This decline, from 1946 to 1962, was significant and resulted primarily from four events that forced changes in the traditional Hollywood structure: (1) the rise of television, (2) the hearings before the House Un-American Activities Committee, (3) the Supreme Court "divorcement" ruling, and (4) the emergence of a vigorous international film movement. By the early 1960s, the American film industry was experiencing significant declines in admissions, the number of films produced, and the number of theaters.

Following this period there emerged, both in America and internationally, a strong film revolution. From 1963 to 1975, films began to express the needs of a changing society, a society in which relevance, awareness, and freedom of expression became watchwords. Motion pictures were no longer a product to be consumed passively by a mass audience; they became vehicles by which creative artists could experiment and communicate messages of depth and intensity. The most recent period of film history, from 1976 to the present, is identified primarily by industrial merger and creative conformity. Films have become more expensive to produce and the corporate structure of the film industry has been collapsing; film companies have been absorbed by other corporations. The creative ferment of the 1960s and early 1970s began to fade. The last ten years have been characterized primarily by fewer films with bigger budgets and an emphasis on creating financial success through packaging.

The scope of motion pictures, although diminished, continues to be significant. The motion picture remains a primary recreational outlet. Despite declining admissions in the mid-1980s, box-office receipts have been rising. California, specifically Hollywood, remains the global capital of motion-picture production. The American film audience has changed considerably, with almost 75 percent of the audience under 34 years of age.

The motion-picture industry is divided into three major parts: (1) production—the making of films; (2) distribution—the supplying of films to markets; and (3) exhibition—the displaying of films to the public. The organization of these three aspects of the industry has changed considerably in the past 30 years. Originally, all three occurred within one company; while production, exhibition, and distribution are handled by a variety of industrial units, there is a return to integrated control.

The motion picture today has several characteristics and roles, which have changed considerably over the past 30 years. Motion pictures now serve as the primary source of content for videos and television. Nevertheless, motion pictures continue to hold a unique place in American leisure patterns. It is a selective medium, catering to the tastes of a young audience, and contemporary film themes clearly reflect this audience's ambitions and tastes. Films have high technical quality that demand strong involvement. The motion picture remains the most international of mass media and has become an important component to the conglomerate communicator.

REFERENCES

1. Robert G. Toll, *The Entertainment Machine: American Show Business in the Twentieth Century* (New York: Oxford University Press, 1982), 17.
2. Ibid., 30.
3. Richard Schickel, "The Crisis in Movie Narrative," *The Gannett Center Journal* (Summer 1989), 5.
4. Diane Shah, "The Producers," *The New York Times Magazine*, October 22, 1989, 27.
5. Neal Gabler, "The Moguls," *The Gannett Center Journal* (Summer 1989), 18.
6. *Variety*, January 8, 1986, 6.
7. "As Big Becomes Huge, a Hollywood Shuffle," *The New York Times*, October 22, 1989, H47.
8. "The 'Vision' Thing," *Newsweek*, October 2, 1989, 37.
9. Robert Atwan, Barry Orten, and William Vesterman, "VCRs: Impacts on the Film, Television, and Cable Industries," in *American Mass Media: Industries and Issues*, 3d ed. (New York: Random House, 1986).
10. Dennis Kneale, "Vestron's Missteps After 'Dirty Dancing' Show Pitfalls of Crowded Video Market," *Wall Street Journal*, August 28, 1989, B1.
11. Hans Fantel, "The Living Room Is Now the Stage," *The New York Times*, December 31, 1989, 20.
12. Richard Gold, *Variety* (Cannes Festival Special Issue, 1989), vol. 335, no. 3, 35.

Recorded Music

No mass medium has had a more volatile or unsettled history than the recording industry. The industry has changed from a leisure-time novelty enjoyed by the middle class into a force for social and cultural expression. The industry is an entire status system; from the inner-city rapper to the upscale jazz aficionado, the music we listen to, the stereo we buy for the house or the car, or the performer on whom we base our style of hair or clothing are significant ways of expressing ourselves. The first part of this chapter gives an overview of the history of recorded music and leads us to the edge of its future. Recent issues in the industry, such as censorship and the rise of rap music, are then discussed, along with the structure and economics of what is now a multibillion-dollar industry.

HISTORICAL PERSPECTIVE

There are five major periods in the history of the recording business. The period from 1877 to 1923 saw the birth of sound recording, and since then the industry has been through two main periods of decline and revitalization.

INVENTION, EXPERIMENTATION, AND EXPLOITATION: 1877–1923

Research by Leon Scott de Martinville and F. B. Fenby, who is credited with having coined the word *phonograph* (from the Greek word for "soundwriter") preceded the actual "invention" of practicable recording machines. In the United States, Thomas Edison and his machinist, John Kruesi, were apparently the first to actually build, in December 1877, a functional device that recorded and played back sound. This phonograph used a hand-cranked metal cylinder wrapped in tin foil for recording purposes, but Edison applied for patents on a disc system as well as on the cylinder. The Edison Speaking Phonograph Company, formed in 1878, built several hundred machines, and salesmen hit the vaudeville circuit. Audiences flocked to hear the demonstrations, but the novelty wore off quickly, and the company suspended business.

In 1885, Alexander Graham Bell, working with Chichester Bell and Charles Tainter, patented a device called the graphophone, which used cardboard cylinders coated with wax. It has little volume but better quality sound than Edison's phonograph. Edison, in 1886, then developed the phonogram, a reusable wax cylinder that ran for 2 to 4 minutes, and in 1889, he issued the first commercial recordings. The Automatic Phonograph Company's nickelodeon, invented by Lewis Glass in 1890, appeared as an entertainment machine in arcades, and the public became enthralled with the forerunner of the jukebox.

Figure 14.1. Thomas Edison poses with the tinfoil-cylinder photograph that he invented in 1877. The photograph was taken by Civil War photographer Mathew Brady in Washington, D.C., on April 18, 1878.

By the mid-1890s, the phonograph was in the parlors of many American homes, while another American, Emile Berliner, was experimenting with a system that used flat discs instead of cylinders. The disc could be mass-produced from an etched negative master, whereas each early cylinder had to be an original. Made from shellac, the disc was harder and more durable than the wax cylinder, which made the disc easier to store. And the disc also produced greater volume and better sound quality from a simpler machine.

In 1901, Berliner and Eldridge Johnson formed the Victor Talking Machine Company and started selling "Red Seal" one-sided recordings made by opera stars. In 1906, the Victrola was born; its distinguishing feature was a speaker horn. The Columbia Phonograph Company used the Odeon two-sided discs (introduced by Germany's Odeon Company in 1905) for its music. The disc business, with 10,000 outlets, became profitable and thus respectable. Edison, who refused to accept "platter reality," continued with his work on wax cylinders and thus faded from the field that he had invented. Assets for Victor grew to over $30 million by 1917, with Americans buying 25 million two-sided discs a year. After an initial coolness toward the medium, famous artists turned to the phonograph as a means of expanding their audiences. Enrico Caruso did more than any other artist to legitimize the medium, and over the years, fans rewarded him with more than $5 million, tax-free, from sales of his records. The industry became worldwide, as interlocking patents permitted the sale of records everywhere.

From 1905 to 1923, few significant technical changes took place. Although the speaker horn of the Victrola was soon enclosed in the cabinet, the scratchy quality persisted. Many musical instruments could not be used to make recordings because they did not record well. Artists stood in front of a huge bell or horn and shouted their songs onto masters. It was a far cry from the concert hall. Things went well enough until the radio came along to end the ''golden age'' of tenors.

TECHNICAL IMPROVEMENT BUT FINANCIAL DISASTER: 1924–1945

The 1920s were expected to be a boom time for the recording industry. Low-cost, reliable phonographs were available, and people had the money to buy them. Although developments in electronic-radio technology (microphones and speakers) led to significant improvements in the technical quality of the phonograph, the public acceptance of radio created an economic recession for the recording industry. Radio broadcast ''live'' rather than recorded music, produced a better sound, and best of all, provided the music free. In financial desperation, the phonograph industry moved into ''radio recording.''

The first commercial, electrically produced recordings were marketed by both Victor and Columbia in 1925 to open an entirely new aural dimension. The electrical-recording process expanded the frequency range, could be played back louder with ''blast,'' allowed musicians to work in a studio setup that approximated the physical arrangements of live performances, and improved the home phonograph with a dynamic loudspeaker. That same year, the Brunswick Company marketed a low-cost electric phonograph with speakers of brilliant quality compared with the quality of earlier mechanical horns. By 1926, whole symphonies and operas were being recorded on albums of up to 20 discs.

Despite the technical progress, the medium continued to lose ground—first to radio, then to talking pictures. In 1928, RCA purchased Victor and discontinued the production of record players in favor of that of radio receivers. The Great Depression hit the recording industry harder than it did any other medium. Record sales dropped to one-tenth of what they had been, and few playback devices were marketed. In 1932, only 6 million records were sold and 40,000 phonographs produced. The phonograph seemed headed for extinction. The end of Prohibition led to the one bright spot in the record business. In the new bars and clubs of the 1930s, the jukebox found a home and turned gathering places into ''juke joints.'' By 1940, more than 250,000 ''jukes'' were using 15 million records a year made by bands of the ''swing era.'' Despite this public consumption of popular music, the record business was still dominated by classical music, limited by drained financial resources, and hindered by unimaginative marketing.

Several business changes stimulated the medium's growth. Jack Kapp and E. R. Lewis bought and reorganized U.S. Decca. They produced 35-cent records to compete with the 75-cent versions of their major competitors. By 1939, Decca was the second-ranking company (behind RCA Victor) and sold 19 million records. In 1940, RCA and Decca sold two of every three records.

Columbia, in serious financial difficulty, was purchased by CBS in December 1938 and restructured to almost corner the popular-music market. The price of Columbia's classical albums was cut to $1; overnight, sales jumped by 1,500 percent. By late 1941, a revitalized Columbia helped the industry sell 127 million discs. Radio-phonograph combinations were also selling well. RCA Victor was selling a record player for less than $10. Music, helped by big bands and the ''swing era,'' was back in business.

Figure 14.2. Radio technology improved the sound quality of recordings and of live music that was broadcast, but siphoned off audiences during the 1930s. The jukebox helped offset drops in home sales and thus supported the industry during its roughest years.

World War II destroyed all hope for the industry's immediate rebirth. Shellac, required for disc production, became unavailable, and electronics manufacturers turned to war work. And on July 31, 1942, the American Federation of Musicians (AFM), headed by James Caesar Petrillo, refused to allow its members to cut any more records. The AFM was concerned that "canned" music would cut back employment opportunities for musicians. The record companies initially refused to negotiate, but a year later, economic pressure forced both Capitol and Decca to allot up to 5 cents per record sold to the AFM's funds for unemployed musicians. The AFM gains were wiped out in 1947, however, when the Taft-Hartley Act made it illegal to collect royalties in this fashion.

THE RENAISSANCE OF RECORDS: 1946–1963

Following World War II, five major forces revolutionized the phonograph industry: (1) technical achievements in electromagnetic recording; (2) improvements in records and playback systems; (3) changes in marketing procedures; (4) television's destruction of radio's old format; and (5) a dramatic change in the content of the medium.

Electromagnetic Recording. Electromagnetic recordings had been experimented with as early as 1889 when a Danish engineer, Vladimir Poulsen, produced a recording on steel wire. Later, paper was used; later still, plastic tape.

In July 1945, John T. Mullin, then in the Army Signal Corps, came across a sophisticated magnetic tape recorder in a Radio Frankfurt station in Bad Nauheim, Germany, where the American Armed Forces Radio Network was supervising a German staff. This magnetophone was a truly superior sound system, without the background noise so typical of phonograph recordings. Mullin brought two machines and 50 rolls of tape to the United States and demonstrated the system to engineers and to entertainer Bing Crosby. Before long the machines were improved and the 3M Company started producing tape.

Real-time performances gave way to multitrack, engineered-time performances. By 1949, most major studios were using noise-free tape recordings for masters, which were then edited and transferred to discs.

The 1950s saw extensive use of reel-to-reel tapes, and technical experiments during these years led to a tape bonanza in the 1960s. Today, there are two basic tape systems.

1. Reel-to-reel systems, which can be edited and have both playback and record capability. High-quality units are fairly large, even in portable models.
2. Cassette systems, which were introduced in 1964. These are portable but cannot be easily edited. They have record capability, however, and dubs can be cheaply made on inexpensive blank tape.

Another tape system, the eight-track cartridge, was introduced in 1958. However, it did not offer recording capability to the buyer, and after a brief period of success, production of eight-track cartridges ceased in 1983.

The introduction of tape-improved sound quality provided detailed aural separation of instruments, allowed for the most minute editing (for example, deleting coughs and miscues), and led to the engineer's becoming a vital force in the "mixing" of the final product. Modern production methods are increasingly using the direct-to-disc process, eliminating the tape-to-disc transfers. Computers and digital recording are being used with great frequency, further enhancing the quality of recorded sound.

Record and Record-Player Improvements. In 1948, Columbia introduced the microgroove 33⅓-rpm long-play (LP) record, which had been developed by Peter Goldmark. It could accommodate almost 25 minutes of music a side because of its slower speed, larger size, and narrower grooves, whereas the 78-rpm record produced only 3 to 5 minutes of music. Made of plastic "biscuits," they were so resilient that they were called "unbreakable."

Rather than submit to a coup by Columbia, RCA Victor, in 1949, brought out its 7-inch 45-rpm records in both single and extended-play (EP) versions. The center hole was far larger than that on either the 78s or 33⅓ LPs. This meant that the consumer needed both a large spindle and a lower player speed to adapt to the 45s.

The "battle of the speeds" lasted for 2 years, until 1950, when record sales dropped to $50 million below the 1947 level. The consumer, uncertain as to which of the two systems would be adopted, bought neither. The companies reached a compromise that established the 33⅓ LP album as the vehicle for recording classical works and collections by pop artists; the 45-rpm record was for pop singles. By 1955, 78-rpm records were no longer in production.

Advances in electromagnetic recording techniques led to a 10-year hi-fi boom. Stereophonic, or multichannel, sound systems, demonstrated in 1957 and marketed in 1958, made monaural systems obsolete. Today, all LPs produced by the major companies are hi-fi stereo albums, and even the 45 is a total stereo production.

Marketing Procedures. At the end of World War II, the major companies controlled the industry and released 40 to 100 records each week. Local dealers marked up the records by about 40 percent. There was a "straight-line" marketing system from manufacturer to distributor to retailer to consumer. It was a tight, profitable system for everyone except those outside the system. The real crack in the majors' armor was the profit motive. The majors controlled the talent and the music, the studios and the manufacturing, as well as the distribution. They were secure, so they rented studios to the independents.

Soon independent producers began to make stars of unknown performers. This development meant that small retailers were faced not only with the speed war and with pricing and stock-duplication headaches, but also with an increasing number of "off brands." The widening variety of musical types forced retailers to make larger investments or suffer the consequences of an inadequate inventory. In addition, promotion people replaced salespeople. The promotion staff worked with radio stations, and retailers were left to their own devices.

The patterns of selling records changed in the mid-1950s as (1) discount outlets (low-margin retailers) offered significantly reduced prices on all popular records; (2) the major record producers, noting the success of small record societies, started their own record clubs; and (3) rack jobbers rented space in dime stores, drugstores, grocery stores, and anywhere else one would be likely to buy a record on impulse. All these marketing innovations hurt the traditional retail-sales outlets—record and department stores. But business was so brisk that the traditional dealers' complaints carried little weight with the record companies. Today, rack jobbers and national record-store chains dominate retail record sales.

The Dawn of Television and the Death of Network Radio. As local radio stations developed new, more economical programming to counterattack the growth of television after 1952, music was the dominant element in the mix. But now it was recorded music that the stations played, providing free exposure to the record industry's products to a huge, affluent, young audience of potential buyers. The boom was on.

The two industries, once fierce rivals, now work very well (and very profitably) together.

The Birth of Rock. Popular music in the United States reflects the diversity of America's "melting-pot" culture. This was not always the case. The four major (RCA Victor, Columbia, Decca, and Capitol) and three emerging companies (MGM, Mercury, and London) produced essentially three kinds of music: white popular, classical, and show (theatrical). Each company had an all-powerful *artist-and-repertoire (A&R) person*, who was, in effect, the company's record producer. This individual selected all the songs to be recorded and all the artists to record them and decided when a "take" was acceptable. Each major company also told its artists which potential hits on the other labels they would "cover" (they would react by recording that hit using their own artists). In effect, a very small number of people controlled the music industry. It was the independent record producers who generally spearheaded new musical trends.

In the early 1950s, these independents created a musical form that shook the music industry to its foundations. Nowhere was the cultural gap between young and old so evident as in the controversy over the sound that Cleveland disc jockey Alan Freed named rock 'n' roll. Rock has never been rock *and* roll. Grammar is not its forte.

Rock music is indigenous to the electronic media. The recording is the original, and live performance is the imitation. *Rock 'n' roll* has been defined best by music expert Richard Penniman (Little Richard), in his hit song "Tutti Frutti," as *Awop-bopaloobopalopbamboom*. If we cannot offer definition, we can identify its characteristics.

1. Rock is a *heavy beat*.
2. Rock is *loud*. It is tactile and insulates listeners from problems.
3. Rock is *electric* music. It is plugged in and we are turned on.
4. Rock is traditionally *simple* (but not simple-minded).
5. Rock is *blatant*. It is the most sexually up-front of any musical form.
6. Rock is a *rejection* of adult sensibilities, an assault on the status quo, and a sign of alienation.
7. Rock is *committed* to social change. It was, and is, the voice of the young during times of war, recession, and cultural upheaval.
8. Rock is *people music*. It is the most "pop" of pop cultures.

Figure 14.3. The "King," Elvis Presley, reigned supreme at the dawn of rock. He made crossovers from country and western, through rock-a-billy, back through country rock to white pop.

9. Rock is *young*. The young make it, buy it, and listen to it; every teenager is a potential star.
10. Rock is *unpredictable*. Who knows what will be popular tomorrow?
11. Rock is *immediate* music that depends on high turnover. Today's hit is tomorrow's "golden oldie."
12. Rock is *dance* music.
13. Rock is *international* and has fans worldwide.
14. Rock is very *big business*.

Rock comes from five traditions in American music.

1. *Rhythm and blues* (R&B) provided the horns, the black beat, and a frank approach to the sexual experience. R&B was rural music that became urbanized for southern blacks who had migrated to northern cities. The form was influenced by jazz, boogie, and the blues. Gospel traditions of "rocking and reeling" were critical in its development. The independents were the major source of R&B records because it was considered to be "race" music by the majors. They introduced whites to the black R&B sound.

2. *Country and western* (C&W) provided the first "stars," the basic instrument (the guitar), and "songs of life and pain." Jimmy Rodgers, "the father of country music," fused the blues with country. Then western swing bands took the "hillbilly" out of country music. The music spoke to the lower class (now the middle class) about poverty, a hard life, and the sadness of "sneakin' around." It held to traditional values and was slow to change.

3. *White popular* ("pop") music provided sentimentality, the "crooner" sex symbol, and industrial know-how. "Pop" was money, power, status, and respectability. It was the music for most Americans until the rock 'n' roll revolution.

4. *Folk* provided the tradition of untrained writers who performed their own music, the participation of the audience, and the rebellion against those in power. Folk music was "people" music, by and for them.

5. *Jazz* provided high-quality trained musicians, improvisation, and a tradition of integration. It developed from a fusion of both black and white musical traditions and innovations that spawned "swing," "bop," "cool," and so forth.

A sixth influence new-waved in from England and out of Jamaica: *Reggae*, the Caribbean version of rock 'n' roll.

MONEY AND POLITICS: 1964–1978

The exact span of years that can be labeled the golden age of rock 'n' roll is in dispute. To set the record straight, the golden age of rock 'n' roll is whenever *you* become aware of the music; rock is what makes puberty, high school, and parental mistakes bearable.

In the mid-1960s, several factors rocketed the record business into the economic stratosphere: (1) the increasing popularity of FM radio; (2) the potential to earn big money; and (3) the politicization of music.

The FM Phenomenon. Radio stations in the FM band had faced tough sledding until they married themselves programmatically and, therefore, economically to rock 'n' roll. In 1964, the British invaded America, led by the boys from Liverpool—the Beatles. Rock flowered, and FM became economically viable with the new, energized, multifaceted sounds of top-40, album-oriented rock (AOR), urban contemporary, soft rock, country rock, folk rock, soul, and fusion. FM stations sold demographics and because of their inherent sound quality, ran roughshod over their AM brethren. And radio—FM radio—was selling millions of records and tapes.

Economic Excesses. Everybody in the music business was making big money. The major companies bought up the independents, whence the innovative music had always come. Rockers earned big money and became stars. Stars made bigger money and became superstars. Everyone thought that the boom would go on forever. So when the record companies bid against one another for stars, contracts got out of hand. Enormous salaries were paid to stars who had lost their audiences, and a lot of new talent failed to get noticed and promoted because the radio stations were locked into tight formats with limited play lists. And the independents were not out there pounding on doors. The business, and the audience, got old quickly and did not even realize that it was in trouble.

In 1964, with little fanfare, the cassette was introduced. Unlike the eight-track-cartridge machines, the cassette has recording capability. Nobody noticed because rock money was growing on trees. Who cared that the audience was home listening to the music—an album at a time on AOR radio. However, they were also taping it. And the boom times were about to end.

Cultural Involvement. There was also the Vietnam War. Rock was a vital part of the antiwar movement. Rock became a marching song and a call to political action, righting cultural wrongs. Theatrical movies and TV dramas avoided mention of the war. Newspapers, books, and magazines were controlled by the Establishment. The only medium to which youth had access was the recording industry, and they sang their polemic loud and clear. After the war, there was Watergate. Then the music died a little. It was less fun. It had gotten self-righteous.

Yet in 1978, there were more gold (193) and platinum (102) albums than ever

Figure 14.4. The Beatles, inspired by Elvis, stormed ashore in 1964; Bob Dylan typified the protest movement of the Vietnam War era.

before. The industry sold 726.2 million recordings for $4.1 billion. The music business was in the big time, and the FM stations were in format heaven.

MTV AND CDs, THE REBIRTH OF THE INDUSTRY: 1979 TO THE PRESENT

The Recording Recession. The bottom fell out in the late 1970s as the United States went through a cultural and an economic recession. America lost much of its creative leadership and innovativeness in the rock business to the Europeans, especially to the second British invasion of punk, new-wave, and new-music bands. Europeans were going out to dance clubs nurturing new musicians and styles while Americans were home listening to "Stairway to Heaven" for the umpteenth time or taping one another's old records. The disco craze swept America in the late 1970s, but it was short-lived and left little in the way of enduring trends in music.

The economic recession was also a hard reality in the music business. In 1978, the music business had reached its zenith in units sold. In the decline from 1979 to 1982, the industry raised prices dramatically to shore up profits, and home cassette taping increased dramatically in an effort to save money (see Table 14.1). In 1983, unit sales stabilized, largely because of one album, Michael Jackson's *Thriller*; 1984 was very strong because of the rejuvenation of the business via music videos (MTV). As the boxed feature illustrates, MTV had much to do with the industry's rebirth; it exposed young Americans to the new trends in music that Europe had already caught on to.

Music Videos. Music videos first flowered in Europe's dance clubs, where state-operated radio and TV limit pop-music performances in broadcasting. The European record companies used videos to expose consumers in clubs to new artists and to new songs by established artists. The videos then flowed through corporate channels to the United States, where publicity departments sent copies to cable outlets to be used as fillers between movies and by pay services like HBO's "Video Jukebox."

In August 1981, Warner-Amex put Music Television (MTV) on the satellite, which bounced it into cable homes. The pictures were accompanied by an FM stereo signal that could be connected to sophisticated home sound systems. MTV, a 24-hour basic cable service, has revolutionized music merchandising by introducing "new music" to the hard-to-reach American heartland and has single-handedly broken the sterile grip that album-oriented radio (AOR) stations had on musical taste in America.

When FM radio was young and hungry, it married itself to rock music. As FM radio became profitable, it became cautious and musically entrenched. Radio sells "numbers" and "demographics" to advertisers. Air time is generally not available to the new musical ideas being tried out in cities, at free college concerts, and on music video. AOR stations were the rage in the early 1980s, and their personnel smugly assumed that they knew what rock music sounded like; their audience (predominately young white males) would always listen to Led Zeppelin's "Stairway to Heaven." In the summer and fall of 1983, some of the new music made the charts, and top-40 stations made it on the radio. The AOR and other "old" formats got trounced in the ratings. Stations made wholesale changes in music formats to play the songs heard on videos. The same songs that listeners had phoned in to request and that had been rejected were now staples. Radio began to ape rock 'n' roll television.

After MTV hit New York and Los Angeles cable services, the record companies believed what retailers in the Midwest had been saying—MTV sells records.

Production costs for early music videos averaged $10,000 per cut. Increasing production values are driving up production costs. Most music videos are shot in 33-mm film, transferred to tape, and edited digitally on video with all the "bells and whistles." Originally, video-production costs were absorbed by the record companies and budgeted as promotions. Today, contracts call for videos to be paid for out of joint profits, and new groups sometimes pay the entire video bill. MTV is not the only game on television. VH-1 is an all-music video channel in competition with MTV. The "Nashville Network" plays country-and-western videos on cable channels throughout America.

Compact Discs. After many years of near-stagnation, compact discs arrived in 1985 to revive the industry's sagging technical spirits. The CD's high-quality sound, very clean and distinct even at high-volume levels, is possible because the digital code is read by a laser beam without loss of sound quality. There is no record wear, and damaging CDs in normal circumstances is very difficult. Some 22.6 million CDs were sold in 1985, despite their high price ($15). By the end of the decade, compact discs had become the major growth market of the music business. As the average price dropped, the annual sales growth rate reached an explosive 184 percent. The positive effect of CD sales is represented by the $6.3-billion industry revenue in 1988, an 11 percent growth rate since 1983. However, the CD explosion also meant a significant decrease in the production of LPs and

Figure 14.5. Compact discs are produced in a dust-free environment. A laser beam etches pits in a glass master; then the master is silver-coated and electro-formed to make a nickel negative. From the negative are made multiple positives, which, in turn, are used as stampers in the molding process. Under heat and pressure in a vacuum chamber, the disc is molded and metalized with an extremely thin, reflective aluminum layer. The disc then is lacquered while spinning and has its hole carefully aligned, labeled by direct printing, packed in a plastic box, packaged, and shrink-wrapped.

W hen MTV first appeared in August 1981, its creators probably had no idea of their network's power to influence American culture. Now almost 10 years old, the fast pace and flashy style of music video has left its mark on fashion, television, movies, and advertising, not to mention changing the way that people appreciate music and performers.

Video has made music a visual as well as an aural medium. It is almost unheard of now for a rock group to release a hit album without doing videos. MTV allows rock singers to show off new styles and attitudes. Pop stars like Cyndi Lauper and George Michael became hot because their looks were just as popular as their music. Anyone who likes a singer's music can dress just like their idol. Music videos, originally rather cheaply produced affairs, have become intricately staged and choreographed. Michael Jackson broke ground with *Thriller* in 1983. Directed by John Landis, it was a 20-minute ghost story featuring zombies, vampires, and werewolves that cost over $1 million. Artists followed his lead by putting together lavish and expensive video clips. Other directors, like Brian DePalma and Martin Scorsese, have also done videos. Videos by Paula Abdul and Bobby Brown are extensively choreographed dance numbers. Performers like Peter Gabriel and Dire Straits, use the latest in animation and video techniques to accompany their music.

Music video combines the sound of radio, the imagery of television and film, and the pace of advertising. It is not surprising that MTV has had a tremendous impact on these other media. After "Miami Vice" imitated music video's meshing of substance and appearance, almost every action television series now uses music

hits as a backdrop to its chases and shoot-outs. Films like *Top Gun* and *Back to the Future* blur the boundary between themselves and music videos; images accompany the movie soundtrack, which can then be turned into a video to promote the film. Television advertising has probably been influenced the most by MTV. Madonna and Michael Jackson entered their songs into the cola wars, while ads for candy or beer can easily be confused with music videos without the stars.

Now that the novelty of music video has worn off, MTV's producers have introduced news segments, comedy series, and dance programs to supplement the ever-present videos. MTV has always raced, in a constant attempt to stay on the cutting edge. Anyone interested in knowing the latest in fashion or music looks at MTV first and waits for the rest of the media to catch up.

45s, the old staples of the business. By 1990, some record companies had announced plans to phase out records. It may be too early to say, but the birth of the digital compact disc could mean the death of the long-playing record.

CD players are available for autos, home stereos, portable stereos, and even Walkman-type radios. CDs have gone beyond the early stage of an expensive status symbol to become a new standard in the music industry.

Space-Age Technology. The synthesizer has had enormous effect on rock. "Digital synths" are replacing guitars as the lead instrument, and the percussionist is being usurped by a "drum box." Eliminated are entire string, woodwind, and brass sections. New music requires new sounds and new colorations of old familiar sounds.

It all began with the invention of what came to be called "the moog," a modular synthesizer developed by Robert Moog and Donald Buchla. The moog was intended for classical music and was popularized by Wendy Carlos in the film *A Clockwork Orange*. Rock innovators—the Moody Blues and Emerson, Lake, and Palmer—used it early on. Synthesized music was further developed by Kraftverk and by Tangerine Dream and then went through "techno pop" with Howard Jones and Erasure. Its widest popular acceptance was in disco. It is also widely used to score commercials and, by Vangelis, Giorgio Moroder, and others to make motion-picture sound tracks.

Now, one artist, working alone and at home, without the special acoustics of a recording studio, can create music that goes straight from the synthesizer through a computer to a digital recorder using an electrical code. The sound-to-microphone step is no longer necessary. Northeastern Digital's Synclavier is part of the new wave of instruments that actually can add harmonics to the sine wave. Precise sounds can be called up from memory and repeated ad infinitum. Timbre, vibrato, and attack can be duplicated to resemble almost any instrument. Even complete systems of multiple instruments costing $250,000 can pay for themselves over a short period by eliminating the cost of studio rental and studio musicians.

Recent Issues in the Recording Industry

The music industry has changed along with the social climate surrounding it. More than 30 years after the negative reaction to early rock music, 1985 saw a resurgence of criticism against rock's sexual and violent explicitness. Parents and social groups, with Tipper Gore as their spokesperson, accused heavy metal bands of encouraging teen suicide with their lyrics, while singers like Prince and Sheena Easton were attacked for their songs' sexual overtones. MTV, whose videos featured strong violent and sexual imagery to accompany the lyrics, was also criticized. Congressional hearings about rock lyrics were held in 1985 to determine if the lyrics should be censored, or at least rated in a system similar to the one used for movies. Among the oddest images this created was the heavy metal band Twisted Sister testifying before a subcommittee dressed in their full regalia and wearing makeup. No form of regulation emerged, but the threat of censorship was enough to lead some performers to tone down their message.

In 1990, the controversy over lyrics erupted and led to court cases. A shop owner in Alabama was the first to be convicted of selling obscene recordings (2 Live Crew's "As Nasty As They Wanna Be," which a court in Florida later found obscene). Although the Alabama case was overturned on appeal, retailers' concerns about legal fees and community stigma have a real effect on the industry. Legislators in several states had been drafting bills to require labeling of recorded music. The issue, linked to First Amendment freedoms, was hotly debated in press and broadcast media across the country. Much of the steam was released by the recording industry's decision to increase the labeling that had begun in 1985 with warnings. An 800-member organization of retailers and wholesalers pressured the Recording Industry of America, the manufacturing trade group, to adopt a uniform sticker ("Explicit Lyrics—Parental Advisory"), uniformly placed, under the shrink wrapping.

The record industry lobbied heavily in the early 1980s for surcharges on sales of blank tape to offset the loss of revenue from home taping; 80 to 90 percent of all blank tape is used to duplicate copyrighted material. Some manufacturers spoke of producing cassettes that could not be dubbed. The lobbying effort was unsuccessful because of the combined counterefforts by tape suppliers and equipment manufacturers. The industry's efforts died out in 1987 when CBS, the leader of the fight, was bought out by Sony.

On a more positive note, the 1980s also witnessed an increased social awareness on the part of the industry. In an effort to provide famine relief for Ethiopia, Bob Geldolf in Great Britain formed Band Aid, and Quincy Jones in the United States put together *USA for Africa*, each project a combined album of songs by many rock superstars. Their concert in 1985, called Live Aid, combined the two groups in a

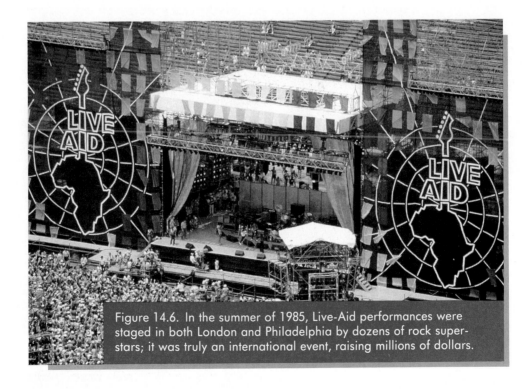

Figure 14.6. In the summer of 1985, Live-Aid performances were staged in both London and Philadelphia by dozens of rock superstars; it was truly an international event, raising millions of dollars.

massive performance that raised millions of dollars in relief. Later projects by musicians to raise money for causes included Farm Aid and Hands Across America.

The 1980s saw an increasing trend toward conglomeratization and commercialization in the music business. By the end of the decade, six corporations—MCA, Time Warner, CBS, Philips, Thorn EMI, and the Bertelsmann Music Group—accounted for over 90 percent of sales. Smaller companies such as Virgin Records or Motown were bought by the majors because the larger labels had the ability to market their music to a national audience successfully. Some critics have said that "corporatization" of music will stifle creativity as the majors may become reluctant to look for new musical trends. However, the major labels, well aware of the danger of stagnation, have remained diversified by purchasing smaller labels but giving them creative independence.

MTV's success prompted corporations to hire rock musicians to make music videolike commercials. Adam Ant and Grace Jones sold Honda scooters; David Bowie and Tina Turner hyped Diet Pepsi. Some performers were too hot for their own commercials; in 1989, Pepsi hired Madonna but then canceled the advertisement because of the controversy caused by her song "Like a Prayer." Groups (The Who, the Rolling Stones, and Eric Clapton) began turning to large corporations for sponsorship of their tours. Ironically, many of these groups had scorned such large companies and their profits in the 1960s.

THE RISE OF HEAVY METAL AND RAP

The 1980s saw the rise of two new styles of rock, both of which captured the rebelliousness and anger of their audience—heavy metal and rap. The roots of

Figure 14.7. Budweiser sponsored the Rolling Stones' 1989 world tour.

heavy metal can be traced to groups like Led Zeppelin or Iron Butterfly in the 1960s. Heavy metal is harsh, grinding music, relying heavily on screaming guitars and violent imagery. Heavy metal performers such as Ozzy Osbourne or Guns 'n' Roses feature outlandish hairstyles and costumes, accompanied by violent stage acts. Their songs are often heavy with inferences to violence and satanic worship, a cause of criticism and proposed censorship. But they capture feelings of dissatisfaction in their young listeners, and heavy metal's critics miss the most important point: The bands are popular only because young people identify with what they are singing.

In the 1980s rap music grew from a small segment of the industry into a popular and successful style. Disdaining the instruments and complexity of conventional rock, rap emphasizes simple but forceful lyrics backed by a steady rhythmic beat. Most rap performers come from the inner city, and their songs reflect their origins. Strong, boastful, and angry, they sing about the violence, drugs, and poverty they face. While some groups, like Run D.M.C. and L.L. Cool J., have been signed by major labels and achieved some success, most rap performers join small record companies or produce their own albums.

Not surprisingly, rap continues to be controversial. Rappers sing against drugs

Figure 14.8. Above, Ozzy Osbourne, a heavy-metal singer. Below, The Fat Boys, a rap group appearing on "Square One," an educational math program. The 1980s saw the rise in popularity of heavy metal and rap as new forms. Harsh, rebellious, and even violent, these new forms were successful because they expressed the feelings of their young audiences.

and racism, but their lyrics suggest that violence is the best solution. Performers such as Public Enemy and N.W.A. have been accused of encouraging violence in their lyrics. Rap concerts have been the scenes of drug dealing and gang fights, leading many auditoriums to ban rap performances. Most mainstream radio stations refuse to play rap because of its lyrics, rekindling the old controversy over programming bias. Rappers have to succeed without big record contracts, heavy airplay, or large concerts.

But rap has become a social statement. While rap lyrics are often disturbing with their disrespect of women and authority and condoning violence, they are the feelings of inner-city youth. Movies like *Do the Right Thing* and *Colors* used rap in their soundtracks to capture the feel of the inner city. To condemn the lyrics is to condemn the situation that the lyrics come from. In response to their critics, rappers say that they are merely expressing feelings that are already there, providing a safe expression of their audience's anger.

THE STRUCTURE AND ORGANIZATION OF THE RECORDING INDUSTRY

Before a record can be a success, several groups must support it: (1) the creative element; (2) the business element; (3) the information and distribution element; and (4) the consumer element. No single element can create a hit or prevent one (see Figure 14.9).

THE CREATIVE ELEMENT

The artist-musician creates the material. The engineer-mixer-technician manipulates the inherent qualities of the medium to create recorded music. Performers are aided, guided, and supervised by a business consultant, generally called an agent. Performers also have managers to handle details and run concert tours. Both agents and managers are paid a percentage of the performer's income, usually 10 percent. Artist-and-repertoire (A&R) people serve a similar function for production companies. The record producer often also serves an A&R function, although his or her task is not to select the groups but to get them taped in a satisfactory manner.

THE BUSINESS ELEMENTS

There are two subcategories: internal, individuals within the record company; and external, groups outside the record company that have a significant impact on the music business.

Internal. Decisions to exploit the creative element are made by high-level corporate officers who approve the financial appropriations that are considered to be essential to the successful marketing of the record. They provide the capital and reap the greatest portion of profits. The marketer-promoter-sales representative devises the best way to get visibility for the record. Since all the company's records cannot be pushed with equal effort, the field representative must promote one unit in preference to another. The advertising and public-relations staffs pre-

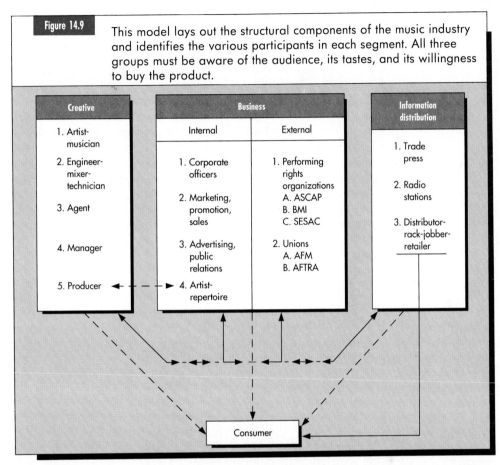

Figure 14.9

This model lays out the structural components of the music industry and identifies the various participants in each segment. All three groups must be aware of the audience, its tastes, and its willingness to buy the product.

pare trade announcements for radio stations, distributors, and retailers, as well as consumer advertisements for the general public. Most of the effort and money is spent on trade materials. In effect, records are "pushed" through the distributor-retailer by the trade press and air play, rather than "pulled" through by consumer demand.

External. Publishing-rights organizations collect performance payments, which come primarily from radio and TV stations. Under the copyright law of 1976, each jukebox pays an annual tax in order to play records. The three organizations that handle publishing rights are the American Society of Composers, Authors, and Publishers (ASCAP), which has about 18,000 members and collects 67 percent of the fees; Broadcast Music, Inc. (BMI), which has over 21,000 writers and 9,500 publishers as clients and accounts for 32 percent of all fees; and SESAC, a small, family-owned company that does about $2 million in business annually for its 200 publishers and 375 catalogs. Broadcasters normally subscribe to both ASCAP and BMI.

The two major labor unions in the recording business are the American Federation of Television and Radio Artists (AFTRA) and the American Federation of Musicians (AFM). Record companies are closed shops, in that vocalists and musicians must join a union in order to record. Union-scale wages are set for every aspect of the business—from studio sessions to club appearances to concert tours.

THE INFORMATION AND DISTRIBUTION ELEMENT

This area has three participants: the trade press; radio-station programmers; and distributors, rack jobbers, and retailers.

The Press. The trade press serves as a general information and evaluation source. Five major publications serve this function. *Billboard, Cashbox,* and *Record World* are reliable sources of business and creative information helpful to the retail industry. The radio industry uses another publication extensively—*Radio and Records*, which publishes the play lists of 250 selected contemporary hit radio stations in large (P-1), medium (P-2), and smaller (P-3) markets. These play lists document the songs that are getting airplay and the heaviness of their rotation (the number of plays daily). *Rolling Stone* concentrates on creative evaluation and has a wide public and trade readership. All five periodicals function as gatekeepers; they aid in the selection process by featuring articles on those records that are expected to be successful. These "trades" cover industry news, trends, and new releases.

There are also tipsheets, such as *Album Network*, the *Brennerman Report, Friday Morning Quarterback,* and the *Hard Report*, which anticipate breakouts and report what is going to happen rather than what is currently popular. Fringe music and new artists are covered by the *Contemporary Media Journal* and *Rookpool*, which help with data on specialty and college markets.

The Programmers. If the local disc jockeys do not play the records, the public cannot become acquainted with them, and audiences are less likely to buy them. Only a handful of the 200 singles and 10 LPs received each week ever get extensive airplay, which is more valuable than any advertising. Stations are serviced by independent record promoters who are paid fees or commissions by the record companies for their success in getting new songs on the air. In the mid-1960s, "NBC Nightly News" broadcast a story that money was paid by the independents to radio program directors for adding new songs to their rotation and reporting these additions to *Radio and Records*. The scheme was called *papering* when the program directors reported adding a song but did not actually play it. After the report, many record companies distanced themselves from the independents, but rumors persist of payoffs in the form of cash, drugs, and favors to disc jockeys to get airtime.

MTV and other video services have replaced radio as the primary influence on consumers' decisions regarding music purchases, thus resulting in the rise of new music from Europe and the rebirth of visual heavy-metal style.

The Distributors. The distributors, rack jobbers, and retailers are also crucial to the recording industry. If a record is not in stock, it cannot be bought. And since the life of popular music, especially singles, is short, it is crucial that the record be available immediately on public demand.

THE CONSUMER ELEMENT

Ultimately, there is the omnipotent audience, the consumers who purchase records, cassettes, and CDs. The record buyer decides whether a group will become stars or a record will become a hit. The Recording Industry Association of America certifies gold, platinum, and multiplatinum records.

1. A gold album must sell 500,000 albums, cassettes, and CDs or generate $1 million in wholesale sales at one-third of the list price. Gold singles must sell 1 million copies. (Sales of 45s and of 12-inch dance remixes are added together. The 12-inch records count as two single sales in the computation, which means that a record could sell 500,000 45s and 250,000 dance singles and be certified gold.)
2. A platinum album must sell 1 million copies or generate $2 million in wholesale income. Platinum singles must sell 2 million copies using the same formula for 45s and dance remixes.
3. A multiplatinum album must sell 2 million copies or generate $4 million in wholesale income. Singles must sell 3 million copies.

The audience can select only from those recordings that are available. Each element can block or hinder the recording communication process. Nevertheless, even if the industry elements all support a given record, the public can, and often does, prefer to buy something else. There is no accounting for taste. Do we know *anything* about record consumers?

1. We know that they spend $6.5 billion a year for more than 700 million records.
2. We know that they buy more cassettes than albums. In fact, they spend six times as much for tapes as for albums.
3. CDs are what they buy, and are growing steadily, although the prices are still somewhat high.
4. We know that they are dancing again because dance remixes are doing well.
5. We know how they spend their money:

Albums	10%
CDs	20%
Cassettes	60%
Cassette singles	3%
Singles	7%

This means that cassettes are dominant but that CDs are also very profitable and digital audio tape is growing.
6. We know that they make 52 percent of your purchases at record and tape outlets, and one in four purchases is a gift.
7. We know that the music audience is aging and was spending significantly less on rock and more on pop and easy listening in the first 5 years of the 1980s, both in retail purchases and through record clubs.
8. We know what they buy by age, race, sex, and region of the country. For example, 64 percent of rock is bought by consumers 24 or younger; 96 percent, by whites; 58 percent, by men; and 57 percent, by northeasterners and southerners. The rock target profile is young, white, male, and East Coast. On the contrary, country music customers are older (70 percent over 25), white (97 percent), female (54 percent), midwesterners and southerners (57 percent). Table 14.1 outlines consumer spending. It has very broad categories and breaks down the target audiences for sound recording. Profiling of consumers is done in much greater detail—perhaps as specific as zip code and last record purchases—by marketing departments in order to reach specific target markets not only for general types of music but also for specific artists.

Figure 14.10

These charts show percentage of dollar volume spent on music type and on the format of recording. Rock dominates the market. Cassettes make up over half the dollar volume; LPs are on the way out. The drop in volume for compact discs may be attributed to the lower prices of CDs.

Configuration Purchased
Percentage of dollar value

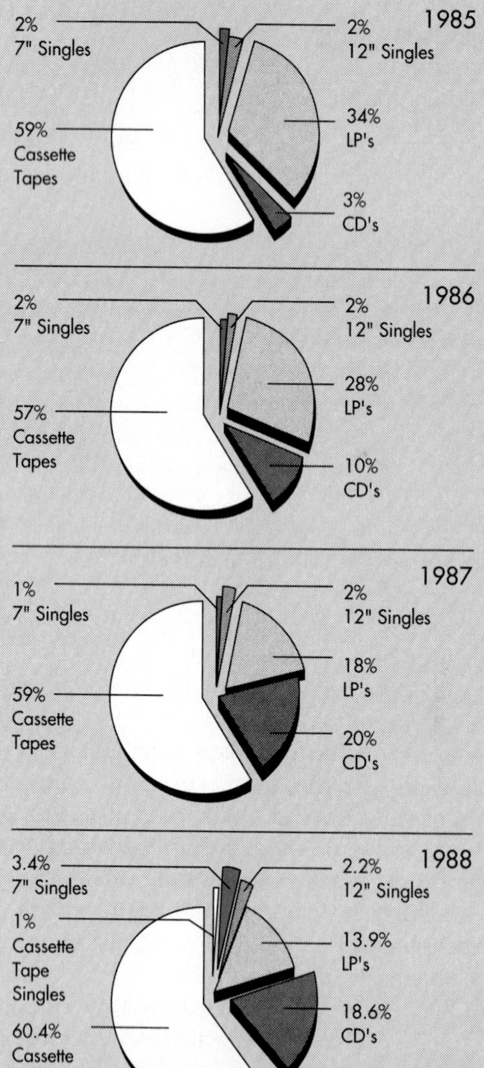

1985

2% 7" Singles
2% 12" Singles
34% LP's
3% CD's
59% Cassette Tapes

1986

2% 7" Singles
2% 12" Singles
28% LP's
10% CD's
57% Cassette Tapes

1987

1% 7" Singles
2% 12" Singles
18% LP's
20% CD's
59% Cassette Tapes

1988

3.4% 7" Singles
2.2% 12" Singles
1% Cassette Tape Singles
13.9% LP's
18.6% CD's
60.4% Cassette Tapes

(Due to rounding, figures may not add up to 100%)

9. We know that they are often impulse buyers and love to be among those getting a CD first. Then they let their best friends make a tape of it and hope it is returned.

THE ECONOMICS AND FUTURE OF THE RECORDING INDUSTRY ....

In the industry, there are both large, self-distribution companies, such as Columbia and RCA, and independent-label companies, which usually specialize in one kind of music and use regional distributors and national networks to sell their product to retailers and then consumers. New movements like early rock and today's rap and street music are usually independent projects because they adapt to changes rapidly. As this music is popularized, independents are often bought out by larger groups when specialized music tastes become part of the mainstream.

Record clubs are another source of sales for the company. Clubs have become important components of the conglomerate mix. When Time Warner and Sony were negotiating for the move of the hot producer team of Jon Peters and Peter Guber to Sony's Columbia Pictures, the *New York Times* reported:

> By far, the most valuable piece of the deal for Time Warner is the stake in Sony's CBS Record Club. In the year ended last March [1989], the record club generated cash flow from operations of roughly $70 million on revenues of about $500 million. Independent record clubs have rarely been sold, but analysts estimated it could be valued at $560 million to $700 million. Thus Time Warner's 50 percent would be worth $280 million or more.[1]

Sound recording is a tough, competitive business in which 8 of every 10 recordings do not make money. In the classical field, 95 percent of the albums lose money; this field is subsidized by the government and foundations in their grants to orchestras. Big new hits and the work of established artists pay most of the company overhead.

To break even, a single must sell about 50,000 copies; an album, 145,000 copies. When an artist has a hit, the individual group can earn a royalty of from 5 to 15 percent on the list price. Under the 1976 copyright law, songwriters get 2.75 cents for each sale. A single that sells 1 million copies, therefore, can earn a writer over $30,000.

The economics of the industry work out so that the producer earns from 40 to 50 percent of the retail price; distributors get from 15 to 25 percent; the retailer gets the remaining 20 to 30 percent, depending on the mark-up. The rack jobber pays the record company 40 to 50 percent, and the retailers pays a flat fee of 10 to 15 percent of total sales, which means that the jobber keeps 35 to 40 percent of every record he or she markets.

The individual artist or group is usually advanced money to produce an album. The advance must also cover touring expenses, which for groups can cost $7,000 a week. For example, say that a group gets $100,000 for an album. Production costs are roughly $50,000 for audio and $30,000 for a video clip, which leaves $20,000 to tour for an average of 10 weeks. If the group is new, it can expect to earn only $1,000 to $3,000 a week. If the album sells 100,000 copies, the group's royalty is $63,000, which the company keeps to cover part of the advance. This leaves the group in arrears $37,000 for the advance, in debt for the tour, and in need of money to produce a second album. The company does a bit better. At 94 cents an album, it earns $94,000 on album sales plus $63,000 in artist royalty, for a total of $157,000, which gives it $57,000 above the advance. The economics of the recording industry notwithstanding, rock superstars earn from $2 million to $6 million each year from song royalties, concerts, singles, albums, promotions, and tours.

The outlook for the future predicts a healthy recording industry into the 1990s. Revenue of almost $9 billion has been forecast for 1993, almost entirely from sales of CDs and cassettes. Table 14.1 shows both short-term and long-term patterns for new releases in terms of recording format.

1. Singles. Sales of singles, the good old 45, were down an average of 12 percent per year. Release of singles may end altogether by 1992.
2. CDs. CD sales have grown an annual average of over 100 percent in the 1980s. Sales will begin to taper off in the 1990s, but CDs should still be the format with the most growth.

Table 14.1.

Manufacturers' Unit Shipments (Millions Net After Returns)

	'79	'80	'81	'82	'83	'84	'85
Disc Singles	195.5	164.3	154.7	137.2	124.8	131.5	120.7
LP's/EP's	318.3	322.8	295.2	243.9	209.6	204.6	167.0
CD's	—	—	—	—	.8	5.8	22.6
Cassettes	82.8	110.2	137.0	182.3	236.8	332.0	339.1
CD Singles	—	—	—	—	—	—	—
Cassette Singles	—	—	—	—	—	—	—
TOTALS**	701.1	683.7	635.4	577.7	578.0	679.8	653.0

Manufacturers' Dollar Value ($ Millions of Suggested List Price)

	'79	'80	'81	'82	'83	'84	'85
Disc Singles	275.4	269.3	256.4	283.0	269.3	298.7	281.0
LP's/EP's	2136.0	2290.3	2341.7	1925.1	1689.0	1548.8	1280.5
CD's	—	—	—	—	17.2	103.3	389.5
Cassettes	604.6	776.4	1062.8	1384.5	1810.9	2383.9	2411.5
CD Singles	—	—	—	—	—	—	—
Cassette Singles	—	—	—	—	—	—	—
TOTALS**	3685.4	3862.4	3969.9	3641.6	3814.3	4370.4	4387.8

Source: RIAA MARKET RESEARCH COMMITTEE
* 1987 figures represent six month sales only.
** 1978–87 totals reflect inclusion of discontinued configurations not itemized on the table.

3. LPs. Sales of LPs have fallen an average of 20 percent per year, and they are predicted to make up less than 1 percent of total sales before long.
4. Cassettes. Cassettes have become, and will remain, the number-one format in terms of sales and new releases. They are predicted to have a 7 percent annual increase in sales in the future.
5. Eight-Tracks. In 1983, eight-tracks ceased to be released.

In the 1980s new developments affected music through a combination of technology and stylistic innovations. The future should be no different. We conclude by turning to the heads of three record companies, who recently speculated about where the industry is heading.

Bob Krasnow, the chairman of Elektra Records, commented:

We have the emerging climate of world music. It's no longer strange to hear a record in a foreign language anymore. At the same time that we've been finding more receptivity in the world market for American music, we're importing music

'86	% Chg. '85–'86	'87	% Chg. '86–'87	'88	% Chg. '87–'88	'89	% Chg. '88–'89
93.9	−22%	82.0	−13%	65.6	−20%	36.6	−44.22%
125.2	−25%	107.0	−15%	72.4	−32%	34.6	−52.20%
53.0	+134%	102.1	+93%	149.7	+47%	207.2	+38.42%
344.5	+2%	410.0	+19%	450.1	+10%	446.2	−.95%
—	—	—	—	1.6	NA	−.1	−105.95%
—	—	5.1*	NA	22.5	+341%	76.2	+239.14%
618.3	−5%	706.8	+14.3%	761.9	+8%	800.7	+5.09%

'86	% Chg. '85–'86	'87	% Chg. '86–'87	'88	% Chg. '87–'88	'89	% Chg. '88–'89
228.1	−19%	203.3	−11%	180.4	−11%	116.4	−35.48%
983.0	−23%	793.1	−19%	532.3	−33%	220.3	−58.61%
930.1	+139%	1593.6	+71.3%	2089.9	+31%	2587.7	+23.82%
2499.5	+4%	2959.7	+18.4%	3385.1	+14%	3345.8	−1.16%
—	—	—	—	9.8	NA	−.7	−108.90%
—	—	14.3*	NA	57.3	+301%	194.6	+239.68%
4651.1	+6%	5567.5	+19.7%	6254.8	+12%	6464.1	+3.35%

Music Videos*

1989		Percent Change	
Units	Dollar Value	Units	Dollar Value
5.96	115.380	—	—

* Market Research Committee reported this information on music videos for the first time in 1989.

from places like Bulgaria, France, and Brazil that either celebrate a great ethnic tradition or a life style.

Music video should represent a third of our dollar volume by the mid-90's. We've had a lot of success with home videos. By the mid-90's, you should be able to buy a video in a compact disc form and be able to play it either as a video or as an album.[2]

"Rap is going to be around for a while, though it may develop into a pop hybrid that involves more music and singing and less pure rapping. Lyrics in the '90's are going to mean everything, since people will be looking not only for new rhythms but for important messages. I think the '90's could be the most inspired decade for pop in the last 30 to 40 years," said Tommy Mottola, the president of CBS records.[3] Clive Davis, who began Arista Records: "Music video has been very valuable as a promotional item, and I think it's here to stay. Long-form videos have shown that they have commercial appeal and that they are no threat to the compact cassette. The record business itself is healthy, and I think it will continue to grow. The technology of the compact disc and the portability of the cassette have insured that."[4]

SUMMARY ....

The record industry is composed of audio reproduction on a variety of materials—vinyl records, magnetic tapes, and digital compact discs.

The history of recording breaks down into five major historical periods: (1) 1877–1923, when the basic experiments, inventions, and exploitation occurred; (2) 1924–1945, when the technical improvements, financial disasters, and consumer ambivalence occurred—all in relation to the new radio medium; (3) 1946–1963, when network radio died and records became the content of local stations, the technology and marketing of recordings were radicalized, and rock and its audiences came alive; (4) 1964–1978, when FM came to dominate radio, the music industry lost all sense of fiscal responsibility, and music became a cultural force and political instrument; and (5) 1979 to the present, when the bottom fell out of the industry but CDs and music video came along to revive the medium and put it on strong ground for the future.

The industry made major technical advances in the 1980s. Music has become more portable. Radios, cassettes, and CD players can be carried in one hand and powered by batteries. Car stereos can be just as good as home stereo systems. CDs are a tremendous advance in sound quality and durability. Long-playing records and 45s are on the way out, surpassed by the superior sound and convenience of cassettes and compact discs.

The current music industry has evolved through these periods to become a complex industrial structure that integrates creative processes with the business, information, and distribution systems to serve the consumer. This structure has many participants, with subindustries and other media involved in the recording communication process. All play important specialized roles.

The recordings flow to the consumers through a variety of channels that participate economically and facilitate the growth and success of the home-entertainment conglomerate. This industry has been affected by changes in the 1980s: the threat of censorship, a resurgence of social awareness by music artists, a narrowing of the industry to a few very large corporations, and the popularity of new music styles that capture the voice of youth, often in disturbing ways.

All of this leads to a medium that is massive, with sales of over $6 billion; international in scope; dominated by youth; portable, yet of high quality; a major socialization instrument committed to social causes; and having extremely high turnover of talent and content.

Of all the media, it is the most difficult to discuss; it is changing the fastest, will be more powerful in the future, and puts control of content and time in the hands of the consumer.

REFERENCES

1. Geraldine Fabrikant, "Sony and Warner Settle Suit Over Producers," *The New York Times*, November 18, 1989, D1.
2. Stephen Holden, "The Pop Life," *The New York Times*, January 3, 1990, C18.
3. Ibid.
4. Ibid.

CHAPTER 15

Books

Book-publishing firms have been significant components in the sequences of merger, conglomeratization, and globalization of mass media that have made headlines in the past few years. This was true when the acquisitions of Bertelsmann, which had purchased RCA Records in 1987, encompassed what is now known as Bantam Doubleday Dell, a merger of three well-established book publishers. Begun in the nineteenth century as producer of a small religious list, closed by the Nazis during World War II, and leveled in 1945, Bertelsmann reemerged first as a European and then as a global communications leader with sales of $6.6 billion. In 1989, this sum took second place to the $10 billion total made by a merger of Time Inc. and Warner Communications; the various book operations of *these* two multimedia firms accounted for close to $1 billion of their 1988 revenues.

Such mergers and acquisitions promise a broader (more profitable) play of creative product and talent and indicate a movement toward media systems. Book authors continue a strong tradition of supplying "product" (books lead to films, audio- and videocassettes, miniseries, and talk-show material on TV and radio, and magazine and newspaper excerpts), all the while extending the lifespan of their books through paperback and book-club sales. More and more, specialists in the new conglomerates and outside packagers and agents are hired to develop and expand properties for *cross*-media use. Access to book publishing provides both a resource and an avenue, a channel, to be used in various ways by modern communicators.

Nevertheless, some people may not classify books as a mass medium at all. It is true that like other media, books have developed from elite to mass to specialized forms. Best-selling books have reached mass audiences, but except for a few best-sellers, most of the books published each year reach relatively small audiences. Overall, the book industry has the lowest gross income of all the mass media. Almost 60,000 new books—new releases and new editions combined—are published each year in this country. Virtually every one of these new books needs a customized introductory marketing strategy as well as its own production plan. Each book must be uniquely estimated, typeset, printed, and bound. It's definitely not like producing boxes of cereal. Further, costs of paper and labor are soaring, and the possibility of returned merchandise (a problem for books as for no other mass medium) ever looms. The impact? As the big publishing houses get bigger, and fewer in number, there is an equally dramatic growth of the "small presses"—literary, specialized, regional or local publishing. Only they can regularly afford to take a gamble on worthy but marginal books, poetry, new voices, books with limited appeal geographically—all important but risky endeavors.

In spite of their relatively weak economic position, books probably have the most long-term power and influence among the mass media. The book is still the

Figure 15.1.
This poster by illustrator Mary Engelbreit points out the special quality of reader accessibility that books possess.

medium used to communicate the most important thoughts of a society, the medium most used to stimulate change, and the medium most used to educate—from preschool to postdoctoral and adult education programs. Libraries are often the central room in primary schools, the focal point of campuses. Nineteenth-century English author and social critic Thomas Carlyle said: "In books lies the soul of the whole past time." This is the kind of worshipful tone with which we have revered the book, as a medium and as an institution. Books offer self-help as well as entertainment. And in spite of the advent of electronic media, the book is still the most convenient and permanent way to package information for efficient storage, rapid retrieval, and individual consumption.

Of all the media, the book has changed least in its coding and format. We begin with a look at its rich history; from there, we will look at the special problems of audience and distribution that confound the builders of media systems, at the trends to watch, and at the changing role of books in mass communications.

HISTORICAL PERSPECTIVE ....

The book was the first portable medium of communication. As far back as 2400 B.C., clay tablets about the size of shredded-wheat biscuits were used as we use books today. In 700 B.C. an entire library of literary works written on such tablets existed in Nineveh in Asia Minor. Paper has an even longer history as writing material, found as papyrus in Egypt as early as 4000 B.C. and used to form rolls (of papyrus or parchment, made from animal skins) that were wound around wooden rods. These scrolls, *volumen*, were difficult to handle and impossible to index or shelve for ready reference.

THE FORMAT EMERGES

In the fourth century A.D., the Romans developed a form of binding called *codex*, in which scrolls of paper were cut into sheets tied together on the left side between boards, forming the kind of book we still use. Codex binding opened a new world for readers, who could leaf through books and find the passages they wanted; they could begin to compare passages and could create a table of contents, an index, and some logical arrangement of material.

The most important innovation for book publishing was the invention of the printing press and movable type. Having developed paper from flax and hemp at the end of the first century A.D., the Chinese were also the first to develop printing. The oldest known printed book is *The Diamond Sutra*, printed in China in 868 and made up of seven sheets pasted together in a 16-foot scroll. The Chinese did not carry their invention much further, and although there was movable type in Korea a half century before it appeared in Europe, we believe that Johannes Gutenberg on his own put together a wine press and movable type to make a usable printing system: The first dated printing was of a papal indulgence in Mainz, 1454. Gutenberg was unsure of the viability of his invention, but the craft of printing spread rapidly in Europe, and more than 30,000 books were produced for a total of 15 million copies within 50 years. Most of these books were religious or ancient classics, printed in Latin or Greek. As more people came into contact with books and learned to read, printers slowly began to produce crude versions of these classics in vernacular languages, and they began to publish books on more popular subjects, such as history, astronomy, and supernatural phenomena.

The first printed books looked much like the hand-copied volumes produced during the Middle Ages. The style of type was Old English, which resembled the handwriting of the monks who had copied manuscripts in florid letters. (A number

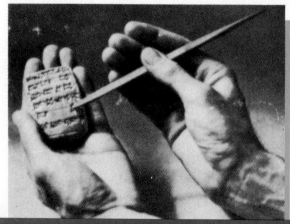

Figure 15.2. Cuneiform characters get their distinctive triangular shape from the reed stylus used to impress lines and wedges on wet clay, which is then baked so it can be preserved.

of newspapers use this in their logos, to suggest something well established.) As more people began to read books, type style itself began to be "vulgarized," or simplified. Gothic type, characterized by black, bold, square letters, was easier to read and expressed a feeling of simplicity and directness. Roman type was a combination of Old English and gothic, with some ornateness and some simplicity in the design of the letters, much like the type styles in widest use today.

Each development in the production of books—whether in paper, binding, printing, typography, or broader distribution through popular translations—brought the book closer to the common person.

BOOKS IN EARLY AMERICA

Nineteen years after the Pilgrims set foot on Plymouth Rock, Stephen Daye became the first printer in North America, establishing himself at Cambridge; and a year later, in 1640, he published his first book, *The Whole Book of Psalms*. The first American Bible was published in 1663; it was soon translated into the languages of the Massachusetts Indians for use in missionary work. In the young United States, books allowed explorers to pass along their discoveries, and they accelerated the accumulation and distribution of many areas of knowledge.

Popular works began to appear, the most famous being *Poor Richard's Almanack*, published by Benjamin Franklin every year from 1732 to 1757. Franklin wrote the *Almanack* under a pseudonym, Richard Saunders, and filled the books with wise and witty sayings that were set between meteorological reports. In 1731, Franklin started the first subscription library in America, the Library Company of Philadelphia. One of the first American inventors, a scientist as well as an eminent statesman, Franklin was one of America's pioneer mass communicators.

Until the nineteenth century, books were relatively scarce, and since the elite and affluent were most likely to possess or read them, a family's library was often a mark of its place in society. The aristocrats of Virginia, for example, prided

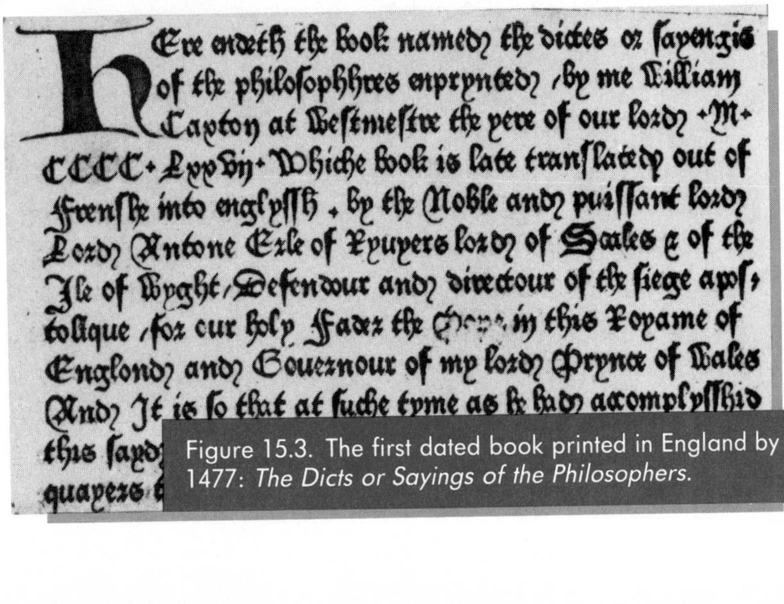
Here endeth the book named the dictes or sayengis
of the philosophhres enprynted, by me William
Caxton at Westmestre the yere of our lord .M.
CCCC.Lxxvij. Whiche book is late translated out of
Frensshe into englysshe, by the Noble and puissant lord
Lord Antone Erle of Ryuyers lord of Scales & of the
Ile of Wyght, Defendour and directour of the siege apos-
tolique, for our holy Fader the [illegible] in this Royame of
Englond and Gouernour of my lord Prynce of Wales
And It is so that at suche tyme as he had accomplysshid
this sayd
quayers

Figure 15.3. The first dated book printed in England by Caxton in 1477: *The Dicts or Sayings of the Philosophers*.

themselves on their leather-bound volumes of classics. One of the best collections belonged to Thomas Jefferson; his personal library of 6,500 books was purchased by Congress in 1815 to start the Library of Congress.

DEVELOPMENT INTO A MASS MEDIUM

For the first 350 years of printing, the production of books changed very little. The type was set by hand, the paper was handmade, and the wooden press was hand operated. At the beginning of the nineteenth century, such slow production did not matter, because only about 10 percent of the population of the United States was able to read. But by the end of the nineteenth century, 90 percent of Americans had become literate, and the demand for books soon exceeded the supply.

The current drive by book manufacturers to have the state-of-the-art capabilities to produce quantities of quality at great speed began with the invention in France in 1798 of a machine that could make paper in a continuous roll rather than single sheets. Press innovations were made about the same time, as we saw in Chapter 9. These developments in technology were accompanied by rapid change in the editorial side of book publishing. A number of major publishers began to emerge.

Figure 15.4. Serialized adventures await beyond the flashy full-color cover of this early entry in the "dime novel" category.

They sought writers to produce quickly for the new market, as well as editors and business people with a clearly defined sense of organized operations.

The nineteenth century saw the emergence of books for the masses, cheaply produced and often sensational treatments of popular themes, either fiction or nonfiction. The faster printing and cheaper paper that had been developed opened the way for the "dime novels" at the turn of the century. These serialized adventures enticed the reader with brightly colored, realistic covers, an approach not unlike the one used for contemporary romances. Thus the world of books—which had been devoted primarily to works of philosophy, religion, literature, and science—also became inhabited by popular heroes of romance, the Wild West, and Horatio Alger success stories that broadened the horizons of possibility for millions. Books came to be judged by the book industry not so much on their literary merits as on their popularity: How many copies were sold? How much money did they make? This best-seller concept would become basic to all mass media.

The Book in the Twentieth Century

Until the end of World War II, book publishing in the United States remained essentially the same kind of industry that it had been in the late nineteenth century. Most firms were still relatively small, family-owned publishing houses, usually specializing in one type of book, such as adult trade books (the novels and general nonfiction available through retail bookshops), professional books (medicine, law, science, etc.), or textbooks.

In this century, changes began to take place that resulted in the sustained growth of book sales. From 1952 to 1970, the book industry grew at a rate of more than 10 percent each year. In the 1970s, the industry grew by 16.5 percent a year. By the close of the 1980s, the gross sales of books were more than $14 billion a year, with school and college textbooks accounting for the largest single category. Table 15.1 shows the breakdown of the totals estimated by the Association of American Publishers for 1989.

This growth can be attributed to four specific developments within the industry and American society: (1) the development of book clubs, (2) the emergence of paperback books, (3) the boom in American education, and (4) new directions in the organization of publishing firms, a complex and constantly changing picture that will be sketched later in this chapter.

Developing the Interest in Books

Unlike magazines and newspapers, which are largely supported by subscription sales, the purchase of a book is usually a one-time transaction to fill a specific need. The book club helped change that process and became a new distribution technique that revitalized book publishing and brought books to the then considerable number of towns with no book outlet. Book clubs began to develop in the 1920s, providing a kind of automatic subscription for books and regular ordering each month through the mail in a habit-forming pattern. A leader, the Book-of-the-Month Club (BOMC) currently boasts 3 million members; to keep their loyalty in an increasingly

Table 15.1.	AAP Estimated Industry Sales 1988–1989		
	Millions of Dollars		
	1988		**1989**
	·$	**$**	**% chg from 88**
Trade (Total)	3036.4	3623.5	19.3
Adult Hardbound	1433.0	1745.4	21.8
Adult Paperbound	852.2	976.6	14.6
Juvenile Hardbound	558.4	665.1	19.1
Juvenile Paperbound	192.8	236.4	22.6
Religious (Total)	675.9	737.1	9.1
Bibles, Testaments, Hymnals & Prayerbooks	185.9	201.0	8.1
Other Religious	490.0	536.1	9.4
Professional (Total)	2411.9	2592.8	7.5
Business	446.0	*NA	*NA
Law	833.0	NA	NA
Medical, Technical, Scientific, & Other Professional	687.0	NA	NA
Book Clubs	690.2	704.0	2.0
Mail Order Publications	697.7	796.8	14.2
Mass Market Paperback Rack-Sized	1006.9	1094.5	8.7
University Presses	198.1	227.0	14.6
Elementary & Secondary Text	1783.8	1983.6	11.2
College Text	1716.8	1842.1	7.3
Standardized Tests	111.4	119.4	7.2
Subscription Reference	473.9	509.4	7.5
AV & Other Media (Total)	207.9	*NA	*NA
El-Hi	166.7	NA	NA
College	15.0	NA	NA
Other	26.2	NA	NA
Other Sales	218.2	NA	NA
Total	13229.1	14665.2	10.9

* *Not available*

fragmented and special-interest-oriented market, now served by proliferating bookstore chains, BOMC has evolved since 1925 from one main monthly selection to a wide range of offerings.

A new dimension was added to book publishing in the mid-1970s: the "managed book." Publishers began to put books together in the same way that magazine executives assemble their products, in editorial boardrooms, using demographics and opinion polls instead of relying on an author's imagination. They look at social, economic, and cultural trends (the growing popularity of gardening, for example) and decide what kind of book is needed and what format will sell. They then contract various pieces of the work to be efficiently produced by specialists. Good examples of this type of publishing are the series produced by Time-Life Books; like book-club offerings, these are sold by direct mail on a subscription arrangement.

MASS-MARKET PAPERBACKS

The dime novel was a precursor to the explosion of adventure and information, romance and inspiration, made possible by the appearance of the first ten 25-cent Pocket Books, in May 1939. Full-length paperback books were developed in Germany as early as 1809, and though they spread through Europe, notably as the still-flourishing Penguins in England, the feeling had been that "cheap books" were viewed by cultured Americans as inferior. Pocket Books's adoption of Gertrude the Kangaroo as its logo heralded something different: inventive design, artistic covers, carefully chosen literature (the 1939 debut of the 10 titles was the result of extensive research and a test-marketing of 2,000 copies of *The Good Earth*, which later that year earned Pearl Buck the Nobel prize), and reliable advice, including the all-time best-selling paperback, Dr. Benjamin Spock's *Pocket Book of Baby and Child Care*

Also different was the method of distribution. The book became part of a sociocultural movement; it was now available not only in bookshops but drugstores, depots, groceries, and hotels. Nontraditional book outlets are even today on the increase. Paralleling the use of the pulp novel as entertainment for soldiers since the Civil War, the new paperback found its stride when servicemen in World War II needed inexpensive portable reading material. The book industry distributed special editions as part of the war effort, and by 1945 some 123,400,000 copies of 1,324 titles had traveled to Americans around the world.

The general audience for books was enhanced by all this. By 1948, approximately 49 million people in the United States over the age of 15 read at least a book a month, and many other publishers of mass-market paperbacks appeared to capture particular corners of the market. In the 1950s, a new breakthrough was Doubleday's Anchor paperbacks of intellectual importance, which led to "quality" or "trade" (larger format) paperbacks, papercover textbooks, and all in all a larger and more diversified book-buying audience.

THE GROWTH OF EDUCATIONAL PUBLISHING

A most important development in book publishing has been the boom in American education. There are more than 50 million students in primary and secondary schools; about 11 million students in colleges, universities, and technical institutes; and more than 25 million adults enrolled in evening courses, on-the-job training, or home-study programs. This represents a giant audience for textbooks, workbooks, supplementary materials, reference works, and laboratory manuals. It should be pointed out that here the ultimate consumer does not make her own selection: Textbooks are usually "adopted" by the instructor for an entire class or in some cases by an administrator or board for a district or statewide system.

Textbooks now account for at least one quarter of the total gross sales of books; if we add together all books falling generally within the educational category, including encyclopedias and professional books, they would account for about half of book sales.

"These School Books combine the rare advantages of superior intrinsic merit, typographical beauty, cheapness, and extensive uniformity of adoption and use." That was written in the introduction to one of the famous McGuffey readers published in the 1850s. Ever since, publishers have been striving for that superior merit in a competitive but lucrative marketplace (the Book Industry Study Group estimates sales of college texts alone will rise to $1.8 billion by 1992). To win the adoption of school books by large states like Texas or California, firms like McGraw-Hill and Wiley spend huge sums on development of a product, all "on spec." To answer demand for college texts that mesh with specific syllabi, one publisher in 1989 announced its capacity to apply new computer technology to custom-edit books for orders as small as 10 copies. Another important segment of educational publishing—even more significant with this country's rapidly changing demographics—is English as a second language.

The Structure and Organization of Book Publishing

The book publisher is essentially an intermediary between reader and author, who is paid a percentage of sales (called royalty) and usually given an *advance* against earnings when a contract is signed. In most small firms, the publisher contracts for all the services necessary for the production and distribution of the publications—including the work of artists, designers, copy editors, paper dealers, printers, binders, sales representatives, and distributors. Even some of the largest book publishers use outside services for some production aspects, and only a handful of major publishers have their own printing facilities.

The larger the firm, the more specialized each individual's function must become. (See the boxed work flow.) Editors themselves have increasingly specialized tasks. Executive editors are responsible for planning publishing programs. These editors are decision makers, deciding what books to publish, which authors should write the books, and how the product should be packaged and promoted. Production editors are technical experts, overseeing the steps necessary to convert a manuscript into a finished book. This includes such tasks as copyediting, design, proofreading, and indexing. The other jobs in book publishing are also specialized, whether in selling, promoting, distributing, or producing. Artists, designers, advertising copywriters, and promotion specialists are of increasing importance and concern.

Because of fixed costs, salaries, and production expenses, books with small runs have a high per-copy cost. The amount needed to cover editorial, design, typesetting, preparation for, and actual work at the press remains the same, no matter how many copies are printed; paper and binding materials are the major variables. It can cost $250,000 to develop and produce an art book (this does not include the cost of advertising and promoting it). If textbooks seem expensive, bear in mind that the unit cost of the physical package could be $10. The price a student pays must cover marketing, distribution, book seller profit, etc. Total book sales are now in the $14-billion-plus range annually, but the profit margin is rather small.

The more than 1,400 distributors, regional wholesalers, national jobbers, and the 21,600 bookstores in the United States and Canada sell 2 billion copies of the 60,000 titles issued each year by approximately 20,000 publishers. Publisher, distributor, and bookstore owner face the reality that only 20 percent of the books published earn a profit. A few titles must support the rest, and because of infor-

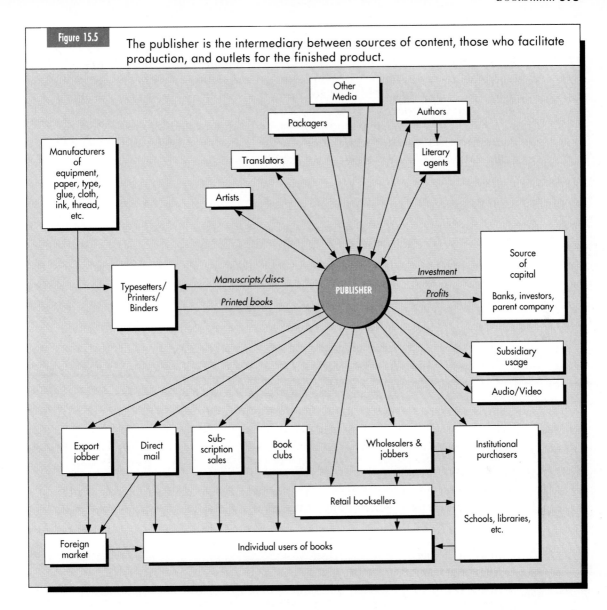

Figure 15.5 The publisher is the intermediary between sources of content, those who facilitate production, and outlets for the finished product.

mation obsolescence, nonfiction books must be revised every few years, especially texts and professional books.

Without the library market, many titles would never be published because 9 of every 10 books sell fewer than 20,000 copies. More than half of these 20,000 books are purchased by 29,000 libraries that buy 1 of every 10 books sold—usually higher-priced, hard-cover, limited-sales editions.

With all the risks it faces, book publishing has become an arena of the small and the giant. During the 1970s and 1980s, independent publishing firms, especially the midsize, were fair game for takeovers. We began this chapter with a look at two examples from a long list of mergers and acquisitions. Hearst bought William Morrow, Rupert Murdoch bought Harper & Row, Newhouse absorbed Random

Book publishing is distinguished by the proportion of involvement in the process of the individual communicator, the author, and his or her sponsoring editor, who oversees the finances and general progress. Being an assistant to such acquiring or executive editors is still, despite low entry (and higher-level) pay and the threat in recent years of job elimination through mergers, a promising route for college graduates and affords a view of the entire process. Procedures vary from house to house and with the degree of computerization used, but *basically* what happens is

Book proposal submitted
↓

Proposal/sample reviewed by content experts and, often, marketing experts
↓

Contract
↓

Development of manuscript
↓

Complete ms arrives and is reviewed by editors
↓

Ms prepared by editorial assistants
to be turned over to production
↓

The managing editor assigns the manuscript to a production editor, who supervises production process from manuscript to bound book.

Production editor prepares a design survey for book based on its various elements (headings, tables, boxes, chapter apparatus, etc.)

↓   ↓

Design survey is passed to designer, who writes specs (specifications for type, size, etc.)

Copy editor is contracted to read ms. for errors of grammar, spelling, capitalization, documentation, and to serve as "naive" reader.

↓

Ms. and specs are sent to compositors or typesetters for estimates of pages, costs.

Art is prepared. Proofs of line drawings and figures are sent to author for approval.

Cover is designed and produced.

Copy is written for cover, catalog, and other promotional materials. Author often assists in promotion.

Any advertising or marketing support plans finalized.

↓

Sample copies sent to reviewers.

↓

Copyedited ms. sent to author for review; is sent back to production editor with any corrections.

↓

Copyedited ms. and type specs sent to typesetter who sets ms. into proofs.

↓

Proofs are sent to author, to freelance proofreader and to production editor. All corrections are coordinated into one set that is sent back to typesetter for correction and preparation of final camera-ready pages.

↓

These final repros proofs are checked and sent to printer. Printer sends blueprint proofs of film of book to production editor for checking.

↓

Book is printed and bound and shipped, to wholesalers, distributors, bookstores.

↓

Reaches the individual end user.

Turnover or launch meeting is held: editors, manufacturing and marketing representatives discuss any unusual situations and fix production schedule.

Specialists try to sell rights to other media and special sales outlets, book clubs, etc.

If a freelance indexer is hired, a set of page proofs is also sent to him or her. Author reviews.

House. . . . With this has come to book publishing, the (comparative) ivory tower of the media, pressure to be more businesslike and accountable.

Conglomerate managers used to other product lines or other national cultures have perhaps put inappropriate pressure on their book-publishing divisions. An industry that introduces 60,000 different "programs" or distinct presentations of content in 1 year has very different challenges from those faced by newspapers, television, or even films. If global conglomerates are attracted by the pipeline of media content that books represent, they may have to adapt their financial expectations of individual publishing companies and realize that bigness is not necessarily conducive to success when it comes to books.

BOOK AUDIENCES

Trade-book readers are, even more than magazine buyers, clearly more than cable viewers, most typically interested in specialized niches. Thinking back to our economic model in Chapter 3, we realize that the choice is not a matter of deciding to watch television or select a magazine or newspaper that will provide a variety of reading matter, but determining that a subject area is of interest, a particular writer's style is engaging, the product is accessible, the considerable amount of time needed to consume the book is available, and the price is affordable. All these factors must work together for the selection of each book. The number of audiences theoretically available for books is higher than for any other medium.

Mass market paperback publishers can no longer count on their audiences, built up over a span of 50 years. Insiders observe that there are simply too many titles (many of them the result of the copycat syndrome) to accommodate in existing rack space or attract enough consumers to gain back a publisher's investment; returns of unsold product from the bookstores—the bane of book publishing—are especially high and damaging in this category. Carole Baron, of Dell, points out that the splintering of the mass audience has finally hit paperbacks: "There's no mass market, just a lot of smaller ones."[1]

NICHES AS A MAINSTAY

Only 13 percent of Americans purchase trade or general-interest books, the kind found in chain and nonspecialized book outlets, according to a study by the Association of American Publishers. Although there would appear to be a possibility of developing a larger "market share" of all media consumers for novels, biographies, and such, only a few genres promise enduring strength. Self-help books, for example, are bought by one-third of all Americans.

Publishers divide the titles they publish into a *frontlist*, the new entries for that season, and the *backlist*, the titles that remain in print and sell year after year to account for up to one-third of sales. Classics, how-to's, and home reference books are the staples of most firms. Just as Hollywood studios were acquired for their film libraries, the jewel in the crown of a publishing acquisition is often the backlist. One of the few independent publishers, W. W. Norton, survived on the depth of its 2,500-title backlist. This body of titles is also important to independent book-stores, accounting for at least 50 percent of their sales. The backlist is a rare predictable element in book publishing and requires a minimum of the promotion needed to launch a new book.

Occasionally one category takes off for a while but perennially there are certain kinds of backlist books that carry a house, and the leaders sell millions over several decades:

cookbooks (the top three best-selling hardcover books from 1895 to 1975 were in this category);

gardening, home improvement and "dream books" of design, selling for $50 or more;

child raising (pregnancy titles are the best-sellers);

financial planning, a sure bet in any economic climate;

health and fitness, an increasingly specialized field;

"celebrity" books—by or about.

Although we cannot live by bread alone and need the escape, inspiration, or beauty of novels, memoirs, history, or poetry, the numbers demonstrate that we are not buying as many of these as publishers would like, or need to survive: General or trade-book divisions of large firms have folded during the last 2 years at a rate to alarm analysts.

JUVENILE PUBLISHING

One of the brightest spots in the changing world of book publishing is claimed by juvenile books, which is on the way to surpassing $2 billion in sales annually. There are several reasons for its remarkable growth: (1) the baby boomers are now having their own children (the number of those 12 and younger is projected to rise to 50 million by 1995); (2) many of these parents are more demanding in looking for books to supplement school reading; (3) schools are swept up in the "whole language" movement in which "real" literature such as novels, biographies, and so on are used in class work; (4) new technologies allow graphic artists to design exciting children's literature (the category is especially focused on fiction at all levels); (5) there are more outlets for these books (some independent booksellers now carry *only* children's books).

Juvenile publishing has always been geared to the backlist, so books remain in print long enough—10 years or more—to earn high production costs (most of these books are in full color). Dr. Seuss has been part of the American scene for over 50 years, and rights to just two of these titles were certainly a treasure sought by Random House when it acquired the publisher, Vanguard Press.

Especially with conglomerates buying rights, paperbacks as well as hardbound editions are readily available. The price seems right: The top 20 all-time best-selling paperbound children's books sold well over 2 million copies, led by *The Outsiders* by S. E. Hinton (5,855,085 copies). Across the board, title output from 1980 to 1988 rose 73.3 percent; absolute success and stellar performance in comparison to other areas of publishing have won juvenile publishing its own best-seller lists in many publications. The period 1988–1989 saw store sales of juveniles increase 19.1 percent compared with 1.8 percent for adult hardcover sales.

THE RISE AND FALL OF THE MEGASELLERS

Total book sales more than doubled in the past decade, to some degree because of rising per-unit prices and growth in the educational market. The picture also reflects book publishing's participation in a boom period for the trade book—one that led to dramatic examples of how the competitive nature of the mass media is not in the long run a healthy thing for the peculiarly privatized world of books.

Competitive bidding for rights to the blockbusters led to giant leaps in advances, the money paid to authors against future royalty earnings, to get them to sign contracts to write one or more books. At the start of the 1980s, a $1-million advance made trade news; by the close of the decade, authors like Stephen King were commanding $30-million. King did author five of the top 20 best-selling novels of the period (see Table 15.2). In other instances, however, more money did not garner more attention and more sales. Even the good track record of historical novelist John Jakes (*Kent Family Chronicles* et al.) could not guarantee his twelfth book, *California Gold*, success; bought for $4.3 million and heavily promoted, it did not do as well as expected. Book publishing remains the least predictable of the mass media; its distribution system and its intrinsically fragmented market does not permit timely feedback—if feedback is available at all. Although it is the oldest of the mass media, it is only now entering the age of modern technology.

Publishers were on the big-book bandwagon for most of the 1980s as 13 novels and 12 nonfiction books, far more than ever before, topped 1-million-copy sales. High hopes led to high print runs, which led to high outlays of money and the introduction of high-tech high-speed presses. Bill Cosby's third book, *Love and Marriage*, came off the press at a rate of 13,000 copies per hour in a 600-foot-long totally integrated production line that occupies 40,000 square feet in a plant owned by Bertelsmann Book Manufacturing Company. It took 1 minute and 20 seconds from the time the paper left the roll until a finished book appeared. Some of these dazzling facilities are not as busy, now that the sobering swing of the pendulum has returned the book-publishing industry to its norm. The game of Can you top this? went on long enough to do several houses in. Megasellers, like mass-market paperbacks, suffer significantly from returns (which exceeded 30 percent in 1989, according to *Publishers Weekly*).

The 1990s are seeing a leveling off of dependence on a few big blockbusters and more attention to the diversity of tastes and the backlist. "Publishers will have to realize that independent [booksellers] aren't selling thousands of copies of Michener's *Caribbean*; we're selling fives and tens from thousands and thousands of titles," said bookstore owner Michael Powell.[2]

Along with all this is the small but steady increase of small publishers as well as nonchain outlets, each in ideal positions to serve the hallmark of today's media public: diversity. The dominance of rapidly growing nationwide bookstore chains such as Waldenbooks and B. Dalton (between them, 1,800 stores and $2 billion in 1989 revenue) in the early 1980s had contributed to concentration on a dangerously small number of megasellers, but too few of these could actually support themselves or the rest of the publisher's list.

SMALL PRESSES AND REGIONAL PUBLISHING

Always part of the spectrum of book publishing and the original issuers of book-length volumes, smaller companies targeted at consumers of specialized or regional

Table 15.2.	Bestsellers of the 1980s

A. Fiction Bestsellers

1. **Clear and Present Danger.** Tom Clancy (Putnam, 1989); 1,607,715
2. **The Dark Half.** Stephen King (Viking, 1989); 1,550,000
3. **The Tommyknockers.** Stephen King (Putnam, 1987); 1,429,929
4. **The Mammoth Hunters.** Jean M. Auel (Crown, 1985); 1,350,000
5. **Daddy.** Danielle Steel (Delacorte Press, 1989); 1,321,235
6. **Lake Wobegon Days.** Garrison Keillor (Viking, 1985) 1,300,000
7. **The Cardinal of the Kremlin.** Tom Clancy (Putnam, 1988); 1,287,067
8. **Texas.** James A. Michener (Random House, 1985); 1,176,758
9. **Red Storm Rising.** Tom Clancy (Putnam, 1986); 1,126,782
10. **It.** Stephen King (Viking, 1986); 1,115,000
11. **Kaleidoscope.** Danielle Steel (Delacorte Press, 1987); 1,065,355
12. **Zoya.** Danielle Steel (Delacorte Press, 1988); 1,000,319
13. **Star.** Danielle Steel (Delacorte, 1989); 1,000,119
14. **Patriot Games.** Tom Clancy (Putnam, 1987); 957,400
15. **Misery.** Stephen King (Viking, 1987); 875,000
*16. **The Sands of Time.** Sidney Sheldon (Morrow, 1988)
17. **The Talisman.** Stephen King and Peter Straub (Viking, 1984); 830,000
18. **Leaving Home: A Collection of Lake Wobegon Stories.** Garrison Keillor (Viking, 1987); 817,000
19. **The Satanic Verses.** Salman Rushdie (Viking, 1989); 766,000
20. **The Icarus Agenda.** Robert Ludlum (Random House, 1988); 753,967

* Sales figures were submitted to *PW* in confidence, for use only in placing the title in its correct position on the list.

B. Nonfiction Bestsellers

1. **Iacocca: An Autobiography.** Lee Iacocca with William Novak (Bantam, 1984); 2,572,000
2. **Fatherhood.** Bill Cosby (Doubleday/Dolphin, 1986); 2,335,000
3. **The 8-Week Cholesterol Cure.** Robert E. Kowalski (Harper & Row, 1987); 2,250,000
4. **Fit for Life.** Harvey and Marilyn Diamond (Warner Books, 1985); 2,023,000
5. **In Search of Excellence: Lessons from America's Best-Run Companies.** Thomas J. Peters and Robert H. Waterman Jr. (Harper & Row, 1982); 1,375,000
6. **All I Really Need to Know I Learned in Kindergarten.** Robert Fulghum (Villard, 1988); 1,280,000
*7. **Jane Fonda's Workout Book.** Jane Fonda (Simon & Schuster, 1981)
*8. **The Frugal Gourmet.** Jeff Smith (Morrow, 1985)
9. **A Brief History of Time.** Stephen W. Hawking (Bantam Books, 1988); 1,130,000
*10. **Yeager: An Autobiography.** General Chuck Yeager and Leo Janos (Bantam, 1985)
*11. **Nothing Down.** Robert Allen (Simon & Schuster, 1980)
*12. **Time Flies.** Bill Cosby (Doubleday/Dolphin, 1987)
13. **A Day in the Life of America.** Rick Smolan and David Cohen (Collins Publishers, 1986); 960,000
14. **Cosmos.** Carl Sagan (Random House, 1980); 887,462
15. **The Frugal Gourmet Cooks with Wine.** Jeff Smith (Morrow, 1986); 860,963
*16. **The Rotation Diet.** Martin Katahn (Norton, 1986)
17. **Motherhood: The Second Oldest Profession.** Erma Bombeck (McGraw-Hill, 1983); 846,000
18. **Trump: The Art of the Deal.** Donald W. Trump with Tony Schwartz (Random House, 1987); 835,091
19. **Loving Each Other.** Leo Buscaglia (Slack/Holt, Rinehart and Winston, 1984); 830,587
*20. **His Way: The Unauthorized Biography of Frank Sinatra.** Kitty Kelley (Bantam, 1986)

* Sales figures were submitted to *PW* in confidence, for use only in placing the title in its correct position on the list.

Source: Publishers Weekly, January 5, 1990, 24–25.

Figure 15.6. Chains concentrate on best-sellers and illustrated gift books they can sell by the stack.

subjects—alternative health, gay literature, Texan home cooking, or divorce proceedings in the state of Washington—are flourishing amid the fragmentations of markets witnessed by all the mass media. Hand in hand with focused publishing has been the growth of decentralized distribution, which is often faster and more audience-responsive than what is provided by large headquarter operations. Michael Raymond, writing for *Publishers Weekly*, sums it up:

> The growth of regional book publishing during the past twenty years has been dramatic and the expansion has profoundly contributed to the development of trade wholesaling in the U.S. Along with the increase in the numbers of publishers, books printed and sold, and retailers, it has been estimated by the AAP that wholesaling now accounts for more than 38% of the total sale of books. Undoubtedly crucial to this burgeoning is the simultaneous growth of two segments of the book industry: regional publishers and regional wholesalers. Their identities are so intertwined that each has ensured the other's stake in the future of the industry.[3]

Many specialized publishers, often using desktop publishing and relying on freelancers, are profitably able to concentrate on topics that the big houses must pass by because of economic constraints; another factor is the greater freedom of viewpoint that an independent publisher can afford. Such small presses don't try to do it all but avoid much of the infrastructure diagrammed in Figure 15.6 and concentrate on editing and marketing. Enter the regional wholesaler. One firm in Denver has an inventory of 77,000 titles, 3,000 of them from 200 Rocky Mountain and western publishers. Bookpeople, a well-established California wholesaler, has 20,000 titles from 1,500 small and regional publishers, and serves customers throughout the country and the world.

By sticking to what they do best, small houses have found not only respectable profit but recognition. At the 1989 presentation of the book industry's prestigious Carey-Thomas awards, John Baker, editor-in-chief of *Publishers Weekly*, pointed out that "all the winners, not just some, are smaller or, as we like to call them, independent presses. As larger publishers have become more generalized, more focused on big budget, would-be bestsellers, we find more of the chance-taking,

Figure 15.7. Displays at small press fairs attest to the continuing diversity of American book publishing.

the really creative approaches, that Carey-Thomas was designed to award, coming from smaller publishers." Those honored included Thunder's Mouth Press for its "real service to American culture" (alternative fiction, neglected works of black writers, etc.), Curbstone Press, specializing on Latin America, and Seal Press, publishing from the Pacific Northwest writer's movement.

GLOBAL REALIGNMENTS

On the other end of the spectrum is globalization. Because books have so long occupied a sacred position in cultures, they have tended to be more protected as national resources. Some American educators have worried about foreign ownership of textbook publishers. As publishers join television and recording communicators in thinking of Europe as one market, the influence seems to be more a question of economics than content. One view is that "European, eventually world publishing, could become similar in pattern to that in the U.S., with large 'federal' publishers thinking globally and small specialist publishers thinking regionally."[4]

American ownership of British and other publishers is on the increase. Simon & Schuster, largest U.S. publisher (see Table 15.3), says it is the fifth largest publisher in the U.K. Random House and Houghton Mifflin are among those that have acquired prestigious London publishers. The impact has been not so much changing the profile of the books published but pooling editorial and financial capability, improving distribution and bookselling avenues, and launching coordinated marketing initiatives. On the other hand, large conglomerates that have entered the U.S. marketplace have learned to leave the idiosyncrasies of our audiences alone. Bertelsmann, which includes 30 general and technical publishing houses and

Figure 15.8. Henry Hirschberg, of Simon & Schuster, the fifth largest publisher in the U.K.

Table 15.3. Leading U.S. Publishers			Revenues (in 000s)		
Company	Employees	Titles	Latest	Previous	% Change
1. Simon & Schuster	9000	N/A	$1300 (est.)	$1200	8.3%
2. Time Inc. Book Co.[1]	N/A	2283	988	891	10.8
3. Harcourt Brace Jovanovich	4313	4961	879.7 ('88)	802.5	9.6
4. Random House[2]	N/A	c.1720	800 (est.)	500 (est.)	60.0
5. Reader's Digest[3]	2700	35	N/A	780 (est.)	—
6. McGraw-Hill	N/A	N/A	727.2 ('88)	706.4	2.9
7. Encyclopaedia Britannica[4]	2300	13	624	590	5.8
8. Bantam Doubleday Dell[5]	1400	c.1400	600	549	9.3
9. Times Mirror[6]	3000	N/A	520	425	22.3
10. The Thomson Corp.	N/A	N/A	500	475	0.5
11. Harper & Row[7]	2329	2600	450	398	13.0
12. Grolier	5800	N/A	443.3	443.3	0
13. Western Publishing[8]	2500	750	450	N/A	—
14. Houghton Mifflin	2150	715	368.3 ('88)	343.4	7.3
15. World Book Encyclopedia	650	N/A	310	N/A	—
16. Maxwell Macmillan[9]	N/A	700	300 plus (est.)	N/A	—
17. John Wiley[10]	1800	640	259	240	7.9
18. Penguin USA[11]	N/A	c.1830	225	N/A	—
19. Putnam Group	809	1088	200	176	13.4
20. St. Martin's	350	1200	161	133	21.0

[1] *Time Inc. Book Co. results projected for 1989 include Warner Boooks as well as BOMC; Scott Foresman, a major element in these results, was sold in December.*
[2] *Random declined to give sales figures. Figures given are estimates of sales before and after Crown acquisition.*
[3] *Reader's Digest is going public, and thus cannot give current figures. Previous year was published estimate. Employees are U.S. only.*
[4] *EB figures are for a fiscal year ending in September.*
[5] *BDD results show estimated worldwide sales for a fiscal year ending June 30, and do not include Literary Guild sales.*
[6] *Times Mirror employees are book employees only. Results for both years are estimates for book operations only.*
[7] *Harper results include Canadian sales.*
[8] *Western Publishing expects a loss in 1989, but is unable to release specific figures before year's end.*
[9] *Macmillan estimated sales are of books only and do not include journals or book club sales.*
[10] *Wiley figures are for fiscal year ending in April.*
[11] *Penguin figures do not include results from Addison-Wesley, which is also part of the Pearson group.*
Source: *Publishers Weekly, December 15, 1989, 25.*

whose foreign sales account for 68 percent of its total revenue, failed to launch a book club here formatted after a highly successful model in Europe.

On both sides of the Atlantic, eyes are on 1992, when the nations of the European common market become one consumer base, larger than the United States and Japan combined, with more than 320 million consumers and a GNP of $4 trillion. More recently, attention has gone to the lessening of censorship and a freer marketplace that resulted from all the changes in Eastern Europe. Shop windows in Budapest feature bios of Elvis, Leon Uris's novel *Exodus*, and *Zen and the Art of Motorcycle Repair*; *1984*, *Dr. Zhivago*, and *Fanny Hill*, long forbidden, are selling in huge numbers throughout Eastern Europe. Another trend is suppliers' reaction: Printers are acquiring bases in several countries, with a geographic division of labor. Technical problems—lack of paper and expertise—plague the publishers of formerly Communist-dominated countries, but perhaps Maxwell and Murdoch et al., who already acquired media properties there, will change the possibilities of book publishing too.

THE FUTURE OF THE BOOK

As we have discovered, it is difficult to generalize about the health of this industry since each of its segments has a distinctive set of problems and possibilities. Common to all areas of publishing, however, is a tendency to swing quickly from gloom to optimism, to doubt, to positive prediction. The death of the industry has been announced regularly since the advent of the phonograph record. Actually, projections show a continuing rise in total book sales, to $29.4 billion by 1993, according to investment banker Veronis, Suhler & Associates, with strengths in certain categories, the leader being professional books (texts of information, assistance, and reference useful to various careers and areas of special study).

Trade books and other segments dependent on a mass market *are* in serious trouble, and in recent years there have been newsmaking cutbacks of personnel, curtailments of publishing lists, closings, and controversies over the proper place of "business types" in an industry where risk is inherent and the aims of communicators sometimes more noble than profitable. In an address to the Book Industry Study Group in July 1988, Houghton Mifflin's chief executive officer, Harold Miller, declared:

> *In the final analysis, publishing is still a gut business, and to capitalize on all the attractive numbers, someone has to have an idea, and someone else has to recognize whether the idea will fly.*

Those agreeing had a champion when in 1990 the managing director of Pantheon Books was forced out, reportedly because he refused to cut his annual list of quality literature although, as in many other houses at the time, there were heavy losses. It remains to be seen if this decade will include a lasting balancing of accounting concerns and gut feelings.

Until very recently, links with the elusive audience(s) were especially tenuous in the case of books. In large part due to bottom-line pressures, publishers have been playing catch up with the twentieth century, not to mention the twenty-first. Some examples:

Publishers are learning to become managers of "account communications" or to work with marketing specialists on tracking publicity and telemarketing, further developing electronic ordering and sales-pattern updates.

Satellite transmission of author appearances are replacing expensive, complicated author tours, and author videos are being used to sell books to the publishers' sales reps, booksellers, and public.

Innovations are being tested to sell books in different ways: chains are opening rental libraries like video stores and are introducing frequent-buyer plans so consumers can accumulate coupons for discounts; books can be personally ordered by fax.

Even more personalized interactions with books are occurring through flexible contents and formats possible through new technology.

Consumers affected by demands on their time due to proliferating media are being catered to through more condensed versions of content.

Cross-media usage is being expanded, so that immediate release of audio cassettes, for example, creates synergies; video publishing is being explored by heretofore traditional book publishers.

Demographics are being studied more closely: The graying of America creates a market for a more diversified list of large-type books, for example.

Still, the book format that emerged from the days of volume is not going to disappear. Electronic books and data bases will continue to aid academic and business research, and even paperback romance novels may become credit-card discs to be inserted into the portable players developed by Sony. But few envision the end of the bound book, either in physical form or stylistic, handcrafted format: "All the factual data on the 14th century stored in all the data banks around the globe will not convey the magic, vision, virtuosity, and style that Barbara Tuchman gives us in *A Distant Mirror*."[5]

SUMMARY

Books have gone through development stages from elite to mass to specialized forms, and the publishing industry is still very much in a state of flux—and turmoil. In this century, especially significant to the development of the medium were the creation of book clubs, the emergence of the mass-market paperback around World War II, and the steady growth of educational publishing, which now accounts for almost half of the publishing revenue.

Technological developments since the invention of movable type have made the mass production of books possible, enabling many to become best-sellers. In recent years, the megaseller phenomenon led to excesses in author advances and eventually caused the collapse of some general-book-publishing sectors.

The publisher is the link among the author, the suppliers, and technicians who produce the book and the readers who buy it. Although total book sales surpass $14 billion, profit margins are small because of fixed costs and the expenses of paper and printing. The industry has become one of small presses, able to take risks on subjects of specialized appeal, and giant conglomerates.

The audience for books is increasingly "nice"-oriented. Some categories such as self-help, cookbooks, homestyle, child care, and celebrities, are sales leaders year after year and help support the rest of the list. Backlist books do not need the considerable customized promotion that frontlist or new publications do. Juvenile books and regional publishing have been very strong, and specialized distribution systems have been created to serve these markets.

Books are probably more individualized than the other media, not only because they are produced in great variety, often for small numbers of readers, but also because the book-reading experience is personal. We read books alone, usually not in groups, and immerse ourselves more deeply in the process. New technology is finally coming to this, the first of the mass media, but the book as we know it will surely remain a significant part of our culture.

REFERENCES

1. Quoted by Liz Hartman and John F. Baker, "State of the Art," *Publishers Weekly*, May 26, 1989, S32.
2. *Publishers Weekly*, January 5, 1990, 40.
3. "Going to Market," *Publishers Weekly*, October 20, 1989, 22.
4. *Publishers Weekly International*, March 16, 1990, S2.
5. John P. Dessauer, "Why Books Won't Die," *Publishers Weekly*, November 26, 1979, 25.

THE FUNCTIONS OF THE MASS MEDIA

············ ═══ ············

In Part 1 we recognized that each medium has a natural affinity for certain coding and formatting and that the same story presented as novel, film, broadcast, or recorded drama will be altered by the medium. One could say that not only content but function varies with the medium and that certain media perform certain functions more effectively than others. In the United States, television and radio generally emphasize the entertainment function, while newspapers consider themselves primarily conveyers of information. In Part 3 we learned that the evolution of each media industry had an effect on its relationships with its audiences, on what it does for them.

But as we have seen throughout this book, distinctions of formats and functions are not always clear. A standard categorization of mass-media functions includes news and information, analysis and commentary, entertainment, persuasion, and education and instruction. However, from the early history of media, we see overlaps. Newspapers also entertain; television also informs. Sometimes they intend to perform these functions, and sometimes the other functions simply evolve. The present trends of conglomeratization, media proliferation, and the concurrent competition for fragmenting audiences are accelerating the pace of blurring.

The most overlaid function of mass media is entertainment, and some critical voices have been raised about this. News as entertainment has been one notable issue of recent years. We should understand, however, that *each* of the functions is legitimate and can be value-free. That is, media do not need to be any more embarrassed about carrying entertaining content than audience members should be about attending to it. We *need* diversion and relaxation through entertainment, and the media provide efficient mechanisms to communicate that entertainment. Less altruistically, it is entertainment that generally draws large audiences to the mass media in the first place. Information or education, viewpoints, or socialization can be imparted only when the audience member is tuned in, and it may take entertainment to command attention—and really to communicate and reinforce significant content. Few would deny the benefit of using docudrama to increase understanding of world history or universal afflictions such as AIDS or retardation, or of using skits and cartoons to enhance preschool learning. One television news consultant, justifying his service of jazzing up local television newscasts, said, "You can't save souls in an empty church."

Thus the broad areas of entertainment and information especially have become overlapping and mutually supportive functions in our mass-media system. Indeed, the mass media could not have gained the popularity and stature they have if it were not for these essential, interrelated functions.

The chapters that follow study four main functions (persuasion, as part of the mass communication process, was covered in Part 2). Beginning with news and information, we naturally progress to analysis and commentary. There, too, there is often subtle blending of functions, from which come new forms of journalism. We then focus on education, in all its forms except socialization (the spreading of cultural information and values), which is explored more fully in Part 5 under "Social Effects."

The fourth function studied is entertainment. First we look at the controversy that has gone on for centuries about the value of popular or current culture. Its importance would not be denied by anyone save the most narrow-minded elites. We offer a more thoughtful and, we hope, thought-provoking look at how media content (particularly entertainment) affects us. It points out the different ways content is evaluated and how its meaning and artistic value are analyzed by scholarly critics and journalistic reviewers, who are, of course, special communicators in their own right. This final chapter in Part 4 is thus two-pronged: It shows how critics view the entertainment function, but it also lets us consider another function of the mass media—criticism. Criticism by mass-media communicators does not mean only reporters watchdogging government or television programs advocating social reform. Criticism *of* the media's output is also a valuable contribution. Knowing how it works will suggest means by which you can become a more involved critical consumer.

Each of the chapters in Part 4 raises a number of issues, such as the gatekeepers' roles in transmittal of news and how much such gatekeeping is determined by audience preferences and, therefore, by marketing considerations. We leave for Part 5 discussion of broader social and cultural issues.

CHAPTER 16

News and Information

The power and influence of the mass media are nowhere more apparent than in the communication of news and information. Interestingly, this originally was an incidental function of the media. For example, newspapers began as political broadsheets and commercial publications and television began almost solely as an entertainment medium before it developed a news function.

The news function, however, has become indispensable to the maintenance of our complex society; its impact is felt on every level. All of us have private networks or communities from which we draw information, but we depend on the mass media to keep us aware of dangers and opportunities on the horizon. The journalist is a tree climber, a person who tries to get the broadest view of what is happening in the world. We rely on accurate news accounts—from foreign news to local politics to weather—for the actions we take and the way we think about the world. Consequently we blame the news media themselves for the ills of society. In ancient times, the bearer of bad news was slain as a carrier of bad luck. In this century, though no politician would claim that the news media won World War II, many have accused them of losing the war in Vietnam.

By and large, the media merely report what has transpired, whether the event is political, social, economic, meteorological, or personal. Most reporters make every effort to be objective and fair; their charge is to maintain a clear separation between opinion and the facts of the story, and print and electronic media structure presentations so as to keep editorial content separate from news. The media do influence the way events are perceived, however. Their gatekeepers decide, from the millions of daily occurrences and events, which are newsworthy and which may be ignored, which are important and which are only moderately so. Reporters and editors thus do play a role in shaping the course of those events, as attention is focused on a problem.

Many charge that the news media sometimes use this influence self-servingly, passing on supposedly objective accounts that are in fact biased toward a particular social, political, or business interest. Perhaps this is not always deliberate. The failure, for lack of time or whatever reason, to check out the accuracy of public-relations handouts or video news releases, for example, can also lead to slanted or incomplete reports. The effect is the same, nonetheless. The impact of the news media is such that the self-appointed watchdog of government and big business is now highly scrutinized itself to ensure that all points of view are heard and that the business interests that control the media do not use the media as a shield.

The extent of the media's influence may never be fully quantified or substantiated, but as we increasingly rely on the media for news and information, that impact can only grow in significance. The changes taking place in the media affect the function of delivering news and information. The critical consumer needs to

Figure 16.1. At 203 Broadway, New York City, *The Mail and Express* (June 1908) posted news of the Spanish-American War, the fires of which were fanned by newspapers of the time. Today's satellite communications bring full coverage nationwide within hours.

understand these charges. This chapter will step back from the preceding close looks at media industries to consider the nature of news and what issues are at the center of the debate about the generation and gathering of it. The specific changes in reporting procedures that are being effected by technological advancement will be explored in Chapter 25.

WHAT IS NEWS? WHO NEEDS IT?

News covers a surprising range of subject matter. A national survey by the American Newspaper Publishers Association found more than 40 general categories of news in daily newspapers. The survey found that more space is devoted to sports than to international news, more space is given to crime than to cultural events and reviews, and more space is accorded to news of interest to men than news of interest to women.

Different media emphasize different categories of news. Newspapers tend to give more coverage to news of crime and justice than do local and national television. National TV gives more coverage to news of government and politics than do newspapers or local television. National TV also gives more coverage to foreign affairs, whereas newspapers give more space to domestic policy. Local TV gives more coverage to economic and social issues and to human-interest items than does national network television.

No medium will survive if it forgets who its audience is and what it needs. The *Philadelphia Inquirer* emerged the victor from a battle with its 134-year-old rival through its editor Gene Roberts's realization that "people have appetites for news on a lot of levels . . . if you pander to readers you end up insulting them . . .

[succeeding] is understanding the full complexity of the area being served, and understanding that you can't take any shortcuts."[1] Research on news attentiveness is vital to advertisers as well as media communicators. Broadcast-news programming, which accounts for 40 to 50 percent of a station's profit, tries through attractive anchors and correspondents to appeal to the largest segment of 18–54-year-olds, the group that will bring in premium advertising rates.

The same news and information content can affect various audience segments in very different ways. Research on news impact tells us that the power of news to set the public agenda—to determine what people will be thinking and talking about—depends on which audience you have in mind. In their book *News That Matters*, Shanto Iyengar and Donald R. Kinder conclude:

> *Television coverage is particularly effective in shaping the judgments of citizens with limited political resources and skills. Those who rarely get caught up in the world of politics find network news presentations particularly compelling. Partisans, activists, close observers of the political scene, on the other hand, are less apt to be swept away. The more removed the viewer is from the world of public affairs, the stronger the agenda-setting power of television news.*[2]

WHEN DOES INFORMATION BECOME NEWS?

In the terminology of the communicator, news is what an individual is willing to pay for with time and money. In other words, news must have some intrinsic value to the individual. Wilbur Schramm, who was professor of communication at Stanford University and influenced media research, categorized news as fulfilling either an "immediate reward" or a "delayed reward" to a felt need.

Immediate-reward news provides instant satisfaction for the recipient, who laughs, cries, sympathizes, thrills, or muses. Schramm placed in this category news such as crime and corruption, accidents and disasters, sports and recreation, and social events.

Delayed-reward news has an impact that does not affect the consumer until later. Such news includes information about public affairs, economic matters, social problems, science, education, weather, and health. Often, delayed-reward news may bring an unpleasant consequence for the reader, listener, or viewer, while the immediate reward can bring instant gratification. Schramm concluded that most news consumers spend more time with, find more satisfaction in, and give greater attention to immediate-reward news than to delayed-reward news.

A great deal of information about many subjects is available, but information does not become news unless it fits the criteria of:

timeliness,
proximity
prominence,
consequences, and
human interest.

The criteria for such decisions help editors decide not only what news to communicate, but how prominently to display a news item and how long to follow a story.

TIMELINESS

Certainly one of the most important criteria for news is its newness. We say that "nothing is as old as yesterday's newspaper," but actually the length of time for which a piece of information continues to be newsworthy depends on the medium. For radio, a story may lose its timeliness after an hour. Television news may have a slightly longer lifetime, from an hour to a day. Daily-newspaper news has a day lifetime; after that, the story must be rewritten with new information. By *today's* standards it is difficult to comprehend, but in colonial times news "flashes" covered events that had taken place a year earlier in the mother country.

PROXIMITY

Geographical factors are also important to news judgment. Relatively speaking, the nearer an event occurs to the people who hear about it, the more newsworthy it is. The election of the governor of Oklahoma is much more important to Oklahomans than it is to Texans. An automobile accident in which two local people were killed might seem more significant to the audience of a small Vermont town than renewed fighting in a Central American war.

PROMINENCE

The more widely known the participants in an occurrence, the more newsworthy the event. If the president of the United States hits a hole-in-one on the golf course, it could be national news. If the mayor does the same, it probably would be news

Figure 16.2. This elaborate eavesdropping system is supposed to have been developed by the ruler of Syracuse from 405 to 367 B.C.; it condensed sound waves to give him the latest news of court gossip and rebellion. (This engraving by Athanasius Kircher shows a baroque setting.) It was the forerunner of public-address devices and later means to deliver timely news.

only in his town. If the golf pro does it, it might be news only for the newsletter at the country club. Actually, prominence has a snowball effect on newsworthiness, since the mass media make famous people more prominent.

CONSEQUENCES

The consequences of an event have a direct bearing on its newsworthiness. A war in Central America might be more newsworthy in a small community in southern Florida that is receiving a wave of political refugees as a result. Scholars who analyze content and the outside influences on what content gets presented can relate coverage (of economic issues, for example) rather precisely to how events (a local factory closing or recession) hit home. Frequency and length of coverage and placement of a story within a news presentation can be charted. Often the conclusion to be drawn is: Bad news is better copy.

HUMAN INTEREST

Finally, there is a criterion that we can refer to only vaguely as human interest—matters that catch and hold our attention because of physical and emotional responses that they elicit. A number of elements provide human interest, including adventure and conflict, humor, pathos and bathos, sex, the odd and the unusual, and self-interest. A high percentage of each day's news reflects these qualities. A 1990 Times Mirror Center study found even regular news readers are more likely to remember President Bush hates broccoli than any details about Earth day.

THE CRITERIA OF NEWS QUALITY ....

Now that we have some benchmarks of news content, we should explore ways of determining the relative quality of that news. Although the Constitution guarantees the right of anyone to operate a news medium, the "profession" of news reporting in the United States has developed certain standards by which to judge the reporting of news. While not legislated, these standards did grow out of legal battles. The news media frequently defend themselves against charges of libel and bias by claiming their reports are truthful—objective, accurate, and balanced or fair. In countries with government-controlled media, such principles are not always upheld.

OBJECTIVITY

News is supposed to be a factual report of an event as it occurred, without the bias of the reporter or an attempt on the part of the journalist to make any one view more influential than another. In the United States, the journalist attempts to play a nonpartisan role—passing on facts for their own sake, allowing the individual to draw conclusions and make interpretations. The journalist is supposed to disavow the role of promoter or persuader.

As William Allen White, late editor of the *Emporia Gazette* and media philosopher, put it, good journalism is "the facts fairly and honestly presented; truth will take care of itself." Until the 1920s journalists tended to take this criteria for granted. But as skepticism became part of the general mood of the country, journalists consciously presented objectivity as an ideal.

Journalists can in actuality never wholly divorce themselves from their work; their emotions and opinions are apt to influence their perceptions of facts and events, whether they think they will or not. Moreover, no journalist ever sees the whole of any situation, and in the rush to meet deadlines, all the implications and complexities of a story may be simplified to report the main facts. In the 1970s, a school of thought called the New Journalism held that the messenger will *inevitably* alter the message. Such new journalists argue that the reader or viewer will be better served, better able to judge and evaluate events, if he knows the biases of the messenger and is made aware that he is hearing one view of the situation. Many of these journalists wrote in the first person to accomplish this.

In any case, the people have a right to know—that is a basic tenet of a free society—and news ought to provide the necessary factual basis for forming sound opinions. The reporter who wishes to fulfill this responsibility through objective reporting is supposed to work at it diligently.

Accuracy

Reporters are supposed to be constantly vigilant for detail and perpetually skeptical of those who would deceive or exaggerate in order to twist and distort the truth.

Who validates accuracy is a real problem, illustrated in headline-making style in 1989 when CBS News relied on a part-time reporter ("stringer") for filmed coverage of the Afghanistan war and was accused of faking bombings. The correspondent described the difficulties in getting anyone to get the story and asked how CBS could reasonably check it:

> CBS elects to cover the war as best it can. On his own initiative, Dan Rather takes the risk, as he did in Vietnam, and goes into Afghanistan. The others do not. Using stringers will always be risky business. But the danger of not using stringers is greater: no coverage. If there is no coverage, genocide remains invisible.[3]

There are many instances of the danger inherent in the changes taking place in how television covers news: The cry for immediacy and the pressure to cut costs force networks to buy amateur's videotape, and these freelancers can be checked to an even lesser degree than professional stringers. Enter the individual judgment within the conglomerate communicator.

Balance and Fairness

Telling all sides of the story is so much a part of American journalism that reporters sometimes seem to be unpatriotic, unwilling simply to accept the pronouncements of presidents or bureaucrats as the only statements on a matter. In war, this becomes particularly difficult for leaders to understand, since the press and the electronic media seem bent on reporting the successes of the enemy as well as the failure of compatriots. But the journalist is supposed to be dedicated to the proposition that only from balanced reporting of both sides of a story will the people be able to discover the whole truth.

Figure 16.3. At the center of the attention of a pack of journalists, a belligerent baseball celebrity, Pete Rose, who felt his side of gambling accusations was not being told.

Each of these criteria is of course not an abstraction but part of the human fabric that makes up each journalist. These traits and others of character and integrity have been explored in detail in a major essay by Michael J. Kirkhorn of New York University. In "The Virtuous Journalist" he writes that journalists who contribute to the "articulation of our time" reveal to us "something which seems truthful, and quite often the act of revealing requires that, among other intervening deceptions, they must sweep aside a clutter of inferior and obscuring journalism . . . they help us remember, or remember for us, what we need to know."[4]

ISSUES IN NEWS SELECTION ....

Judgments about news—what to report and how to report it—may constitute some of the most important decisions made in our society. Some media researchers have found that media news is *the* educator, mover, and shaper of the American people. Not always understanding the exact mechanisms that constitute its function, critics take the media to task for not doing their job of providing unbiased information well enough. They—and we—need to examine the problems that arise in the process of news selection.

AUDIENCE REACTION

Since news decisions are consumer-oriented, news often overemphasizes immediate-reward types of information in order to sell media. Crime and violence almost always outweigh and outdraw stories of good deeds, constructive action, peaceful progress, and orderly dissent. The aberrations of society—the odd, the unusual, the unique—are more often the subject of news than the normal events. Tabloid journalism lends itself to this kind of selectivity. *New York Times* television critic Walter Goodman has observed that although a news style may not be racially *motivated*, the content and images are often grist for the mill of racial provocateurs.

Local news as well as national has no time to cover the large segments of law-abiding, hard-working minorities.

Dr. Glenn T. Seaborg, Nobel Prize–winning nuclear scientist and former chairman of the Atomic Energy Commission, warned that people are so constantly reminded of evil and corruption in the world by the news media that they may sink into a hopeless morass of gloom and despair, not realizing that the world is still a beautiful place with much more good about it than bad. Not just depression but fear and hysteria can sometimes result from a small detail of the news. An initial television report in 1989 that a small portion of U.S. apples had been contaminated with a chemical, Alar, led to widespread fear that all red apples were contaminated. Across the nation, supermarkets and grocery stores removed red apples from their shelves, and apples were dropped from school-lunch programs. Though the actual scientific evidence was inconclusive and limited, public perception of danger escalated quickly, fanned by more news reports about the public's fear. Federal officials complained that once the story broke, they were unable to get across the less alarming scientific evidence and stem the reaction. The mass media's ability to reach millions of people instantly means that incomplete stories and inaccuracies may be repeated many times before they are corrected. Complicated stories with many qualifications may be unfairly simplified as reporters and the public focus on potential dangers.

An even more dramatic, now classic example of this is the famous Orson Welles radio broadcast, "War of the Worlds," in 1938. The Welles radio program was a dramatization of a science-fiction story about Martians invading Earth, told in the form of a news program, with bulletins interrupting a music show. Perhaps a million of the 6 million people who heard the broadcast believed it was a real newscast and reacted as if there were a real invasion. Police and radio stations were besieged with calls, and many hurried to flee the area. As a result, the code of the National Association of Broadcasters (NAB) adopted a resolution forbidding dramas to be presented as news programs. Given the potential consequences, editors must weigh carefully the communication of alarming information.

Journalists cannot control public reaction, however, and they traditionally defend the publication of "bad" or controversial news by saying that people prefer to read such stories and that exposing corruption and danger does more good for society than praising constructive action. As always, balance is required.

THE IRONY OF OBJECTIVITY

Another consequence of news selection is the distortion caused by the attempt to be objective and fair. The unprincipled person can tell a lie to make news and have it reported with the same weight as the truth. This is especially true of people in authority, who can make news simply by holding a press conference or anonymously leaking scandalous but self-serving information to an eager reporter. The media's principle of objectivity can leave itself open to manipulation.

Perhaps the best historical example of this problem involves Senator Joseph McCarthy of Wisconsin, who in the early 1950s used the exposure of Communists in government for his own political ends. The senator made charges, most of which he was never able to substantiate, that sometimes ruined people's careers and lives. The news media objectively reported the fact that Senator McCarthy had charged Mr. A with being a Communist, and Mr. A, if available, denied the

Figure 16.4. Orson Welles and Mercury Theatre on the Air inadvertently provided researchers with an extraordinary opportunity to study the effects of "news" delivered by mass communication. The radio adaptation of H. G. Wells's *War of the Worlds* was received by many listeners as straight news and caused panic and injury across the country.

charges. Both sides of the story were told, so the news media were giving a fair and balanced coverage of news. But the reporters could not inject their opinion that the senator was lying, and thus irreparable public damage was done to the accused.

Ultimately the truth will win out, if we believe English poet and essayist John Milton's theory that we should put truth to the test in the open marketplace of ideas. And ultimately, in the case of Senator McCarthy, it was the news media that continued to give him coverage until his distortions became so apparent that his colleagues in the Senate finally censured him.

JOURNALIST BIAS

While it is important to look at the consequences of what the news media decide to print or broadcast, it is equally important to be aware of what does not become news. Many minorities and alternative political groups feel they are inadequately covered by the mainstream media. Often they point to the social, political, and economic backgrounds of the journalists as the reason for this, as well as the economics of the media business itself as another focus of blame.

Conservative critics have said that the media are too liberal to be fair to their views or objective. The Vietnam War is one major example used by conservatives to point out the media letting liberalism influence coverage. A study in the mid-1980s found that the mainstream media were composed mostly of white males with above-average incomes and a college education; over 50 percent described themselves as politically liberal and only 17 percent described themselves as conservative. This decade-long survey, *The Media Elite: America's New Power Brokers*, also looked at media coverage during the same period and concluded that there was some connection between coverage and personal beliefs. The study did not conclude that the media are always biased to the left, but it said that journalists tend to follow their instincts when there are no other directives.

Some claim that journalists, mostly from upper-middle-class homes, are not attentive to the concerns of the mostly blue-collar worker. Many blacks and other minorities feel they get little attention in the mainstream media for the same reason. They complain that the coverage they get usually falsely portrays them as poor and marginal.

Finally, many socialists and Marxists in the United States charge that journalists merely reinforce the status quo in their reporting—a relatively conservative, capitalist perspective. They claim reporters do not question the system enough, nor examine the economic assumptions on which their own industry is based. One socialist journalist, who worked for the *Wall Street Journal* and the *Los Angeles Times*, wrote:

> *Editors accept capitalist ideology and let its assumptions guide their news judgement. But few are conscious ideologues. Most just want to print good stories and get the paper out on time. In their mind, a good story is one that is read and commented upon, whatever its message.*[5]

In the end, we must say that news is a two-edged sword. Even those who would use it purposely to deceive will sooner or later be exposed by the same media that allow them expression. The consequences of news are enormous, and no one should undertake to deal with news unless he wants to accept the awesome responsibilities for making such decisions. We will further explore how internal and external pressures affect the ethics of all media in Chapter 21.

THE PROCESS BEHIND NEWS DECISIONS

Of the millions of events that occur in the world each day, and of the thousands of people who do something interesting, who decides what goes on the front page of the newspaper or which will be the top story on the 11 o'clock TV news?

The executive editor may have the last word, but he usually has a lot of help in reaching a decision. At most newspapers and television stations, news decisions are made in regular conferences among reporters, editors, news directors, and producers.

At the *New York Times* and the *Los Angeles Times* news conferences, the managing editor begins by conducting an informal inquiry of editors from the metropolitan, national, foreign, and financial departments. There are generally two such inquiries: an early one involving primarily assistant editors, and a later one involving senior editors. From the two conferences and from conversations before and between them, a consensus gradually emerges on the day's major stories, and an executive news editor sketches in the actual placement of the stories on a dummy (a layout form of design) during the second conference. The dummy is often distributed to all the major desks and bureaus of the newspaper, and the editors are encouraged to challenge it. At the *Washington Post*, the managing editor goes over the dummy at a final news conference, asking the appropriate editor to comment on each story already tentatively sketched in. The editors may suggest changes, and late-breaking events can force additional changes throughout the day.

Different editors and different publications and broadcast operations make different judgments about the news. *Time* and *Newsweek* often come up with the same cover story, partly because they are aiming at the same general audience and partly because it is often easy to arrive at a consensus on the number-one national story of the week. Such consensus is much rarer from one metropolitan newspaper to the next, and even from one TV newscast to the next.

A study of the front pages of the *New York Times*, *Los Angeles Times*, and *Washington Post* reveals great differences in judgment, interest, style, scope, and tone among the papers. Only 28 times over a 155-day period did the newspapers agree on the most important story of the day. On 56 days (one-third of the time), each paper had a different lead story. On 33 days (one-fifth of the time), there was not a story that appeared on the front pages of all three papers. Only on 32 days did the three front pages have more than two stories in common.

Another study of newspapers in more than a dozen cities on 50 selected days showed an even greater diversity in front-page selection. Local stories generally dominated the front pages, leaving room for only one or two, if any, national or foreign stories.

Newspapers that develop different editions for distinct geographical or ethnic groups find themselves presenting one day's news in various lights. Note the difference in emphasis and tone between the English- and Spanish-language editions of the *Miami Herald* (Figure 9.11).

If each of us feels overwhelmed by the output that we are invited to take in, consider the plight of the gatekeepers, editors, and managers. In the last half century, they have seen wire-service reports increase from a few thousand words daily to the point where modern technology allows transmission of close to 10,000 words a *minute*. One can easily see why syndicates include among their offerings digests of current stories. The New York Times Company includes a syndication service that offers not only material from its own and other leading U.S. papers but approximately 150,000 words each week assembled from newspapers around the world. Thus the decisions about what to print may be facilitated by businesses that serve media businesses, but ultimately each newspaper and magazine (or broadcaster) has to make the calls for its audience.

INVESTIGATIVE NEWS REPORTING

One of the most important developments in news and information has been the increase in investigative reporting. Indeed, some investigative reporters have become the modern heroes of American journalism. Others, such as Don Bolles of the *Arizona Republic*, have been assassinated by the enemies they created in uncovering inside information. Investigative reporters make news by going beneath the surface situation to find the real cause or purpose of an event. In their book *All the President's Men*, Robert Woodward and Carl Bernstein, the *Washington Post* team that cracked the Watergate coverup by the Nixon administration, gave an unusual glimpse of the world of investigative reporting: wheedling secrets from confidential sources, talking their way into private homes and offices in the hope of getting new facts, meeting contacts in dark parking garages to glean morsels of information, and building a case, piece by piece, until a larger picture is formed.

To satisfy the journalistic need for speed and thoroughness, investigative reporting is often done best by teams of reporters. Jack Anderson, who bills himself as an investigative reporter in Washington, employs a small staff of aides who serve as researchers and investigators for his column.

Investigative journalists are also beginning to use computers with information data bases to analyze vast amounts of data quickly. Recently, newspapers have even hired reporters trained as social scientists to perform this kind of work. Stories that once would have been virtually impossible to research are being made available through the use of computers.

It is interesting to note that many of the 1990 Polk Journalism Awards were given for investigative reporting:

> CAREER AWARD: Mr. Hechinger for 45 years of reporting and commenting on education. He also won awards in 1949 and 1950.
>
> FOREIGN REPORTING: Mr. Kristof and Ms. WuDunn for coverage of the upheaval in China last year that ended in a violent crackdown against the democracy movement by the Government.
>
> INTERNATIONAL REPORTING: Mr. Engelberg and Mr. Gordon for disclosures of plans by European and American companies to increase the proliferation of chemical weapons-producing technology in the third world.
>
> NATIONAL REPORTING: Rick Atkinson of the *Washington Post* for a three-part series on the Stealth bomber.

Figure 16.5. Jack Newfield personifies the investigative reporter. His pieces in the *Village Voice* in New York had wide impact.

POLITICAL REPORTING: Andrew Melnykovych of the *Casper* (Wyo.) *Star-Tribune* for exposing collusion between the Federal Government and 12 major oil companies to cut back on royalty payments to Wyoming.

REGIONAL REPORTING: Miranda Ewell and David Schrieberg of the *San Jose* (Calif.) *Mercury News* for a three-part series about the inadequacies of court interpreters and the effect on the judicial system in California.

LOCAL REPORTING: The *Hartford* (Conn.) *Courant* for its articles on the recording of suspects' conversations with their lawyers by the police and the effect of that on civil rights in Connecticut.

MEDICAL REPORTING: John M. Crewdson of the *Chicago Tribune* for a 50,000-word exploration of the intensely competitive response of the scientific and political communities to the AIDS crisis.

NETWORK TELEVISION REPORTING: CBS News for its coverage of the upheaval in China.

LOCAL TELEVISION REPORTING: WCSC-TV in Charleston, S.C., for its coverage of Hurricane Hugo.

TELEVISION INVESTIGATIVE REPORTING: Jonathan Kwitny for "The Kwitny Report" on WNYC-TV, a series of analyses of international and domestic events.

RADIO REPORTING: Robert Knight, senior producer of "Undercurrents," a nationally syndicated investigative news program originating at WBAI-FM in New York, for its coverage of the United States invasion of Panama.

RADIO AND TELEVISION AS NEWS MEDIA ....

For almost forty years the country has had the benefit of network television news—not just its regularly scheduled news broadcasts, but its special coverage of elections, conventions, summit meetings, and those grim and terrible times when one of our leaders has been the victim of an assassin's bullet. The benefits which have come from an open reliable flow of information during a time of crisis are almost incalculable. For a large and diverse nation based on a concept of consensus, it's been a remarkable service, all the more remarkable when you realize that this service has had to coexist on that small plate of glass in your home with car chases and sitcoms, with football games and soap operas. It moves from remarkable to amazing when you realize that the ultimate responsibility for the network news divisions has rested in the hands of the same businessmen who have shaped the rest of American television as it exists today.[6]

These words, from former head of CBS News Ed Joyce, only remind us what we as media consumers know: The majority of people in the United States depend on broadcast news. In many parts of the world, electronic journalism is *the* source of information for populations with low literacy rates; in other places, government control of the press has led to "underground" communication via videotaped news and information programs from the free world. Some political analysts attribute much of the rapid spread of Eastern Europe's pro-democracy movement to circulation of such tapes.

The major broadcast networks and cable news services have large operations to gather and edit news and information, including correspondents around the world. ABC, for example, maintains 12 bureaus in the United States and 17 abroad. The clear leader in comprehensive news coverage is cable. CNN provides round-the-clock news to 55 million households here, more than five million in Europe, and more than two million households elsewhere in the world. It delivers programming to 500,000 hotel rooms around the world.

Local television stations continue to increase their news coverage, especially in the mornings and early evenings. Local radio news has also increased, mostly on AM, as the number of stations has increased. In recent years, however, radio stations forced to cut costs have cut back on their news operations: 15-minute newscasts used to be the rule; now radio usually provides news in short 5-minute bursts every hour. Several 24-hour, all-news formats have been successfully aired on AM radio in recent years. Most of those that survive tend to be all-sports or all-business formats; an all-weather format had to be abandoned in Minneapolis. A stronger trend is all-talk radio, such as WCBS in New York City, with frequent news updates; length of coverage (also by the station's correspondents) is determined by the event. Radio is a dominant news medium in the morning and in the middle of the day, and the growing popularity of these programs indicates the revival of radio as an expanding medium for news and interpretation.

One radio network in the mid-1980s that was doing extensive news on radio, with in-depth reports using correspondents stationed around the world for documentaries and news-magazine features, was National Public Radio (NPR), a service of the Corporation for Public Broadcasting. It produces more radio programming than does any other network, and its listenership is growing rapidly. NPR produces "Morning Edition," which provides its network stations with 3 hours of news each morning; "All Things Considered," a 90-minute news mag-

Figure 16.6. NBC's Chet Huntley and David Brinkley first became nationally important communicators through their comprehensive election coverage. Incoming data and correspondents' reports have become steadily more sophisticated, and today CNN is a leader in thorough, continuous team coverage as well as direct transmission of news around the globe.

azine that is broadcast in the evening and is probably the most influential news program on radio; and "Weekend Edition," a Saturday and Sunday news magazine. Recently introduced is NPR's "Latin File," a 14-minute daily news service to Hispanics.

Broadcast television news has generally settled into a format of network news in the morning, some local news at noon, local and network news in the evening, and local news in the late evening. Audience needs (personal schedules) dictate the varying composition of news programs throughout the day—quick takes in a hurried morning, more profiles and human-interest pieces when we can put our feet up at day's end. The trend toward late-night in-depth analysis is symbolized by ABC's "Nightline," begun in 1980 (modes of analysis and commentary are studied in the next chapter). Networks have wanted to get into hour-long early-evening news programs, but affiliate opposition (and turning to cable suppliers for alternative programming that would better suit local needs) has made this impractical.

ELECTRONIC NEWSGATHERING

One of the most important developments in broadcast news has been the introduction of electronic news gathering—or ENG, as it is called in the trade. ENG is possible because of the perfection of minicams—miniature hand-held television cameras. Minicams can be used either for videotape or for live transmission, doing away with the time-consuming jobs of developing and editing movie film. A crew travels *to* an event in a van that has a microwave relay dish on top of it to send the signal directly to the TV station, which puts the live picture on the air. The television viewer can witness a fire, for example, while it is happening and listen to the reactions of persons on the scene.

For the communicator, ENG presents not only opportunities but challenges:

> When network television covers a major news event the challenges are unique to electronic journalism. The process is an odd mixture of journalism and something which is best analogized in military terms, "the movement of men and matériel." For every correspondent the public sees, there are numerous camera crews, producers, and technicians who are essential for converting an unfolding news event into understandable, accurate news reports.[7]

In the 1950s, the use of film and the lack of satellite transmissions and jets could mean there was as much as a day between shooting and broadcasting, a time lag unheard of today. Because ENG involves a minimum of setup time and no film-development time, the newsday can run from early morning to late at night. The 1989 San Francisco earthquake gave proof of how we have come to take for granted smooth transmission of superbly edited news spots and features. ABC's Ted Koppel voiced the frustration clearly shared by colleagues as he viewed for hours pictures without sound (and vice versa) and poor-quality broadcasts that were themselves upsetting; things must be bad if network TV news is out of control. However, it was one of CNN's finest hours, which gave it the largest audience in history. According to Nielsen, the coverage gained its highest average 24-hour audience (1,273,000) and highest quarter-hour audience (3,622,000) ever.

Among problems ENG poses for broadcast journalism are the ethical questions of live coverage. ENG reporters often have no editors judging the news for the viewers before it is transmitted. Whatever happens live happens on the screen as well. Do cameras in courtrooms and government chambers interfere with the business at hand, turning justice and legislation into a show? Is it valid news or merely sensationalism to bring pictures of war and intense human suffering into the living room? Each new technology brings with it exciting possibilities as well as new dangers for abuse or misuse.

THE BROADCAST COMMUNICATORS

In previous chapters we considered the influence and possible interference of the conveyor of the message. We saw that the visible communicator, the person who looks into our homes via the television camera, is increasingly groomed as a performer. One scene in the film *Broadcast News* embodies this fact. Suave anchor-on-the-rise Tom is rehearsing the solid reporter Aaron, who aspires to visibility, for a chance to do the weekend news. Tom counsels: "When you feel yourself reading, *stop*—sell yourself a little more."

The audience and the medium bear equal responsibility for magnifying the role of the anchor. Tom Brokaw, Peter Jennings, and Dan Rather ("I was trained to ask questions") like getting into the field. We want to depend on what they say they find there; Walter Cronkite became for a generation "the most trusted man in America" (therefore, when we saw his reports that the Vietnam War was a disaster, it mattered). Maybe we expect too much of those who climb the trees; they are to be reliable reporters and all-knowing evaluators, as well as personable. Figure 16.8 illustrates the comparatively high level of trust we place in televised news.

Again, the requirements of the medium directly affect the effectiveness of the

Figure 16.7. The film *Broadcast News* gave viewers an inside look at the operations and politics of network journalism. The producer (played by Holly Hunter) excels at pulling together the pieces at a frenetic pace, often on-air, while new anchor (William Hurt) is groomed and coached by the less flashy Aaron (Albert Brooks).

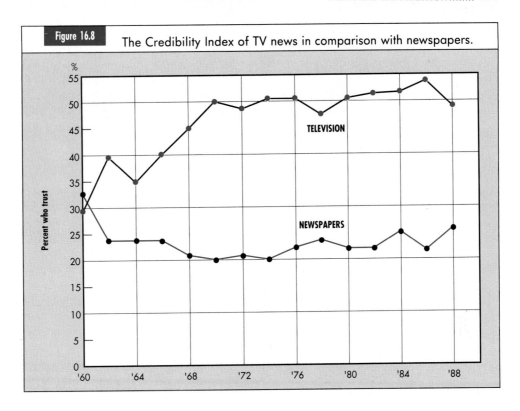

Figure 16.8 The Credibility Index of TV news in comparison with newspapers.

communication. Dan Rather, who has frequently said he's a natural reporter not a natural anchor, comes across differently on his radio spots of news and commentary and his nightly news show, sitting behind a desk reading copy. Ed Joyce points out that few realize the combination of skills needed to be a broadcast communicator—ability to communicate meaning from a rolling sheet of paper with conviction, clarity, and personality, coupled with "the training and instincts of the journalist . . . interviewing, interaction with reporters, the ability to receive new information through an earpiece and translate it for viewers in some coherent fashion."[8]

MEDIA DIFFERENCES IN THE PRESENTATION OF NEWS ....

Because of coding, format, and audience response factors, communication of news that is designed to be viewed must be structured in quite a different way from that designed to be heard or read.

In writing for the print media, an important principle is that the eye is likely to be attracted to the first part of the page or the story or the paragraph or the sentence; the eye then is attracted elsewhere. Since the purpose of news is to transmit information as efficiently as possible, it must have a style and structure that permit quick and effective communication. Language must be clear, simple, and to the point. Syntax must be direct and concise. Organization must be logical. The writing must have clarity and brevity.

The news story must be organized and written in such a way that others can work on it easily; it might be compared to a racing car with easily accessible parts that allow for rapid repair by all mechanics at the pit stop. Copyreaders, announcers, editors, directors—all must be able to work with the news copy quickly and cooperatively.

In newspaper news, the "inverted-pyramid" structure is usually used to organize the story. As we saw in Chapter 4, on Coding, this method of reporting serves two important functions. First, it gives the hurried newspaper reader the most important information immediately. Second, it allows the editors to cut a story at the end, if there is competition for time or space (as there usually is), without losing the essential facts of the story.

Unlike the eye, which focuses immediately, the ear needs time to become accustomed to sound. So news copy for radio and television generally backs into a story, giving the ear time to listen for the important element of the sentence. A radio or television news story needs a phrase or something to prepare the audience. A lead-in might begin, "According to the latest figures, George Bush has won the election."

The broadcast media usually have time only to skim the surface of the news. A 15-minute newscast contains only about 1,800 words and about 25 stories. An average daily newspaper has more than 100,000 words and a compendium of different news items. Radio must tell the news in terms of effective sound. Television must tell the news in terms of vivid visual images. During the week in October 1989 when the media heavily covered the San Francisco earthquake, a geologist who had been asked to contribute briefly to several TV shows' background reports admitted relief at being invited to go on a radio talk show: The format allowed him to go into greater detail, whereas television limits the use of static "talking heads."

While a story about a hurricane lends itself to video pictures of the destruction, a complex story of industrial tax fraud does not; in this case, television may lead with the exciting visual story, while a newspaper might headline the tax story, complete with an economic analysis.

Television's need to sum up a story quickly has led to what is known as the *sound bite*, a phrase or two that encapsulates an event or viewpoint. An analysis of 280 weekday network newscasts from Labor Day to Election Day in 1968 and 1988 revealed the reduction of the average length of a sound bite from 42.3 to 9.8 seconds; in 1968, political candidates spoke for a minute without interruption in 21 percent of all newscasts whereas this was *never* the case 20 years later. In recent elections, savvy politicians have manipulated the sound bite and the vivid visual image, and turned legitimate coverage into virtual commercials shedding more heat than light. Print news is less susceptible though not immune to this kind of abuse, simply by virtue of its style of presentation.

Entertainment does play a part in the presentation of news especially but not exclusively on television; we've noted an increase in "infotainment"—happy talk, newscast cosmetics, faster pace, eyecatching graphics, and adaptations of tabloid journalism for television, with reporters "using little more than inflammatory narration."[9]

Figure 16.9. KTLA Los Angeles made history on April 22, 1952, when it did a remote live broadcast of an atomic bomb test.

While there is some blurring of formats from one media to another, there are media differences. In the future, media news coverage may become even further differentiated. The print media will no doubt continue to stress in-depth coverage, interpretation, explanation, and analysis, while the broadcast media will specialize in headline and spot-news responsibilities, the "extra editions," and perhaps more of the light, dramatic, and human-interest elements of the news. While there are those who abuse freedom of the press, most reporters are acutely aware of what society expects and what it truly needs. The basic role of analysis, opinion, interpretation, and commentary in print and electronic media is the focus of the next chapter.

SUMMARY

News is one of the most important functions of the mass media. As our world grows more complex, we depend more and more on information about what is happening around us in order to function in society. The news media have the ability to get quicker and more complete and accurate news than can the ordinary citizen.

News, however, is relative to the interests of the audience. What is news for one person may not be news for the next. We do expect certain qualities in all news, including objectivity, accuracy, balance, and fairness. Journalists use certain criteria—including timeliness, proximity, prominence, consequences, and human interest—to select news that they believe to be of interest to their audiences.

News interests vary with age and socioeconomic status. However, most people are usually more interested in information that gives them some immediate satisfaction than news whose consequences are less obvious. Since sensational news is usually of more interest than nonsensational news, news can actually distort reality by overemphasizing the weird and evil in society. Even objective and balanced reporting can be distorted by those who wish to manipulate the news, and it is important to be aware of what does *not* appear in the news. Both news reporters and news audiences must be constantly aware of how news selection affects coverage.

The style and structure of news varies from medium to medium. Investigative reporting has become important to print media, while electronic newsgathering (ENG) is an essential element of television news. The differences in the style and structure of news provided by the various media may increase in the future as each medium develops its own way of presenting news and information.

REFERENCES

1. Quoted by Michael Fancher in "The Metamorphosis of the Newspaper Editor," *The Gannett Journal*, Spring 1987, 75.
2. Shanto Iyengar and Donald R. Kinder, *News That Matters: Television and American Opinion* (Chicago: University of Chicago Press, 1987), 60.
3. Mike Hoover, "CBS Film Flap: No Stringers, No News," *The New York Times*, October 16, 1989, A21.
4. Michael J. Kirkhorn, "The Virtuous Journalist," *The Quill*, February 1982, 9.
5. A. Kent MacDougall, "Boring from Within the Bourgeois Press: Part Two," *Monthly Review*, December 1988, 13.
6. Ed Joyce, *Prime Times, Bad Times* (New York: Doubleday, 1988), xi.
7. Ibid., 123.
8. Ibid., 142.
9. *Broadcasting*, November 6, 1989, 63.

CHAPTER
17

Analysis and Commentary

It is essential to have facts, but facts often have to be interpreted. The reporter who climbs the highest tree and looks out over the horizon may send back an accurate and objective report, but may not be communicating all the information necessary to make the right decision. A black cloud may turn out to contain locusts, not rain. Friendly-looking visitors may prove to be hostile. Even the fair and objective account of an occurrence may be misleading. At no time in American history was the insufficiency of straight reporting better illustrated than during the years of student unrest and political protest over the Vietnam War. The American government often gave a daily "body count" of the North Vietnamese soldiers killed in action. The next day, the news media duly reported the government's "body count" as an objective fact. The impression left with the American people was that we were killing more of their men than they were of ours, so we must be winning the war. It took some time for Americans to realize that we were not winning the war.

Hedley Donovan, a *Washington Post* reporter and *Fortune* writer, became Henry Luce's successor as editor-in-chief of *Time* and has recounted his 40 years in journalism in *Right Place, Right Times*. He tells of what happened to him and others visiting Vietnam to see for themselves: Unable to continue endorsing the domino theory that if Vietnam fell, so would Southeast Asia, or to accept the real casualty toll, he wrote an opinion essay in *Time*, which included: "We must all begin by recapturing some sense of astonishment that the U.S. is still engaged in this war." Something similar happened to broadcast journalist Walter Cronkite, who is regarded as fostering the first real movement in government circles as well as in public opinion toward seeing that the war made no sense.

During this wrenching time, groups practiced manipulation of the news media to serve their own political purposes. The era is symbolized by student protests. The term *media event* was coined to describe a "happening" staged to attract maximum media coverage. As dissenters became increasingly street smart in dealing with people and savvy about what reporters and broadcasting crews looked for in a news story, they orchestrated confrontational events strong in visual "copy." Today, such techniques are used by those who demonstrate against capital punishment, nuclear weapons, abortion, pollution, toxic-waste dumps, fur coats, and much more. Globally this practice has variations but many similarities. Activists provide photo opportunities and spokespersons and force the media to discuss feelings as well as facts in a story.

Those who wish to express a particular point of view—whether establishment

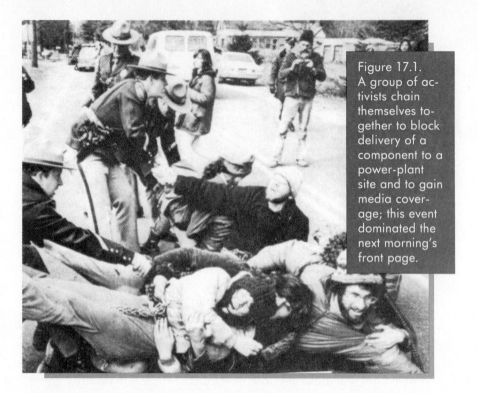

Figure 17.1. A group of activists chain themselves together to block delivery of a component to a power-plant site and to gain media coverage; this event dominated the next morning's front page.

or radical—can use the *news* function of the media to communicate their ideas. To balance the use and abuse of news, the media must also be used to fulfill the need for *analysis and interpretation*—to put facts into perspective, to tell what an event means, to explain, to argue, to persuade, to express expert opinion about what happened, and to provide a forum for the expression of conflicting opinions.

Commentators have ranged from the profoundly influential, like the legendary Walter Lippmann, to arbiters of fashion and taste. Although it is often difficult to draw a distinction between news and commentary, there are a number of genres special to the area of analysis and interpretation, forms of communication that allow a mirror to be held up to society in a way different from reporting. This chapter looks at the history and the present influence of some of those forms.

THE SEPARATION OF FACT AND OPINION

Actually, the role of persuader, the act of molding opinion, came earlier in the historical development of media than did the role of informer. Early newspapers and magazines were often more a collection of editorials and advertisements than of news stories. It was not until the mid-nineteenth century that news assumed great importance in mass communication. Then the tradition grew that news and opinion should be communicated separately. The reporter has been taught not to editorialize, not to express ideas and opinions and feelings about what happened, but to tell simply what happened. This practice is not followed by journalists in all countries; in many European countries, journalists are expected to bring their interpretation to the news they report.

The usual practice among American newspapers is to place editorial comment and opinion on a separate editorial page, often printed toward the end of the first section of the paper, and to leave the front page and first inside pages for the publication of "straight" news. Another practice is to label clearly intepretative analysis or comment. Sometimes the line between the two areas is a very fine one. In a 1989 survey by the professional standards committee of a national editorial writers association, 45 percent of the editorial-page editors at the 82 largest daily papers in the United States confirmed the need to maintain a wall of separation between news and editorial departments (39 percent said some communication should be included and the rest said no wall should exist). Editorial editors reporting to a news editor are twice as likely to deny the need for rigid separation as are those reporting to a publisher. As chains buy up newspapers, the philosophy toward editorial/news separations can cause problems, but local autonomy and freedom of editorial writers from business or publisher interests have been priorities with at least two of the largest chains, Gannett and Knight-Ridder.

The political affiliation of a newspaper or the bias of its staff may sometimes seem to affect its "objective" political news coverage. News magazines have a particular problem because although they conceive of their mission as a weekly "interpretation" of the news, their stories are not individually labeled as interpretation, and many readers accept these stories as unbiased news accounts. The blurring of fact and opinion in the news media has become an increasing problem, requiring more critical attention on the part of the consumer.

Radio and television also have a special problem in interpretation and analysis. For many years, the Federal Communications Commission prohibited editorializing on the somewhat nebulous ground that broadcasting is such a powerful medium that it should not be allowed to influence opinion; it should only report facts. The FCC later tried to regulate the editorial function of broadcasting through the so-called Fairness Doctrine, no longer in operation, to assure the presentation of contrasting views. Currently much of the balance found in print and electronic journalism must come from the standards and ethics of a media organization or individual practitioner.

April 20, 1952, was a milestone in twentieth-century news programming. The first prime-time broadcast of Edward R. Murrow's series "See It Now" featured simultaneous images of contrasting viewpoints and live interviews, and served for many years as the prototype of quality network-news documentaries. It is remembered for pioneering in giving the American public its first simultaneous live glimpse of the Atlantic and Pacific oceans, but more significantly it gave reporters an "entirely new weapon in journalism," in the words of CBS's Fred Friendly. Each program focused on one or two stories in search of explanation and gave meaning to important issues of the day.

Ted Koppel, whose "Nightline" is watched by 5 million to 7 million American households each weeknight, is a newsman by his own definition and background and likes to take on a neutral or an Everyman demeanor that makes him "the beneficiary of a certain public acceptance that I would not have if I were, let's say, a commentator who expressed his own views on subjects, or a politician."[1] He nevertheless is highly adept at choosing subjects and approaches that will do what editorializers aim for: the "day's last decoder" (in the words of communications

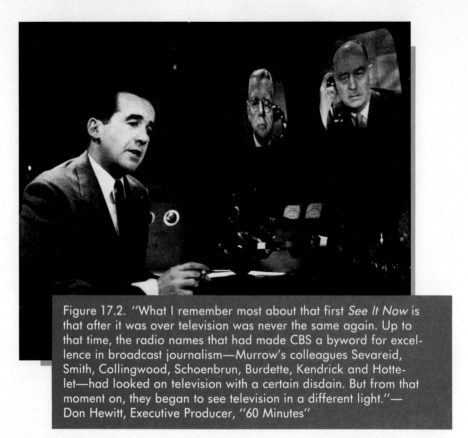

Figure 17.2. "What I remember most about that first *See It Now* is that after it was over television was never the same again. Up to that time, the radio names that had made CBS a byword for excellence in broadcast journalism—Murrow's colleagues Sevareid, Smith, Collingwood, Schoenbrun, Burdette, Kendrick and Hottelet—had looked on television with a certain disdain. But from that moment on, they began to see television in a different light."—Don Hewitt, Executive Producer, "60 Minutes"

expert Marshall Blonsky). He has us examining our consciences and those of our leaders as we consider what is happening in the world. There are, in other words, many ways for communicators to make comments; here we look at means that are clearly labeled as opinion and analysis.

MEDIA INSTITUTIONS THAT INTERPRET AND ANALYZE

Many forms of commentary, such as cartoons, column-essays, and crusading editorials, have been with the American media from their earliest days. As a matter of fact, we wouldn't have to search much further than Benjamin Franklin to find political cartoonist, social reformist, editorial writer, and influential publisher all in one. One of his earliest pieces was the anonymous satirical "Dogood Papers" that appeared in the *New-England Courant*; his first book was *A Modest Inquiry Into the Nature and Necessity of a Paper Currency*.

EDITORIALS

Print. Editorials have become a standard feature in American newspapers and in some magazines and on television programs as well. Generally, editorials do not have bylines. They are written by writers who represent the medium's management. The editorial-page staff begins each day by deciding which issues require editorial statements. Members of the editorial staff discuss the general treatment of these issues and, with guidance from management on crucial issues, determine the stand that the newspaper will take. The editors, the publisher, and the reporters who may have strong opinions about the news they are covering may contribute a relevant editorial judgment.

Furthering the tradition set by seventeenth-century English essayists, the writers and printers of the American colonies used the editorial form to further political causes. The first, though short-lived, magazine here was *The American*, which was subtitled "A Monthly Review of the Political State of the British Colonies." Later publications, Noah Webster's *The American Magazine* and *The American Museum*, published, respectively, the *Federalist Papers* and Thomas Paine's *Common Sense*. David Shaw has chronicled the life of the editorial in "The Death of Punditry," a paper prepared for the Gannett Research Center. Historian Allen Nevins in *American Press Opinion, 1785–1927* points out that an 1884 editorial by William Cullen Bryant, published in the *New York Evening Post*, led to the creation of Central Park. The power of the American press in the late nineteenth century did effect social benefits as well. James Russell Lowell observed that newspapers had largely "supplanted the pulpit, . . . even the deliberative assembly and had come to wield an influence without precedent hitherto in American history."

The forceful editorial voice in our times lacks the dominant role it played in the nineteenth century. Reese Cleghorn, president of the *Washington Journalism Review*, commented that

> *dramatic displays of conviction have gone the way of the Linotype. The final touch to a wimpy performance by the press in the 1988 presidential race was the abstention by about half of the country's daily newspapers from endorsing any candidate.* Editor & Publisher *informs us that the number of newspapers that were undecided or that have a no-endorsement policy in presidential races has risen steadily since 1932, when 7.45 percent of the dailies adopted this posture. . . .*
>
> *I attribute this year's editorial wimpiness to the increased corporation of newspapers and their loss of the personal imprimatur of editors whose strong views were well known. Many editors hang back now because of a fear that readers will think they are being dictatorial, as well as concern that an editorial endorsement will suggest they are biased in their news coverage.*
>
> *The growth of group ownership also may be a factor. Few groups today send out the message at election time to endorse Candidate A, and that is to the good; but too many manager-editors down below lack strong views on what is happening to the country and what should be done about it.*[2]

Addressing a convention of editorial writers in 1988, the *Fort Worth Star-Telegram*'s publisher Richard Connor expressed similar concern:

> *Our editorial pages today have become pages of consensus. More often than not, we simply outline problems, examine issues and ponder topics—but we really don't tell anybody what we think about those problems and topics. We don't take a firm, unequivocal stand on issues of vital importance.*
>
> *I'd like to see a return to editorial pages that inspire, provoke, anger, make people happy, make people laugh, make people cry—editorial pages that make people react.*[3]

Figure 17.3. The *Miami Herald*'s special section of opinion typifies the modern editorial page.

Broadcast. The broadcast media have not yet unanimously embraced their right to air their opinions. A survey by the National Association of Broadcasters (NAB) indicated that only slightly more than one-half of the stations in the country (57 percent of radio and 56 percent of television) regularly broadcast editorials (following the NAB's definition of an editorial as an on-the-air expression of the opinion of the station licensee, clearly identified as such, on a subject of public interest).

But the editorial function is growing in broadcasting. The larger stations are more apt to editorialize, which bears out the journalistic theory that the stronger the medium, the more courageously it accepts its responsibilities. Four out of 10 television stations now put editorials on the air every day; 2.5 out of 10 radio stations do the same. Listeners or viewers are typically invited to express their responses to the views expressed by the local station or some named individual.

Public Access

Media scholar J. Herbert Altschull points out that the publications of Benjamin Franklin's time were actually conceived of as communicators of opinion; in 1730 it was too early to think of newspapers (indeed, the term used then was *paper*) as sources of general news.[4] Franklin, a businessman as well as writer, felt that printers like himself should "chearfully serve all contending Writers that pay them well, without regarding on which side they are of the Question in Dispute" (column space was for sale).[5]

Public access to mass media has since become a critical issue. Some forceful pressure groups advocate open access to the media. In his book *Freedom of the Press vs. Public Access*, Benno C. Schmidt, Jr., describes some of the rights claimed by those who advocate access: the right of political candidates to advertise or appear in the media in which their opponents appear; the right of a person to respond to an attack or criticism; the right to advertise competing goods, services, or ideas in a medium that accepts advertising; or the right of anyone to have his or her views published or news covered on subjects about which the medium has carried its views or news. Recently there has been some renewed interest in reestablishing equality of access that was known as the Fairness Doctrine.

The FCC regulations on cable television, adopted in 1972, required each new cable system in the top 100 markets to keep available an access channel for use by the general public, educational institutions, and local government. This channel was to be available without charge at all times on a first-come, first-served non-discriminatory basis. Live studio presentations of less than 5 minutes were to be subsidized by the cable system, but other production costs were to be paid by the user. The public-access channel caused some problems in cities where it was in use, such as New York, where the programs tended to appeal to narrow and special-interest groups, such as homosexuals or transcendentalists, and the channel had trouble attracting audiences and financing.

In the late 1970s, in an effort to reduce restrictions on the growth of cable television, the FCC removed the open-access-channel regulation for cable-television systems. Now, no mass medium must provide access to outsiders to its properties. No one can walk into a radio or TV station and demand to go on the air with his or her version of the news or opinions. And no one can demand that any newspaper, magazine, or book publisher accept his or her ideas and put them into print.

Figure 17.4. The press had been barred from covering the invasion of Grenada during the Reagan administration, but these easily photographed and televised placards conveyed Florida students' opposition to the military action.

Further definitions of access rights came about as a result of the most celebrated access case of the 1970s, *Miami Herald Publishing Co. v. Tornillo.* In 1972, the *Miami Herald* ran an editorial that opposed the candidacy of a Florida union leader who was running for the state house of representatives. The candidate, Pat L. Tornillo, Jr., wrote a reply, which the *Herald* refused to publish. The case ultimately reached the Supreme Court, which ruled that the newspaper did not have to publish the reply. The Court's decision in the *Miami Herald* case was a firm rejection of the idea that anyone has a constitutional right to force a publisher to print something against the publisher's will. The Court held that such a ruling would do greater damage to freedom of the press than access would help freedom of expression.

Nevertheless, the mass media have an obligation to encourage uninhibited public dialogue and freedom of expression for everyone. And today, the mass media voluntarily accept this responsibility in larger measure than ever before. For example, newspapers are providing more space for letters to the editor. The editorial-and-opinion ("op-ed") page of a newspaper or magazine or special sections of other publications provides a forum for input, feedback, and frequently a dialogue between distant members of the audience. The social upheavals of the 1960s forced newspapers to open their pages to new, "outsider" voices. The new format of The *New York Times* op-ed page, which debuted on September 21, 1970, announced an era in which readers could voice themselves extensively.

Since the people who write letters to the editor do not represent a true cross section of the public, the media cannot publish or broadcast all the letters that come into their offices, and selection and judgment—gatekeeping and agenda setting—are key elements in communicating the public's opinions. Some newspapers, such as the *Salt Lake City Tribune*, have a "common carrier" column for outsiders and pay a community panel to screen the contributions. The reporters on "60 Minutes," the popular CBS investigative news program, conclude the show each week by reading letters of reaction to earlier shows. Other media have appointed ombudsmen to deal with readers' and listeners' complaints. These are all signs that mass-media leaders are concerned about public access at the same time that they enjoy their essential rights to use their own franchise freely.

Figure 17.5. Network news commentators have long been looked to for background reporting. Walter Cronkite, who told America "the way it is," is shown on an early broadcast of "Meet the Press."

During World War II, it became apparent that objective news reports about the war were often influenced by Allied and Axis propaganda activities. American concern about the effects of international propaganda prompted the establishment of a high-level group to study the problems of free communication in modern society. The Commission on Freedom of the Press carefully investigated and analyzed the passive objectivity of news reporters and concluded, among other things, that "it is no longer enough to report *the fact* truthfully. It is now necessary to report *the truth about the fact.*"[6]

The news media are increasingly developing specialists who know as much about their subjects as the experts and can add their own expert opinions to give their audiences a fuller understanding of the situation. Even the wire services, long the staunchest defenders of straight, objective news reporting, are making more use of background and interpretative reports.

SUMMARIES AND INTERPRETATIONS

Weekly newsmagazines, Sunday-newspaper supplements, and some weekly newspapers also fulfill the need for interpretation and analysis. They regard their role as summarizers and explainers, putting the news into historical, political, or scientific perspective. *Time*, especially, has perfected the technique of "group journalism," in which facts are sent to New York headquarters by many reporters who cover different angles on a given story. These facts are scrutinized by editors and specialists, who then put together a final summary that synthesizes, interprets, and analyzes the facts from a broad perspective. A few publications, printed in weekly-newspaper format, have been started for this purpose alone. One is *Barron's*, a national weekly financial review published by Dow Jones & Company.

DOCUMENTARIES AND CRUSADES

The documentary has often been a powerful force for the interpretation and analysis of events that often cannot be better communicated in any other way. Using historic film footage and current interviews, it can provide a vehicle to review recent history and put confusing events into clearer perspective.

Some intepretative programs and documentaries, done primarily as public-service efforts, have been "tucked away at unwanted hours" of Sunday mornings or afternoons, the so-called Sunday ghetto of broadcasting. The networks use special documentaries that preempt regularly scheduled shows whenever an event of major consequence occurs—an earthquake, a space launch, a riot, or the death and funeral of a great person. When the space shuttle *Challenger* exploded shortly after lift-off in January 1986, the networks devoted many hours to specials and documentaries and panel discussions, replaying the scene in slow motion, investigating the probable causes, and examining the event from every angle.

The same techniques have been used to probe, analyze, and interpret great issues—race relations, drug addiction, court procedures, political campaigns and elections, espionage, island invasions, and war. Local news staffs of both radio and television stations have used the documentary to expose local police corruption, poverty, hunger, housing, shortages, and education problems.

The documentary can have a powerful effect because it can use sounds and pictures together to move people. William S. Small, former network news executive, describes one of the most impressive CBS News efforts, the 1968 documentary "Hunger in America," an hour of emotional broadcasting that opened with film of a baby actually dying of starvation in front of the camera. "The broadcast had tremendous impact," says Small,

> *particularly on the then Secretary of Agriculture, Orville Freeman, who bitterly attacked it and demanded equal time. He called it "shoddy journalism" that blackened the name of the Agriculture Department. Even as Freeman attacked, he was taking official steps that CBS interpreted as conceding the broadcast's main points: The Department abandoned its ceiling on food stamp programs, sharply expanded the number of counties with such programs, enlarged the quantity and variety of surplus food and sought (and won) Senate approval for an additional $200 to $300 million for food programs.[7]*

In 1989, WGBH (Boston) and Central Independent Television in England presented through PBS a 13-part series "War and Peace in the Nuclear Age," 5 years in the making and complemented by a book by John Newhouse, published by the trade-book publisher Alfred A. Knopf. It was a television history of the people, events, issues, and decisions that brought us from Roosevelt and Stalin to Reagan and Star Wars. Thus it set out both to chronicle *and* interpret the effects of nuclear weaponry on foreign relations and on contemporary thinking. Its producers did not want to present any single point of view. Its goal was "to displace the feeling that the management of nuclear affairs is beyond public influence or understanding."

In 1971, CBS's "The Selling of the Pentagon," a documentary on the public-relations efforts of the military, became an editorial issue in its own right. Supporters and detractors used the media to praise or attack the production. The program's format eventually caused an attempt by the House Commerce Committee, chaired by Harley O. Staggers, to issue a contempt citation against CBS president Frank Stanton. Stanton refused to submit "outtakes" (film not actually used in the program) for committee analysis. The committee was concerned that two personal interviews shown in "The Selling of the Pentagon" may have been used out of context. Eventually, the issue about whether Congress should become the arbiter of what is *truth* in programming was settled. The FCC ruled that the program had met all the criteria under the Fairness Doctrine then in effect. Some cynics regarded the criticism of the documentary as an attempt by Pentagon supporters to cloud the issue or prevent future media disclosure of military-industrial activities for fear of reprisals.

Another documentary that got great media attention was the 1989 PBS look (a sympathetic one) at the Palestinian revolt against Israeli occupation of the West Bank. A New York City station scheduled to air it backed out, calling it "propaganda." Retitled from "Days of Rage" to "Intifada: The Palestinians and Israel," it was lengthened from 90 minutes to a new 2½-hour package that had an added framework of wider perspective. The wraparound material was designed, said PBS programmer Barry Chase, "to provide some clear indication that this is not your normal documentary, that it is more in the nature of an editorial or a commentary column."[8] PBS later aired a program giving the Israeli point of view, "A Search for Solid Ground: The Intifada Through Israeli Eyes."

Figure 17.6. A segment of the documentary series "War and Peace in the Nuclear Age" shows artist Barbara Donachy assembling her ceramic miniature of the U.S. nuclear arsenal—27,000 cones representing the number of U.S. nuclear warheads in 1986.

Documentaries sometimes include advocacy. *Crusades* always do. More common to print media, a crusade often starts with a news story that uncovers some problem in society. The newspaper editors and reporters seek more facts, they decide how they will treat the story, and may publish the material in a series of news stories or interpretative reports; sometimes they follow up with sidebars and features on various aspects of the problem, and conclude the crusade with an editorial or a series of editorials in which the newspaper presents its conclusions and recommendations. The *Washington Star*, for example, undertook a crusade against fraudulent used-car sales practices and forced the government to improve regulations. Crusades have been the hallmark of courageous journalism since the early days of the media.

THE INDIVIDUAL VISION AND THE SOLE VOICE

Individual vision, investigation, concern, and expression are behind all of the forms of analysis and interpretation we have just surveyed, where the media organization and the audience interact. Sometimes it is not the media organization or its institutionalized means of expressing opinion that we are most aware of but the personality of one writer, artist, or commentator.

COLUMNISTS AND COMMENTATORS

The media provide an opportunity for experts and specialists to analyze and interpret public problems in their fields on a regular basis through the column, a byline feature. Many newspapers and magazines have staff columnists who write on local or special interests. But most columnists are handled by national syndicates, to which the publications subscribe (see Chapter 2). On one Friday, the *Philadelphia Inquirer*, apart from its "Weekend" supplement of human-interest and entertainment features, included the following items by nonstaffers as analysis, commentary, and background: a piece labeled "Analysis" from the *Boston Globe*, an in-depth piece on Nicaragua from AP and Reuters, several human-issues articles that were "specials" to the paper, a syndicated column by Ann Landers, business advice and commentary from AP and Knight-Ridder, an automotive piece from AP, nine letters to the editor, two op-ed commentaries, book reviews picked up from other papers, and more.

Columnists typically have great latitude to handle material in their own way, with a light or heavy touch, with sarcasm, satire, or humor. Individuals with certain political or attitudinal bents and the owners-managers of publications find each other so that the individual contributor's stance generally fits into the paper's or broadcaster's framework. Occasionally individuals are reined in by management's gatekeepers. A celebrated example occurred in 1990 when the syndicated columnist and "60 Minutes" commentator Andy Rooney had remarks that offended blacks and homosexuals attributed to him by a newspaper reporter. CBS News quickly suspended Rooney from the program, and for the first time in 12 years, "60 Minutes" lost its number-one place in the ratings. His reinstatement, complicated by the fact that the remarks could not be definitely attributed, was accompanied by the commentator's statement, "Do I have any opinions that might irritate some people? You're damn right I do. That's what I'm here for."

The format of 15-minute radio commentaries by strong personalities has vanished: Individuals with strong political commitments, such as Gabriel Heatter, Raymond Gram Swing, and Fulton Lewis, Jr., or persons with strong interpretative-reporting talents, such as Elmer Davis, H. V. Kaltenborn, and Edward R. Murrow, are gone and have not been replaced.

Most stations now use a variety of reporters and correspondents, some of whom might comment on and analyze local news, but often not as personalities. The networks have commentators, but they, too, are more likely to be reporters than persuaders—anchors such as CBS's Dan Rather, NBC's Tom Brokaw, and ABC's Peter Jennings. Paul Harvey, on radio, still falls into the category of the strong personality with definite political commitments.

The mass media also assume a responsibility to provide critical analysis of public performances, particularly in the popular arts. Books, movies, concerts, recordings, and dramas are public performances that need to be reviewed. Reviews help a potential audience find the right performance and the performer play to the right audience, aiding the artist in perfecting a craft and the public in making decisions. This form of commentary is explored in Chapter 19.

PHOTOJOURNALISTS

We must mention the men and women behind cameras as individual communicators who provide commentary on their times. Photographers like Henri Cartier-Bresson stand out as having (it seems) been present at every important event of the last 40 years, from Gandhi's assassination to the conflict in Northern Ireland. Dorothea Lange is among those who brought attention to human suffering in this country. Robert Capa, who was killed while at work, practiced advocacy journalism, conveying messages about ordinary people as well as significant events. *Life* brought us virtually everything suggested by its title, from movie stars to famine, from world war to invention. Each day, the wire services and leading newspapers bring us images, many of them with similar potential to move or provoke us.

EDITORIAL CARTOONS

The editorial cartoon has been a force on the American editorial page since 1754 when the first cartoon appeared in the *Pennsylvania Gazette*, accompanying an editorial written by Benjamin Franklin. It pictured a snake, cut into 13 pieces, representing the British colonies, and it was entitled "Join or Die."

Effective editorial cartoons use the art of caricature, employing a few swift lines to exaggerate a character, personality, or feature to make a point. A few strokes of the pen can communicate much meaning. Herblock's grim, five-o'clock-shadowed hydrogen bomb expressed widely shared opinions about banning nuclear weapons. The economies of time and space that are permitted by the editorial cartoon give it particular force for mass communication.

Thomas Nast's first drawings were published in Frank Leslie's *Illustrated Newspaper* when he was only 15. He won national attention during the Civil War, contributing to *Harper's Weekly*'s unionist stance. His legendary role is due, however, to his tireless assault on government corruption, especially personified by New York Democratic party boss Tweed and his creation of continuing symbols of political power, such as the Republican party's elephant, shown in Figure 17.7. Frederick Opper's publisher, William Randolph Hearst, was strongly opposed to President William McKinley and his influential manager Mark Hanna. Figure 17.8 is typical of a drawing done for clear understanding by the average newspaper reader. Theodore Roosevelt and William McKinley, identifiable in the caricatures, are right in the pockets of the powerful trusts that cared little for the common people in the audience for this cartoon.

In a profile of cartoonist Tom Toles, *Washington Journalism Review* editor Clint O'Connor wrote:

> *Despite the homogenized, chain-dominated newspaper world of the 1980s, the art form of editorial cartooning lives. At its best, one of those little three-by-four-inch boxes can say more than 100 Safires and Wills, and although the press has been heavily criticized for perhaps allowing President Teflon [Ronald Reagan] to dance merrily to his own tune these past eight years, that cannot be said of a handful of cartoonists who have actually been saying something amongst all that gray, opinion-page prattle.*[9]

Doonesbury creator Garry Trudeau reflected on the delicate position of the editorial cartoonists in remarks to the American Newspaper Publishers Association:

"ANOTHER SUCH VICTORY, AND I AM UNDONE."—Pyrrhus.

Figure 17.7.

"Now, Willie, you and Teddy can have a nice game of peek-a-boo. Papa likes to see little boys enjoy themselves.

Figure 17.8.

"Satire is *supposed* to be unbalanced. It's supposed to be unfair. Criticizing a political satirist for being unfair is like criticizing a 260-pound nose-guard for being physical. . . . All the tools of his trade—distortion, caricature and ridicule—mitigate against fairness and endearment."

THE IMPACT OF ANALYSIS AND INTERPRETATION

Finally, we must ask: How effective are the media in fulfilling a role as interpreters and analysts in our society? Most readership studies show that more people read comic strips than editorials.

In its study of the impact of broadcast editorials, the National Association of Broadcasters concluded that awareness of and actual exposure to editorials are more prevalent among men, young adults, and college-educated people. The NAB's survey showed that about 66 percent of the public felt that broadcasting stations should editorialize. A large majority of those who have seen or heard editorials (83 percent for television, 73 percent for radio) remembered instances in which an editorial made them think more about a particular issue. And about half (54 percent for television, 47 percent for radio) reported that these editorials helped them make up their minds about issues.

Do editorials change minds? Probably not as much as editorial writers would like. During political campaigns, editorial endorsement of political candidates does not seem to make a great impression on voters according to most studies. Frank Luther Mott's analysis of the power of the press in presidential elections showed that candidates who had been supported by newspapers were beaten more frequently than they triumphed. Doris Graber's studies of media and politics show how people process or screen out much of news and analysis.

Yet there is much tangible evidence of the immediate impact of the mass media's analysis and interpretation, from editorials, columns, commentaries, crusades, and documentaries, including legislation passed, injustices corrected, individuals aided, tasks completed, and political victories won.

Well-informed citizens, who alone can make democracy work, require news, information, analysis, and interpretation. They should get their facts, and the truth about the facts, from as wide a selection of media as possible. They should have access to as many different reporters and interpreters for any given event or issue as possible. Otherwise, they will be like the blind men who touched only one part of the elephant and falsely interpreted it as the whole.

SUMMARY

The analysis and interpretation functions of mass media, although not given as large a role as news and information or entertainment and advertising, are nevertheless important and may be becoming more so with the growing complexity of modern life. Many studies have shown that facts can be manipulated and news can be distorted. The media have an obligation to provide a fuller interpretation of the truth.

The American tradition has been to present fact and editorial opinion separately. Newspapers follow this format for the most part, but news magazines usually do not pretend to provide facts without their own interpretation and analysis. Radio and TV have not been as active in expressing editorial opinion, in part because the FCC formerly regulated against it.

Today, the media present analysis and interpretation in a variety of forms: interpretative and background reports, editorials, weekly summaries and interpretations, editorial cartoons, documentaries, crusades, columnists and commentators, criticism and reviews, and letters to the editor.

Increasingly, the public is concerned about its own ability to express a variety of opinions in the mass media. A growing number of mass communicators agree that an obligation to provide a forum exists for all mass media, and the responsibility is more ethical than legal at this time.

Syndicates are the chief means whereby newspapers and, to a lesser extent, broadcasting can provide interpretative and analytical material on a broad range of subjects. In the end, however, studies show that even though interpretation and analysis are vital to the public's complete understanding of events, people do not read editorials as much as they read news and entertainment, and the opinions expressed by the mass media have not been as persuasive as communicators might hope.

REFERENCES ....

1. Quoted in Marshall Blonsky, "Ted Koppel's Edge," *The New York Times Magazine*, August 14, 1988, 35.
2. Reese Cleghorn, "The Editorial Wimp-Out," *Washington Journalism Review*, December 1988, 5.
3. Richard L. Connor, "Let's Put Some Bite Back into Our Bark," *The Masthead*, Winter 1988, 18.
4. J. Herbert Altschull, *From Milton to McLuhan: The Ideas Behind American Journalism* (White Plains, N.Y.: Longman, 1990), 108.
5. Ibid., 107.
6. Zechariah Caffee, Jr., *Government and Mass Communication* (Chicago: University of Chicago Press, 1947), 50.
7. William S. Small, *To Kill a Messenger: Television News and the Real World* (New York: Hastings House, 1970), 39.
8. Richard Zoglin, "Ruckus Over *Days of Rage*," *Time*, September 4, 1989, 70.
9. Clint O'Connor, "Cartoonist Tom Toles: A Quirky Light in the Murk of Politics," *Washington Journalism Review*, December 1988, 24.

Instruction and Education

The educational function of media encompasses (1) the use of media in formal settings; (2) informal (usually individual-oriented) instruction and self-improvement; and also (3) education in its broadest sense. This last, known as socialization, enables us to participate in society (by reinforcing cultural norms), and affects social attitudes and increases general knowledge. The much-researched and hotly debated social effects are discussed in detail in Part 5's consideration of issues. This chapter looks at the use of media in formal and informal instruction.

The three aspects of education cited above are interrelated. Although the mix of media in each individual's learning experience is different, some general patterns are evident in the amounts and kinds of formal instruction, informal education, and socialization in which Americans participate. We begin with a look at the most structured aspect, formal instruction in schools and workplaces.

FORMAL EDUCATION

The burgeoning numbers of narrowcast opportunities through cable TV and classroom and personal use of new technologies, not to mention the ubiquitous videocassette, are all giving the educational capabilities of media new meaning and new life. Although public-television programming finds diverse usage, attempts to use major network *broadcast* channels to deliver instruction to special-interest audiences have not been successful. This comes as no surprise when we recall our economic model of supply and demand. An example makes this clear.

In 1982, the CBS-TV network and New York University announced the end to one of TV's grand experiments in formal education, "Sunrise Semester." After 25 years, the televised college course, on which some of the university's most distinguished professors reached an early-morning audience of credit and non-credit students, was being canceled. The numbers told the story: CBS indicated that in 1981, only 42 of its 200 affiliated stations carried the program and only 47 students were enrolled for credit.

With the single exception of books, media and formal education have had a checkered history. Each side is apt to blame the other for everything from lack of vision to lack of money. In the case of "Sunrise Semester," the problems were familiar ones to the media–education dialogue: primarily, a minimal investment in production. And on camera, lectures without visual and production support—

mere "talking heads"—make for dull education. On the other hand, fusing entertainment with instruction has already proven successful, as evidenced by the longevity of PBS how-to programming.

Chapter 15 showed us that at least one-half of all book sales fall into the general education category. This figure alone is impressive, but the potential of media participation in education is only beginning to emerge. Overall, professional and instructional communication is one of the fastest-growing areas within our study.

BOOKS AND VIDEOS

The most influential medium in formal instruction is the book, which also plays an important role in socialization and informal education. Books are successful because their coding and format allow them to adapt so well to the individual needs and habits of the students who use them.

A specialized form of the book has evolved in the school environment. The textbook provides an exposition of one subject area and serves as the content core of a class. Several other kinds of books are specifically designed for the classroom; they include teacher editions of the text, consumable workbooks used in conjunction with the text, and manuals and trade books used to supplement and reinforce textbooks. Paperbacks are used for a variety of purposes—from supplementary reading in primary grades to core texts in higher education.

Societies have created a separate institution just to house their books. Libraries provide long-term storage and easy retrieval of information. In order to make efficient use of the information stored in the library, a separate class of books was developed. Reference books, despite their limited numbers, account for 8 percent of book revenue each year. Some of the content has been transferred to or replaced by data bases, but the bound reference book shows no signs of disappearing.

The book is a useful learning device because it is compact, portable, low in cost, and reusable; it does not require special equipment; it does not disrupt nonusers; it allows for individualized learning since people can set their own rate of learning; it has easy reference capacity. There is renewed awareness among educators that print has communication benefits that broadcast and electronic media do not. Another reason for the importance of books in the classroom stems from the whole-language–integrated-learning perspective that has been catching on in educational thinking. It stresses the use of trade books—novels, biographies, general nonfiction—instead of reliance on textbooks; the idea is to show students that learning and writing travel across the curriculum and continue as a lifelong experience. Universities have developed Literature for Reading courses in their education departments, and booksellers are among those developing in-service programs for teachers to help blur the distinctions between schoolroom, library, bookstore, and home.[1]

Literature studies are reinforced and brought to life through the playing of excerpts from videos of films, PBS, or commercial broadcasts of novels, documentaries, or educational series. Language arts and speech are increasingly depending on videotapes, including playbacks of student performances. These two applications and similar ones in social studies, social sciences, foreign languages, and even science will be found in all levels of education. A typical high school student may in a week consume the following: videotapes of scenes from *The Scarlet Letter*; a program from the PBS "Story of English" series; a filmstrip on Nathaniel Hawthorne; clips from *Cry Freedom*; newspaper articles on current events in South Africa; a video on a French painter; tapes from the nightly news in Paris; a *Nova* biology segment; and a newsmagazine's coverage of a museum show.

MAGAZINES, JOURNALS, AND DATA BASES

The *Standard Periodical Directory* lists around 70,000 titles of periodicals published in the United States and Canada. In the educational system two kinds of periodicals are more important than the others: the more scholarly journals, which print the latest research and other information in a given field; and the trade journals, which offer the latest information about the application of new research.

As a field expands, the number of scholarly and trade journals proliferates as well. For example, almost 2,000 periodicals deal with education, about 1,000 cover library science, and more than 500 deal with media and media-related activities. It is almost impossible to stay abreast of the information in these fields, so special reference services, which cover a given area, have emerged. For example, *Topicator* is a periodical guide to a select group of magazines that deal with radio and television.

The magazine plays a minor role in the primary grades of public schools because few magazines of the quality of *Highlights* are published for elementary pupils. Publishers find that subscribers outgrow their material rapidly, and it is too expensive to resell their product to each generation. For middle school–junior high students, magazines do not have the volume of the number-one publication, a tabloid newspaper (see Table 18.1).

We have read of the inroads being made by Whittle Communications in producing mass media designed around advertising; the issue of advertising directed at students is indeed a thorny one. *Young American* has strict limits on types of ads it will accept, but many school districts still feel advertising is not suitable children's fare. In high school, when term papers become part of assignments, many students who want to search periodical literature use the public library. Thus students making the transition from high school to college sometimes have difficulty adjusting to the increased emphasis placed on the periodical. Although the book is easier to find and use than the journal, a large library's periodical collection can and should expand the amount of data available to researchers.

Table 18.1.	Circulations of Young People's Publications		
Publication	Ages	Circulation	Frequency
Young American	6–14	4,600,000	21 a year*
Boys' Life	7–14	1,392,535	Monthly
Junior Scholastic	12–14	717,481	Biweekly
Sports Illustrated for Kids	8–13	600,000	Monthly
Barbie	6–12	500,000	Quarterly
3-2-1 Contact	8–14	442,026	10 a year
Kid City Magazine	6–10	309,358	10 a year
Games Junior	6–12	250,000	Bimonthly

* It became a bimonthly in April 1990.
Sources: Welsh Publishing Group, October 1989.
Standard Rate and Data Service, *Consumer Magazine and Agri-Media*, September 1989.

Electronic publishing is more compatible with the structure and function of journals (to communicate the results of ongoing research) than with the structure and function of books. Rather than subscribe to a journal, an instructor will have on-line access to a data base that "publishes" information in a format unique to that instructor. The whole concept of information input, storage, and delivery is changing rapidly, and although books, magazines, and newspapers will not die, their methods of publication will change the way they are used, especially in formal education.

NEWSPAPERS

Newspaper organizations increasingly think of themselves as educational institutions rather than merely businesses. The editorial staff of a daily newspaper is essentially in the business of developing and communicating knowledge, researching facts, and packaging them for the paper's audience. Some newspapers approach this task with the same seriousness that universities bring to the development of knowledge, allowing their staff sufficient time, freedom, and security to pursue knowledge and even establishing a sort of tenure and sabbatical-leave system for expert writers and specialists on the staff.

Without doubt, newspapers provide a wide variety of information necessary for day-to-day living, as well as an increasing number of facts and ideas to round out the informal education of a well-informed citizen. Newspapers have also become source materials for some academic disciplines, particularly the social sciences.

Although the daily newspaper is heavily used in the socialization of members of society, and newspaper promotion departments devise campaigns to encourage classroom use, it remains the least-used mass medium in formal instruction. Again we need to think in terms of modern media addressing the needs of target audiences. *Young American* is one example (see Figure 18.1). Founded by Michael Forzley in 1983, it is the nation's fastest-growing newspaper, distributed as a supplement to 59 metropolitan and community newspapers to foster early newspaper reading and delivered, along with a curriculum guide for teachers, directly to elementary and middle schools in urban and suburban areas. Its average penetration of the 6–14-year-old audience was 22.8 percent in 1990.

Focus groups, reader surveys, and classroom visits constitute the market research behind the editorial content of the four-color tabloid; it also has eight student correspondents reporting from various parts of the country. One topic dominates each issue and regular features include

News Flash—New briefs about current events, contests and holidays.
Where in the World?—A descriptive map of a city, state, nation or planet currently in the news.
At Issue—A forum for *Young American* readers to express their ideas and opinions.
You and the News—Articles about the things kids are doing and about things that directly impact them.
YA Sports Stars—Stories about kids making sports news.
New Releases—An introduction to new movies, television shows and music.
Bill Nye, the Science Guy—A humorous approach to answering readers' science questions.

Figure 18.1.

Money, Money—Economics for kids.
Upstarts—A special page for beginning readers.

Each issue also contains large ads for toy cars, the National Guard, discount stores, etc.

All in all, it is a far cry from the more sober weekly readers of world affairs that these students' parents and grandparents grew up with. Its combination of entertainment, news and information, commentary, education, and persuasion have won it not only strong sales but awards from the Educational Press Association of America, from Parents' Choice (a group concerned with children's media), and the President's Excellence in Private Sector Initiatives award. Literacy advocate First Lady Barbara Bush has lent her endorsement.

SOUND RECORDINGS

Eighty-five percent of all colleges and universities use some form of audio in their instructional programs. Perhaps the most rapidly growing general use of audio media is for self-paced instruction; the recorder and playback machine can serve as a *very* patient tutor while an accelerated student can skip ahead or increase the pace of his or her instruction.

For music classes, records and tapes can be used to introduce new material or to provide musical accompaniment. In preschool and primary grades, tapes and records can be used for developing rhythms, telling stories, playing games, and acting out stories. In social studies, tapes and records can bring into the classroom the voices of people who have made history.

One special application of prerecorded audio media is the Talking Books Program that has been set up by the American Printing House for the Blind to make as much material as possible available to the visually impaired. At present, over 11,000 book titles are available, along with recordings of several current periodicals.

American corporations are using cassettes as inexpensive extensions of sales training and for personnel development. An executive of the Gillette Corporation estimates that the company's sales representatives in rural areas spend the equivalent of 18 to 25 weeks a year in their cars. During that time they can be receiving production information, sales leads, and customer information. Some companies have exploited the dramatic capabilities of the audio medium in management-training programs that deal with conflict resolution and stress management.

Motion Pictures

Before the development of videotape and the VCR, 16-mm and 8-mm films were a familiar instructional tool for most primary- and secondary-school teachers. As video projection reaches the point where large-screen images are sharp and faithful in color rendition, the last major obstacle to using video rather than film in the classroom will have been overcome. Of course, by that time, videodisc may have replaced videotape as the most popular format. Because they can be mass-produced like phonograph records, videodiscs are considerably cheaper than videotape. Recorded moving images will always have a firm place in instruction. However, with the exception of certain types of instruction, such as film-history courses, film will play a limited role in the future.

Radio and Television

The formal-education function of radio in the United States is expensive and fairly ineffective. For a number of years, some of the more than 1,100 public radio stations served as little more than classical jukeboxes for an elite audience within the total society. National Public Radio, formed by a joining of 90 stations in 1970 and government and foundation subsidized, is gaining momentum and diversity, described under "Informal Education." Attempts have been made to use educational radio as a means of formal instruction, but despite its potential, radio is rarely involved in classroom instruction.

Television in the Classroom. Despite many efforts, the history of television in the classroom has been less than a success story, especially when money spent and successful results are compared. Much of this limited success was due to the manner in which television was used and the forms that it assumed. Until the mid-1980s, television and formal instruction were, at best, unwilling and ineffective partners. Television was essentially a remote, expensive, restricted business whose primary interest and appeal was as a medium for the masses—"television of abundance," as it was called.

Television is now easily accessible for use in education, not only through over-the-air broadcasts but also by means of closed-circuit and cable-TV systems, all of which may be linked by satellite relays. Programs are now available on videocassette and videodisc, making TV materials nearly as available as audiotapes and records. Furthermore, camcorders enable instructors—and their students—to create their own materials.

Educational applications of cable proliferate. Schools can pick up area programming and produce and broadcast their own daily news shows, communicate with other schools and share instruction in low-enrollment courses, use a video-taped lesson when a teacher is absent, and share with the community the school plays and academic achievements its tax dollars are funding. With satellite dishes they access worldwide programming; about one-fifth of the nation's 15,577 school districts have satellite equipment. With hands-on studio or camcorder work, they invite students to become more critical consumers of media in general. One high school media coordinator, Michael Witsch of Mamaroneck, New York, observed, "They understand that the cameraman is making a decision about what is shot and what is not shot. They look at TV a bit more warily."

The complex electronic technology that affords television so many of its advantages is also, in a sense, a disadvantage. The technology allows many possibilities for noise, for disruption of the communication flow. Programs may be poorly produced, even in sophisticated studio surroundings. Atmospheric conditions may disturb broadcast signals or satellite reception. Classroom receivers may malfunction. Costs are another limiting factor. Even basic equipment can be expensive, but some of this is being ameliorated as local cable companies offer free cable hookup and transmission to schools in their areas. In doing so, they promote the increasing number of educational programs available on cable (including C-SPAN, The Discovery and the Learning Channels, A & E, and Black Entertainment TV).

Perhaps television's most serious limitation as an instruction tool is that under typical conditions, it is a one-way channel of communication. A feedback loop can be provided by means of push-button student-response systems or even "talk-back" arrangements. But in normal practice, one-way communication is still the rule.

Alternative education programs designed to keep students from dropping out of school have been especially creative in use of the media. CNN's "Newsroom" program, a 15-minute capsule of daily events, is used to stimulate informal discussion in such settings. An alternative recently developed is "Channel One," a faster-paced version of the news offered by Whittle Communications, complete with commercials. Although the very existence of commercials sprinkled throughout the 12-minute newscast, which debuted March 5, 1990, upset many educators and parents, Chris Whittle argues that his program "—a mix of MTV-style graphics, new factlets and features on subjects like steroid-hooked teens—[is] the perfect teaching tool for kids who think 'the Ayatollah Khomeini [was] a Russian gymnast.'"[2]

A television corollary to the use of novels and other nontextbooks in the classroom is the CBS Television Reading Program, developed by that broadcast group's Educational and Community Services. It is a nationwide television script-reading project designed to utilize elementary- and secondary-school students' enthusiasm for television to improve their reading skills and their motivation for further reading, learning, and creative thinking. Students receive matched-to-broadcast scripts of upcoming CBS prime-time network programs, which they read and often act out in class, and then use to enhance TV viewing; teachers receive packets of curriculum material to guide activities and discussions. Local CBS affiliates are the coordinators of selection and airing of programming and distribution of classroom materials, which are printed by local newspapers interested in promoting literacy (and, of course, future newspaper readers). We will take another look at this project under "Informal Education."

The availability and use of Instructional Television (ITV) has been documented as a result of a series of surveys conducted by the Corporation for Public Broadcasting (CPB) since 1977. Its usage is small (no more than 30 percent of teachers regularly use ITV, and takes up less than 2 hours per week). A far greater impact is made by incorporation of off-air PBS programming into the normal curriculum.

Higher Education and Telecommunication. In higher education, the use of television for instruction appears to be widespread but quite conservative. More than 80 percent of colleges and universities used video for instruction during the 1984–1985 school year, according to a study by the Corporation for Public Broadcasting and the Department of Education. About 32 percent of schools offered telecourses, which make substantial use of video, in 1985. Only a few courses are usually offered via television and only about 14 percent of the total college TV effort is devoted to off-campus course work.

No single source provides the educational and telecommunications communities with objective, reliable information about what the new technologies are, where they are being applied, and in what settings and for which learners particular technologies seem most effective. There is, however, some centralization of efforts now under way through regional and national initiatives to provide programming services, to facilitate teleconferencing networks, to gather information on the use of telecommunications in higher education, and to assist colleges and universities in implementing technology within courses and curricula.

Vocational Training and Business Television. Vocational training has made efficient usage of television and has been noticeable. For far-flung industries, teleconferencing by satellite keeps individuals current and motivated. One example of business television is the Law Enforcement Television Network, which began programming by satellite to 900 stations in all 50 states in the middle of 1989 to train police officers. Encoded so that would-be criminals cannot access the program, it offers techniques and basic methods through realistic scenes involving potential suicides, wiretapping, police applications of facsimile machines, and so forth. The president of the Dallas-based network describes the format, pacing, and tone of the segments as targeted to officers whose first learning experience was "Sesame Street." Course credit as well as discounts on insurance are rewards for regular viewing. The series was created by Westcott Communications, whose Automotive Satellite Television Network has been beaming training programs to new dealerships since 1986.

PBS's National Narrowcast Service offers businesses, agencies, and colleges a wide range of human resource development programming via satellite and other delivery systems. On a monthly basis, NNS offers its subscribers up to 40 hours of video-based training courses, live seminars, and teleconferences. NNS programming is available on a pay-per-program basis through off-air recording licenses. Live special event teleconferences allow NNS to reach into communities so that managers in all sizes of business can participate in important informational

Figure 18.2. Nonbroadcast/industrial television is a fast-growing and already major media industry. The Law Enforcement Television Network is one example of training by satellite.

programs such as "AIDS: A Matter of Corporate Policy," "EEOC and the Laws It Enforces," "Peat Marwick's Annual Tax Briefing for Executives," and "Ethics: Tough Questions and Complex Answers."

The total annual program output of video by corporations themselves is far greater than the combined output of the major commercial-television networks, and total usage has increased each year.

Adult Learning. The PBS Adult Learning Service (ALS), created in the fall of 1981, is the ongoing result of the first nationwide effort to provide coordination of adult learning through television. A series of local partnerships, among more than 1,400 colleges and universities and 96 percent of all public TV stations, offers college-credit courses to more than 200,000 tuition-paying students each year. The ALS catalog offers 35 courses that are also available during prime time for the enjoyment of the general audience.

All this began when publisher and philanthropist Walter H. Annenberg announced his intention to donate $150 million over a 15-year period toward the improvement of telecourse programs. In 1984, the first wave of Annenberg-funded programs included the 26-program series "Congress: We the People," in which veteran TV journalist Edwin Newman hosts an inside look at how Congress works. A more "typical" telecourse is "The Write Course," a 30-lesson series consisting of video lessons closely integrated with textbook readings, study guides, and writing assignments—a one-semester college-level course in composition. By means of television broadcasting, learners can be reached at home, making "open learning" a reality. At the same time, this mass medium is becoming an individual medium. The development of small, inexpensive home-video recorders makes it feasible for students to view video materials on an individually prescribed basis.

INSTRUCTION WITH THE NEW AND EMERGING MEDIA

Electronic Publishing. New technology has its impact on the oldest medium, books, particularly in education. The sociologist Ithiel de Sola Pool observed in his article "The Culture of Electronic Print": "Virtually all handling of text . . . and also publishing, will be done within computers. . . . Printing the text onto paper will be for the convenience of the reader alone."

Videodiscs promised to be able to compress the contents of the entire Library of Congress into a medium-size room. Among Sony's recent projects: Data Discman, a portable, palm-size device that can do data searches and store 100,000 pages of data optically (it can also play small CDs when you tire of reading).

Traditionally, the book is a fixed unit in which certain ideas are presented. Electronic publishing can alter this concept because a group of authors can write and edit on computer networks. As each author modifies, edits, and expands the content, the text changes from day to day. In addition, the teacher in the classroom can use the text in new ways. Even if she did not have access to a text on-line, a more conventionally published textbook can be, as we saw in Chapter 15, edited on demand for each class syllabus. The student can also make modifications, so reading becomes an interactive dialogue with the teacher and authors.

Interactive Video. Interactive video has become the latest "buzzword" in media instruction. The possibilities for branching, collecting data, using computer-generated text and graphics, and creating personalized message systems make this linkage between computer and video technology one of the most flexible mediated systems of instruction in use today.

As Diane Gayeski, a professor at Ithaca College, points out: "One of the simplest, but most powerful, techniques using the random accessibility of video segments is showing people what they're interested in. This can be done by providing a menu in print, through computer generation, or in the tape or disc itself, by which a participant can select a topic."[3] The difference between random-access video and traditional linear video is like the difference between a book and a scroll. With a book or random-access device, you can locate just the "page" or "chapter" you want, without having to "scroll" through the whole program.

Training and information can be provided by the branching capabilities of interactive video. By asking questions, the teacher can determine whether a trainee has grasped an important concept. If not, remedial segments can be shown that correct misunderstandings. Such programs can present the information in different terms. Many computer-based programs are able to keep track of patterns of responses and to branch to a specific style or level of explanation accordingly. Other systems include printout or record-keeping options, providing useful information about the user's progress, as well as the program itself.

Interactive video can increase the effectiveness of testing and assessment, allowing for immediate scoring and/or feedback and supplementary instruction, if necessary, as part of the test. Instead of being limited to print or diagrams to present test items, video can present dramatized scenes, moving parts, and realistic sounds, adding to the scope and face validity of the assessment.

Instruction for Those with Impairments. Interactive video is being made available to those with special needs through advancing technology. The blind can "read" a screen of menu thanks to IBM's Personal System/2 Screen Reader, which announces aloud any customized selection of information determined by the user.

Figure 18.3. IBM's InfoWindow can be used by children and adults as a tool in training, educating, informing, and selling. It coordinates with a range of multimedia, self-paced, personalized presentations.

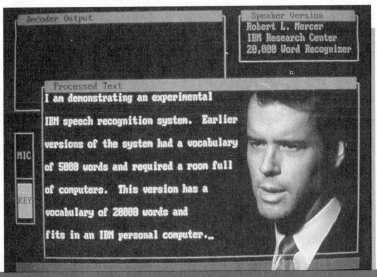

Figure 18.4. An experimental IBM speech-recognition device indicates the potential of future communication. This system can transcribe sentences from a 20,000-word vocabulary with 95% accuracy; a digital signal processor performs 30 million operations per second in transcribing the spoken word for people with handicaps.

The deaf are served by an experimental IBM speech-recognition system (Figure 18.4) that can transcribe sentences from a 20,000-word vocabulary with more than 95 percent accuracy. A digital-signal processor performs 30 million operations per second in speeding transcription of the spoken word. SpeechViewer vocalizes sound for the deaf so they can learn to communicate more effectively.

The Future. Much of the excitement about these new technologies is centered on their potential to improve the quality of education for students both off and on campus. Collaborative thinking about the content and how to teach it offers a chance that the quality of teaching will improve. Also, with large data bases to draw on, the student may be able to tackle problems and concepts as an undergraduate that previously were regarded as appropriate for only graduate students.

Embedded within the technologies is the potential for helping students to see ideas differently and to manipulate them more effectively. Some students, for example, find it difficult to visualize abstract mathematical or scientific concepts when aided by only static drawings and the printed page. But with computer simulations or video representations, some of which can be electronically manipulated so that the student can "see" the concept from different perspectives, the ideas can be made more comprehensible.

Yet as one student of the use of information technology in education remarks, "Society and schools and most students are not about to change. But it's easy to get smoke in your eyes."[4]

Among the issues that have had a negative impact on the use of electronic media in schools are:

Society's general attitude is that electronic media are for entertainment, not for education.

Teachers are often print-oriented and have little free time to develop the skills and attitudes necessary to use electronic media in the classroom.

Local "in-house" materials do not reach the production standards that people have become accustomed to in commercial radio and in TV films.

Software content ages rapidly and is difficult to maintain professionally and economically.

The question is not, ultimately, whether the new technology will be deployed; it is whether the door that separates the dedicated and imaginative teachers, the brilliant psychologists, the human philosophers, and the creative software designers from the world of misuse, indifference, suspicion, and hostility will be unlocked.

As Marilyn Kressel, founder and former director of the Center for Learning and Telecommunications of the American Association for Higher Education, stated,

> *The quality and evaluation of technology-based instruction continue to plague educators and policymakers. Software is being cranked out everywhere from obscure garage-top attics to high-tech production facilities. A critical analysis of what works and what doesn't work when delivered by television, radio, computer, telephone, or any other technology is simply unavailable. . . .*
>
> *Will these systems address the issues of educational quality and thrive, or will they go the way of so many other innovations, fizzling into a footnote in educational textbooks? Might we be left with dormant, 1960-vintage university and college production studios and warehouses filled with obsolete PC's and bins full of floppy*

discs? Those of us who have seen the potential for technology to instruct and excite when integrated into educationally sound delivery systems would hate to be accused of such faddism. The scenario is preventable, but who will marshal the necessary resources to ensure good practice?[5]

An answer is offered by the 1989 report of the Congressional Office of Technology Assessment, "Technology and the American Economic Transition." It found that the productivity of American schools has been declining largely because education invests a smaller portion of its resources in labor-saving technology than any other major industry, whereas 30 percent of the $50 billion spent by American employers on training programs goes into computer-based instructional systems. Vendors of such systems point to the benefit of having time for enrichment programs because technology can compress the time needed on basic learning. Teachers in primary and secondary education are increasingly appreciative of television's own enrichment possibilities. "I don't like competing with television, but I like using it as a tool. Television isn't the enemy anymore if you use it not as a babysitter, but as an extension of the lesson," commented high school English teacher Mary Curtiss.[6]

The 1989 congressional report asked for the establishment of a federally supported learning research institute to promote greater use of technology in formal education. So far, the most innovative uses of the communication revolution and instructional techniques are not in the "halls of ivy" but in the "real world" of work. Advanced uses of media learning are invading the home and the workplace before they are seen in school.

INFORMAL EDUCATION

Examples of material that informally increases our knowledge abound and overlap with what educates us in other ways. Our approach here will be to look at several basic categories of media content that, in contrast to what we have previously considered, is not *primarily* generated or coordinated by an institution that also serves as its gatekeeper. We will consider programming that is offered for general consumption: Selection is left to the individual (by and large), and such programs must compete among news, commentary, and entertainment for an audience.

DOCUMENTARIES

Documentary films were first developed as a conscious film form in the 1920s by filmmakers Robert Flaherty in the United States and John Grierson in England. Grierson defined the documentary as a creative treatment of actuality. Grierson, Flaherty, and others developed the concept of the documentary as a socially significant film form rather than merely a vehicle for showing newsreel footage and "travelogue" material. The documentary flourished in the 1930s and 1940s when it was used to communicate messages to a variety of audiences about the Depression and World War II. "Documentary" now denotes many media forms other than programs designed to interpret human problems. The travelogue and nature program remain popular informative and entertaining presentations, less today as

Figure 18.5. The Emmy-winning documentary "The Tunnel" brought political events to the living room by showing how West Berlin students dug a passage under the Berlin Wall to rescue 50 men, women, and children. In the house from which digging started, an NBC correspondent and cameraman flank one of the students.

part of museum or community lecture series than as widely available television broadcasting.

Television is the prime influence on the continuing development of documentaries that come under the public-affairs umbrella. The commercial networks, primarily through their news departments, and the Public Broadcasting Service occasionally produce and broadcast significant documentaries that are later released in 16-mm-film and video form. Programs such as "Vietnam: A Television History," the architecture series "Pride of Place," "War and Peace in the Nuclear Age," and the Jacques Cousteau and *National Geographic* specials are examples of outstanding TV documentaries that have wide use in education.

Informally, we educate ourselves about food, art, sharks, language, and much more through television and/or purchase or library loan of program tapes, audio cassettes, and books. In effect, our informal education occurs before, during, and after our school years. It is the means by which we stay intellectually and emotionally alive. It is also the area of media use least easily documented. There are, however, statistics like those in Table 18.2.

DOCUDRAMAS

Normally, the documentary's point of view is not too difficult to ascertain. A relatively new development, however, the "docudrama," has complicated the process. In general, the docudrama is a dramatization of current newsworthy events and trends rather than creative reportage. Although the makers of docudramas insist

Table 18.2.	The All-Time Most-Watched Public Affairs Programs on PBS		
Title		**Date**	**Cumulative Audience***
SHOAH (Part 1)		4/87	9.8%
FRONTLINE: "An Unauthorized History of the NFL"		1/83	9.2%
VIETNAM: A TELEVISION HISTORY: "Roots of War"		10/83	8.7
"Hiroshima Remembered"		8/85	8.3
FRONTLINE: "Death of a Porn Queen"		6/87	8.2
"Democratic Presidential Debate"		1/84	8.0
CHILD SEXUAL ABUSE: WHAT YOUR CHILDREN SHOULD KNOW: "A Program for Parents"		9/84	7.4
FRONTLINE: "Memory of the Camps"		5/85	7.2
FRONTLINE: "The Real Stuff"		1/87	7.1
VIETNAM: A TELEVISION HISTORY: "Tet, 1968"		11/83	7.0
"Visions of 'Star Wars': A NOVA/FRONTLINE Special Report"		4/86	6.8
VIETNAM: A TELEVISION HISTORY: "The First Vietnam War (1946–1954)"		10/83	6.8
FRONTLINE: "88 Seconds in Greensboro"		1/83	6.7
FRONTLINE: "The Earthquake Is Coming"		2/87	6.6
SHOAH (Part 2)		4/87	6.5
VIETNAM: A TELEVISION HISTORY: "America's Mandarin (1954–1963)"		10/83	6.4
FRONTLINE: "AIDS—A National Inquiry"		3/86	6.1
VIETNAM: A TELEVISION HISTORY "The End of the Tunnel (1973–1975)"		12/83	6.1

* *Cumulative audience: the percentage of U.S. TV homes viewing at least 6 minutes of a program.* Data as of 1988; *The Civil War* would be top now.

that their films are dramatizations of fact, not fiction, the line between "docu" and "drama" may sometimes be difficult for the viewer to draw. The evaluation of the point of view may also be comparatively difficult.

The film *Death of a Princess*, a dramatization of the search by an English journalist for the truth behind published reports that a young Saudi Arabian princess and her lover had been publicly executed for adultery at the instigation of her royal father, is a prime example of the docudrama genre. Shown on PBS, the film generated considerable controversy, and with an audience draw of 13.8 percent remains one of their all-time most-watched drama programs. But did it document Saudi Arabian ruling-class mores and Islamic legal principles? Or did it dramatize them in such a way that fiction prevailed over fact?

Media as History Educators. Motion pictures and television shows, in recent years especially, have become our history teachers. Wars of all sorts lend themselves particularly well to the visual media. We know more than we would have about the Civil War (*The Blue and the Gray*, *Glory*), World War II (*The Winds of War*), the Russian Revolution (*Dr. Zhivago*, *Reds*), violence in Latin American politics (*Missing*), the American Revolution (*George Washington*), and the drug wars.

All this activity is no accident. After the 1985 miniseries on the Civil War, *The Blue and the Gray*, scored well in ratings, network officials felt that audiences would respond to other historical subjects. "The American public likes to be taken into the landscapes of the past," said Marian Brayton, vice president–dramatic specials for CBS Entertainment.

CBS's lineup of historical specials especially improved its reputation among educators, members of the clergy, and others who are often critical of network programming.

The benefits of increasing the knowledge base of the American people are obvious. Yet because movies and television, through their unique coding of visual images, have enormous power to shape perception, they are suspect and singled out for scrutiny. When the extent of the artistic license taken by filmmakers and producers goes beyond careless or intentional modifications of costuming or pacing, to enhance a story, the media have the potential to manipulate opinion and falsify history. Few in the audience may be equipped to notice, say critics. Once again, the overlaid function of entertainment is at the core of the issue. The exact depiction of events rarely makes for enjoyable or, from a communicator's standpoint, feasible content. Something *will* be lost when a 659-page book about race and class in America becomes a 2-part television program.

THE CULTURAL HERITAGE

All media contribute to reinforcing the fabric of American society, cultural achievement, and specialized audiences' ethnic heritages. An ongoing function of the mass media, even in this day of increasingly fragmented audiences, is the spread of appreciation for the literacy and musical heritage of American civilization, which of course includes that of Europe. Recently, concerted efforts have been made to widen the appreciation of black and native-American culture and history; some states are mandating adequate coverage of such achievements in history textbooks.

Americans have been brought closer to fellow citizens and the rest of the world through programs such as National Public Radio's "Performance Today" (a daily 2-hour arts information show), "New Sounds" (contemporary music), or "World of Opera" and PBS's "Great Performances," sharing theatrical productions, world dance championships and presentations of ballet, opera, symphonies, and historical events, culture, and spectacles. The Saturday-afternoon broadcasts from the Metropolitan Opera in New York City are fascinating examples of the interrelationship of media and media functions, including the whole gamut of education and socialization. While clearly entertaining, these live nationally broadcast performances, complete with on-air synopses and intermission quizzes, are instructional for the 5 million who listen each week of the season. The formality of the presentation is especially targeted to the cultural filters of dedicated opera buffs; the musical education function is reinforced through the Metropolitan Opera Guild's weekly magazine *Opera News*, which contains pictures, descriptions of narrative and musical developments, and background on the opera and the performers. For more than 50 years, this program has also been a public-relations gem. Sponsor of the radio broadcast since 1931 and supporter of the PBS-televised "Live From Lincoln Center" is Texaco, whose surveys indicate it is a factor in consumer selection of its gasoline. The role of gatekeepers (who is to decide what of so-called "high culture" should be communicated as public service?) and market research (what do we know of audience segmentation, and how much of an interest base can we rely on?) come into play. Many of the "worthy" programs shown by net-

Figure 18.6.
A *TV Guide* ad
for an opera
via "Great Per-
formances."

works on early and golden-age TV have succumbed, only to have cable and video gladly and profitably pick up the slack. Kultur Video, the leading supplier of classical music videos, grew 1000 percent between 1983 and 1987 and continues to expand.

SELF-IMPROVEMENT AND INSTRUCTION

In this area we see the most dramatic example of the privatization of media in all its forms. There is no need to cite the enormous knowledge the individual reader seeks and receives from books. A phenomenon of bookselling has been the steady growth of audio- and videocassettes, with each season bringing lower prices.

Videos. There are at least 40 audio publishers and scores of video producers with aggressive marketing and packaging strategies to convince book retailers to give up precious display space and urge readers to buy electronic versions of books. Often audios are condensed versions or adaptations, such as multivoiced dramatizations, on one or more cassettes convenient for car or jogging listening. Recent releases ranged from *How to Be Your Own Therapist* to *Webster's New World Power Vocabulary*, to *No Man's Land*, a Western written by Louis L'Amour.

Videos are struggling to find their role in the overall bookstore mix, but there is a solid track record in how-to's, fine arts, travel, popular movies, and performances of all kinds. HomeVision, a successful producer of such videos, has, as Public Media Video, entered special-interest programs for the general market. Their first offering was *Vintage: A History of Wine*, based on a PBS series; cross-promotion plans are a key to success in this exploding market. "Joseph Campbell and the Power of Myth, with Bill Moyers" was a PBS series based on Campbell's books and sold over 125,000 videocassettes (40 percent in bookstores).

Marketed also in direct-mail catalogs originating with organizations like AT&T (to sell "information packages"), American Express, and gift merchandisers, videos are sometimes the communicator's format of choice. Producers tout what makes them better than other media: complete with birdcalls and computer-animated range maps, Audubon Society's Video Guides "give you a truly multi-dimensional view of 505 North American species in their natural habitats. That's something no book or field guide can do!" Or they incorporate the best of other media: Little League's official how to play baseball by video's easy-to-follow segments are "enhanced with network-style slow-motion and stop-action demonstrations. . . ." An example of a series that combines entertainment, special-interest how-to, and enhancement of cultural knowledge is *Art Under Foot*. Ten programs explore not only the practical aspects of buying and caring for oriental rugs but their origins and profiles of rug makers "to link the people who make them with the people who buy them."

National Public Radio. Both out-and-out how-to and a widening circle of programming geared to individual edification and information are offered on National Public Radio. More than 350 stations are now autonomous partners with the Washington, D.C.–based NPR production center, which has as its mission to provide a "touchstone—for clarity, continuity, a renewed sense of community" to over 6 million listeners.[7] Its efforts have been recognized by scores of prestigious journalism and service awards. Weekday and weekend news programs, using its own widely traveling commentators, emphasizes in-depth and analytic coverage that helps listeners get inside political, social, and health issues. Hallmarks are their unique blending of report, interview, satire, commentary, features, and other newsmagazine elements, held together by the personality of hosts such as "Weekend Edition's" Scott Simon. *Los Angeles Times* columnist Steve Weinstein commented: "For a growing number of adults across the country, Scott Simon's ability to induce both common people and major newsmakers to stumble and stammer and finally puzzle out their lives at his microphone has provided an intelligent and often irreverent alternative to the traditional Saturday-morning menu of mindless stimulation."[8]

A leader among call-in radio shows is "Car Talk," originating with WBUR-FM, Boston, which has become one of National Radio's hottest properties. Diagnosis of automotive maladies and general car-industry news is served up with intelligence and humor by two brothers, Ray and Tom Magliozzi (tip: "How hard you accelerate from a dead stop is more important than changing your oil, getting a tune-up, rotating your tires, anything. That's why one car with 50,000 miles on it runs great, and another is ready for the junkyard").

PROGRAMMING FOR CONTINUING LEARNING

Almost 20 percent of PBS programming is labeled educational (in addition to the 24 percent "cultural" and 56 percent "public affairs" subject areas). Obtained through individual public-television stations and independent U.S. and foreign producers, the national institutions offered via PBS are of course led by "Sesame Street," produced by the Children's Television Workshop for over 20 years, and now increasing school readiness in 80 countries, and "Mister Rogers' Neighborhood," out of WQED-TV, Pittsburgh, where Fred Rogers stumbled into children's

Figure 18.7. Education, informal and formal, is perhaps the most fertile field for the introduction of entertainment as an overlaid function. "Car Talk," carried by National Public Radio, is a successful mix of irreverent patter and sound advice.

television in 1954 after he "watched people throwing pies at each other" on TV and decided to work to improve a corner of the medium. Seven million homes now tune in each weekday, new generations finding guidance in emotional development and "growing up caring" above all else.

Entertainment techniques to instruct are utilized on several other popular shows, including "Square One TV," also an Emmy winner, designed to increase the nation's 14 million 8–12-year-olds' interest in math. Game shows, animation, music videos, and parodies of popular television shows and commercials all have serious teaching goals and demonstrate the value of math in everyday life. Mathman, a video-game character who "eats" correct answers, was an early hit.

Public television remains the pioneer and the transmitter of most educational programs for children, whereas adult learning and documentary series are often snatched away by cable. Here is a typical list of PBS offerings other than "Sesame Street" and "Mister Rogers' Neighborhood."

Captain Kangaroo shows are meant to be both fun and educational. Several segments of the series were videotaped in Milwaukee's own Discovery World Museum.

Zoobilee Zoo Ben Vereen stars in this lively series that appeals to youngsters' creativity, imagination, and interest in the arts to promote social development.

Shining Time Station Ringo Starr is Mr. Conductor, an 18-inch man with magical powers, in this series designed to entertain young children while supporting their social, creative, and artistic development.

Reading Rainbow LeVar Burton hosts this series that encourages children to continue

Figure 18.8 Tempestt Bledsoe of "The Cosby Show" plays a time-keeper in a music video, using arithmetic to check employees' comings and goings on "Square One TV," Children's Television Workshop's math series for 8–12-year-olds. The program skillfully uses skits, game shows, rap music, sitcoms, and other media successes to hold attention.

reading during the summer when beginning readers may lose their newly acquired skills.

Long Ago and Far Away James Earl Jones hosts this series that captures the magic of storytelling for children as well as adults. Award-winning animated and live action films from around the world are featured.

3-2-1 Contact works to improve children's observational skills, stimulate their interest in science, and promote science as a career.

Knowzone is a science series based on *Nova* episodes, but is tailored to a younger audience, covering topics from dinosaurs to tornadoes.

ColorSounds Music videos, featuring the best in pop, country, and rhythm and blues, are presented with captioned lyrics to teach reading, phonics, parts of speech, and grammatical structure.

Newton's Apple is a family science series that answers viewer questions, and provides imaginative and entertaining science demonstrations.

Degrassi Junior High is a drama series that explores the lives of junior high students, and the joys and heartbreaks of growing up today.

The Power of Choice Comedian and counselor Michael Pritchard talks with teens about peer pressure, self-esteem, parent relations, pregnancy, drugs, and alcohol.

Soapbox With Tom Cottle Psychologist Tom Cottle talks with teenagers about issues they face today, including drugs, sex, suicide, and divorce.

CBS, as we have seen, has long been an outstanding network in educational efforts. Their Educational and Community Service sends out comprehensive packets of curriculum guidelines for teachers and suggested background reading for selected programs. Another effort was "CBS Storybreak," a series of Saturday-morning animated specials bringing quality books to television, produced for 1989's Year of the Younger Reader.

Many of the various study guides are produced by Kidsnet, a clearinghouse for children's broadcasting in Washington, D.C. It connects viewers with other agencies in the special needs, literary, and communication network. CBS/Broadcast Group also offers "Television Worth Teaching" awards to educators for innovative use of *commercial* television. A long way from "talking heads," television and other media recognize that entertainment teaches.

The CBS/Library of Congress "Read More About It" project celebrated its tenth anniversary in 1989, with over 250 programs chosen by the library to contain announcements of CBS book lists available to all viewers; the first was *All Quiet on the Western Front*. For "The Moon Above, the Earth Below," a CBS News Special on the twentieth anniversary of the moon landing, CBS provided information on resources, activities, and discussions for sciences, math, social studies, career awareness, arts and tech centers. Their late afternoon "Schoolbreak Specials" are amplified by study guides.

SUMMARY

The educational function of media encompasses not only the use of media in formal and informal settings but also in education in its broadest sense.

The most influential medium in formal instruction is the book; it adapts well to the individual needs and habits of the student. The book is cheap, compact, portable, and reusable, and it allows individualized learning. Textbooks are the staple of classroom learning, although many educators have begun to combine novels, biographies, and nonfiction books with texts to give a wider selection of ideas.

The textbook is complemented by other media in the classroom. Videos enhance the instruction of history, science, literature, and foreign language. Periodicals are published more frequently than books, so are more current and contain more specialized information. Newspapers have not yet found a niche in formal education, although newspapers have been developed that encourage reading among young people. Sound recordings are effective because they allow self-paced instruction and are good for drill work. Cable television is developing as a means of communication in classrooms at all levels.

Informal education by the media is very different from formal education: Material is offered for general consumption by the public, so selection is left to the individual who must choose it over news, commentary, or entertainment.

Motion pictures and television have very recently become history teachers by offering programs like "The Blue and the Gray" and movies such as *Glory*. However, a viewer must be careful to sort out fictional plot elements from historical fact.

The media contribute to communicating and reinforcing American social and cultural achievements, along with specialized ethnic heritages. Recent efforts have focused on widening the appreciation of black and native-American culture and history.

Self-improvement and instruction are a wide market for the media. The individual reader can receive an enormous amount of knowledge from books in fiction, nonfiction, self-help, and journalism. Videos offer a solid lineup of how-to's, travel, performances, and popular movies. National Public Radio has a wide selection of programming geared to individual edification and information. On television, PBS features "Nova," "National Geographic," and "Masterpiece Theatre." Educational programming on the other networks is harder to find, although CBS offers many family specials and literary dramatizations.

The future of formal and informal media education focuses on data bases, which will allow easy storage and retrieval of massive amounts of information; interactive video, which will allow self-determined video instruction; and attempts to bring the new technologies into the classroom on a more universal level. Just how far the technology goes in the field of formal education is hard to predict; it will have to overcome barriers in both budgets and attitudes among conservative educators to become effective.

REFERENCES

1. Sheila Wilensky-Lanford, "Children's Booksellers and Teachers: Partners in Literacy," *Publishers Weekly*, January 20, 1989, 101.
2. Joshua Hammer, "A Golden Boy's Toughest Sell," *Newsweek*, February 19, 1990, 52–53.
3. Diane Gayeski and David Williams, "Interactive Video—Accessible and Intelligent," *E-ITV*, June 1984, 31–32.
4. Hyman H. Field, "Issues in Financing Higher Education Telecommunications," *National Forum* (Summer 1986): 12.
5. *USA Today*, March 3, 1984, 12.
6. Quoted in "The Second Blackboard," *Newsweek*, April 2, 1990, 48.
7. Douglas J. Bennet, "What's Different About National Public Radio?"; NPR brochure.
8. Steve Weinstein, "An Alternative to Saturday Blahs," *Los Angeles Times*, July 2, 1987.

CHAPTER

19

Entertainment and Art

Media entertainment serves as the primary source of what has come to be called popular culture, the chosen art of the people. Music, films, television, novels, and magazines improve the quality of life in our intense, crowded, increasingly urbanized·society. A significant factor is that entertainment is used to shrug off the world of work and refresh us at the end of the day.

Entertainment, whether or not the fact is appreciated by critics, may well be the single most important role of mass communication. The introduction to a book that reprints an essay on comedy by English novelist George Meredith and a treatise by French philosopher Henri Bergson concludes:

> *Bergson says that comedy can make us human and natural in the midst of mechanical societies. And Meredith implies that comedy can enlighten us and redeem us from our worst stupidity—the original sin or pride, or complacency. Both, in sum, believe that comedy is a premise to civilization. . . . that comedy is not only a social game, but art.*[1]

Of course, these gentlemen wrote long before sitcoms, but the point is still valid: Entertainment answers a primal and a societal need, and when it approaches art, it brings a redeeming and beautifying element to humankind. It seems obvious, and yet the cause and effect are elusive (Bergson's essay was based on a lecture entitled ''Why does one laugh?'').

With the introduction of the mass media, the number of listeners or viewers increased, and the growth of the middle class and the spread of communication through affordable channels did much to homogenize tastes. Later the maturing of the media and the cumulative education of audiences led to an ever-greater diversity of interests and tastes. This chapter considers the shifting position of entertainment in our society, and focuses on ways scholars and critics have found to analyze this complicated and pervasive media function. Their methods include a variety of tools we can all use to become more thoughtful and critical consumers in the media marketplace.

Consultant and authority on this chapter's discussion of the analysis and interpretation of entertainment is Arthur Asa Berger.

CRITICISM AND DEFENSE OF MASS CULTURE...

Considerable debate has taken place over the value and effects of mass-media entertainment-art on our culture and society. Cultural anthropologists, sociologists, and critics have tended to group cultural artifacts into three categories, which have been given various names. Van Wyck Brooks, a media critic, coined the terms *highbrow*, *middlebrow*, and *lowbrow* to describe these categories.

Highbrow, or high, *culture* is composed of cultural artifacts that can be appreciated by only an educated and intellectual elite. Examples include Shakespeare's plays, T. S. Eliot's poems, Beethoven's sonatas, Matisse's paintings, the journal *Daedalus*, and Ingmar Bergman's movies.

Middlebrow culture has pretensions of being refined and intellectual but also has wider human appeal. Examples include *Horizon* magazine, Neil Simon's plays, Amedeo Modigliani's paintings, Ogden Nash's poems, and Norman Mailer's novels.

Lowbrow culture consists of those artifacts that have massive appeal to the largest possible audience, an appeal that is usually visceral rather than cerebral, emotional rather than rational, crass rather than aesthetic. Examples include soap operas, TV situation comedies, advice-to-the-lovelorn newspaper columns, sex-and-violence movies, and pulp novels.

There are problems with such a categorization. For one thing, entries in one of the three classifications must be specific and must be subject to change. If we use these categories over a period of time to measure audience perception of film as a medium, for example, motion pictures as a whole have moved from lowbrow in the 1890s to middlebrow in the 1940s to highbrow in the 1980s.

Also, there is in this analysis an elitism that verges on snobbery. It seems more reasonable to adopt a method of analysis that is more objective and a classification based on the medium, the techniques, the function of the content, and the success of the content. We will be exploring such an approach later in this chapter.

Much criticism of the mass media has been inspired by a former work ethic that praised labor and condemned idleness. The feeling was that if readers or listeners or viewers were not being informed, enlightened, persuaded, or educated, their time was being wasted. Today we recognize that recreation is vital to personal happiness and self-development. Much mass-media fare that has been designed specifically to provide recreation has been scorned by segments of the intellectual community, but none of us should overlook the importance of emotional escape, fantasy, and catharsis, all necessary to the renewal of the human spirit. Also, entertainment as one of the ways to tell stories fulfills an important cultural function.

The *interaction* of the media artist, the mass medium, and the audience creates a film's ultimate "worth." Along the way there can be some bumpy spots. A communicator's standards stemming from the medium and genre—how well a work uses its codes and format—and his or her own values may lock horns with the marketplace. We saw this in Chapter 2's discussion of the reluctance of filmmakers to accept changes in their work dictated by preview feedback. Originality and tradition or audience expectation are often in conflict. *Barry Lyndon*, a film by Stanley Kubrick based on a minor novel by William Makepeace Thackeray, goes against the grain of Kubrick's traditional films. His originality was misunderstood by his movie audience. The beauty, elegance, and grace of *Barry Lyndon* are a joy.

Figure 19.1. Entertainment as an overlaid and needed function is heralded on the front page of the November 9, 1876, edition of *The Daily Graphic* ("An Illustrated Evening Newspaper"); the engraving is captioned "A Happy Relief From Politics. . . . Now we shall have a newspaper pleasant and profitable to read and take home with us. Politics is well enough for down-town in the morning, but we want something else for evenings at home."

The photography, sets, music, and acting are remarkable. But audiences were less responsive to the film because it lacks the story, the liveliness, and the hype of *2001: A Space Odyssey* or *A Clockwork Orange*.

Perhaps Stanley Kubrick was ahead of his audience. Mass-audience rejection or acceptance of a film is not necessarily the measure of its worth. Many films that were undervalued by contemporaries are revered later as objects of lasting significance and beauty. The films of Charlie Chaplin and Buster Keaton are prime examples. The status of these men has been elevated from media clown to film artist. Nonetheless, movies are made for a "now" box office and not for tomorrow's critical credos.

Each medium has technical, cultural, and economic limitations that determine how much and what kinds of entertainment it can provide. Some media are essentially purveyors of mass culture; others, of more elite culture. The media and the audiences tend to be selective and to seek each other out. The audience must be an active participant. Great artists improve the tastes of audiences, but not all producers of media content are great artists. It is this dichotomy that leads to intense criticism and defense of mass culture.

The crassest expression of the mass-culture position is that of the media entrepreneur who says, "Give the fools what they want. If people will pay for comic books but not poetry, give them comics. If the audience demands burlesque, don't give them Lady Macbeth." Media owners are first and foremost businessmen who must sell a product to as many customers as are necessary to make a profit. Popular culture is big business and therefore suspect. But as is usually the case, there are other sides to the story.

For example, the economic and technical problems in filling the time and space of the mass media are very real. Enormous quantities of content produced at equally enormous costs are the facts of life in mass communication. Although quality and quantity are not theoretically impossible to produce in tandem, the timetable that producers set for themselves makes it a difficult feat to accomplish.

One argument in defense of mass culture maintains that both good and bad exist in "class" culture and in mass culture and that class and mass not only coexist in a society but also enrich and enliven each other. There are pretentious elements

Figure 19.2. Charlie Chaplin is now well established as a comic genius, typically with a poignant or sharp-eyed message. *Modern Times* uses entertaining visuals to show the effects of industrialization on the individual.

of class culture, just as there are products of genuine quality that emerge from mass culture.

"Class" products and artifacts that reach a mass audience through the mass media—Jacques Cousteau's TV documentaries, James Reston's newspaper columns, or Stanley Kubrick's films—prove that a growing number of people have a taste for quality at a price they can afford. By the same token, mass-produced or mass-communicated culture that acquires unexpected quality—Charlie Chaplin's little tramp, Red Smith's sports columns, the Beatle's rock recordings, or Rod Sterling's "Twilight Zone" TV series—proves that what moves the masses often has genuine and long-lasting quality.

Popular culture, or popular arts, might be best regarded as *current* culture. In every culture, much of what came to be considered as art began as entertainment. New movements in art emerged out of a rejection or modification of the art that came before it. It always takes a period of time before any new art is accepted. New art forms are often enjoyed by audiences long before they are recognized by critics. So it is with the content of mass communication.

ANALYZING WHAT ENTERTAINS US

One scholar, Michael Real, has suggested that we live in a "mass-mediated culture." A central question suggests itself here. How do we make sense of the mass media that bombard our consciousness and vie for a portion of our day? More specifically, how can we analyze, interpret, and understand the works presented by the media—what critics call *texts*?

The kinds of interpretation and analysis that scholars make of films, television programs, and books are not of interest of most people. What does interest them is whether a film is worth going to or a television program is worth watching or taping. In the case of films, for example, most people rely on the work of reviewers, primarily journalists, who tell their audiences something about a new film—who's in it, what it's about, how good the acting is. As convenient as these types of reviews and news stories are to us as consumers, they rarely focus on the larger picture. It is the kind of criticism that studies and describes things such as aesthetics, psychological effects, social values, and other elements contained in media art that helps us see and evaluate the effect of content on us. It can educate audiences, make constructive response to communicators, and in general help define what has "worth" for us as individuals and as a culture.

There are, it should be pointed out, a number of controversies and sources of confusion that relate to how we criticize texts and the media. The term *text* will be used here primarily to refer to a specific work of popular art—a film, television program, radio show, novel, or even a commercial. The term *genre* will be used for *kinds* of texts. Genres will be discussed later in this chapter. At this point, it is enough simply to remember that in the case of television, for example, we find news shows, sports programs, game shows, talk shows, soap operas, action-adventures, commentaries, dramas, documentaries, and many other genres.

Even the term *criticism* is somewhat vague and misunderstood. Being "critical" doesn't mean being negative (a common connotation of the word). As we shall understand it, *criticism involves any means of evaluating, analyzing, or interpreting a work of art, a genre, or the media.*

Evaluation

It is relatively easy to evaluate a work—we like it or we don't like it, and there is no disputing taste. All of us are critics, as when we see a film, for instance, and talk about it with our friends. We usually give a general evaluation of the film and talk about specific aspects of it—the acting, the plot, the dialogue, the theme, and what it reflects about society, among other things. We may like part of the film and dislike other parts; we may be confused by the film; we may consider the emotional impact of the film. This is a personal kind of criticism and tends to be based on preferences and unconscious emotional reactions. The same applies to other experiences we have—attending rock concerts, football games, plays, or reading romance novels or detective stories.

This kind of criticism is not far removed from that found in newspapers, radio, or television—journalistic criticism. Journalistic reviewing ranges from relatively short articles in daily newspapers and comments on radio to long sophisticated reviews in weekly magazines such as *The New Yorker*. (There are also a number of journals devoted to film reviewing and criticism, such as *Film Quarterly*, which are often quite recondite.) Reviewers and columnists primarily evaluate the *performance* qualities of specific works or events, such as a concert or a television show. They address us as consumers of culture and have an effect on our decisions whether to see a film, buy a book or a recording. It might even be suggested that critics function as "advertisers" of texts in one respect and as entertainers in another, even when they are hostile and give negative reviews. Many people rely on critics, but what do we do when critics disagree with one another, which often happens?

Actually, in the largest sense, it is not terribly important whether we *like* a text or not. What is important is whether we can discover *the way the text generates meaning, how it works as a creative effort*, and whether we can say anything interesting about its social, political, and cultural implications and effects. We need to look at criticism on a more scholarly level. Such criticism does not destroy our appreciation of texts but enhances our appreciation of them since it reveals the complexity of works of art and the remarkable ways they achieve their effects. It does this by using specific techniques of analysis and interpretation.

Analysis

Analysis involves taking something apart and examining the different pieces to see how they relate to and function with one another. When critics talk about analyzing a text, such as a situation comedy, they usually mean looking at an episode of the show (though some critics argue that the text is really the series itself). In analyzing a situation comedy (and by extension, any filmed or broadcast text) when we function as critics, we look at such matters as acting, dialogue, action, attitudes and values, setting, lighting, sound, and other aesthetic aspects. We decide what are the most important *elements* in a particular kind of text and then examine them in detail.

Consider, for example, Stanley Kubrick's celebrated and controversial film *2001*, which has been dealt with in a slender book, *Filmguide to 2001: A Space Odyssey*

Figure 19.3. *2001* is a fascinating subject for criticism. The use of silence alone has been studied so that we can intellectually grasp what it is that entertains.

by Carolyn Geduld. She discusses the film in a long essay, fittingly entitled "Analysis," and deals with everything from Kubrick's fascination with the number 4 to the music, cutting, kinds of shots, and themes found in the film.

INTERPRETATION

Analysis is different from interpretation, which involves the application of some discipline, methodology, or body of knowledge to a text to show how the text communicates to people, to draw inferences about how it might *affect* them (both as individuals and as part of society), to consider its ideological messages or ethical status; one could go on and on.

Different kinds of critics, with different methodologies, interpret texts in different ways. At times, as a matter of fact, even critics with the same discipline or methodology see different things in the text. This is because texts are so incredibly complex and the process of creation and communication so involved that there is room for many interpretations.

A classic example of this would be *Hamlet*. Countless books and articles have been written by historians, philosophers, psychiatrists, Marxists, to cite just a few, that attempt to understand why Hamlet acted as he did and why the play has such an impact upon people. Another example would be James Bond, the hero of a number of spy novels and films. Marxist critics have focused on Bond as an ideological spokesman for capitalism; psychoanalytic critics have dealt with the Oedipal relation between Bond and "M"; while feminist critics have been primarily interested in Bond's relationships with women.

Critics, then, always have some kind of a *position or belief structure* that informs or animates their work. One doesn't just criticize. You are a psychoanalytic critic, a semiotic critic (semiotics is the study of signs and representations), sociological critic, a Marxist critic, a Freudian or Jungian critic, an ethical critic, a feminist critic, or some combination of disciplines such as a Freudian-Marxist or a semiotic-feminist-Freudian. Why one rather than another? Because each critic believes that a particular method or combination of methods most completely and satisfactorily explains what is going on in a text.

CRITICISM IS AN ART, NOT A SCIENCE

There is no science of criticism, just as there is no science of creativity. What complicates matters even more is that the creators of texts don't completely understand what they are doing or what they have done. Creativity is as much a mystery to creative people as it is to psychologists and other researchers who study creativity and to critics who interpret their works.

Most of the scholars in universities focus their attention on the so-called elite art forms, which have high status. Scholars in communications departments (and allied departments such as journalism and broadcasting) investigate "popular" art forms, which have, because of the aesthetic limitations of many of the texts they study, little status in the academic world. It might however be argued that some texts carried by the mass media pose more complicated problems than literary texts since we often have to deal also with auditory and visual phenomena. In any case, the important point is, all critics—regardless of orientation—use a similarly thorough method. Let us consider some of the basic critical approaches, bearing in mind we are here studying specific programs or texts, not the medium per se. Each of these in turn sharpens our perception of codes, of communicators' motivations, of manipulation of the pictures inside our heads, and of the synergies among communicator, content, and audience.

SEMIOTIC ANALYSIS

Semiotics is the science of signs, a *sign* being anything that can be used to represent or stand for something else. Facial expression is a sign. Some other signs are teeth, hair color, hairstyle, clothing, body language. Words are signs, and of course we conventionally understand as signs objects with drawings and letters on them. In truth, for semioticians, everything is a sign, and men and women are sign-generating, sign-interpreting animals. As might be expected, some signs are more important than others.

Semiotics attempts to discern the way people use signs and to offer a science that explains how signs function. From this perspective, a film or television show (or any text) is a collection or system of signs; not just words but setting, costuming, lighting, editing, and camera shots all communicate messages to viewers.

It is generally agreed that the modern science of semiotics is based on the work of two men—the Swiss linguist Ferdinand de Saussure and the American philosopher Charles S. Peirce. They had different systems of analysis, but their interest in signs led to the development of semiotics as we now know it.

SAUSSURE AND THE NOTION OF CONCEPTS

Saussure divided signs into two parts: the *signifier*, a sound-image, and a *signified*, a concept. A smile, for example, would be a good signifier of "happiness," its signified. The relationship between the *signifier* and *signified* is arbitrary and based on convention. This means that a word and what it stands for are related only by convention; there is no natural or logical connection between them. That explains why dictionaries are always changing. Word usage changes as time passes.

Since this relationship between sounds or images and what they stand for is

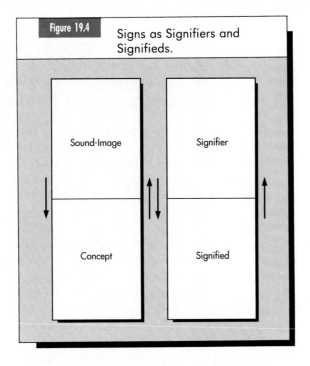

Figure 19.4 Signs as Signifiers and Signifieds.

Sound-Image

Concept

Signifier

Signified

conventional, a communicator can encode a message with some confidence. A code is a system of rules or conventions that tells us how to interpret signs. We learn about "power dressing," the clothes to wear for interviews or similar occasions. From a semiotic perspective, this is an example of code in action. A film or television director uses these codes to cue viewers into certain attributes of his performers. To cite an obvious example, if a male actor opens his mouth and we see two fangs, we know we are dealing with a vampire figure. And the lighting is a powerful sign; horror stories generally take place in the dark and are full of mysterious shadows and forms, while situation comedies are more brightly lit.

Saussure offers another important insight. Concepts do not have meaning by themselves; their meaning is based on some established system of relationships. And the most important relationship, for all practical purposes, is that of opposition. That is, a concept is defined by what it is not, contrasted to other concepts. "Rich" has meaning only if there is "poor," "sad" if there is "happy," and so on. In making these oppositions, one must find a true opposition, not a negation such as "happy" and "unhappy."

Peirce's System of Signs

Peirce suggested that there are three kinds of signs—icon, index, and symbol—and that each communicates in different ways.

Kind of sign:	ICON	INDEX	SYMBOL
Signify by:	resemblance	causal connection	convention
Process:	can see	can figure out	must learn
Examples:	pictures, photographs	smoke/fire	flags, words

Figure 19.5.
Nothing more
needs to be
said.

An icon communicates by resembling something (for example, a photo resembles a person); an index communicates by establishing some kind of a causal connection between things (for example, smoke indicates fire); and a symbol communicates by convention (one must learn what a given sign, such as a flag or word, means).

Peirce differed with Saussure in believing that icons and indexes were not arbitrary; only symbols were arbitrary. His system is particularly useful in analyzing texts that have visual components. For example, advertisements and commercials are full of signs that are used to communicate various meanings to viewers. Thus, smiles on the faces of people using a given product are indexes of happiness and satisfaction. When someone holds up a package of cereal for us to see, that is iconic communication. Using semiotics, we can understand how these signs function with much greater precision than we could before this science developed.

Signs can be looked upon as means of conveying information quickly and economically. Thus a large Mercedes Benz is associated with wealth, and a person shown driving one is assumed to be wealthy. Signs can lie, and the person driving the car may have stolen it or may be leasing it. We always have to be on guard when interpreting signs. When using these methods, one relies upon the store of information people have in their minds to do much of the work. Most people know that a Mercedes Benz costs a great deal of money, which means that only wealthy people can afford them, so they function as signifiers of wealth. This is very useful for companies advertising products that are ''upscale,'' products directed to elite elements in the population. That is why advertising uses metaphors, to communicate by comparison, a great deal of the time. It is very efficient . . . as long as the audience can "decode" the commercial correctly.

Peirce believed that everything in the universe functions as a sign, which means that semiotics becomes the master discipline for discerning meaning. Before the development of semiotics, film and television texts tended to be analyzed primarily in terms of their sociological and political content. Content tended to be the main focus, and the *ways* particular films or television programs communicated were neglected.

Semiotics gave critics a new topic—how meaning is generated in life and by extension, in works of art. This has become a central focus in literary study and in mass-media criticism (though semiotics is often used in conjunction with other methodologies or domains such as psychoanalytic, Marxist, or feminist thought). The focus, then, is on how a text generates meaning and the various ways people "read" or "decode" the text. Not everyone decodes a text the same way or as the creator of the text expected, and this problem of aberrant decoding is particularly

Figure 19.6. This illustration is both icon and symbol. It is clearly a resemblance of the top of a house, but the device on top illustrates a symbol graphically: it is an alphabet letter as communicated by an optical telegraph invented by Claude Chappe during the French Revolution.

Figure 19.7. The use of sophisticated art brings the message of airline service to its target audience.

problematic with mass-mediated texts. Some critics, such as the Italian semiotician and novelist Umberto Eco, argue that the role of the "reader" is crucial and that audiences play a more important part in the creative process than they have been given credit for in the past.

PSYCHOANALYTIC CRITICISM

This method uses the insights of Sigmund Freud and other thinkers such as Carl Jung and Erik Erikson. These thinkers all had theories about how the human mind functions; these theories can be used to interpret such matters as the creative process and the motivations of characters in stories.

Psychoanalytic critics assume that the human psyche is divided into three spheres: consciousness, preconsciousness, and the unconscious. An iceberg would be a good way of representing this, as is shown in Figure 19.8

The realm we describe as consciousness is that relatively small element of the iceberg that shows above the water. It is the part of our psyches that we are aware of. Just below it is the thin preconsciousness area, which is somewhat perceptible. But the major part of the psyche is the unconscious, which is not accessible to us. All of our experiences are stored there and have an effect on us. From the psy-

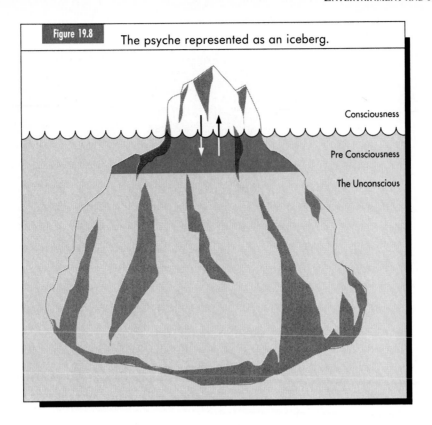

Figure 19.8 The psyche represented as an iceberg.

choanalytic perspective, works of art resonate with this unconscious material, and it may be that works of art communicate from the unconscious of the artist to the unconscious of the artist's audience.

THE OEDIPUS COMPLEX

One celebrated example of this may be cited. Freud believed that we all experience in our early years (around the age of three) "Oedipal" strivings: We wish to have the undivided attention and love of our parent of the opposite sex. He called this phenomenon the Oedipus complex because it resembled what was shown in the myth of Oedipus, the Greek hero who unwittingly killed his father and married his mother. In most people, these Oedipal strivings, which are unconscious, are resolved and do not cause trouble. But in some people, they are not resolved and have a major impact on their lives. These buried strivings, Freud suggests, explain why we are so moved when we see Sophocles' play *Oedipus Rex*, which is based on the Oedipus myth, or works where the connection is not as evident, such as Shakespeare's *Hamlet*. We *recognize* the compulsions the characters feel because we've "been there" ourselves.

This theory is controversial, and many people regard it (and Freud's theories in general) as sheer nonsense. On the other hand, the Oedipus complex has been used by critics to interpret a wide range of media entertainment. For example, as Mark Rubinstein has stated in "The Fascinating King Named Kong":

Figure 19.9. Through the centuries, staging of classics such as *Hamlet* and *Oedipus Rex* have striven to reflect contemporary interpretations and psychological overtones.

It should be clearer now, at least to those who have seen the movie of 1933, why the story of King Kong has the power to move us the way it does. It not only retells certain basic myths of human society and religion, but it also recounts stories of our childhood passions and development.[2]

The Id, Ego and Superego

In later years, Freud developed another theory of the psyche based on an unconscious conflict that goes on, he argues, in all people—between the id and superego aspects of their personalities. The id, described by Freud as "a cauldron full of seething excitations," is characterized by impulse and the desire for sensual gratifications of various kinds. The superego is represented by parental influence, conscience, and restraint. The id says, "I want it now," and the superego says, "Don't do it, or you'll be sorry." The id provides energy and is necessary, but if it is not restrained, we cannot accomplish anything. The superego provides restraint, but if not controlled, overwhelms us all with guilt. All these forces operate, generally speaking, at the unconscious level.

Mediating between the id and superego is the ego, that agency in the human psyche that, Freud says, "stands for reason and good sense." It helps us relate to the environment and preserve ourselves. If the ego can maintain a decent balance between id and superego, all is well, but if either the id or superego becomes dominant, all kinds of problems follow.

DEFENSE MECHANISMS

The ego uses a number of different "defense mechanisms" to maintain a semblance of balance and ward off anxieties. In making a psychoanalytic interpretation of a text, we presumably see the characters using a number of these mechanisms. Some of the more important of them are

Ambivalence: feeling opposite emotions, such as love and hate, for the same person at the same time.

Avoidance: refusing to deal with subjects that distress us because they are connected to unconscious aggressive or sexual impulses.

Fixation: an obsessive attachment to something or someone, usually as the result of a traumatic experience.

Identification: a strong attachment to and desire to become like someone.

Projection: attributing to someone else our hostile or negative feelings.

Reaction Formation: a flip-flopping of feelings that involves suppressing one element of an ambivalent attitude and maximizing the other.

Repression: unconsciously barring instinctual desires from consciousness; generally considered the most basic defense mechanism.

Suppression: consciously deciding to put something out of mind; this is the second most basic defense mechanism.

Rationalization: offering reasons to justify behavior that is motivated by unconscious and irrational forces.

Regression: return (generally for short periods) to earlier stages of development to avoid stress and anxiety.

Understanding these concepts and theories gives us ways of understanding the behavior of characters in drama and fiction as well as interpreting other kinds of mass-mediated texts. For example, in "Star Trek," we find three main characters, each of whom tends to represent one aspect of the psyche. Thus Spock, who has no emotions and represents pure rationality, can be seen as an ego figure. McCoy, on the other hand, is very emotional and is an id figure. And Captain Kirk, who runs things, is a superego figure. (His name is, interestingly, close to the German word for church, *kirche*.) Cop shows and films deal with police (superego) figures and criminals (id) figures. Darth Vader, the horrible villain in *Star Wars*, has repressed his paternal feelings about his son Luke and his humanity, and is fixated on gaining power. James Bond deals with villains who are usually fixated on controlling the world; they tend to be older men who capture Bond and torture him but are ultimately defeated by Bond, who then makes love to a beautiful woman. The Oedipal aspects of these relationships are obvious.

Psychoanalytic criticism rests upon the assumption that we are not aware of all that is in our minds and that we are often governed by forces and motivations beyond our consciousness. Freud's goal was a noble one; he wished to rescue us from being dominated by unconscious id forces, which often function in destructive ways. He summed this up in his famous statement "Where Id was, there Ego shall be." He created a science of psychoanalysis that has been used by sociologists, historians, anthropologists, and critics of both "elite" literature and the mass media.

Figure 19.10. "Star Trek" not only has generations of viewers, but invites a variety of critical approaches.

MARXIST ANALYSIS

This kind of criticism applies the basic ideas of Marx and Engels (as well as other Marxists) to texts and to media in general. Marxist thought, like all thought, is constantly being reinterpreted, but there are certain concepts that most Marxists would agree are central to his philosophy. Here are key ideas that are most relevant to our study of the mass media.

DIALECTICAL MATERIALISM

It is the economic relations in a given society and the institutions that stem from these economic relations—education, the church, the legal system, and the arts—that shape people's consciousness. As Marx wrote:

> *The mode of production of material life determines the general character of the social, political and spiritual processes of life. It is not the consciousness of men that determines their being but, on the contrary, their social being determines their consciousness.*[3]

Materialism argues that social arrangements, not ideas, are crucial. Other thinkers, known as "idealists," have argued that ideas play the major role in determining how societies develop.

Marx recognized that ideas play an important role, but he suggested that these ideas don't arise spontaneously but are consequences of economic, political, and social arrangements.

Class Conflict

Marx saw society as made up of two classes at war with each other. These are the *proletariat*, the great mass of workers who have nothing but their labor to sell and are grievously exploited, and the *bourgeoisie*, who exploit the masses, own the means of production, and want to maintain the status quo. Eventually, Marx believed, things would get so bad that the proletariat would revolt, destroy the bourgeoisie, and create a classless society in which the means of production are owned and managed by the masses.

Marx wrote: "The history of all hitherto existing society is the history of class struggle."[4] Socioeconomic class is the central aspect of social relations. The bourgeoisie tries to convince the proletariat that stratification and inequality are natural (unchangeable), and not the result of historical accident or chance. Or, as in America, the so-called ruling class tries to convince the masses that everyone is "more or less" middle class and that we live in a classless (all middle-class) society. How does it do this? In great part through the mass media, which the ruling class controls and which it uses to spread "false consciousness."

False Consciousness

According to Marx, "the ideas of the ruling class are, in every age, the ruling ideas; i.e., the class which is the dominant *material* force in society is at the same time its dominant *intellectual* force."[5] This means that the ruling class, by controlling the media, has a profound influence on the ideas of the masses. According to this thesis, the ideas people have are the ideas the ruling classes want them to have, and people only have the illusion that their ideas are their own. Marxists use the term *ideology* to stand for a coherent body of social and political beliefs that explain how society operates. What the media spread (even though those who work in them may not be doing so consciously) is an ideology that is always favorable to the ruling classes.

Alienation

Capitalist societies can produce goods in great abundance, but they also generate a great deal of alienation since they pit everyone against everyone else. Alienation is seen as the central problem of capitalist societies; people become estranged from one another and, ultimately, from themselves. They indulge in various attempts to escape from alienation but cannot succeed in doing so.

This produces a sense of misery and unhappiness that is functional for the ruling classes since the masses try to assuage their unhappiness by compulsively buying things and this generates great profits for the ruling classes. This phenomenon is called consumer lust, one of the ultimate consequences of alienation. All of this is not directly recognized by the people afflicted. And alienation afflicts all elements of society, according to Marx. It is not limited to the proletariat.

Many people are "bought off" by being able to purchase things, but the gap between the rich and the poor keeps widening, and revolution ensues. What the ruling classes attempt to do is hold off the revolution, which they are able to do for a while. But ultimately there must be a revolution and the end of classes and the ideological domination of one sector of society over the general public.

EXAMPLES OF MARXIST CRITICISM

When Marxist critics analyze a text or speculate about the media in general, they look for the ways the ideology of the ruling class is embedded and hidden in films, television programs, newspaper stories, sports, and various other aspects of popular and elite culture. They believe ideology indoctrinates people when they consume mass media. Some Marxist critics have suggested, for example, that Disney creations have, without their readers and viewers of the cartoons being aware of it, spread American capitalist ideologies all over the world. According to this notion, as spelled out in a book by Ariel Dorfman and Armand Matellart, *How to Read Donald Duck* (International General Publishers), the values found in Disney's comics and other creations are unconsciously absorbed by people and ultimately shape their view of politics and life. Others have suggested that "Star Trek" has a hidden capitalist bias; the ship is called the *Enterprise*, and it travels the cosmos "freeing" captive peoples and spreading American-style democracy and values.

It is the function of Marxist media critics to point out to people that they are being indoctrinated and to show how this insidious process works in particular texts. Marxist critics do not necessarily believe in violent revolution; they simply find Marx's concepts useful in criticizing texts and the media, often in conjunction with other methods of analysis such as semiotics or psychoanalytic thought. There is good reason to argue that all texts have ideological dimensions to them, even though the creators of these works aren't aware of what they are doing and the consumers of these texts aren't aware that an attempt is being made to indoctrinate them with bourgeois ideas and values.

SOCIOLOGICAL CRITICISM

Sociology focuses its attention on groups and institutions, and is concerned with social interactions of people or collectivities rather than the psyches of individuals, the realm of psychology. Of course, there are many aspects of sociology: deviant behavior and processes of social control, the family, social mobility, population, social change, race and ethic relations, power—and of particular interest to us, collective behavior and mass communications.

Sociologists have developed a number of concepts which can be used to analyze and criticize the media texts or the media in general. A sociological critic would interpret a dramatic production, for example, in terms of the roles of the characters (and whether they are stereotyped), their values, the social classes of different characters and how that social class is portrayed. When looking at the media in general, sociological critics might make content analyses to determine such things as how groups are portrayed, what groups are underrepresented or overrepresented, and the roles that women are given.

MAIN CONCEPTS

Some of the sociological concepts relevant to the mass media are discussed below.

Anomie. This is based on the Greek term *nomos*, which means "norms." Anomic people lack norms and don't accept the conventions of society. They are not necessarily alienated since they may belong to strong groups. Urban gangs are anomic but not alienated.

Class. A class is a group with something in common. As we conventionally use the term, we are concerned with socioeconomic class, which involves where a person or group of people belong in the class structure. The standard indicators of class are wealth, education, occupation, and family. Class is important because it is connected to lifestyles, values, and status. We tend to feel that once we locate people in a particular class, we know a good deal about them.

"All in the Family" is a good example of the way working-class (in this case, lower-middle-class) people are often portrayed on television. Archie Bunker was a "lovable bigot," and though the show was created to ridicule racism, sexism, and anti-Semitism, surveys showed that large numbers of people said they agreed with Archie Bunker. Upper-middle-class professional people tend to be overrepresented in television, and ethnic minorities, working-class people, and women have been underrepresented; this, many sociologists believe, gives these people negative self-images.

Ethnicity. This refers to the various groups that share origins abroad or other distinguishing characteristics. For many years (and still, to varying degrees), ethnic groups were presented in negative and stereotyped ways in the media, in contrast to white Anglo-Saxon Protestants (WASPs), who were portrayed as the standard to which everyone should aspire.

Race. This refers to the genetic heritage of people. Physical anthropologists suggest that there are three broad classes of races: Negroid, Mongoloid, and Caucasoid. Different racial groups, especially blacks, have until very recently been portrayed in negative and destructive ways in the media.

Sex. When we discuss sex sociologically, we are really talking about gender,

Figure 19.11. "All in the Family" has been closely watched by sociology-minded critics.

whether one is a male or a female. The development of feminism in recent years may be thought of as an attempt by women to change the patterns of expectations many people (women as well as men) have about how women are supposed to behave, what roles they are to play. Feminists are incensed about the sexism that pervades society, especially how women are treated and seen by males and the inequality that exists in the workplace.

Thus, sociologist Gaye Tuchman has written an essay, "The Symbolic Annihilation of Women by the Mass Media," that argues that television proclaims that women don't count for much.[6] Other critics have commented about the "sexploitation" found in programming, in many print advertisements, television commercials, and, most particularly, in MTV. Since some young girls "model" their behavior on the images of women they see in television and films, these images have profound social consequences.

Social Role. As we grow up in society, we are "socialized," or taught to play specific roles in various situations. Thus a person may play the role of student in the morning, worker in the afternoon, and parent in the evening. Roles are based on expectations shaped by a person's place in society or some group. Thus, an instructor plays a different role in a university than a dean, and women are given certain kinds of roles in the media that many people find destructive and demeaning.

Status. Status always involves some kind of ranking within some organization or entity and the prestige and power that is associated with one's ranking. Status is different from role, though role is obviously affected by status. A general obviously has much more status than a private and plays a different role. Status is generally connected to occupation. The occupations with the greatest prestige in American society are professional—doctors, lawyers, bankers, and professors. Status is not strictly based on money; a plumber may make more money than a clergyman, but that doesn't confer higher status.

We see people with high status playing major roles in many soap operas such as "Dallas" and "Dynasty," which are about the lives of rich and powerful (often unscrupulous) business people. Programs such as "The Cosby Show" and "thirtysomething" are peopled with doctors and lawyers, business leaders and others with high status; we don't have many television programs about low-status people such as plumbers or factory workers (except, perhaps, in situation comedies such as "Roseanne" where the characters tend to be people we laugh at).

Stereotypes. Stereotypes (parts of the "pictures inside our heads") are images of groups or categories of people that are widely shared. These stereotypes tend to be negative and often are destructive, though there are some stereotypes that are positive (the selfless country doctor from the good old days). Many Americans share ridiculous notions about blacks, Jews, Asians, women, doctors, and lawyers, to name some of the more commonly stereotyped groups. Stereotypes commonly involve occupations, ethnicity, gender, and race, and are based on generalizations that do not take individual differences into account.

Topical Analysis. Often sociological critics take some topic, such as violence or stereotypes of Jews or blacks, to investigate. Content analysis is a research technique that usually involves counting the amount of something in some sampling of the media. It is assumed that this sampling is representative so that valid generalizations can be made from an analysis of the results. It is further assumed that we can know about people by analyzing the content of the media they consume.

Values. This term refers to general beliefs and attitudes about life—what is good and what is bad, what is important and what is unimportant. Values are important because they help shape our behavior. Sociologists studying the media would concern themselves with the values of the main characters in various texts. What are these values? Are they positive and worth inculcating in young people, or are they negative and destructive?

As an example, consider the values of J. R. Ewing in "Dallas." He is unscrupulous, he lies and cheats, he abuses people, and his relationships with women are unsatisfactory to say the least. He is the main character in one of the most popular American television programs of recent years, one that is seen all over the world (and that may lead to stereotypes about what Americans are like). He is presented as a villain, of course, but he is the center of attention, and it is possible that many young people find him and his lifestyle appealing.

CRITICISM TAKES EFFORT

Readers of works in print and broadcast and film audiences are often not aware of all that transpires during their experiences with texts. When we watch a film, we want to be entertained, and thus we don't subject the film to the kind of effort it takes to make a critical interpretation. And the kinds of things discussed by semioticians, Marxists, psychoanalytic, and sociological critics seem farfetched to many people. This stems from a lack of training in the various methodologies used in making serious interpretations of texts and from the fact that this discipline often uses terminology that is arcane and far removed from the everyday concerns of the average person. But the concepts we've explored here can at least begin to arm you to be more perceptive about specific works. Now we turn to genres, or kinds of works.

ASPECTS OF GENRE CRITICISM

Generally speaking, when we discuss film, television, or radio, unless we are dealing with the aesthetics or social impact of these media, we are talking about the *kinds* of programs or films associated with them—that is, about specific genres. There are a limited number of kinds of programs or genres, and many of those found on television were found earlier on film and radio. In the early days of moviemaking, certain types of presentation evolved both because the public enjoyed westerns, melodramas, action films and because studios needing to produce one or two features a week depended on formulas. We have seen how radio came of age with the first serial, "Amos 'n Andy," which spawned dozens of formula comedies and soaps, the continuing backbone of television programming.

The focus of the genre critic is to gain better insights into the nature of genres in general and specific genres, whether romances or talk shows. Genre is one of the more important ways we have of understanding texts and the media that carry them. Knowing the conventions of a genre helps make sense of a work within it. Network television genres are especially rich in conventions; because programs are directed toward large audiences, they cannot be too inventive. Each genre, has certain elements of form, content, and style that are expected and that distinguish it from others.

In *The Six-Gun Mystique*, John Cawelti deals with one of the most important genres of the 1960s, the western. Westerns, he says, are very formulaic; they take place at a certain location (on the edge of civilization) at a certain time period; have specific kinds of heroes, heroines, and villains; and have certain plot characteristics (the chase, the gunfight) that most everyone is familiar with. He suggests that the difference between popular genres and avant-garde art works involves the matter of convention versus invention. Avant-garde works are high on invention and low on convention, and thus pose "problems" to audiences. Popular genres are high on convention and low on invention, and thus are easily understood by large numbers of people. There are various subcategories of westerns, but in the days when westerns were popular (and they once dominated television), people learned these subcategories rather quickly.

There is also a logic to all narratives or dramas that we learn from one of our earliest experiences with them—fairy tales. There are heroes who have to do some task or defeat a villain (or both); there are heroines who inspire the heroes; there are helpers for the heroes and the villains, and various other characters who appear and reappear, even though they may have slightly different roles.

A Russian scholar, Vladimir Propp, made a study of a number of Russian fairy tales and discovered that they were all similar. From these stories he elicited a number of "functions," which he defined as an act of a character seen in terms of its significance for the story. These functions, Propp suggested, were the building blocks of all narratives. He found more than 30 of these functions in the stories he examined. And they can be found, in modified form, in contemporary stories that have nothing to do with kings and queens, heroes and princesses.

Some of the main functions Propp listed were:

Initial Situation: members of family or hero introduced.
Absentation: a member of family absents self from home.
Interdiction: a member of family is told not to do something.
Villainy: villain does something to member of family.
Mediation: villainy is discovered; hero is sent to fix things.
Difficult Task: a difficult task is proposed for the hero.
Receipt: hero gets a magical agent from a donor figure.
Struggle: hero and villain struggle.
Solution: task is resolved.
Victory: villain is defeated.
Wedding: hero is married, ascends to throne.

With relatively minor modifications, one can apply these functions to a typical James Bond story. He is sent on a mission by M; he is given a "magical agent" (a new gun, a car that flies); he struggles with a powerful villain (usually an older man) who is eventually defeated; and he then makes love with a beautiful woman. The reason Propp's theory works with the Bond stories, and others as well, is that Propp discovered what might be described as the basic elements of narratives.

Dealing with genres is often a complicated matter. Consider, for example, the

Figure 19.12. James Bond takes on new meaning through Marxist, psychoanalytic, and sociological criticism.

number of genres found in a typical newspaper. We find news reports, editorials, opinion essays, comics, sports articles, columns, horoscopes, cartoons, film reviews, art criticism, how-to articles, science reporting, and advertisements, to cite the most common. Thus all media present many different genres to their audiences, who must learn what to expect from each genre and subgenre. As consumers of media who spend enormous periods of time with them, we are all "critics," whether we are aware of it or not.

Focal Points in the Study of Media

We have discussed various ways of analyzing and interpreting texts—works of art carried by the media. We have clarified what we mean by textual criticism. But there are areas other than the work or genre and genre criticism that might be considered, as Figure 19.13 shows.

These include, besides the work of art, the artist (or creator) of a text, the audience of the text, America (or the society in which the text is created), and the medium that carries the work of art. As the diagram shows, all of these focal points can interact with one another, either directly or indirectly.

The Work

The focus here is on the text and the elements in it. As we have seen, various techniques of interpretation are used by critics to explain how the text relates to

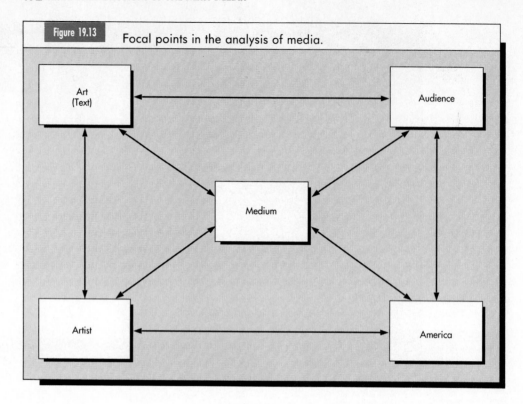

Figure 19.13 Focal points in the analysis of media.

its genre and generates meaning, and to deal with such things as its psychoanalytic and ideological content, and what it reflects about society.

AUTHOR

Critics who focus on the authors of texts are essentially biographical critics who are interested, among other things, in the creative process and in the way texts are produced. In some cases, such as the novel, authorship is not a problem. But who is the real author of a film, a collaborative art form? The screenplay may have been written by three or four people, and it is not what is crucial in films as far as authorship is concerned. Generally speaking, critics have concluded that it is the director who is the "author" in films, and there is a French term used to suggest this—"auteur" criticism, as we have noted.

AUDIENCE

Audiences tend to be studied by sociological critics and other kinds of social scientists. They attempt to determine what effects a text may be having on a given audience (and by implication, society in general). The focus in this kind of media research is directed away from texts to those who "read" and "decode" the texts.

Some researchers do various kinds of content analysis. They assess the degree of violence on television or study images of women, blacks, Jews, or some other group. Generally speaking, it is assumed that the media are powerful and that material carried by the media has important effects on audiences, though much research does not support such conclusions. The subject is one that is continuously debated in scholarly journals.

AMERICA (SOCIETY)

There is a good deal of concern by some critics about how specific texts and the media affect society in general (we explore this in Chapter 23). It is possible to study certain films or television shows that achieve incredible popularity and offer generalizations about what these texts reflect about society and how they may be affecting it. Generally speaking, however, critics dealing with society focus on the media themselves—and particularly on television, the dominant medium of the last 40 years. There have been thousands of books and articles written on various aspects of television, and in 1978 a book, *Television and Human Behavior*, appeared that summarized the findings of 2,500 scientific studies. Since the publication of the book, countless other scientific studies have been made. Researchers seem pretty well convinced that television plays a major role in American society, but when you get to specifics, there are many disagreements.

MEDIUM

There are other critics interested in the media per se. These critics, who tend to focus on film and television, might best be described as media aestheticians. They investigate how different kinds of shots, lighting, and camera work, for example, give a work a distinctive quality. And they are concerned with how viewers react to particular kinds of camera shots, lighting, color, sound, and editing. One important book that focuses specifically on media aesthetics is *Sight, Sound, Motion* by Herbert Zettl. Another, which deals with the subject more broadly, is Arthur Asa Berger's *Seeing Is Believing: An Introduction to Visual Communication*. And there are two classic works by the Russian film director Sergei Eisenstein, *Film Form* and *Film Sense*, which deal with film aesthetics. The main thrust of these books and others like them is that *the medium plays an important role in texts. The channel of communication is not simply a mode of transmission.*

PROBLEMS OF CRITICISM ....

One problem critics face is that when it comes to evaluating and interpreting texts, there are no touchstones or criteria that everyone will accept. People don't even agree about what *art* is. So critics of each persuasion are on their own, making their analyses and interpretations and hoping to show that their approaches and insights are so powerful that they command acceptance. In other words, criticism is like feudalism—there's no central authority that runs things; critics have their own little fortresses and sally forth to interpret texts as they please.

But this is entirely reasonable, since works of art—elite and popular—are complex, and the way they work and their effects are difficult to fathom. When we get really complex works—films and television programs where we have everything to consider, from plot structure to facial expressions of the characters, from dialogue to lighting, from editing techniques to the effects of music—you can see how much a critic has to know and how complicated criticism can be.

Furthermore, tastes change from period to period, as do how we relatively value the various media. And there are considerable differences in taste in any society at any given time, due to such things as levels of education and sophistication, socioeconomic class, ethnicity, and differences in generations. As people get older, their individual tastes sometimes change. The teenager who listens to rock and roll all day may end up liking symphonies and opera or listening to "elevator-music" radio stations when older. In theory, the critical methodologies discussed above should be able to offer insights to explain why we like what we like when we like it. But understanding people and their tastes is even more difficult than understanding media or art.

Another issue is the difference in the "tools" we bring to analysis, interpretation, and evaluation. The more we know, the more we "see" in works of popular culture. For example, if we do not know history, we miss allusions to people and events in the past, and if we haven't read much literature, we don't notice parodies of famous works or references to famous characters from mythology, literature, or other arts. If we lack information about psychology and politics, we often cannot understand why certain characters in stories act as they do.

There's a very funny film called *Der Dove* that is a spoof of the work of Ingmar Bergman, the great Swedish film director. If you've never seen any of Bergman's films, you can't fully appreciate *Der Dove* and see how it parodies Bergman's style. *Apocalypse Now*, based on *The Heart of Darkness*, a work by the English novelist Joseph Conrad, has also been parodied in a film called *Porklips Now*. If you don't know the Conrad work, you can't understand everything that happens in *Apocalypse Now*, and if you've not seen *Apocalypse*, you can't appreciate *Porklips Now*.

Figure 19.14. The film *Apocalypse Now* generates tremendous power by not stereotyping the Vietnamese. This document of the Vietnam War, which is based on Joseph Conrad's novel *Heart of Darkness*, is itself parodied in *Porklips Now*.

There are some critics who argue that all works are based on and draw their inspiration from works that were created earlier, a theory known as *intertextuality*.

The moral of this story is that critics have to know a great deal about history, literature, social thought, and the arts to make sense of the mass media and the texts they carry. Critics must be able to see how specific works are connected to works and genres, and to social and political events. Media criticism is an exciting enterprise and somewhat like a game; critics are like detectives, searching for clues that will reveal the "true meaning" of texts and the way these texts reflect and affect the societies in which they are found. The works carried by the media may seem simple and may be limited from an aesthetic viewpoint. But if looked at in terms of the way they generate meaning and their impact on individuals and society, they pose profound and very complicated problems for the critic of the mass media.

SUMMARY

Americans use the media as entertainment in periods of recreation and leisure. Considerable debate has taken place over the value and effects of mass-media entertainment/art in our culture and society. Each medium has limitations that determine how much and what kinds of entertainment it can provide. Some media are essentially purveyors of mass culture, others of more elite culture. The media and the audiences tend to be selective and seek one another out. Traditionally, media critics have talked about lowbrow, middlebrow, and highbrow culture, with the popular media usually relegated to the lowest level. An objective opinion, however, would judge entertainment by its overall qualities, not by how large an audience it attracts. Criticism involves any means of evaluating, analyzing, or interpreting a work of art, a genre, or the media. All of us are critics; our reactions to a media product are shaped by our individual tastes. Journalistic critics assist us in making consumer decisions. But scholarly critics are not concerned with whether they like a product. What is important to them is the way the product generates meaning as well as how it works as a creative effort.

Analysis involves taking something apart and examining the different pieces to see how they relate to one another. Interpretation is the application of a certain methodology to criticize a product. Critics have a belief structure already in mind as they consider a work, one that they believe is most effective in considering what goes on in a text.

From the semiotic perspective, a text (a specific work) is a collection or system of signs: In addition to the performers' words, there is setting, costuming, lighting, editing, camera work—all of which communicate a message to the viewer. Signs are a method of conveying information quickly and economically, but a communicator must remember that not everyone decodes signs the same way.

Psychoanalytic critics apply the insights of Sigmund Freud and others who assume that the human psyche is divided into the conscious (which we are aware of), the preconscious (which is somewhat perceptible), and the unconscious (which is not accessible to us). These critics believe that most media affect us through the subconscious, where our "real" forces and motivations are stored.

Marxist analysis applies the basic ideas of Marxist thought—that society is made up of two classes at war with one another, the proletariat (the great mass of workers with nothing but their labor to sell) and the bourgeoisie (who own the means of production, exploit the workers, and want to maintain the status quo). Marxist critics analyze a text by looking for ways in which this ideology is embedded and hidden within it.

Sociological critics are concerned with the interaction of groups of people rather than the psyches of individuals. They consider how groups of people are portrayed by the media—for example, does a movie show blacks, women, or homosexuals in a poor light?—and how the media's images of groups shape our own beliefs.

Genre criticism involves the grouping of texts into various genres, or types; examples of genres are westerns, dramas, and comedies. Knowing the characteristics of a genre helps to make sense of a work within it.

Critics must consider more than the work itself. There are a number of other analytical focal points, including the creator, the audience, the society in which the work is created, and the medium. Critics must consider how these focal points interact with one another to influence how the work is put together and how it is accepted by the audience. Unfortunately, critics do not know all the answers. Critics disagree with one another, even if they share the same methodology. This is because individual tastes, beliefs, and experiences are different. Understanding the orientations of critics allows us to apply their critical evaluations to our own views of a text, a genre, or the media that produced it.

REFERENCES

1. Wylie Sypher, "Introduction," in *Comedy* (New York: Doubleday, 1956), xvi.
2. In Arthur Asa Berger, *Media USA*, 2nd ed. (New York: Longman, 1990).
3. Karl Marx, *Selected Writings in Sociology and Social Philosophy*, T. C. Bottomore and M. Rubel, eds. (New York: McGraw-Hill, 1964), 51.
4. Ibid., 200.
5. Ibid., 78.
6. Gaye Tuchman, Arlene Kaplan Daniels, and James Benet, eds., *Hearth and Home: Images of Women in the Mass Media* (New York: Oxford University, Press, 1978).

MEDIA ISSUES

T his book opened by pointing out that the changes taking place in the mass media—such as the sheer numbers of competing messages and the pattern of consolidated ownerships—make it even more imperative that we become critical consumers. Concern with the influence of the mass media is not a new development. It has led to formal governmental regulation to varying degrees throughout the world. And it has in this century prompted media institutions and organizations to formulate codes as self-regulation and as efforts to publicize a sense of responsibility. The increasing presence and power of mass media and new forms of communication that we use and interact with does give new importance to a number of basic issues.

The current merging of media organizations and blurring of formats—and the holistic, integrated approach of this book—are borne out through the inevitable interjection of issues into all the preceding chapters. What this final part of *Mass Media VI* does is to put them into perspective for more focused consideration and, we hope, to launch you toward continuing awareness and examination of media effects, of communication that goes beyond the successful delivery of coded content.

We begin with a look at what end users and communicators know is "legal" in the way mass communication operates. Constitutional, federal, state, and local laws and regulations are studied in Chapter 20. From a notion of the freedom of the media we go to what's "right," the personal and organizational decisions that have to incorporate but expand upon rules to approach "wisdom."

In the next two paired chapters, we introduce the complex subject of what we know about the effects of the output of the mass media. These discussions document why limits on press and entertainment freedom can be important. A brief history of communication research leads into views of "mediated" or media-influenced behavior on the individual and society.

Obviously such issues as the power of the media take on larger proportions as global conglomerates become more of a basic factor of the mass media. The concerns raised in Chapter 24 range from border crossing of content and media marketing to the precarious role of national voices and values. We need a sense of comparative media freedoms to be sensitive as well as successful communicators.

We close, appropriately, with an eye to the future. Not only does our concluding chapter synthesize and expand what individual chapters have revealed of emerging technologies—it raises the special issues, notably access and responsibility, inextricably tied to the borderless, lightning quick, often expensive new technologies.

This final part, then, is (just as school graduation is) more properly a commencement.

CHAPTER

20

Government and the Media

It is no surprise that over the years there have been a number of controversies and other legal entanglements involving the mass media and the U.S. government. After all, no other institution is offered the kind of legal protection that the First Amendment to the Constitution provides the press. What regulations there are aim to protect society from damage by the mass media and protect the rights of some media from damage by competing media, individuals, or the state itself.

Freedom of the press is the result of a long struggle for individual rights and freedoms under Anglo-Saxon law. The way was paved by such documents as the Magna Carta of 1215, the Petition of Rights of 1628, the English Bill of Rights of 1689, and the American Declaration of Independence of 1776. In the New World of the American colonies, where both communication and independence were important, freedom of speech and of the press became key elements in the sociopolitical fabric.

The first provision in the 1791 Bill of Rights has provided the basic legal framework for protecting freedom of expression in the United States:

> *Congress shall make no law respecting an establishment of religion, or prohibiting the free exercise thereof; or abridging the freedom of speech, or of the press; or the right of the people peaceably to assemble, and to petition the government for a redress of grievances.*

More exact definitions of "freedom of the press" have been left for courts to decide. And the courts have been more than willing to do so. Through a number of decisions and opinions, they have, for example, expanded the definition of the term *press* to include virtually all the mass media as we know them today. This chapter surveys the landmark decisions that have collectively told us "what's legal." It thus starts our exploration of media issues with a foundation in what the mass media may and may not do. We can then begin to understand what they should and should not do, and why.

INTERPRETATIONS OF THE FIRST AMENDMENT

Just as the courts have refined and clarified the definition of *press*, they have also had to address more substantive issues inherent in this amendment. The range of opinions and views on this topic run from the "absolutist" view that the First Amendment means exactly what it says (i.e., "no law") to those far more willing to accept some laws that could punish the mass media for some types of content, such as potentially libelous or obscene material.

Consultant and authority on content for this chapter is James Hoyt.

Few American jurists have stated the *absolutist position* more strongly than the late Justice Hugo Black. To Black, the words of the amendment were clear, fundamental, and absolute. He interpreted the First Amendment as a command forbidding any restraint on speech and press:

> It is my belief that there are ''absolutes'' in our Bill of Rights, and that they were put there on purpose by men who knew what words meant and meant their prohibitions to be ''absolutes.''[1]

The views of Black and other like-minded justices have been widely embraced by the mass media.

Despite the inherent appeal of such a clear and simple interpretation of the First Amendment, over the years the absolutist view of Justice Black and others has been a minority opinion. The predominant view has been that the First Amendment means somewhat less than it says, that despite its ''no law'' wording there *are* some areas, such as libel, where it is appropriate for action to be taken against the press without clear-cut First Amendment protections.

The prevailing view of these *more limited* First Amendment protections was well articulated by Justice Shirley Abrahamson, of the Wisconsin Supreme Court, at a conference at the University of Wisconsin:

> When I read the First Amendment as an absolutist I find that the amendment only establishes the issues, not the solutions. . . . On its face the amendment restrains only the actions of Congress. That can't be true. We know the First Amendment also restrains the executive and judicial branches of the federal government and it restrains state government. That's because the courts have so interpreted the Constitution. Which laws abridge free press and which do not? Does imposing minimum wage laws or antitrust laws on the press abridge free press? . . . There are laws 1, 2, 3, 4 or 10 stages removed from the central theme of the First Amendment . . . but we cannot deny that each of these laws might have an impact—directly or indirectly—on what is published. What laws which govern all of us should also govern the press?

Figure 20.1. Shifts in societal standards can be reflected in court decisions. Works of art as well as media content were scrutinized in the late 1980s for violation of obscenity and pornography laws.

Because the prevailing legal view is that we should be willing to accept some appropriate limitations on mass-media freedoms, a series of legal actions and other controversies have evolved over the past 200 years. Behind these cases, however, stands a legal presumption that before a legal action can be brought against the mass media, the objectionable material must first have been published or broadcast. That is, the media must first disseminate the potentially libelous (or obscene) message to the public before any legal action becomes appropriate.

But this is not always the case.

CENSORSHIP AND PRIOR RESTRAINT

Censorship, whether prior restraint or suppression of communication by the government, has been held unconstitutional, except regarding motion pictures. Government agencies, both local and national, have from time to time attempted to censor communication, sometimes for the best motives. The Minnesota legislature, for example, passed a "gag law" in the 1920s aimed at restricting newspapers that were "public nuisances," specifically scandal sheets that made scurrilous attacks on the police and minority racial groups. But in its interpretation of the First Amendment, the U.S. Supreme Court found this law illegal. In another ruling, the Supreme Court struck down a state law that would have imposed a tax *only* on newspapers and other publications. The justices said that taxes imposed on other businesses may also be imposed on newspapers and other publications, but taxes that single out the press can be a potential tool for censorship that abridges freedom of the press.

THE QUESTION OF NATIONAL SECURITY

When governments can label communication as a threat, freedom of speech and of the press is in danger. Among the first laws passed by the Congress were the Alien Acts of 1798 and the Sedition Act of 1798. The Sedition Act made it a crime for a newspaper to criticize the government, on the theory that such criticism could harm the new government. This philosophy prevails in many newly independent countries today. But Thomas Jefferson and many others felt that the Alien and Sedition Acts were a clear violation of constitutional rights, and when Jefferson became president, the law expired. The courts have steadily upheld the impunity of the press as goad and critic of government.

Between the demise of the Alien and Sedition Acts and the outbreak of World War I, the American government was reluctant to pass laws that would limit freedoms in order to protect national security. However, as the United States has become a national power with much to protect, as wars have become world wars, and as threats to national security have increased, the American people have allowed the government to make exceptions to freedom of speech and the press during wartime. During World War I, Congress passed the Espionage Act, which made it a crime to publish information that could be used by the enemy against America. The law lapsed when the war ended. A similar act was enacted during World War II, and it too lapsed at war's end. However, with the dawn of the cold war and the nuclear age, Congress felt that national security was again vulnerable, and in 1950, it passed a law that makes it a crime to disclose communications intelligence or to publish classified information concerning the communications-intelligence activities of the United States.

The Pentagon Papers Case

The well-known Pentagon Papers incident in 1971 clearly illustrates the issue of prior restraint. A multivolume Department of Defense study, entitled *History of U.S. Decisionmaking Process on Viet Nam Policy*, although classified as top secret, was leaked to the press. Both the *New York Times* and the *Washington Post* decided to publish stories and excerpts based on the material in the 47 volumes. The Department of Justice obtained a temporary court injunction to prevent publication of the material. Because of its significance, the case quickly went to the Supreme Court. In a 6–3 landmark decision, the Court ruled in favor of the newspapers and freedom of the press.

Although the Court's decision clarified the First Amendment, it did not broaden the protection of freedom. The newspapers hoped that the Court would rule that the First Amendment guaranteed an *absolute* freedom. However, in the Pentagon Papers case the Court held that the government simply had not provided sufficient evidence to justify prior restraint of the publications. This decision, al-

Figure 20.2. The front page of the *Washington Post* the day after the Supreme Court's decision in the Pentagon Papers case.

though widely hailed at the time as a major victory for the press, left the door open for courts to decide how much justification the government must provide to censor a publication.

THE PROGRESSIVE MAGAZINE CASE

Those prior-restraint limits were tested again 8 years later. In 1979, a small magazine, *The Progressive*, based in Madison, Wisconsin, accepted an article from a freelance writer named Howard Morland. The article contained the attention-arresting title: "The H-Bomb Secret: How We Got It, Why We're Telling it." During the prepublication reviewing process, while the article was being checked by various experts for factual accuracy, a copy of the article was sent to the U.S. Department of Justice. In a short time, that department obtained, through a Wisconsin federal judge, a restraining order prohibiting *The Progressive* from publishing the article.

The grounds for the order was that the article contained classified information, in violation of the Atomic Energy Act of 1954, which contains language forbidding all disclosure of nuclear secrets. The magazine, while agreeing to withhold publication, defended the article on the grounds that the information it contained was obtained from public sources and that the article was really about false security and secrecy in the thermonuclear-weapons program; it was not a how-to guide to making an H-bomb.

The magazine was confident in its defense, but it did not have a chance to demonstrate it in court. At the urging of some of the attorneys responsible for prosecuting the case, the Justice Department withdrew the case, and the magazine proceeded to publish the article. In this case, although there was not a formal legal resolution of the charges, the precedent stood that the government, when inclined, could obtain a restraining order that could force a medium to withhold publication, at least for a period of time. That precedent still stands.

In 1985, the government successfully prosecuted its first case against an individual who had disclosed classified information to the media. In this case, a government employee was found guilty of having sold three classified spy-satellite photos to a British defense magazine. As government has grown more cautious about its secrets, it has turned again to the 1950 law, which is still on the books. In 1986, William Casey, director of the CIA, informed the *Washington Post*, the *New York Times*, and NBC News that they could be charged with espionage if they published or broadcast information that was being leaked to the press as a result of several spy trials. It was the first time that a government official had made such an overt official threat against the press and indicates the growing problems in this area of government restriction.

RESTRICTIONS ON ENTERTAINMENT

In 1915, the Supreme Court, in *Mutual Film Corporation v. Industrial Commission of Ohio*, upheld the right of individual states to censor motion pictures, on the ground that they are "a business, pure and simple." They are a "spectacle or show and not such vehicles of thought as to bring them within the press of the country." However, in 1952, a Supreme Court decision changed this ruling somewhat and

Figure 20.3. *The Last Tango in Paris*, with Marlon Brando and Maria Schneider, strained views of what was permissible and was banned in some areas following its release in 1974.

laid the groundwork for increasing freedom for motion pictures. In *Burstyn v. Wilson*, which involved the film *The Miracle*, the Supreme Court stated:

> *We conclude that expression by means of motion pictures is included within the free speech and free press guarantee of the First and Fourteenth Amendments. To the extent that language in the opinion in the Ohio case is out of harmony with the views here set forth, we no longer adhere to it.*

Decisions since then have continually weakened efforts to censor movies. Not a single state now has a movie-censorship board. Of the last four states to have such a board, New York, Kansas, and Virginia phased theirs out in the 1970s, and Maryland's was abolished in 1981. Only a few cities still require motion pictures to be submitted to a board for examination prior to public showing.

When we speak of movie censorship, we are referring primarily to censorship of obscenity, and obscenity is not protected by the First Amendment. For example, Section 223 of the Federal Communications Act makes it illegal for anyone who uses the telephone to make comments or statements that are "obscene, lewd, lascivious, filthy, or indecent." In any case, censorship of obscenity does not give government the right to revoke broadcast licenses. In 1982, a small town in Utah passed an ordinance prohibiting the transmission of pornographic and indecent material over cable TV. A federal judge struck down the ordinance, calling it "overbroad" because it would have threatened revocation of the cable company's license for broadcasting such films. However, in 1983, a Cincinnati cable firm was indicted on obscenity charges for having broadcast adult movies on the Playboy channel.

The Supreme Court has upheld the right of local courts and legislatures to forbid the sale of obscene material. A person who violates a local ordinance against the sale of such material is subject to arrest and punishment. The government has generally held that the morals of the community should be protected by restricting the importation, distribution, and sale of certain types of pornographic communication.

There is widespread confusion over terminology. *Erotica* in the mass media is sexually oriented content that has as its purpose the physical and emotional arousal of the consumer. Books, magazines, and films are the traditional mass media for erotica, but sound recordings, cable television, and videocassettes are active in the distribution process. *Erotica* is a cultural term, whereas the word *pornography* has a legal, albeit vague and arbitrary, definition at times.

Pornography is any obscene material. *Obscenity* is based on legal criteria. In *Miller v. California*, the Supreme Court declared the determination of the existence of obscenity is based on "(a) whether the average person, applying contemporary community standards, would find that the work, taken as a whole, appeals to the prurient interest; (b) whether the work depicts or describes, in a patently offensive way, sexual conduct specifically defined by the applicable state law, and (c) whether the work, taken as a whole, lacks serious literary, artistic, political, or scientific value."

If a book or movie is shown to possess all three characteristics, it is legally obscene; in some communities, the distributor, exhibitor, and seller are liable for prosecution for making such material available to the public. A major change in dealing with pornography was the ruling by the Supreme Court in 1973 that "community standards" are local, not national. This means that something can be erotica in San Francisco but pornography in a small town in the Midwest. In 1987, the Court once again broadened the definition of *community* and implied a national standard.

Pornographic content falls within the definition of erotica, but not all erotica is obscene. The intensity of erotic stimuli varies from mild "cheesecake" photos to explicit "stag films."

The application of local standards gained national implications in 1990 when Home Dish Satellite Corporation, which distributed hard- and soft-core sex films throughout the country, was indicted (along with GTE and other major companies involved in satellite transmission) by the district attorney of Montgomery County, Alabama, for obscenity. States had been prosecuting people on obscenity charges since the early nineteenth century, but this was the first case where local laws affected programming carried nationwide. Since a network carrying only R-rated films was also indicted, the Satellite Broadcasting Communications Association saw "potential trouble for all the major cable companies like HBO, Cinemax, and the Movie Channel."[2]

The Customs Bureau of the Treasury Department has the right to impound obscene material or gambling and lottery information, and thus keep such materials from being imported into the United States. But a Supreme Court decision in the late 1950s declared unconstitutional the role of Customs in restricting the importation of propaganda materials. In 1938, Congress passed the Foreign Agents Registration Act, which provides that any person who represents a foreign government must register with the Justice Department and that any foreign publication that contains propaganda to influence the American public must be labeled as propaganda. In 1983, the Justice Department attempted to restrict three Canadian films by forcing them to be preceded by a message stating that the films were political propaganda and expressed views not supported by the United States. The films were *If You Love This Planet*, an antinuclear film that was nominated for an Academy Award, and two films exposing the problems of acid rain, said to come from America: *Acid Rain: Requiem or Recovery* and *Acid From Heaven*.

The U.S. Postal Service exercises the right to restrict the distribution of obscene publications or lottery advertisements through the public mails. However, the Postal Service has greatly reduced its fulfillment of this responsibility in the past decade. It requires shippers of obscene materials merely to put them in plain wrappers and label them accordingly. This supposedly protects those who do not want to be exposed to pornography. The Postal Service also requires shippers of pornography to remove from their mailing lists the names of anyone requesting it.

It is important to note that in all cases of such restrictions by the Customs Bureau, the Postal Service, and local authorities, none has the right to censor, or *prevent* publication. It should also be noted that social mores are changing rapidly.

Although a number of state and local authorities, sometimes inspired by pressure groups, passed increasingly restrictive laws concerning the sale of pornographic material in the 1980s, these laws have been frequently challenged as violations of First Amendment rights, and the Supreme Court has been active in further defining the constitutional limits of the law. For example, at the urging of women's groups, Indianapolis passed an ordinance banning the sale of pornography on the ground that it discriminated against women by portraying them as sex objects. The ordinance allowed any woman who said she had been harmed because of the sale of pornographic material to seek damages from businesses that sold or exhibited it. In 1986, the Court ruled such an ordinance unconstitutional.

In 1985, Virginia passed a law barring newsstands from displaying such magazines as *Playboy* and *Penthouse*. In 1986, the Supreme Court ruled that such a law is too sweeping. Laws can prevent businesses from selling pornography to minors, said the Court, but laws that force sellers to hide such material unreasonably interfere with adults' ability to exercise free choice in the purchase of material. But the Court has upheld the constitutionality of laws that force sellers to keep pornography "behind the counter" or away from shelves on which food products are displayed. And in *New York v. Ferber*, stricter definitions were outlined for child pornography. At the turn of the 1990s the burning issue was the alleged obscenity of heavy metal and rap lyrics (see Chapter 14).

LIBEL

Civil libel, or *defamation*, is a legal issue frequently faced by journalists and others in the mass media. Contrasted with criminal libel (false and malicious attack), it is the broadcast, or publication, of a message that harms someone else's reputation. The potential for libel actions exists simply because there are so many stories written about so many people by so many reporters. Add to this the fact that much reporting involves stories that are critical of some individual or official, and we can understand the frequency of libel disputes.

There is evidence that the number of libel actions is related to the historical reluctance of the mass media in the United States to take criticism very seriously. A study of libel plaintiffs during a 10-year span in the 1970s and 1980s found that 75 percent of them would have been satisfied if the newspaper or broadcast station had simply published or broadcast a correction, retraction, or apology. The failure to agree on such modest resolutions resulted in the libel actions.

Libel cases against the news media can be filed by anyone who believes that his or her reputation has been harmed. The plaintiff must prove that the offensive material was published or broadcast, that it was false, and that it injured his or her reputation. As in many other kinds of legal actions, libel verdicts are frequently determined by whether the plaintiff can meet a specified burden of proof. Just what is such a burden of proof in a libel dispute?

One of the most far-reaching Supreme Court decisions was its 1964 ruling in *New York Times v. Sullivan*. The case came about as the result of an advertisement that appeared in the *Times* in 1960. The ad was placed by an ad hoc coalition of civil-rights leaders. The text of the ad charged some public officials in the South with using violence and other illegal tactics to try to stop the generally peaceful civil-rights movement. It was claimed that the ad libeled, among other individuals, L. B. Sullivan, then the Montgomery, Alabama, police commissioner. Although the charges contained in the ad were generally true, it did contain a number of factual errors.

Sullivan won the case in the trial court, but the verdict was appealed to the Supreme Court, which unanimously reversed the decision. The Court ruled that the media have a right to publish defamatory falsehoods about public officials *if* the statements are made in good faith, concern the official's public life, and are not made with "reckless disregard" for the truth.

The result of the decision was that public officials (a term broadened by the Court in later decisions to include "public figures") had to meet a substantially higher burden of proof than a private citizen to win a libel case. That is, whereas you or I would need only to prove that the false statement published was made with negligence, a public official or public figure would have to prove that it was published with "malice." The Court defined *malice* as advance knowledge that the published material was false or reckless disregard for the truth or falsity of it.

Perhaps the most famous libel suit of the 1980s was brought by television star Carol Burnett against the *National Enquirer*. The *Enquirer* had published a story that Burnett had been drunk and disorderly in a Washington restaurant. She proved the description false and libelous, and a California court awarded her $1.6 million in damages, which was subsequently lowered to $750,000 by an appeals court. In another famous case, *Time* produced a cover story on the war in Lebanon that accused Israeli Defense Minister Ariel Sharon of having encouraged acts of atrocities against Palestinians in refugee camps. *Time* admitted that it had accepted the report of a correspondent without double-checking it because of the pressures of deadline, but it contended that it had not maliciously defamed the Israeli general. The court ordered *Time* to pay $1 for its offense.

In the area of libel, the Supreme Court is essentially saying that it is so important for the mass media in the United States to report on the public acts of public officials that occasional factual errors can be tolerated. In effect, if the media had to double- or triple-check every fact, they would censor themselves to the point of being ineffective government watchdogs.

TRIALS AND OTHER CONFLICTS WITH THE JUDICIAL BRANCH ....

When a crime is committed, most of us learn about it through the mass media. Unless the criminal act is something we witnessed or participated in personally, other than hearing second- or third-hand accounts from friends, we depend on radio, television, and newspapers to report the details. Of course, in most cases the media are quite free to report such information because the First Amendment protects their right to obtain and to publish or broadcast such material.

But occasionally such reporting by the media can intrude in the criminal justice process and perhaps interfere with another constitutionally guaranteed right, the right to a fair trial. The Sixth Amendment, often called the fair-trial amendment, says, in part: "In all criminal prosecutions, the accused shall enjoy the right to a speedy and public trial, by an impartial jury. . . ." What if the reporting of some crime details (protected by the First Amendment) compromises the right to a fair trial (protected by the Sixth Amendment)? When two amendments conflict, which has priority? Because the answer depends on the circumstances of each case, the answer is not obvious, and the topic becomes a fertile one for legal battles between the media and the judiciary.

PRETRIAL PUBLICITY: TO PROTECT THE JURY

Even though the majority of criminal cases don't result in a trial before a jury, at the time the crime is committed, it must be assumed that any citizen in the vicinity is a potential juror who could be asked to determine the guilt or innocence of the accused. And of course those same citizens constitute the audience of the various mass media, so the stories about the crime carried by those media clearly could affect the ability of the jury to remain impartial. Because of this prospect, our criminal justice system pays careful attention to the types of pretrial publicity available to potential jurors.

Of potential damage to a defendant are information about confessions (or even alleged confessions), stories about the defendant's previous criminal record, statements about the defendant's character, and comments about the defendant's performance on various tests or refusal to take such tests. Although many newspapers and broadcast stations voluntarily restrict reporting this kind of information prior

Figure 20.4. The First Amendment offers journalists the guarantees of freedom of press and speech, and in most cases this extends to court coverage.

to a trial, they are free to report, should they choose to do so, because of the First Amendment.

The law and our criminal justice system have developed a number of remedies designed, among other things, to compensate for the effect of the broadcast or publication of prejudicial pretrial publicity:

Continuance, or delay of trial, to permit the effects of pretrial publicity to subside.

Voir Dire, a normal part of the jury-selection procedure in which the prospective jurors are questioned prior to being impaneled in an effort to discover any bias, including that generated by the media, relevant to the case being tried.

Change of Venue, to minimize the effects of local pretrial publicity by moving the trial to a distant community where the jurors know less about the details of the crime. Such a process is expensive; it requires moving the judge, prosecutor, court officials, attorneys, witnesses, and other trial participants. Some states permit a variation on this plan, simply importing a jury from a distant community.

Admonition by the judge after the jury is impaneled and before the start of the trial itself, to reach a verdict exclusively on the basis of the evidence presented in the courtroom. No one knows whether this final attempt to minimize the effect of pretrial publicity is effective, but judges generally believe that jurors take such instructions seriously.

Gag Orders—Contempt of Court

Judges are concerned that trials conducted in their courtrooms may be successfully appealed based on the negative effects of media publicity surrounding the trial. Thus it is not surprising that some judges have attempted to limit further the freedoms of the press by restricting the media's ability to report details of a crime prior to the time it goes to trial.

So-called gag orders, enforced by a judge's contempt-of-court authority, can be addressed either to the media, ordering them not to publish or broadcast certain specific details about a case prior to trial, or to the trial participants, ordering them not to disclose such information to the media. A 1975 Nebraska case brought this issue to the Supreme Court.

Erwin Simants was arrested in North Platte, Nebraska, and charged with the murder of six members of one family. The local judge, Hugh Stuart, responded to numerous press requests for information about the case by issuing a gag order prohibiting the broadcast or publication of a wide range of information that he said would be prejudicial to Simants. The Nebraska Press Association appealed Judge Stuart's action, and in 1976 the Supreme Court ruled unanimously that the judge's order was unconstitutional.

The Court's decision did not, however, provide the definitive answer to the gag-order issue. While agreeing that the order in the Simants case was improper, five members of the court did suggest that gag orders *may* be acceptable if there is unusually intense and pervasive publicity about a case and the judge is convinced that there is no other means available to keep prejudicial information from potential jurors. The remaining four members of the Supreme Court, by the way, said that gag orders would not be constitutional under any circumstances. As a result of this decision, the number of gag orders issued dropped dramatically, but they have

Figure 20.5. *New York Times* reporter Myron Farber was sent to jail for 40 days for contempt of court. His reporting had convinced a New Jersey prosecutor to reopen a murder case, and Farber was subpoenaed to testify about his knowledge of the case. His refusal to name sources cited in his articles brought him the contempt citation.

not disappeared completely. Of those that have been successfully issued in recent years, more are the type directed at trial participants than at the mass media.

In 1983, a U.S. district court judge issued gag orders barring CBS's "60 Minutes" from broadcasting a story about a New Orleans criminal case, saying that it would prejudice the case. But a U.S. court of appeals in New Orleans postponed the trial so the effects of the publicity would not affect the jury, and the Supreme Court refused to change the ruling. Such battles between the courts and the press will no doubt continue.

Journalists as Sources of Information in Court Cases

Another right granted by the Sixth Amendment is the right of defendants "to have compulsory process for obtaining witnesses." This refers to the subpoena power of a court, the authority to issue an official court order summoning witnesses to appear and testify. Because the primary job of journalists is to gather information, they tend to retain considerable details, some of which they report and many of which remain as notes and other unpublished material. This information is frequently deemed important to the trial itself. Thus reporters, and occasionally editors, periodically find themselves as the subjects of subpoenas asking them to provide details to which they have special access.

Because reporters often obtain information by guaranteeing that the identity of the source will be kept confidential, these cases often result in legal battles that place journalists at odds with the judicial system. Reporters generally hold that maintaining such confidences is essential to their profession, that they would be unable to do their job effectively if their news sources thought that their every word would be revealed to prosecutors or other legal authorities.

Confidential News Sources. Twenty-six states have laws that provide some protection of a journalist's right not to reveal confidential sources of information.

In a 5–4 decision in 1972, the Supreme Court ruled that journalists have no *absolute* privilege to protect their sources of information if they are subpoenaed to testify in court proceedings, unless there is a state law giving them such protection. The decision distinguished journalists from medical doctors, who do not have to reveal the nature of their relationships with their patients; from lawyers, whose contacts with their clients are similarly privileged; and from ministers, whose contacts with parishioners can remain confidential.

The Supreme Court case involved three journalists—Paul Pappas, of WTEV-TV in New Bedford, Massachusetts, who had refused to tell a grand jury what he had seen in a Black Panthers headquarters; Earl Caldwell, of the *New York Times*, who had also refused to testify about a Black Panther case; and Paul M. Branzburg, a reporter for the *Louisville* (Kentucky) *Courier Journal*, who had refused to tell a state grand jury the names of individuals he had written about in a drug story.

The Court suggested that if these journalists wanted to have such a privilege, or shield, from government subpoenas, they would have to obtain it through law, not through the First Amendment. As a result of the decision, about half (26) of the states have passed some form of a "shield" law to do just that. The number may be deceptively high because virtually all of the state shield laws are qualified, in that they specify conditions under which they do not apply, as when the information needed from the journalist is central to the case and cannot be obtained from any other source. There have even been some unsuccessful attempts to encourage Congress to enact a federal shield law. The issue remains controversial, and even the ranks of journalists are split on the topic.

Since the Supreme Court decision, a number of journalists have gone to jail for contempt after they refused to divulge information in court proceedings. For example, Peter Bridge, a former reporter for the *Newark* (New Jersey) *News*, was sentenced to an indefinite jail term for having refused to answer a grand jury's questions that went beyond his story about an alleged bribe attempt. He was ultimately released. In Fresno, California, four journalists from the *Fresno Bee*—

CAPITOL GAMES   **By James Stevenson**

Figure 20.6.

the managing editor, the newspaper's ombudsman, and two court reporters—went to jail in 1976 for an indefinite term for having refused to tell a judge the source of secret grand jury testimony used in a news story. In 1981, the Supreme Court let stand an order that a *Philadelphia Inquirer* reporter be jailed for having refused to answer questions about her source for a story about the government's Abscam operation.

Congress can also cite journalists for contempt, as it did in the 1976 case of Daniel Schorr, then a CBS News reporter, who refused to tell the House of Representatives how he had obtained a copy of a congressional committee's report on intelligence activities. Congress ultimately decided not to punish Schorr.

Search Warrants. Prosecutors, and other law-enforcement officials, have also occasionally resorted to a somewhat more extreme method to obtain information from journalists—a search warrant to enter a newspaper office, broadcast station, or reporter's home to locate information relevant to a legal action, information that they have generally been unable to obtain elsewhere.

The Supreme Court addressed this issue in 1978 in *Zurcher v. Stanford Daily*. The case stemmed from a 1971 student demonstration at Stanford University in which students occupied some administrative offices. When police entered the building, a fight occurred in which several police officers were seriously hurt. The fight was photographed by a student, and the pictures were published in the student newspaper, the *Stanford Daily*. Law-enforcement officers then obtained a search warrant to try to locate additional pictures of the fight in the newspaper's files to help them identify the students involved. The unsuccessful search was conducted even though there were no allegations that any members of the newspaper's staff were involved in the fight.

The newspaper challenged the constitutionality of the search, arguing that such a search threatened the freedom of the press and jeopardized the ability of the press to do its job, that because of such searches, journalists' jobs would be disrupted, confidential sources (afraid that their identities would be revealed) would refuse to cooperate with reporters, and reporters would not keep their notes or tapes out of fear that they would be discovered. The Supreme Court, however, in a 5–3 vote, disagreed with the newspaper's position.

As a result, to this day, search warrants can be used by law-enforcement officials, although there has been some protection for journalists added by the 1980 Privacy Protection Act. This federal law places some limits on the *ways* law officers and other government officials can search for material that is the property of the mass media or other individuals who expect to distribute the material by print or broadcast.

MEDIA ACCESS TO INFORMATION ....

The problem of a free press versus a fair trial also extends to the courtroom. In the courtroom the most controversial issues involving the media have dealt with whether (a) court proceedings, including pretrial sessions, can be closed to the press and the public, and (b) whether cameras and other electronic equipment can be used in the courtroom by journalists covering the trial. The issue of closed court proceedings is related to our earlier discussion of gag orders and other built-in safeguards to reduce the effects of pretrial publicity in that the goal of such closures is also to minimize the potentially prejudicial information that gets into the public domain. The question of cameras in the courtroom deals primarily with the effects of such technology on the conduct of a fair trial.

Access to Court Proceedings

The Sixth Amendment guarantee that defendants have the right to a "speedy and public trial" has long been interpreted as a right of access to court proceedings for both the public and the mass media. About the time *Nebraska Press Association v. Stuart* (the case involving the trial of accused murderer Erwin Simants) was being decided by the Supreme Court in 1976, a number of judges, attempting to guarantee a fair trial, had begun to experiment with actually closing some pretrial proceedings. Many of these judges had been encouraged by a portion of the decision in *Nebraska Press Association* that suggested that closing some preliminary hearings might be necessary to protect the trial from the potential dangerous effects of prejudicial pretrial publicity.

When the issue of closing such pretrial proceedings reached the Supreme Court in 1979, the Court, to the surprise of many, decided that such closures were acceptable. In *Gannett v. DePasquale*, the Court ruled 5–4 that the judge (DePasquale) had acted properly when he ordered a reporter to leave his courtroom during a pretrial hearing. The Supreme Court was far from united in this case, as evidenced by the 5–4 vote and the fact that the nine justices wrote five opinions. Nevertheless, the majority offered a new interpretation of the Sixth Amendment right to a "public" trial: This right is a right to protect the defendant, and if the defendant chooses to waive that right (as occurred in this case), the courtroom can be closed.

Gannett v. DePasquale provided such a dramatically different interpretation of the Sixth Amendment than had been used up to that time that judges throughout the country immediately began to use it as a rationale for closing pretrial proceedings and in some cases, trials. At least in part because of this response to the decision, the Supreme Court almost immediately accepted another case that involved a very similar issue. It almost appeared that the Court wanted an opportunity to clarify its 1979 decision. When this new case, *Richmond Newspapers v. Virginia*, was decided in 1980, journalists and other mass-media personnel experienced relief. The Court reaffirmed, on a vote of 7 to 1, the principle that the right of the public and the press to attend criminal trials is guaranteed by the First Amendment. Although the decision was not nearly as unanimous as the vote suggests, the leading opinion was firmly based in the First Amendment and considered trials public assemblies where the business of government is transacted. The justices did *not* go so far as to say that the First Amendment is an absolute roadblock to closed trials; they did admit that in some unusual circumstances, a trial judge might bar the public and the press from a trial to guarantee the fair administration of justice.

Cameras in the Courtroom

Newsreel cameras were permitted in the courtroom during the 1934 trial of Bruno Richard Hauptmann for the kidnapping and murder of the infant son of the American hero Charles Lindbergh. The judge, however, had ordered that participants

Figure 20.7. Television cameras in the courtroom are becoming a more common sight as technology reduces the levels of disruption once common to broadcast trial coverage.

were to be photographed only before or after the trial each day or during recesses. Despite this limitation, the newsreel company, operating a "pool" camera (providing film for all other companies), tricked the judge by attaching a remote-control device to its camera. When the judge discovered that the trial was actually being filmed despite his order, he kicked cameras out of the courtroom for the remainder of the trial, and the entire episode led state after state to ban cameras in their court systems. After the Hauptmann trial the American Bar Association (ABA) passed Canon 35 of its Code of Judicial Conduct, to serve as a model policy for states if they wanted to ban cameras from courtrooms.

The successful lobbying efforts of the ABA led to virtually all of the states enacting such a ban. Such efforts were further enhanced in 1965 when the Supreme Court reversed the Texas conviction of Billie Sol Estes on bribery charges. The reason: Estes's trial was televised over his objection. This 5–4 decision reasoned that Estes had not received a fair trial and that the mere presence of the television cameras in the courtroom creates a presumption of unfairness. Texas, one of the few states that had not formally adopted Canon 35, soon did so. In the late 1960s and into the mid-1970s, virtually all states banned cameras and other recording devices from their courts.

Throughout much of the 1970s, media professional organizations sought to convince state supreme courts that the *Estes* case had been unusual, that new technology no longer required large cameras or additional lighting, and that the First Amendment did not distinguish between media in defining their freedoms. Some of these lobbying efforts began to succeed by 1977 when a few states, including Florida and Wisconsin, permitted experimental uses of cameras in their courts. Today, all but four or five states have rules that permit and direct the use of cameras in their courts.

Overall, the national experience with cameras in courtrooms has been an overwhelming success. To be sure, some judges, lawyers, and prosecuting attorneys have expressed concerns, but in state after state those concerns have turned out to be unjustified. Prosecutors were afraid cameras would make already reluctant witnesses even more reticent to testify, but the fact that in most states they can request cameras to be turned off has made this a nonissue. And in Wisconsin, Florida, and the few others that permit judges to make the determination, compelling reasons for turning cameras off have been recognized.

Judges were concerned that prosecutors, up for reelection, would play to the cameras, and attorneys have worried that judges would do the same. As it has turned out, neither worry was well founded. It appears that the public, looking through the lens of the camera, has effectively constrained legal and judicial behavior so that trials have run just as smoothly with cameras present. And just as groundless have been fears that trial participants would be distracted by the cameras. Compared to the newspaper reporter taking notes during vital testimony or the flamboyant sketch artist who performs from the first row behind the bar, a silent, almost hidden video camera in the back corner of a courtroom can hardly be considered distracting.

In 1981, the Supreme Court received its opportunity to decide the constitutionality of courtroom photography over the objection of a participant. *Granger v. Florida* involved two off-duty Miami police officers convicted of burglary who appealed their case on the ground that they failed to receive a fair trial because it had been televised over their objections. The Supreme Court ruled unanimously that the televising of trials, even over the objection of the defendant, is within the

Figure 20.8. Government action on all levels is open to public and media viewing, except for a few special instances of security or privacy. Federal bodies have been made especially accessible to us via cable (C-SPAN), and the actions and debates of state legislators, such as these from New York, are regularly reported.

bounds of the Constitution. This landmark ruling neither endorsed nor opposed television in the courtroom; it simply said that it was not unconstitutional.

So almost all state court systems, along with the U.S. Senate and the U.S. House of Representatives, permit their deliberations to be televised. Only the federal court system has yet to approve rules and procedures permitting television and other cameras access to their sessions.

ADMINISTRATIVE AND EXECUTIVE BRANCHES

When journalists report on activities in executive branches of government, the issues and controversies they encounter are quite different from those they typically face when reporting on the judicial branch. The disputes are more likely to involve the media's right to access to government information in the first place. All branches of government, but especially the executive, create and retain vast amounts of information. Even though most of this information is generally considered "public" and it is assumed that the public and the press have access to it, the government is often reluctant to release sensitive information, requiring some sophisticated efforts by the media to obtain it.

THE FREEDOM OF INFORMATION ACT

Prior to 1966, if journalists (or the public) were denied information they were seeking from the government, there was little they could do in response. Even government-compiled information such as the results of product safety tests and various economic reports were unavailable to reporters if government agencies chose not to release the information. Often such reports were withheld because they would have revealed information embarrassing to the government, evidence of inefficiency or wrongdoing. However, after many years of hearings and testimony, Congress adopted the Freedom of Information Act (FOIA), designed to open government records and files that had previously been closed to the public and the media. Currently, hundreds of thousands of requests are made each year to obtain information under the terms of the FOIA.

The Freedom of Information Act remains one of the most controversial pieces of federal legislation that affects the press. It was signed, reluctantly, by President Lyndon Johnson in 1966, and in virtually every congressional session since, bills have been introduced to modify the law. The debates tend to cover the same points each time. The government, often represented by federal agencies, believes the FOIA is too stringent and should be weakened. And just as predictably, the news media believe the law is too weak and needs to be strengthened. Although some changes have been passed since 1966, the law still exists in much the same form. Requests must be disposed of within 10 working days, and no justification need be provided when making a request.

The main problem reporters tend to have with the FOIA is that an administration unwilling to comply with a proper request can interfere with its use. For example, over the years, various federal agencies have responded to FOIA requests by claiming the documents have been lost or transferred, by claiming to be too short-staffed to meet the request, or by purging critical information from a file before releasing it. Although the FOIA assumes that requested information will be made available, it does include a number of specific exemptions, including the following:

Classified national-defense or foreign-policy documents;
Agency personnel rules and practices;
Information permitted to be kept secret by other laws;
Confidential trade secrets and financial information;
Information involved in private litigation;
Personnel and medical files;
Information compiled for law-enforcement purposes;
Information related to the regulation of financial institutions;
Geological information and maps concerning oil wells.

The Reagan administration made strenuous efforts in the 1980s to reduce the effectiveness of the Freedom of Information Act and to increase the penalties for government employees who leaked information to the press. The Intelligence Identities Protection Act of 1982 makes it a crime to expose the identities of American intelligence agents. The Defense Department in 1982 also broadened its practice of giving employees lie-detector tests, in an effort to prevent leaking information, and the Reagan administration unsuccessfully urged Congress to pass a law making all government employees subject to lie-detector tests for the rest of their lives.

Despite the many controversies regarding its application, the FOIA has proven a useful asset for journalists covering the federal government. In addition, it has served as an example for the states in adopting their own versions of the FOIA. In fact, every state in the nation has some kind of open-records law, although they vary in specificity, exemptions, and enforcement provisions.

OPEN MEETINGS

In 1976, Congress passed and the president signed into law an important bill that became known as the "Government in Sunshine" Act, a federal open-meetings law. This law applies to about 50 federal commissions, agencies, and boards appointed by the president. The requirements of the law are quite simple and straightforward: Such public bodies are required to conduct their business meetings in public, must provide notice of those meetings 1 week in advance, and must keep careful records of their meetings. As with the FOIA, news media have been filing legal challenges against agencies that appear to be violating the Sunshine Act. As a result of such litigation, federal agencies appear to comply more readily with provisions of the law.

All 50 states have specific statutes that require open meetings. Some of these laws are rigorous and are taken seriously; others are weak and lack strong enforcement. But many of the states have good laws with strong sanctions available for use against public officials who violate the legal provisions. Most state open-meetings laws provide an exemption for executive sessions, such as meetings at which personnel problems are discussed.

In general, both the federal government and the state governments take seriously their respective provisions for open records and open meetings. In the United States, it is assumed that the government's business is also the people's business and that the people have a right to know what government is doing.

Although controversies between the government and the media continue to occur in these areas, both sides seem to recognize the necessity of a clear policy for the proper release of government information to the public through the mass media.

PROTECTION OF PROPERTY AND COPYRIGHT ....

The government has sometimes invoked the right or protection of property as a means of restricting media access to a news event. In a few cases, the media have been cited for trespass in covering events like fires. The news media contend that they should not have to obtain the permission of a property owner to enter the scene of a news event, but court rulings on such cases have not yet established clear precedents.

The government also regulates communication by protecting the property rights of communicators. The present copyright law was revised in 1976 for the first time since its passage as a federal statute in 1909. The copyright law protects the property rights of authors, composers, artists, and photographers, and establishes a system of penalties and redress for violations of those rights. Among other restrictions, the 1976 revision also limits the amount of photocopying that can be done on copyrighted works and extends the life of a copyright to 50 years after an author's death. It is important to note that facts and ideas cannot be copyrighted, only the order and selection of words, phrases, clauses, and sentences, and the arrangement of paragraphs.

Copyright laws were the center of attention in legal battles fought by the mass media in the 1980s. One was the debate over whether manufacturers of home video-recording equipment must pay copyright royalties to producers of TV programs because video-recorder owners tape movies and shows that are aired on television. Sony argued that owners of video recorders have a First Amendment right to copy publicly aired programming and replay the tapes as often as they like for their own private use. Universal City Studios and Walt Disney Productions countered that there is no such right allowing wholesale free taping of copyrighted films. They contended that the practice illegally deprives them of fair compensation for use of their movies. If viewers cannot record the programs, they have to watch television, and the producers receive royalties each time a program is aired. The Court ruled that the public has a limited right to record video programs for personal use, but not for resale. Off-the-air taping has cost the media $100 million in lost revenues in the last decade.

Another battle was over the ownership of syndicated television films. FCC rules have prohibited the three major networks from directly owning most programming and syndication rights since they are the prime distributors of the films. The networks sought the ownership rights, while the film and independent television studios in Hollywood claimed that they should own the rights to TV films and syndicated programs. The Court said the producer is the copyright holder.

A third case involved a controversial ruling drastically curtailing the use an author may make of primary source materials. The Supreme Court declined to review a court of appeals ruling in New York, the center of book publishing in the United States, that traditional research materials—diaries, letters, and other unpublished documents—are protected by copyright (until 2003) and quotation of them without formal permission is infringement. This would technically allow the descendants of the Founding Fathers to sue for violation of copyright.

Especially with globalization of the media, an ongoing problem is international recognition of copyright law. Piracy is prevalent in books and records in some parts of the world. And with the reuse of content, such as film libraries, ownership of material has become an even thornier issue. One recent ruling imposed a further obligation on media to honor original copyright holders, such as the writer of the short story upon which the Hitchcock film *Rear Window* was based. Briefs before the Supreme Court in this case indicated that 1,000 or more films might be similarly involved and the studios liable for continuing damages unless they withdraw their products from distribution. The question of what is a "derivative" work will continue to be a tricky one, but in any event, authors who feel they have long been exploited by the repackaging of their ideas may have literally had their day in court.

SUMMARY

The First Amendment sounds like an absolute statement; "Congress shall make no law . . . abridging the freedom of speech, or of the press. . . ." However, various court decisions over the years have interpreted the First Amendment to have a more limited meaning. It is commonly agreed that some types of laws that limit freedom of speech and press, such as libel laws and obscenity laws, are constitutional.

In most cases, legal action can be filed against the press only after the information has been published or broadcast. However, there are limited circumstances in which the government has been able to restrain publication of disputed material in advance. In both the Pentagon Papers case and *The Progressive* case, the government was successful in obtaining a restraining order delaying publication of articles.

The most common legal issue faced by journalists and others in the mass media is libel, the broadcast or publication of untrue information that harms someone else's reputation. The courts have ruled that public officials and public figures must prove that the libelous information was published with *malice*; that is, they must be able to establish that the reporter knew the information was false before publishing it. Or they must establish that the information was published with "reckless disregard" for whether it was true or false.

Our criminal justice system includes a number of safeguards to minimize the prejudicial effect that pretrial publicity might have on a person's ability to be an unbiased juror. These procedures—such as continuance, voir dire, change of venue, and admonition—are normal components of the trial process. Judges who have been convinced that these procedures would be ineffective have occasionally resorted to using a gag order, a judicial order restraining the media from publishing or broadcasting about the case or restraining trial participants from talking to the media about the case.

The Supreme Court has ruled that the First Amendment does not exempt reporters from providing confidential information they have obtained while covering a story, but about half the states have passed shield laws to protect them from such requests. The Supreme Court has also held that unannounced searches of newspaper or broadcast offices are not a threat to freedom of the press and that search warrants can be used, with some limits added in 1980.

Courtrooms in the United States are generally open to both the press and the public, according to the Supreme Court. However, not all journalists are permitted to use the tools of their trade inside the courtroom. Only within the past 10 years have cameras been regularly permitted in the various state court systems. Today, about 45 states permit some kind of camera and microphone coverage of their courts. The federal court system, however, remains closed to cameras. The Supreme Court ruled, in 1981, that the televising of a trial over the defendant's objection does not cause that trial to be unfair.

Administrative or executive branches of federal, state, and local governments face frequent requests from reporters and the public for access to government records. The federal Freedom of Information Act specifies rules and procedures. Government meetings are also generally open to the press and the public under the terms of the 1976 federal Sunshine Law. In addition, all 50 states have specific statutes requiring open meetings.

Property rights affect the media, too. The most significant issue will continue to be about who owns communications. Copyright law has protected authors since 1909. As cross-media usage of contents grows, so does concern that the originator of a story or artistic work receive due compensation for repackaging of a creation. Ownership of media programming is a growing problem for highly competitive conglomerate communicators.

REFERENCES

1. "Justice Black and First Amendment 'Absolutes': A Public Interview," *NYU Law Review* 37 (1962):548.
2. Neil A. Lewis, "Obscenity Law Used in Alabama Breaks New York Company," *The New York Times*, May 2, 1990, A23.

Media Ethics

Those who wrote the Constitution and Bill of Rights thought that a plurality of communicators would guarantee that the truth would surface. The dynamics of media-audience relationships have grown far more complex than the Founding Fathers could have imagined. We have many more messages bombarding us today, in ever more more sophisticated ways, while there are a steadily diminishing number of independent communicators. The burden is on us to sort it all out, but we simply cannot do it alone. We have to depend on the judgment, standards, and responsibility—the ethics—of those who generate and shape what we see and hear.

Ethics attempts to outline what's "right." If the law encourages a number of interpretations, the notions of what constitutes ethical behavior are even more diverse. In fact, even determining what *ethics* encompasses may not be a simple task. A respected commentator on the issues of journalism, John C. Merrill, has defined it as the "branch of philosophy that . . . is very much a normative science of conduct, with conduct considered primarily as self-determined, voluntary conduct. Ethics has to do with 'self-legislation' and 'self-enforcement.'"[1] In *Ethics and the Press*, Merrill and coauthor Ralph D. Barney noted that "journalistic ethics . . . should set forth guidelines, rules, norms, codes or at least broad principles or maxims that will lead, not *force*, the journalist to be more humane and not necessarily more human."[2]

Now consider this:

Every journalist who is not too stupid or too full of himself to notice what is going on knows that what he does is morally indefensible. He is a kind of confidence man, preying on people's vanity, ignorance, or loneliness, gaining their trust and betraying them without remorse. Like the credulous widow who wakes up one day to find the charming young man and all her savings gone, so the consenting subject of a piece of nonfiction writing learns—when the article or book appears—his hard lesson. Journalists justify their treachery in various ways according to their temperaments. The more pompous talk about freedom of speech and "the public's right to know"; the least talented talk about Art; the seemliest murmur about earning a living.[3]

Thus began Janet Malcolm's trenchant critique of author Joe McGinniss's relationship with Dr. Jeffrey MacDonald, a physician and former Green Beret who stood accused of stabbing and beating his wife and two children to death. The story of the case became McGinniss's best-seller *Fatal Vision*. The critique itself stirred lengthy controversy; the *Columbia Journalism Review*, for example, surveyed 20 prominent journalists—writers and broadcasters—and printed their reactions

---

Consultant and authority on content for this chapter is Robert Drechsel.

and views on their uses of sources in the July-August 1989 issue, under the title "Dangerous Liaisons."

MacDonald, steadfastly maintaining his innocence, had given McGinniss exclusive and total access to him and his legal defense team so that he could write the book (and share the proceeds with MacDonald). Apparently, he assumed from the beginning that McGinniss would produce an account that confirmed his innocence, even after the jury found him guilty. When the book portrayed MacDonald as a vicious murderer, he was stunned. Until the day *Fatal Vision* was published, MacDonald had expected his "friend" and confidant to produce a flattering account.

What MacDonald hadn't known—because McGinniss never let on—was that as the case unfolded, McGinniss had become convinced that MacDonald was guilty. Yet, as McGinniss himself put it: "I liked MacDonald. During his seven-week trial, I laughed, jogged and drank beer with him, browsed through bookstores with him and saw him surrounded by dozens of people who believed totally in his innocence."[4] In fact, for months after the trial, McGinniss conceded that he "reached out to him (MacDonald) through a series of compassionate letters—as I would to any friend in despair—suspending not disbelief, but, in this case, belief."[5]

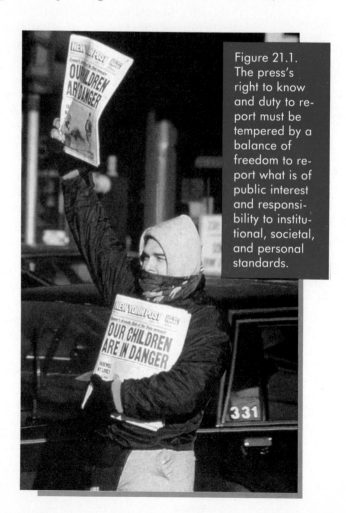

Figure 21.1. The press's right to know and duty to report must be tempered by a balance of freedom to report what is of public interest and responsibility to institutional, societal, and personal standards.

Is Janet Malcolm's generalization about the moral indefensibility of journalism thus correct? Are journalists really inherently con artists whose deceptions are morally unjustifiable under all circumstances? If not, under what circumstances is it justifiable for journalists to deceive sources into trusting them? In her critique of McGinniss, Malcolm failed to disclose that she was being sued by a source who claimed that many of the quotes she attributed to him in a *New Yorker* story were fabricated.[6] Was this failure to disclose morally defensible? When we ask whether such acts or omissions are "morally defensible," we are asking whether they are ethical. There are no easy, cookbook answers to most ethical questions; indeed, media ethics may be more a matter of procedure than a result. But the procedure can be an enormously valuable exercise. This chapter will provide a brief overview of media ethics—it offers the background needed for an understanding of contemporary concerns, some of the sources of ethical standards, and a sampling of the types of ethical issues commonly facing people in the media.

PERSPECTIVES

Although media ethics has received particular attention during the past decade, concern about ethical issues is hardly new. One of the most prominent codes of journalistic ethics, the Statement of Principles of the American Society of Newspaper Editors (ASNE), was first adopted in 1923. One study found that more than 25 percent of U.S. newspapers display some code of ethics on their premises, and the ASNE statement is the code of choice in 58 percent of those instances. (It is reprinted in its entirety in Chapter 5, where we considered the role of gatekeepers' standards.) The Standards of Practice of the American Association of Advertising Agencies is another well-established code: It dates back to 1924. And those are examples of only the most formal manifestations of concern about media ethics.

The sometimes outrageous behavior of the partisan press in the United States two centuries ago has been well documented. Chapter 9 chronicled the emergence of the penny press in the 1830s; it and the so-called yellow journalism of the Hearst and Pulitzer heyday later in the century stimulated considerable criticism both within the media and from outside. As early as the late 1820s, there were complaints that the highly colorful—and popular—reporting by some newspapers of police-court activity was tasteless, indecent, and possibly a stimulant to crime. Some of the criticism sounded remarkably like Janet Malcolm's in 1989. Horace Greeley, the editor and publisher of the *New York Tribune*, complained in the early 1840s that reporting about courts was becoming reckless, unprincipled, and immoral under the hypocritical pretense that the press was duty-bound to keep the public informed.[7] Meanwhile, James Gordon Bennett and his *New York Herald* became the object of a "moral war" by those upset with the content of his newspaper.

The first quarter of the twentieth century saw the publication of books devoted to newspaper ethics and serious discussion of the need for "professionalizing" the press. The concerns of that era are still the relevant ones: Should press freedom be defined as a right for those who own the presses or as a right of readers, as a right to know? What social and moral obligations does journalistic professionalism imply? What provisions should ethics codes contain? Should codes be enforceable? Are they useful primarily as tools for deflecting public criticism of the media, or are they genuine mechanisms for assuring that the media operate in the public interest? The two leading proponents of the ASNE's Statement of Principles, for example, disagreed fundamentally on whether the Principles should be used as a mechanism for expelling undesirables or only as a set of ideals toward which journalists ought to aspire.

THE DEBATE OVER RESPONSIBILITY

What underlies such debate is nothing less than the question of how best to balance freedom and responsibility. One might take the extreme libertarian position that society is best served by imposing no responsibilities on the media and allowing them to operate virtually free of coercion. According to this argument, as each medium (and communicator) freely does what it wishes—even though some may behave irresponsibly—the result will be a cornucopia of information and opinion that rational members of the audience can use to make informed decisions. In other words, this view holds that freedom to communicate is best defined as freedom for the speaker or, for all practical purposes, freedom for those with meaningful access to a medium of mass communication.

On the other hand, one might believe that freedom inherently entails certain moral, if not legal, obligations. A proponent of this view might argue that the rights of the audience are ultimately more important than the unqualified rights of newspapers, reporters, broadcasters, advertisers, or public-relations practitioners. Thus, the media are free—free to be *responsible*.

This concept of social responsibility is perhaps best reflected in the work in the 1940s of the Commission on Freedom of the Press, a group of renowned scholars formed primarily under the auspices of Time, Inc., and chaired by Robert M. Hutchins of the University of Chicago. The Hutchins Commission, as it came to be called, issued a series of reports pertaining to freedom and responsibility in mass communication. The commission's work received a chilly response from the media, perhaps because it contained statements like this:

> . . . the conditions affecting the consumer's freedom have radically altered. Through concentration of ownership the flow of news and opinion is shaped at the sources; its variety is limited; and at the same time the insistence of the consumer's need has increased. He is dependent on the quality, proportion, and extent of his news supply not alone for his personal access to the world of thought and feeling but also for the materials of his business as a citizen in judging public affairs. With this situation any community in which public opinion is a factor in policy, domestic and international, must be deeply concerned.
>
> Clearly a qualitatively new era of public responsibility has arrived; and it becomes an imperative question whether press performance can any longer be left to the unregulated initiative of the issuers. . . .
>
> Since the consumer is no longer free not to consume, and can get what he requires only through existing press organs, protection of the freedom of the issuer is no longer sufficient to protect automatically either the consumer or the community. The general policy of laissez faire in this field must be reconsidered.[8]

To a committed libertarian, these are ominous words. The media have moral obligations to society? What obligations should the media have? Obligations to

DEAN YOUNG
225 EAST 45TH STREET
NEW YORK, N.Y. 10017

December 18, 1985

Ms. Colleen Last
538 Fifth Avenue South
Clinton, Iowa

Dear Ms. Last:

I was most distressed by your comments concerning my "BLONDIE" daily comic strip of October 28th regarding adopted children. I was even more distressed (devasted!) by the hundreds of letters I have received from around the world, verifying your accurate and astute opinion. You, of course, were quite correct in your assertions as to my insensitivity and ignorance on that particular Friday in October.

Each day I try to transcend the imaginary world of "BLONDIE" and bring only wholesome fun and laughter into an all-too-real world already over-burdened with pain, tragedy, and despair. In the fifty-five year history of the strip, this has always been our credo. Our main focus is to win smiles, not enemies!

But in this instance a mistake (on my part) was made. And I accept total responsibility for it and am quite deserving of the wrath perpetrated by it.

I assure you that the mistake was made without malice and in blind innocence, a poor excuse, admittedly -- but one which I will beg your forgiveness for. Please know that the realization of what I have done, hurts me...as much as anyone.

Hoping that you will accept my apologies and assurances that it will not happen again and that your continued readership will justify the truth in what I have said, I remain,

With heartfelt apologies,

DEAN YOUNG

DY:vm

CC Des Moines Register

Figure 21.2. Demonstrating that creators of comic strips are indeed sensitive to issues of media ethics, Dean Young wrote this public letter apologizing for his comic-strip treatment of and comment on adopted children.

whom? Who should decide what these obligations are? Who should enforce them and how?

The social-responsibility view still has its committed and articulate critics. Professor J. Herbert Altschull has complained that *social responsibility* is a term "so vague that almost any meaning can be placed upon it."[9] Professor John Merrill, whose views on self-responsibility we quoted earlier, has warned that social responsibility is costing American journalism its freedom:

Most American journalists think they are free. Actually, they are giving up their freedom, adapting to institutionalism and professionalism, and demeaning their individuality and rational self-interest. They are escaping from freedom and self-

responsibility into the comfortable sanctuary of social ethics and fuzzy altruism. American journalists, like most journalists in the Western world, while still chanting the tenets of libertarianism, are marching into an authoritarian sunset under the banners of "social responsibility."[10]

As Merrill suggests, it does appear that the media have largely gotten over their concerns about the Hutchins Commission's views and have embraced the view that they have important societal or ethical obligations. We can see this acceptance in journalists' acknowledgement that journalists are public trustees. The social-responsibility concept is also reflected in some of the ethical principles and practices by advertisers and public-relations practitioners, although they appear to apply it more cautiously than journalists.

CREDIBILITY AND CONFIDENCE

Of course, social responsibility may be more readily embraced to the degree that media ethics can be linked with media credibility and public confidence in the media. A survey by the *Los Angeles Times* in the mid-1980s found that only 23 percent of the respondents considered journalism in America "basically ethical."[11] (See Figure 21.3.) A study by the American Society of Newspaper Editors found that 78 percent of the respondents agree that reporters "are just concerned with getting a good story, and they don't worry much about hurting people."[12] And

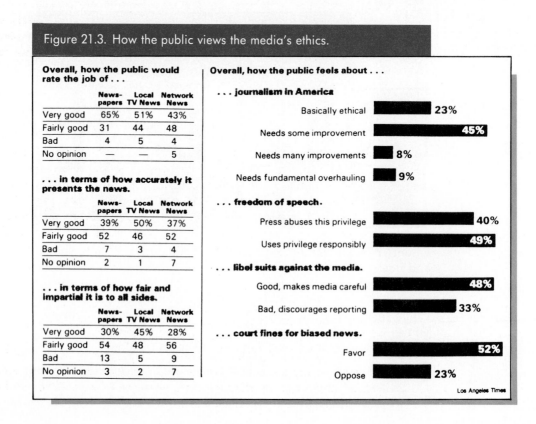

Figure 21.3. How the public views the media's ethics.

Overall, how the public would rate the job of . . .

	News-papers	Local TV News	Network News
Very good	65%	51%	43%
Fairly good	31	44	48
Bad	4	5	4
No opinion	—	—	5

. . . in terms of how accurately it presents the news.

	News-papers	Local TV News	Network News
Very good	39%	50%	37%
Fairly good	52	46	52
Bad	7	3	4
No opinion	2	1	7

. . . in terms of how fair and impartial it is to all sides.

	News-papers	Local TV News	Network News
Very good	30%	45%	28%
Fairly good	54	48	56
Bad	13	5	9
No opinion	3	2	7

Overall, how the public feels about . . .

. . . journalism in America
- Basically ethical — 23%
- Needs some improvement — 45%
- Needs many improvements — 8%
- Needs fundamental overhauling — 9%

. . . freedom of speech.
- Press abuses this privilege — 40%
- Uses privilege responsibly — 49%

. . . libel suits against the media.
- Good, makes media careful — 48%
- Bad, discourages reporting — 33%

. . . court fines for biased news.
- Favor — 52%
- Oppose — 23%

Los Angeles Times

another national poll asking the public to rate the honesty and ethical standards of 25 professions and occupations has found television journalists in 9th place, newspaper reporters 12th, and advertising practitioners 23rd. Automobile sales-people finished at the bottom.[13] So it would hardly be surprising if professional communicators assumed that appeals to ethics will enhance credibility and public confidence.

That is precisely what Professor Philip Meyer, of the University of North Carolina, concluded after he surveyed publishers, editors, and other staff members in a study of ethics for the American Society of Newspaper Editors: "[E]thics is treated as a public relations problem. When strong stances are taken, such as a prohibition against concealed recordings, it is done more to avert criticism than because of any thoughtful weighing of the consequences for basic values. And those values remain unclear."[14] Even if Meyer is correct, such cynical use of ethics may be doomed to failure. The results of acting ethically may not be inherently popular.

The bottom line is that media ethics may be more usefully thought of as a process rather than a result. The crucial question for the communicator is: "How should I go about deciding what I *ought* to do in any given situation?" The results of morally justifiable actions may be as unpopular as those of knee-jerk actions that cannot be morally justified. More than once, the subjects of news stories have committed suicide, apparently because of the stories—and while journalists may be able morally to justify publishing such stories, the results are unlikely to be praised. Conversely, morally unjustifiable behavior may sometimes be extremely popular. A newspaper may publish a barrage of highly prejudicial publicity about the accused in a particularly heinous crime; publishing the prejudicial material may not be justifiable, but it may be highly popular in a community thirsty for revenge.

SOURCES OF ETHICAL STANDARDS

Ethical problems present themselves in an infinite variety. How, then, is a mass communicator with a commitment to ethical behavior to resolve them in some consistent manner? The first step is so obvious that it may easily be overlooked: Give the problem careful thought. But analytical thought is difficult in a vacuum; it needs a framework, a set of principles to be referred to. There are at least two such sources: general moral theories and formal or informal media codes. (Media codes, of course, may themselves be judged in terms of moral theory, but that would go far beyond the scope of this chapter.)

THE THEORY OF UNIVERSALITY

Moral theory is clearly an enormous subject; we will focus on how some moral theories apply to mass-media decisions and operations. Some philosophers have asserted that our actions will be morally justifiable only if we act according to rules that we would be willing to make universal. It's one version of the Golden Rule. Would we want an application of our standards to be made in any and all areas, eventually to affect us in turn? This can be an extremely demanding standard, one that might easily lead to unpopular results.

We began this chapter with the issue of whether journalists ought to deceive sources to win their trust and cooperation. To answer this question, the journalist might ask whether she would want deception to be a universal rule. Since no one would want everyone in the world to engage constantly in deceptive behavior, the journalist would conclude that it is *always* wrong to deceive a source. Or consider an advertiser pondering whether it is ethically appropriate to create a toy advertisement aimed at children that makes the toy appear larger and capable of more movement than it is. Such deception—and certainly the deception of those who are the most vulnerable—would, by the same line of reasoning, *always* be wrong.

This approach can be criticized precisely because it is so inflexible. Should we really consider deception always wrong? What about cases in which a journalist can uncover irrefutable evidence of wrongdoing by someone in a position of public trust only by lying to a source? Certainly we would not want lying to be universally practiced. But what about the harm that will continue if the wrongdoing is not exposed and the good that will accrue to individuals and society if the wrongdoing is exposed? The point is that the type of ethical theory we have just sketched is *not* based on the consequences of behavior, and under such a theory, lying is always wrong, even if more good might sometimes result from lying than from telling the truth.

The Theory of Utilitarianism

Another moral theory does consider consequences. *Utilitarianism* asserts that the morally correct rule or course of action is that which yields the greatest good for the most people. Professors Clifford Christians, Kim Rotzoll, and Mark Fackler summarize the utilitarian approach succinctly in their book on media ethics:

> [W]e first calculate in the most conscientious manner possible the consequences that would result from our performing the various options open to us. In making this estimation we would ask how much benefit and how much disvalue would result in the lives of everyone affected, including ourselves. Once we have completed these computations for all relevant courses of action, we are morally obligated to choose the alternative that maximizes value or minimizes loss. Knowingly to perform any other action would result in taking an unethical course.[15]

Journalists' invocation of the "public's right to know" also has utilitarian overtones. A wide range of journalistic behavior—from reporters' stakeout of Senator Gary Hart's town house to obtain evidence of a possible extramarital affair during his 1988 presidential campaign to stories that trigger suicides—has been justified by journalists in the name of providing information beneficial to the public. Things are complicated by a distinction between supplying information that is *in the public interest* and that which may *interest the public*, such as the scandalous. What is it that makes coverage of the homosexuality of a legislator newsworthy? Its sensational aspect or its relevance in assessing the performance of a congressman?

The very fact that so much seemingly questionable conduct can be justified by the utilitarian approach becomes a source of objection to it. As Professor Edmund Lambeth has put it: "Who counts the 'greatest number' and who measures the 'greatest good' are questions that ring painfully in the ears of the citizenry as well as sensitive observers of the press."[16]

Further, it is no simple matter to determine in advance what the consequences of any act may be. And one of the temptations of utilitarianism is the ease with which it can be applied after the fact, used in hindsight. Communicators making ethical decisions on utilitarian grounds ought to be doing their analysis before they act, not grasping for a justification afterward. Yet, even the most well reasoned utilitarian decision might be subject to tremendous public criticism if the consequences turn out to be more harmful and the benefits less useful than the communicator anticipated.

DECISION BY MEANS OF PROJECTION

Still another theory holds that decisions are best made if we imagine ourselves stepping out of real life, outside of our social, economic, and other roles and characteristics. We then further imagine that when we return to "real life," we might emerge in someone else's position. Thus, when we make our decision, we have an incentive to choose the course of conduct protective of the most vulnerable party.

Consider our advertiser pondering whether to design an ad aimed at children that portrays a toy as larger and more capable than it is. In deciding what to do, our communicator "projects" or imagines that he no longer occupies the role of advertiser and that he might emerge from this imaginary world as a child. Would the communicator favor designing a deceptive advertisement if he might be its victim?

PUTTING THEORY TO THE TEST

We have traced just three of many general approaches to making ethical decisions, and we have simplified even these. But different ethical theories can yield different results, and reasonable people can differ, even when applying the same theory. This can be graphically illustrated if we pause and take a short multiple-choice "test," one that has been administered to readers and editors in at least four cities.[17] Of course, there are no right or wrong answers in the way there are right and wrong answers on an objective exam in a class. And your options are artificially restricted by the yes-no format. But think through the justification you use in reaching your own conclusions and then turn to p. 540 at the end of the chapter to see how newspaper editors and their readers responded. You might be surprised at how responses can differ (or in some cases, not differ) from city to city and between editors and readers.

Case No. 1. A woman county commissioner is raped. The afternoon newspaper reports she was hospitalized following an assault but does not indicate it was a sexual attack. A conservative and antifeminist, she has blocked the expenditure of funds for a rape crisis center at the local hospital. This has been a much publicized local controversy for the past 6 months. But now she tells you that she plans to rethink her position on the crisis center. She also makes clear the deep personal trauma she is suffering as a result of the assault and asks that you not say she was raped.

Would you ...

1. Go ahead with the full story, including her change of mind, recognizing that the shift is a significant public-policy development?
   Yes ( )   No ( )

2. Say no more than the afternoon paper did?
   Yes ( )   No ( )
3. Refer to the attack simply as an assault but report that the convalescing board member is rethinking her position on the crisis center, thus suggesting the nature of the attack?
   Yes ( )   No ( )
4. Report the assault and say nothing about the rape now, but decide when she actually votes for the rape crisis center you will report the reasons for her change of mind, whether or not she wants to talk about it?
   Yes ( )   No ( )

Case No. 2. A mayor is a hard-liner on crime. He has made drug enforcement a major issue. You learn that his 19-year-old son, who lives at home and attends junior college, has been arrested for possession of a small quantity of marijuana, a misdemeanor.

Would you ...
1. Run the story on his arrest?
   Yes ( )   No ( )
2. Run the story if the arrest were for selling a pound of marijuana?
   Yes ( )   No ( )
3. Run the story if the arrest were for using cocaine?
   Yes ( )   No ( )
4. Run the story if the arrest were for selling cocaine?
   Yes ( )   No ( )

PROFESSIONAL CODES

The ethics codes of various media organizations and associations provide another source of guidance for mass communicators facing ethical decisions. One might think codes would provide recipes for ethical behavior that make decision making easy. Most of them have provisions on truth telling, fairness, conflict of interest, and good taste. Review the codes for newspapers, broadcast news, public relations and advertising included in Parts 1 and 2 of this book. A closer look quickly reveals that the codes provide no easy solutions. Sometimes their provisions seem to conflict with each other. More significantly, virtually all of them leave room for broad interpretation, and that is probably for the better. First, it is simply impossible to write a code that covers every situation and does so unambiguously. Second, elaborate codes that are excruciatingly specific may actually foreclose thoughtful consideration of problems when they arise, leading communicators to do what the code says without considering why. Nevertheless, it would be a mistake to dismiss codes as useless. They have frequently become the context for thoughtful debate about issues facing communicators and their media, they provide a set of ideals for the media and communicators, and they highlight the general types of issues to which communicators ought to be sensitive.

Most codes have a strong flavor of social responsibility, as we see in the first article of the ASNE's Statement of Principles:

> The primary purpose of gathering and distributing news and opinion is to serve the general welfare by informing the people and enabling them to make judgments

Figure 21.4. Network news is especially apt to be analyzed for fairness and responsibility. The movie *Broadcast News*, starring William Hurt, took us to the other side of the camera as well.

on the issues of the time. Newspapermen and women who abuse the power of their professional role for selfish motives or unworthy purposes are faithless to that public trust.

The Code of the Society of Professional Journalists (SPJ) begins with an affirmation that:

We believe . . . in our Constitutional role to seek the truth as part of the public's right to know the truth.

We believe those responsibilities carry obligations that require journalists to perform with intelligence, objectivity, accuracy, and fairness.

The Declaration of Principles of the Public Relations Society of America (PRSA) states that "a member shall conduct his or her professional life in accord with the public interest." The organization defines *public interest* "primarily as comprising respect for and enforcement of the rights guaranteed by the Constitution of the United States of America," a definition that may imply a libertarian approach as much as one of social responsibility. The American Association of Advertising Agencies (AAAA) standards seem to take a narrower view and reflect different priorities in asserting that "a responsibility of advertising agencies is to be a constructive force in business" and that "to discharge this responsibility, advertising agencies must recognize an obligation, not only to their clients, but to the public, the media they employ, and to each other." Under the AAAA approach, whatever public-interest obligations advertising practitioners have flow from their obligations to business rather than vice versa. On the other hand, the public-relations and advertising codes go beyond the journalistic codes in the area of enforcement. Violations can lead to expulsion from the PRSA or AAAA. Journalistic organizations, by contrast, have long and sometimes heatedly debated whether they ought to do the same, and thus far, the forces opposing such enforceability have prevailed.

Nowhere has the enforceability issue been more hotly contested recently than in the Society of Professional Journalists. In the mid-1980s, some members of the organization vigorously argued in favor of adding enforcement provisions that would allow local SPJ chapters to adjudicate complaints about ethics violations. Ultimately, the organization not only rejected such proposals but repealed the portion of its code that had urged journalists: "Actively censure and try to prevent violations of these standards. . . ." Among the reasons offered for rejecting enforcement were fear that accused ethics violators might bring libel suits and fear that enforcement might encourage the use of the ethics standards as evidence in lawsuits against the media. Apparently for similar reasons, the Radio Television News Directors Association also dropped a provision from its code that had given the association authority to censure violations.

INSTITUTIONAL ETHICS

Individual media organizations have developed their own standards, at first unwritten, with most tenets a matter of common understanding. However, because of the increased interest in program and print standards and a desire that their practices and their degree of corporate responsibility be generally known, many organizations have published booklets of their guidelines. The major TV networks, for example, have a department of program practices or standards separate from entertainment, news, or other divisions. We have included here excerpts from the CBS/Broadcast Group Program Practices publication, which begins by describing the components of the media environment and proceeds to explain that, "program standards must not only articulate important principles of responsibility to our audiences, they must do so in a manner which does not inhibit the responsiveness, dynamism, creativity and innovation of the programs we are to present."

General Standards
A CBS television program is a guest in the home. It is expected to entertain and enlighten but not to offend or advocate. CBS entertainment programs are intended to conform to generally accepted boundaries of public taste and decorum. . . .

Language
The language in a broadcast must be appropriate to a public medium and generally considered to be acceptable by a mass audience. Coarse or potentially offensive language is generally avoided. . . . Blasphemy and obscenity are not acceptable for broadcast.

Nudity and Sexuality
If consonant with prevailing societal standards, used for legitimate dramatic or historical purposes and not perceived as exploiting the body for prurient interests, certain degrees of undress are acceptable. The depiction of sexual intercourse is unacceptable for broadcast. . . .

Characterizations
Creative imperatives of the script will dictate the behavior and mannerisms of all characters. Character portrayals must be carefully crafted and sensitive to current ethnic, religious, sexual and other prominent social concerns and unacceptable

stereotypes. Care is also to be exercised when depicting characters subject to physical or mental disabilities to ensure that such persons are not demeaned.

Accuracy and Misapprehension

. . . Programs or scenes containing elements whose technical accuracy is important to maintaining public confidence in the integrity of a profession or institution must strive to be accurate in all material regards. Consultation with qualified advisers is encouraged.

Presentations which could convey the misapprehension that a dramatized or prerecorded event is occurring "live" or in the form of spontaneous news coverage of a contemporary event are not permitted. Use of words such as "bulletin" or devices such as a "horizontal crawl" are unacceptable and reserved solely for the use of CBS News. . . .

Violence

As a component of human experience, the dramatic depiction of violence is permitted. Here, violence is defined as "the use of physical force against persons, or the articulated, explicit threat of physical force to compel particular behavior on the part of a person." Accidents and incidents of comic violence are not included in this definition. Any depiction of violence must be relevant to plot and/or character development. It should not be gratuitous, excessive or glamorized. Violence should not be used exploitatively to entice or shock an audience. . . . The use or portrayals of animals shall conform to accepted standards of humane treatment.

Substance Abuse

Character portrayals and scenes depicting the consumption of alcohol, drugs, cigarettes and similar substances must be thoughtfully considered, essential to plot and role development and not glamorized. When the line is crossed between normal, responsible consumption of a particular substance and abuse, the distinction must be clear and the adverse consequences of abuse specifically noted and explored.

Children and Television

Protagonists, "heroes," should exemplify the most positive elements of social and personal codes of conduct such as honesty, fairness, compassion and respect for authority. Attitudinally, such characters should show respect for important societal institutions, concern for distinguishing right from wrong and commitments to such ideals as justice, ethics and humanity. Characters which represent unacceptable social and personal conduct need not be avoided but must clearly be portrayed as undesirable.

Violence should not be portrayed as a socially acceptable means of conflict resolution. It should not be glorified, made to seem fascinating, amusing or palatable. While villains may exhibit some violent behavior, this action should not be imitatable, horrific or extended in its presentation. Acts which carry the potential for violence should be clearly set in the realm of fantasy. Human beings should not be severely harmed or killed. . . . Characters should not be placed in circumstances that provoke excessive or prolonged anxiety, or suggest gratuitous psychological pain. Characters should not be placed in hopeless situations and those in peril should be presented with ways to overcome their predicaments. . . . Program content and commercial messages must be clearly distinct.

Network standards, therefore, are not run on the whim or fancy of the person in charge of a program. Rather, the ethical system is an agreed-on set of values that combines personal, professional, and institutional values. In 1983, General William Westmoreland brought a libel case against CBS following a documentary that accused the general of involvement in a conspiracy to underestimate enemy strength in Vietnam for political purposes. CBS had commissioned an internal study of the documentary and its preparation, and the resulting review was quite critical of the procedures that had been used. They were, as Ed Joyce points out in his memoirs of his years with CBS News, violations of the institution's own codes.[18]

Although almost 60 percent of the management personnel of news organizations who responded to a recent survey of media ethics said that their organizations have formal written policies, not all institutional ethics evolve from or into written form. In 1984, for example, the *New York Post* banned from its pages all advertising of pornographic films, burlesque houses, and topless bars. This decision was made by a "consensus at an upper management level" at the paper. This "consensus," in effect, is an institutional ethical system at work.

Ethics and the Law

It is tempting when considering an ethical issue to ask first whether a course of action is legal or illegal. But it is no answer to conclude that something must be ethical merely because it is not illegal. Nor is something inherently unethical because it is illegal. For example, "puffery"—expansive hyperbole such as "the very best chocolate," "the finest beer," or "works wonders"—is not illegal in advertising, but it is at least arguable whether puffery is ethical. Or there may be situations in which a journalist has no legal right to withhold the name of a confidential source, but withholding may be the ethical thing to do. At the very least, to equate ethics and law is to risk avoiding some important thinking about *why* something is or is not ethical.

Critics of social-responsibility theory have long been concerned that it may be a sort of authoritarianism in disguise. If mass communicators concede that they have assumed the obligations of public trustees, the argument goes, it is only a short step to holding them legally responsible for failure to satisfy what otherwise might be regarded as only moral obligations. In fact, some legal commentators have suggested that in libel cases journalists should be found legally negligent if they violated the ASNE or SPJ code of ethics in preparing the allegedly libelous material.

It is not unusual for plaintiffs' lawyers to subpoena ethics policies and codes or to seek documents involving internal reviews done by the media after complaints that a mistake has occurred. General Westmoreland's case against CBS provides an excellent example. Westmoreland's lawyers subpoenaed the network's internal report, hoping to use it in court as evidence against CBS. The network resisted the request but was required to turn over some of the material. Although the judge found most of the report irrelevant, he rejected CBS's contention that such internal reviews should never have to be disclosed.[19]

In at least one other case, a court has held that a newspaper's failure to follow its internal policy of never naming sexual-assault victims could be construed as negligence for which the newspaper could be sued.[20] A woman was abducted by

Figure 21.5.
In *Absence of Malice*, Sally Field stars as an overzealous newspaper reporter who, in her eagerness to get a story, ignores basic ethical concerns. The film is a good, albeit dramatized, illustration of media ethics (or absence of them) at work.

a man who she believed intended to assault her sexually. She jumped from his car and went to the police, who made their records on the incident available to reporters and did so while the man remained at large. After a newspaper reported her name and address, the man harassed and terrorized her. Such cases, though not everyday occurrences, illustrate how difficult it can be to keep legal and moral responsibilities distinct, and how high the stakes can become when they are merged.

TYPES OF ETHICAL PROBLEMS

Mass communicators face so many types of ethical dilemmas that generalizing about them is difficult, but we can try to compress the types of issues into five categories: conflict of interest; truth/accuracy/honesty; gathering information; privacy/propriety; and physical and other harm. Keep in mind that such categorizing is artificial; it does not exhaust all the possibilities, and some issues clearly overlap categories. There is one other area we should mention here—the concept of "image ethics," or the responsibilities inherent in using the new technology of digital retouching of photographic images. It is a growing concern, and we will illustrate the visual technology behind it in Chapter 25.

CONFLICT OF INTEREST

Conflict of interest is an issue of divided loyalty. It can take many forms, and there have been some spectacular examples. One was so serious that it led to a *Wall Street Journal* reporter being convicted of violating fraud and securities laws. The reporter, R. Foster Winans, wrote a regular column about stocks called "Heard on the Street." Despite the *Journal*'s stringent policy requiring that the content of such columns be kept confidential until publication, Winans provided advance information about the content of his columns to brokers who used it to make a profit on stocks affected by the column. Winans was quickly fired. In court, the government alleged that Winans had defrauded the *Journal* of confidential business information. Winans's criminal conviction was upheld by the U.S. Supreme Court.[21]

Winans's culpability is virtually beyond debate. But in many other situations, the issue is more ambiguous, as was the experience of Linda Greenhouse covers the U.S. Supreme Court for the *New York Times*. While the Court's decision was pending in its controversial decision on the constitutionality of a Missouri law regulating abortion, Greenhouse (and several other reporters and editors) marched in a massive demonstration in Washington, D.C., in favor of abortion rights. After the Court's decision came down and it appeared that some states might enact more restrictive laws on abortion, a reporter for a Florida newspaper sent letters and small wire coat hangers to 160 legislators in that state.

Greenhouse said she considered marching in the demonstration to be an anonymous act similar to voting. "It's not as if I was marching under a banner that said 'New York Times Reporter for Choice,'" she was quoted as saying. "I was just another woman in blue jeans and a down jacket."[22] The Florida reporter, Vicky Hendley, said she didn't think her position as a reporter required her to give up her personal involvement in a cause she believed in. She also said that during her 2 years as an education reporter for the *Vero Beach Press-Journal*, the

Figure 21.6. The conflict-of-interest issue was applied to reporters' participation as private citizens in the antiabortion rally in March 1986.

issue of abortion never came up.[23] Greenhouse continued to report for the *Times*; Hendley was fired.

This chapter is not the appropriate forum for debating the appropriateness of the journalists' actions or the responses of their employers. Rather, ask yourself what basic ethical questions you think these types of situations raise, how you think the people involved ought to have behaved, and (most importantly) *why* you think what you think. Perhaps you will refer back to our brief discussion of general ethical theory as you grope for a principled answer. Perhaps the media codes will be helpful. But remember, your reasoning should allow for consistency. If, for example, you think a reporter in Greenhouse's position behaved ethically in marching but the Florida reporter did not behave ethically in sending the letters and coat hangers, you ought to be operating on the basis of a principle that applies consistently in both cases. In other words, if the cases are distinguishable, they must be distinguishable in a consistent, principled way.

Philip Meyer, whose work we have quoted, asked respondents to his media ethics survey whether reporters' personal backgrounds or experience are likely to help or hinder their coverage of various fields. He found that the respondents generally agreed it would be a help if a reporter assigned to cover agriculture was raised on a farm. But the respondents generally thought it would be a hindrance if a reporter whose parents run an independent oil-exploration business was assigned to cover energy. Why should journalists be so accepting of the former and critical of the latter? If bias, or even the appearance of bias, is a concern, why shouldn't this be as much a problem for the agriculture reporter as for the energy reporter? The answer, Meyer suggests, is that informal rules about conflict of interest are less absolutist than formal rules. He concludes that the real standard journalists use is that the "seriousness of an apparent conflict increases in proportion to the degree that it antagonizes news sources."[24]

Meyer is skeptical of absolute rules in the realm of media ethics:

> *Prohibiting all that merely appears evil along with the activities that are in fact evil can certainly save time and discussion. Such a shortcut may, however, come at some cost. It may be that painstaking reflection and weighing of values is exactly what newspaper people need, and a code of ethics that holds that* looking *bad is as much to be enjoined as* being *bad may short-circuit the process.*[25]

Consequently, Meyer doesn't see the seeming inconsistency between the agriculture and energy reporters as inherently wrong. But it is wrong, he asserts, for journalists to treat conflict of interest with the "rhetoric of absolutism," rhetoric that "hides from view the shadowy areas where the real ethical struggles are waged."[26]

Conflict-of-interest issues can easily arise at the institutional level as well. Consider, for example, what happened while Attorney General Edwin Meese was considering whether to approve an antitrust exemption allowing the merger of business operations of the separately owned *Detroit News* and *Detroit Free Press*. The *Free Press* took a cautious editorial stance in its comment on Meese. The newspaper did not run editorial cartoons about Meese done by its own cartoonist. The *Miami Herald*, a major newspaper owned by one of the companies seeking the Detroit agreement, also acknowledged that it had tempered its treatment of Meese. The *Herald*'s editorial page editor was quoted as saying that he told a staff cartoonist not to draw any editorial cartoons about the attorney general.[27]

Institutional conflict-of-interest issues also surface in the context of advertising. There have been complaints that the print media have been "soft" on the tobacco industry and the health dangers of smoking for fear of alienating one of their largest advertisers. Recently, for example, a company planning to begin national advertising for its stop-smoking system was unable to place its ads in *Time, Newsweek, Sports Illustrated, Life,* and *US* magazines. The company's vice president of sales and marketing told the *New York Times* that "across the board, national magazines have rejected the ad, telling us specifically that they did not want to upset their cigarette advertisers." Not all the publications confirmed that assessment, but the advertising director of *US* did acknowledge that he had rejected the ads for the economic reason that "it would put us in an awkward position to run an anti-smoking ad in the same issue as cigarette ads."[28]

Truth/Accuracy/Fairness

Journalists, public-relations practitioners, advertising people—all have publicly proclaimed their devotion to accuracy and truth. If there is any area of ethics in which we might expect issues to be black and white, this would seem to be it. But even in the area of truth, accuracy, and honesty, matters become complex. For example, truth and accuracy are not necessarily the same. A journalist can quote a source who is lying; the quote is accurate but untrue. Sometimes journalists feel it is necessary to lie to get the truth. Sometimes the truth can hurt people. Is truth so important a value that it overrides all other considerations? What about problems of omission? In the dispute between General Westmoreland and CBS over the documentary asserting that Westmoreland had conspired to underestimate the strength of the enemy, the record showed that CBS had omitted and edited material that would have supported Westmoreland's position. But does that mean the conclusion of the documentary was untrue or merely that the documentary was one-sided? Is there a difference?

Sometimes journalists have resorted to the use of composite characters in their stories without saying so. That is the behavior that cost Janet Cooke her Pulitzer Prize in 1981 when it was discovered that the 8-year-old heroin addict about whom she had so compellingly written did not exist. Cooke left the *Washington Post* in disgrace. But when similar allegations were made about the work of Alastair Reid, a long-time writer for the *New Yorker*, Reid did not resign, nor was he fired. He staunchly defended his undisclosed use of composites as helping him to capture the truth. More recently, ABC came under fire for a video segment on "World News Tonight" that seemed to show a U.S. diplomat handing a briefcase to a Soviet agent. In fact, the scene was a reenactment but was not labeled as such. ABC subsequently apologized.

Advertisers and public-relations practitioners almost inherently face difficult issues of truth and honesty in much of what they do. Indeed, it was impossible not to touch on ethical questions in Chapter 8's discussion of the criticisms directed toward advertising.

What issues of truth and fairness are raised by advertising approaches intended to give people good "feelings" about products but that provide virtually no information? Or advertising intended to give people good or bad feelings about political candidates without providing any information of substance or drastically simplifying or distorting issues? What of the situation in which advertising is technically accurate but not necessarily truthful about what it implies? Is it ethically justifiable, for example, to tout a food product, accurately, as "cholesterol free" when the product is also loaded with saturated fat that presents a serious health risk?

Advertising and public-relations practitioners, more than print and broadcast journalists, face problems of conflicting loyalties. Their primary clients are manufacturers, service providers, organizations, and even government agencies and political candidates—and these clients control the message. When it comes to truth telling, full disclosure, and honesty, how should such communicators balance these loyalties with obligations to the public to which their messages are directed? Is it a satisfactory answer to say that people are not fools and will not be manipulated?

GATHERING INFORMATION

Issues involving the *collection* of the information that finds its way into the media also involve all types of communicators. For journalists, the issues range from when it is appropriate to grant and violate the confidentiality of sources to whether it is appropriate to be a party to deception, harassment, or even lawbreaking in the process of gathering information.

Imagine, for example, that you are a reporter and that you receive a call from the director of public relations for the advertising agency handling the ad campaign for a gubernatorial candidate. He says he has highly significant information about an opposing candidate but that he will provide it only if you promise you will not identify him in any story you write. You promise the confidentiality, and he hands you documents showing that the opposing party's candidate for lieutenant governor had been arrested twice more than a decade ago—once for petty theft and once for unlawful assembly. The theft conviction had been vacated shortly thereafter, and the other charge had been dropped. When you return to the office, however, your editors conclude that the real story is less the relatively minor arrests than the political dirty trick. Consequently, over your vehement protests, they decide to break your promise and publish the source's name. As a result, the source loses his job.

This is no imaginary scenario. It happened in Minneapolis–St. Paul when two newspapers broke their reporters' promises. A wire service used the material and kept its reporter's promise. A television station promised confidentiality but never ran the story. Most journalistic ethics codes place a high, if not absolute, value on maintaining promises of confidentiality. In fact, this case came before the courts, and, before the decision was reversed on appeal, the two newspapers were ordered to pay the source $700,000 damages on the basis that they broke a contract with him. The judge ruled that the case was not about freedom of expression. But who was *morally* correct here? The reporters? The newspaper editors? The wire service? The television station that refused to do either the story about the arrests or the attempted dirty trick? What was the moral culpability of the source?

The granting and withholding of confidentiality is only one technique used in newsgathering. Journalists have also deceived people in a variety of ways. They have "attacked" sources with so-called ambush interviews, they have disguised themselves, they have accepted stolen information, they have paid for information, and they have occasionally broken the law. Lest this sound like a litany of activities that are obviously wrong, recall that the famous Pentagon Papers (the classified documents constituting the government's secret history of American involvement in Vietnam) were unlawfully taken by a source and leaked to newspaper reporters who kept this secret until publication began.

In other words, journalists can often quite reasonably argue that important public interests are served by the publication of information obtained in a questionable manner. Columnist and investigative reporter Jack Anderson had one of his people pass through security checks in the Capitol with a plastic handgun while Anderson carried a bullet. Anderson then walked into Senator Dole's office and showed him the gun and bullet—all to expose how vulnerable Congress is to terrorism. The technique was "legitimate and necessary to demonstrate flaws and wrongdoing," Anderson was quoted as saying in defense of his action. "I was trying to save lives on Capitol Hill."[29] Two correspondents for a French network tried to sneak fake bombs into airline baggage compartments to test security measures at John F. Kennedy Airport in New York. Although an airline employee noticed one of the packages and summoned police, authorities later said the package might have made it aboard. The *Milwaukee Sentinel* sent a 17-year-old and a 14-year-old into a variety of stores to buy state lottery tickets. It is illegal to sell tickets to people under 18, yet the underage teenagers were successful in buying tickets.

Nor do issues involving information gathering implicate journalists alone. The news media have frequently experienced pressure from advertisers to cover or not cover certain stories, and sometimes the media have given in. But what are the ethics of exerting such pressure to benefit a business or organization? Journalists are also frequently offered "freebies" of various kinds: trips, sample merchandise, books and recordings to review, tickets to athletic and cultural events, Christmas gifts, and the like. Many newsrooms have adopted strict guidelines forbidding or limiting acceptance of such offerings, but only the wealthiest media can afford to pay all of the expenses necessary for all types of coverage. For that matter, what issues might you see raised by public-relations practitioners' staging of "pseudo-events" merely to attract media attention? What are the ethics of designing political campaign activities for the primary purpose of getting a candidate's image on television screens? And what are the ethical issues for journalists as they decide whether or how to cover such activities?

Privacy/Propriety

Perhaps no ethical issues have been more controversial in recent years than those involving journalists' alleged invasions of privacy and the propriety of some news coverage, advertising, and entertainment. How much privacy should journalists accord to public figures, including political candidates and officeholders? How should journalists cover tragedies? Should they show victims of crashes, killings, drownings, and the like? How should they treat grieving survivors? Is "tabloid journalism" becoming an oxymoron? How explicitly should sexual images, violent images, and even crude language be communicated in the media? These are the types of questions that face communicators daily, even hourly.

As we saw earlier in the example of Colonel Higgins being hanged, media gatekeepers may have tough calls to make. In California, a photographer at the scene of a drowning took a dramatic photograph showing the 5-year-old victim in a body bag with his face visible. The boy's father was kneeling, weeping; the boy's

Figure 21.7. Pennsylvania State Treasurer R. Budd Dwyer holds a pistol in his hand before inserting the barrel into his mouth and pulling the trigger in front of news cameras during a news conference in his state capitol office in Harrisburg. Reporters and editors often must make quick decisions about their coverage of such gruesome events.

brother was crying out in grief. The photographer's newspaper ran the photograph, as did newspapers around the country. After strenuous complaints from readers, the local newspaper's managing editor publicly apologized, but he also said he intended to nominate the photo for a Pulitzer prize. Early in 1987, the state treasurer of Pennsylvania put a revolver in his mouth and killed himself during a news conference. The entire incident was captured on videotape, which some television stations broadcast.

A new problem regarding explicit language has arisen in connection with the coverage of AIDS. Despite the danger to public health, the news media have often been reluctant to use words such as *intercourse, rectum, penis, oral sex, semen,* and more colloquial terms. Some newspapers describe the danger as occurring when there was an "exchange of bodily fluids." Some newspapers and broadcasters have refused to accept public-service advertising urging people to engage only in "safe sex" for fear that the material is too blunt and might be offensive. Only recently have the media begun to develop guidelines for handling AIDS coverage. The breakdown of taboos clearly affects commercial advertising as well. Ironically, the media appear far less squeamish when it comes to fictional portrayals of sex and real and fictional portrayals of violence.

Physical Harm and Other Harm

There are numerous ways communicators' actions can raise ethical questions. Tobacco and alcohol advertising aimed at residents of poor urban areas has been criticized as leading to physical harm. Subtler are psychological effects. For example, advertisers have been accused of stereotyping women and minorities, portraying women largely as objects of sexual interest, and portraying minorities in secondary or subservient roles. The Miller Brewing Company found itself in the midst of a major public-relations problem when it produced a 16-page "Beachin' Times" insert for campus newspapers before the spring-break season in 1989. The insert not only emphasized scantily clad females but included pointers on "sure-fire ways to scam babes." "Follow these tips and you can turn spring break into your own personal trout farm," the copy proclaimed. Readers' anger turned both to Miller and to the newspapers that accepted the insert. The brewer stopped further distribution of the advertising and apologized. Similarly, the trade journal *Electronic Media* apologized after it ran an advertisement for "Crime Diaries." The ad showed a man holding a knife to the neck of a terrified woman, with copy saying, "Women like the romantic intrigue. Men like the realistic action." (The show never aired.)

The news media, too, have had their share of complaints about insensitive handling of stories about women and minorities, if not for ignoring minority issues altogether. In addition to being accused of covering criminal cases so sensationally as to destroy a defendant's possibility of a fair trial, they are chastised for ignoring other serious risks allegedly created by their reporting. There has been concern that reporting on suicides, particularly teenage suicide, may stimulate more such suicides. Sources have threatened and even proceeded to commit suicide in response to stories about them. A superior court judge in Washington committed suicide after a *Seattle Post-Intelligencer* reporter called to inform him that the newspaper was about to publish exclusive stories detailing allegations about his sexual misconduct with teenage boys. The judge had already announced that he would not seek another term. It might be viewed as a demonstration of the effect of utilitarianism; the newspaper justified its decision on grounds that the story was far more than a story about the judge but a story about the failure of the state judicial-conduct commission to handle serious problems adequately. According to

Figure 21.8. The question may be: What is the best way to right a wrong?

the newspaper, the judiciary and the bar knew about the judge's illicit sexual contacts with juvenile offenders but did nothing.

Journalists have also been criticized for conduct less threatening of life. The *New York Post* once obtained and printed the answers to a New York Regents test on chemistry. The newspaper did so as part of a story on how easy it is to cheat on the exam and reported that it took only 15 minutes and a couple of phone calls to get copies of several exams and the answer sheet.[30] The chemistry exam was then canceled hours before 80,000 students were scheduled to take it. Similarly, a newspaper in Madison, Wisconsin, published a story on cheating in the state lottery and included photographs and text by a reporter explaining precisely how to cheat.[31]

We could continue with examples of media behavior that raises ethical questions, but the point is simply this: Ethical issues come in a fantastic range of shapes and forms, but before communicators can deal with ethical questions, they must recognize them and define them. It is easy, particularly under time pressure and organizational pressure, to overlook ethical questions until it is too late. Perhaps the simplest advice for the professional communicator is this: Imagine that you receive a telephone call from an irate person demanding to know why you have acted as you have. If you cannot quickly and rationally answer, and feel yourself struggling for reasons and excuses, you probably have not recognized or sufficiently thought through the moral issues implicit in your actions. And be sure to engage in this imaginary conversation before you act, not after.

SUMMARY

In this survey of the landscape of media ethics, we have seen that moral questions about mass communication have long been with us. We have asserted that media ethics is more a process than a result, that there is no absolute answer to the question whether any given type of communication behavior is ethical. Rather, the process of reaching a morally principled decision is of the utmost importance.

After the era of yellow journalism, there were concerted efforts in the early twentieth century to formulate and formalize professional and institutional codes of ethics. Results include the Statement of Principles of the American Society of Newspaper Editors, the Standards of Practice of the American Association of Advertising Agencies, the Declaration of Principles of the Public Relations Society of America, and the Standards of Practice of the American Association of Advertising Agencies. We have seen that most discussion of media ethics today seems to fit within the social-responsibility approach to media freedom, but public-relations concerns are also involved.

Several general moral theories are useful background to media ethics, especially the benchmark of universality, the Golden Rule; utilitarianism; and projection, or putting ourselves in someone else's shoes. Of more specific guidance are the organizational statements of ethics, and we reviewed the substance of CBS/ Broadcast Group policies. In practice, the media have to balance a sense of responsibility with a need to permit creativity. The interaction of ethics and legalities is a complicated matter: A violation of ethics may or may not make a media practitioner legally liable.

Responses to the Cases on Page 540 (Percentage Who Said Yes to Each Option)				
Case No. 1:	Charlotte, NC	St. Paul, MN	Miami, FL	Hartford, CT
1. Readers	31%	33%	35%	32%
Editors	8	22	39	20
2. Readers	30	54	22	not asked
Editors	75	41	18	not asked
3. Readers	32	35	30	49
Editors	13	30	14	40
4. Readers	5	16	18	12
Editors	4	12	29	0
Case No. 2:				
1. Readers	61	58	64	61
Editors	42	48	75	60
2. Readers	83	50	92	82
Editors	75	89	100	100
3. Readers	70	72	78	67
Editors	54	74	86	70
4. Readers	83	93	94	87
Editors	83	96	100	100

Five types of ethical problems were surveyed: conflict of interest, truth/accuracy/honesty, gathering information, privacy/propriety, and physical and other harm. We realize that communicators look not only to general ethical theory and media codes but to their own sense of rightness for guidance in making ethical decisions.

We began this chapter with the case of Joe McGinniss and the deception of Dr. Jeffrey MacDonald. We raised some of the questions that incident suggests, but we did not answer them. We hope you will be able to wrestle with them more thoughtfully now.

REFERENCES ....

1. John Calhoun Merrill, *The Imperative of Freedom* (New York: Hastings House, 1974), 164.
2. John C. Merrill and Ralph D. Barney, eds., *Ethics and the Press* (New York: Hastings House, 1975), X.
3. Janet Malcolm, "Reflections: The Journalist and the Murderer," *The New Yorker*, March 13, 1989, 38.
4. Joe McGinniss, "My Critic's Cloudy Vision," *The New York Times*, April 3, 1989, 23 (national edition).
5. Ibid.
6. *Masson v. The New Yorker Magazine, Inc.*, 881 F.2d 1452 (9th Cir. 1989).
7. Willard G. Bleyer, *Main Currents in the History of American Journalism* (New York: Houghton Mifflin, 1927), 215.
8. Ibid., 124–25.

9. J. Herbert Altschull, *Agents of Power: The Role of the News Media in Human Affairs* (New York: Longman, 1984), 302.

10. John C. Merrill, *The Imperative of Freedom: A Philosophy of Journalistic Autonomy* (New York: Hastings House, 1974), 4.

11. David Shaw, "Media: High Ratings Are Tempered," *Los Angeles Times*, reprint of story published August 12, 1985, 9.

12. These results and others are summarized in D. Charles Whitney, *The Media and the People* (working paper) (New York: Gannett Center for Media Studies, 1985).

13. Ibid.

14. Philip Meyer, *Ethical Journalism* (New York: Longman, 1987), 178.

15. Clifford G. Christians, Kim B. Rotzoll, and Mark Fackler, *Media Ethics: Cases and Moral Reasoning*, 3rd ed. (New York: Longman, 1991), 16.

16. Edmund B. Lambeth, *Committed Journalism: An Ethic for the Profession* (Bloomington: Indiana University Press, 1986), 10.

17. The scenarios and results from Charlotte, N.C., St. Paul, Minn., and Miami, Fla., can be found in Richard A. Oppel, "Readers' in the Editor's Chair' Squirm Over Ethical Dilemmas," *ASNE Bulletin* (October 1984): 5, and from Michael J. Davies, "In the Editor's Chair, Readers Face Tough Choices," *Hartford Courant*, April 1, 1984, B3.

18. Ed Joyce, *Prime Times, Bad Times* (New York: Doubleday, 1988).

19. *Westmoreland v. CBS*, 601 F. Supp. 66 (S.D. N.Y. 1984).

20. *Hyde v. City of Columbia*, 637 S.W.2d 251 (Mo. App. 1982).

21. *U.S. v. Carpenter*, 108 S. Ct. 316 (1987).

22. Quoted in Stephanie Saul, "Judgment Call: Do Reporters Have a Right to March?" *Columbia Journalism Review* (July/August 1989):51.

23. Quoted in Debra Gersh, "Question of Conflict," *Editor & Publisher*, August 19, 1989, 11.

24. Meyer, *Ethical Journalism*, 71–72.

25. Ibid., 19.

26. Ibid., 74.

27. Mark Fitzgerald, "Treading Softly," *Editor & Publisher*, July 30, 1988, 12.

28. *See* Randall Rothenberg, "Antismoking Product's Ad Stirs Debate," *The New York Times*, November 11, 1988, D17.

29. George Garneau, "Anderson's Gun Incident Has Journalists up in Arms," *Editor & Publisher*, June 24, 1989, 22.

30. Andrew Radolf, "Post Takes Heat for Printing Stolen Test Answers," *Editor & Publisher*, June 24, 1989, 14.

31. "Lottery Cheating Child's Play," *Capital Times* (Madison, Wis.), September 20, 1988, 1.

Mass Media Impact on the Individual

Why do there need to be certain limits on the freedom of the media? What is the importance of media ethics? Media must be free from widespread external controls in order to protect and correct society; however, they must also be responsible to that society because the mass media do make differences in our lives, not only through performing specific describable functions but in more subtle ways.

That the media have the potential to exercise enormous power has fueled the growing, still young field of media research. Because it spills into other areas of concern, scholars in various disciplines engage in parallel research. One study often contradicts another, and many feel that we are far from being able to distill the input of mass communication research into truths. One perspective continues to be that the media are *not* as powerful as we assume.[1] We nevertheless keep looking for answers. The media are pervasive and cannot be underestimated. All researchers have in common the realization that there is much work to be done and that a better understanding of the effectiveness of communicators becomes even more crucial in an era of privatization and globalization.

There are many useful books that give more detailed looks at the state of research on media impact than this one can provide. Examples include the latest editions of Melvin DeFleur and Sandra Ball-Rokeach's *Theories of Mass Communication* and Shearon Lowery and DeFleur's *Milestones in Mass Communication Research*, which point up increased awareness of the role of the mass media in *constructing* individual and shared meaning.[2] This chapter must restrict itself to summarizing the progress of mass-communication research in the past few decades and introducing findings regarding impact on the individual. Chapter 23 takes a wider view. We thus base our discussion generally on one of the several approaches to the issue of effects: division of impact into short-term effect (generally the influences on individual behavior) and long-term effect (socialization, or the imparting of knowledge and values to a cultural group, and social and political change).

TRADITIONAL CONCERNS OF MASS-COMMUNICATION RESEARCH

In 1948, Bernard Berelson framed his famous and cogent reply to questions about the effects of communication: "Some kinds of communication of some kinds of issues, brought to the attention of some kinds of people under some kinds of conditions, have some kinds of effect."[3] As to delineating these effects, Berelson, in conjunction with Morris Janowitz, commented:

The effects of communication are many and diverse. They may be short-range or long-run. They may be manifest or latent. They may be strong or weak. They may derive from any number of aspects of the communication content. They may be considered as psychological or political or economic or sociological. They may operate upon opinions, values, information levels, skills, taste, or overt behavior.[4]

Given the problems of mass communications research, why do we persist? Because it is a fact that a causal relationship exists between exposure to the mass media and human behavior, even though it is impossible to establish absolute relationships for every individual in every instance.

METHODOLOGIES

Media science is beginning to gather the wherewithall to emerge as an independent social science. What we think we know about the effects of mass communication has come from numerous field studies and laboratory experiments. Three basic methodologies have contributed to the current body of knowledge:

1. *Historical research* investigates past and current media events in order to make comparisons; recently, content analysis has broadened that endeavor.
2. *Survey research*, using representative, random, or stratified samples of audiences, has assessed media effectiveness in the diffused environment of the "real world" to determine who watches, listens to, and reads what the media produce.
3. *Experimental research*, done in the controlled environment of the laboratory, has contributed much toward determining specific short-term changes in behavior and attitudes as they relate to mass media content.

As should be expected, differences in design, methodology, and manipulation of the data have produced some disagreement among researchers and practitioners.

Figure 22.1. In television's early days, those without sets would gather in public places for communal viewing of important events. Nevertheless, the impact of content remains a highly individual experience and leads to many different effects.

Mass communication research has had to face up to a serious deficiency: Most of what we have done is short-term rather than long-term. This is the case because longitudinal studies are (1) *costly*, and funding is inconsistent; (2) *topical*, and data have been collected to prove a point; (3) *time-consuming*, and researchers in the academic setting are pressed to produce results that can be published quickly; (4) *difficult to sustain* when human subjects are required for a study of sensitive issues, such as violence or erotica; (5) *subject to methodologies that change*, and some collected data cannot be compared with information gathered at an earlier date; and (6) *evaluated by very powerful pressure groups* that dispute answers that conflict with their position on the issue, affect their economic base, or both.

Research on the effects of mass communication has focused primarily on three general areas:

Cognition and comprehension,
Attitude and value change, and
Behavior change, including both antisocial behavior (negative change) and pro-
  social behavior (positive change).

We consider each before proceeding to major studies and then to the subject areas of specific ongoing research.

Cognition and Comprehension

The communication process begins with gaining an audience's attention, then proceeds to generating awareness (cognition), and finally—optimally—results in comprehension. In mass communication, cognition is affected by the fact that the individual does not read all pages of a newspaper or listen to every minute of a newscast with equal attention. Yet by constant, repetitive exposure, the media can become highly effective on a wide variety of issues.

Comprehension (as with all media effects) is, in large measure, the result of the interaction of media content with the direct, personal experiences of audience members. A person's ability to recall a media event also depends on repeated exposure to the stimulus and some reinforcement via interpersonal relationships. For example, if a person has a brother who is living in a Middle Eastern country that becomes a trouble spot, the very mention of that area will increase the person's awareness because he needs that information and is gratified by it.

Although Americans have one of the best overall information systems in the world, considerable misunderstanding occurs because people misinterpret, fail to hear, or refuse to accept the facts. Evidence also suggests that audience members' predispositions on a given issue create subtle, unconscious misconceptions in spite of repeated exposure to messages that contradict these notions.

Wilbur Schramm pointed out that "the mass media can widen horizons. . . . They can let a man see and hear where he has never been and know people he has never met."[5] Obviously, this is an important effect of mass media in developing societies in terms of the diffusion of innovations, but it is also relevant in any society caught up in rapid growth and change.

Attitude and Value Change

In media research on attitudes, there is general agreement that the mass media affect the values of a society and the attitudes of individuals. The extent, speed, and longevity of the effects remains in question.

Most research evidence supports the hypothesis that mass media can create opinions more easily than they can change opinions. The mass media set agendas: They determine what we think about and what actions may be taken by us or by our leaders.

Reinforcement of existing beliefs is the main effect of most mass communication experiences. One reason for this reinforcement is the tendency of humans to protect themselves by means of selective exposure, selective perception (note the use of filters), and selective retention. We tend to expose ourselves only to messages that agree with our opinions. When exposed to messages with which we disagree, we tend to perceive only those elements that fit our preconceptions. Finally, we tend to retain facts and ideas that agree with our opinions. Psychologist Leon Festinger studied this phenomenon and named it *cognitive dissonace* or *inconsistency*. This theoretical view is said to conclude that there are *limited or null effects*. Festinger's main hypothesis is that the psychologically uncomfortable existence of dissonance motivates a person to try to reduce it. For example, a man who continues to smoke, even though he knows that smoking is harmful, may rationalize that if he stopped smoking, he would put on weight, which could be equally bad for his health.

Considerable research has also verified the "bandwagon effect": People adopt opinions because they are, or seem to be, the opinions of a large number of other people. This social conformity is most commonly demonstrated in advertising, which frequently uses such phrases as "9 out of 10," "more people use," or "mil-

Figure 22.2. Subtle or forthright, advertising's thrust is often to increase individual desire to share benefits others have—and if possible, go one better.

lions recommend." Studies also show that small, cohesive minority groups have an unusual amount of resistance to the bandwagon effect but that most people, lacking the support of a strong, active reference group, simply go along with the majority.

We have seen in earlier chapters that the mass media, especially those using images, can make an event or a person more important to us. This prestige enhancement is known as *status conferral*, and the news media confer it not only on persons in the news, but also on those who report the news. News "stars" are considered to be very powerful in terms of generating attitudes about events as well as providing information about them.

News may also be dysfunctional and cause an effect that was unintended. According to some sociologists and psychologists, news, which is invariably about deviations and abnormalities in society, may actually create anxieties among readers, listeners, and viewers; feeling overwhelmed by the news, they may react by turning inward to a private life over which they have more control. There is considerable support for the idea that heavy users of mass media develop negative attitudes about the world.

BEHAVIOR CHANGE

Research has investigated both antisocial (negative) and prosocial (positive) changes in individual behavior to determine what the media's influences are on specific kinds of behavior. This more tightly focused research has become popular in the last two decades in response to dissatisfaction with the minimal-efforts theory. Among the behaviors studied are *play patterns, voting behavior*, and *aggression*.

Mass media dominate leisure-time activity in our society. Certain media usually generate much public interest if participation in them requires no skills (TV viewing, radio listening, and moviegoing). In effect, mass communication experiences are so attractive and rewarding that the individual consciously gives up or modifies other activities in order to partake of them. But the media do not make a person more passive unless he or she has a very strong predisposition to be so anyway.

Studies have investigated various aspects of family-life patterns. In general, the media studies—specifically of television—indicate that television has not had a marked effect on family lifestyles. At a superficial level, members of a family spend slightly more time together (not necessarily interacting with one another) viewing television as a group—until a second TV set is purchased. The specific fear that TV viewing negatively affects schoolwork seems to be unfounded.

Considerable research has been devoted to the effects of mass communication on voting behavior. The mass media seem to be relatively ineffective in converting a voter from one party affiliation to another. Few voters seem to be influenced by specific political commercials for a candidate they dislike. The critical role of the media apparently is to reinforce political attitudes.

It takes considerable time for people to adopt specific behaviors, and depends on several factors, including the number of people involved in the decision; the economic and social risk necessary; the future ramifications of the action; the extent of departure from current practices; and the *compatibility* of the new behavior with the personality, values, and motives of the individual. The *interaction* of media exposure and other personal experiences becomes the critical force in behavior change.

Figure 22.5 and the summary to this chapter outline the interactive nature of the communication process. The eight elements of the model break into two groups: (1) the five variables that interact to produce (2) the three reactions, or effects of exposure, to mass communication. The modification of individual variables in any one of the sets affects the particular experience on specific individuals. The levels of arousal, short-term effects, and long-term impact depend on the nature of the environment, the type of content, the style of the medium, the personalities of the audience members, and the kinds of social interactions before, during, and after exposure.

MAJOR STUDIES OF THE MASS MEDIA . . . .

Since the 1930s, numerous studies have been reported, but unfortunately not enough of them have been replicated. In addition, articles have appeared in the popular press that misrepresent or misinterpret study results and stress sensational or unsubstantiated findings. However, several of the studies deserve a brief review.

EARLY STUDIES OF MOTION PICTURES, RADIO, AND COMIC BOOKS

The Payne Fund studies, conducted from 1929 to 1932, evaluated the influence of motion pictures on children. These 13 studies, published in 10 volumes, focused on audience composition and content analyses of themes. Results suggested that movies can affect information acquisition, modify cultural attitudes, stimulate emotions, and disturb sleep. Results even suggested that some films can produce negative "morals" and behaviors in some children. This report reinforced existing public concern and led to an industry self-censorship system that lasted until the 1960s.

The "Invasion from Mars" study was hastily done after the Orson Welles radio drama "War of the Worlds" was broadcast on October 30, 1938, and panicked an estimated 1 million listeners, who believed the drama to be real. (We chronicle this event in Chapter 16.) The major findings were these:

1. The excellent quality of the production, designed around fictional news reports, contributed to the panic.
2. People who tuned in too late to hear disclaimers and who could not verify the broadcast's authenticity from another source were most likely to panic.
3. Individuals with "weak" personalities, lower education levels, and strong religious beliefs were most susceptible to panic.
4. Once frightened, people stopped listening altogether or refused to believe that all was well despite the fact that other stations were on the air.
5. Political tension in Europe and a depressed economy at home created cultural conditions that contributed to the overall panic.

In the aftermath of the broadcast, standards were mandated to prevent similar broadcasts. The power of radio was real.

The Wertham "Comic-Book" studies, published in 1954, analyzed the effects of selected sexually oriented or violent comic books on emotionally disturbed children.[6] Wertham's findings were based on his clinical work; he observed and solicited reports that such content contributed to the negative behavior of children with problems. The sensationalism of the media's coverage of Wertham's studies led to severe economic problems for comic-book publishers and the imposition of an industry "seal of approval" self-censorship. Interestingly, the hardiest survivors among comic books today are the types that Wertham condemned.

RESEARCH ON THE INTERACTION OF REACTIONS

The studies discussed thus far found a variety of effects of mass communication and led to public consternation and strict self-regulation of motion pictures, radio, and comic books. This body of work strongly suggests that the media can have an impact on comprehension, attitudes, and behaviors and that different individuals react differently in the same situation. This conclusion negates the *magic-bullet theory*, in which the exposure to one media experience is the sole cause of a specific response. It supports the belief that interpersonal interaction before, during, and after a media event is one, if not *the*, major determinant of the effect of that particular mass communication experience. Research on propaganda is relevant here.

The "People's Choice" study analyzed voting predispositions in the 1940 presidential election. For the first time, the tools of the social scientist were used in a large-scale field study of communication. The study found that political propaganda persuades voters to remain loyal to their political beliefs rather than change parties. Variables such as religion, socioeconomic status, age, occupation, and urban versus rural residence were identified as important. The study also suggested that media content moves through a "two-step flow," in which opinion leaders influence less active information seekers, and these interpersonal social contacts are more important than exposure to the media. This is illustrated in Figure 6.5.

Project Revere, conducted between 1951 and 1953, studied military propaganda but also was interested in airborne leaflet distribution to contact soldiers and noncombatants behind enemy lines. Results demonstrated that messages are *leveled* (shortened to fewer words), *sharpened* (emphasized selected ideas), and *assimilated* (understood) as they pass along interpersonal channels after the initial contact with the leaflets (medium).

The book *Interpersonal Communication Research* by Carl Hovland and Elihu Katz, working with Paul Lazarsfeld, had an impact on our understanding of mass communication effects in the 1940s and 1950s. The authors examined information and opinion exchange within social groups and shed light on the influence of source credibility, fear appeals, order of presentation, and explicit and implicit message variables. They also presented a more thorough analysis of the *"two-step flow"* theory. These studies found that there are many different opinion leaders, depending on the content of a communication. Most important, interaction among people influences the effect perhaps more than the content.

EARLY STUDIES OF TELEVISION

Since the early 1950s, most research on the effects of mass communication has focused on television, especially the effect of television on children. A review of some of the significant work of the 1950s and 1960s reveals a variety of important information.

Television and the Child by Hilde Himmelweit, A. N. Oppenheim, and Pamela Vance was suggested by the British Broadcasting Corporation (BBC) and funded by the Nuffield Foundation to assess the impact of television on children in England.[7] Begun in 1954 and published in 1958, this field study matched children aged 10 through 14 in four cities in England. The study utilized questionnaires, observational techniques, mothers' diaries and viewing habits, interviews, personality measures, teachers' opinion studies, and school performance to gather information. It even compared children prior to television's coming to town and after its arrival. The 11 studies found the following:

1. Age, sex, emotional maturity, and personal need reflect taste and lead to program selection.
2. The more active, more intelligent, and more socially interested child needs television less.
3. Parental example is significant as to what and how much is viewed on television.
4. TV viewing influences children's ideas about jobs, success, and social surroundings.
5. TV dramas can frighten children, especially if they depict realistic violence and are viewed alone and in the dark.
6. Parental viewing with children reduces fright, but most children enjoy the excitement.
7. Knives are more fearful than guns; fisticuffs have little impact; and verbal aggression is often more frightening than physical acts of violence.
8. TV viewing takes time away from other leisure activities but does not seem to have an impact on learning or school performance.
9. Viewing violence on television has little impact on the normal, active child but does seem to affect the emotionally disturbed, heavy viewer.
10. Television affects children, but not to the degree that they are fundamentally changed.
11. Supervision of viewing and interaction with children by adults is the critical

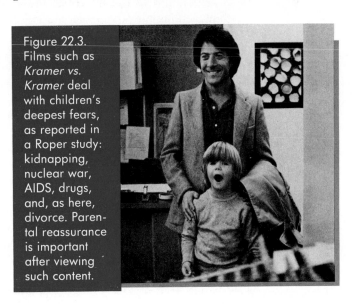

Figure 22.3. Films such as *Kramer vs. Kramer* deal with children's deepest fears, as reported in a Roper study: kidnapping, nuclear war, AIDS, drugs, and, as here, divorce. Parental reassurance is important after viewing such content.

intervening variable in short-term and long-term effects of television on children.

The book *Television in the Lives of Our Children* by Wilbur Schramm, Jack Lyle, and Edwin Parker included 11 studies funded by the National Television and Radio Center that were conducted from 1958 to 1960. They used the *uses and gratification approach* and focused on the functions that television served. They found:

1. No harmful physical effects (eyestrain, loss of sleep) result from watching television.
2. Television helps children acquire information and stimulates their interest in subjects about which information is not otherwise available.
3. Children who are passive, under stress, possess inferior social skills, or are less intelligent make greater use of television.
4. As brighter, socially active children age, they watch television less.
5. Children watch television for thrills and play and seem to like being mildly frightened.
6. Adults and children alike seek out and use TV content to gratify certain needs.

The major conclusion of the studies was this:

> *For some children, under some conditions, some television is harmful. For other children, under the same conditions, or for the same children under other conditions, it may be beneficial. For most children, under most conditions, most television is probably neither harmful nor particularly beneficial.*[8]

The Effects of Mass Communication, a book by Joseph Klapper, was suspect because of Klapper's association with the TV industry as an employee of CBS and his role as a defender of and apologist for industry positions on the effects of violence.[9] Klapper's work is a summary of previous research and advocates the *"phenomenistic" approach* to television effects, that is, that television and other mass media must be viewed as *only one of many factors* rather than as the only factor in any consideration of the effects of the mass communication process on human behavior. Among his other observations: (1) children's reactions to television vary, based on use, gratification, and group association; (2) when mass media do have an impact, it often is a result of other variables being inoperative or because the individual is actually desirous of change; (3) media have measurable psychophysical impacts, but these are probably of short duration.

Experimental and field studies done in the 1950s and 1960s demonstrated that violent TV content, regardless of the existence of other variables, led to aggressive behavior in children. The "Bobo" doll experiments done by Albert Bandura and his colleagues tested Bandura's social-learning theory and suggested that children learn personalities. These experiments were concerned with modeling, or imitative behavior, stimulated by TV violence, whether that violence was rewarded or punished. Bandura argued that TV violence has both a learning and a motivating effect. Bandura's much publicized article in *Look* magazine (1963) went beyond what his data demonstrated; many felt that it strayed back to the "magic-bullet" approach. Nevertheless, the research did demonstrate a relationship between TV violence and aggression in children in the laboratory setting.

The aggression-machine experiments of Leonard Berkowitz used a button-pushing situation in which helping or hurting could be simulated. The "hurting" consisted of pushing a button that supposedly administered an electric shock to another person. Both college students and children exhibited more aggression, as measured by the length of shocks they administered, after they were exposed to TV violence. Berkowitz suggested an *instigation theory*, according to which media violence somehow triggers aggressive behavior, especially when the violence appears to be justified.

The catharsis experiments conducted by S. Feshbach in 1955 posited the opposite result from that of Berkowitz. Feshbach concluded that TV violence reduces aggression by defusing the need and predisposition to act aggressively. When these experiments were replicated researchers who believe that TV violence stimulates violent behavior, they found nothing to corroborate cathartic effects. In the 1960s, Feshbach continued work in support of his theory and found TV violence to decrease aggression in aggressive boys but increase it in nonaggressive boys. This finding was also challenged by other researchers.

Comparing these milestone field studies and experiments presents a confusing, if not conflicting, picture of the effects of television. The experimenters demonstrated that TV violence does not make a difference in aggression, regardless of the other variables. The books by Himmelweit, Oppenheim, and Vance; Schramm, Lyle, and Parker; and Klapper argue that TV violence is one of many factors in the environmental mix and that other factors may be more powerful than the content of television when it comes to negative attitudes or antisocial behavior. Events across America caused other researchers, especially those employed by the government, to take other looks.

GOVERNMENT INVOLVEMENT IN MEDIA RESEARCH ....

Throughout the 1950s and 1960s, politicians were uneasy about the impact and power of the mass media, especially television, and about that medium's effects on children. Senators Estes Kefauver (1954), Christopher Dodd (1961), and John Pastore (1968) held hearings on subjects related to the mass media and social ills. When cities exploded in riots in the 1960s, the violent and pornographic content that was widely available in the mass media was suspect as a contributing cause. Three large-scale governmental investigations sought answers to, and possibly scapegoats for, America's ills.

VIOLENCE

In June 1968, President Lyndon Baines Johnson created the National Commission on the Causes and Prevention of Violence in America to evaluate conditions that had led to the domestic turmoil: assassinations, anti-war protests, inner-city riots. A portion of the report submitted by the Media Task Force in December 1969 was a huge volume titled *Violence and the Media*. The report suggested that portrayals of violence on television dominated the schedule (80 percent of programs) and refuted the networks' claim that violence had been reduced. The report implied that violent TV content was a contributor to turmoil in the streets. George Gerbner's *violence index*—a technique for counting the number of violent acts on a TV show—was the measurement used.[10] It was and remains a controversial instrument be-

Table 22.1. TV Violence, 1989	
Show (Network)	Violent acts per hour
America's Most Wanted (Fox)	53
Hardball (NBC)	47
Tour of Duty (CBS)	45
The Young Riders (ABC)	40
Booker (Fox)	37
Hunter (NBC)	33
Mission Impossible (ABC)	30
Alien Nation (Fox)	25

Source: National Coalition on Television Violence.

cause of its all-inclusive definition of violence; it includes comic action and does not adequately adjust for the explicitness or degree of the violent act and its outcome. Table 22.1 shows a tally for 1989.

Further political discussion and public disturbances led to *Television and Social Behavior: The Surgeon General's Report*, which was completed by the Surgeon General's Scientific Advisory Committee on Television and Social Behavior to study TV violence as a public-health hazard. The committee's selection, research decisions, and summary report were all controversial. The political debacle that followed the report involved the blackballing of social scientists by the TV industry; the revelation of questionable funding practices; and the publication of the much-criticized, politically compromised summary volume (*Television and Growing Up: The Impact of Televised Violence*), which many of the researchers felt misrepresented the findings of their 23 reports. In the studies, Gerbner continued to find high levels of violence in his content analyses; other researchers found that television can teach aggressive behavior; still other researchers decided that TV viewing decreases with age and developed a sociocultural description of those prone to excessively violent behavior; and content analyses described how the media portrayed an America with few blacks and Hispanics and depicted traditional stereotypes of women. In effect, the report seemed to repeat previous work and appeared to be an unwise expenditure of funds.

PORNOGRAPHY

In 1967, Congress established through Public Law 90-100 the Commission on Obscenity and Pornography, which, on September 30, 1970, submitted its report. The report contradicted many strongly held beliefs of politicians and citizens alike. The findings of the commission have been attacked, and the report's proposed legislation has been ignored.

The members of the Commission on Obscenity and Pornography were unable to reach unanimous agreement on the effects of obscene material. The findings of the majority are these:

1. In the nonlegislative area, the major media involved in providing pornographic materials are paperback books, magazines, and films; however, with the advent of the new cassette videotape units, pornographic materials have become available more readily for use in the home.

2. In the legislative area, all local and state laws as well as federal statutes (Statutes 18 U.S.C. Sec. 1461, 1462, and 1465; 19 U.S.C. Sec. 1305; and 39 U.S.C. Sec. 3006) prohibiting the sale of pornographic materials to consenting adults should be repealed, because

    a. There is no empirical evidence that obscene materials cause antisocial attitudes or deviant behavior, although the material is sexually arousing.

    b. Increasingly, large numbers of persons (most frequently middle-aged, middle-income, and college-educated males) use pornography for entertainment and information, and these materials even appear to serve a positive function in healthy sexual relationships.

    c. Public-opinion studies indicate that the majority of Americans do not support legal restriction of adult uses of pornography and legal attempts to control the distribution of obscene material have failed.

    d. Obscenity laws are an infringement on Americans' constitutionally guaranteed right to freedom of speech.[11]

The commission also stated that although the empirical evidence suggests that pornography is in no way harmful to children, on ethical grounds, obscene material should not be made available without direct parental consent to persons under 18. The commission also argued that unsolicited mailings and public displays should be prohibited.

Research in the field is in its infancy because of social pressures and other difficulties in conducting it and because of problems in obtaining financial support. In general, mild erotica seems to generate a pleasurable emotional state in subjects, but there appears to be a link between erotica and aggressive behavior. There may also be a systematic transfer of sexual energy to negative kinds of behavior if other release is not possible. Interestingly, the higher the arousal level, the more likely it is that the material will be judged pornographic. Studies also indicate that satiation occurs with repeated exposure, and the subject loses interest. Recent studies also seem to indicate that male and female responses are growing more alike and that exposure to erotica and the resultant arousal levels affect how subjects perceive attractiveness in others and the receptiveness of others to their own sexuality. Limited research has been done relating erotica to anxiety, guilt, socially threatening situations, liberal or conservative views, and intellectual versus anti-intellectual variables. Without question, additional research is necessary.

CURRENT CONCERNS

Before the 1970s, there were approximately 300 research titles relating to media effects. In that one decade another 2,500 works appeared. About 90 percent of the research on media effects is recent, and most of that work revolves around three key words: *television* (the dominant medium); *violence* (common to many television formats and programs); and *children* (an especially vulnerable segment of the audience). Other related areas of research interest are the effectiveness of television in imparting prosocial attitudes and behaviors and the effects of TV advertising on children. In fact, the whole area of image effects is one of growing importance.

Televised Violence and Children

For over 30 years, researchers have studied the use of television as babysitter. There can no longer be any question that TV violence is arousing and that arousal can lead to aggressive behavior in normal children. The research overwhelmingly substantiates these premises.

Among children, there is also a correlation between heavy TV viewing and lower socioeconomic background, and children from disadvantaged homes rate violent behavior as more acceptable and more enjoyable to view on television than do youngsters from more economically advantaged backgrounds. In addition, children whose parents are heavy TV viewers invariably imitate that behavior.

Socially deviant children who are prone to violent behavior enjoy violent TV content, and their exposure to TV violence stimulates antisocial behavior in the real world. Unquestionably, the viewing of TV violence by emotionally disturbed youngsters must be viewed as a *catalyst* for, if not a cause of, aggressive, antisocial actions. The correlation is stronger in boys than in girls.

The research literature indicates that the single most important intervening variable in mitigating the negative effects of television is the parent (or older sister or brother or other adult), who acts as an opinion leader. Adults can take positive action regarding children's TV viewing by controlling the amount of time spent viewing, supervising the kinds of programs viewed, and viewing television with children and interacting with them before, during, and after the exposure. A child does not have an inalienable right to view as much television as he or she wants.

Research, unfortunately, indicates that most parents do not worry about their children's TV viewing; it may be that parents do not know how much television their children watch. Yet, even as parents fail to supervise their own children, more than one-half of American adults express the opinion that excessive TV viewing is responsible for the poor state of education in the United States.

Television Advertising and Children

Political-action groups have had limited success in changing TV advertising directed at children. Action for Children's Television (ACT) prodded the National Science Foundation into sponsoring a review of research about the effects of advertising on youngsters. The findings, which appeared in 1977, reported the following:

1. Children do not understand that the primary intent of advertising is to sell.
2. Children do not understand disclaimers.
3. Commercials on television are effective in developing active consumerism in children.
4. As a result of seeing TV commercials, children attempt to persuade their parents to make certain purchases, which sometimes leads to conflict between parents and children.

5. Very strong evidence exists that TV advertising generates product awareness but that children become less accepting and finally skeptical of advertising claims by the time they reach their teens.

6. Very young children have difficulty perceiving the difference between advertising and program content.

This report and other actions by ACT contributed to the following changes in TV advertising directed at children:

1. Children's vitamin ads were discontinued.
2. Characters in shows no longer sell products.
3. Advertising time is limited on weekends.
4. Premiums in association with breakfast cereals were discontinued.

Recently Congress has renewed focus on the need for regulation of what young children are exposed to.

PROSOCIAL LEARNING

If TV content can lead to antisocial behavior, it has the potential to be used to educate and socialize children in positive ways. Studies show that TV programs help children's cognitive process at the three levels from *perceiving* to *comprehending* to *remembering*. Researchers have found that the process improves with age but that the very young do not understand much of what they view and tend to forget the little that they do understand. Specialized program content can lead to imaginative play and positive behaviors, such as altruism, friendliness, and self-

Figure 22.4. "Sesame Street" has for decades been both an individual and group socialization experience for children around the world.

control. And studies have shown that special "diets" of controlled TV programs can result in prosocial behaviors among behaviorally disturbed children.

The development of prosocial learning content is suspect because it is associated with cultural "mind control." Some people believe that the imposition of selected socially acceptable, middle-class values may actually be a handicap to the disadvantaged children they are designed to help. In the next chapter, we will look more closely at imparting social values.

The Impact of Images

A 1989 PBS series led by Bill Moyers pulled together current thought in academic circles on the communicators' uses of the power of the visual. Its conclusion: We are not only *affected* by images that are the basis of our expectations, views of the world, and values, but we are "intimately managed" by mass-produced images. A whole industry has sprung up to offer the research and technology of visual communication. Demographic studies focus on audiences' filters, so a magazine like *Self* can create an editorial spread that will sell "a look" as effectively as advertising does. Experts electronically monitor our subtlest reactions to what we see on TV, primarily for the benefit of advertisers and ad agencies responsible for 32,000 commericals a year. Besides all this, technicians manipulate what is presented for public view, as we will see in Chapter 25.

The obvious object of all this attentiveness is advertising and public relations, but just as entertainment has merged with news, so has persuasion infiltrated a range of media content. Professor Stuart Ewen of Hunter College and others on the "Consuming Images" segment of the PBS series point out that the "if people buy it, it's right" attitude has affected news programs that "construct" coverage of events to create the largest audience (rating).

Figure 22.5. Director Alfred Hitchcock was master at the use of film techniques and characters to draw in the spectator: film angles and plot details that lead from an ordinary day to increasing horror are effective in *Psycho*.

Robert Pittman, a Time Warner executive, opened a floodgate of debate when he advocated using the one language this country's "TV babies" can understand—powerful television images—to get them interested in "a host of societal ills." While some decry the spread of an MTV culture, the principle *is* being widely adopted. It can be used to facilitate caring. But the use of the image as the message needs further study. A spate of recent films, including *Last Exit* and *The Cook, the Thief, His Wife and Her Lover*, have left interpretation of the images solidly up to the audience. Film critics call such films "cool" or recessive, contrasted with "hot" high-action genres that offer "the thrill of being a participant in mostly implausible melodrama while remaining safely outside of it." Such arousal is far simpler than that of the cool films that involve us by demanding that we fill in the blanks and make judgments for ourselves. Perhaps amidst the escalating media clutter and copycat syndrome, this mode of communication will prove a more effective one.

SUMMARY: THE MODEL OF MEDIA EFFECTIVENESS ....

The best way to understand the effects of mass communication is to summarize what we know into the Model of Media Effectiveness (Figure 22.6). This paradigm contains eight sets of elements. Five variables—environment, content, medium, audience, and interaction—lead to three types of reactions—arousal, short-term effects, and long-term impact.

VARIABLES

There are five primary sets of variables in our model.

Environment. Environmental variables include the political, economic, and social conditions that exist at the time of exposure to a mass communication message. The radio broadcast "War of the Worlds" created panic partly because of the troubled economic situation and the dangerous international conditions in the

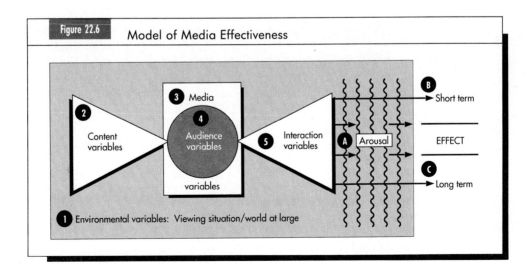

Figure 22.6 Model of Media Effectiveness

1930s. The environment itself also contributes to a medium's impact. The motion-picture theater, with its comfortable seats, large screen, and controlled environment, is relatively free of interruptions. But a dark house on a stormy night can be fearful for a child (or an adult) with or without TV violence.

Content. Content variables are manipulated by media artists. Most of the frightening films or TV programs we view use the following variables to arouse fear: explicit violence; a combination of erotic elements and violence; realism in the violent acts and settings; weapons of violence (knives are more threatening than guns or fist-fights); verbal aggression and threatening action, which have a strong impact on children; sympathetic villains, who are more difficult to understand than the traditional division between "good guys and bad guys"; identification of the audience with the characters, which makes violence directed at the characters more real (violence directed at youngsters and animals is the most fear-inducing for children); vulnerable characters; familiarity with continuing characters; and a relative powerlessness on the part of characters to control the situation.

Medium. Media variables refer to the style of the stimulus material using the inherent codes of a given medium. Loud music and flashy visual techniques—such as unusual camera angles, deep-shadow lighting, erratic camera movement, and rapid editing—contribute to arousal, regardless of content.

Audience. Audience variables are very significant because they involve the personality characteristics of individual audience members. Individuals who have had previous experiences with certain stimulus material react differently from those who are unfamiliar with it. Normal people respond differently from disturbed individuals. Any one person responds differently to even the same content based on his or her physical health or the degree of tension, anxiety, or stress he or she is experiencing.

Interaction. Interaction variables are dependent on the presence of others in the audience with whom we communicate before, during, and after the experience. Most of us have been "set up" by our friends to be frightened before a film begins. We have held hands or tried to defuse tension by yelling or laughing. We have talked afterward to release our tension or have hidden around the corner and jumped out to startle others or have been startled by them. We know that children are less affected by violence when their parents also view the show and interact with them.

REACTIONS

The Model of Media Effectiveness also visualizes the reactions that the interacting variables produce as a result of the mass communication experience.

Arousal. Arousal is a straightforward, measurable response to a stimulus. Unquestionably, exposure to erotic content is biologically and sexually arousing for both men and women. In addition, exposure to fear-inducing and violent content stimulates human biochemistry and emotional reactions. That level of arousal is physiologically measurable. Anyone who has seen *Psycho* or *The Shining* or *The*

Terminator or *Rambo: First Blood, Part II*, or *Aliens* can attest to sweaty palms and shortness of breath and increased heart rate and tension in the pit of the stomach. Films such as these definitely arouse and frighten audiences. And most users of erotic and fear-inducing content seek out that material for the stimulation it provides.

Short-Term Impact. Short-term changes in comprehension, attitudes and values, and behavior have been observed, and much of that research has been corroborated by subsequent studies that have replicated the original work. Audiences laugh at cruelty because much humor is based on inhumane actions—from pratfalls to tasteless ethnic jokes. We cover our eyes, grab hold of the person next to us, scream out warnings to the hero, and cheer the demise of the villain in the throes of physical agony. The audience loves the class clown, who "smarts off" during a tense moment so that we can release our built-up tensions. Children in this heightened state have been observed to act out mild antisocial behaviors in laboratory experiments where there is no prosocial adult intervention. There is also evidence that a causal relationship exists between exposure to violent content and negative aggressive reactions in disturbed or emotionally confused adults. There is a link between exposure to nonsexual violent content and aggressive sexual behavior.

Long-Term Effects. On this issue, there is *some* evidence that repeated exposure to *some* kinds of content, in *some* kinds of environments, on *some* kinds of audience members leads to *some* kinds of long-term changes in behavior and attitudes. Long-term changes such as the civil rights, women's, and gay movements occur; we recognize them historically, but we have problems measuring them. The difficulty remains in isolating mass media involvement from the other cultural currents at work in our personal lives and in our society. This brings us to our next chapter.

REFERENCES

1. A survey of research that reflects this point of view is found in William J. McGuire's article "Who's Afraid of the Big Bad Media?" published in Arthur Asa Berger's *Media USA*, 2nd ed. (White Plaints, NY: Longman, 1991), 272–80.
2. Melvin L. DeFleur and Sandra J. Ball-Rokeach, *Theories of Mass Communication*, 5th ed. (White Plains, NY: Longman, 1989), xiii.
3. Bernard Berelson, "Communications and Public Opinion," in *Mass Communication*, ed. Wilbur Schramm (Urbana: University of Illinois Press, 1949), 500.
4. Bernard Berelson and Morris Janowitz, eds., *Reader in Public Opinion and Communication*, 2d ed. (New York: Free Press, 1966), 379.
5. Wilbur Schramm, *Mass Media and National Development* (Stanford, Calif.: Stanford University Press, 1964), 127.
6. Frederic Wertham, *Seduction of the Innocent* (New York: Rinehart, 1954). Wertham's work is not documented by subject description and is difficult to apply beyond the two qualifications noted in the text: (1) violent and sexually oriented content; and (2) emotionally disturbed children. Yet press reports and personal appearances and writings by Wertham attempt to expand his work to include all comics and all children. His studies from 1948 to 1954 do not seem to justify this expansion.

7. Hilde Himmelweit, A. N. Oppenheim, and Pamela Vance, *Television and the Child* (London: Oxford University Press, 1958). This book was the first major longitudinal study of TV's effects and makes a significant contribution to our understanding of the emergence of a new medium in a modern industrial society—in this case, Great Britain.

8. Wilbur Schramm, Jack Lyle, and Edwin Parker, *Television in the Lives of Our Children* (Stanford, Calif.: Stanford University Press, 1961), 13. This was the first of many studies about the influence of television on children, and it remains a major contributor to our understanding of this process.

9. Joseph T. Klapper, *The Effects of Mass Communication* (Glencoe, Ill.: Free Press, 1960), 8–9.

10. George Gerbner, Larry Gross, Michael Morgan, and Nancy Signorielli, "The 'Mainstreaming' of America: Violence Profile Number 11," *Journal of Communication* 30, no. 3 (Summer 1980).

11. *The Report of the Commission on Obscenity and Pornography* (New York: Bantam Books, 1970), 53–72.

12. Vincent Canby, "Is Violence in the Eye of the Beholder?" *The New York Times*, May 13, 1990, H22.

Mass Media and Society

The mass media serve as the central nervous system of the United States, the critical information chain that vibrates without pause, and also provide ongoing socialization—the spreading of information, values, and attitudes. The government and the governed, the opinion leaders and the general citizenry, inform and shape each other using mass communication.

Take, for example, the enormously expensive operation that put an astronaut on the moon. Why were American taxpayers willing to put billions of dollars into that venture rather than, say, clean up the inner cities or build low-cost housing? Part of the answer may be that the space program benefited from compelling use of the mass media.

NASA encouraged full coverage of the space effort. Television, radio, and the other mass media were there when the first American rocketed into orbit on February 20, 1962; one little girl later wrote to Colonel John Glenn that she listened to his heartbeat during the media's tracking of his pioneering flight. Mass communication stimulated public interest, allowing NASA to build its case with Congress, the president, and the people. By the time of the first manned *Apollo* flight in 1968 and the landing on the moon the year after, 528 million people around the world participated in space exploration. In nations where home TV sets were not yet common, great crowds gathered in public squares to watch the events communally. James Clayton, a *Washington Post* writer, referred to the *Apollo 11* flight as the most massive publicity effort in the history of the world.

We elect presidents who have the ability to harness media power. Presidents Gerald Ford and Jimmy Carter, both bright and good men, failed to kindle enough public support to retain their offices. President Ford lacked "media magic," and the failure of President Carter's administration to solve the Iranian crisis, played out live and in color on television, was undoubtedly a major reason for *his* failure to win another term. President Carter's fall from power was not measured in loss of political clout but in his disappearance from the front pages and television screens of America. The most powerful office in the world was media-vacant for the last 3 months of the Carter administration. Ronald Reagan was already the focus of the news, with media skills second to none, not even John F. Kennedy, who was the darling of the news establishment. George Bush may not have Reagan's charisma, but he knows well the power of the media and personally checks on what the Fourth Estate has to say about him.

The media themselves are neither saviors nor destroyers of society; it is those who gain access to and make skillful use of mass media who determine both positive and negative media contributions in this country. We have much to learn about how American public opinion is shaped by the ideas, information, and analysis provided through mass communication. This chapter introduces a number of

Figure 23.1. The American public has walked in space, landed on the moon, and grieved at the loss of the *Challenger* crew. We have participated in those experiences "live" via the mass media.

important fields where research is being done and documents some of mass media's longer-term social effects.

HISTORICAL PERSPECTIVE

The very forms of the evolving mass media and their common availability have changed the way we think of ourselves and relate to others, even the way we think and perceive our world. The media have given us a heightened sense of potential involvement.

THE POWER OF THE PRINTED WORD

The most influential communication development prior to the twentieth century occurred in 1450: Johannes Gutenberg's invention of movable type. Before the invention of the printing press, only the privileged few owned hand-copied Bibles and had great power to interpret the word of God for their own benefit.

The printing and distribution of the Bible changed the power of the church and brought about a religious revolution. A Catholic priest, Martin Luther, felt that all people should be able to read the word of God for themselves and conduct themselves according to their own consciences, not according to the dictates of a priesthood. He translated the Bible from Latin into vernacular German (virtually inventing the German language in the process). Martin Luther understood the impact of the printed word, and he devoted much of his life to using it for his purposes. He was the most prolific serious writer in history; one edition of his works exceeds 100 volumes. George Will, writing in 1983 on the five-hundredth anniversary of Luther's birth, called him "the first great life bound up with mass communication. . . . Luther showed how the tangible (a new technology, printing) can shape the intangible (the idea of an institutional church)."[1]

The printed word made possible the rise of science by allowing facts and observations to be gathered and shared, so that new and more valid conclusions could be drawn about the universe. Books could carry the message that the world was round, not flat. Less than 50 years after the invention of printing, Christopher Columbus set sail across the Atlantic and did not fall off the edge of the earth.

The printed word also made possible the transfer of economic and commercial information necessary to the conduct of business. A new mercantile class, armed with information, arose to challenge the economic and political monopolies of the landed aristocracy. Out of the mercantile class came the middle class, which profoundly changed the economics and politics of Western civilization.

The printed word also brought about the political revolution that replaced monarchical and authoritarian governments with democracy and libertarianism. Citizens became more informed and began to demand that governments serve their needs rather than the needs of the governors. Indeed, without mass media, America as we know it would not exist. It was the printed word—broadside and pamphlet—that induced masses of Europeans to immigrate to the New World. Without the colonial weekly newspaper, the war against the British Crown would probably not have been fought or, if fought, would probably not have been successful. Later, antislavery publications, such as *Uncle Tom's Cabin*, did much to foment the Civil War, as did the newspaper editorials of Horace Greeley and James Gordon Bennett.

ACOUSTIC SPACE, THE ALPHABET, AND ELECTRIC CIRCUITRY

Marshall McLuhan, who startled and inspired the intellectual world of the mid-twentieth century with his ideas that media are more important than the messages they carry, also suggested that human history can be divided into three great stages, each of which is caused by the dominant medium of the time.

In the first stage, the pre-alphabet, pre-written-language age, people lived in *acoustic space*. They know only what they could hear and see in their immediate environment. Their world was small and tribal, governed by the group's emotions of the moment, a world of mystery and communal participation. Even today, in the few primitive societies that remain on earth, in which there is no written or mass communication, the inhabitants live in a culture of good and evil spirits rather than of laws, of feeling and emotion rather than of ideas and information.

The second great stage was marked by the *development of alphabets*, forcing people to think in logical terms. The advent of writing as the dominant mode of communication made people think in a linear, connected, and continuous fashion. One could think for oneself; become an individual separate from the tribe; and develop a rational universe, governed by laws based on logic, and a logical pattern of thought that could lead to science, invention, technology, an industrial society, the assembly line, and mass production.

The third great stage, according to McLuhan, came with the *development of the electric media*, starting with the telegraph in the nineteenth century. The electric media changed the linear way of thinking, making the aural and tactile senses important again in the perception of messages. High-speed information, sent over far distances by means of electronic waves, are changing our sense of time and space, reasoned McLuhan.

The electronic media may well be changing not only our perceptions but also our thought patterns, our lifestyles, our values, and even our way of governing ourselves. We can slow down or speed up our recording of reality and thus change our perceptions of physical phenomena. Using high-speed film, we can photograph a drop of water falling into a glass and observe the spire of water that rises as a result, with a small ball on the top. The electronic media can give us "instant replay," allowing us to observe a football play, for example, from many different angles—in slow motion or fast motion.

Indeed, football is a good example of a sport that is uniquely suited to color television. And baseball is a sport that is uniquely suited to newspapers. Baseball is a linear sport; generally, one thing happens at a time: The pitcher winds up and then throws the ball; the batter swings, hits the ball, and runs to first base. Football, on the contrary, is inherently more explosive than linear. Each of the 22 men on the playing field has his own assignment on any given play. It would be impossible to do football complete justice by writing about it in the old-fashioned newspaper style. But television can use a variety of cameras to capture the action, with instant replay, different angles, reverse angles, zooms, stills, and slow motion.

THE ROLE OF THE MASS MEDIA IN SOCIALIZATION

Socialization is a learning process and lets us gain membership in society. Interpersonal communication is usually more important than mass communication for most socialization. Children's social values are well on the way to being established before they have sufficient social experiences to have any rational perceptions of radio or television. But as our media environment grows larger and more pervasive, media impact becomes more significant.

Gerhart D. Wiebe, former dean of the School of Public Communication at Boston University, has sharpened the definition of socialization by breaking the communication process into three zones on a continuum.

Directive messages command, exhort, instruct, persuade, and urge in the direction of learning and new understanding. They must, says Wiebe, come from authoritative figures and call for substantial and conscious intellectual effort by the learner. Most studies show that messages that intend to direct performance or change behavior in children do not succeed unless they tie in to a structured, face-to-face, teacher-pupil relationship. Thus the media enrich rather than totally replace formal education.

Maintenance messages tell us what to do in the everyday business of living: where we can find food, what dangers we should avoid, when we should pay our taxes, how we can get a driver's license, and whom we should regard as friend or foe. Such messages call for relatively little conscious intellectual effort. The mass media play an extensive role here through the communication of new information, analysis, interpretation, persuasion, and sales promotion. Wiebe maintains that three conditions must exist before communication messages will have an impact on main-

Figure 23.2. Cicely Tyson's joy at the birth of the child who grew to become the protagonist of *Roots* was shared by millions in the miniseries that offered several messages or functions.

taining social norms: (1) the audience must be predisposed to react along the lines indicated in the message; (2) social provisions must exist for facilitating such actions; (3) the message itself must have audience appeal.

Restorative messages renew and refresh the human capacity for productive social relationships. They include fantasies, which allow us to escape the realities of life; humor, which allows us to relieve the tensions of the day; and drama and violence, which can provide catharsis for frustrations and anxieties. In their communication of restorative messages, the mass media play perhaps their most important role in the socialization process.

Television is the medium that contributes most to the socialization of Americans because it is the medium used by more people more of the time; one study found that the average high school graduate will have spent more time in front of the TV set than in the classroom. For young children, it has an increasingly powerful effect, demonstrated not only by preschoolers' ability to count but also in developing concepts such as friendship and emotions. "Mr. Rogers' Neighborhood" has become a national institution in this regard. For older children, the electronic media are important in modifying attitudes and lifestyles, and various book series provide needed insight into common problems such as divorce, cliques, and substance abuse.

As adults, we look to the media for the opportunity to understand events and consequences so we can form opinions and take appropriate action for ourselves and our institutions. In some of the events that have shaped our present—civil rights, women's rights, sexual and human rights, and war—the mass media played and continue to play key roles, not only through news reports that wielded tremendous impact but through entertainment, documentaries, advertising, and the propaganda of rock music. The media were there with the events more often than some of us wanted.

THE MASS MEDIA AND SIGNIFICANT SOCIAL ACTIONS ....

SOCIAL JUSTICE

If you are white, compare your feelings about blacks with those of your parents and grandparents. If you are black, how does your self-concept differ from that of your parents and grandparents? The TV spectacle "Roots" opened the eyes of many white Americans and encouraged black Americans to take pride in their African heritage. Film and other mass media reflect the times in which they are made as much as the historical period they cover. Sometimes, media critics note that programs are ahead of their times; "Living Color" in 1990 was cited as an example. Media are both agents of change and reflections of what society wants to believe at a particular time. Political and economic groups that control the media can also control the images on the screen.

Events in the news and entertainment media have become the conscience of America. The media continue to expose the resurgence of bigotry—such as the 1987 problems of integrating the all-white county of Forsyth County, Georgia, and the deaths of young black men chased by white youths in Brooklyn, New York, and the intimidations and attacks on Asian Americans by blacks.

In the 1950s television was a major news instrument used by black Americans to carry their grievances to the American body politic. As the effectiveness of such coverage became clear, marches, speeches, boycotts, sit-ins, freedom rides, and other demonstrations were staged for the media and the white power structure.

A blossoming TV news industry was ready to bring dramatic events into 8 of every 10 American homes when a black woman, Rosa Parks, refused to surrender her seat on a Montgomery, Alabama, to a white man. The Montgomery bus boycott of 1954 and 1955 was one of the first successful mass challenges to public segregation. It also produced a black leader for the news media, especially for television. The Reverend Martin Luther King, Jr., was a master propagandist. His low-key, reasoned, Gandhi-inspired approach to nonviolent protest was perfect for the news. Television helped make Dr. King a symbol of change, also in his violent death. Murdered whites and blacks became martyrs under the glare of television. The civil-rights movement was a media movement.

Because civil-rights protests were covered by the media, the federal government and the people of America were moved to action in the 1960s. A protest is worthless unless the people and the power structure know what is happening. The freedom rides organized by the Congress of Racial Equality (CORE); the marches led by the Southern Christian Leadership Conference (SCLC); the manifestos, posturings, and programs of the Black Panthers; the urban riots in Harlem, Watts, Newark, and Detroit—mass media highlighted them and pressured politicians to act.

The entertainment industry also played a role. The blatant racism of *The Wooing and Wedding of a Coon*, the "Sambo" and "Rastus" series, *The Nigger*, and *The Birth of a Nation* were supplanted in the 1920s and 1930s by black "fools" and "mammys." The tragedy of such great talents as Stepin Fetchit, Willie Best, and Mantan Moreland was not that they played buffoons but that these were the only roles available to them and the only blacks that movie audiences saw. With a few notable exceptions—*Hallelujah, Heart in Dixie, Green Pastures*, and *Cabin in the Sky*—the screen was lily white. Few white Americans knew that a black B-film industry was

Figure 23.3. Witnessing civil-rights leaders roughly treated during peaceful marches had wide influence.

flourishing under the talents of Oscar Micheaux and other independents throughout the 1940s.

The watershed year for black images in white media was 1949, when four problem films were released; one of them, *Intruder in the Dust*, is notable as the first Hollywood portrayal of an independent black man. In the 1950s, one black star, Sidney Poitier, saved dozens of whites, emerged as a visible hero, and improved white impressions of blacks. He won an Academy Award for best actor (in *Lilies of the Field*). By the mid-1960s, the "age of Poitier" had paved the way for a number of black talents, including Lou Gossett, who won an Academy Award for best supporting actor in *An Officer and a Gentleman*.

As we saw in Chapter 13, an economically viable black urban audience made it possible for "black exploitation" films to emerge. A TV breakthrough came in 1965. After a virtual "whiteout" since the early 1950s, Bill Cosby starred in "I Spy" and proved that black stars can attract high ratings; he won two Emmy awards doing it. Many syndicated TV shows have featured black characters, and "Julia," an often maligned series that starred Diahann Carroll, was important because it offered the example of a black professional woman making it in a white man's world.

In the late 1970s, "Roots" and "Roots II" validated early breakthroughs. The public acceptance of "Roots" was evidenced by the highest ratings ever achieved by any program to that time. The combined miniseries dealt with many issues that just a few years earlier would have been impossible to portray on television.

Clearly the classic example, although not a completely uncontroversial one, of awareness raising through entertainment is "The Cosby Show." While some critics feel the well-to-do Huxtables are not typical of black or even many white families today, no one disputes the explicit role models offered by the series or the more subtle reinforcement of the value attached to black culture, in terms of the novels referred to, the art on the walls, the black colleges discussed, and so on.

Blacks have found acceptance by white audiences in a wide variety of roles. No longer invisible or stereotyped, they began 20 years ago to live and breathe, and become heroes and villains. It was not a revolution but it was a big step forward, and entertainment continues to be part of the process of change. Popular, fresh talk-show star Arsenio Hall recently told interviewer Connie Chung: "I'd like to be the Martin Luther King of comedy" to bring people together.

Black ownership of broadcasting stations started to increase in the 1970s, and black radio has become a viable instrument in the advertising marketplace. In addition, special-interest magazines have continued to serve black readers. Perhaps in no other medium does black artistic input dominate as it does in the recording industry. Traditionally the entertainment entry point for blacks, records made by blacks, as well as those by Hispanics, now reach most white audiences. In all media, the fact that minorities appear part of "the system" is a major change of the past 25 years. Tokenism still exists in mass media, but affirmative action is a reality.

Without mass media, the progress made in civil rights may still have occurred, but not with the speed and impact that it did. Mass media have access to and influence on the power elites of this society. The media have challenged the old saw that you cannot legislate cultural change. Mass media have not done it on their own, but attitudes and behaviors on racial issues have changed because of what all of us read, heard, and saw in the media.

SEXUAL POLITICS

It is fruitless to argue over whether mass media changed society's attitudes toward women or whether a changed society modified the media's portrayal of women. A vital interaction took place. Most assuredly, a relationship exists between how men and women view themselves and each other and what media culture holds up as role models.

For the most part, the women's movement has made better use of the print media than it has of the electronic media. Women have had easier access to print, print costs are lower and offer a wide range of media vehicles, and more women are trained to write than are trained to use radio, television, and film. Simone de Beauvoir's *Second Sex*, Betty Friedan's *Feminine Mystique*, Kate Millett's *Sexual Politics*, magazines such as *Ms.* and *Working Woman*, and myriad other media vehicles were involved in observing, redefining, and advocating new roles for women in society. Even such traditional magazines as *Cosmopolitan*, *Redbook*, and *Woman's Day* have moved in new directions. Counterproposals to women's liberation ideas have also been mounted in the print media, most notably *The Total Woman*, which advocates a more conservative approach to male-female relationships.

The news media have assisted and resisted women's groups when staged events and other protests have occurred. By any measure, women's-rights events are covered more sparingly and less enthusiastically than were civil-rights stories in the 1960s. This is, in part, because the women's movement is *decentralized*, which makes it difficult for journalists to cover several groups that often seem to be at ideological odds; *localized*, made up of essentially independent local groups so that the news media cannot always identify important issues; not *hierarchical*, which does not give media a leader to focus on; *not ritualized*, so that mass media sometimes cover events that make "poor news," such as conferences, women's studies, and women's centers; and *internally opposed*, with some women's groups in public opposition to the goals of the movement—for example, passage of the Equal Rights Amendment.

The most significant progress in electronic journalism has been the increasing number and responsibilities of newswomen. The cumulative effect of TV appearances by Judy Woodruff, Connie Chung, Diane Sawyer, and Jane Pauley (whose departure from "The Today Show," to make room for the younger Debbie Norville, irritated women viewers and immediately led to the show's departure from top rating) has been important in consciousness-raising and affects the attitudes of men and women on a wide range of issues.

The independent, intelligent women portrayed in sitcoms are a far cry from the earlier stereotypes of TV women in "I Love Lucy," "My Friend Irma," and "Father Knows Best." The new TV women can take care of themselves and, if they have to, can handle the bad guys in "Police Woman," the first successful adventure series with a woman (Angie Dickinson) in the title role. Even daytime soap operas are now peopled with career women involved in the business and professional worlds. Commercials project an image of women as attractive, childless, and wage earners, with male friends and husbands who are "liberated" as well as good-looking.

In the motion-picture and sound-recording industries, the opportunity to express opinions corresponds with the ability to sell tickets and records. Barbra Streisand's "The Women in the Moon" was a political message as powerful as Helen Reddy's "I Am Woman," and similar songs may have had more cultural impact than the amateur "librock" bands of the 1960s because Streisand and Reddy reach audiences outside the women's movement. In the early 1980s, Streisand expanded

Figure 23.4 Kathleen Turner brings a modern strength to the characters she plays; she's shown is *Crimes of Passion*, costarring Anthony Perkins.

her roles, becoming actress, composer, director, and producer of *Yentl*, a widely successful Hollywood film.

The very late 1970s and early 1980s saw the rebirth of "women's movies." The significant difference was that the women's roles included new stereotypes and themes that are traditionally the province of male stars. The films starring Jane Fonda, Meryl Streep, and Cher display a broad range of heroines, many of whom deviate from older Hollywood types. Many films—*Norma Rae*, *Coal Miner's Daughters*, *The Turning Point*, *Terms of Endearment* and *Steel Magnolias*, among others— offered fine women's parts. Media images and media opportunities for women are growing at a rapid rate. The feistiness of Roseanne—and the success of her series— attest to how far we've all come.

HUMAN RIGHTS

The sexual revolution that has taken place in our society in the past 30 years was begun, as was the women's movement, not by the mass electronic media, but by the more specialized print media. But in both cases, and in the case of civil rights as well, the electronic media no doubt changed Americans' perceptions of civil rights, women, and sex to make possible the acceptance of the radical ideas espoused by the more specialized print media.

The sexual revolution really started with writers of books for very narrow and specialized audiences. Their notions of sexual freedom finally found their way into men's magazines that reached a national audience with *Playboy*, which was started in the mid-1950s. The "*Playboy* philosophy" of sexual permissiveness and frank sexual pleasure had considerable influence on other magazines and books, but it did not creep into such mass media as newspapers, radio, television, or publicly shown motion pictures until a decade or two later.

In 1972, ABC produced a prime-time drama called *That Certain Summer*, which examined a homosexual relationship. Yet it was not until 1980 that a sitcom, "Love, Sidney," could deal with homosexuality with some ease. In 1974, *A Case of Rape* was the first major TV drama to investigate that crime from a woman's point of view. It was not until October 1983 that a network soap opera, "All My Children," used a continuing character who was clearly a lesbian. In 1983, NBC produced *Princess Daisy*, a tentative look at a brother-sister sexual relationship. And in 1984, ABC produced a two-hour drama, *Something about Amelia*, which was the first frank and honest treatment on national prime-time television of an incestuous father-daughter relationship.

The gay-rights movement has been largely confined to specialized print media. There are now newspapers and magazines that cater to gays. But most daily newspapers and national TV programs still treat homosexuality as an aberration in society, not as normal behavior. The film industry has produced some feature films with gay central characters—*Suddenly Last Summer*, *The Fox*, *The Boys in the Band*, *Reflections in a Golden Eye*, *Fortune and Men's Eyes*, *The Ritz*, *Outrageous*, and *My Beautiful Laundrette*. But in most TV shows, only a very infrequent episode alludes to "the problem." A scene on "thirtysomething" showing two men in bed caused an uproar and advertising withdrawal. A sizable portion of the specialized erotic-film industry, however, does exploit this sexual preference in films produced for urban markets.

With increasing numbers of activists, the gay-rights issue is bound to receive increasing coverage in the mass media. Unlike resistance to civil rights and the women's movement, which is subtle and diffuse, open resistance to gay rights is a reality.

Today, the mass media are moving to explore the AIDS epidemic as a heterosexual disease. AIDS is "out of the closet," and ads for condoms are gaining media acceptability as a preventer of disease as well as a contraceptive device. However, American mass media still have not persuaded most Americans that AIDS is anything other than a disease that affects gays, drug users, and an occasional unfortunate soul who contracts the disease via a blood transfusion. The entertainment media are just beginning to probe the dramatic possibilities of the medical/sexual emergency, and news programs are attempting to get behind the headlines.

An ABC San Francisco affiliate, KGO-TV, devoted a once-a-week segment to a visit with a former entertainment reporter dying of AIDS. This electronic diary shared more of the affliction than hard news could convey and evoked intense personal reaction (overwhelmingly favorable) among viewers. (Nevertheless, the station slotted the spot so it was announced before a commercial, leaving time for anyone not wishing to see it to avoid it.)

As the 1990s dawned and Barbara Bush brought a new down-to-earth image of a First Lady, television led the way in reflecting what was happening in society and in schools, where people with handicaps were entering the mainstream. Retarded and physically disabled individuals were featured on sitcoms and dramatic series; dramas deepened understanding of diseases like Alzheimer's and Tourette's syndrome; and realistic scenarios of working-class problems, spousal and child

Figure 23.5. Christopher Burke, an actor who is retarded, has encouraged viewer understanding of the handicapped in his role on "Life Goes On."

abuse, environmental issues, and single-parent families raised awareness in society at large and spoke out to viewers who were caught up in these problems.

MILITARY CONFLICT

Electronic communication has certainly changed the nature of both war and politics since the mid-twentieth century. War has now become a media event, covered in color video from helicopters as though it were a movie in the making.

Before the Vietnam War, the U.S. government maintained wartime security measures over news dispatches that were sent from the front lines, and as a result, news readers never received the full gruesome details of war. The Vietnam War, however, was never officially declared as a war, so there were no official censorship procedures. In addition, TV networks had pressed very hard for uninhibited coverage of the war, and politicians needed television to convince the American public of the rightness of the war. As a consequence, the Vietnam War was the first to be reported, often live and in living color, without any government restraints on the coverage. For the first time, the American people could really see the gory details of war, and, ironically, the government could not hide the futility of its efforts. Indeed, it may never again be possible to have a war such as the one in Vietnam as long as television is permitted to cover it freely and fully.

When Great Britain went to war with Argentina in 1982 over ownership of the Falkland Islands, Prime Minister Margaret Thatcher kept the British news media away from the war zone, so the battle could not be covered live. The British government reasoned that it would be easier to win the war without the "prying" press providing coverage that might stir up negative public opinion. The negative public reaction was still widespread, however, despite what many Britons viewed as a form of press censorship.

Figure 23.6. Only one feature about the Vietnam War was made while it was being fought, *The Green Berets*, starring John Wayne. Shown is a scene from *Platoon*, a powerful personal reappraisal of the conflict; it uses entertainment to convey an important message.

During the U.S. invasion of Grenada in October 1983 to evacuate American students and oust a Cuban-backed, Russian-supplied government that had murdered its elected leader, the American press corps was kept "out of action" by the Reagan administration. Fuming journalists caused congressional leadership to invoke the War Powers Act and have a study group fly down to determine whether the invasion was justified. American public opinion thanked an enormously popular president by bolstering his high ratings.

Who lost? Certainly not the president—and, in the long run, not the news media. We, the people, lost because a serious precedent had been set that abridges our freedom of communication. Why were Americans not more concerned? Perhaps because we had won quickly and turned out to be the good guys for a change. And perhaps because we have become somewhat less than enamored of the egotistical exercise of power by some reporters, news stars, ambush journalists, and the news apparatus in general.

If those two engagements had been long, drawn-out battles, the media and the public would no doubt have insisted on full coverage. The lessons that have been learned from all this, it seems, is that war can succeed if it amounts to quick skirmishes away from the limelight of media coverage. And wars of the future might be like that.

The electronic age has also spawned another kind of war—terrorism—in which the terrorist strikes in order to gain national or international publicity for political purposes. The taking of American hostages in Iran was an example. A radical hijacks an airplane full of civilian passengers, not to get a free ride to his destination but to get reporters to give some coverage to his point of view. An elderly gentleman fills a van of dynamite and drives it up to the Washington Monument, threatening to blow it up, not to satisfy some irrational or insane motive, but to warn the world of nuclear war.

MASS MEDIA AND AMERICAN POLITICS

It is far easier to trace the interrelationship of the mass media and specific social and political movements than it is to discuss the role of the mass media in politicization—changes in general political awareness and participation. Media scholars do agree that two of the basic processes of political socialization—imitation and political education—are facilitated by the mass media. News and entertainment media provide examples of individuals and groups exercising political rights. They, *more than anything else*, inform us of those rights and the values being expressed, and show us how we can vote, demonstrate, or otherwise support a point of view.

But as Doris Graber has expertly reported, the pitfalls and unexplored areas of research on media and politics are numerous.[2] Largely due to the ad hoc nature of public opinion polls, we don't *really* know the extent of media influence. The suspicion is there are too many different reactions of political content to constitute a measurable net effect. Reporters of news are basically honor-bound not to interject interpretation, and thus the audiences, who generally lack the means to judge the accuracy of coverage and sort out the truths from video releases and other political public relations, must come to private conclusions.

We do recognize the power of the media as agenda setters, guiding us to learn about and think about certain topics, and as gatekeepers. Content analysis is still a fledgling specialty, confined mostly to page one and top of the news stories, but through it we can track things like the greater attention given to a candidate's image than to his or her positions. The issue of how critical media consumers actually are continues to be a burning one. Some analysts feel we have put too much stress on the uses and gratifications approach introduced in the preceding chapter. They feel the audience is viewed by pollsters as active seekers and users of media content (pollsters ask: "Why did you choose this program, article, book, etc.?") whereas they are actually more typically passive absorbers. The crucial question is: Who determines the political education needs (for information, perspective, example) that are gratified or satisfied by the programs and publications produced by the media?

Research on media and politics has suffered somewhat from the academic orientation of researchers. Political scientists tend to reinforce Gerhart Wiebe's notion that the media cannot create, only reinforce, an attitude. Professor Graber finds that many political scientists continue to slight media impact. The research horse does not shed its blinders readily, especially since the design of many political science studies serves to minimize media impact. Media influence is acknowledged only when messages presented by news stories reach audiences directly. When media messages are transmitted in multiple-step processes, as often happens when they are diffused through interpersonal contacts, researchers routinely fail to credit the media as the original source of the information. Similarly, media influence has been slighted when it involves a chain of attitude changes. For example, media emphasis on a candidate's political party affiliation may make partisan concerns salient to audiences. In turn, attention to partisan concerns may change votes.[3] She feels concentrating research at the microlevel of media effects on individuals should be shifted to long-neglected macrolevel systems effects. Obviously there is a long, hard road ahead before more scientific conclusions can be made, but the interrelationship of individual and conglomerate communicators, individual end user, and opinions within that individual consumer's circle (as introduced in Part 1 of this book) will continue to be to the fore.

FREEDOM OF COMMUNICATION AND THE CRITICAL CONSUMER

The greatest danger we face is not someone conquering us and taking away our freedoms but our giving them up unknowingly because we fail to realize we have them, do not understand their value, or believe someone else might abuse the privilege, especially the news fraternity.

The purpose of freedom of speech, freedom of assembly, and freedom of the press is to guarantee the citizen's freedom of communication and create the potential for an informed electorate, one that is capable of making educated decisions, to emerge. "Free" speech, assembly, and press are not without costs. Maintaining these freedoms often involves struggle. A free press, for example, may step on the toes of members of powerful interest groups.

Or the climate in Washington becomes a factor. In its first 2 years, the Reagan administration

Sought to limit the scope of the Freedom of Information Act (F.O.I.A.).

Barred the entry into the country of foreign speakers, including Hortensia Allende, widow of Chilean President Salvador Allende, because of concern about what they might say.

Inhibited the flow of films into and even out of our borders; neither Canada's Academy Award-winning "If You Love This Planet" nor the acclaimed ABC documentary about toxic waste, "The Killing Ground," escaped administration disapproval.

Rewrote the classification system to assure that more rather than less information will be classified.

Subjected governmental officials to an unprecedented system of lifetime censorship.

Flooded universities with a torrent of threats relating to their right to publish and discuss unclassified information—usually of a scientific or technological nature—on campus.[4]

THE SPECTER OF CENSORSHIP

Censorship in time of war is accepted as essential to national survival. The censorship of unpopular views in time of peace endangers the survival of our democratic ideals, if not our very democracy. Censorship need not come from Washington. More frequently, the pressure to censor comes from political-action groups, and it is often directed at libraries and schools. Unfortunately, it is successful more than 50 percent of the time.

Let us consider one example of an attempt at containing the impact of the media. On November 20, 1983, ABC's movie *The Day After* blew the lid off the TV ratings; 48 million homes, or 62 percent of the viewing audience, were tuned in to the program. Yet this $7-million production had difficulty finding sponsors because it focused on the controversial subject of the aftermath of a nuclear war, and advertisers that sponsored the program were threatened with boycotts of their products. The threat came from the Reverend Jerry Falwell and the Moral Majority as part of their campaign against politically sensitive programs. Falwell's request for equal time was refused by ABC. The network did broadcast a discussion of the issues raised by the film and included nationally recognized authorities with differing viewpoints in the discussion.

Censorship of the program failed, although in some areas the action succeeded. Pressures that TV networks can withstand with relative impunity are often too strong for a school system to fend off. *The Day After*, viewed at home by millions of children, usually with their parents, was unacceptable in classrooms in Pinellas County, Florida, and elsewhere—even with parental approval and adult supervision in a course related to the show's subject.

POTENTIAL PROBLEMS IN MEDIA POWER

High costs and enormous profits have led to a concentration of media power and information control in the hands of a limited number of sources. Critics have spoken of an "elite" that controls media content. They have expressed fears that these

Figure 23.7. *The Day After* may not be great and lasting art, but it had the potential to generate the kind of discussion that is important to a free society.

"media barons" exercise undue influence on the social, economic, and political structure of the United States.

For example, the 1980s were a "boom time" for the businesses of mass communication, and the mass media influenced the American economic and social viewpoint that there will always be more of everything for everyone. The news, as well as the entertainment media, glorified economic growth, consumerism, and financial hedonism in the form of the "Yuppie ethic." What do "Lifestyles of the Rich and Famous," *Money* magazine, "Wall $treet Week" (on PBS), or the movie *Trading Places* tell us about the real values in the world today? Marxist-oriented critics say the mass media are the tools of capitalism, in terms of both trumpeting the rewards of those who "make it" and validating that American economic dream.

The media not only tell us to dream big, but also are active participants themselves. They invest huge sums of money and gamble that they will make a profit. But how does the system work for all of us?

Because of the enormous sums risked in the media marketplace, the media in general have become more competitive in trying to capture the largest, most valuable audience available instead of attempting to meet the special needs of all segments of society. Some media investors refuse to take anything other than mild positions on sensitive issues and feel that coverage of radical and reactionary positions is threatening.

The rise of media giants and corporate conglomerates is an understandable consequence of our economic system, but it is bothersome. It smacks of too much control by a small minority that is also driven by the profit motive. The alternative seems to be government ownership and control of the media, and this is unacceptable in our society. Access and responsibility are the key issues in media today.

The state of the mass media may not be as dire as some people think, however. Cheaper means of publication and production are becoming available. In many towns and cities in America, new publications, most of them weeklies, are getting established on low budgets through offset printing. Even the electronic media are becoming less expensive. Hand-held cameras and videotape equipment are being manufactured at prices that many people can afford. This has brought about so-called people's television—neighborhood and inner-city groups that produce closed-circuit telecasting for local viewers.

And in spite of the economic warnings (explored in Chapter 3), mass media in the United States are more varied in their ownership and ideological commitment than are media in any other country in the world. One study, undertaken in the greater Washington, D.C., area, found more than 250 discrete information media available to the average citizen. These media included daily and weekly newspapers, regularly published local newsletters and magazines, AM and FM radio, and commercial and educational television. The average American can choose among a vast array of media. It is of increasing importance that *both* average citizen and mass communicator make their choices with a sense of responsibility.

SUMMARY

The mass media are truly powerful institutions in American society. They are involved in every aspect of our economic, political, and cultural systems. American public opinion is shaped by what we read, watch, and listen to in the mass media.

Historically, we can trace the influence of the media. Marshall McLuhan divides human history into three eras characterized by the relative importance of the media: pre-alphabet "acoustic space" where feelings rather than thoughts dominated; the alphabet and linear thinking; and the electric media, which again changed our perceptions and thought processes. Certainly Johannes Gutenberg's printing press did more than make books; it remade how people thought about the world. Martin Luther reshaped Christian theology as the first media minister—a tradition that America's television clergy participate in fully.

The media are revolutionary instruments because they massage the very societies that give birth to them. The press parented in Great Britain came to the colonies and turned our ancestors into rebels and founders of a new nation. The peace movement, the civil-rights movement, and the women's and gay-rights movements were all revolutionary and used the mass media to reshape the world to make it a better nation for all to live in.

The more abstract functions of the mass media—socialization and politicization—are currently debated areas of research. Television, the most pervasive and powerful of the media, is the most studied. Although researchers often disagree as to the actual ability of media content to form opinions, all agree on the need for carefully designed studies on systems or macrolevels as well as microlevels.

Freedom of communication must include access and responsibility; the mass media output should not be controlled by the very few. If we are to have social justice today and freedom for the future, you—the critical consumer—must participate fully in the mass-communication process. You must manipulate the mass media, or they will manipulate you.

REFERENCES

1. George Will, "Luther's Quest," *Washington Post*, November 10, 1983, A21.
2. "Media and Politics, A Theme Paper," delivered at 1989 Midwest Political Science Association Meeting, Chicago, April 13–15, 1989.
3. Ibid., p. 10.
4. Floyd Abrams, "The New Effort to Control Information," *The New York Times Magazine*, September 25, 1983, 22–23.

CHAPTER 24

Media Issues in the Global Village

Never before has the old saw that "knowledge is power" been more appropriate. As a twenty-first-century communication worker, you'll find it easier than ever to gather *information* because technologies make access easier, but finding the *knowledge and wisdom* on which power is based will be more difficult because you'll be required to become a citizen of the world.

In this chapter we will provide a world view of mass media, to encourage insight into (1) the issues accompanying the trend toward global economic concentration in mass-media industries, (2) the effect of the various philosophies under which press systems operate, (3) levels of freedom in various countries around the world, and (4) specific issues and the questions relating to global ethics. All of these will influence the work of communicators to an increasing degree. To the key issues raised in the preceding chapters—freedom, access, and responsibility—we add that of control.

What is true for any one nation's media system is amplified in the international marketplace. Too much economic power in the hands of a few media owners may create barriers to entry by smaller media companies that wish to add their points of view to the marketplace of ideas. Too much economic power concentrated in the hands of a few world-class media companies may lead to predatory pricing so that advertisers and media consumers pay more than a fair price for access. Moreover, too much concentration may encourage the media monopolies to emphasize the most profitable "products or services" such as entertainment at the expense of other services such as news and analysis that may be less profitable. Let's begin our survey of global issues by looking at patterns of ownership and the potential influence of these.

GLOBAL CONCENTRATION OF MEDIA INDUSTRIES

Media companies can be very profitable for individual and institutional investors; the general market trend in the 1980s toward mergers, and acquisitions, and leveraged buyouts has characterized the media industries as well.

In 1988, the total return for the Standard & Poor 500 Composite Stock Index was around 17 percent (appreciation in value of the stocks and a modest dividend

Consultant and authority on content for this chapter is Lowndes F. Stephens of 3.5 percent). Common stockholders in several media-industry stocks were doing as well or better than the average investor. According to Media General, the return on stockholders' equity for newspaper companies was 15.8 percent; 8.9 percent for broadcasting companies; 39.3 percent for book-publishing firms; 19.6 percent for motion-picture companies; 17.1 percent for magazine publishers; and 28.1 percent for advertising agencies. The Dow Jones Equity Market Index (base year 1982 = 100) in July 1989 was 312; stock prices were up 212 percent in 7 years, or 30.3 percent on an annual basis.[1] The media-industry performance was among the leaders at 562 (66.0 percent on an annual basis). Advertising company stocks had also exceeded the overall market performance with an index of 384 (40.6 percent on an annual basis).

Chapter 3 explored the effects of vertical integration and studied various companies and industries in terms of structure, conduct, and performance. Here we cite a few of the globally significant developments in media business. The American market continues to attract global media barons. The largest media acquisition in 1988 was Rupert Murdoch's News Corp.'s purchase of Triangle Publications (*TV Guide*, *Seventeen*, *Daily Racing Form*, and *Good Food*) from founder Walter Annenberg for $3.2 billion. With that acquisition, Murdoch's News Corp., based in Sydney, Australia reported total media revenues in 1988 of $1.68 billion, up 35 percent from 1987, making it the thirteenth-largest media company.

Thomson Corp., Toronto, the seventeenth-largest media company operating in the United States, owns 96 daily newspapers in the States, accounting for a

Figure 24.1. Content for the 15 different language editions of the monthly *Reader's Digest* is determined through joint editorial input by locally based editors and headquarter general editors.

combined circulation of 1.48 million. Thomson is the fifth-largest magazine publisher in the United States, specializing in technical trade journals such as *Medical Economics*, *American Banker*, and *Communications Engineering and Design*.

Hachette Publications, Paris, is the forty-eighth-largest media company operating in the United States, with all its U.S. media revenues in the magazine field (*Woman's Day*, the largest in terms of advertising revenues). Hachette S.A., is the world's largest magazine producer—74 in 10 countries, including *Elle* and *Paris-Match*. It is also the world's largest publisher of reference books, among them the *Encyclopedia Americana*, obtained when the company purchased Grolier's in 1988. This French company accounts for 30 percent of the books bought in that country, and it recently acquired Salvat of Spain, which offers the largest distribution network for printed works in the Spanish-speaking world. Media critic Ben Bagdikian believes Jean-Luc Lagardere, the arms manufacturer who purchased Hachette in 1980, intends to combine a major television operation with the company's Europe 1, the largest radio network in Europe.

Reuters Holdings, P.L.C., London, is the fifty-third-largest media company operating in the United States, with 1988 revenues of $351.3 million. Reuters exceeds the media revenues of its wire-service rival in the United States, the Associated Press, which reported 1988 revenues of $261.6 million.

Reader's Digest, a global publisher, and one of the world's leading direct-mail marketers, had $1.8 billion in annual worldwide revenues, more than half from international operations for the fiscal year ending June 30, 1989. Operating from world headquarters in a suburb of New York, it has 7,400 employees in 54 locations around the world and publishes its magazine in 15 languages for 39 national editions, reaching 100 million people. More than 21 million Condensed Books volumes in 10 languages are sold in 17 countries, and its own line of books is published in 19 countries. It is half owner of Dorling Kinderseley, a London-based global publisher, and is also involved in music, video recordings, and various special-interest magazines.

The merger of Time, Inc., and Warner Communications, Inc., in 1989 created the world's largest media firm, worth $18 billion, a sum that exceeds the combined gross domestic products of Jordan, Bolivia, Nicaragua, Albania, Laos, Liberia, and Mali. Time Warner is truly a global giant, with subsidiaries in Australia, Asia, Europe, and Latin America. It is the world's leading direct marketer of information and entertainment, the largest magazine publisher in the United States, with a worldwide readership of 120 million. The new company is one of the world's largest book dealers; subsidiaries include Warner mass-market paperbacks; Scott, Foresman; Little, Brown; Time-Life Books; and the Book-of-the-Month Club. Time Warner is the world's second largest record company (WCI). Time Warner is the second largest cable operator in the United States. Its cable subsidiaries include American Television and Communications Corporations, Home Box Office, and Cinemax pay channels. With Warner Brothers, it is a major player in motion-picture production.

The German firm, Bertelsmann A.G., with properties in 15 countries on four continents, is another member of what Bagdikian calls the "Lords of the Global Village." Bertelsmann is probably second only to Time Warner in terms of its worth. When Bertelsmann exceeded the market-share standards for print media set by the Federal Cartel Office (Federal Republic of Germany), the company expanded, first throughout Europe. In this country Bertelsmann owns Doubleday Bantam

Dell and the Literary Guild book club as well as RCA and Arista records. Gruner & Jahr, a subsidiary, publishes more than 40 magazines, including *Parents* and *Young Miss* in the United States.

One media baron preparing for a unified Europe in 1992 is London's Robert Maxwell. An example of his acquisitions was signing to buy a 40 percent stake in a leading Hungarian newspaper on the day Hungary declared itself a republic, October 23, 1989. Maxwell Communications Corporation, owner of the respected Macmillan publishing house in the United States, launched *The European* in May 1990, a 64-page weekend broadsheet aimed at affluent, mobile Europeans. The English-language paper sells for about 82 cents an issue and will look somewhat like Gannett's *USA Today*. The economics of such a gamble are staggering. Maxwell will spend $16.4 million in 1990 promoting the paper in Britain and on the Continent and will give roughly 1 million promotional copies to households in Britain. He is shooting for a circulation of 300,000 and expects to break even in 3 years. It took Gannett 4 years to get the *USA Today* international edition to its current circulation of 38,000.

New information technologies like fiber optics and satellites make it easier to publish and broadcast across borders. North America, Europe, Asia, and Australia are being strung with fiber-optic cable, and by 1992 more than 16 million miles of it will be in place. In many countries, especially in Western Europe, government broadcasting monopolies are turning to the private sector, and advertisers are aiming at megamarkets that extend beyond country and continental boundaries.

In 1989, when WPP Group of London made a successful but hostile bid for

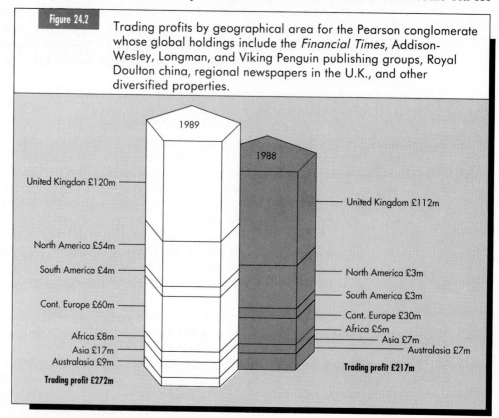

Figure 24.2 Trading profits by geographical area for the Pearson conglomerate whose global holdings include the *Financial Times*, Addison-Wesley, Longman, and Viking Penguin publishing groups, Royal Doulton china, regional newspapers in the U.K., and other diversified properties.

1989
United Kingdon £120m
North America £54m
South America £4m
Cont. Europe £60m
Africa £8m
Asia £17m
Australasia £9m
Trading profit £272m

1988
United Kingdom £112m
North America £3m
South America £3m
Cont. Europe £30m
Africa £5m
Asia £7m
Australasia £7m
Trading profit £217m

the ad agency Ogilvy Group, one of the world's largest, Ogilvy's stock rose 53 percent. Such a merger has made WPP the world's largest agency, with billings of $13.5 billion and operations in 53 countries. It provides international advertising and related marketing services to clients in as many countries. Over 50 percent of its revenues and 55 percent of its net income in 1988 came from foreign operations. This transnational corporation provides worldwide advertising, public-relations, direct-marketing, promotion, and market-research services. It has the clout to affect market power. For example, in 1989, the company (then Ogilvy Group) signed an agreement with Omnicom's BBDO and DDB/Needham for a joint media-buying venture, primarily in Europe.

Saatchi & Saatchi of London is the world's second largest advertising agency, with offices in 80 countries, annual revenues of $5.7 billion, and a 5-year earnings growth rate of 22 percent. While 80 percent of Saatchi's operating income is generated by its communication units such as the advertising agency of Backer Spielvogel Bates, 20 percent of Saatchi's income comes from its consulting division. This division of eight firms includes human-resource consultants such as the Philadelphia-based Hay Group, Inc.

BBDO Worldwide has 121 overseas agencies in 50 countries. J. Walter Thompson Co., already in the WPP Group fold, reported 1988 non-U.S. billings of $2.1 billion, up 31 percent. Other global advertising agencies include Leo Burnett Co., Chicago, with 1988 non-U.S. billings of $1.1 billion, up 20.6 percent. D'Arcy Masius Benton & Bowles, New York, has majority interests in 43 foreign agencies and reported non-U.S. billings of $1.6 billion in 1988, up 34.8 percent. McCann-Erickson Worldwide, New York, with foreign billings up 34.5 percent to $3.1 billion in 1988, has 144 agencies in 67 countries. Young & Rubicam, New York, with 127 offices in 44 countries, had non-U.S. billings of $2.6 billion in 1988, up 13 percent.

Advertising spending continues to rise. Ad agency McCann-Erickson expected a 10 percent increase, Saatchi a 10.9 percent increase, for overseas spending in 1989. Saatchi forecast increases in ad spending for 1989 of 18.4 percent in Thailand and 15.3 percent in Taiwan; it predicts South Koreans' ad spending will reach $3 billion by 1991, making it the eleventh-largest advertising nation in the world. Saatchi also expects ad spending to increase dramatically in the People's Republic of China. In Europe, Spain is its number-one pick, expecting increases in ad spending of 23 percent.

The companies in free-market countries that own newspapers attempt to become "full-service" information providers, so they typically own other media properties. For example, 92 of the 100 American media companies with newspaper properties in 1988 also made money in other media industries. Newspapers' share of the advertising dollar is eroding as cable television continues to grow and cultural literacy levels continue to decline. The Cabletelevision Advertising Bureau estimates that 70 percent of America's households will have cable by 1994, up from 55 percent in 1988.

The book-publishing industries in the United States and Great Britain demonstrate that media conglomerates don't always reach economies of scale by buying out other companies. Sometimes the results of takeover mania are dismal for art and money, as *The Economist* reported in a book-publishing profile in 1990. The "artists" or editors at these houses don't get along with the "bean counters." But the fact is that even though American book sales rose by 25 percent in each of the two decades prior to 1985, profits are tougher to make today.

Among English-language publishers, The News Corporation (Australia) accounts for $1.42 billion in worldwide book sales, the most of any of the conglomerates. In 1990 Murdoch's company consolidated previously separate U.S. publishing units under a new imprint: Harper & Row and Scott, Foresman joined the U.K. Harper Collins. Paramount Communication's Simon & Schuster imprint accounts for about $1.3 billion in sales. Hachette of France owns Groliers in the United States, which accounts for worldwide sales of $1.1 billion.

The fourth-largest book publisher based on 1989 data is Reed (Great Britain), followed by Pearson, another British conglomerate, both with sales in excess of $900 million. Maxwell Communications Corporation (Great Britain), owner of Macmillan (U.S.) and two British houses, accounts for $593 million, enough for twelfth place.[2]

The conglomerates (e.g., Murdoch, Maxwell, Newhouse, Time Warner, Bertelsmann, and Hachette) paid as much as 25 times the existing profit margins of these target companies when they purchased them. Some of the houses are still run like cottage industries, and they are inefficient. We have seen that the industry is saddled with very high fixed costs, and it has been depending on a few hits to cover all the misses. The publishing houses' share of the cover price of books has dropped from 30 percent to 20 percent, and profits are down to about 5 percent of the cover price. The booksellers like Dalton and Waldenbooks will get 50 percent of the cover price, the author 15 percent, and the printer 10 percent. Marketing and promotion costs may account for about 5–10 percent. Foreign rights sales and copublishing deals help, so authors who have "global appeal" are especially valuable. Books by Gore Vidal, John Le Carré, and Gabriel García Márquez sell worldwide, says *The Economist*, like records by Michael Jackson or Pavarotti.

Figure 24.3. American megahits are designed for international marketing. Here is *Batman*'s final confrontation scene, with Michael Keaton and Jack Nicholson.

Today, then, considerable market power is concentrated into a very few hands. Transnational corporations are the big players in this global information economy. These companies operate for the most part in countries where freedom of the press and political rights are respected by the government.

PERSPECTIVES ON PRESS THEORIES ....

Classifications of the world's press systems ultimately reflect how much or little control constrains the operations of the news media. Most recognize that the press serves the needs of the nation-state to some degree and that the needs of the collective (the government) may not be in the best interest of a majority of individual citizens. Differentiations of press-system types are often made on the basis of the extent to which the political rights and civil liberties of citizens are respected by the government, on the extent to which the press is allowed to challenge government constraints on these freedoms.

In a sense, all political philosophies are either *libertarian* or *authoritarian*. A libertarian political philosophy basically holds that the individual is most important in society; the state, government, and media exist to serve the needs of the individual. If they are not serving these needs, the individual can change them. An authoritarian political philosophy basically holds that some higher order has authority over the individual. That higher order may be the church, the state, a political leader, a teacher, or a parent. In an authoritarian society, the individual exists to serve the needs of the higher order.

These descriptions are two extremes at either end of a political continuum, but no society is as simple as either-or. Nations can be analyzed for degrees of freedom and/or control of mass media.

One method used to describe, analyze, and compare different media systems and their political philosophies was outlined in the mid-1950s by Frederick Siebert, Theodore Peterson, and Wilbur Schramm in their book *Four Theories of the Press*. They reasoned that throughout the world, all media systems can be broken down into four basic types: (1) the authoritarian system; (2) the Soviet communist system, a derivative of the authoritarian; (3) the libertarian system; and (4) the social-responsibility system, a derivative of the libertarian. We will describe this model before considering other perspectives.

THE AUTHORITARIAN SYSTEM

The authoritarian system is as old as humankind. Throughout history, governments have controlled public expression. As soon as the printing press was developed in fifteenth-century Europe, those in power realized that it had to be controlled. The authoritarian system is based on the political assumption that absolute power should rest in the hands of a monarch, a dictator, the ruling church, or the aristocracy.

Under this system, the mass media may be privately owned (although the broadcast media are often owned by the state), but they are directly controlled by the government through laws and licenses. Direct criticism of the government by the media is usually forbidden because the media is supposed to support the state.

Figure 24.4. Western correspondents are sometimes kept out of authoritarian countries. A freelance photographer made it to a frontier post at Bazargan on the Turkish-Iranian border.

Media owners can have their property taken away, and they and their editors and writers can be put in jail, if their products detract from or compete with the power of political authority.

Much of the noncommunist world—including many countries in Latin America, Africa, the Middle East, and Asia—still operates under this system. The fascist regimes in Germany and Italy were modern European examples. Adolf Hitler expressed the basic idea of the authoritarian system when he said:

> *Our law concerning the press is such that divergencies of opinion between members of the government are no longer an occasion for public exhibitions, which are not the newspapers' business. We've eliminated that conception of political freedom, which holds that everybody has the right to say whatever comes into his head.*[3]

THE SOVIET COMMUNIST SYSTEM

Despite the dismantling of the Communist party in Eastern Europe, several countries still operate the media under this political philosophy. The Soviet communist system is an extension of the authoritarian system. It developed from the application of Marxist-Leninist-Stalinist philosophy to mass communication in the twentieth century. Its basic assumption is that the individual needs to be changed so that he or she will share with and support society as a whole.

In its purest form, the mass media are owned by the state, and the media communicators are loyal party members because they must interpret all communication from the party's point of view. Owning and operating a private printing press under this kind of system is as serious a crime as printing counterfeit money is in the United States. Lenin expressed this philosophy in a speech he gave in Moscow in 1920:

> *Why should freedom of speech and freedom of the press be allowed? Why should a government which is doing what it believes to be right allow itself to be criticized? It would not allow opposition by lethal weapons. Ideas are much more fatal things than guns.*[4]

When the Communist revolution succeeded in Cuba, the first act of the new regime was to take over all institutions of communication and education, including newspaper, magazine, and book-publishing companies and radio and television stations.

THE LIBERTARIAN SYSTEM

The libertarian system struggled into existence in seventeenth- and eighteenth-century Europe as a revolutionary act against the repressive authoritarianism of the established monarchies. John Locke and John Milton gave libertarianism its most eloquent rationale. They argued that the state exists to serve the needs of the people. Governments that are not responsive to their citizens can be overthrown. Individuals have the right to seek and know the truth, and to express their ideas and opinions.

To ensure complete freedom of expression, the media should be privately owned. Indeed, the mass media under a libertarian system should function as watchdogs of government. The only restraints on media should be laws designed to protect the rights of individuals, such as libel laws to protect people's reputations and privacy laws to protect them from the media's invasion of their privacy.

The Founding Fathers, especially Thomas Jefferson and Benjamin Franklin, were imbued with the philosophy of the Enlightenment, libertarianism, and democracy. James Madison, signer of the Declaration of Independence, framer of the Constitution, and fourth president of the United States, expressed the essential argument for libertarianism in this manner:

> *Nothing could be more irrational than to give the people power and to withhold from them information without which power is abused. . . . To the press alone, checkered as it is with abuses, the world is indebted for all the triumphs which have been obtained by reason and humanity over error and oppression.*[5]

SOCIAL-RESPONSIBILITY SYSTEM

The realities of mass society have caused many thoughtful people to conclude that absolute freedom for the individual may no longer be possible; too many people live close to one another and are dependent on one another for survival. After World War II, the nongovernmental Commission on Freedom of the Press was established in the United States to discuss the relationship between the press and society in a cold war world. Under the leadership of a Harvard philosophy professor, W. E. Hocking, the commission issued a two-volume report that concluded that freedom of the press should be preserved but that it can be maintained only if the mass media accept their responsibility to society as a whole.

In a libertarian system, the freedom of people to do whatever they want often prevails, as was the case in 1979 when the government withdrew its case against a Wisconsin magazine, *The Progressive*, allowing it the legal right to publish an article on how to build a hydrogen bomb (see Chapter 20). Under the social-responsibility theory, such an article would probably not be allowed to be published. The mass media are still privately owned and operated under the social-responsibility theory, but they operate with the sanction of society. If they do not serve the interests of society or if they threaten the security of society, they can be taken over by the government to ensure public welfare and safety.

The social-responsibility theory exists in the United States to some extent in the broadcast media, but not in the print media. Radio and TV stations in the United States are privately owned, but they are licensed by the government. Because broadcasters use public property, the airwaves, the public has a right, through its government, to exercise some control over broadcasting. And if the government, through the Federal Communications Commission, finds that a broadcaster is not serving the public interest, the broadcaster's license can be revoked or not renewed, or a fine can be levied.

CONTEMPORARY PRESS PHILOSOPHIES

In *The World News Prism* (1987) William Hachten expands the preceding typology to include two concepts or press philosophies that better represent what is going on in Third World countries; his classification terms are *authoritarian*, *Western*, *communist*, *revolutionary*, and *developmental*. The communist and developmental concepts are variations of the authoritarian philosophy. The Western and revolutionary concepts are similar only in that the press tries to operate outside government controls.

Hachten eloquently captures the essence of the debates over the issue of press freedom:

> *The world's system of distributing news can be likened to a crystal prism. What in one place is considered the straight white light of truth travels through the prism and is refracted and bent into a variety of colors and shades. One person's truth becomes to another, biased reporting or propaganda, depending on where the light strikes the prism and where it emerges. As we understand and accept the optics of a prism for measuring the spectrum of light, so must we understand and accept the transecting planes of different cultural and political traditions that refract divergent perceptions of our world.*[6]

J. Herbert Altschull's market, Marxist, and advancing press systems classification parallel the First, Second, and Third World designations used by international relations scholars. He believes press systems throughout the world share many characteristics, what he calls the Seven Laws of Journalism:

1. Press systems are agents of those in political and economic power.
2. Their content reflects the interests of those who finance the press.
3. All journalists believe in free expression (though they may define it differently).
4. All journalists believe in social responsibility and public access.
5. Journalists believe the other press doctrines (other than the doctrine they follow) are deviant.

Figure 24.5. Press at a "stakeout" for news of the hijacking of Kuwait Airways plane in Algiers in April 1988 have to decide how much of the propaganda to relay.

6. Journalism schools transmit the value systems and ideologies of the larger society.
7. Press practices always differ from theory.

Robert Picard calls democratic-socialist a Western subtype of press philosophy that allows for legitimate government intervention in press affairs to ensure plurality of press ownership, social accountability, and public access. Denis McQuail also sees a Western subtype he calls democratic participant theory, which puts emphasis on the rights of citizens to relevant information, to answer back, and to use the means of communication for interaction in small groups.

Elizabeth Schillinger thinks there are three assertions one can make about the relationships among press, government, and society. First, the press, the people, and other national institutions in a nation-state (country) share primary motives—*survival*, *ideology*, and *market*. Secondly, one of them will be predominant at any given time and influence the behavior of the government, press, and society. Finally, nation-states and their press systems vacillate continually from one prevailing primary motive to one or both of the other two.

The survival motive relates to building, preserving, and defending the nation and government. The press plays the role of government partner when the survival motive is dominant (Uganda, 1976–1988; People's Republic of China, June 1989). During times of crisis (U.S. military operation in Grenada and press blackout, dealing with terrorists), the press in traditional democracies, where the primary dominant motive is the market, may be censored by government because the survival motive may become temporarily dominant.

When the dominant motive is ideology, the press is charged with propagating and popularizing the ideology, demonstrating its application to everyday life and supporting ideological leaders and their political agents (USSR, 1928–1940, 1964–1982; Iran, 1980–present).

The market motive is about protecting, maintaining, and encouraging private enterprise and free-market activity. The role of the press is to serve private enterprise and protect it and the public from government controls. The press is a "marketplace" of ideas and a watchdog of government (USA, 1802–1860, 1890–1914). Schillinger has taken Altschull's press laws, modified them somewhat, and added another—that press behavior and effectiveness is influenced by the level of technology and economic resources available.

All this helps us understand the remarkable movements toward a market economy in Poland and the Soviet Union, and the crackdown in the People's Republic of China after a period of more liberal economic and military reforms. Schillinger believes the press systems in the United States, Europe, and Japan are vacillating between the market and ideology motives in the 1990s, cognizant of the need for some government controls as they continue to recognize the importance of capitalism.

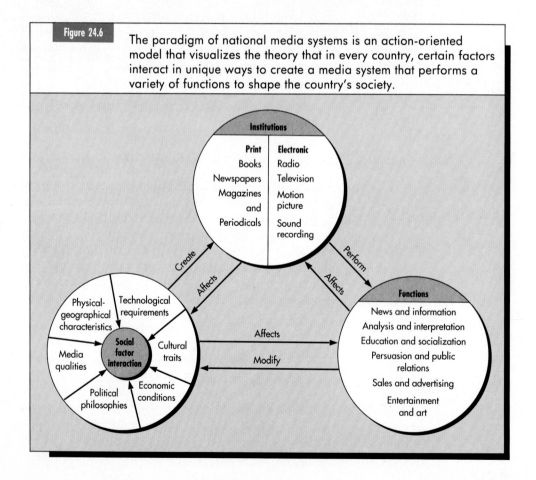

Figure 24.6 The paradigm of national media systems is an action-oriented model that visualizes the theory that in every country, certain factors interact in unique ways to create a media system that performs a variety of functions to shape the country's society.

THE ROLE OF ECONOMICS

Futurists Alvin and Heidi Toffler believe the major powers of the world are vigorously pursuing master plans for survival in the next century. As we closed the decade of the 1980s, pro-democracy movements in Eastern Europe and elsewhere changed the political philosophies under which many nation-states will operate. Opening up new markets, now available in Eastern Europe, and encouraging international trade are part of the "grand designs" in Europe, the Soviet Union, the People's Republic of China, and Japan. For example, in 1992, the integrated economy of Europe calls for opening post and telecommunication services to competition and establishing "pan-European" standards for products, services, and safety, which the European Community believes will add 2 million jobs, result in price reductions of 6 percent, and increase gross national product by 5 percent.

While these developments might expand the free flow of information across borders, some observers are concerned that too much global economic concentration in the media industries might widen the knowledge gap between "information-rich" and "information-poor" countries. American entertainment media keep and increase their dominance in films and television programming, to the point where some European countries talk of import quotas. One important tenet of the social-responsibility doctrine is that the press should link "buyer" and "seller"—in other words provide a free marketplace for ideas, economic products, and services.

So it is important for us to keep up with who owns the media: We can then make informed judgments about the conduct of the media regarding the functions shown in Figure 24.6.

PRESS FREEDOM, PROSPERITY, AND MEDIA USE ....

According to The International Bank for Reconstruction and Development, commonly known as the World Bank, about 52 percent of the world's population live in countries where the GNP per capita per year is less than $500 (U.S.), most in the developing Third World nations of Africa and Asia. From 1980 to 1987, there has been no growth in the per capita output of the economies of 61 countries, representing about 14 percent of the world's population. On the other hand, GNP per capita output has exceeded 3 percent in the People's Republic of China (9.1 percent), Pakistan (3.3 percent), and 21 other countries, representing 29 percent of the world's population. These levels of productivity are the highest rates among 185 countries followed by the World Bank.

What does this have to do with media issues?

Economic prosperity is significantly more pronounced in countries where government respects the political rights and civil liberties of its citizens.
Access to a free and responsible press is a civil liberty accorded to citizens who live in free states.
Mass media are more widely available in free states than in nonfree states.

We do not intend the following analysis as a recommendation for one form of political system over another, but it does demonstrate a significant association between economic prosperity and freedom.

INDICATORS OF MEDIA AVAILABILITY

Freedom House, a New York-based organization interested in strengthening democratic institutions, has conducted an annual Comparative Freedom Survey since 1972. The map in Figure 24.7 reflects data it developed on factors such as the degree to which fair and competitive elections occur, individual and group freedoms are guaranteed in practice, and press freedom exists. In some countries, the category reflects active citizen opposition rather than political rights granted by a government. Freedom House's categorization of the world's nations for 1990 is given with the map.

The Associated Press, the Inter-American Press Association, and the International Press Institute also conduct annual assessments on gains and losses in press freedom, and some of these are published in the Stanley Foundation magazine *World Press Review*. Freedom House's survey is used because scholars are involved in making the assessments, which include overall assessments of changes in political rights and civil liberties. The most-free states are ranked 2; the least-free states are ranked 14. It is possible to plot the Freedom House ranking on a graph in relationship to the relative purchasing power of the countries and the availability of media (in terms of daily newspaper circulation and number of radio, TV, and telephone sets per 1,000 population). The data are provided in Table 24.1. We can see that the least-free nations have significantly lower levels of real buying power (about $2,000 per capita versus more than $11,000 per capita on average for the most-free states). The median per capita real buying power among countries

Table 24.1.	Freedom, Prosperity, and Media Use in 159 Countries					
	Number of Countries	Purchasing Power	Newspaper Circulation	TV	Radio Sets	Telephone
			(Per 1,000 Population) (Average by Freedom Category)			
Freedom Ratings (Freedom House)						
2 (Most Free)	26	$11310	322	436	1135	524
3	11	5328	112	449	1029	452
4	11	2889	91	259	317	84
5	9	2390	50	33	138	20
6	5	2785	47	44	94	26
7	11	3907	111	190	374	111
8	3	5145	96	15	28	11
9	7	1737	86	82	199	20
10	11	4571	150	85	171	34
11	20	2305	80	255	403	101
12	14	4459	31	77	86	27
13	12	1287	12	69	76	22
14 (Least Free)	19	1792	29	10	23	1
Rating of Press System						
Free	56	7277	212	240	574	240
Partly Free	28	3730	114	102	215	59
Unfree	75	2490	49	24	43	6

Source: Lowndes F. Stephens.

in this analysis is $1,957 (half are above and half below this figure). Among the 26 most-free states, the range is from $3,111 to $17,615 (the United States is the highest), and the average is $11,310. Overall, Qatar ($23,956) and Nauru ($19,512) rank above the United States.

Among the 19 least-free states, the range is from $195 (Equatorial Guinea) to $11,142 (Bahrain); it should be noted that the $195 is Gross Domestic Product per capita (PPP not available). Significant variation accounts for the relatively high average ratings for the three states rated as partly free: Bangladesh ($883), Morocco ($1,761) and Singapore ($12,790). The average purchasing-power parities for the 56 countries rated "free" by Freedom House is $7,277, compared to $3,730 for countries rated "partly free" (28) and $2,490 for countries judged "unfree" (75).

Media penetration is significantly greater in the most-free states. Median newspaper circulation is 58 per 1,000 population for all countries in the analysis, compared to an average of 322 for the most-free nations and 29 per 1,000 for the least-free nations. The number of television sets varies from an average of 436 per 1,000 among citizens of the most-free countries to a low of 10 per 1,000 among citizens of the least-free countries. Exactly similar patterns characterize the diffusion of radios in these countries, with people owning about twice as many radios as they do television sets (from 1,135 sets per 1,000 population in the most-free to as few as 23 per 1,000 sets in the least-free nations). Finally, the availability of telephones shows the most dramatic variability. In the most-free states, there are 524 phones per 1,000 population versus only 1 phone per 1,000 people in the least-free states.

Newspaper circulation and telephone penetration accounts for the most significant and positive variation in purchasing power. Television and radio penetration are modest but negative predictors of purchasing power. Other modest but positive predictors of purchasing power are literacy, population size, and press-freedom ratings. These factors together accounted for about 92 percent of the variance in purchasing power (reflecting adjustment for sample size) in this analysis. Let's look now at variations in freedom among countries in our analysis.

Freedom Index

The most-free states are located in North America, South America, Europe, and Australia, the *least-free* states in Africa, the Middle East, and Eastern Europe. Pro-democracy movements in 1989 were the catalyst for improved freedom ratings in 45 countries, but antidemocracy movements in the People's Republic of China and crackdowns on journalists' reporting conflicts in South Africa, Nigeria, El Salvador, and Suriname led to declining freedom ratings in 30 countries.

In terms of Freedom House's press-system ratings, 56 countries were judged as having a free press in 1990, 29 were judged partly free, and 74 countries were judged to have unfree news and information systems. Despite the gains in press freedom in Algeria, Botswana, Chile, Gambia, Hungary, Paraguay, Poland, Tunisia, East Germany, and Czechoslovakia, 73 journalists were killed in 24 countries in 1989, up from 46 deaths (22 countries) in 1988. The total number of all cases of attacks and harassments against journalists more than doubled to 1,164, reported from 84 countries.

How do these assessments by Freedom House compare with the actual perceptions of government officials from these countries? Media scholar John Merrill interviewed information-press officials at UN missions in New York and embassy

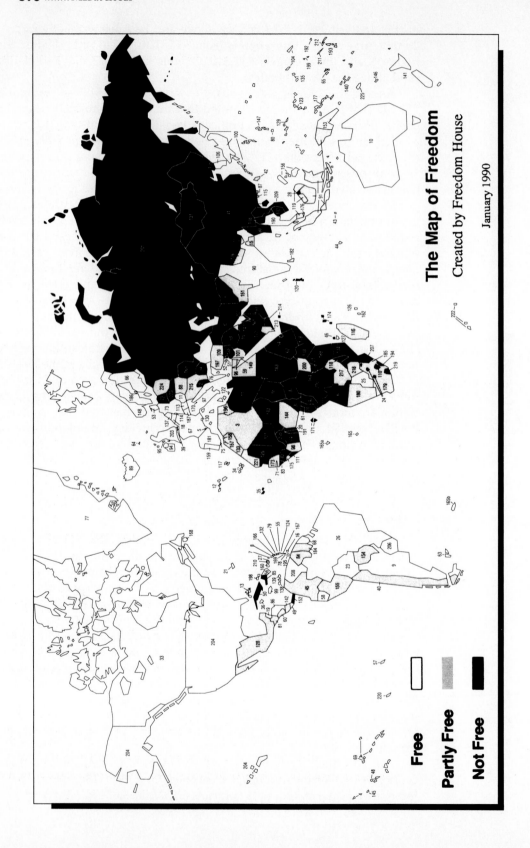

The Map of Freedom

Created by Freedom House

January 1990

Free

Partly Free

Not Free

Figure 24.7 The Map of Freedom

Free States

8	Antigua & Barbuda
9	Argentina
10	Australia
11	Austria
13	Bahamas
16	Barbados
18	Belgium
19	Belize
23	Bolivia
25	Botswana
26	Brazil
33	Canada
49	Costa Rica
51	Cyprus (G)
52	Cyprus (T)
53	Denmark
55	Dominica
56	Dominican Republic
58	Ecuador
66	Finland
67	France
71	The Gambia
73	Germany (W)
76	Greece
78	Grenada
86	Honduras
89	Iceland
90	India
94	Ireland
96	Israel
97	Italy
99	Jamaica
100	Japan
104	Kiribati
106	Korea (S)
114	Luxembourg
122	Malta
126	Mauritius
135	Nauru
137	Netherlands
141	New Zealand
148	Norway
153	Papua New Guinea
156	Philippines
159	Portugal
166	St. Christopher-Nevis
167	St. Lucia
169	St. Vincent and the Grenadines
177	Solomon Isls.
181	Spain
186	Sweden
187	Switzerland
190	Thailand
195	Trinidad & Tobago
199	Tuvalu
203	United Kingdom
204	United States
206	Uruguay
140	Vanuatu
208	Venezuela
212	Western Samoa

Related Territories

4	Amer. Samoa (US)
5	Andorra (Fr-Sp)
7	Anguilla (UK)
138	Aruba (Ne)
12	Azores (Port)
21	Bermuda (UK)
27	Br. Vir. Isls. (UK)
34	Canary Isls. (Sp)
36	Cayman Isls. (UK)
157	Ceuta (Sp)
39	Channel Isls. (UK)
43	Christmas Is. (Austral.)
44	Cocos (Keeling Isls.) (Austral.)
48	Cook Isls. (NZ)
57	Rapanui/Easter Is. (Chile)
63	Falkland Is. (UK)
64	Faeroe Isls. (Den)
68	French Guiana (Fr)
69	French Polynesia (Fr)
222	French Southern & Antarctic Terr. (Fr)
75	Gibraltar (UK)
77	Greenland (Den)
79	Guadeloupe (Fr)
80	Guam (US)
95	Isle of Man (UK)
113	Liechtenstein (Swz)
117	Madeira (Port)
127	Mahore (Fr)
123	Marshall Isls. (US)
124	Martinique (Fr)
158	Melilla (Sp)
129	Micronesia (US)
130	Monaco (Fr)
132	Montserrat (UK)
139	Ne. Antilles (Ne)
225	New Caledonia (Fr)
145	Niue (NZ)
146	Norfolk Is. (Austral.)
147	No. Marianas (US)
17	Belau (Palau) (US)
220	Pitcairn Islands (UK)
160	Puerto Rico (US)
162	Reunion (Fr)
165	St. Helena and Dependencies (UK)
165a	Ascencion
165b	Tristan da Cunha
168	St. Pierre-Mq. (Fr)
170	San Marino (It)
192	Tokelau (NZ)
198	Turks & Caicos. (UK)
210	Virgin Isls. (US)
211	Wallis & Futuna Isls. (Fr)

Partly Free States

3	Algeria
14	Bahrain
15	Bangladesh
22	Bhutan
40	Chile
45	Colombia
59	Egypt
60	El Salvador
65	Fiji
81	Guatemala
84	Guyana
88	Hungary
91	Indonesia
98	Ivory Coast
101	Jordan
107	Kuwait
116	Madagascar
119	Malaysia
128	Mexico
133	Morocco
180	Namibia
136	Nepal
142	Nicaragua
144	Nigeria
151	Pakistan
154	Paraguay
155	Peru
224	Poland
173	Senegal
175	Sierra Leone
176	Singapore
179	South Africa
182	Sri Lanka
184	Suriname
185	Swaziland
42	Taiwan (China)
193	Tonga
196	Tunisia
197	Turkey
200	Uganda
213	Yemen (N)
215	Yugoslavia
217	Zambia
218	Zimbabwe

Related Territories

87	Hong Kong (UK)
115	Macao (Port)
221	Western Sahara (Mor)

Not Free States

1	Afghanistan
2	Albania
6	Angola
20	Benin
28	Brunei
29	Bulgaria
205	Burkina Faso
30	Burma
31	Burundi
102	Cambodia
32	Cameroon
35	Cape Verde Isls.
37	Central African Republic
38	Chad
41	China (Mainland)
46	Comoros
47	Congo
50	Cuba
223	Czechoslovakia
54	Djibouti
61	Equatorial Guinea
62	Ethiopia
70	Gabon
72	Germany (E)
74	Ghana
82	Guinea
83	Guinea-Bissau
85	Haiti
92	Iran
93	Iraq
103	Kenya
105	Korea (N)
108	Laos
109	Lebanon
110	Lesotho
111	Liberia
112	Libya
118	Malawi
120	Maldives
121	Mali
125	Mauritania
131	Mongolia
134	Mozambique
143	Niger
150	Oman
152	Panama
161	Qatar
163	Romania
164	Rwanda
171	Sao Tome & Principe
172	Saudi Arabia
174	Seychelles
178	Somalia
183	Sudan
188	Syria
189	Tanzania
191	Togo
201	USSR
202	United Arab Emirates
209	Vietnam
214	Yemen (S)
216	Zaire

Related Territories

24	Bophuthatswana (SA)
219	Ciskei (SA)
149	Occupied Territories (Isr)
194	Transkei (SA)
207	Venda (SA)

press attachés in Washington. He asked them the extent to which they believed the following controls should be applied to journalists: (1) in-country licensing; (2) international licensing; (3) identification cards or accreditation; (4) university education; (5) in-country codes of ethics; and (6) international codes of ethics. He evaluated the responses on an ordinal scale ranging from 4 (very much in favor) to 0 (very much against), and he summed the items into a Control Inclination Index (CII).

Countries favoring "strict control" (CII scores of 20–24) are East Germany, Iraq, Peru, Cuba, the People's Republic of China, Syria, Tunisia (24); Bulgaria, Jordan, and Paraguay (23); Ethiopia, the Soviet Union, Lebanon (22); Angola, Czechoslovakia, Egypt, Yugoslavia, Panama (21); the Central African Republic, Kuwait, Bolivia, Zimbabwe, Malaysia (20).

Countries favoring "moderate control" are the Ivory Coast, Hungary, Guyana, Pakistan, Ecuador, Argentina (19); Nigeria, Poland, Portugal, Bangladesh, South Korea, Indonesia (18); Austria (17); Denmark, Turkey, Chile, Costa Rica, Guatemala (16); Sudan, Finland, Spain (15).

Finally, the countries favoring "little control" of the press are South Africa, the Philippines (14); New Zealand (13); Norway, India (12); Sweden, Australia, Japan (11); the Netherlands, the United Kingdom, West Germany, Mexico (10); Greece, Canada (9); the United States of America (8).

A sense of comparative press freedom has become a vital tool in the communicator's "kit bag." It defines further the condition of the U.S. media, and it gives us a notion of the wider context in which the conglomerate communicator works today.

Global Media Issues

What issues will be faced by communication workers in the twenty-first century?

The Flow of Information

One issue is how developed countries will respond to growing demands of Third World governments for a more balanced flow of international news and information, and a more comprehensive representation of life in the developing world. The developing world of "have-nots" are interested in a New World Information and Communication Order (NWICO), formulated by UNESCO, and they also seek a New World Economic Order, or more justice, in the way the world's communication resources and economic wealth are distributed.

The developed countries assume a greater burden in funding World Bank reconstruction and development loans to these countries and in funding the cultural, educational, and scientific programs of UNESCO. But Third World countries in Latin America, even so-called newly developed countries, are increasingly unable or unwilling to repay the principal or interest on these loans. In the 1980s, the United States pulled out of UNESCO and has defaulted on payments to this organization because it believed the organization was Marxist in orientation and inefficiently managed. The new director-general of UNESCO, Federico Mayor, a Spanish biochemist, has worked for 2 years to reorganize the group and to tone down the NWICO rhetoric or earlier directors, a reaction to "media imperialism."

The emphasis is now on a "balanced dissemination of information without any obstacle to the freedom of expression." Even the International Organization of Journalists, long on record favoring the licensing of journalists and a NWICO, is toning down its rhetoric and allowing correspondents to report unconventional views (such as the fact that some Third World leaders are saying it is inconsistent to argue for a NWICO when several developing countries don't practice political democracy).

The developing world worries about the distorted view of Third World countries depicted in the news of Western news agencies, news that focuses mostly on conflict, poverty and despair, crises. These world news services or wire agencies include the Associated Press, United Press International, Reuters, Agence France Presse, and TASS, from the United States, the United Kingdom, France, and the Soviet Union; the Deutsche Press Agentur in West Germany and the Kyodo News Service in Japan.

They also are troubled by the paucity of international news in general in American media. As we have seen, the costs of maintaining one print correspondent overseas for 1 year can easily amount to $300,000, and much more for a television reporter and cameraman. So there are only about 420 foreign correspondents today working full-time for U.S. news organizations versus about 2,500 during World War II. Some huge media chains such as Gannett and Thomson don't have any permanent foreign correspondents, relying instead on the wire services. According to a 1986 report by the American Newspaper Publishers Association (ANPA), out of 1,676 dailies in the United States, only 23 accounted for the total of 186 permanent overseas newspaper correspondents working for American dailies. The international news hole in U.S. papers has never been very high, laments the Center for Foreign Journalists in Washington, around 10 percent in the 1970s and 6 percent in the 1980s, but one recent study by Michael Emery of 10 of America's most distinguished newspapers put the cumulative international news hole at 2.6 percent of total space in the newspaper. Interestingly, Emery notes that only 37 percent of the space in these papers is devoted to nonadvertising content.[7]

But we live in a global village today and what happens in Somewhere, World, impacts Mainstreet, U.S.A., and vice versa. So Third World debt *is* a story that should play in Omaha because if Latin Americans can't buy food produced by grain belt farmers, those farmers may also default on bank loans. Destruction of an ecosystem in the United States, Brazil, and other places around the world, affect all citizens of the world. On the other hand, John A. Hamilton, author of *Main Street America and the Third World* and *Entangling Alliances*, argues that there are important international stories in our own backyards. As state governments expand their economic-development programs in other countries, there will be more local angles on foreign news.

CULTURAL ILLITERACY

A related global issue is the increasing level of cultural illiteracy among American citizens. E. D. Hirsch, Jr., author of *Cultural Literacy: What Every American Needs to Know*, believes a truly literate citizen must be able to grasp the meaning of any writing addressed to the general public. He notes that "all citizens should be able for instance to read newspapers of substance," a point made by Thomas Jefferson 200 years ago when he said:

Were it left to me to decide whether we should have a government without news-papers, or newspapers without a government, I should not hesitate a moment to prefer the latter. But I should mean that every man should receive those papers and be capable of reading them.[8]

Unfortunately, Americans show little interest in international news, in part because they lack the functional and cultural literacy skills that would be needed to recognize the significance of events in places unknown to them. An international Gallup Poll for the National Geographic Society in 1988 of 10,000 adults in the United States, Japan, France, West Germany, the United Kingdom, Sweden, Italy, Canada, and Mexico found that Americans know comparatively much less about the world than citizens of these other countries and considerably less than Americans knew when the survey was first conducted in the 1940s. Consider these findings from the survey of American adults:

1. Fifty-six percent don't know the population of the United States.
2. New York State was correctly identified from a map of the 48 contiguous states by only 55 percent of the respondents, and 37 different states—from Maine to Florida, and from coast to coast—were identified as New York.
3. Fourteen percent could not identify the United States from a world map (projects to 24 million adults).
4. Only 50 percent knew of the fighting in Nicaragua between the Sandinistas and the Contras.
5. One in three Americans cannot name *any* of the members of NATO; 16 percent bestow NATO membership on the Soviet Union.
6. Fifty percent cannot name *any* Warsaw Pact nation; 11 percent named the U.S. as belonging to this alliance.
7. Twenty-five percent cannot identify the Soviet Union or the Pacific Ocean on a world map (projects to 44 million).
8. The typical American respondent could identify (from outline maps) 6 of 10 U.S. states; 4 of 12 European countries; 3 of 8 South American countries.[9]

In his controversial best-seller, *The Closing of the American Mind: How Higher Education Has Failed Democracy and Impoverished the Souls of Today's Students*, Allan Bloom, classics professor at the University of Chicago, asserts a serious life means being fully aware of alternatives, thinking about them with all the intensity one brings to bear on life-and-death questions: reason–revelation; freedom–necessity; democracy–aristocracy; good–evil; body–soul; self–other; city–man; eternity–time, being–nothing. In his chapter on "Our Ignorance," Bloom's metaphor captures the essence of what it means to be cultural illiterate:

We are like ignorant shepherds living on a site where great civilizations once flour-ished. The shepherds play with the fragments that pop up to the surface, having no notion of the beautiful structures of which they were once a part. All that is necessary is a careful excavation to provide them with life-enhancing models. We need history, not to tell us what happened, or to explain the past, but to make the past alive so that it can explain us and make a future possible. This is our educational crisis and opportunity.[10]

Programs like the Cable News Network's "CNN World Report," begun in 1987 by Turner Broadcasting, are helping to provide Americans an unedited and un-censored report from around the world. This, the largest global news exchange and global newscast, works as an open repository of foreign-news feature reports from around the world. Even the United Nations (UN Television) provides film reports to CNN. Countries and news organizations that contribute to the repository can also take from it, free of charge. CNN is beamed to one-third of the earth's surface by a satellite built and controlled by the Soviet Union. Cable News Network is watched in most foreign embassies around the world, by foreign ministers and heads of state.

ACCESS TO TECHNOLOGY

Who controls the technologies of freedom is another important global issue. Who will control high-definition television? Who will control the airspace for communication satellites? Who will control the technologies for beaming propaganda to foreign audiences and the technologies for defending against these broadcasts?

Figure 24.8. The CNN Newsroom in Atlanta, Georgia, links the global and space villages.

The BBC estimates that more than 60 countries broadcast programming for external consumption. The USSR, the United States, the People's Republic of China, the United Kingdom, India, Albania, Iran, Australia, Spain, the Netherlands, France, Turkey, Bulgaria, Poland, Czechoslovakia, Canada, Sweden, Italy, Romania, Portugal, Yugoslavia, and Hungary have been doing so since 1950.

The International Telecommunications Satellite Organization (INTELSAT) was established in 1964 to manage international satellite communications. More than 120 countries belong to the consortium. COMSAT is the U.S. member of INTELSAT. The satellites are owned by INTELSAT, but most of the ground stations are owned by the member nations.

The International Telecommunications Union (ITU), established in 1934, is the arbiter of who gets radio frequencies. At the ITU's 1971 World Administrative Radio Conference (WARC) for Space Telecommunications, nations agreed to do all in their power to reduce their broadcasting across borders via satellites unless they have reached a prior agreement with those countries. Satellites have been put in the sky on a first-come–first-serve basis by countries without asking anyone for permission. At the 1979 WARC, the allocation of the radio spectrum first became an issue because the numbers of satellites in the geostationary orbit were projected to exceed the number the orbit could accommodate (about 250) without the satellites creating electromagnetic interferences with other satellites and users of the radio spectrum. The geostationary orbit is located at a distance of about 22,300 miles above the equator. Some equatorial nations such as Colombia and Indonesia claim exclusive jurisdiction to the airspace above them, including the corridor intersecting the geostationary orbit; hence, they want no satellites in their airspace unless they have given permission. Moreover, the ITU's first-come–first-serve rule has meant that "latecomers," mostly developing countries late in the satellite procurement game, are not permitted to put satellites into orbits that would interfere with the paths of existing ones. These satellites already in orbit have been launched primarily by First World countries.

It is easy to understand the controversy when you realize that a wide variety of programming can be received with an inexpensive backyard satellite dish. From the WESTAR-5 satellite, for example, one transponder may bring X-rated movies, another the Financial News Network, yet another, a sports channel. An early generation satellite, COMSTAR, had a capacity of 18,000 two-way telephone circuits, or 24 television channels. As larger-capacity satellites are launched by developed nations seeking larger markets, cries of "cultural imperialism" by Third World nations may get louder because their citizens can easily pirate the programming, using cheap backyard dishes.

In the developing world, television systems were often initially sought as status symbols; the lack of indigenous programming led to dependency on First World countries for content. The new technologies (to be discussed in the next chapter) make it easier for citizens to circumvent the protective hands of Big Brother. There are an estimated 50,000 subscribers to underground video in Chile, and 250,000 camcorders in Czechoslovakia played a role in upheavals there. Interestingly, the increased call for relaxed immigration laws (because the demand for emigration from East bloc to West bloc, from Southern Hemisphere to Northern Hemisphere countries, is increasing) may be tied to the exportation of television programs and movies. Many countries welcome skilled workers, especially those who are able to contribute to the information economy. It's a public diplomacy argument that may be the reason the United States and other developed countries have objected to any calls for the ITU to tighten its regulation of the geostationary orbit.

But the messages that travel across borders are not just news stories, propaganda, and entertainment programs. Advertising messages help pay the freight, and advertising has become a transnational affair. Some advertising agencies, such as N.W. Ayer, Inc., have entered into joint ventures that have the ad agencies producing TV movies and miniseries. Ayer clients (e.g., American Telephone & Telegraph, Gillette, and General Motors) help finance and sponsor TV movies. Ayer has a joint venture with World International Network (WIN), an organization representing TV networks in 106 countries. WIN's member stations would pay to air the movies in their countries, thus spreading production costs around, because the movies would be shown in the United States as well as other countries.

POSTMATERIALISTIC VALUES

Another issue is the apparent culture shift in advanced industrial societies from materialistic to postmaterialistic values, which could influence public expectations of democratic institutions, including the press. Political scientist Ronald Inglehart reaches such a conclusion from analysis of extensive studies from developed countries in North America, Western Europe, and the Pacific basin.[11] Inglehart and his associates base their research on two decades of survey studies from the Euro-Barometers projects of the Commission on the European Communities, World Values Surveys in 1981–1982 conducted in 25 countries, and a three-nation panel study from 1974–1981 (United States, West Germany, and the Netherlands).

Inglehart argues that our values are shaped by (1) socialization and (2) scarcity. In the short run, our values reflect *present* socioeconomic conditions; in the long run, they are based on the socioeconomic environment that existed during our *pre-adult years*. Secondly, we value what we missed during childhood (scarcity hypothesis). Today, because many younger adults in these countries were raised during periods of economic prosperity and physical security (free of war), we are finding that these adults are more nonmaterialistic in their outlook than are older adults who may have experienced economic deprivation and war during their formative years.

Materialists are focused on physiological needs, physical and economic security. They want maintenance of a strong military force, strong law enforcement, economic growth, stable prices. Materialist elites include many corporate executives, government bureaucrats, agricultural decision makers, and the general public in the United States. Postmaterialists, on the other hand, are focused on social and self-actualization needs (aesthetic, intellectual, belonging, and esteem). They value individual liberty and freedom but see themselves as stewards of the environment and the community, so they are other-directed. They want government to help create a more humane society, and they want strong participatory democracy. They also want more say on the job. Postmaterialist elites include many media representatives, public-interest-group leaders, labor leaders, policymakers, and research-center executives.

Postmaterialists have more permissive attitudes on abortion, divorce, extramarital affairs, prostitution, euthanasia, and homosexuality. Postmaterialists are embracing new social movements such as the ecology, anti–nuclear power, anti-war, and peace movements. Postmaterialists in Europe, for example, are more inclined to embrace a notion of European citizenship than they are a narrowly defined kind of country-specific nationalism. On a Sunday in January 1990, some 50,000 people joined hands in the main square of Bulgaria's capital, swayed, and sang "We Are the World." The signs of transnationalism are everywhere. As the superpowers relinquish front-stage status, we may see a greater emphasis in advanced industrial societies on cleaning up the environment and improving the prospects of freedom in the Third World. But we must be prepared to redistribute the world's wealth more equitably because these nations are likely to remain materialistic, given their years of economic deprivation.

Harvard philosopher John Rawls's ideas may strike a responsive chord for world communicators in the twenty-first century. In *A Theory of Justice*, he argues that injustice results because some of us are blessed with good fortune by birth. To resolve the injustice, we should act as "ideal observers" behind a "veil of ignorance," with all facts of inequality eliminated from our moral thinking. Behind this veil of ignorance, we will be better prepared to provide everyone with an equal right to maximum freedom and permit inequality only to the extent that it serves everyone's advantage and only as it comes about under conditions of equal opportunity.

GLOBAL ETHICS

Finally, it may be time to think about a global ethical code for journalists. The ideals we considered under Media Ethics take on new significance. In 1989, the World Association for Christian Communication convened an international conference, attended by representatives from over 80 countries, and produced "Communication and Community: The Manila Declaration." Among other things, the declaration notes the following:

> *Mass media and the information industries are structures of power. They are intertwined with national centres of political, economic and military power and are increasingly linked at the global level. Ordinary people are victims of media power and are treated more and more as objects rather than subjects. This is particularly true for women, manual labourers, indigenous minorities, senior citizens and children. Great efforts are required to reverse this trend.*[12]

Ethicist John Merrill says there are principles or maxims on which journalists from all over the world should be able to agree. First we should be *empathic*—have a deep desire to understand the perspectives, needs, and hopes of people of other countries. We should share a desire to focus our energies on *substantive issues*. We should be *honest, forthright, sincere, and clear in our presentations*. We should be *respectful of sources and audiences*, not prone to turn argument toward the person or the political system. Moreover, we should be *dedicated to our own ethical standards that are culture bound but flexible when it is important to be.*

A more humane world-communication environment might evolve if communicators adhere to Merrill's "Kantian Supermaxim":

> *TREAT THE PEOPLE OF OTHER NATIONS—NOT AS OBJECTS TO BE MOVED, USED, CHANGED OR MANAGED—BUT AS SUBJECTS WITH BASIC PERSONAL DIGNITY—SUBJECTS AND CONSUMERS OF JOURNALISM WITH THEIR OWN MINDS AND VALUES, CAPABLE OF DECISIONS AND ACTION. RECOGNIZE THEM AS MEMBERS OF HUMANITY WHO CAN SENSE A UNIVERSALITY IN MANY OF THE MAJOR*

*DIMENSIONS OF MORALITY AND WHO RECOGNIZE THAT WHILE ETH-
ICAL PRINCIPLES ARE TIED TO THE TRADITIONAL MORES OF A PEO-
PLE THEY ARE MORE THAN SIMPLY ETHNOCENTRIC WHIMS.*[13]

SUMMARY

A global perspective has become essential to communicators heading toward the twenty-first century. Recent economic trends—mergers, acquisitions, and vertical integration—have heightened concern about control of the world's media by a powerful few. Foreign ownership has become a factor in the United States, and new technologies such as fiber optics and satellites connect us in a global village.

Transnational corporations find fertile ground in countries where freedom of the press is greatest. There are many ways to analyze a nation's mass communication system. One of the most important is the impact of political philosophies on mass communication. Although a variety of political philosophies exist, four major theories of political/media systems have emerged. These are summarized in the book *Four Theories of the Press* and include: (1) the authoritarian system, in which government controls public expression; (2) the Soviet Communist system, in which the purpose of mass communication is to support the Communist party in its efforts to revolutionize society; (3) the libertarian system, which holds that the state exists to serve the needs of the people and that there should be complete freedom of expression; and (4) the social-responsibility system, which asserts that freedom of the press can be maintained only if the mass media accept their responsibility to society as a whole.

Media scholars have been building upon this base to represent what is happening in Third World countries, to reflect gradations in the spectrum of relative freedom, and to explain the movement of a nation's economic and press system from one mode to another.

Studies using Freedom House rankings show us that access to a free and responsible press is more widely available in free and prosperous states. Each nation has evolved its own mass-communication system based on unique conditions and factors. Although this text is concerned primarily with the American system of mass media, it is important to look at the media systems of other countries and try to understand why they are different from both the American system and one another.

Differences among systems and growing concentration of media ownership among Western nations contribute to several issues: (1) a need for a more balanced flow of news information and representation of developing countries; (2) cultural illiteracy; (3) control of access to technological breakthroughs; (4) cultural shift from materialistic to postmaterialistic values; and (5) need for global ethics.

REFERENCES

1. For further explanations and information, see Christine Ammer and Dean S. Ammer, *Dictionary of Business and Economics*, rev. ed. (New York: The Free Press, 1984), 403.
2. ''Book Publishing: The Diseconomies of Scale,'' *The Economist* 7–13 (April 1990):25–28.

3. "Hitler's Secret Conversations," in *The Great Quotations*, comp. George Seides (New York: Lyle Stuart, 1966), 321.

4. Quoted in H. L. Mencken, comp., *A News Dictionary of Quotations on Historical Principles from Ancient and Modern Sources* (New York: Knopf, 1966), 966.

5. Quoted in *Speaking of a Free Press* (New York: ANPA Foundation, 1970), 15.

6. William A. Hachten, *The World News Prism: Changing Media, Clashing Ideologies*, 2nd ed. (Ames: Iowa State University Press, 1987), xvii.

7. Michael Emery, "An Endangered Species: The International Newshole," *Gannett Center Journal* 3:4 (Fall 1989):151–65.

8. E. D. Hirsch, Jr., *Cultural Literacy: What Every American Needs to Know* (New York: Houghton Mifflin, 1987), 12.

9. National Geographic Society, 1988, 3:3.

10. Allan Bloom, *The Closing of the American Mind: How Higher Education Has Failed Democracy and Impoverished the Souls of Today's Students* (New York: Simon & Schuster, 1987), 239–40.

11. Ronald Inglehart, *Culture Shift in Advanced Industrial Society* (Princeton, N.J.: Princeton University Press, 1990).

12. *Media Development* (April 1990):21.

13. John C. Merrill, *The Dialectic in Journalism: Toward a Responsible Use of Press Freedom* (Baton Rouge: Louisiana State University Press, 1989), 223.

The Impact of Emerging Technologies

It used to be that thousands of years would pass before a new development in communications would occur. As time went by, major developments happened once every few centuries, and then within decades. Now new processes and techniques are being developed almost yearly, even daily. So much has happened recently that mass-communication researchers labeled the 1980s as the *beginning* of the communication revolution. Who knows what the 1990s will bring? The future is now.

Up to this point, we have been looking at the process, participants, and the industries of the mass media as they exist today. In this chapter, we'll look at some of the more important developments of recent years that are beginning to have significant effects on the world of mass communication. Future technological developments and processes and future implications will be surveyed. By the end of this chapter, you should have a good understanding of the role that equipment and processes play in the changes taking place in the mass media.

To comprehend how fast the possibilities and the issues presented by new technologies are being altered, it is sometimes useful to start with a look at the past. It is interesting to see how mass communication came about and how slowly it progressed until recently. Then we can appreciate the rapidity of developments today.

HISTORICAL PERSPECTIVE

The Sumerians of the Middle East in 3500 B.C. preserved signs and symbols in wet clay tablets by using cylinder seals and then baking the tablets in the sun. Not much happened in the area of communication until 2,000 years later when the Phoenicians introduced symbols for sounds and created an alphabet. Over two millennia passed before the publication in China of the first book printed from blocks. Then came Johannes Gutenberg's introduction of printing from movable type in 1450; by 1490, every major European city had at least one printing press. This printing revolution paved the way for a shift from an oral and scribal transmission of culture to a printed one and from elitist control of knowledge to wide dissemination.

Consultant and authority on content for this chapter is Lucinda Davenport

Figure 25.1. A labor-intensive printing industry has drastically changed through computerization.

The example of the pace of change in the newspaper industry is a useful one. The Gutenberg printing press continued to be a common way of publishing until Ottmar Mergenthaler's Linotype machine was first used at the *New York Tribune* in 1886. Over the years, other media forms have intruded upon the newspaper's traditional sphere of influence and for the first time gave people a choice of a news medium. But while automobiles, airplanes, radio, and television were developed, newspaper printing techniques remained the same.

After continuing unchanged for so long, technical developments such as visual display terminals and now computers are commonly seen in print and broadcast newsrooms. Many newsrooms no longer have teletype machines or news wires but receive information from satellites 22,300 miles above the earth, transmitting more than 10,000 words a minute. As the age of electronics develops, mass-media executives are uncertain about the future of gathering, producing, presenting, and distributing news and information. Significant issues confront both the individual and conglomerate communicators as well as the consumer of media content. We cannot begin to digest them until we are comfortable with the vocabulary of the processes.

COMPUTERS AND SOFTWARE

Where would we be without computers and their software? They are the cause of the communication revolution. Computers are in businesses and in homes; they're used for transferring information and finances and for playing games; some old computers are as large as a room, and newer ones are tiny microchips located within your watch and credit cards. People are corresponding with computers in place of typewriters, figuring finances with calculators, conferencing long distance.

About every type of technology discussed in previous chapters and in this one includes the use of microchips, computers, and software. Computers are in print and broadcast newsrooms and production studios, performing far more tasks than most people realize. After we see how they are used in writing and presenting news, we will delve into the integration of computers with other types of technology for gathering, researching, and disseminating information.

BROADCAST ORGANIZATIONS

Major departments in radio and television organizations include newsroom, production, and management functions. Computers have helped produce a new generation of equipment and have automated many functions in each area.

From a list of menu items appearing on the first screen, reporters can instruct the computer to assist them in a task of their choosing. They might want to check their electronic mailbox for fresh information. Or the reporter who has just come back from shooting an exciting event might want to use the scriptwriting function to write the story. Using a split screen, the scriptwriting software automatically sets margins, columns, and headings, and standardizes video and production-room cues. Thus, reporters can devote time to *thinking* about the story and writing it for the audience instead of interrupting their thought processes to type routine directions and details. The syndicated news wire can be keyworded, shown on one-half of a split screen while the reporter's rewrite appears on the other half.

The completed story is stored until the editor has a chance to call it up on his or her computer for review. Once edited and in final form, the story is transmitted automatically to (1) a printer, so that the anchors have a chance to preview the story and make notes on a hard copy before the newscast and (2) the teleprompter for anchors to read while on the air. The computer controlling the teleprompter is told which anchor is reading what story and automatically sets the type size and reading speed most comfortable for each announcer. The electronic story is also sent to (3) the electronic morgue, where all stories, past and current, are stored electronically and used later as background information for another story.

Meanwhile, assignment editors handle areas from the main menu where assignments are listed, personnel schedules recorded, and rundown sheets (containing the order and times of news stories) are regularly revised and timing recalculated automatically.

Data-base and spreadsheet applications from the main menu are used commonly by management for budgeting personnel salaries, equipment costs, and inventory. Other software applications in a broadcast organization include programming packages that act as a detailed guide scheduling commercials, news breaks, and programs for the complete broadcast day and accounting packages for figuring payrolls, billing, and other bookkeeping records. The advertising staff might use the computers to record research on audience demographics. They can duplicate their results on computer discs sent to clients who might want to advertise only during the programs that engage a targeted audience.

In the future, many broadcast-station operators and announcers will use computers with a touch screen to fade in and out automatically a number of equipment devices such as cart machines, cassette decks, audio feeds, recorders, and on-air telephones and microphones.

PRINT NEWS ORGANIZATIONS

Many computer applications functioning in a print news organization are the same as those in broadcast. A reporter types a story on a terminal and sends it to a central computer, while journalists working away from the newsroom write with portable lap computers and transmit stories to the central computer via a telephone hookup. Then, at the editor's convenience, stories are transmitted from the central computer to the editor's terminal for reviewing and headline writing. Often these stories appear on a split screen—the reporter's original or wire story on one side and the revision on the other—and after approval, the story is sent to a photo typesetting machine that can print it at a rate of 2,500 lines or more per minute on paper strips to be pasted up. Some advanced newsrooms have "pagination":

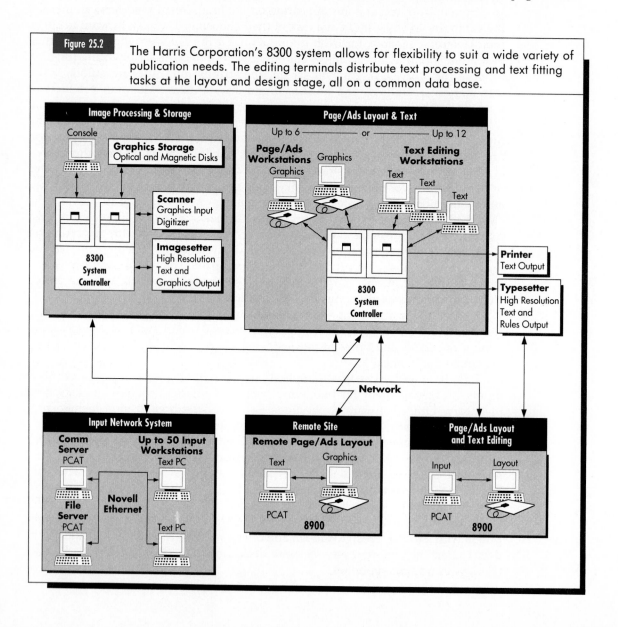

Figure 25.2 The Harris Corporation's 8300 system allows for flexibility to suit a wide variety of publication needs. The editing terminals distribute text processing and text fitting tasks at the layout and design stage, all on a common data base.

The entire page is composed on a terminal screen and is sent directly to a printing plate. With only a few people doing most of the work with computers and terminals, these technological advances invariably have eliminated personnel (and created problems for management and labor unions).

CHANGING PRINT INFORMATION TECHNOLOGIES...

More and more people, including reporters, writers, and publishers, are getting their information from electronic sources. Instead of searching for and reading information and news appearing in the traditional print form of books, newspapers, and annual reports, people are getting the same information faster when it is stored electronically. Electronic information is not for the casual reader, but rather for those who are looking for particular bits of information. The main difference between electronic and traditional print users is that the electronic ones can obtain the same information that is found in a newspaper but do not have to read the whole newspaper to find it.

Electronic storage of information is usually referred to with the generic term of *electronic data base* and includes *videotex, online data bases, electronic bulletin boards, teletext, cabletext,* and *audiotext*. Other electronic news sources are stored in *CD-ROM discs* or are sent to fax newspaper subscribers.

VIDEOTEX

Videotex is the process of transmitting millions of bits of information from a mainframe or "host" computer for presentation on one's computer screen. The two largest videotex systems are CompuServe Information Services, owned by H & R Block, with about 600,000 subscribers, and Prodigy, a joint venture of IBM and Sears. Prodigy has a flat fee of about $10 a month; CompuServe charges for the time one is connected to the service.

The name "videotex" comes from "video" and "text" because the first subscribers read the "text" information (graphics were too primitive and took up too much memory power) from video display terminals or television screens before computers became affordable. In England, where videotex was first developed, their generic term is *viewdata*, as in "view" the "data" on one's screen.

Equipment includes

1. a mainframe computer, where the desired information is stored,
2. transmission lines, usually telephone, to send information between one's personal computer and the mainframe,
3. telecommunication software enabling your computer to dial the mainframe, and
4. a modem to change the *digital information* (the way information is stored and presented in the mainframe and the personal computer) to *analog* (the way information is transmitted along telephone lines).

Videotex systems have two-way interaction between the subscriber and the mainframe. Two most commonly used videotex applications are *information retrieval* and *electronic messaging*; however, other uses include *transactional services*, *polling*, *computing*, and *telemonitoring*.

Information retrieval includes, but is not limited to, the knowledge found in local and national newspapers, periodicals, newsletters, annual reports, reference books, catalogs, directories, and timetables. Electronic messaging, the other common use, is completed simply by typing a note on the computer and sending to another videotex user on the same system or one that is connected with that system. Subscribers use transactional services to shop in electronic malls, conduct their banking business, pay bills, and make travel or hotel arrangements. With polling, people can make their opinions known in market research, and maybe someday, political races. Computing helps one with management information and financial figures, and the last application, telemonitoring, continually checks a building's security points and energy systems.

ONLINE DATA BASES

Connecting to an online data base requires the same equipment as connecting to a videotex system because it involves the same process. The main difference between the two is that an online data base is not transactional, or two-way, and is used only for obtaining specialized information. Each data base usually deals with a particular area of information, and several data bases can be accessed with one phone call to an online service, or vendor, handling the data bases. Today, there are about 450,000 data bases handled by about 500 online services.

Usually businesses, rather than the average person, can afford to subscribe to an online service because the information is so specialized and thus expensive. Monthly bills can run from several hundred to several thousands of dollars. Some of the largest online services include Mead Data Central's Lexis (for legal information) and Nexis (for general news), Knight-Ridder's VU/Text (newspapers only), BRS (for bibliographic information), and Dow Jones Retrieval Service (for financial news).

ELECTRONIC BULLETIN BOARDS

Electronic bulletin-boards systems (BBS), just like online data bases, have only one or two of the applications found on a videotex service. They also have the same connection process. Electronic bulletin boards do not require a big mainframe computer and are usually run from a personal computer with a "hard drive." Exactly how much power is needed depends on how complex or large the system operators want it to be. In addition, electronic bulletin boards allow two-way communication, whereas online data bases are one-way (information retrieval only). People with similar interests "gather" on these boards to discuss specific topics. They can carry on threads of conversation through their computers by exchanging electronic messages or "conferencing" in real time. They can also find specific information stored in the board's various "data libraries."

About 5,000 electronic bulletin boards are found around the country. Although most of these boards are operated by private individuals from their homes, a large number are operated by small businesses, ranging from graphics companies to newspapers, as a means of promoting their products or services. Electronic bulletin boards are usually free to the caller, who is often paying a long-distance telephone charge to the board.

TELETEXT, CABLETEXT, AND AUDIOTEXT

The same logic holds for the other "text" terms as for videotex: Teletext is information broadcast from a television station to one's television screen or is sent by cable (cabletext). Audiotext is information received through the telephone receiver.

With teletext and cabletext, television viewers receive news usually found in the daily or weekly local newspaper. This one-way information is preselected for the viewer and silently appears in "pages" on the screen in the same continuous rotating order. How many pages of information are offered depends on the local broadcast or cable station. Teletext piggybacks the regular television signal and needs a decoder because it appears in the same area used for closed captions for the hearing impaired, whereas cabletext uses no decoder because it uses a cable channel.

Audiotext is an easy way to find information. Simply pick up your touch-tone telephone and dial one number for an update on television soap programs and another number for football scores. By dialing hundreds of numbers, a caller can receive information from a computer "voice" instead of watching it on a television or computer screen.

All three services are free to the user. However, one must rent or buy a decoder to receive teletext, subscribe to a cable company to receive cabletext, and have a telephone to receive audiotext (unless the number is long distance).

CD-ROM

CD-ROM stands for "compact disc—read-only memory" and means that the prerecorded information cannot be altered. It's a different method of accessing similar information found in an online data base: Instead of calling to a mainframe computer, one must have a CD player connected to a personal computer. Some feel that a CD-ROM is easier to use than connecting to a host computer. A difference between the two is that the CD-ROM is not updated quickly and a subscriber usually receives monthly or quarterly updates. Thus, while online data bases are best for up-to-the-minute news, CDs are used for research needs.

CD-ROM discs are also extremely advantageous for archival purposes: Less room is taken up on one's bookshelves when a complete encyclopedia set can be encoded on a single CD with room to spare. (To expand on this example, some say that libraries will become one-room CD storage houses in the future.) Information or programs that take up about 1,000 floppy discs can be recorded on one CD and transferred to the computer when needed. The expense of one CD is much less than 1,000 discs. Similar to an online data base, the cost of an information-filled CD-ROM varies depending on the information it contains. Most CDs are less expensive than online data bases; however, again, the information is not as up-to-date.

The CD-ROM is a type of optical disc, which is a light-based type of technology. Other light-based technologies discussed later in this chapter include fiber optics, over-the-air laser and compact disc variations such as digital video-interactive (DV-I) and videodiscs.

FAX NEWSPAPERS

In addition to these electronic communication processes and computer-encoded information technologies, there are fax newspapers. Some news organizations have contracts outlining particular news interests of clients, and as the news of the day is composed, only certain articles are sent in the form of fax newspapers to the client's business or home at a prearranged regular time, which is usually very early in the morning so that the client is prepared for his or her business day.

Instead of being bought at the newsstand or being delivered to one's doorstep, the newspaper is sent over a fax machine and consists of two or three legal-size pages listing only those articles of interest extrapolated from that day's news. The cost is more than a newspaper because of the technology it takes to select individualized information and send it long distance.

The innovative communication technologies mentioned here are the ones of immediate concern to mass-communication organizations for their reporters' use in the newsroom for gathering information but also for presenting and distributing their information in a different format other than the traditional newspaper or broadcast structure. The next section discusses modern methods used to transmit news and information to media organizations and individuals.

CHANGING INFORMATION AND ENTERTAINMENT TRANSMISSION ....

Our focus shifts now to those communication technologies affecting the traditional broadcast industry. However, times are changing, and these technologies are used by all mass media because they are ways of obtaining and sending information.

Great inroads have been made with the advent of new technologies developed to speed up and improve the quality of news and information. Some of the new transmission technologies include *satellite*, *microwave*, *fiber optics*, and *ISDN* transmission, or a combination of each.

SATELLITES

As we saw in the preceding chapter, satellites have helped to shrink the world. A satellite hovers more than 22,000 miles above the earth and travels at the same speed that the earth rotates. It obtains energy from the large array of solar panels on its "wings" or cylindrical-shaped body, and battery backups are used during solar eclipses. In addition, thrusters expending short streams of gas enable the satellite to maintain its position in space for more than a decade. The information transferred between satellites and ground stations is virtually error-free. And as the power of satellites increases, the diameters of newly built receiving dishes decrease.

Those relay stations hanging in space are affecting mass-media industries in a variety of ways. One that the consumer doesn't usually think about is that satellites allow for the immediate exchange of information *between* news organizations

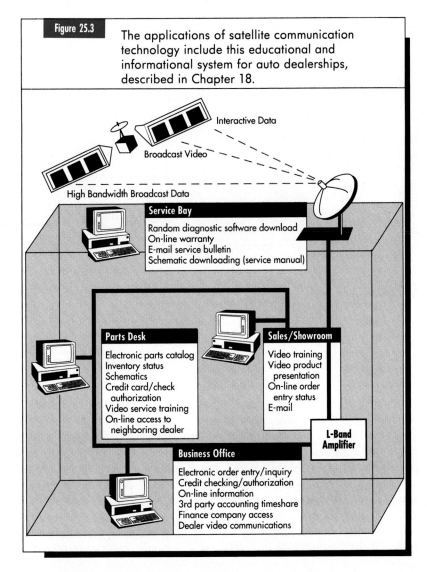

Figure 25.3 The applications of satellite communication technology include this educational and informational system for auto dealerships, described in Chapter 18.

and between syndicator and client as well as delivery of content from communicator to printing plant. A second advantage of the satellite for news organizations appears in the area of investigative reporting. Pictures of and information about other countries obtained via satellite can help reporters make independent observations about an event or issue instead of relying on outside, sometimes suppressed, sources.

A news station's common method of "live remote" reporting is a third advantage made possible with the development of satellite technology. Producers are no longer limited to in-house visuals, nor do reporters have to race back to the station with film footage to be edited before the broadcast. With the help of a truck containing satellite equipment and a secured dish on its roof, camera operators can shoot video and audio of almost any event, send it (uplinked) via microwaves to a satellite their news station is leasing, and have it beamed down (downlinked) to the station for broadcast to viewers' homes.

Figure 25.4. This Skylink mobile satellite transmission unit, used by WXIA-TV in Atlanta, enables a reporter to broadcast live from any location. The signal can also be sent instantly to other television stations owned by WXIA-TV's parent company.

A fourth, and perhaps most important, area where satellites have made a change is in the cable industry. Without satellite technology distributing programs, the cable industry would not be where it is today. And there would be no HBO, Showtime, or Turner Broadcasting. Using a variety of technologies, these and other programmers have been able to carve out a lucrative niche for themselves: To receive something like HBO, movies and other programs from a headquartered land station are sent via microwave to a satellite above the earth's atmosphere. There the satellite reinforces the signals and redirects them to the many cable subsidiaries or cable companies subscribing to the service. Then the cable companies redistribute the signals through fiber optic cables to individual subscribers' homes where the programs are seen on the television screen.

For a while, in the mid- to latter 1980s, Direct Broadcast Satellite (DBS) transmission was threatening the cable programmers' business. Private individuals with satellite dishes could receive programs free, straight from a satellite without subscribing to cable stations. Satellite dish sales went up but then plummeted when angry cable programmers began scrambling their signals to prevent unauthorized viewing. After much deliberation, cable programmers decided to offer home dish owners packages lower in price than those offered cable subscribers. Now satellite system sales are increasing again.

Smaller antennae and a higher-powered transmission process used in other countries are being developed for the United States. With this advanced technology, media experts predict that about 12 million home satellite systems will be in place before the end of the 1990s. In addition, several communication conglomerates plan to invest about $1 billion to broadcasting to napkin-size flat dishes by 1994.

MICROWAVE AND OVER-THE-AIR LASER

Satellites using very high microwave frequencies are good for long distance and one point to multipoint transmission. Microwave is also used for terrestrial transmission *within* cities. Both microwave and over-the-air laser transmissions can relay a wide range of information and are more cost-effective than land lines, such as traditional wiring or cabling. In addition, the nature of over-the-air laser technology prohibits information stealth. On the downside, the efficiency of these two transmission methods is dependent on weather conditions. In heavy rains or even smog, the information bits might be dropped or misdirected, so that the line-of-sight transmission does not reach its destination.

Both terrestrial microwave and over-the-air laser are efficient means of relaying information relatively short distances. However, if one were to send information from one side of the country to the other, satellite would be the most cost-effective, efficient, and secure method in the long run.

FIBER OPTICS

Fiber optics employs the use of light waves to carry information through thin tubes of glass surrounded by a noncorrosive coating. These are much smaller than the traditional telephone or television cables but carry many times the amount of audio, video, graphics, and text (digital and analog) information.

Another advantage to fiber optics is that it is the most secure method of data transportation. With fiber optics, information cannot be tapped as it can be with satellite and some cable, does not encounter electromagnetic or radio-frequency interference, and does not have the same constraints as line-of-sight transmission methods. In addition, unlike terrestrial microwave, cable, or broadcast, fiber-optic transmissions can travel great distances without repeaters to strengthen a signal. And one can send two-way information with fiber optics, whereas satellite is one-way.

Fiber optics is slowly being integrated into present communication technologies and methods. The delay is due to the fact that this innovative process is not needed for unique data transmission. It does what present processes do, only better. When methods and equipment start to break down and need restoring, they will probably be replaced with fiber optics.

ISDN

The telephone company has been thinking for several years about building an *integrated services digital network* (ISDN). Instead of having one channel of information for the telephone, one for computer data, and yet another for video, ISDN would digitize and combine audio, text, and video into one network. This type of network would carry hundreds of millions of bits of information per second to every customer on demand.

The idea is that instead of calling someone to say that you'll be hanging up to send an article via computers and modems, the text can be sent as you are talking. Visuals can be sent simultaneously. The telephone company would be providing digital bits on demand and wouldn't care whether the bits are being used for voice, image, or text.

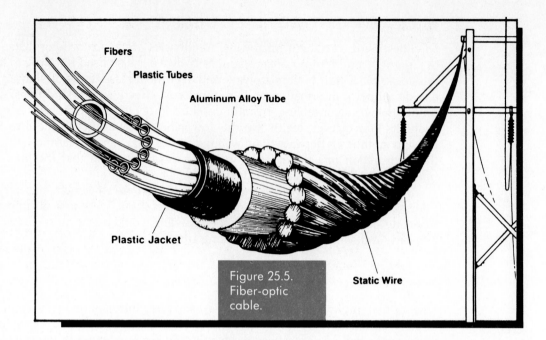

Figure 25.5.
Fiber-optic
cable.

Although many communication specialists are talking about the possibility of ISDN, it has yet to be developed. Implementation problems include finding a national and international technical standard that is satisfactory to all countries and determining future amounts of information flow.

Changing Information and Entertainment Presentation...

No longer are we bound by broadcast, cable, and telephone methods of moving information (image, voice, audio, and text) from one place to another. There are new developments in how that information is being packaged once it arrives at its destination.

For a long time, when one obtained information, it was either read in a printed publication, heard on the telephone, or viewed on television. Then inroads were made with the presentation of information on a computer screen. More innovations are being developed in the areas of *HDTV*, *VCRs* and *Super-VHS* and *Videodiscs* (optical discs) to make the presentation of information cleaner, clearer, more efficient, and comfortable to the receiver.

HDTV

When most people think of high-definition television (HDTV), they think only of sharper pictures. But there's much more. Characteristics of HDTV include (1) improved resolution, (2) more realistic color, (3) a more natural horizontal and vertical viewing ratio, and (4) digital multichannel sound.

The television standard in the United States is 525 scanning lines and 60 pictures per second. To make images sharper, high-definition standards are 1,125 lines at 60 frames per second. This change, as well as the color improvement, is not easily detected with a regular-size television but is clear with large-screen sets. Our present color system was developed many years ago when sets were 16 to 21 inches and color was used to fill in the vacant spots in the black-and-white programs. Thus, the inadequacies of these outdated standards are magnified when programs are watched on large-screen television. HDTV technology will improve color range and fidelity to match that of 35-mm film.

Another characteristic of HDTV, the shape of the screen, will change from a 4:3 to a 5:3 ratio to reflect a wide, more natural viewing pattern because our vision is more horizontal than vertical. In addition, HDTV will introduce digital multi-channel sound because consumers today expect high-quality digital sound, as evidenced by the lucrative compact-disc industry.

As with most new technologies, the transformation from one communication process to another will take time. And HDTV is not different. The average person will have to justify buying a different or modified television set, but the technology used in producing the programs and distributing the signal will change. In addition, the television industry will have to agree on national and worldwide technical and transmission standards. Some analysts feel HDTV could revitalize this country's role in the electronics industry, but with a lack of backing from the Commerce Department for focused U.S. initiative, American firms have begun cooperation with Japan.

OPTICAL DISC

As noted in our earlier discussion of CD-ROM, optical discs are a light-based technology. Most optical compact discs (CDs) are small round discs slightly larger than the palm of a hand. Laser light encodes information on the disc by cutting minute grooves to represent information, then this information is played back when the light beam is reflected off the disc, varying the length of the beam as it passes over the different grooves.

CD-ROM (compact disc—read-only memory) is used regularly for archival purposes. Information is encoded on the disc, and no one can modify it, no matter how often the disc is used.

CD-WORM (compact disc—write once read many) is used often in conjunction with a computer for business purposes, such as financial records. Information can be encoded on a daily basis, but once it is written on the disc, it cannot be altered. One can continue to read and add to, but not change, the data.

DV-I (digital video—interactive) is still a relatively new concept to many people. It acts very much like hypermedia software—software that combines text, pictures, audio, and animation. In fact, once a piece of hypermedia software is developed from a computer, it is then transferred to a compact disc because CDs have great durability. Using a compact-disc player and a computer, a user can experience the DV-I's full-motion, full-screen video display, which can present new information continuously for about an hour. Most often, DV-I's are used for games or educational purposes, where the user can interact with the information.

DV-I's will eventually be popping up in people's homes because the compact-disc player is used for several reasons: retrieving CD reference information, keeping financial records, and now interactive educational purposes. In addition, society is becoming more accustomed to software (which the DV-I replicates) and communicating interactively with computers.

Videodiscs, another type of optical disc, also present a full-motion, full-screen video display, but are the size of LP (long-playing) records. Developed before the DV-I, videodiscs are used for encoding and distributing movies. Their main competition in this area is the VCR; however, videodiscs have superior audio and video quality. Also, it is possible to stop a videodisc and view a single frame without damaging the disc, whereas stopping a VCR tape progressively ruins the tape and the heads. Although videodiscs have been on the market for about as long as VCRs, they have not caught on because of the additional expense of the equipment attached to a television needed to play a videodisc. VCRs were found to be more desirable because they could be used in a variety of ways: to play one's home movies, to show rented movies, and to record television programs.

Good things come with optical discs. They are relatively inexpensive, depending on the information they contain, are durable because of their plastic coating, and last for 10 years or more, regardless of how often they are used.

CHANGING VISUAL COMMUNICATION TECHNOLOGIES ....

One of the most exciting areas of new mass-media technologies involves visual communication. After staying relatively the same for more than 100 years, great strides are being made in the equipment and materials used for capturing and

Figure 25.6. Harris Corporation's IMAGES system (left) is an electronic darkroom that is hardware independent and based on industry standard system software. Sony's MVC-2000 Hi-Band Pro-Mavica™ Still Video Camera (right) allows images to be captured in new ways.

processing images. And as with most of the new communication technologies presented in this chapter, visual innovations also are being made with the digitization of information.

Although they look similar, 35-mm cameras are slowly being replaced by still video cameras. Instead of using light-sensitive film, images are recorded on magnetic media such as 2″ × 2″ videodiscs that look like standard small personal-computer discs and hold up to 50 shots. The discs can be slipped into still video recorders for "soft" viewing while one decides which image to produce in "hard" copy by a still-image printer. This process can be analogized with searching for or looking at a word-processed article on the computer screen (soft viewing) and then deciding to print it out (hard copy). When a photojournalist wants to send an image back to the home office, the digital image is changed from analog (telephone transmission signals) to digital and displayed for soft or hard viewing by a still-video transceiver.

Recently introduced is the Image Management and Graphic Enhancement System (IMAGES) that Florida-based Harris Corporation has designed to be especially useful for the newspaper industry. Picture input can be received from analog photo wire services, digital wire services, scanners (remote, local, foreign), and files, and a user can output to layout systems, imagesetters, wire services, and many other devices. Up to 32 different images can appear on a screen, selected, and edited. Technology *is* changing communication.

Another new technology is the video transfer stand or scanners, which transfers original 35-mm slides or prints to electronic still video for disc storage.

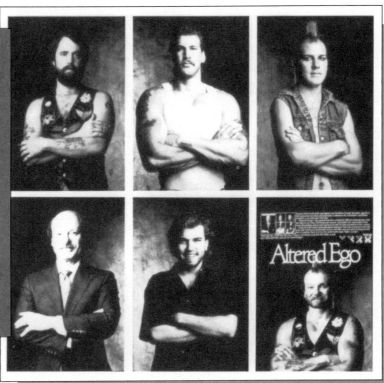

Figure 25.7. Digital technology allows seemingly endless manipulation of images: removal of unwanted objects or people, rearrangement of nature or individuals, creation of new entities. Five separate photographs were combined using Scitex 350 Response System.

IMAGE MANIPULATION

Once received and brought out of storage, the image goes to the electronic dark-room (ED) or electronic picture desk (EPD) for editing and, in some cases, complete manipulation. Here images are viewed on the computer screen, and the complete picture or just parts of the image are cropped, contrasted, lightened or darkened, rotated, reversed, sharpened, flipped, zoomed, and caption-added.

Once in the ED, it doesn't matter if the original image was an illustration, graphic, or photograph because they have similar digitized appearances on the screen. In many cases, it is difficult to discern a completed computer-generated graphic from a photograph. Not only is it easy to retouch these visuals, but they can be taken apart, reassembled, and altered. Also, certain images in the visual can be moved around; for example, changing a tree from one side of the road to the other or removing the tree altogether. In addition, a composite photograph can be made from several. For example, two individuals from two different photographs can be combined into one image to make it appear as if the two people had their picture taken together.

This kind of image manipulation can shake public trust and even discredit the use of photographs as court evidence. Newspapers are trying to find guidelines between "improving" an image and completely altering it. However, print shops and advertising agencies, with a different objective than newspapers, have been manipulating images for some time now.

Once the desired image has been selected, the ED editor can send the picture, with other graphics and articles, to the main pagination system for electronic page layout. Complete pages are assembled on screen and then output to a laser plotter to produce a finished page negative in one piece.

Whether the process begins with the still camera or starts with scanning 35-mm film for ED processing, digital imaging has many advantages: Companies save thousands of dollars in ink, paper, chemicals, and other supplies, as well as time. The electronic procedure is quicker than film processing, and digital data are transmitted 10 times faster to the home office than in the traditional analog mode. Deadlines are no longer held up or missed because of photo production time. In addition, whereas the quality of the photograph is dependent on the quality of the transmission (telephone lines and receiver equipment), digital images experience no loss of image quality. Also, it is just as easy to have color as black-and-white when dealing with this new equipment.

A drawback to still cameras, but not digital processing, is that the resolution quality is not as good as 35-mm film. However, as with traditional color television, the quality of resolution is not as readily apparent in small visuals as in large ones. This negative aspect is secondary to many companies because the photos are now able to hit deadline time and the photos and graphs can be handled as quickly as words and stored in a variety of ways.

A particular consideration is that many photographers feel that they have lost their autonomy in visual judgment when others are deciding the fate of (manipulating) their images. Some traditional photo personnel positions might be streamlined or eliminated. And photojournalists may become more like television-news camera operators, merely holding a place in the chain of news production. Meanwhile, many graphic artists might be turned into computer operators.

CLASSROOMS OF THE FUTURE

Schools are implementing many of the new technologies for their information needs, to keep pace with the industry, and to educate their students better. They must keep pace with industry so that they may continually give their students the best training by providing them with up-to-date career skills and new information. Thus, upon graduation, students can immediately begin their new work instead of spending time training on the job.

Not only are technologies being used in the classroom, but the classroom of today and the future can be anywhere. Students and teachers can take advantage of new technologies in a single or combined manner. New transmission technologies and video allow teachers at school to communicate with one or more students in their homes. Students can see the instructor and the other students. Another way for teachers and students to interact is through videotex and electronic bulletin boards. Lesson assignments and questions can be exchanged electronically. Or everyone can be online at the same time in a conference mode.

At times, students might not need the instructor. These self-paced courses can be learned with the use of digital video-interactive optical discs or hypermedia software. Students react to the technology and it, in turn, responds to the students' answers using animation, graphics, voice, and text. Students will no longer have to go to hundreds of different sources in the library to find background material for a project or research information for a paper. Text and graphics online data bases and CD-ROM discs can be keyworded to find information instantly.

Schools are also using these communication technologies for advancement of the academic institution itself. Schools communicate with researchers, teachers, and professionals worldwide, using a variety of technologies, such as videotex and electronic bulletin boards. To respond to information quickly, they use microwave and satellite transmission. And they will be using libraries of CDs and online data bases.

NEW TECHNOLOGIES AND LEGAL AND ETHICAL ISSUES

It is difficult to predict the use of an innovation. On one hand, some technologies are developed on the theory that as soon as everyone finds out about it, it can't be produced fast enough. Sometimes the idea or product has caught on so quickly that it has brought about problems not thought about or previously encountered. On the other hand, if a technology simply improves an existing process or device but does not fill a need, it is not universally accepted until existing equipment needs replacing.

Policymakers are now grappling with legal and ethical issues concerning technology. Historically, laws once made for newspapers and print publications had to be modified to include or exclude broadcast. Then broadcast policy had to be altered to include or exclude cable. And so it goes. With so many new communication technologies being developed, the boundary lines of traditional media are being blurred. To formulate a policy for some media and not others is difficult, especially when one doesn't know what uses to expect in the future. Some of the more apparent legal problems include *industry standardization, ownership, copyright, privacy*, and *security*. Some societal and individual issues deal with *equal access* and a *change in work structure and equal opportunity*. These are only a few of the issues sitting atop the iceberg; there are many more.

INDUSTRY STANDARDS

America's capitalistic ideal often makes the general public adaptation of a technology difficult. Companies are worried about sinking too much of their resources into research and development if consumers don't want to waste their money on one technology in case it quickly becomes obsolete in favor of another. One example is the eight-track versus cassette, and a second example is beta versus VHS.

The videotex technology has grown rapidly in countries where the government owns the communication systems and has supported one type of technical standard. In the United States, however, we are trying to find a videotex standard. We are trying to figure out what to do with HDTV as well. As with many technologies, once a standard is found within the industry of a country, an international standard will have to be agreed upon. Sometimes it's the other way around: Once an international standard has been found, national industries follow. Then transmitting and receiving information will be simpler and more prevalent, creating a global village.

OWNERSHIP

Ownership has become an important topic because the lines of communication are no longer clear. For example, the telephone company owns transmission lines, telephone receivers, and AT&T personal computers. What if the phone company wanted to know about and control everything that went out over its lines? What if the phone company became an information provider performing and then replacing the newspaper? It would have a monopoly on the information, the transmission lines, and the receivers. This is a worrisome thought to some countries and individuals. It does, however, merit careful thought about how much one company can own or regulate.

COPYRIGHT

Another question concerning ownership or copyright relates to the information itself. For instance, a newspaper has published a story on government spending. It prints it in the newspaper. It is also on an online data-base service. Then, a CD-ROM company packages sections of the online data base of which this story is a part. Whose information is it? And who is to blame if the information is false?

Is it breaking the law to intercept information or entertainment from a cable or broadcast company's satellite? Is it stealing? What about copying software? And what of videotape recorders copying television programs? These are questions that are being resolved bit by bit.

PRIVACY AND SECURITY

A worry for users of electronic information is that others will be able to break into their system or data-storage area and steal the company secrets. Unfortunately, this happens often. Computer literates are faking companies' electronic records and stealing money. Computer science students have found ways to break into top-secret government files online and private satellite transmissions; and newspaper reporters have been able to steal stories from previous employers.

Companies and organizations are worried; so are individuals. Subscriber profiles can be compiled by recording movements such as individual transactions, how or where time is spent online, the types of movies watched, or what products are bought from a cable shopping channel or an online electronic mall. Often these profiles are sold as target audiences to other companies or advertisers. Unfortunately, this intrusion suggests that Big Brother could be watching and that people cannot lead private lives.

EQUAL ACCESS

From small communities to the world, there is inequality. Some people have more than others because they have more money. Others are able to learn progressively difficult lessons because they have obtained an education from which to start their learning theories. Both of these situations contribute to the inequity of access and new technologies issues.

A well-informed public is essential to participating effectively in societal decisions. What if most of this information is located on software or CD-ROMs or in online data bases, which is (1) costly to obtain and (2) requires prior knowledge to use the technology? How will disadvantaged groups be guaranteed access to information that would guide their decisions? Or will others decide for them? Will the information-rich get richer? Will there be a bigger gap between the haves and the have-nots? Again, we are looking for the answers.

CHANGE IN WORK STRUCTURE AND EQUAL OPPORTUNITY

Optimists note that with so many new communication technologies, the workplace will become smaller and the work force dispersed. Employees will be able to "telecommute" by working on personal computers at home and transmitting their completed tasks to the office. People won't have to conform to the eight-to-five office hours, and they can watch their children while working at home. In addition, telecommuting might help ease the problems of smog and jammed traffic.

While these are good thoughts, pessimists say that those who are not at the workplace tend to be forgotten when it's time for promotions and raises. Those working at home and watching their children will succeed only in increasing the workday because the activities cannot be done simultaneously. People will go stircrazy.

Probably the most important aspect of telecommuting and new technologies concerns equality. On one hand, with telecommuting, there is no conscious or subconscious discrimination because face-to-face communication is not necessary. Thus pay should be equal to the work completed. On the other hand, equal-opportunity ground gained could be lost. The handicapped would be kept out of sight, the elderly could conceivably stay indoors, and difficulties with work and parenting would not be evidenced. In other words, inequality and social problems would be out of the public eye. Computer networks are also changing the way Americans build social relationships, participate in civic affairs, and seek entertainment. The term *electronic communities* is cropping up more and more, and there seems no end in sight for the ramifications of the emerging technologies or for their influence on existing technologies. Ithiel de Sola Pool, M.I.T. political scientist, has said that "networked computers will be the printing presses of the 21st century."

SUMMARY

New communication technologies are being developed or improved every day. It is no longer easy to keep up with the mass-media industries. Whereas new printing techniques used to appear once every few centuries, computers are now revolutionizing the world. Every innovation presented in this chapter has developed with the help of microchips, and more developments are happening now.

If this chapter had been written 10 years ago, topics would easily have been grouped into sections such as print, broadcast, and graphics. With the blurring of boundary lines between the various technologies, the divisions are more difficult to discern. For example, references once found only in "print" (books and newspapers) are also found by the electronic means of videotex, online data bases, and optical disc. "Broadcast" used to be the most common means of transmitting information over the air without the use of wires. Today, transmission processes come in various ways—satellite, microwave, terrestrial microwave, and over-the-air laser. Whereas *broadcast* automatically implied television, now the term includes cable. And cabling could be copper or fiber optic. Even the term *movies* has changed. Once it meant going out to the cinema; today, people sit at home and watch movies transmitted by satellite and cable, or picked up at a video rental store. With the blurring of boundaries, it is easier to think not of the product—newspaper, television—but in terms of the activity being accomplished, such as "information sources or storage," "transmission processes," and "presentation methods."

The communication processes and equipment discussed in this chapter are by no means comprehensive. They are, however, some of the more significant ones that are now having an important effect on the decisions newsroom executives and communication managers are struggling with today.

Because the essence of this chapter has been a succinct overview of complex technologies, it is not possible to summarize content in detail here. We should, however, point again to the impact of all this—the emerging issues such as image manipulation, implications of the changing classroom, industry standardization, ownership, copyright, privacy, security, equal access, and changes in the workplace. These are not future predictions. The future is now.

Glossary

....

AAAA. American Association of Advertising Agencies. A national trade organization that is influential in developing self-regulation in advertising, specifically in developing standards of ethical practice. p. 210–211

ABC. *See* Audit Bureau of Circulation. Also, American Broadcasting Company. p. 143

access. Ability of audience members to use the various media for communication of their messages. Also, ability of communicators to get information from sources, particularly the government. pp. 63, 437

account group. Various specialists in advertising agency headed by an account executive or supervisor who collectively serve the needs of a client advertiser. p. 194

A. C. Nielsen (Also, Nielsen Media Research). A company that specializes in broadcast ratings using an audimeter and diaries. It supplies ratings for network-television programming, among other services. p. 138–141

ACT (Action for Children's Television). A consumer group that is dedicated to pressuring television, especially the networks, to produce better children's programming and to reduce and, eventually, eliminate what it considers to be harmful advertising aimed at children. p. 107

Acta Diurna. The earliest form of newspaper. In 59 B.C., the Romans posted these public news sheets. p. 218

Ad Council (Advertising Council). Nonprofit organization that produces and places public-service advertising campaigns nationwide, on behalf of the AAAA and Association of National Advertisers. p. 182

ADI. A broadcast-ratings term meaning "Area of Dominant Influence." Television stations use this concept, developed by Arbitron, to define their markets for advertisers. A station's ADI is made up of the counties that cluster around its signal. p. 268

advertising. Messages designed to inform and persuade consumers to buy a particular product or service. The sender/sponsor is identified. p. 178

advertorial. Position statement by an individual, group, or corporation, on some controversial subject, by means of advertising. p. 182

affiliate. A broadcast station that airs programs produced by or belonging to a national or regional network. p. 34

agenda setting. Ability of the media to direct attention to certain issues. p. 411

alternative press. A form of newspaper, often called the *underground press* in its early (1960s) days. It is characterized as much by its form and style as by its content. Printed by inexpensive offset methods, these papers are often sold in the streets and often deal with radical politics and sexual topics. p. 238–239

amplification. The process of boosting a message so that it stands out from other messages and commands audience attention. Amplification is achieved primarily by strong signals, repetition of message, and endorsement. p. 126–127

AM radio. A form of radio transmission in which sound waves modulate the amplitude (length) of the carrier wave. p. 280

ANPA. American Newspaper Publishers Association. p. 95

AP. *See* wire services.

ARB. American Research Bureau, former name of **Arbitron.**

Arbitron. A major broadcasting-ratings service that is especially important in local-market radio. p. 138

ASNE. American Society of Newspaper Editors.

audience. Receivers of media content who are active participants in mass communication, as distinguished from the *public*, which is the total pool of available people and a passive entity. p. 111

audimeter. An electronic research device used by Nielsen to record television listening and viewing times and stations. It is used to determine national television-program ratings. p. 135

audio books. Spoken books, usually condensed, available on audiocassettes. p. 463

audiotext. Information carried via telephone lines connected to a computer. p. 615

audio visual media. A combination of electronic media's capabilities and the design capabilities of print to offer both verbal and nonverbal messages. p. 81

Audit Bureau of Circulation (ABC). An organization that validates the circulation statements of member newspapers and periodicals. p. 129

aural media. Media that are completely dependent on sound. p. 81

auteur theory. A theory drawn from French film criticism and popularized in the United States by film critic Andrew Sarris that posits the director as artistically preeminent in the creation of a motion picture. Each director, according to the theory, has a recognizable touch or characteristic style. p. 13, 492

authoritarian theory. The oldest theory of the press, which asserts the government's control over the press, using such techniques as licensing, censorship, and imprisonment. p. 589

bandwagon effect. Phenomenon that occurs when people adopt opinions because they are the opinions of a large number of other people. p. 549

barter. A term used in broadcasting to mean an agreement between stations and advertisers to use products or services by the advertiser in lieu of full or partial payment for air time. "Barter time" is often arranged through the services of a barter broker. p. 36

bicycling. The passing along of a program tape from one station to another. p. 36

billings. Amount of money represented by the advertising placed by an agency for a client. Billing also refers to the list of credits for a film or TV program. p. 191

blacklisting. An insidious method of preventing suspected Communists from working in radio, television, and motion pictures in the 1950s during the so-called Red Scare period. p. 336

black press. Begun in 1827, black-owned newspapers continue to serve the needs of many black Americans. p. 222–223

block booking. The practice of requiring a theater owner to take several films produced by a studio in order to get one or two good ones; now illegal. p. 347

blockbuster. A huge hit; most often used for films. p. 339

broadcasting. Sending messages via radio or TV transmission for open reception by the public. p. 119

broadsheet. Type of newspaper; a large sheet of paper printed on one or two sides, often folded. p. 411

cable television (CATV). Community antenna television. A service subscribed to by the viewer and transmitted to the viewing location by cable from a central receiving point. p. 271–275

call letters. A broadcasting station's identifying letters—for example, WICB—assigned by the FCC. The letter *W* is usually the first letter in call signs of stations east of the Mississippi; the letter *K* begins most call signs of stations west of the Mississippi. p. 291

campaign. A coordinated series of different ads in different media. p. 197

Canons of Journalism. A code of ethical behavior adopted by the American Society of Newspaper Editors in 1933; it is strictly voluntary, with no means of punishment or enforcement. p. 227

Canon 35. A voluntary guideline for the American Bar Association that prohibits cameras and audio-recording equipment from courtrooms during trials. p. 284

CD (Compact disc). Developed in the mid-1980s, the CD—a digital sound recording—provides high-quality sound and will not scratch or wear out because of the laser stylus, which does not touch the disc. p. 369–372

censorship. The systematic deletion of a message or parts of a message in order to prevent it from being received by the audience; it is prior restraint or suppression. p. 501

chain ownership. Ownership of a number of newspapers by one group. p. 232

channel. A band of frequencies in the UHF or VHF spectrum assigned by the FCC to a given television station or stations within which they must confine their broadcast signals. p. 2–8

circulation. The number of copies of a publication sold by subscription or counter sales. p. 143

clear channel. A radio frequency usually reserved for a single, high-powered station to operate at night. Clear-channel stations broadcast on 50,000 watts. p. 285

clutter. The virtually overwhelming number of competing messages in any medium. p. 122–123

code. A media's symbol system; its language. In motion pictures, visual symbols, and the way they are conveyed (camera angle, e.g.), carry much of the message; in newspapers, print symbols, such as typeface, create meaning. p. 13–14

codex. An early (fourth century A.D.) form of book in which sheets of parchment were cut and tied together on the left side between boards. p. 388

comic. A particular form of magazine and newspaper content that can be a cartoon, comic strip, or comic book. A comic usually develops a narrative, uses continuing characters, and incorporates dialogue or description. p. 318–319

commercial speech. Messages, especially conveyed by advertising, that are subject to regulation. The right to express these is, however, protected by the Constitution. p. 103

common carrier. A communications form that offers its services to the public and is regulated by the FCC. Ownership of the medium is divorced from control of the messages carried. Telephone is a common carrier; broadcast television is not. p. 101

communicator. The sender or initiator of a message. In mass communication, the communicator is rarely one individual acting alone. The media communicator is a complex network of people, each of whom has different functions and responsibilities. p. 12–13

compositor. Person who sets type or keyboards copy for the print media. p. 396

conflict of interest. An ethical issue of divided loyalty, which often occurs in mass communication. It frequently takes place when a reporter has a personal relationship with a subject being written about. p. 535–538

conglomerate. A large corporation or holding company that owns a variety of businesses. In mass communication, a conglomerate may own media companies as well as industries totally unrelated to the media. p. 54

consent decree. Agreement between the government and the film studios to break up the production and distribution monopoly; the

studios could no longer distribute to their own theaters. That arrangement is being reinstituted, however. p. 207

controlled circulation publication. One that is sent, often free of charge and unsolicited, to a targeted audience. p. 322

controlled message. Advertising and other messages paid for by a sponsor. p. 179–180

cooperative advertising (Co-op). Local advertising run in conjunction with a national sponsor, which usually provides the advertising materials and shares costs and mentions with the local advertiser. p. 188

coproduction. The preparation and delivery of content through the coordinated effort of more than one media organization. p. 403

copy. Matter, as a manuscript or illustration, to be published. Copy is the content of the print media; it can also be the message prepared for delivery on the air. p. 78

copycat syndrome. Also known as the sequel syndrome, the tendency of competitors to imitate each other's successes. p. 25

copyright. Legal protection granted to the owner(s) of literary, musical, dramatic, pantomine, choreographic, pictorial, graphic and sculptural works; motion pictures; and other audiovisual works and sound recordings. The fundamental rights given by the law include reproduction, preparation of derivative works, distribution of copies, public performance of work, and right to publicly display the work. p. 518–519

corrective advertising. Advertising required by the FTC to correct prior advertising that made false or misleading claims. p. 207

cost efficiency. Often referred to as cost per thousand (CPM) to place an advertisement before its actual or potential audience. p. 141

counter programming. In broadcasting, the airing or scheduling of a program designed to appeal to a different segment of the audience from that of competing stations, the same audience as that of the competition, or an entirely new or different audience from that of the competition. p. 57–58

CPM. Cost per thousand; a comparative tool to evaluate the efficiency of particular media. p. 141

crossmedia ownership. Control of more than one medium by one company. p. 232

C-SPAN. Cable Satellite Public Affairs Network. p. 515

cumulative audience. The total number of individuals reached by successive issues or broadcasts. Also called *cume*, it is especially important in radio ratings. p. 138

daypart. In broadcasting, a standard portion of the day. p. 138

DBS. Direct broadcast satellite transmission, in which a television signal is delivered directly to a home receiving dish by satellite. p. 274

decode. To receive and understand a message sent by a communicator or encoder. p. 116

delayed-reward news. News that provides context and background for the receiver and does not affect the consumer until later—for example, public-affairs, education, and economic news. p. 413

demographics. Usually computer-assisted ability to analyze audiences, subscribers, or consumers in terms of where they live, affluence, age, sex, and such, in order to target advertising or public-relations campaigns. p. 180

deregulation. The process of reducing or eliminating government regulation in business and industry. It has become especially important in broadcasting in the 1980s. p. 69

diary. A rating system in which audiences keep written records of their TV and radio usage. It is used by Arbitron for radio ratings and by Nielsen for TV ratings. p. 135

directive messages. Messages that command, exhort, or persuade in the direction of learning and new understanding. p. 568

direct mail. A method of advertising and/or public relations that uses the postal system to send a message to potential readers who have something in common (target audience). p. 162

disclosure of sources. An ethical issue involving the right of news reporters to maintain confidentiality of sources versus the right of the public to know the source of information. p. 511–512

divorcement ruling. A major Supreme Court decision in 1950 that broke up the vertical monopoly of the major motion-picture studios by requiring them to "divorce" exhibition, production, and distribution. p. 336–337

docudrama. Fictionalized treatment of actual, usually current events, on television. p. 460–462

documentary. An electronic media form that combines interpretive reporting and usually editorial comment, via selection of historical footage, current visuals, and interviews. p. 439–441

downlink/uplink. Jargon for a satellite earth station for receiving (downlink) or sending (uplink) satellite signals. They are also used as verbs. p. 617

drive time. A radio term referring to the time when most people commute to and from work, normally from 7:00 to 9:00 A.M. and 4:30 to 6:30 P.M. Radio has its largest audience at these times, especially in urban areas. p. 295

DV-I. Digital video-interactive. Software that combines text, pictures, audio, and animation most often used for games or educational programs. p. 621–622

electronic mail. Personally targeted messages relayed through computers or fax machines. p. 162

electronic media. Broadcasting media—radio and television—derived from their method of transmission. The term *electronics* describes the area of technology dealing with currents of free electrons, as opposed to transmission through currents in wires only, which is generally termed *electric*. p. 81

electronic news gathering (ENG). The use of compact videotaping systems (minicams) to record news events and stories in the same manner as traditionally done with film cameras. p. 425–426

encode. To prepare messages for sending by selecting the appropriate symbols, style, etc. p. 71

equal time. A provision by the FCC stating that stations selling or giving time to one candidate for public office are required to sell or give equal time to all legally qualified candidates for the same office. News programs are excluded from this provision. p. 102

erotica. Sexually oriented content, the purpose of which is physical and emotional arousal. p. 505

ethnic press. Newspapers designed for a particular ethnic group, such as German-Americans or Spanish-Americans. They often are printed in the group's language and are confined to urban centers containing a significant percentage of a particular group. p. 240–241

external public relations counsel. A firm or individual providing independent advice on public relations. p. 155–157

Fairness Doctrine. The obligation imposed by the FCC on broadcasters to cover controversial issues. It stipulated that broadcasters must seek out and present contrasting points of view on controversial issues. No longer in effect, it is the subject of re-evaluation toward re-implementation. p. 102

FCC Federal Communications Commission. A U.S. government agency established in 1934 that regulates broadcasting, including licensing broadcast stations. It regulates all forms of broadcasting, including citizens'-band, marine, and police radio. p. 101–103

feedback. Audience reactions that come back to the sender. Feedback is essentially communication in reverse and is ultimately designed to influence the sender and his or her future communication. p. 128

fiber optics. An information transmittal system using light waves carried through thin glass tubes. p. 619

filter. A frame of reference through which audiences receive messages. Four types of filters—informational, physical, psychological, cultural—affect an individual's perception and reception of media content. p. 116–121

First Amendment. The constitutional guarantee of press, speech, and religious freedom. It reads: "Congress shall make no law respecting an establishment of religion, or prohibiting the free exercise thereof; or abridging the freedom of speech, or of the press; or the right of the people peaceably to assemble, and to petition the government for a redress of grievances." p. 499–501

FM radio. A form of radio transmission in which sound waves modulate the frequency of the carrier wave. FM frequencies have higher fidelity (88–108 megahertz) and are subject to less interference than AM frequencies. p. 285

focus group. A small group of people, led by a market researcher, gathered in an informal setting to discuss a product. p. 199

format. General plan or organization of a channel of communication. p. 74

format radio. Often called formula radio, radio formats are carefully constructed combinations of music, talk, and advertisements designed to appeal to a specific group of listeners. p. 37–38

fourwalling. A system whereby film distributors rent theaters for carefully planned simultaneous release of a new motion picture for a limited time. p. 348

fragmentation. The splintering of audiences into diverse specialized smaller parts. p. 25–26

frame of reference. A set of previously held ideas, preferences, and conclusions through which we interpret a message. p. 8

freedom of information (FOI). Specifically, the Freedom of Information Act of 1966, which gives the media and members of the public access to federal government agency files. p. 516–517

freeze. A four-year period between 1948 and 1952 when the FCC "froze" all further television station licensing in order to allow the medium to solve some technical and economic problems. p. 253

frequency. A particular number of radio waves per second. p. 285

FTC Federal Trade Commission. A U.S. government agency that regulates unfair and misleading advertising as well as other unfair competitive business practices. p. 206–207

gag orders. Directive to media or trial participants to prevent disclosure of details of a case prior to the trial. p. 509–510

gatekeeper. An individual or individuals who can determine and affect the information or entertainment received by an audience. A gatekeeper can block information, add to it, or alter it. p. 14

genre. A category of artistic work, such as a mystery or a sitcom. p. 473

global village. A term popularized by the communications scholar Marshall McLuhan. It refers to the "shrinking" of the world society because of the ability to communicate via mass media. p. 17

group journalism. Reportage by a team of researchers and writers blended to fit a certain style. p. 439

happy talk. TV news that features entertainment and personable anchors. p. 262

hard news. Traditional straight news as contrasted to "softer" human interest pieces. p. 262

HDTV (High-definition television). Television reception characterized by sharper pictures and improved resolution due to larger number of lines per inch as well as digital multichannel sound. p. 620–621

highbrow culture. Category of cultural artifacts that is designed to appeal to an educated and intellectual elite. p. 470

HUT (Homes using television). The percentage of homes viewing TV during a given time period. p. 138

hype. Hyperbole, or an exaggerated message. p. 534

iconic sign. A sign that communicates by resemblance. p. 477–478

iconoscope. The first electronic television camera tube, invented by Vladimir Zworykin in 1928. p. 249

image manipulation. The changing of a photograph in an electronic darkroom process that adds, deletes, or retouches visual content. p. 624

immediate-reward news. News that provides instant satisfaction for the receiver—for example, sports, fire, and crime news. It is also characterized by its transitoriness. p. 413

implosion. the opposite of explosion. A media-audience concept that describes the audience at the center being bombarded by media messages that converge on the individual. p. 123–126

independent. Also, "indie." Especially designating those television stations that are not network-owned or affiliated. p. 34

indexical sign. A sign that communicates by establishing some kind of causal connection between things. p. 477–478

information subsidies. Public relations handouts to the media, such as video and print news releases. p. 159–160

in-house agency. Part of the advertiser's own company; the agency workers are employees of the advertiser. p. 195

institutional advertising. Advertising whose primary objective is not to promote a specific product or service, but to gain public goodwill or prestige for the advertiser or sponsor. p. 180

institutional ethics. Media ethics that are informal and often associated with gatekeepers within media institutions. p. 532–534

interactive. Referring to those technologies that permit users' participation, such as two-way cable, videotex, and certain optical videodiscs. p. 456

internal communication. Communication within a company or organization in the form of employee newspapers, annual reports, etc. p. 155

intertextuality. A theory stating that all creative work is based on and inspired from other works. p. 495

invasion of privacy. Published or broadcast information that violates an individual's right to be let alone or damages one's peace of mind. p. 540–541

inverted-pyramid structure. A method of news presentation that presents the most important facts, together with the necessary explanatory material, in the first paragraph (summary lead) of a news story and then moves into the detailed portion of the story (body) in descending order of importance. p. 80

investigative news reporting. A style of reporting that goes beneath surface situations to probe the real cause or purpose, often to expose wrongdoing. It stresses careful assembling of facts in developing the story. p. 421–423

ISDN (Integrated Services Digital Network). A service proposed by the telephone companies that would digitize and combine audio, text, and video into one network. p. 619–620

jazz journalism. Style in the popular press of the 1920s and after that was characterized by colorful reporting. p. 227

JOA (Joint Operating Agreement). Agreement whereby competing newspapers in the same regional market share some production expenses so that each may survive. p. 66–68

kinescopes. Films used in the early days of television for network programming. p. 329

kinetograph. The first motion-picture camera, invented by Thomas Edison and his assistant William Dickson in 1888. p. 329

libel. A defamatory communication that is published or broadcast. Before libel is created in a communication, three conditions must exist: publication (published or broadcast); identification of the person, persons, or entity; and defamation (attack on a "good" name). p. 506–507

libertarian theory. The theory of the press that asserts that since the public is essentially rational, the government need never interfere in the free and unfettered competition of the various elements of the media. p. 589

Linotype. A machine invented in 1884 by Ottmar Mergenthaler that molds and sets type from hot metal. It replaced hand setting of type and had a major impact on newspaper and book publishing. p. 221

lowbrow culture. A category of cultural artifacts that appeal to the largest possible audience; usually implied is crass, emotionally oriented content. p. 470

LP (Long-playing record). First developed in 1948, the record is made and played at 33-⅓ rpm, providing up to 25 minutes of music per side. It is being replaced by CDs. p. 363

magic bullet theory. The theory that assumes that everyone in the audience will experience a similar effect from specific media content. p. 552

maintenance message. Content that aids people in coping with their daily lives. p. 568–569

marketing. All the various activities of sales promotion, advertising, and public relations designed to sell goods or services. p. 157–158

market segmentation. The breakdown of a market by demographics and consumer needs. p. 61

market share. The percentage of tool shares or audience in a defined market that is won by a product, service, or media organization. p. 200

mass communication. The process whereby mass-produced messages are transmitted to large, anonymous, and heterogeneous audiences. p. 6

mass media. The institutions of public communication that have as their physical channel of transmission a mass medium— television, radio, motion pictures, newspapers, books, magazines, and recordings. p. 3

media acculturation. The process by which mass communication creates cultural consensus and understanding among individual components of society and brings people together on some common issues. p. 565

media event. An event specifically staged by an individual, group, or corporation to attract media coverage. p. 431

media-support system. The means by which a particular mass medium finances production, distribution, and exhibition of content. There are basically four types of support: audience; advertiser; audience and advertiser; and public and/or public subsidy. p. 178

media-systems paradigm. An action-oriented model that visualizes the theory that in every country, social factors interact in unique ways to create a national media system to perform a variety of functions that participate in reshaping that society. p. 594

message. The information being delivered to the receiver by the communicator. p. 6–9

micromarketing. Marketing effort, especially by a medium, to receive an extremely targeted or localized audience. p. 311

middlebrow culture. A category of cultural artifacts that have pretentions of being refined and intellectual but also have wider appeal. p. 470

monopoly. Control of a market by one owner, thereby eliminating competition. p. 57

Motion Picture Association of America (MPAA). A primary gatekeeper of the motion-picture industry. Its 1968 rating code classifies movies into G, PG, PG-13, R, and X categories. p. 97

muckraking. Exposing political and social wrongdoing; synonymous with *investigative news reporting*. Although the term dates back to the seventeenth century, it was popularized mainly by Theodore Roosevelt. p. 226

multiplexing. Sending or receiving simultaneously two or more messages or signals over a common circuit. Also, use of multiscreen movie theaters. p. 291

multistep flow theory. A process that suggests that the effects of mass media alone do not alter opinion or belief; rather, the media's message flows through and is filtered by a network of opinion leaders. p. 116

narrowcasting. Reaching certain categories of viewers or listeners. p. 119

National Public Radio (NPR). A network of approximately 200 noncommercial radio stations funded in part by the federal government through the Corporation for Public Broadcasting (CPB). p. 262

network. Two or more radio or television stations connected by wire, microwave, or satellite to broadcast the same programs, usually—although not necessarily—simultaneously. p. 31–35

new journalism. A style of journalism that emerged in the 1960s in which writers expressed their feelings and values and used techniques usually found in fiction. p. 416

news hole. Space devoted to news apart from advertising and set features. p. 235

newsletter. A specialized form of print media. Written in letter form, it contains a wide variety of specialized and specific information for particular target audiences. It normally carries no advertising. p. 316–318

New World Information Order. A philosophy emanating from several studies done in the late 1970s that postulates the communication integrity of every nation of the world. It is essentially a reaction by many Third World countries against what they term American and Western "media imperialism." p. 600–601

noise. In mass media theory, anything that interferes with clear communications—from technical problems of reception to clutter in presentation to information overload. p. 122–126

objectivity. A dominant theme of the journalism profession, to report events in a factual way, uninfluenced by attitudes or values of reporters, editors, or publishers. p. 415–416

obscenity. Content that is judged to be lewd, indecent, or designed to incite depravity. p. 504–505

oligopoly. Control of a market by a small number of owners. p. 57–58

op-ed page. A publication's editorial section devoted to opinions and essays submitted by contributors or the general audience. p. 438

owned-and-operated (O&O). Broadcast outlets owned and operated by the networks. By FCC rules, each network is allowed only seven O&Os, no more than five of which can be VHF stations. p. 265

pass-along reader. Person who reads a publication that he or she did not buy. Readers within households subscribing to the publication are included in the definition of *primary readers*. A periodical's total audience consists of both primary and pass-along readers. p. 113

payola. Reward in cash, goods, or services for the performance of undeserved favors; doing for pay what should be done without charge. The term originated in the 1950s to describe the practice of paying to have records played on radio. p. 378

pay-TV. A system in which a viewer pays a per-program fee or a monthly fee to view specific programs or programming not available on regular television channels. HBO is a pay-TV channel for cable subscribers. p. 59

PBS. (Public Broadcasting Service.) Established in 1970 as the corporate voice of "educational and public" broadcasting in the United States, PBS manages programming, production, distribution, and station interconnection. p. 275–276

penny press. The first mass newspaper medium. Originating in the 1830s, the papers sold for a penny and offered news for less-educated, ordinary citizens. p. 221–222

people meter. Device used by Nielsen to measure audience attendance to television programming. p. 130

periodical. A magazine or journal published at regular intervals. p. 304

persistence of vision. A phenomenon in which the eye retains an image for a short time after the object has been removed from view. Motion pictures are possible because of this phenomenon. p. 328

playlist. List of current songs being played by a radio station. p. 378

point. A national rating unit equalling 921,000 households. p. 22–23

pornography. Any obscene material, as legally defined by dominant theme; must appeal to a prurient interest in sex; material must be patently offensive and affront community standards; material is without socially redeeming value. p. 505

press agent. A public relations practitioner engaged in getting publicity for a client, especially a celebrity. p. 152

prime time. The time when television stations have their largest audiences; generally 7:30 to 11:00 P.M. on the East and West coasts and 6:30 to 10:00 P.M. elsewhere in the United States. p. 269

print media. All those media that communicate with printed matter: books, newspapers, magazines, newsletters, etc. p. 26–27

prior restraint. *See* censorship.

professional book. A book to serve the special or technical needs of various professions, such as law, medicine, education. p. 391

professional ethics. Media ethics characterized by a system of codes and, in some cases, regulations that specifically "spell out" ethical practices and/or conditions. p. 95–96

propaganda. Information spread by official means to sway public opinion for or against something; it may be based on truth or fallacy. p. 505–506

PRSA (Public Relations Society of America). A professional trade association established to elevate and professionalize the practice of public relations. p. 149

public. The total pool of available people, as distinguished from an *audience*, which is defined by the individuals who actually use the media content. p. 111

public relations (PR). A management function that obtains, assesses, and evaluates public attitudes toward an organization, advertiser, or individual; a program of action is executed to develop public understanding, goodwill, support, and acceptance. p. 149

rack jobber. An individual or firm that supplies records or publications to display stands in nontraditional outlets such as drug stores. p. 364

rate card. A list or card giving important information concerning the medium's policies on its advertising, including space or time rate, plus data on mechanical requirements, closing dates, commissions, rate protection, spot length, color, rate inclusions, and so on. p. 34

ratings. Estimates of the number of people or households, usually expressed in percentages or percentage, who view or listen to a program or broadcasting station from a sample of homes or people with (*but not using*) television or radio. p. 138–140

receiver. The target of the message sent by the communicator. p. 6–9

recording. A generic term referring to a variety of sound-reproducton systems, including records, reel-to-reel tapes, cassettes, and videotape-music productions. p. 362–363

regulators. An individual or organization that exists *outside* the media institutions and is capable of altering, modifying, or stopping media content from reaching an audience—for example, the FCC and the Supreme Court. p. 14

restorative message. Content that renews human capacity for productive social relationships. p. 569

ROP. Run-of-press advertising. A sales promotion activity that involves inserting coupon brochures, store circulars, and catalogs into newspapers. p. 188–189

sample. A portion of the total population involved in a survey, of whom questions are asked. To be valid, a sample should be representative of the total population involved. p. 129–130

semiotics. The study of the role of signs and representations. p. 476

sender. A communicator. p. 6–9

sensationalism. Intentional production of excitement or shock employed by tabloid newspapers and others by the use of photographs and stories with sexual or violent slant. p. 417–418

share. An audience-measurement term usually referring to a percentage of homes *using* television that are tuned to a particular program. p. 140–141

shopper. Local newspaper with advertising the dominant component; ad revenue supports the publication that is free of charge and often unsolicited. p. 233–234

small press. Independent, specialized publisher. p. 24

soap opera. A major form of daytime network television programming that features continuing stories and characters in a strip (five-day-a-week) format. The form was popular on network radio for almost 30 years. p. 260

social-responsibility theory. The theory of the press first presented in 1947 by the Commission on Freedom of the Press. It developed from the basic assumptions of the libertarian theory, but emphasized the need of occasional government encouragement of media idealism and performance. p. 524–526

soft news. Human interest or entertainment-slanted feature as opposed to hard, straight news copy. p. 428

sound bite. Broadcast news term to designate the encapsulating of news content into a succinct bit. p. 428

spectrum band. The narrow band of radio waves on which radio stations transmit. Because of the limited nature of the spectrum band, the FCC must regulate stations' use of frequencies. p. 65

spinoff. The development of another media property, such as a book, from the original one, such as a motion picture. p. 386

strategic releasing. A process by which a content source regulates communication by strategically timing and packaging the message for maximum effect. p. 103

stereotype. Derived from a printing term meaning a mold made from a printing surface, it applies to a mental picture one might have acquired from a general pattern of opinion. p. 120

strategic withholding. A process by which a content source regulates communication by blocking the media from receiving a message or parts of a message. p. 104

stringer. An unsalaried reporter or photographer, not regularly assigned to a news organization, who acts as a local contact on an irregular basis and who initiates story ideas and does photography and/or reporting. Stringers work on retainers, word rates, negotiated article rates, or a combination of these methods of payment. p. 24

superstation. A local TV station whose signal is available by satellite relay to cable systems across the country. WTBS-TV in Atlanta is the original. p. 272

syndicate. A corporation that owns a group of newspapers or magazines or a group of radio or television stations. Syndicates also refer to organizations that sell comic strips and special columns to newspapers and magazines. p. 31

syndication. The sale of television or radio programs and series or newspaper features directly to individual stations or papers. Commercial television networks, for example, place successful series into syndication following their network runs. p. 36–37

tabloid. A newspaper of small page size, usually 5 columns wide and 16 to 18 inches deep, about half the size of a regular newspaper. It often is characterized by a great deal of photography, topical reporting, and emphasis on sensational headlines. p. 417

target audience. In advertising, the audience most likely to buy a particular product. In more general terms, a specific audience most likely to view, listen to, or read a particular media content. p. 113

teletext. A system for sending printed information to home television screens using scanning lines that are not needed for receiving TV programs. p. 615

textbook. A book prepared specifically for classroom use. It usually provides exposition of one subject area and serves as the content core of a given class. p. 393–394

trade book. A book produced for the mass market and usually sold through bookstores. p. 391

ultrahigh-frequency television (UHF). Television channels 14 through 83. p. 252–253

underground press. *See* alternative press. p. 238–239

UPI. *See* wire service. p. 29–31

utilitarianism. A philosophy that advocates a course of action that yields the greatest good for the most people. p. 528–529

vertical integration. One company's exclusive ownership of the means of production, distribution, and presentation of a product or service. p. 47

very-high-frequency television (VHF). Television channels 2 to 13 on the lower end of the broadcasting band. p. 252–253

VHS (Video Home System). The more popular of the two videocassette formats, it uses ½-inch tape; the other form is Beta. p. 620

videodisc. A disc containing (potentially great amounts of) visual and aural information. It can be used to play back content, like a recording, and can be connected to a computer and function in an interactive mode. Television programs, motion pictures, or other visual materials can be played. p. 456

video display terminal (VDT). An electronic typewriter and television screen connected to a computer. It is used by journalists and other writers to create and edit material. p. 613

video magazine. New hybrid form of communication; a periodically released video designed for a targeted audience. p. 324–325

videotex. A system that transmits information from a mainframe to one's own computer screen. It can be used for information storage and retrieval, in-home banking, and shopping. p. 613–614

volumen. Ancient scrolls of writing material made from animal skins. p. 388

wire service. An organization that gathers news stories, prepares them in a convenient form, and sends them (by wire or satellite) to newspapers and broadcasting stations around the country that pay for the service—for example, AP (Associated Press) and UPI (United Press International). p. 29–31

yellow journalism. A derogatory term for sensation-mongering, irresponsible journalism. Reputedly short for "Yellow Kid journalism," it alludes to the cartoon *The Yellow Kid*, in the nineteenth-century *New York World*, a newspaper especially noted for its sensationalism. p. 225–226

Bibliography

What follows is a selective bibliography, especially designed to provide a range of books under general subject areas that will take you to the *next* tier of knowledge about topics explored in this text. (Few books cited below have also been cited as chapter references.) More exhaustive bibliographies are mentioned below; our list of the best of current literature and some important classics aims for a nonduplicative extension of the understanding and information established by *Mass Media VI.* We begin with a few titles that are basic reference tools. Included are periodicals of general interest; under specific subject areas you will find specialized publications and other sources.

GENERAL AND REFERENCE

Barnouw, Erik; Gerbner, George; and Schramm, Wilbur, eds. *International Enxyclopedia of Communications.* 4 vols. New York: Oxford University Press, 1989. Scholarly and authoritative alphabetical coverage by hundreds of expert contributors of ideas, concepts, and practices; views a range of events, social processes, etc. in relation to mass communication. Bibliography with each article.

Blum, Eleanor, and Wilhoit, Frances Goins. *Mass Media Bibliography: An Annotated Guide to Books and Journals for Research and Reference.* Champaign, Ill.: University of Illinois Press, 1990. Over 200 entries, including indexes and *other bibliographies.*

Channels magazine year-end Field Guide issue on all media industry developments.

Connors, Tracy Daniel. *Longman Dictionary of Mass Media and Communication.* White Plains, NY: Longman, 1982. All major terms (7000), abbreviations, organizations, etc. of daily interest to the practitioner, with important variants of meaning from one context to another.

Hudson, Robert V. *Mass Media: A Chronological Encyclopedia of Television, Radio, Motion Pictures, Magazines, Newspapers, and Books in the United States.* New York: Garland, 1987. Covers 1638 to 1985.

Literary Market Place (LMP): The Directory of the American Book Publishing Industry. New York: R. R. Bowker, yearly. Information on associations, suppliers, reference sources useful for all print media.

PaineWebber. *Annual Conference on the Outlook for the Media.* New York: PaineWebber, yearly.

Rivers, William L.; Thompson, Wallace; and Nyhan, Michael J. *The Aspen Handbook on the Media.* New York: Praeger, 1977.

Sterling, Christopher H. and Haight, Timothy R., eds. *The Mass Media: Aspen Guide to Communication.* New York: Praeger, 1977.

Sterling, Christopher H., ed. *Trends,/1978,* and *Electronic Media: A Guide to Trends in Broadcasting and Newer Technologies, 1920–1983,* New York: Praeger, 1984.

U.S. Industrial Outlook. Washington, D.C.: U.S. Department of Commerce.

Ward, Jean, and Hansen, Kathleen A. *Search Strategies in Mass Communication.* White Plains, NY: Longman, 1987. Instruction in obtaining information for use in communication and in enhancing knowledge of the media; specific data bases, indexes of media output, and a range of other reference aids.

Weiner, Richard, ed. *Webster's New World Dictionary of Media and Communications.* New York: Simon & Schuster, 1990. 27 media and performance fields covered; weighted toward print.

Indexed daily newspapers with regular media industry coverage include *The Wall Street Journal, The New York Times, Los Angeles Times.*

In addition to the specialized journals and publications listed under the subject areas following, of general interest are: *Communication, Communication Quarterly, Communication Research, Critical Studies in Mass Communication, Gannett Center Journal, Journal of Communication,* and *Journal of Mass Media Ethics.*

PROCESSES AND PRACTICES OF MASS COMMUNICATION

Arnheim, Rudolf. *Visual Thinking.* Berkeley: University of California Press, 1969. The psychology of visual effects, artistic and informational.

Becker, Lee B., and Schoenbach, Klaus, eds. *Audience Responses to Media Diversification: Copying With Plenty.* Hillsdale, NJ: Erlbaum, 1989. Data-filled study of how audiences in 11 countries react to dramatic and proliferation of electronic communication.

Berner, R. Thomas. *The Process of Editing.* Boston: Allyn & Bacon, 1991. A guide to copyediting, layout, and design for journalists; its principles and concepts useful for anyone interested in encoding and gatekeeping functions.

Beville, Hugh M., Jr. *Audience Ratings: Radio, Television, and Cable,* rev. ed. Hillsdale, NJ: Erlbaum, 1988. Comprehensive coverage of broadcasting feedback.

Crowley, David, and Heyer, Paul, eds. *Communication in History: Technology, Culture, and Society.* White Plains, NY: Longman, 1991. Essays on communication's role; each new technology seen as extending basic human communication.

Garvey, Daniel E., and Rivers, William L. *Broadcast Writing.* White Plains, NY: Longman, 1982 (2d ed. in prep.). Complete process for all forms.

Kindem, Gorham. *The Moving Image: Production Principles and Practices.* Glenview, IL: Scott, Foresman, 1987. Techniques and aesthetic considerations involved in video and film; background to help communicators and editors make decisions.

Montgomery, Kathryn C. *Target: Prime Time: Advocacy Groups and the Struggle Over Entertainment Television.*

New York: Oxford University Press, 1989. Media activism vs. networks, 1950s on.

Schramm, Wilbur. *The Story of Human Communication: Cave Painting to Microchip.* New York: Harper, 1987. By a leader in communication research, an easily comprehended chronicle of processes and technology.

Severin, Werner J., with Tankard, James W., Jr. *Communication Theories: Origins, Methods, and Uses,* 2d ed. White Plains, NY: Longman, 1988. Theories of perception, learning, and attitude change as they affect media practitioners.

Shook, Frederick. *Television Field Production and Reporting.* White Plains, NY: Longman, 1989. The language of television and creative approaches taken by practitioners.

Swann, Alan. *Layout Source Book.* Secacucus, NJ: Wellfleet Press, 1989. The relationship between type and images in 100 years of magazines, books, and advertising, profusely illustrated.

Practitioners' Roles: A Sampling

Armer, Alan A. *Directing Television and Film.* Belmont, CA: Wadsworth, 1990. From the logic behind script analysis to the actor-director collaboration.

Biagi, Shirley. *Newstalk I: State-of-the-Art Conversations with Today's Print Journalists.* and *Newstalk II: Conversations with Today's Broadcast Journalists.* Belmont, CA: Wadsworth, 1987. Interviews with professional journalists, such as David Brinkley, Sam Donaldson, Judy Woodruff, and samples of their work.

Fink, Conrad C. *Inside the Media.* White Plains, NY: Longman, 1990. Lively introduction to media organizations via behind-the-scenes looks at specific firms, possible career tracks for communicators and executives, and advice from practitioners.

Gans, Herbert. *Deciding What's News: A Study of CBS Evening News, NBC Nightly News, Newsweek* and *Time.* New York: Random House, 1979. An influential work by an eminent sociologist on the gatekeeping role.

Lavine, John M., and Wackman, Daniel B. *Managing Media Organizations.* White Plains, NY: Longman, 1988. Operations, functions, planning, budgeting, and leadership principles and techniques.

Madsen, Roy Paul. *Working Cinema: Learning From the Masters.* (*See* Film)

Shoemaker, Pamela, and Reese, Stephen. *Mediating the Message: Theories of Influence on Mass Media Content.* White Plains, NY: Longman, 1991. Unique synthesis of recent/content research and thinking about media effects *on* the message; study of roles of agenda setters and gatekeepers, largely within media organizations.

Verna, Tony. *Live TV: An Inside Look at Directing and Producing.* Boston: Focal, 1987. With contributions by practitioners of news, sports, special events, and entertainment programming; emphasis on collaborative nature of mass media.

Economics

Bagdikian, Ben H. *The Media Monopoly,* 2d ed. Boston: Beacon Press, 1987. An important study of what the author finds as the lack of diversity and the increased concentration of control in the mass media.

Besen, Stanley M.; Krattermaker, Thomas G.; Metzger, Jr., A. Richard; and Woodbury, John R. *Misregulating Television.* Chicago: University of Chicago Press, 1984. Examines the failures of FCC regulation and recommends less rules to lead to better economic performance.

Caves, Richard. *American Industry,* 6th ed. Englewood Cliffs, NJ: Prentice-Hall, 1987. An introduction to the structure, conduct, and performance model of economic analysis.

Compaigne, Benjamin J., ed. *Who Owns the Media?* White Plains, NY: Knowledge Publications, 1982. This valuable book examines the structure, conduct, and performance of the media industries at the beginning of the 1980s.

Dunnett, Peter J. S. *The World Newspaper Industry.* New York: Croom Helm, 1988. A study of economic structure.

Gomery, Douglas. *The Hollywood Studio System.* New York: St. Martin's, 1985. An economic study of the film industry.

Levin, Harvey. *Fact and Fancy in Television Regulation: An Economic Study of Policy Alternatives.* New York: Russell Sage, 1980. Levin relates possible corrections to improve performance.

Poltrack, Dale. *Television Marketing.* New York: McGraw-Hill, 1983. The author, who has long worked at CBS, lays out the conduct of the television business.

Scherer, Frederic M. *Industrial Market Structure and Economic Performance,* 2d ed. Chicago: Rand McNally, 1980. The bible for methods to understand the economics of structure, conduct and performance.

Webb, G. Kent. *The Economics of Cable Television.* Lexington, MA: Lexington Books, 1983. A bit dated with all the recent changes, this book remains the only book length study of this important subject.

Public Relations

Broom, Glen, and Dozier, David. *Using Research in Public Relations.* Englewood Cliffs, NJ: Prentice-Hall, 1989. Comprehensive guide by 2 leading public relations educators and researchers.

Center, Allen H., and Jackson, Patrick. *Public Relations Practices: Managerial Case Studies and Problems,* 4th ed. Englewood Cliffs, NJ: Prentice-Hall, 1990. The "best and the worst" cases of recent public relations programs (all types) detailed.

Grunig, James E., and Hunt, Todd. *Managing Public Relations.* New York: Holt, Rinehart and Winston, 1984. Begins with concepts for 4 models of public relations; looks at various aspects of public relations practice.

Hiebert, Ray Eldon. *Precision Public Relations.* White Plains, New York: Longman, 1988. Essays by leading educators and practitioners moves reader through the process; concludes with look at the future of the practice.

Howard, Carole, and Mathews, Wilma. *On Deadline: Managing Media Relations.* Prospect Heights, IL.: Waveland Press, 1988. Written by 2 corporate media relations professionals; ranges from what is news and spokesperson training to measuring effectiveness.

Olasky, Marvin N. *Corporate Public Relations: A New Historical Perspective.* Hillsdale, NJ: Erlbaum, 1987. Lively analysis, attacking the commonly-held view that

American public relations has improved progressively since the era of press agents like P.T. Barnum.

Pavlik, John V. *Public Relations: What Research Tells Us.* Newbury Park, CA: Sage, 1987. Valuable synopsis; also, critique of what needs to be done, and a look at system theory as an emerging paradigm for public relations.

Public Relations Research Annual. Hillsdale, NJ: Erlbaum, yearly. Scholarly articles exploring such topics as applying role, systems or ethical theory in public relations. Published by the Public Relations Division of the Association for Education in Journalism and Mass Communication (AEJMC).

Tucker, Kerry, and Derelian, Doris. *Public Relations Writing: A Planned Approach for Creating Results.* Englewood Cliffs, NJ: Prentice-Hall, 1989. Techniques driven by a strategic plan for bottom line results.

Toth, Elizabeth Lance, and Cline, Carolyn Garrett, eds. *Beyond the Velvet Ghetto.* San Francisco: International Association of Business Communicators, 1989. Follow-up to a 1986 research study focussing on fact that the field was becoming a predominantly female profession; describes subtle and not-so-subtle discrimination as well as strategies for addressing disparities.

Key periodical resources: *Communication World, Public Relations Journal, Public Relations Review* (relates to social sciences).

ADVERTISING

Arlen, Michael J. *Thirty Seconds.* New York: Penguin Books, 1981. Insightful and humorous description of the conception, development, and execution of American Telephone and Telegraph Company's "Reach Out and Touch Someone Campaign."

Fox, Stephen S. *The Mirror Makers: A History of American Advertising and Its Creators.* New York: Morrow, 1984. Highly readable.

Gartner, Michael G. *Advertising and the First Amendment.* New York: Priority Press Publications, 1989. Former newspaper editor and now president of NBC News argues forcefully that "restrictions on commercial speech are ineffective as social policy and dangerous to our democracy."

Jones, John Philip. *Does It Pay to Advertise?* Lexington, MA: Lexington Books, 1989. Based on many years at J. Walter Thompson; a series of case studies.

Ogilvy, David S., *Ogilvy on Advertising.* New York: Vintage Books, 1983. One of the most famous names in advertising history criticizes advertising and offers advice on how to make it better.

Roman, Kenneth K., and Maas, Jane J. *How to Advertise.* New York: St. Martin's Press, 1976. Slim volume by leading advertising executives, full of helpful, practical advice about strategy, what works in advertising, how to get better production and better media plans.

Sandage, Charles H.; Fryburger, Vernon; and Rotzoll, Kim. *Advertising Theory and Practice,* 12th ed. New York: Longman, 1989. Classic introductory advertising text; comprehensive and well illustrated.

Schudson, Michael M. *Advertising: The Uneasy Persuasion.* New York: Basic Books, Inc., 1984. A professor of sociology concludes, advertising is not as important or effective as many critics believe.

Periodicals to follow: *Advertising Age, Adweek, Agency* (new quarterly from AAAA), *Marketing & Media Decision.*

NEWSPAPERS

Bagdikian, Ben H. *The Media Monopoly.* (*See* Economics)

Cose, Ellis. *Inside America's Most Powerful Newspaper Empries—From The Newsrooms To The Boardrooms.* New York: Morrow, 1989. Perhaps intended to update two earlier trade books, *The Kingdom and the Power* by Gay Talese and *The Powers That Be* by David Halberstam, this chronicles new generations of management at America's leading newspapers.

Fink, Conrad. *Strategic Newspaper Management.* Carbondale, IL: Southern Illinois University Press, 1988. Comprehensive survey of the evolving structure of the modern newspaper.

Fry, Ronald W., ed. *Newspapers Career Directory.* Hawthorne, NJ: Career Press, 1987. Advice from top practitioners in newswriting, advertising, management, marketing, etc.

Giles, Robert H. *Newsroom Management: A Guide to Theory and Practice.* Indianapolis: R. J. Berg & Co., 1988. In-depth application of modern-management (behavioral science) techniques to the newsroom; sensitive to individuality of communicators.

Goulden, Joseph C. *Fit To Print: A. M. Rosenthal and His Times.* New York: Lyle Stuart, 1988. Profile of the leader of news operations at *The New York Times* and thus of the influential paper itself.

Prichard, Peter. *The Making of McPaper: The Inside Story of USA Today.* Kansas City, MO.: Andrews, McMeel & Parker, 1987. Authorized but entertaining account by a Gannett insider of the birth and growth of the pioneering newspaper.

Thorn, William J., with Mary Pat Pfeil. *Newspaper Circulation: Marketing the News.* White Plains, NY: Longman, 1987. Historical and present roles played by circulation, followed by description and case studies of marketing problems and systems.

Aspects of newspaper history are covered in:

Bryan, Carter R. *Negro Journalism in America Before Emancipation.* Journalism Monograph 12. Lexington, KY.: Association for Education in Journalism, 1969; Chalmers, David Mark. *The Social and Political Ideas of the Muckrakers.* Secaucas, NJ: Citadel, 1964; Leonard, Thomas C. *The Power of the Press: The Birth of American Political Reporting.* New York: Oxford University Press, 1986; Mills, Kay. *A Place in the News: From the Women's Pages to the Front Page.* New York: Dodd, Mead, 1988; Schudson, Michael. *Discovering the News: A Social History of American Newspapers.* New York: Basic Books, 1978; Smith, Jeffery A. *Printers and Press Freedom: The Ideology of Early American Journalism.* New York: Oxford University Press, 1988; Udell, Jon G. *Economic Trends in the Daily Newspaper Business: 1946 to 1970.* New York: American Newspaper Publishers Assn., 1970.

Good general histories are:

Altschull, J. Herbert. *From Milton to McLuhan: The Ideas Behind American Journalism.* White Plains, NY: Longman, 1990.

Emery, Michael, and Energy, Edwin. *The Press and America: An Interpretive History of the Mass Media,* 6th ed. Englewood Cliffs, N.J.: Prentice-Hall, 1988

Mott, Frank Luther. *American Journalism.* New York: Macmillan, 1964.

Current developments are reported in the weekly *Editor & Publisher*, which also publishes an industry yearbook. The *ASNE Bulletin* and *Masthead* are useful for both news and reflective pieces; *See also* News and Analysis.

BROADCASTING AND CABLE

Barnouw, Erik. *A History of Broadcasting in the United States.* 3 vols. New York: Oxford University Press, 1966, 1968, 1970. A masterful history of how radio and television became an integral part of American life; detailed narrative, entertaining vignettes, and a look at trends.

Blum, Richard A., and Lindheim, Richard D. *Primetime: Network Television Programming.* Boston: Focal, 1987. Comprehensive look by insiders at whole process of creating and marketing specific programs.

Comstock, George. *The Evolution of American Television.* Newbury Park, CA: Sage, 1989. By author of a seminal work, *Television in America*, thoughtful exploration of the medium's power in recent years.

Douglas, George H. *The Early Days of Radio Broadcasting.* Jefferson, NC: McFarland & Co., 1987. Remarkably detailed account of the personalities and industrial developments from the first station through "Amos 'n' Andy".

Fielding, Ken. *Introduction to Television Production.* White Plains, NY: Longman, 1990. Clear presentation of the total process and specific hands-on techniques to accomplish programming goals effectively and efficiently. Good for nontechnical communicators as well.

Greenfield, Jeff. *Television: The First Fifty Years.* New York: Abrams, 1977. Pictorial history, recapturing the development and great moments and series or shows of the medium.

Head, Sydney W., and Sterling, Christopher H. *Broadcasting in America: A Survey of Electronic Media.* 6th ed. Boston: Houghton Mifflin, 1990. Set a standard as best single volume on American technology, distribution, and legal factors.

Hilliard, Robert L. *Radio Broadcasting: An Introduction to the Sound Medium*, 3d ed. White Plains, NY: Longman, 1985. Thorough coverage of all aspects, managerial, technical, and performing.

Jacobs, Jerry. *Changing Channels: Issues and Realities in Television News.* Mountain View, CA: Mayfield, 1990. Practices within local, national, and international organizations.

MacDonald, J. Frederick. *Don't Touch That Dial: Radio programming in American Life from 1920 to 1960.* Chicago: Nelson, 1979. Brings back the "theater of the mind"— especially its role in shaping values in the U.S.

O'Connor, John E., ed. *American History/American Television: Interpreting the Video Past.* New York: Ungar, 1983. Fourteen historians use examples of TV programs as artifacts in important critical study of the medium.

O'Donnell, Lewis B., and Hausman, Carl. *Radio Station Operations: Management and Employee Perspectives.* Belmont, CA: Wadsworth, 1989. Daily workings of radio as a business.

There are many other relevant titles listed under Processes and Practices of Mass Communication, Practitioners' Roles, and Media Effects. Specific works on cable include:

Baldwin, Thomas E., and McVoy, D. Stevens. *Cable Communication.* Englewood Cliffs, N.J.: Prentice-Hall, 1983.

Brenner, Daniel L. et al. *Cable Television and Other Nonbroadcast Video: Law and Policy.* New York: Clark Boardman Company, Ltd., 1988.

Ferris, Charles D. et al. *Cable Television: A Video Communications Practice Guide.* 3 vols. New York: Matthew Bender & Company, 1988.

Jesuale, Nancy et al. *CTIC Cablebooks, vol. 1, The Community Medium; vol. 2, A Guide for Local Policy.* Arlington, VA: The Cable Television Information Center, 1982.

U.S. House of Representatives. *Cable Franchise Policy and Communications Act of 1984, Report of the Committee on Energy and Commerce.* Washington, D.C.; U.S. Government Printing Office, 1984, Report #98-934.

Weinstein, Stephen B. *Getting the Picture: A Guide to CATV and the New Electronic Media.* New York: The Institute of Electrical and Electronics Engineers Press, 1986.

See also listings under New Technologies. To keep up with rapidly developing changes, consult periodicals such as *Broadcasting, Cablevision, Cable World, Channels, Journal of Broadcasting and Electronic Media*, and *Multichannel News*, as well as BCTV: Bibliography on cable television (index of books, newspapers, journals, etc. from Communications Library, San Francisco). Also: *Broadcasting/Cablecasting Yearbook* and *World Radio and TV Handbook*.

MAGAZINES

Baughman, James L. *Henry R. Luce and the Rise of the American News Media.* Boston: Twayne, 1987. Charts emergence of Time Inc. and its cofounder in context of changes taking place in the media.

Click, J. William, and Baird, Russell N. *Magazine Editing and Production.* 5th ed. Dubuque, IA.: Brown, 1990. Executive and practical aspects of all types of publications, from startup to design and marketing.

Fry, Ronald W., ed. *Magazines Career Directory*, 2d ed. Hawthorne, NJ: Career Press, 1987. Facts and advice by professionals in editorial, promotion, design, production, and management.

Mott, Frank Luther. *History of American Magazines.* New York: Appleton, 1930. Classic study of U.S. magazine publishing up to the Depression.

Gill, Brendan. *Here at The New Yorker.* New York: Random, 1975. An insider's chronicle of the first 50 years of an American institution.

Paine, Fred K., and Paine, Nancy E. *Magazines: A Bibliography for Their Analysis, with Annotations and Study Guide.* Metuchen, NJ: Scarecrow Press, 1987. Arranged by content, audience, writing, history, advertising, business press, type of publication, etc.

Wood, James Playsted Wood. *Of Lasting Interest: The Story of the Reader's Digest.* rev ed. New York: Doubleday, 1967. The development of a global leader, called "the greatest common denominator in communications we have."

There are various directories of publications, such as *The Standard Periodical Directory, The National Directory of Magazines, Oxbridge Directory of Newsletters, Ulrich's International Periodicals Directory*, and *MMP* (*Magazine Marketplace*), an industry directory from Bowker. A leading periodical about periodical management is *Folio*.

FILM

Bogle, Donald. *Blacks in American Films and Television.* New York: Garland, 1988. Overview of blacks' contributions; essays on influential individuals and content.

Bywater, Tim, and Sobchack, Thomas. *Introduction to Film Criticism.* White Plains, NY: Longman, 1988

Eisenstein, Sergei. *The Film Sense.* Trans. by Jay Leyda. New York: Harcourt, 1947. His theories of film, including his celebrated notion of "montage." With its companion, *Film Form,* considered classic in film aesthetics.

Film Review Digest. New York: Kraus-Thompson, yearly. Criticism excerpted from U.S., British, and Canadian reviews.

Giannetti, Louis. *Understanding Movies,* 4th ed. Englewood Cliffs, NJ: Prentice-Hall, 1987. How filmmakers use language and techniques to convey meaning; from specialized cinematic tools to theory, well illustrated.

Gomery, Douglas. *Movie History.* Belmont, CA: Wadsworth, 1990. Applies communication process and media economic aproaches to film history. Analytic framework includes global considerations.

Hamilton, Ian. *Writers in Hollywood, 1915–1951.* New York: Harper, 1990. Auteur theory is challenged as we look at work of scriptwriters, often eminent novelists, during Hollywood's golden age.

Jarvie, I. C. *Movies and Society.* New York: Basic Books, 1970. Sociology of movies: who makes them, who sees them, what is the transaction and appreciation.

Katz, Ephraim. *The Film Encyclopedia: The Most Comprehensive Encyclopedia of World Cinema in One Volume.* New York: Harper, 1990. Esteemed for accuracy.

Leff, Leonard J., and Simmons, Jerold L. *The Dame in the Kimono: Hollywood, Censorship, and the Production Code from the 1920's to the 1960's.* New York: Grove Weidenfeld, 1990. Social and business history in an account of the dynamic between the public and the industry and the subtle connections between art, money, politics, and religion in America.

Levin, G. Roy. *Documentary Explorations: 15 Interviews with Film-Makers.* New York: Doubleday, 1971. Brief history of the form, followed by exploration of the issue of objective reality.

Madsen, Roy Paul. *Working Cinema: Learning from the Masters.* Belmont, CA: Wadsworth, 1990. All aspects of the craft, with input from leading practitioners; principles balanced with behind-the-scenes reality.

Schatz, Thomas. *The Genius of the System: Hollywood Filmmaking in the Studio Era.* New York: Pantheon, 1988. Comprehensive study based largely on primary sources.

Shipman, David. *The Story of Cinema: A Complete Narrative History from the Beginnings to the Present.* New York: St. Martins, 1986. Huge, international history.

Squire, Jason E., ed. *The Movie Business Book: The Inside Story of the Creation, Financing, Making, Selling, and Exhibiting of Movies.* New York: Simon & Schuster, 1983. Forty-two notables share their experience; some players might have changed but the information is still valid.

Wakeman, John. *World Film Directors, 1890–1945.* 2 vols. New York: H. W. Wilson, 1987. Encyclopedia of critical essays on major filmmakers around the world.

Useful periodicals: *American Film, Film Comment, Film Quarterly; Variety* is the movie trade paper.

RECORDED MUSIC

Fornaiale, Pete. *The Story of Rock 'n' Roll.* New York: Morrow, 1987. History of popular culture's phenomenon and its relation to radio and recording industries.

Gelatt, Roland. *The Fabulous Phonograph,* 2d ed. New York: DaCapo, 1977. Evolution of machines, records, and tapes.

Kapan, E. Ann. *Rocking Around the Clock: Music Television, Post Modernism, and Consumer Culture.* New York: Routledge, 1987. Analysis of MTV by a theorist of popular culture; a guide to recent sociological/psychological/semiotic thinking on the relationship between television and viewers.

Shemel, Sidney, and Krasilorsky, William M. *This Business of Music,* 5th ed. New York: Billboard Books, 1985. Survey of operations and individuals behind the labels.

Sklar, Rick. *Rocking America: How the All-Hit Radio Stations Took Over.* New York: St. Martin, 1985. The rock radio revolution by one of the creators of the Top 40; 30 years of behind-the-scenes and analysis; list of songs that got top ratings.

Toll, Robert C. *The Entertainment Machine: American Show Business in the Twentieth Century.* New York: Oxford University Press, 1982. Interesting chronicles of several media; impact of the phonograph.

Billboard Magazine and its publication program, *Downbeat* and *Rolling Store* are ongoing sources of information about popular music (charts included for all categories of recordings). Brochures and other materials are also available from The Recording Industry Association of America in New York.

BOOK PUBLISHING

Altbach, Philip et al., eds. *Perspectives on Textbooks and Society.* Albany: State University of New York Press. Forthcoming. Articles by publishing professionals on the making and marketing of books, with emphasis on the writer-reader relationship.

Dessauer, John P. *Book Publishing: What It Is, What It Does,* 2d ed. New York: Bowker, 1981. Comprehensive description of different types of editors, elements of publishing decisions, straight through to distribution.

Gross, Gerald, ed. *Editors and Editing.* New York: Grosset & Dunlap, 1962. Personal approaches to many facets of editing based on letters, memoirs, speeches, etc. of luminaries of this century.

————. *Publishers on Publishing.* New York: Grosset & Dunlap, 1961. Anthology of writings by those who founded the great American and British publishing firms.

Huenefeld, John. *The Huenefeld Guide to Book Publishing,* 4th ed. Lexington, MA: Mills & Sanderson, 1990. Manual for managers of small publishing houses; tips on making acquisitions decisions, monitoring finances, working with production suppliers, choosing marketing strategies.

Schreuders, Piet. *Paperbacks, U.S.A.: A Graphic History, 1939–1959.* Trans. by Josh Pachter. San Diego, CA: Blue Dolphin Enterprises, 1981. Lively account of the golden age of mass market paperbacks, illustrated.

Smith, Datus C., Jr. *A Guide to Book Publishing,* rev ed. Seattle: University of Washington Press, 1989. Clear introduction to roles in a publishing firm, especially for anyone considering entry.

R. R. Bowker is the publisher of guides and directories for book publishers. The annual *Literary Market Place* (there is an annual international guide) is an invaluable source. Bowker publishes directories of books in print. *Publishers Weekly* is the trade journal of news, listings, ads, and essays on publishing globally, book design and manufacturing, and retailing, its main thrust.

News and Analysis

Altschull, J. Herbert. *Agents of Power: The Role of the News Media in Human Affairs.* White Plains, NY: Longman, 1984. Thoughtful perspective on past and present role of the press as themselves agents of other powers—economic, political, social.

———. *From Milton to McLuhan: The Ideas Behind American Journalism.* White Plains, NY: Longman, 1990. Philosophical foundations of journalism; how press affected by intellectual context.

Boorstin, Daniel J. *The Image: A Guide to Pseudo-Events in America.* New York: Atheneum, 1988. Reissue of classic indictment of the illusionary process of news gathering.

Broder, David. *Behind the Front Page: A Candid Look at How the News Is Made.* New York: Simon & Schuster, 1987. Insights of a leading political reporter.

Bogart, Leo. *Press and public; Who Reads What, When, Where, and Why in American Newspapers,* 2d ed. Hillsdale, NJ: Erlbaum, 1989. How competition and marketing pressures affect the industry and content of newspapers.

Dennis Everette E., and Merrill, John C. *Media Debates: Issues in Mass Communication.* New York: Longman, 1990. Two media scholars debate on a range of topics relevant to journalism.

Does Television Change History? Proceedings of the 2nd National Conference on Television and Ethics, March 6, 1987, Boston. boston: Emerson College, 1987. Look at fine line betwen documentary and docudrama.

Benjamin, Burton. *Fair Play: CBS, General Westmoreland, and How a Television Documentary Went Wrong.* New York: Harper, 1989. Inside-the-craft story. There are many books on CBS News per se, such as *Air Time: The Inside Story of CBS News* by Gary Paul Gates and *Prime Time, Bad Times,* a memoir by Ed Joyce.

Goldstein, Tom, ed. *Killing the Messenger: 100 Years of Media Criticism.* New York: Columbia University Press, 1989. Important provocative thinking about the press.

Keir, Gerry, McCombs, Maxwell E., and Shaw, Donald L. *Advanced Reporting: Beyond News Events.* White Plains, NY: Longman, 1986. Strategies and tactics of coverage, interviews, etc.

Wanniski, Jude, ed. *The 1989 Media Guide: A Critical Review of the Print Media's.* Morristown, NJ: Polyconomics, Inc., 1989. Annual look at how press performed, with opinions, ratings, and profiles of journalists and their work.

Winfield, Betty Houchin, and DeFleur, Lois B. *The Edward R. Murrow Heritage.* Ames, IA.: Iowa State University Press, 1986. Panel of journalists examine the influence of the reporter/commentator and how his ideals of integrity, creativity, and accountability fare in today's media.

Periodicals of special importance: *Columbia Journalism Review, Journalism Quarterly, Nieman Reports, Quill, Washington Journalism Review.*

Analyzing and Evaluating Entertainment

Berger, Arthur Asa. *The Comic-Stripped American: What Dick Tracy, Blondie, Daddy Warbucks and Charlie Bown Tell Us About Ourselves.* New York: Walker & Co., 1973. Analyzes important American comic strips and comic books in terms of what they reflect about American culture, politics and society; uses psychoanalytic, semiotic, and Marxist methods of analysis.

Berger, Arthur Asa. *Media Analysis Techniques.* Beverly Hills, CA: Sage, 1982. Shows how semiotic analysis, psychoanalytic criticism, Marxist analysis and sociological analysis can be used to deal with mysteries, football, advertising and all news radio.

Bettelheim, Bruno. *The Uses of Enchantment.* New York: Vintage Books, 1977. Classic study of fairy tales using Freudian psychoanalytic methods.

Bywater, Tim and Sobchack, Thomas. *Introduction to Film Criticism: Major Critical Approaches to Narrative Film.* White Plains, NY: Longman, 1989. A variety of methods of interpreting film such as journalistic, aesthetic, social-scientific, historical, auteur, and genre criticism.

Dorfman, Ariel. *The Empire's Old Clothes: What The Lone Ranger, Babar, and Other Innocent Heroes Do to Our Minds.* New York: Pantheon Books, 1983. From a Marxist perspective, deals with the ideological content of a number of important characters from the world of media.

Eisenstein, Sergei. *The Film Sense.* (*See* Film).

English, John W. *Criticizing the Critics.* New York: Hastings House, 1979. Considers various critics' theoretical assumptions and how their beliefs affect their work.

Gelmis, Joseph. *The Film Director as Superstar.* (*See* Film).

Geduld, Carolyn. *Filmguide to 2001: A Space Odyssey.* Bloomington, Ind.: Indiana University Press, 1973. Has material on Stanley Kubrick, the director; the production of the film; and a detailed aesthetic analysis of the film itself.

Grotjahn, Martin. *Beyond Laughter: Humor and The Subconscious.* New York: mcGraw-Hill, 1966. A Freudian reading of popular humor and related aspects of popular culture.

Jung, Carl C. *Man and His Symbols.* New York: Dell Books, 1968. A good introduction to Jungian thinking and how this psychoanalytic approach to culture in general can be applied to the arts—popular and elite.

Kaminsky, Stuart M. *American Film Genres: Approaches to a Critical Theory of Popular Film.* Dayton, OH: Pflaum, 1974. Attacks the notion that there are "art" films (which are worth serious study) and "popular films" (which are not worth study). Deals with the nature of genre and important popular film genres such as musicals, horror films, gangster films, and Westerns.

Marx, Karl. *Selected Writings in Sociology and Social Philosophy.* Edited by T. C. Bottomore and M. Rubel, New York: McGraw-Hill, 1964. A collection of classic writings by Marx on politics and society, taken from a number of his works.

McLuhan, Marshall. *The Mechanical Bride: Folklore of Industrial Man.* Boston: Beacon Press, 1976. Short essays on advertisements and comics that McLuhan found significant. Written in the 1940s, it is a pioneering semiotic (though not identified as such) and ideological analysis of American popular culture.

Propp, Vladimir. *Morphology of the Folktale.* Austin, TX: University of Texas Press, 1973. A classic study of the nature of narrative, based on the analysis of common "functions" found in a number of Russian fairy tales.

Seldes, Gilbert. *The Public Arts*. New York: Simon & Schuster, 1956. One of the first books to deal with media and popular culture—and, in particular, the movies, radio and television—seriously.

Vande Berg, Leah R., and Wenner, Lawrence. *Television Criticism: Approaches and Application*. White Plains, NY: Longman, 1991. Essays interpreting all basic television genres are prefaced by the writers' explanation of methodology and are accompanied by marginal notes to lead students through the process of criticism.

LAWS AND FREEDOM

Brenner, Daniel L., and Rivers, William L. *Free But Regulated: Conflicting Traditions in Media Law*. Ames, IA.: Iowa State University Press, 1982. Lawyers, journalists, and researchers examine mass media law.

Brasch, Walter M., and Ulloth, Dana R. *The Press and the State: Sociohistorical and Contemporary Interpretation*. Lanham, MD.: University of Press of America, 1988. A history, from ancient times, of government controls of press freedoms and discussion of ongoing issues.

Dennis, Everette E., Gillmor, Donald M., and Grey, David L., eds. *Justice Hugo Black and the First Amendment*. Ames, IA.: Iowa State University Press, 1978. Articles detailing the opinions of Black regarding the First Amendment.

Ernst, Morris L., and Schwartz, Alan U. *Censorship: The Search for the Obscene*. New York: Macmillian, 1964. A century and a half of major cases revealing what was thought obscene or pornographic.

Final Report of the Attorney General's Commission on Pornography. Nashville, TN: Rutledge Hill Press, 1986. Experts summoned during the Reagan administration speak on the dangers of pornography.

Le Duc, Don R. *Beyond Broadcasting: Patterns in Policy and Law*. White Plains, NY: Longman, 1987. Legal, economic, technological, and political intereactions in federal deregulation policy.

Middleton, Kent R., and Chamberlin, Bill F. *The Law of Public Communication*, 2d ed. White Plains, NY: Longman, 1991. Balanced coverage of law as media practitioners confront it; organized around the functions of the law; includes public relations and advertising.

Powe, Lucas A., Jr. *American Broadcasting and the First Amendment*. Berkeley, CA: University of California Press, 1987. Historical and contemporary situation of FCC regulation, which author feels is not constitutionally justified.

MEDIA ETHICS

Bowie, Norman E. *Making Ethical Decisions*. New York: McGraw-Hill, 1985. Nicely edited selection of readings in philosophy intended to give readers tools for making ethical choices.

Christians, Clifford G., Kim B. Rotzoll, and Mark Fackler. *Media Ethics: Cases and Moral Reasoning*. 3rd ed. White Plains, NY: Longman, 1991. Uses real and hypothetical cases pertaining to all branches of media, including public relations, to raise and discuss ethical issues; the standard text for practitioners facing real problems.

Commission on Freedom of the Press. *A Free and Responsible Press*. Chicago: University of Chicago Press, 1947. The classic expression of social responsibility obligations of the media.

Elliott, Deni, ed. *Responsible Journalism*. Beverly Hills, CA: Sage, 1986. Useful, focused set of readings on the source and practice of journalistic responsibility.

Hocking, William Ernest. *Freedom of the Press: A Framework of Principle*. Chicago: University of Chicago Press, 1947. Stimulating and provocative expression of philosophy of social responsibility.

Hulteng, John L. *The Messenger's Motives: Ethical Problems of the News Media*. 2d ed. Englewood Cliffs, NJ: Prentice-Hall, 1985. Discussions and useful examples of ethical issues.

Jaksa, James A., and Pritchard, Michael S. *Communication Ethics: Methods of Analysis*. Belmont, CA: Wadsworth, 1988. Ways of reasoning through ethical issues, though not focused exclusively on mass communication.

Merrill, John C. *The Imperative of Freedom: A Philosophy of Journalistic Autonomy*. New York: Freedom House, 1990. Spirited critique of social responsibility theory and defense of libertarianism.

Merrill, John C., and S. Jack Odell. *Philosophy and Journalism*. White Plains, NY: Longman, 1983. Useful and readable overview of basic philosophical principles and their application in journalism.

Meyer, Philip. *Ethical Journalism*. White Plains, NY: Longman, 1987. Presents results and thoughtful discussion of survey of editors, publishers and staffers at 300 newspapers.

Rivers, William L.; Schramm, Wilbur; and Christians, Clifford G. *Responsibility in Mass Communication*. 3rd ed. New York: Harper, 1980. Most recent edition of classic text providing overview of media ethics.

EFFECTS

Bennett, W. Lance. *News: The Politics of Illusion*, 2d ed. White Plains, NY: Longman, 1988. How news is reported and consumed in America—for entertainment more than information.

Berger, Arthur Asa. *Media USA: Process and Effect*, 2d ed. White Plains, NY: Longman, 1991. Overview of various effects on individuals and society; contributors analyze specific works.

Dates, Jannette L., and Barlow, William, eds. *Split Image: African Americans in the Mass Media*. Washington, DC: Howard University Press, 1990. Historical essays surveying image of blacks in all media, including advertising.

DeFleur, Melvin L., and Ball-Rokeach, Sandra. *Theories of Mass Communication*, 5th ed. White Plains, NY: Longman, 1989. Authoritative text selecting specific issues in major sociological and psychological theories, linked to mass communication.

Emmert, Philip, and Barker, Larry L. *Measurement of Communication Behavior*. White Plains, NY: Longman, 1989. Methods and instruments of communication and audience research.

Ewen, Stuart. *All Consuming Images: The Politics of Style in Contemporary Culture*. New York: Basic Books, 1988. Author of pioneering *Captains of Consciousness* expands thesis past industries to present seamless *network* of industries.

Fighting TV Stereotypes: An ACT Handbook. Newtonville, MA: Action for Children's Television, 1982. Discusses role of women and minorities.

Fiske, John. *Television Culture*. New York: Routledge, 1988. Audience-oriented study of medium and social framework in which it operates to construct reality.

Gitlin, Todd, *The Whole World Is Watching: Mass Media in the Making and Unmaking of the New Left*. Berkeley, CA: University of California Press, 1980. Role of TV and press in making media celebrities of protesters in the 1960s.

Gumpert, Gary. *Talking Tombstones & Other Tales of the Media Age*. New York: Oxford University Press, 1987. How media techniques, such as use of video and audio tape, blur perception of reality.

Hallin, Daniel. *The Uncensored War: The Media and Vietnam*. Berkeley: University of California Press, 1986. How media played pivotal role in change of opinion.

Harris, Richard Jackson. *A Cognitive Psychology of Mass Communication*. Hillsdale, NJ: Erlbaum, 1989. How our minds create media-based knowledge, which creates behavior.

Hiebert, Ray Eldon, and Reuss, Carol. *Impact of Mass Media*, 3d ed. White Plains, NY: Longman, 1991. Lively collection of views on *all* current controversies.

Iyengar, Shanto, and Kinder, Donald R. *News That Matters: Television and American Opinion*. Chicago: University of Chicago Press, 1987. Important scholarly work using research on media's role in political behavior.

Kinsella, James. *Covering the Plague: AIDS and the American Media*. Rutgers, NJ: Rutgers University Press, 1990. Study of how journalistic prejudices and politics of news gathering have affected perception of the problem.

Kubey, Robert, and Csikszentmihalyi, Mihaly. *Television and the Quality of Life: How Viewing Shapes Everyday Experience*. Hillsdale, NJ: Erlbaum, 1990. Individuals reporting on immediate media experiences lead to analysis of role of media in U.S. society; cross-national studies also.

Liebert, Robert M., Sprafkin, Joyce N., and Davidson, Emily S. *The Early Window: Effects of Television on Children and Youth*, 2d ed. New York: Pergamon Press, 1982. Comprehensive review of the main research and activist concerns at peak of concern.

Lippman, Walter. *Public Opinion*. New York: Macmillan, 1921. Classic work on how perceptions and attitudes can be influenced.

Lowery, Shearon A., and DeFleur, Melvin L. *Milestones in Mass Communications Research*, 2d ed. White Plains, NY: Longman, 1988. Roadmap of communication research, focusing on 13 major studies.

Nimmo, Dan, and Combs, James E. *Mediated Political Realities*, 2d ed. White Plains, NY: Longman, 1990. Shows that few people learn about politics directly and that media can even transform political reality into fantasy.

Tuchman, Gaye, Daniels, Arlene Kaplan, and Benet, James, eds. *Hearth and Home: Images of Women in the Mass Media*. New York: Oxford University Press, 1978. Essays on the images of women on TV, in the press; television's effect on children's socialization.

Globalism and International Communication

Cooper, Thomas W. *Communication Ethics and Global Change*. White Plains, NY: Longman, 1989. Essays from 16 countries, codes of ethics.

Gerber, George, and Siefert, Marsha, eds. *World Communications: A Handbook*. Policy makers and scholars from more than 25 countries sum up issues and roles.

Katz, Elihu, and Wedell, George. *Broadcasting in the Third World: Promise and Performance*. Cambridge, MA: Harvard University Press, 1977. Field research and analysis of ways Western approaches must adapt to regional needs.

Martin, L. John, and Hiebert, Ray Eldon. *Current Issues in International Communication*. White Plains, NY: Longman, 1990. Classic and contemporary essays on theory, policy, and the realities.

Merrill, John C., ed. *Global Journalism: Survey of International Communication*, 2d ed. White Plains, NY: Longman, 1991. Macro view of systems, news flow, and controversies, plus detailed regional descriptions and statistics of media systems, prepared by experts. Extensive bibliography.

Stevenson, Robert L. *Communication, Development, and the Third World*. White Plains. NY: Longman, 1988. Unesco debate over New World Information Order and role of media and telecommunications in developing countries.

New Technologies

Dizard, Wilson P., Jr. *The Coming Information Age: An Overview of Technology, Economics, and Politics*. White Plains, NY: Longman, 1989. Describes developments with eye to implications for international policy.

Donnelly, William J. *The Confetti Generation: How the New Communications Technology Is Fragmenting America*. New York: Holt, 1986. Reminding us of how television affects us unwittingly, author explores ways to control the new technologies.

Gross, Lynne Shafer. *The New Technologies*, 3d ed. Dubuque, IA: Brown, 1990. States of the art and the new interrelationships of media that result.

McLuhan, Marshall, and Powers, Bruce R. *The Global Village: Transformations in World Life and Media in the 21st Century*. New York: Oxford University Press, 1989. Extends visionary early work of McLuhan, applied to today's worldwide integrated electronic network.

Mirabito, Michael M., and Morgenstern, Barbara L. *The New Communications Technologies*. Boston: Focal, 1989. Economic and social implications.

Naisbitt, John, and Aburdene, Patricia. *Megatrends 2000: Ten New Directions for the 1990's*. New York, Morrow, 1989. Updated field guide by leading social trends forecasters, with new global emphasis.

Newberg, Paula R. *New Directions in Telecommunications Policy*. 2 vols. Durham, N.C.: Duke University Press, 1989. Sophisticated essays on issues such as pluralism and regulation.

Negrine, Ralph M., ed. *Satellite Broadcasting: The Politics and Implications of the New Media*. New York: Routledge, 1988. Key cultural issues and effects on existing systems.

Williams, Frederick; Rice, Ronald E.; and Rogers, Everett M. *Research Methods and the New Media*. New York: The Free Press, 1988. Ways to plan and track use of new technologies.

Index

CREDITS ....

1.1. (a) © National Broadcasting Company, Inc.
1.2. Courtesy of KDKA, Radio Pittsburgh
1.3. From *Men, Messages, and Media* by Wilbur Schramm. Copyright © 1973 by Wilbur Schramm. Reprinted by permission of Harper and Row, Publishers, Inc.
1.4. Copyright © 1948, American Telephone and Telegraph Company, reprinted by permission.
1.5. Reprinted with permission of Macmillan Publishing Company from *The Fundamentals and Forms of Speech* by Weaver and Ness. Copyright © 1957, 1963 by The Bobbs-Merrill Company.
1.9. Dana Fineman/Sygma
1.11. Courtesy of The New-York Historical Society, New York City
2.1. O. Franken/Sygma
2.2. Reprinted with permission from T.V. Guide ® Magazine. Copyright © 1989 by News America Publications, Inc. Radnor, Pennsylvania.
2.3. Courtesy of York Graphic Services, Inc., York, Pa.
2.4. From Frederick Shook, *Television Field Production and Reporting*. Copyright © 1989 by Longman Publishing Group, photographer Eric Lars Bakke.
2.6. Wide World Photos; CNN
2.7. © 1987 National Broadcasting Company, Inc.
2.9. © 1986 National Broadcasting Company, Inc.
2.10. *Movie Star News*
Box, ch. 2. Left, all characters © United Feature Syndicate. Used by permission of United Feature Syndicate. Right, reprinted by permission, Tribune Media Services.
3.2. Photograph © Harvey Wang
3.3. Copyright © 1989 Twentieth Century Fox Film Corporation. All rights reserved.
3.6, 3.8. The Museum of Modern Art/Film Stills Archive
3.9. Courtesy of *The Detroit Free Press*; reprinted with permission of *The Detroit News*, a Gannett newspaper, copyright 1989.
Box, ch. 3. Copyright 1989, *Channels* Magazine. Reprinted by permission.
4.2. Museum of Modern Art/Film Stills Archive
4.3. Courtesy Lexus Div., Toyota
4.6. *Movie Star News*, Courtesy of RKO Studios
4.7. From Frederick Shook, *Television Field Production and Reporting*. Copyright © 1989 by Longman Publishing Group, photographer Eric Lars Bakke.
4.8. From Ken Fielding, *Introduction to Television Production*. Copyright © 1990 by Longman Publishing Group.
4.9. Museum of Modern Art/Film Stills Archive
4.10. Terry Smith
4.11. The Paddington Group; agency: Berenter, Greenhouse & Webster
Box, ch. 4. Figure by Alexander Nevsky from *The Film Sense* by Sergei M. Eisenstein, Jay Leyda, copyright © 1942 by Harcourt Brace Jovanovich, Inc. and renewed 1970 by Jay Leyda, reprinted by permission of the publisher.
5.1. From Frederick Shook, *Television Field Production and Reporting*. Copyright © 1989 by Longman Publishing Group, photographer Eric Lars Bakke.
5.2. NBC, *USA Today*, Dec. 3, 1985.
5.3. *Movie Star News*, courtesy of Warner Brothers, Inc.
5.4. Courtesy The Leonard Goldberg Company
5.5. Wide World Photos
5.6. Susan Biddle, The White House
5.7. © 1989 Annie Leibovitz/Capital Cities/ABC Inc.
Box, ch. 5. Courtesy American Society of Newspaper Editors; Radio Television News Directors Association.
6.1. Nielsen Media Research
6.2. Johnson Publishing Co. Inc.
6.10. Courtesy Nike, Inc.; agency: Wieden and Kennedy
6.11. Photo courtesy Sygma
6.12. Nielsen Media Research

6.14. 1989 TIO/Roper Report, reprinted with permission of National Association of Broadcasters, Washington, D.C.
6.15. © 1990 BPI Communications, Inc. Used with permission from *Billboard*.
6.19. Starch INRA Hooper; L'Oreal Hair Div. agency: McCann-Erickson
Box, ch. 6. Courtesy Eveready Battery Company Inc.; courtesy Bugle Boy Industries
7.1. Doug Marlette, New York *Newsday*
7.4. Courtesy Johnson & Johnson, © Ted Horowitz 1982
7.5. Courtesy p.r. newswire
7.6. Courtesy of Ketchum Public Relations, a unit of Ketchum Communications, Inc.
7.7. The Names Project Aids Memorial Quilt. Photo by Mary Gottwald
7.9. Public Relations Society of America
7.10. Reprinted by permission, IABC/Communication World
7.11. Reprinted by permission of The Chase Manhattan Bank, NA
Box, ch. 7. Interpretations courtesy of PRSA, 33 Irving Place, NY, NY 10003
8.1. Courtesy American Express; agency: Ogilvy and Mather
8.2. © 1990 Northern Telecom; agency: J. Walter Thompson, Chicago (creative director Tom DeMint, art director John Siebert, copywriter Carl Ross)
8.3. Courtesy of American Medical Association
8.4. Based on data in *Advertising Age*, May 15, 1989, 24; data prepared by Robert J. Coen of McCann-Erickson advertising agency
8.5. Based on data from *Statistical Abstract of the United States* and *Advertising Age*
8.7. American Express
8.10. © The Arbitron Company. Reprinted with permission.
8.11. Reproduced with permission of © Pepsi Co, Inc. 1989.
8.12. Courtesy of R. R. Donnelley & Sons Company (creative director Gordon Hochhalter, designer Dan Larocca, illustrator Robert Giusti)
8.13. Courtesy of GM Corp. and the Buick Motor Division; agency: McCann-Erickson, Detroit-AGT
8.14. Courtesy Xerox Corporation; agency: Backer Spielvogel Bates
Box 1, ch. 8. Courtesy of Apple Computer, Inc.; courtesy NYNEX Information Resources. Agency: Chiat/Day/Mojo
Box 2, ch. 8. Reproduced by permission of the American Association of Advertising Agencies
9.1. Picture Collection, The New York Public Library
9.3. Courtesy of the New-York Historical Society, New York City
9.5. Courtesy of the Bell & Howell Company
9.6. Copyright 1945, Los Angeles Times, reprinted courtesy of Vis-Com. Inc., Minneapolis
9.7. American Newspaper Publishers Association
9.8. Courtesy of Joan Silbersher
9.9. Veronis, Suhler & Associates, Wilkofsky Gruen Associates
9.11. Courtesy, *Miami Herald*
9.12. Courtesy of The Austin Company
Box, ch. 9. Graphic data from *Advertising Age*
10.1. © 1990 National Broadcasting Company, Inc. All rights reserved.
10.2. *Movie Star News*
10.3. Courtesy of The National Broadcasting Company, Inc.
10.4. The Bettman Archive, Inc.
10.5. CBS Photography
10.6. © 1989 National Broadcasting Company, Inc. All rights reserved.
10.7. ABC News
10.8. ABC News
10.9. (a) © 1989 Fox Broadcasting Co.; (b) TM & © 1989 Twentieth-Century Fox Film Corporation.

10.10. CBS Photography
10.11. (a) Veronis, Suhler & Associates, A. C. Nielsen, Wilkofsky Gruen Associates; (b) *The TV Book*
Box, ch. 10. CBS Photography; Picture Collection, The New York Public Library
11.1. David Sarnoff Research Center Archives
11.2. Courtesy of KDKA Radio, Pittsburgh
11.3, 11.4. The Bettmann Archive, Inc.
11.5. Courtesy of The National Broadcast Company, Inc.
11.6. CBS Photography
11.9. Stan Barouh, National Public Radio
11.11. © 1989 The National Broadcasting Company, Inc.
Box, ch. 11. Reprinted with permission of Broadcast Programming
12.1. Veronis, Suhler & Associates, Wilkofsky Gruen Associates
12.2. Picture Collection, The New York Public Library
12.3. Courtesy The Reader's Digest Association
12.4. *Ebony* cover courtesy The Johnson Publishing Co. Inc.
12.5. *Collier's* and *The Saturday Evening Post* covers reprinted courtesy of Vis-Com, Inc., Minneapolis
12.8. © 1990 Special Reports, Whittle Communications, 505 Market St., Knoxville, Tenn. 37902. Reprinted by permission.
Box, ch. 12. Courtesy *Spy* Magazine
13.2–13.7. Museum of Modern Art/Film Stills Archive
13.8. *Movie Star News*
13.9. Museum of Modern Art/Film Stills Archive, © 1980 by United Artists Corporation
13.11. Courtesy, The Film Society of Lincoln Center
13.12. Simon & Goodman Picture Company
13.13. Forty Acres and a Mule Production Company
Box, ch. 13. Museum of Modern Art/Film Stills Archive; *Movie Star News*
14.1. Courtesy Edison National Historic Site
14.2. Wide World Photos
14.3. *Photoplay Presents*
14.4. The Bettmann Archive, Inc.; *Movie Star News*
14.5. Century 21 Programming, Dallas, TX
14.6. Tom Mihalek/Sygma
14.7. Courtesy Anheuser-Busch; agency: Fleishman Hillard Inc.
14.8. (a) © Theo Westenberger/Sygma; (b) Public Broadcasting System
14.9. Recording Industry Association of America Inc. and Chilton Research Services
Box, ch. 14. MTV: Music Television® is a trademark of MTV Networks, a division of Viacom International Inc.; A. Tannenbaum/Sygma
15.1. Courtesy of Mary Engelbreit Ink
15.3, 15.3. Picture Collection, The New York Public Library
15.5. Adapted from chart in *A Guide to Book Publishing*, with permission of the R. R. Bowker Company, Copyright © 1966 by Xerox Corporation.
15.8. Courtesy of Simon & Schuster
16.1. (a) Courtesy of The New-York Historical Society, New York City; (b) reprinted with permission, Gannett Westchester Newspapers, White Plains, NY
16.3. Melvin Grier/*Cincinnati Post*
16.4. New York *Daily News*
16.5. Photo by Janie Eisenberg, courtesy of the *Columbia Journalism Review*
16.6.(a) © Courtesy of the National Broadcast Company, Inc.; (b) CNN
16.7. Photo Kerry Hayes, © 1987 Twentieth-Century Fox Film Corp. All rights reserved
16.9. Courtesy KTLA, Los Angeles
17.1. Photo by Tom Sobolik
17.2. CBS Photography
17.3. Copyright © 1989 *The Miami Herald*. Reprinted with permission

17.4. Wide World Photos
17.5. CBS Photography
17.6. Copyright © George J. Riley
18.8. Courtesy Young American Publishing, Co., Inc., Portland, OR
18.2. Courtesy Westcott Communications
18.3, 18.4. Courtesy of International Business Machines Corporation
18.5. © 1986 National Broadcast Company, Inc.
18.6. Courtesy Metropolitan Opera Guild, Inc.
18.7. Photo by Richard Howard
18.8. Courtesy Public Broadcasting System
19.1. Courtesy of The New-York Historical Society, New York City
19.2, 19.3, 19.5. Museum of Modern Art/Film Stills Archive
19.7. Courtesy Air France; agency: Laurence, Charles, Free & Lawson, Inc. (artist: Jenkins)
19.9. Picture Collection, The New York Public Library
19.10. © 1986 National Broadcasting Company, Inc.
19.11. CBS Photography
19.12. Museum of Modern Art/Film Stills Archive
19.14. Courtesy of Zoetrope Studios. All rights reserved.
20.1. Cartoon by Paul Szep reprinted courtesy of *The Boston Globe*
20.2. © *The Washington Post*. Reprinted with permission.
20.3. Museum of Modern Art/Film Stills Archive
20.4. From Frederick Shook, *Television Field Production and Reporting*. Copyright © 1989 by Longman Publishing Group, photographer Eric Lars Bakke
20.5. UPI/Bettman Newsphotos, courtesy of the *Columbia Journalism Review*
20.6. Courtesy of the *Los Angeles Times*.
20.7. From Frederick Shook, *Television Field Production and Reporting*. Copyright © 1989 by Longman Publishing Group, photo by Eric Lars Bakke
21.1. Copyright by R. Maiman/Sygma
21.3. Copyright 1985 *Los Angeles Times*. Reprinted by permission.
21.4. Photo Kerry Hayes, © 1987 Twentieth-Century Fox Film Corp. All rights reserved.
21.5. *Movie Star News*, courtesy Columbia Pictures
21.6, 21.7. Wide World Photos
21.8. Courtesy *The Capital Times*, Madison, WI
22.2. Courtesy of Oldsmobile Division, General Motors
22.3. *Movie Star News*, Courtesy of Columbia Pictures
22.4. RCA Corp.
22.6. Museum of Modern Art/Film Stills Archive
23.1. Courtesy National Aeronautics and Space Administration
23.3. Wide World Photos
23.5. © 1989 Capital Cities/ABC, Inc.
23.6. Photo by Ricky Francisco. Copyright © Hemdale Film Corporation 1986
23.7. Copyright Capital Cities/ABC Inc. (Photo Dean Williams)
24.1. Courtesy The Reader's Digest Association
24.3. Museum of Modern Art/Film Stills Archive
24.4. S. Franklin/Sygma
24.5. Thierry Orban/Patrick Orban/Sygma
24.7. Reprinted from *Freedom at Issue*, Jan.-Feb. 1990, with the permission of Freedom House
24.8. Courtesy CNN
25.1. Courtesy Arcata Graphics Book Group, Kingsport, TN
25.2. Courtesy The Harris Corporation
25.3. Reprinted with permission from *Automative News*, November 6, 1989. Copyright Crain Comm. Inc.
25.4. Reprinted by permission of WXIA-TV
25.5. Courtesy NorLight™
25.6. (a) Courtesy The Harris Corporation; (b) Courtesy Sony Corporation of America
25.7. Photography by Hunter Freeman, courtesy of VisiColor, Inc., Denver, Colorado